LANGUAGE AND AREA STUDIES

East Central and Southeastern Europe

LANGUAGE and AREA STUDIES

East Central and Southeastern Europe

A Survey

Edited by

Charles Jelavich

THE UNIVERSITY OF CHICAGO PRESS

Chicago and London

The research reported herein was
performed pursuant to a contract with the
United States Department of Health, Education, and
Welfare, Office of Education (under provisions of
Section 602, Title VI, P.L. 85-864). Copyright
is claimed until 31 December 1976. Thereafter
all portions of this work covered by copyright will
be in the public domain.

Standard Book Number: 226–39615–0

Library of Congress Catalog Card Number: 72–81222

THE UNIVERSITY OF CHICAGO PRESS, CHICAGO 60637
The University of Chicago Press, Ltd., London W.C. 1

Printed in the United States of America

To the memory of

George Rapall Noyes

Scholar and teacher
and
the first Ph.D. in Slavic Studies
in the United States

CONTENTS

viii   *Contents*

PREFACE

The area with which this survey is concerned, East Central and Southeastern Europe [1] — that is, Poland, Czechoslovakia, Hungary, Romania, Yugoslavia, Bulgaria, Albania, Greece, and, where relevant, European Turkey and East Germany — represents a historical mosaic influenced by divergent political, social, economic, religious, cultural, and linguistic developments over the centuries. As a borderland region subject to constant external pressures, this area is a unique political, social, and economic laboratory whose significance for the contemporary world cannot be overestimated. Beginning with the ancient Greeks, whose contributions are evident in all these lands, the 110,000,000 inhabitants of the area, divided into at least a dozen distinct national groups, have been influenced and shaped by the major movements of European civilization: by classical and Christian Rome, Byzantium and the Orthodox church, the Ottoman Turks and Islam, the Renaissance, the Reformation, the Enlightenment, nationalism, socialism, and the industrial revolution. The great neighboring states, Imperial Russia, the Habsburg Empire, Prussia (Imperial Germany), and the Ottoman Empire, have also left their imprint on the area either through direct conquest or cultural penetration.

From a historic point of view it is fascinating to study what happened to peoples subjected to these often conflicting influences. The Romanians, for example, who claim to be of Daco-Roman descent, found themselves in the course of their history faced by Slavic, Byzantine, and Magyar pressures. They retained their identity, yet they also ab-

1. Throughout this volume the term "Eastern Europe" will also be used to designate this area. It does not include the Soviet Union.

sorbed attributes from their neighbors. Yugoslavia, with its Byzantine, Western, and Islamic cultures, offers a similar object of study. All these countries in fact provide an excellent laboratory for the examination of what happens when divergent ideas and cultures either come into conflict or meet and merge.

Although these countries are often overshadowed in world history by their larger neighbors, the Russians, the Germans, and the Italians, and although generally lost in college textbooks, they have nevertheless made significant contributions of their own to European civilization. Eleven Nobel prize winners were born here. The world of music has been enriched by the contributions of Chopin, Dvořák, Smetana, Bartók, Kodály, and Enescu. In literature Mickewicz, Kafka, Čapek, Andrić, Seferis, and Kazantzakis enjoy worldwide reputations. Byzantine mosaics, frescos, and icons and the sculpture of Ivan Meštrović are only a few examples of contributions in the arts. Even in sports the great swimming and football teams of Hungary and the ice hockey and football teams of Czechoslovakia have earned more than their share of honors in worldwide and Olympic competition.

In addition to its past achievements, the area's significance in the contemporary scene is enormous. Today East Central and Southeastern Europe has become a most valuable testing ground for the competing principles of socialism and capitalism. The area possesses characteristics not found in any other part of the world where these two systems confront each other. Within these lands, whose area (498,000 sq. mi., excluding East Germany) is slightly less than double the size of Texas (267,000 sq. mi.), one finds countries in vastly different stages of economic, cultural, and political development. The contrast between the highly industrialized areas of Bohemia and the rural, backward lands of Albania is an apt illustration.

The less developed of these small states face the same problems as the majority of the nations of the world who are not yet on the economic level of Western Europe, the United States, and the Soviet Union. Many of the problems of education, trade, commerce, manufacturing, etc., are common alike to these Eastern European countries and to Africa, Asia, and Latin America. The degree of success achieved in Eastern Europe and the efficiency of their economic models will have an enormous impact throughout the poorer nations. In fact, it has been said that these developments could be much more significant than the accomplishments of either the Americans or the Russians.

Today hundreds of students from Africa and Asia, future doctors, lawyers, economists, engineers, etc., are enrolled in the universities and technical institutes of East Europe. They are being taught by professors and research scholars who have studied in either the U.S.S.R., Western Europe, or the United States, and who are seeking to adapt to their own countries those features of socialism and capitalism which best satisfy the needs of their own state. This development is clearly of major importance for the contemporary world. Some experts on Soviet affairs have even given the opinion that what has happened in Eastern Europe explains some of the changes and the experiments now taking place in the Soviet Union.

In the political as well as in the economic sphere, Eastern Europe has been the center of dramatic developments affecting all of the socialist states. Beginning with Tito's break with Stalin in 1948 and the growth of national communism, all of the states have undergone internal changes in their political structures. The new ideas and attitudes from this area have again influenced the development of other nations.

It is interesting to note that although all of these states are undergoing an active period of growth and reorganization, they have chosen differing roads toward the achievement of the same goal of national prosperity and strength. The area thus provides the scholar and student with a unique laboratory for the study of varying contemporary political and economic theories. Take, for example, the contrasting conditions in the four adjacent Balkan states, Albania, Bulgaria, Greece, and Yugoslavia, with a combined population of 38,000,000 and a total area of 205,000 square miles, which is almost the exact equivalent of the combined population and size of the states of California and New York. All four fell under Ottoman domination in the fifteenth century; they achieved national liberation by 1914. Today, despite certain similarities in their historical experiences, they have developed different political, cultural, and economic systems. Albania is seeking to emulate China; Bulgaria is a classic Soviet-model state; Yugoslavia has combined features of the East and West in her national life; Greece is ostensibly pursing Western principles and a free-enterprise economy with a smattering of government planning. The relative success or failure of each in achieving its aims is not only an interesting subject for comparative study, but will be of great influence in the future on the political and economic decisions of other countries.

Despite the extreme interest and importance of events in Eastern Europe in both the past and present, the area, as this survey indicates, has not been adequately studied. In the opinion of most of those who aided in the project, the two major reasons for this neglect are the immensity of the language problem and the previous preoccupation with Soviet studies. These hindrances are no longer the obstacles they once were. Universities and colleges are showing growing interest in the area for both teaching and research; their demands for qualified instructors and scholars in the field cannot be satisfied by present graduate programs. Increased attention and support from the universities, the foundations, and the government are thus necessary if the needs of the nation are to be met for the next decade. The purpose of this survey is to indicate the strengths and weaknesses, the accomplishments and the failures in American training and scholarship, and to indicate the direction in which the participants in this project would like to see research and training in this field move in the future.

In 1965, the Joint Committee on Slavic Studies (JCSS) of the American Council of Learned Societies (ACLS) and the Social Science Research Council (SSRC) decided that a special effort should be made to examine the problems and needs in East Central and Southeast European studies in the United States. The JCSS, which had guided the development of Russian-Soviet studies in America, and which also was entrusted to perform the same function for the East European area, recognized that whereas Russian-Soviet studies had made great progress since 1945, the East European area lagged far behind in development and accomplishments. It became its purpose, therefore, to remedy this situation. Thus the JCSS appointed a Subcommittee on East Central and Southeast European Studies (SECSES)[2] whose goal was to be, according to Professor Chauncy Harris, then chairman of the JCSS:

> . . . to examine the state of American scholarship on the countries and cultures of East Central and Southeast Europe, and take leadership in planning the stimulation and development of such studies. Topics which might appropriately be considered are the state of present studies by discipline or by country, promising lines of development, desirable publications, opportunities for field research or study in the area, possibilities for American participation in international congresses, scope and nature of programs in universities, existing or desirable exchange programs, and critical needs of scholarship and scholars on the area.

2. The membership of SECSES has been as follows: John C. Campbell (Council on Foreign Relations), 1965– ; Istvan Deak (Columbia University), 1967– , William Harkins (Columbia University), 1967– ; George Hoffman (University of Texas), 1965– ; Andrzej Korbonski (University of California, Los Angeles), 1967– ; John M. Montias (Yale University), 1965–66; Alexander Schenker (Yale University), 1967– ; Edward Stankiewicz (University of Chicago), 1965–67; Benjamin Ward (University of California), 1966–67; Serge Yakobson (Library of Congress), 1965– ; and Charles Jelavich (Indiana University), 1965–68, chairman.

In April, 1965, SECSES met in Chicago to formulate its plans. The committee devoted considerable time to the question of which countries should be included in the survey. Those scholars who were primarily interested in the recent postwar developments which brought about the establishment of the people's democracies in Eastern Europe believed strongly that East Germany should be included and that Greece and European Turkey should not. On the other hand, those who looked at the area in historical perspective were equally firm in their conviction that these two states could not be omitted if one were to have a proper appreciation and understanding of the forces, factors, trends, and developments which conditioned the evolution of these lands. Therefore, it was agreed to include Greece, European Turkey, and East Germany wherever this seemed appropriate. SECSES then concluded that it should make its own brief introductory survey of the problems and needs of the area. Subsequently, with the information from this preliminary study, the committee drafted a project which had four basic goals. They were to prepare (1) a survey of graduate training and research needs, (2) an evaluation of the role of East European studies in undergraduate instruction, (3) a survey of "the state of the art" in fifteen disciplines, and (4) a two-volume bibliographic and reference guide of 6,000 annotated titles. The American Council of Learned Societies submitted this proposal to the U.S. Office of Education, which endorsed it and agreed to subsidize it.

The project called for the completion of the surveys during the academic year 1966–67, whereas the bibliographic guides would not be ready until early 1969. In October, 1966, the survey directors met in New York to discuss the project, the approach to be used, and its implementation. It was agreed that because of the very uneven state of development among the fifteen disciplines to be surveyed, and their unique problems and needs, it was neither feasible nor possible to produce reports with identical formats. Nevertheless, it was decided that where possible the state-of-the-art survey should not only carefully examine American research in the disciplines, but should also make reference to some of the principal works of West European scholarship. In addition, if any of the East European countries had achieved notable successes in a discipline, this should be mentioned with reference to the appropriate work. The survey therefore was to be thorough in its American coverage, suggestive of Western European achievements, and indicative of any special scholarship in a particular East European state.

In addition, it was stressed that each survey should have, when possible, a brief sketch of the historical development of the discipline in the United States which would stress the state of our knowledge prior to 1941 and what has been achieved thereafter. Each author was then to indicate those areas, subjects, or topics which in his opinion required further investigation, and to suggest new areas for research. Moreover, each author was to make an evaluation of graduate training in his discipline and to recommend steps for its improvement and expansion. During the actual survey it became evident that these goals could not be entirely realized for all the disciplines. Therefore some changes were introduced, but essentially the survey has followed the plan as originally conceived.

It was also understood that no scholar could keep up with the publications and the developments in his own discipline for the entire area from Poland in the north to and including Greece and European Turkey in the south. Therefore each survey was conducted as a cooperative effort of interested scholars. Each survey director commissioned subreports on countries or regions from as many of his colleagues as necessary, which he then incorporated into his general report with the appropriate acknowledgment for the assistance given.

In connection with the reports on undergraduate instruction and graduate training and research, the two survey directors visited numerous colleges and universities to discuss the relevant problems with scholars, students, and university administrators. It was especially important to ascertain the interest of the universities themselves in the further expansion of East European studies and their willingness to give practical assistance in this direction. In addition, much similar information was solicited by correspondence.

Having decided on basic procedures, the committee adopted the following schedule. It was agreed that by March, 1967, each survey would be substantially completed. The directors then prepared a preliminary report, reproduced each in 150 copies and distributed them at the meeting of the American Association for the Advancement of Slavic Studies held in Washington, D.C., in April, 1967. Here our colleagues were requested to read these reports and to submit written observations and suggestions to the appropriate survey director which he could take into consideration in the preparation of his final report. The individual surveys were completed by November, 1967, and were then submitted for further evaluation to a conference of scholars and foundation and government officials in December, 1967, in New York. Thereafter the reports were edited for publication.

Special mention should be made of the bibliographic and reference guide, a monumental task. SECSES deplored the fact that our area of study did not have a standard bibliographic guide, which is the indispensable tool for the student, scholar, and librarian. There was adequate proof that the study of the area had suffered after 1945 at least

in part due to this lack. The preparation of a two-volume guide covering the social sciences and the humanities thus assumed the highest
priority. One volume is to be devoted to Southeastern Europe (the
Balkans) and the other to East Central Europe. The aim is to duplicate
for our area what has been achieved for the Russian-Soviet field by
the two excellent volumes, *Basic Russian Publications: A Selected and
Annotated Bibliography on Russia and the Soviet Union* (1962) and
*Russia and the Soviet Union: A Bibliographic Guide to Western-Lan-
guage Publications* (1965), both published by the University of Chicago
Press and edited by Dr. Paul Horecky, Assistant Chief and East European Specialist, Slavic and Central European Division, Library of Congress. SECSES has been most fortunate in securing Dr. Horecky as
editor of our volumes, which the University of Chicago Press will also
publish. The most encouraging aspect of this undertaking has been the
cooperation given by over 125 American and European scholars. In
fact, when this undertaking was announced, many scholars volunteered
their assistance, a response that attests to the need felt for a bibliographic and reference guide.

A word should also be said about what the project was unable to
accomplish or to undertake. The anticipated survey of library holdings,
and the deficiencies in this field, could not be carried out for many
reasons, the most important of which was the lack of the necessary financial support. However, a committee has been appointed to explore this
problem thoroughly and to make specific recommendations concerning what needs to be done and how it should be accomplished. In
addition, SECSES carefully considered the suggestion that the Baltic
states be included in our project. Although understanding fully the arguments in favor of the proposal, SECSES concluded that these states
did not fall within the sphere of its competence. There were also financial considerations. The question has also arisen why "the arts" in general were not a part of the survey. Given our resources, we had to
establish priorities, which meant that some disciplines, regretfully, had
to be omitted.

As editor of this volume and director of the survey, only I can fully
appreciate the importance of the cooperation given the committee by
our colleagues in the East European field.[3] Whatever merits this proj-

3. I spent several days at each of 14 universities. I discussed our project with
more than 115 scholars, administrators, and librarians at these institutions. Thirty
colleagues wrote extensive reports on the developments at their universities and
made valuable suggestions for our field. More than 125 answered general inquiries
or provided various kinds of statistical information. In addition, I was able to discuss our project with many interested individuals at a number of scholarly meetings during the past three years.

ect may have or whatever future benefits may derive from it is due to those who gave so generously of their time and effort, either by participating directly in the surveys or answering my numerous queries. Particular appreciation must be accorded to Dr. Gordon B. Turner, Vice-President, American Council of Learned Societies, for his constant assistance and encouragement. In the Office of Education, which recognized the urgent need for the survey and which subsidized it, we received valuable support and understanding from Mr. Albert S. Storm, Chief, Language Section, Instructional Materials and Practices Branch, Division of Higher Education Research, and Dr. Carl P. Epstein, Program Officer, Office of Education, Language and Area Research Section, the Institute of International Studies. The Joint Committee on Slavic Studies, under the chairmanship first of Professor Chauncy Harris, University of Chicago, and, subsequently, of Professor John M. Thompson, Indiana University, authorized and consistently supported this project. The burden of the technical aspects rested upon the secretary, Miss Helen McCauslin, who devoted many of her evenings and weekends to meeting various deadlines, preparing reports, and completing the many tasks associated with such an undertaking. Mrs. Ruth Hougland typed the entire manuscript with dispatch and great care. As usual, I express my deepest thanks to my wife, Barbara Jelavich, for her assistance which, among other things, included the reading of the manuscript and proofreading the volume.

In the transliteration of the Slavic languages, the Library of Congress system has been followed with minor modifications. Since this survey was completed in January 1968, it was not possible to obtain full and accurate statistical information for 1966–67. Some figures, however, were available and these are noted in the reports. Therefore most of the statistical data is valid only through 1965.

CHARLES JELAVICH

April 19, 1968

CONTRIBUTORS

CONRAD M. ARENSBERG, author of the chapter "Anthropology," is Professor of Anthropology, Columbia University. He has written "The Old World Peoples: The Place of European Peoples in World Ethnography," *Anthropological Quarterly* 36 (1963): 75–99, and, with Solon T. Kimball, *Culture and Community* (New York: Doubleday, 1965).

HOWARD I. ARONSON, author of the chapter "Survey of West and South Slavic Languages," is Associate Professor of Slavic Linguistics at the University of Chicago. He has published *Bulgarian Inflectional Morphophonology* (The Hague: Mouton, 1968) and "The Grammatical Categories of the Indicative in the Contemporary Bulgarian Literary Language," *To Honor Roman Jakobson* (The Hauge: Mouton, 1967).

DAVID E. BYNUM, co-author of the chapter "Folklore and Ethnomusicology," is Assistant Professor of Slavic Languages and Literatures, Harvard University. He has written "Kult dvaju junaka u kulturnoj istoriji Balkana," in *Anali filološkog fakulteta* (Belgrade: Rad, 1966), and "Themes of the Young Hero in Serbocroatian Oral Epic Tradition," *PMLA* (1968).

JOHN C. CAMPBELL, author of the chapter "International Relations," is a Senior Research Fellow in the Council on Foreign Relations, New York. He has written *American Policy toward Communist Eastern Europe* (Minneapolis: University of Minnesota Press, 1965) and *Tito's Separate Road: America and Yugoslavia in World Politics* (New York and Evanston: Harper & Row, 1967).

PAUL DEMENY, author of the chapter "Demography," is Associate Professor of Economics, University of Michigan. He is the co-author, with A. J. Coale, of *Regional Model Life Tables and Stable Populations* (Princeton: Princeton University Press, 1966) and *Methods of Estimating Basic Demographic Measures from Incomplete Data* (New York: United Nations, 1967).

KAZIMIERZ GRZYBOWSKI, author of the chapter "Law," is Professor of Law at Duke University. He has written *The Socialist Commonwealth of Nations, Organizations and Institutions* (New Haven: Yale University Press, 1964) and *Soviet Private International Law* (Leyden: A. W. Sijthoff, 1965).

WILLIAM E. HARKINS, author of the chapter "Literature," is Chairman of the Department of Slavic Languages and Professor of Slavic Languages, Columbia University. He has written *A Modern Czech Grammar* (New York: King's Crown Press, 1953) and *Karel Čapek* (New York: Columbia University Press, 1962).

GEORGE W. HOFFMAN, author of the chapter "Geography," is Chairman of the Committee of Eastern European Studies and Professor of Geography, University of Texas, Austin. He has written *Balkans in Transition* (Princeton: D. Van Nostrand, 1963), and he is editor of *A Geography of Europe*, 3d ed. (New York: Ronald Press, 1939).

BARBARA JELAVICH, co-author of the chapter "History," is Professor of History, Indiana University. She has written *A Century of Russian Foreign Policy, 1814–1914* (Philadelphia: J. B. Lippincott, 1964) and *Russia and the Greek Revolution of 1843* (Munich: R. Oldenbourg, 1966).

CHARLES JELAVICH, author of the chapter "Graduate Training and Research Needs," co-author of the chapter "History," and director of this survey, is Professor of History, Indiana University. He is the author of *Tsarist Russia and Balkan Nationalism, 1879–1886* (Berkeley and Los Angeles: University of California Press, 1958) and, with Barbara Jelavich, *The Balkans* (Englewood Cliffs, N.J.: Prentice-Hall, 1965).

KOSTAS KAZAZIS, author of chapter 18, on the non-Slavic languages, is Assistant Professor of Balkan Linguistics, University of Chicago. He has written "On a Generative Grammar of the Balkan Languages," *Foundations of Language* 3 (1967), 117–23, and, with F. W. Householder and Andreas Koutsoudas, *Reference Grammar of Literary Dhimotiki* (The Hague: Mouton, 1964).

GEORGE L. KLINE, author of the chapter "Philosophy," is Professor of Philosophy at Bryn Mawr College. He has contributed "Leszek Kołakowski and the Revision of Marxism," in George L. Kline, ed., *European Philosophy Today* (Chicago: Quadrangle Books, 1965), pp. 113–63, and *Religious and Anti-Religious Thought in Russia* (Chicago: University of Chicago Press, 1968).

LYMAN H. LEGTERS, author of the chapter "Undergraduate Instruction," is Associate Director of the Far Eastern and Russian Institute and Professor of Slavic Studies, University of Washington, Seattle. He has contributed "Karl Radek als Sprachrohr des Bolschewismus," *Forschungen zur osteuropäischen Geschichte* 7 (1959): 1–128, and *Research in the Social Sciences and Humanities* (Santa Barbara: American Bibliographical Center/Clio Press, 1967).

ALBERT B. LORD, co-author of the chapter "Folklore and Ethnomusicology," is Professor of Slavic and Comparative Literature and Honorary Curator of the Milman Parry Collection, Harvard University. He is the author of *Singer of Tales* (Cambridge: Harvard University Press, 1960) and *Serbo-Croatian Heroic Songs*, 2 vols. (Cambridge, Mass., and Belgrade, Yugoslavia: Harvard University Press and the Serbian Academy of Sciences, 1953–54).

IRWIN T. SANDERS, author of the chapter "Sociology," is Vice-President, Education and World Affairs, New York. He is the author of *Balkan Village* (Lexington: University of Kentucky Press, 1958) and editor of the volume *Collectivization of Agriculture in Eastern Europe* (Lexington: University of Kentucky Press, 1958).

NICOLAS SPULBER, author of the chapter "Economics," is Professor of Economics and Fellow of the International Development Research Center, Indiana University. He has written *The Soviet Economy: Structure, Principles, Problems* (New York: W. W. Norton, 1962) and *Soviet Strategy for Economic Growth* (Bloomington: Indiana University Press, 1964).

EDWARD STANKIEWICZ, author of the chapter "Linguistics," is Chairman of the Department of Slavic Languages and Literatures and Professor of Slavic and General Linguistics, University of Chicago. He is the author of *Selected Bibliography of Slavic Linguistics*, vol. 1 (The Hague: Mouton, 1966) and *Declension and Gradation of Russian Substantives* (The Hague: Mouton, 1968).

MILOŠ VELIMIROVIĆ, author of the chapter "Musicology," is Professor of History of Music, School of Music, University of Wisconsin. He has published *Byzantine Elements in Early Slavic Chant* in Monumenta Musicae Byzantinae, 2 vols. (Copenhagen: Ejnar Munksgaard, 1960) and "Liturgical Drama in Byzantium and Russia," *Dumbarton Oaks Papers* 16 (1962): 351–58.

PAUL E. ZINNER, author of the chapter "Political Science," is Chairman of the Department of Political Science and Professor of Political Science, University of California, Davis. He is the author of *Revolution in Hungary* (New York: Columbia University Press, 1962) and *Communist Strategy and Tactics in Czechoslovakia, 1918–1948* (New York: Praeger, 1963).

1/ GRADUATE TRAINING AND RESEARCH NEEDS

Charles Jelavich

Indiana University

DEVELOPMENT OF EAST CENTRAL AND SOUTHEAST EUROPEAN STUDIES

BACKGROUND

American interest in East Central and Southeastern Europe almost spans the life of the American republic. After gaining their own independence in a war against an imperial power, the American people looked with sympathy upon the attempts of others to win their political freedom. Following the successful revolts in South America, attention turned back to Europe and centered on the national movements within the Russian, Ottoman, Habsburg, and Prussian-German empires. First, in 1821, when the Greeks rose against the Turks, American intellectuals and statesmen, recalling the debt of Western civilization to classical Greece, strongly supported aid to the rebellion. With the conclusion of this event in the establishment of independent Greece, interest next turned to the fate of Poland, which had been partitioned at about the time that America gained her independence. The association of the name of Kościuszko with the American struggle was an added bond of attachment. Similarly, the Hungarian revolution of 1848–49 awakened real sympathy; Kossuth on his subsequent visit to the United States was received with warmth and enthusiasm.

The close ties of the American and British academic and intellectual worlds, particularly before World War I, also served as an introduction for Americans to the problems of East Central and Southeastern Europe. Prominent statesmen and historians, in particular, W. E. Gladstone, became interested in the fate of the subject nationalities, especially those of the Ottoman and Habsburg Empires. The books of two

1

writers, R. W. Seton-Watson and Henry Wickham Steed, who were concerned with the Habsburg Empire, became well known in the United States. Thus the American student, both through his past history and his association with England, was first introduced to eastern Europe through the problems of its national minorities. More interest was shown in the struggle of these groups against the dominant nations and institutions than in the policies, organization, and reasons for existence of the great imperial states. This approach predominated in American writing, particularly in history, until the recent period.

The first graduate studies in the area were given at Harvard under the direction of Professor Archibald Cary Coolidge. Two of his first students were Robert J. Kerner and Robert H. Lord, who wrote dissertations on Bohemia and on Poland, respectively. The first doctorate in Slavic Languages and Literatures was granted by Harvard to George Rapall Noyes, who studied with Professor Leo Wiener. Noyes subsequently went to Berkeley, where he introduced courses in all of the Slavic languages. Specializing in Polish, he translated into English the great Polish authors, and also Serbian ballads and Russian plays. Thus by 1914 American academic interest, although small, was nevertheless present.

World War I, the peace settlements, and the events of the interwar period stimulated further interest in the area. In examining the background of the war, scholars inevitably were led to a closer examination of two aspects — the tangled diplomatic controversies after the Congress of Berlin and the problem of nationalism. Thus the events leading to the assassination at Sarajevo became one of the most thoroughly studied problems in modern history. At the same time, the emergence, revival, or enlargement of the new nations — Albania, Bulgaria, Czechoslovakia, Greece, Hungary, Yugoslavia, Poland, Romania, and Turkey — appeared to justify the idealism of those who felt that a national-liberal political solution in Central and Southeastern Europe would provide an answer to the area's basic problems. In particular, the creation of Czechoslovakia, under the leadership of Thomas G. Masaryk, awakened great hopes. Attention was thus devoted to the origins, development, and foreign policy of these states. History and language courses on both the graduate and undergraduate level were expanded. Robert J. Kerner at the University of California, Carlton J. H. Hayes and Philip Mosely at Columbia, S. Harrison Thomson at the University of Colorado, and William L. Langer at Harvard were prominent in encouraging this development.

Again in 1939 the world became engaged in a war whose immediate causes involved issues in this area. The Munich crisis, the invasion of Poland, the subsequent Nazi occupation, and the final victory of socialism in all of these states except Greece and Turkey, made it essential that American knowledge of these nations be widened and deepened. Thus when the American universities moved to meet public, student, academic, and governmental needs by creating institutes and centers for the study of Soviet Russia, in most instances Eastern Europe was included in these organizations. The chief reason behind this decision was the recognition of the necessity of immediately learning as much as possible about communist societies. The international tensions of the Stalin period made this also appear to be a question of national security.

Given the needs, resources, and feelings of the time, the decision to combine East Central and Southeast European studies with those of the Soviet Union was logical and understandable. Moreover, the programs were successful given their purpose at the time. Today, two decades after World War II, our knowledge of Eastern Europe, when compared to that before the war, has indeed increased. The study of East Central and Southeastern Europe is now an accepted part of the academic curriculum of many universities. In addition, every language of the area — modern Greek, Turkish, Albanian, Bulgarian, Serbo-Croatian, Macedonian, Slovene, Hungarian, Romanian, Slovak, Czech, Polish, and even Sorbian — has been taught. Several of these languages have been offered on a yearly basis for over a decade at about six universities.

This development, as well as the association with Soviet studies, has, however, brought up several questions which will be examined in the following pages. Two fundamental problems must be studied. First, do the countries included here — Albania, Bulgaria, Czechoslovakia, Greece, Hungary, Poland, Romania, and Yugoslavia (leaving aside the more controversial question of East Germany and European Turkey) — possess the prerequisites necessary for their inclusion in a single area program in the generally accepted definition of the term? Second, if they do, should these lands be studied in conjunction with the Russian-Soviet programs?

AREA PROGRAMS

A major development in American education has been the introduction of the area programs which now exist for Russia, the Moslem world, Africa, Asia, Southeast Asia, Latin America, and even Western Europe. According to P. E. Mosely, the purpose of these centers is "to help people see a society, a system of power, or an economy or all three interacting together as they do in real life, and to see them both in their interconnections and as a whole." [1] It has been pointed out that although the concerted emphasis on area studies is new, the concept is not. Every child when studying his own country's development, experiences the area approach. He does this by studying all aspects of his nation's past. Moreover,

> . . . for several centuries the interdisciplinary study of ancient Greece and Rome provided the central core for the training of minds in the west, and classical training has today a high prestige in Britain and France. In addition to mastering grammar and vocabulary, a student of the classics must understand the philosophy and logic, the literature and history, the political, economic and social institutions, the religious beliefs and military strategies of the ancient world, and, above all, the interconnections among them. The peculiar feature of classical studies is that they deal with a civilization which in its fully developed form seemed relatively stable for several centuries and which can no longer be studied *in situ* today. In contrast, area studies aim to study and interpret living societies, all of which are developing, some slowly, some tempestuously, but none without profound implications for the future of mankind. [2]

In order for a group of countries to be constituted into an "area," it is essential that they have a common denominator, which may be ethnic, religious, geographic, historic, linguistic, or cultural. The overwhelming majority of the American scholars consulted agree that the one unifying theme connecting the states covered in this survey lies in the postwar establishment of communist regimes. Only at this time were the political destinies and development of these peoples bound so tightly together that there is real justification in joining such disparate countries as, for instance, Albania and Poland or Bulgaria and Czechoslovakia, into a single unit for research and study. This view explains the inclusion of East Germany, but it makes necessary the exclusion of Greece and European Turkey from the "area."

However, the majority of the scholars consulted who specialize primarily on these lands do not agree that the events of the past two decades are the best foundation for the organization of the field. They thus oppose the linking of East Central and Southeastern European studies with those of Soviet Russia. The arguments used stress the fact that the decisive influences exerted in the past have come from other

1. In Harold H. Fisher, ed., *American Research on Russia* (Bloomington: Indiana University Press, 1959), p. 10.
2. *Ibid.*, p. 11.

directions. For the Balkans, Byzantine and Ottoman traditions far outweigh in importance those of Russia; East Central Europe developed in close touch with the great movements of Western Europe — the Renaissance, the Reformation, the Enlightenment, and the industrial revolution. Cultural patterns in Europe moved from west to east, not vice versa. Moreover, once the bond of communism is removed, it is difficult to find a substitute tie linking all of these states together. Religion has been a dividing not a unifying influence. Language has been even more of a problem. In August, 1966, the First International Congress of Balkan Studies was held in Sofia. Here the five accepted languages were English, French, German, Italian, and Russian — but not one Balkan language. In August, 1967, a conference at Bratislava on the Ausgleich of 1867 recognized English, French, German, and Russian, but not Polish, Czech, Slovak, Hungarian, Romanian, Slovene, or Serbo-Croatian, the languages of the majority of the people of the Habsburg Empire.

Because of this lack of a central force, most of the participants in the survey believe that it is preferable to regard these lands as comprising three regions for study rather than one.[3] Although there is disagreement on the exact boundaries, the divisions usually suggested are: (1) the Balkans (Southeastern Europe), (2) East Central Europe (the former Habsburg lands), (3) Poland, either alone or in combination with Czechoslovakia. Even this organization presents great problems. The overlapping of the boundaries of these fields is obvious. For example, Croatia and Slovenia, although a part of Yugoslavia today, were for centuries historically allied with Austria or Hungary, or both. Their historical evolution is thus central European and Adriatic, not Byzantine-Ottoman. Poland, because of her role in European, Baltic, and Russian history, represents an integral unit. Yet this state is closely tied to the developments in the Habsburg and Prussian (German) lands.

Of the external influences exerted upon all three of these regions, there is general agreement that with the exception of the last two decades, that of Russia has been the least significant. In only two countries,

3. When faculty members were asked which was the best approach to graduate study in the field, twenty-two scholars advocated the regional approach, three preferred to emphasize a region-nation combination, and six thought the training should be on a nation alone. On the other hand, twelve scholars chose the area approach, and three favored some form of area-region combination. In other words, thirty-one preferred the narrower region-nation program and fifteen chose the broader area emphasis. Twelve colleagues made other suggestions or did not answer this question.

In reply to the same question, graduate students also preferred the regional emphasis, but on a closer numerical basis. Twenty advocated the regional-national combination, but fifteen stressed the area-region emphasis.

Poland and Bulgaria, is Russian influence of any real significance in comparison with that of the Western nations. In Poland, the people in general looked unfavorably upon their association with Russia and tended to reject whatever came from the east. Although the Bulgarians, particularly in the pre-liberation period, were more favorably disposed toward Russia, the principal influence on their national life was Byzantine-Ottoman. In the case of other nations, for instance Hungary and Albania, the association with Russia becomes comparatively even more tenuous.

In the circumstances previously described, those participating in the survey agree in general that the organization of East Central and Southeast European studies must depend on what the individual university or institute intends to accomplish. Two alternatives are possible. First, if a university wishes to develop an area program centered on communist societies, then it is logical and desirable that East Europe be associated with Russia. In this case, East Germany should be included in the countries studied but Greece and European Turkey should be excluded. This approach also has certain advantages for those specializing in Slavic linguistics or Slavic literatures where the association with Russian is natural. Second, if, in contrast, the purpose is the training of students and scholars in depth and in historical perspective, then East Central and Southeastern Europe should be administered as an autonomous unit. This division was put into effect in 1954 at Columbia University, where the disadvantages of the combination with Russian studies were recognized from the beginning. From the point of view of the number of students trained, the Institute on East Central Europe at Columbia has been the most successful in the United States. Indiana University and the University of Washington have both recently established autonomous East European programs within their institutes.

However, even if the autonomous area program is accepted, the problem remains of the organization of a program covering nations which, as explained before, do not together form a true "area." Again most of those consulted favored the three-part division described earlier. Since it was recognized that few institutions could afford a program covering all three regions, it was believed best that one of the three regions be selected for specialization. Although general survey courses should be given covering all three, graduate teaching, library acquisitions, and scholarly research should center in one. This unity of approach was considered superior to a program which included, for instance, specialists in Polish history, Czech literature, Greek folklore, Yugoslav geography, and Romanian sociology.

Some of those consulted presented strong arguments in favor of yet another solution. They cited the example of several universities which have developed strong programs concentrating on one country rather than on a region or the entire field. Poland and Yugoslavia, the two countries which receive the greatest attention in the United States, are particularly good choices for the national approach. There was also some sentiment expressed that, despite the financial hindrances, there should be at least three area programs, but preferably six — two in the east, two in the midwest, and two in the west — which would encompass all of the ten states in this survey.

In summary, it will be seen that unlike the Russian area there is no agreement among those specializing in East Central and Southeastern Europe on the advisability or possibility of a single area program. Because of the diversity of the region and its historical evolution, most of those consulted believe that each institution should decide what it wishes to emphasize, and then it should formulate a program to meet its individual needs. In short, there are three acceptable choices. First, if the emphasis is on present politics, an area program in association with Soviet studies is feasible. Second, if the study of communist societies is a secondary consideration, then the adoption of a program based on the entire area but with emphasis on one of the three regions (Balkans, Habsburg, or Poland) is recommended. Survey courses for the entire area should be taught, but research and graduate teaching should center in one. Third, in some circumstances, a university may prefer to develop an intensive program in one country.

In addition to the question of area organization, certain other problems have arisen in the postwar decades. How they were met and the successes or failures will be summarized in the next section.

Weakness and Successes in the Postwar Period: Deficiencies

In reviewing the postwar years, satisfaction can be expressed over some of the achievements, which have been indeed impressive, but these accomplishments are overshadowed by the problems and deficiencies which still impede the progress and development of East Central and Southeast European studies. First and foremost is the fact that relatively few scholars have been trained in this field. The figures available are in part misleading. Statistics are hard to acquire; in many instances they were not kept. It is often difficult to distinguish the East European from the Russian specialist. Nevertheless, it appears that between 1945 and 1965, 53 doctorates were awarded in history, 38 in linguistics, 24 in political science, 23 in economics, 16 in international relations, 11 in literature, 7 in sociology, 5 in law, 2 in anthropology, 1 in geography and 4 in other disciplines, or a total of 184.[4] Although again no exact figures are available, it is known that a number of other specialists were trained in each of the following disciplines — anthropology, ethno-musicology, folklore, geography, musicology, and philosophy. When it is remembered that the economists, the political scientists, and to a certain extent those in international relations, are primarily concerned with the postwar period, these figures show the poor state of general East European studies. The scarcity of scholars in literature, a condition which is true also for the Russian-Soviet field, is particularly regrettable because of the importance of this subject for an understanding of the people of the area. Without an increase in the number of students trained, the area cannot expand in the manner it should.

The second major problem concerns the lack of attention given to the non-Slavic people — the Albanians, Greeks, Hungarians, and Romanians. The case of Greece is particularly revealing. Because Greece did not become a communist country, it has been virtually excluded from the programs on East Central and Southeastern Europe. Yet from a historical point of view, through Byzantium, the Orthodox church, trade and commerce, and the position of the Greeks in the Ottoman Empire, these people have exerted more influence on Southeastern Europe than any other in the Balkans.

The study of all the non-Slavic nations has suffered from the difficulties encountered by their languages in finding a "home" in the academic organization of most universities. For years it has been a major question which department should handle Albanian, Greek, Hungarian, and Romanian. Little enthusiasm has been shown by any of the accepted language departments in acquiring a new addition. The classicists appear little interested in modern Greece or even in having modern Greek taught. Romance language departments tend to regard Romanian as exotic and a luxury. Some have even refused to accept it in their curriculum when outside funds were available. Hungarian was virtually ignored until 1956, when it suddenly became an important language. Uralic-Altaic departments were subsequently expanded at Columbia and Indiana. Although these centers are to be welcomed, they have had in part the effect of removing Hungary from inclusion in the East European area organization. Albania has, for all practical purposes, been totally ignored. Recently the problem of introducing these languages into the university programs has in some instances been solved by the creation of a department of linguistics. Nevertheless, even with these de-

4. See table 2 in Appendix at end of this chapter.

velopments, the languages of one-third of the people of the area are not adequately studied.

Third, library resources are still very weak for the majority of the countries. Although Berkeley, Columbia, and Harvard in the prewar years acquired respectable holdings for Czechoslovakia, Yugoslavia, and Poland — at least in history and literature — the collections for the other states were extremely weak or almost nonexistent. The situation has not improved much in the past two decades for several reasons. First, library funds are restricted and those available have usually been directed toward building up Russian-Soviet collections. Second, with the exception of Greece and Yugoslavia, it was difficult to purchase books from these countries for about a decade or longer after the war. Third, prewar publications have disappeared from the market, and some states have introduced laws prohibiting their export. After 1956 the situation improved with respect to Poland and Hungary, but only recently for Romania and Bulgaria. In the case of Albania, the situation has remained the same. The fourth major problem for the libraries has been that of the personnel needed to order, process, and catalog the works from these countries. Here again the Slavic collections have fared better, since a Russian librarian with a little extra effort can handle books in the other Slavic languages. In contrast, the non-Slavic people require a specialist for each language, a luxury which few libraries could ever hope to afford. Although it has not been possible to make a systematic survey of library holdings for these countries, the general information made available confirms that Czechoslovakia, Yugoslavia, and Poland are the best represented. It should be noted, however, that there are two outstanding collections on modern Greece, one at Harvard and the other at the University of Cincinnati.

Fourth, although the universities, foundations, and the federal government have contributed large sums to the development of Russian and East European studies, most of the money has been used for the Russian-Soviet field. This result has not been because of any direct policy of curtailing funds for Eastern Europe or of discriminating against it. On the contrary, various attempts have been made to encourage East European studies, but the field has simply been overshadowed by the international, political, and academic considerations of the Russian area. Moreover, because of the restricted language requirement and the better library and research resources, scholars in the Russian field have been trained more rapidly, have obtained good university positions, have published substantially. Consequently, their applications for fellowships, grants-in-aid, etc., are often more impressive than those of their colleagues in the East Central and Southeast

European area, who work under severe handicaps. In addition, most of the committees established to administer fellowships, grants, and development funds for Russia and Eastern Europe are made up largely of scholars specializing in the Russian-Soviet field. They are understandably in a better position to evaluate a project in their own area than one dealing, for example, with some aspect of Romanian land tenure in the nineteenth century. East Central and Southeast European studies have thus not received the kind of encouragement given to Russian studies in their great period of development after the war. As a consequence, East European studies, even in the most advanced disciplines — history, economics, and political science — have only reached the stage attained by Russian studies in 1955. In other fields the date would be closer to 1950. Our area thus lags more than a decade behind Russian-Soviet studies.

Fifth, the area also suffered because of the curtailment of funds for bibliographic aids. For example, the Library of Congress formerly published the excellent *East European Accessions List*, a companion to the *Monthly List of Russian Accessions*. However, this bibliography only survived ten years before budgetary considerations eliminated it. This was a serious blow to the librarians and scholars in the field.

Sixth, the *Journal of Central European Affairs*, which had been the principal outlet for articles on history, politics, and international relations for twenty-five years, suspended publication in 1964. Although several new publications have now appeared which will fill the need, the area nevertheless was without a journal at the time when interest was increasing and a place was needed where the results of research could be published.

Seventh, in the past four or five years an increasing number of colleges and universities have been willing to commit themselves to expansion in this area but have been discouraged by the lack of qualified candidates for positions. In history, the most developed discipline, there were about a dozen positions open for either Habsburg or Balkan historians in 1965–66 and 1966–67, but only two or three were actually filled by candidates specifically trained in these fields.

ACCOMPLISHMENTS

In contrast to the negative aspects, there are also a considerable number of positive achievements. First, because of the emphasis which has been placed on the Russian language and the general requirement that Russian linguists know two Slavic languages, all the Slavic languages are now taught, although not always on a regular basis. Most popular are Polish and Serbo-Croatian, followed by Czech, with Bulgarian far behind. Even though Russian is taught regularly through the third or fourth year, the other Slavic languages are usually offered only for one year, irregularly for two. This trend is due to the fact that it is believed possible to learn the other Slavic languages in one or two semesters if the student has already had three or four years of Russian. Most institutions have, however, indicated an interest in adding language instructors in Polish, Czech, and Serbo-Croatian.

Second, and closely related to the expansion of the teaching of the major Slavic languages, is the rise in interest in the other languages. In fact, all the major and minor languages of the area have been taught at some time within the last five years — that is, modern Greek, Albanian, Macedonian, Slovene, Hungarian, Romanian, Slovak, Sorbian, and Kashubian. Although these have often been organized principally to fulfill the requirements of the linguist, they are also, of course, of value to the area.

Third, at least twenty universities in the postwar period have committed themselves to the establishment of substantial programs or course offerings in the area. Three of these, Columbia, Indiana, and Washington, seek to cover the entire field. Nine others emphasize the Balkans, six the Habsburg lands and Poland-Czechoslovakia. In some instances there is an overlapping of regions and no clearly defined area of concentration.

In addition, a number of colleges and private liberal arts institutions have developed special summer programs or study tours involving some of these countries, especially Yugoslavia. An increasing number of our most talented graduate students are coming from these institutions.

Fourth, closely connected with the expansion of interest in the area are the excellent opportunities now available for positions for students trained in the field. Those concerned with university administration and placement believe that the prospects for the future will continue to be excellent. Based upon the Columbia and Indiana figures, the majority of those with degrees enter teaching (63 percent with an M.A.; 76 percent with a Ph.D.), but other occupations are also open. The government employed 15 percent of the M.A.'s and 6 percent of the Ph.D.'s. The remaining 18 percent with Ph.D.'s entered such fields as journalism, radio and television, business, private research, the army, law, and library work.[5]

5. It is important, however, to stress that when students were asked what was their career goal, 84 percent indicated research and teaching. Only one, because he believed there were limited teaching opportunities in this field, specifically

Fifth, the American cultural exchange agreements with Bulgaria, Czechoslovakia, and Hungary, in existence since 1963, have been a great stimulus to interest in the area. Now a young scholar cannot only visit these countries, but he can carry on a research program for a semester or a year. This program should be expanded to include Poland and Romania.

Sixth, the Ford Foundation program for Hungary, Yugoslavia, and Poland, has brought many scholars from these countries to study and carry on research in the United States. They have been able to lecture, conduct seminars, and lead discussions on East European problems, especially on the faculty level.

Seventh, a number of American universities have established regular programs in which foreign scholars are invited for a year to give courses and seminars. Chicago has visiting professors in language and literature from Poland. Indiana has a similar arrangement with Hungary and Yugoslavia. Washington has visiting professors in geography from Poland. This practice has been adopted by other institutions on a semester basis. It is especially valuable in the field of literature where American scholars are few. This exchange could be expanded to include other universities and additional countries.

Eighth, one of the most encouraging aspects of the field has been the sudden increase in publication outlets. In fact, in this question the specialist in our area now enjoys certain advantages over his colleagues in the Russian-Soviet field. Not only can he submit material to journals in the United States and Western Europe, but also to certain publications in Eastern Europe. Previously, from 1939 to 1964, the principal publication for the area in the United States was the *Journal of Central European Affairs*, edited by S. Harrison Thomson at the University of Colorado. It published articles in the social sciences and the humanities. The *Slavic Review* (formerly the *American Slavic and East European Review*) also accepted contributions in the field, although the emphasis has always been more on East Europe as a part of Russian-Soviet or Slavic studies. The suspension of publication of the *Journal of Central European Affairs* in 1964 was greatly regretted and for a short time the need for a replacement was acutely felt. Now new journals are appearing, emphasizing different aspects of the area or individual countries.

The first new publication was the *Austrian History Yearbook*, which is devoted to the study of the Habsburg lands. Particularly im-

stressed government service. The other students were not precise in their replies. For placement statistics, see table 7.

portant is volume 3, published in three parts in 1967–69, which contains a thoroughgoing review of the nationality problem of the empire.

In 1967 and 1968, several other new journals commenced publication. The *East European Quarterly*, published at the University of Colorado, appeared in 1967. It has an international editorial board and publishes in English, French, and German. In 1968, the Conference Group on Central European History of the American Historical Association introduced *Central European History*. The emphasis here is to be on German and Habsburg history. On the individual countries, one publication, the *Polish Review*, has been in existence since 1956; this will be joined in 1969 by the *Journal of Rumanian Studies*. The Center for Neo-Hellenic Studies at the University of Texas is considering a similar publication for modern Greece. In addition, the *Journal of Asian History*, which appeared for the first time in 1967, publishes articles dealing with Ottoman domination in Eastern Europe and on general questions of eastern influence on European developments. Another new journal, *Canadian Slavic Studies*, which appeared first in 1967, emphasizes East Europe as well as the Russian field. A regular bibliographical section devoted to new publications in Eastern Europe is included. This will, to some extent, replace the loss occasioned by the suspension of the *East European Accessions List*.

In addition, the submission of articles by American scholars continues to be welcomed by the *Slavonic and East European Review* (London), *Canadian Slavonic Papers* (Toronto), *Südost Forschungen* (Munich), *Jahrbücher für Geschichte Osteuropas* (Munich), *Forschungen zur osteuropäischen Geschichte* (Berlin), *Österreichische Osthefte* (Vienna), and *Balkan Studies* (Thessaloniki). Further, in 1963 the Romanian journal *Revue d'études sud-est européenne* and in 1964 the Bulgarian *Etudes balkaniques* appeared. Both journals accept articles in French, German, or English submitted from abroad. The scholar in the area thus has a wide choice of publication opportunities, both in the United States and Europe.

GRADUATE TRAINING

The survey on graduate training covers three topics: (1) the training of those who are now scholars or graduate students in the field, (2) the subjects, regions, and disciplines which have been emphasized, and (3) the hindrances and difficulties encountered which limit the expansion and development of graduate studies. In conclusion, recommendations for improvement are given. The generalizations in this section are based on statistics provided by the universities, information solicited from scholars and students, and from interviews throughout the country with those concerned with these problems. Specific questions were asked of 77 faculty members, of whom 61 replied, that is, 80 percent, and of 84 graduate students, of whom 44 answered, or 52 percent.

In a discussion of the programs of study followed by graduate students, a distinction must be drawn between two groups. First, those who entered East Central and Southeast European studies immediately after the war suffered from all of the disadvantages associated with an underdeveloped area. They were trained in a discipline, but they did not have available to them a selection of courses, colloquia, and seminars in the East European field. Nor was any kind of area training offered. The emphasis in their course selections for their graduate studies thus of necessity fell outside of the field, chiefly on subjects related to Russia, Germany, or international relations. Upon obtaining positions in a university, they developed their own courses on the basis of published material, often largely obtained from these countries. Many in this group received their complete graduate training in other areas and subsequently began research and teaching in the East European area.

A second group, usually the students of the first, has not met as many difficulties as those encountered by their teachers. Those now in the area have the benefit of more lecture courses, colloquia, and seminars in their own discipline and in the area. The libraries have increased their holdings and more books have been written which aid graduate students. Languages are also taught on a wider basis. However, in many respects these students are following in the path of their predecessors. The emphasis remains on the discipline, and East Central and Southeast European Studies are still at most institutions closely associated with Russian and Soviet programs.[6] In other words, the problem of balancing Western, Central European, and Byzantine-Ottoman influences against those of Russia has been improved, but not adequately met.

Moreover, despite the increase of courses, the number offered does not meet the desires of the students in the area. It is just this condition which, in the opinion of many of those consulted, constitutes the major weakness in graduate training. Although the graduate student in the major centers does have courses, graduate colloquia, and seminars in his discipline, he would like a wider choice, more on individual nations, and,

6. See table 8 in Appendix at end of this chapter.

in history, more emphasis on social, economic, and intellectual topics, with less on political developments. In general, the students are most concerned with the need for increased course offerings in their own discipline, rather than in others.[7]

With the lack of choice within his own field, the student must thus make selections in other areas. Because of the close association of the East European with the Russian-Soviet field at most universities, he usually prefers, or is compelled by departmental regulations, to select Russian subjects instead of those dealing with Western Europe, even when the latter may have more relevance to his particular field of interest. The lack of an adequate number of course offerings thus reinforces the position of East European studies as a kind of adjunct to the Russian area.

In language training, a central part of the graduate student's program, it is apparent that a great majority receive their first introduction to languages of the area in graduate school, unless, of course, they have learned one at home or are natives of the country in question. Most graduate students come equipped with either French, the first language, German, the second, or Russian, the third. In graduate school, they must usually learn, in addition to the language of their major interest, another of the three major languages because of university requirements for a doctorate. This problem will be discussed in greater detail later.

The Emphasis in Graduate Training

The postwar programs were not directed primarily toward East Central and Southeastern Europe. Only from Columbia, the single university which has had an autonomous East European Institute since 1954, do we have anything resembling adequate, detailed statistics. Other institutions — for example, Chicago, Indiana, and Washington — have turned to this area only in the last decade. Their information is thus of more limited value. The following discussion is thus based on the statistics provided primarily by Chicago, Colorado, Columbia, Illinois, Indiana, Michigan, Princeton, Stanford, Washington, and Wisconsin. Figures were not available for Berkeley, and the Harvard report was incomplete. Nevertheless, from even these limited sources, certain conclusions can be made concerning the disciplines and regions which have drawn the most attention in graduate study in the postwar years.

As shown in table 1 (see Appendix at end of this chapter), in the two

7. See table 9.

decades from 1946 to 1965, 375 M.A. degrees were awarded. From 1956 to 1965 Columbia alone awarded 149 M.A. degrees. If the preceding decade is considered (when the figures overlap with those of the Russian area), an additional 127 could be added to make a total of 276. During these two decades, only 99 degrees were given at Chicago, Illinois, Indiana, Stanford, Wisconsin, and Washington. Even if figures were available from Berkeley and Harvard, the clear superiority of Columbia would be little reduced. Of the M.A.'s awarded at the reporting institutions between 1956 and 1965, 50 were in international relations and 68 in history — that is, 54 percent of the total were given in these two related disciplines. Political science was represented with 24 (11 percent), economics with 22 (10 percent), linguistics with 22 (10 percent), and literature with 21 (9 percent). Anthropology, ethnomusicology, folklore, geography, law, musicology, philosophy, and sociology collectively offered about 6 percent of the degrees conferred.

The figures for the doctorates granted (table 2), however, disclose a different pattern. In the period 1945–65, 184 Ph.D.'s have been awarded, with 75 granted at Columbia and 109 at the other universities reporting. However, it is possible to identify at least ten scholars (in folklore, geography, musicology, etc.) who gained degrees who were not trained at any of the reporting institutions. Columbia thus provided about 40 percent of the doctorates. In the percentages referring to the fields of specialization, the order remains much the same except for linguistics, which produced 38 Ph.D.'s,[8] and international relations, which had only 16 doctorates. History had 53 doctorates, political science 24, economics 23, literature 11, sociology 7, and law 5. The other disciplines were almost totally neglected.

From table 3, which refers to the country of specialization within each discipline, it is evident that the prewar emphasis on Poland and Yugoslavia remained constant. These two countries attracted 25 and 21 percent, respectively, of the students — or 46 percent of the total. Czechoslovakia and Hungary each had 14 percent. These four states attracted 74 percent of the students, whereas Greece, Bulgaria, Romania, Albania, and East Germany together only represent 26 percent. (European Turkey was not considered here.)

The figures not only reveal the countries which have gained the greatest attention, but they also show the importance of the language training available. Had it not been for the Hungarian revolution and the establishment of the Uralic-Altaic departments at Columbia and In-

---

8. During 1966 and 1967 an additional thirteen doctorates were awarded in linguistics.

diana, the three Slavic countries, Poland, Yugoslavia, and Czechoslovakia, would have dominated the area, largely because the languages of these nations are widely studied in connection with Russian. In contrast, the other languages are virtually ignored.

The lack of balance between the languages and the subordination of all of them to Russian is indicated in table 4, which lists the NDFL fellowships from 1959 to 1966. Here the weak position of the East European languages in comparison with Russian is most strikingly illustrated. Of the total of 1,497 awards to be divided among Albanian, Bulgarian, Greek, Hungarian, Polish, Romanian, Serbo-Croatian, and Russian, 1,228 (or 82 percent) were finally granted to Russian. There were only 66 grants given to Polish, 61 to Hungarian, and 56 for Serbo-Croatian — together about 12 percent of the total. Czech had 46 (or about 3 percent), whereas Albanian, Bulgarian, Greek, and Romanian had collectively only about 3 percent (Albanian 14, Bulgarian 5, Greek 8, and Romanian 13). These languages, then, excluding Russian, received 269 fellowships. In contrast, Turkish, under the NDFL program, received in the same period 137 awards — or more than half as many as all the East Central and Southeast European languages combined. These figures are a strong indication of why East European studies are so poorly developed. Language is the crucial question in graduate training in the field, yet little support has been received. Where grants have been awarded, the favored states, Poland, Czechoslovakia, Yugoslavia, and possibly Hungary, have received first support, with little left for Albania, Bulgaria, Greece, and Romania.

It will be noted in the above statistics that figures on area certificates have been omitted. As is discussed elsewhere, those who are participating in the survey agree that graduate and undergraduate students should be prepared thoroughly in a discipline, but at the same time they should be encouraged to choose widely among the electives in the field given in other departments. The limited appeal of the area certificate is shown in the figures which we have. For instance, using the example of Columbia and Indiana, where certificates are given in connection with the M.A. and Ph.D. programs, relatively few of those who have received degrees bothered about the certificate. Between 1956 and 1965, Columbia awarded 26 certificates. (There were perhaps an additional ten in the decade prior to 1955 when the records were kept in connection with those of the Russian Institute.) In the same period, however, 149 M.A.'s were awarded. In other words, only 17 percent of those obtaining the degree also received a certificate. At Indiana in the same period, only 8 certificates were given, in comparison to 40

M.A.'s, thus here the figure is 3 percent higher, or 20 percent.[9] These percentages also reflect the developments at other institutions. The area certificate has thus not received wide acceptance among graduate students.

Major Problems in Graduate Training

The principal difficulties encountered by graduate students are: (1) the need for many languages, (2) the inadequate library facilities and the difficulties in acquiring primary materials, (3) a lack of a sufficiently wide choice of courses in their own discipline, and (4) the lack of fellowship support in view of the difficulties in the field.[10] The length of time needed to complete the degree has also been mentioned. The first consideration, the fact that the graduate student in the field must acquire some three to five languages, presents major difficulties, particularly for the average American student who comes to graduate studies poorly prepared linguistically. Once he does commence courses, he meets added problems. The principal complaints of area students as opposed to those of linguistics students in the East Central and Southeast European field concern not only the lack of basic tools — that is, grammars, readers, dictionaries, tapes, etc. — but the type of instruction available. In the past the needs of the East European field have been too often regarded as identical to those of the Russian and Soviet area. Moreover, most language instruction for our area has been carried on in Slavic language departments where the emphasis is upon Russian, with the other languages occupying a secondary position. The larger demand for Russian is, of course, a logical explanation for this development, but it does not improve the position of the student in the East European field, who is now virtually compelled to learn Russian whether he needs it or not. Moreover, in most universities, not only are the other languages only taught for one or infrequently for two years, but the instruction often proceeds on the assumption that the student has taken Russian. In most cases the teacher is a Russian specialist with a lesser interest in the second language. The course is sometimes designed primarily with the interest of the linguist in mind. The area student without

9. If these same certificates are assessed in relation to the doctoral degrees awarded (and the information supplied did not indicate whether the certificate was awarded in conjunction with the M.A. or the Ph.D. or both), the percentages are higher, but still reveal a general lack of acceptance. Of the 75 Ph.D.'s at Columbia, only 34 percent received the certificate, although of the 17 Ph.D.'s at Indiana, 47 percent obtained the certificate.

10. See table 10.

a knowledge of Russian — or without a particular interest in linguistics — thus finds himself at an enormous disadvantage and is often not able to keep up with the course.

Moreover, many students have been led to believe that knowledge of Russian is the golden key to the East Central and Southeast European area, and that their major language problems are solved once they have learned it. Not only is this not true, but the graduate student should understand that Russian is not even the most important of the languages for the area. Forty scholars working in the East European area, representing ten disciplines, were asked to list on the basis of priority the three to five non-native languages which they considered basic for research and teaching in the country of their specialization for the years since 1500. Although this survey was imperfect since in some countries the most important non-native language changed with the centuries, the statistics nevertheless reveal the complexity of the issue. For the four countries principally studied in the postwar period, Poland, Hungary, Yugoslavia, and Czechoslovakia, most of those consulted listed German as the *first* foreign language. The exceptions were the following: for Poland, two specialists in literature named Latin, another French. For Yugoslavia, a linguist and a political scientist cited Russian, an economist, French. For Hungary, a historian chose Latin, but only for the sixteenth to eighteenth centuries. There was unanimous agreement on German for Czechoslovakia.

As for the *second* foreign language, there was a difference of opinion. For Poland, French and Latin predominated, although one answer named Italian. For Hungary, Latin and French were selected; French was chosen for Yugoslavia, but Russian, Latin, and Turkish also received recognition. There was no agreement on the second language for Czechoslovakia, although French, Russian, Polish, and Hungarian were all mentioned. As a *third* language, Russian was named for Poland, and Russian and Italian for Yugoslavia. For Czechoslovakia, Latin was added to the list already given.

Whereas German predominated in these lands, French held *first* position in most replies for Greece and Romania. However, an economist listed English for Greece and a historian chose Latin for Romania. Italian and German shared *first* and *second* place, respectively, for Albania. Only in Bulgaria did Russian rank as the *first* foreign language, but with Turkish and German also named. With a few exceptions, German was chosen as the second language for all three of these states. For the *third* language, French was named for Albania and Bulgaria, with Turkish also important for the former. Turkish and English held third place for Greece. Turkish, modern Greek, and Church Slavonic were in this category for Romania. In response to the same question, the answers of the students followed the same pattern.

These figures show the great difference from the linguistic point of view between Russian studies and those of Eastern Europe. In the former, the Russian language opens the door to research in all disciplines. In the area with which we are concerned, the prospective student is confronted not only with the native language but also with an array of secondary languages vital for research and study in his field of interest. Also, despite popular misconception, Russian is the major non-native language for only one country, Bulgaria; German and French dominate in the other six, with Italian holding this position in Albania.

The second major problem in language training concerns the scheduling and availability of courses for the area student who needs a language as a tool for his research. Most universities with large Russian area programs have been able to offer a graduate course in Russian for those who wish to acquire a reading knowledge in their own field. This is an expensive service which cannot be duplicated for languages in which only a few students enroll. The situation is particularly acute for the non-Slavic languages. Although an institution might be willing at times to offer special reading courses in Polish, Serbo-Croatian, or even Czech, the possibilities are extremely remote that Albanian, Bulgarian, Greek, Hungarian, and Romanian would be given on this basis.

Both faculty members and graduate students indicated strongly that they would be willing to attend summer institutes, if stipends were available, to learn these languages as a tool. When asked to specify which languages they would be interested in studying in such summer programs the faculty made these choices. Twenty-three indicated they would like to study Romanian; 18 selected Serbo-Croatian; 12, Greek; 12, Bulgarian; 9, Hungarian; 8 each for Czech, Polish, and Turkish; 6, Albanian, with the remainder being divided among various other languages. Among the graduate students 14 selected Polish; 12, Serbo-Croatian; 11 each, Czech and Hungarian; 10, Romanian; 4, Turkish; 3, Greek; and 2 each, Bulgarian and Albanian. Thus it is evident that the faculty members wish to expand their linguistic abilities, since they preferred the less-known languages such as Romanian, Greek, and Bulgarian. On the other hand, the graduate student, who at this stage of his career can only afford to study the languages directly relevant to his dissertation, tended to emphasize those languages which have been taught rather regularly, that is, Polish, Serbo-Croatian, Czech, and Hungarian. Yet there was also a strong interest among the students for Romanian.

A third difficulty encountered by the student is that of learning to speak the language of his specialization, particularly when it is taught for only one year with an emphasis on structure and vocabulary. An answer to this problem can probably best be found in the summer institutes and the programs for study abroad which are discussed later.

The language problem is certainly the major block to the expansion of study in the area. The magnitude of this issue is indicated by a unique attribute of East European studies in general. Although it was not possible to make a completely accurate survey, it can be estimated that over 60 percent of the scholars publishing in the area are either emigrants from these lands, where they acquired the basic language tools, or they are the children of emigrants who were able to gain some linguistic competence at home along with an interest in the area. Therefore, in graduate school they had a considerable advantage over those with no direct relationship to the area. In addition, about 90 percent of the second-generation scholars became specialists in the country of their parents' origin. Even though their abilities and scholarship are of the highest quality, they tend to perpetuate the national approach to the study of these lands. These scholars dominate the field, particularly in economics, history, literature, and political science, the most popular disciplines. This trend is not so apparent in linguistics, where most of the scholars are not of East European origin.

After the language question, undoubtedly the major obstacle encountered by the graduate student is the problem of finding books in his field in his university library, unless, of course, he lives near New York, Boston, or Washington. The university libraries considered to have significant collections in the entire area or parts of it are California (Berkeley and Los Angeles), Chicago, Columbia, Colorado, Harvard, Illinois, Indiana, Kansas, Michigan, Ohio State, Princeton, Stanford, Texas, Virginia, Washington, Wisconsin, and Yale. However, even in these libraries, the majority of the material concerns the "favored" nations of Poland, Yugoslavia, and Czechoslovakia and the disciplines of history, political science, and literature. Students not served directly by these central libraries, or who have an interest in the "unfavored" nations and disciplines, have great difficulty in finding adequate material upon which to base the research papers and the thesis necessary for a higher degree. In the past, interlibrary loan has been of enormous significance to East European research. Recently, unfortunately, the entire system has become overloaded. And libraries are becoming increasingly reluctant to lend books which they know cannot be replaced if lost. The time consumed by interlibrary loan procedures now often means that a student who applies for a book one semester will not receive it until the next, if it becomes available at all. Until the library situation is improved, the less-developed disciplines and regions will continue to lag behind the rest.

Equally important is the fact that on certain central problems books simply do not exist. This question is discussed in the chapters on the individual disciplines. The student is thus fully dependent upon unpublished archival material, and he must study abroad if he wishes to complete an important research project. It should be noted that, unlike the situation in regard to the United States and Western Europe, large collections of primary material have not been published in the East European countries. There are, of course, certain notable exceptions. Also, students in literature are not so directly affected. However, for the overwhelming majority of topics, the student will not find in the United States an adequate store of published primary materials for a doctoral dissertation. He must go abroad to finish his research.

The question of the lack of an adequate selection of courses in the disciplines has already been mentioned. It is also a common complaint of the individual student in the area that even when his department offers lectures in East European studies, they are not sufficient to his needs. Often the professor with whom he is working is a specialist in one region, for instance, the Balkans. Courses will be given on Balkan problems, but not on those of the other East European countries. An increase of lecture courses offered, which it can be assumed would also be open to undergraduates, would indeed stimulate interest in the field and attract more students to graduate study. Thus, it is interesting to note that current events (30 percent) and ethnic background (22 percent) have exerted a much stronger role in influencing the present group of graduate students than has undergraduate class experience (20 percent).

The student in our area suffers from an additional major disadvantage. Upon entering graduate school, he soon finds that his studies will take considerably longer than those of his colleagues in the Russian, West European, and other better-developed fields. Unless he comes with an unusual language background, he will need four to six years to complete his degree. The question of time is one of the principal reasons why the suspension of the area certificate has been advised. The length of time necessary to complete work for the doctorate is extremely discouraging for many able students. It is obvious, except in the case of language students benefiting from the NDFL grants, that they will not be able to obtain financial support for this extended period. If they work, the time spent on the degree is further lengthened. Quite a few, particularly those who are married, have become discouraged and have left the university or have shifted to another program.

Many of the problems listed above could obviously be met by increased financial assistance to the area. Certainly much aid has been received in the past. Unquestionably, the progress which has been made so far is directly related to the fellowship programs (tables 5 and 6) of the various foundations, the federal government, and the regular grants given by the universities. At different times the Social Science Research Council (SSRC), the American Council of Learned Societies (ACLS), the Ford Foreign Area Fellowship Program (FAFP), the Institute of International Education (IIE), the Inter-University Committee on Travel Grants (IUCTG), whose functions in 1969 were taken over by the newly created International Research and Exchanges Board (IREX), and the Office of Education through NDFL have all given support to this field. Two of these programs, the SSRC to 1958 and the joint ACLS-SSRC after this date, were primarily of assistance to faculty members, although SSRC did award some graduate fellowships. The Foreign Area Fellowship Program and the NDFL were designed for graduate students, although the former does give some postdoctoral grants. The IUCTG assists both graduate students and faculty. Sources of financial support, therefore, do exist. The question, however, is whether the funds available now are adequate, and also whether the emphasis regarding discipline and area should not be changed. Let us therefore examine the figures for past grants to see where they were awarded.

As far as graduate students are concerned, FAFP awarded a total of 84 fellowships between 1954 and 1965; NDFL gave 193 between 1963 and 1967, the period for which statistics were obtained. The significance of these figures can best be appreciated if we consider separately those grants made for the study of linguistics, language and literature, and the other disciplines. Thus FAFP made only one award in linguistics, whereas NDFL gave 26. FAFP sponsored 7 candidates in literature, but NDFL, in a category classified as "language and literature," aided 97 students. Thus, as is obvious, 64 percent of NDFL's main effort was directed toward some form of language and literature study, while only 10 percent of the FAFP program was in these fields.[11]

If one excludes from the calculations the awards made to graduate students by FAFP and NDFL for the study of language and literature discussed in the preceding paragraph, then FAFP made 76 awards (1954–65) and NDFL 70 (1963–67) for all the other disciplines. Both

11. The statistics for this section are given in table 6.

FAFP and NDFL made the largest percentage of awards to history; the first gave 29 fellowships, or 38 percent; the second 37, or 53 percent. To political science FAFP awarded 13 fellowships, or 18 percent, but NDFL had 7, or 10 percent. The only discipline where there was a great discrepancy between the two institutions was in economics. FAFP granted 12 fellowships, or 16 percent, whereas NDFL made only one award, or 1 percent. As far as the other disciplines are concerned, NDFL and FAFP together made four grants in anthropology, three in geography, one in law, and two in sociology. There were no awards in ethnomusicology, folklore, musicology, or philosophy. NDFL did, however, make 18 awards, or 26 percent, in a general category classified as "area studies."

The figures from other organizations reveal the same trends in the graduate student category. Thus, for example, IUCTG, which has programs with Bulgaria, Czechoslovakia, and Hungary, made only 13 awards between 1963 and 1965, of which 10 were in history. IIE, which emphasizes Poland, Yugoslavia, and Romania, between 1959 and 1965 made a total of 57 awards, but these are collective figures for graduate students and faculty. Of these, 16 were for a category described as the "arts." Of the remaining 41, 16 were in linguistics, 5 in literature, and 11 in history. Most encouraging, however, is the fact that IIE also awarded 3 fellowships to musicology and one to philosophy, disciplines which do not even appear on the other fellowship lists.

It can thus be seen that the same discrepancies exist in the choice of countries and disciplines in which fellowships were awarded that can be found in the library collections. It is, of course, also a question whether the fellowships awarded in the postwar years from these major fellowship funds were sufficient to encourage and develop graduate training adequately, given the difficulties of the field.

RECOMMENDATIONS

Although it is undoubtedly true that many of the difficulties faced by graduate students could be solved by a more generous allotment of fellowship funds, other problems must be met by the universities themselves. The present generation of graduate students in the universities are not satisfied with the selection of courses offered. They would like a wider choice within their own discipline. The problem of languages must also be clearly recognized by the institution offering studies in East Central and Southeastern Europe, and the student should be made aware of the fact that he will be expected to achieve a high level of language competence. Most important is the emphasis which should be placed on undergraduate preparation. Those participating in this survey agree that the best background for graduate studies is an undergraduate degree in the discipline, but the significance of early language instruction is also indicated. The graduate student should be able to work with at least two of the major languages — French, German, and Russian — and preferably two from Eastern Europe, one Slavic and one non-Slavic. Since all academic institutions, whether junior colleges, colleges, or universities, offer French and German, the undergraduate student interested in this field can begin his linguistic preparation even at schools which do not have a strong Slavic language department. If the student is fortunate enough to have learned either French or German in high school, enrollment in Russian upon entrance into the university would be ideal. If he wishes to specialize in an area, for instance Poland, he could instead commence Polish. In graduate school the student can then study another language in the area. His years in graduate school will have been considerably shortened by his previous studies.

For those who must acquire their principal language training as graduate students, the best solution is probably the summer language and area institute. A single additional language can be learned during the academic year along with a regular program of studies in a discipline, but a second puts too great a burden on the student. These summer courses would, of course, be open to postdoctoral as well as graduate students. As mentioned above, great interest has been expressed in these by both graduate students and by those who have completed their degrees, particularly for the study of Bulgarian, Greek, Serbo-Croatian, and Romanian. It is hoped that in these institutes two approaches would be used, one emphasizing reading knowledge for those who require a language as a tool, another stressing idiomatic speech for those who will need to work in the country itself. Some institutions have tried to meet the problem of the spoken language by sending their graduate students to the summer language institutes for foreigners which are now held in Poland, Czechoslovakia, Hungary, Yugoslavia, and Romania. This solution has the great advantage that the student is immediately placed in the proper environment for learning. Since the courses are international, the language of instruction must be the native one, and those in the courses are virtually forced to use it from the beginning. The cost of participation has so far been relatively low. It varies between $600 and $1,000, including overseas travel. The student is also able to become acquainted with the country and to visit scholars in his field.

The question of inadequate library facilities is also one which must be faced by universities with East European programs. Greater emphasis must be placed on building up the collections outside of the major centers. Although it is true that it is now difficult, if not impossible, to acquire the majority of the important books published before World War II, the new photographic techniques allow perfectly adequate copies to be made of materials not protected by copyright. Here the use of Xerox should be encouraged over microfilm or microcard. It is hoped that every library with an Eastern European collection will regularly provide for such photocopying services.

In relation to language instruction and library acquisition, the question has frequently been raised by university administrators and others about the advisability and feasibility of cooperation between universities, particularly those in a given geographic area. It has, for instance, been recognized that it is not possible for all of the fifteen or twenty American universities who are chiefly interested in Eastern European studies to offer a complete program of the languages required by the area. Although the idea of a division of labor is good in theory, it has not proved very successful in practice. Most universities are willing to teach such languages as Polish and Serbo-Croatian, for which the demand is high and which fit well into a program emphasizing Russian, but few institutions have shown much enthusiasm about committing themselves for a long period to the less popular languages where student attendance is irregular. Graduate students are also reluctant to leave their own institutions during the regular academic year to attend a language course at another university. The best field for cooperative effort appears to be the summer language programs. The Committee on Institutional Cooperation (CIC) of the Big Ten universities, together with Chicago, has already taken a step in this direction. A summer language program was held in 1967. The emphasis fell on Polish, Czech, and Serbo-Croatian, again the most popular languages. Although this program has been developed primarily to meet the needs of the CIC institutions, students from other universities were welcomed.

Cooperation is even more difficult in regard to library acquisitions. Scholars working in any of the regions or individual countries require a good collection for the entire field. Moreover, they need more than a collection restricted to one nation or region for their students and their lecture courses. Although some division is possible, an agreement which, for instance, would provide that one library acquire the books for Poland, another for Yugoslavia, and a third for Hungary, is not satisfactory from a practical standpoint. The libraries, like the language departments, are also more interested in specializing in the more popular disciplines and subjects.

In addition to the establishment of adequate language training facilities and good libraries, the universities can aid the graduate student by allowing great flexibility in their East Central and Southeast European programs. Because of the complexity of the area it is almost impossible to recommend a standard program which would guarantee competence in East European studies. And although there is general recognition that East Central and Southeast Europe do not constitute an "area" in the true sense, there is no widely accepted division. The "Poland, Habsburg, Balkan" pattern has been suggested, but here the lines of demarcation are difficult to draw. The national approach also has its advocates. In these circumstances it should be expected, and it is even advisable, that the training given in East European studies will vary throughout the country. There is general agreement that graduate students should be trained in a discipline, with an emphasis on a region or nation in Eastern Europe, but a further definition of the best approach to graduate studies would be difficult to obtain.

Because of these, and, of course, other considerations, most of those consulted have recommended the abolishment of the area certificate, particularly since it seems that the same results can be achieved in other ways. At present there is an adequate body of literature available in the four major disciplines — history, international relations, economics, political science, and possibly in geography and literature — which allows the interested student to acquire the necessary knowledge by reading. Moreover, most graduate programs allow for a wide choice of electives outside of the department of specialization. The only strong defense of the area certificate came from institutions where the area certificate is accepted as the outside field for the doctoral degree.

The purpose of the recommendation to suspend the area certificate and to encourage great flexibility in graduate study programs is not to be interpreted as an attempt to minimize the interdisciplinary approach, but rather to stress it on an individual basis. It is recognized that the needs of the student will depend on the direction of his principal interest; those specializing in the sixteenth century have other requirements than those in the twentieth. Each student, it is generally believed, should in close cooperation with his major professor be permitted to draw up the program best designed to meet his own needs within the general requirements of a department for the degree. It should be the responsibility of the professor to see that the student does take courses and seminars outside of his discipline to widen his understanding of the area.

The final recommendations for graduate study concern the need for increased grants and fellowships. Obviously the individual student can greatly benefit from a wider availability of individual fellowships, preferably offered on a longer than one-year basis. Of the graduate students participating in this survey who have received fellowships, most have stated that they could not have continued their studies without this assistance. Therefore the widening and strengthening of the area as a whole will require the recruitment and training of able students. The availability of scholarship funds will play perhaps the major role here. Special grants for foreign travel and study at the summer language institutes would also be of enormous assistance. In addition, consideration should be given to the establishment of postdoctoral fellowships in Eastern European studies on a wide basis. These should serve two purposes. First, they would allow a young scholar time to convert his thesis into a work which could be published. Second, grants should be made available which would allow the specialist in one nation, or a part of the area, to study in depth another and thus enlarge his perspective. A Slavic specialist, for instance, might choose to work in a non-Slavic area, and vice versa. Postdoctoral grants should also be given for attendance at summer institutes either in the United States or abroad.

It is to be strongly recommended that graduate student fellowships be administered by those in the East Central and Southeast European area and not in combination with Russian studies. The requirements of the East European field are different and separate from those of the Russian field and they should be judged on their own standards.

GENERAL RECOMMENDATIONS FOR THE FIELD OF EAST CENTRAL AND SOUTHEAST EUROPEAN STUDIES

GRADUATE TRAINING AND AREA PROGRAMS

There was almost unanimous agreement among those consulted that Poland, East Germany, Czechoslovakia, Hungary, Romania, Yugoslavia, Albania, Bulgaria, Greece, and European Turkey, all states which today may or may not be included in the field under consideration, do not together constitute an "area" in the accepted definition of the term. Instead these countries form a historical mosaic which can be viewed in different ways. Two alternatives recommended are:

A. If a university wishes to emphasize the study of the recent period, particularly of communist societies, then these countries, excluding Greece and European Turkey, should be studied in association with the Soviet Union. Thus a Russian and East European Institute is a proper and logical structure to encompass the field.

B. If, however, the field is to be studied in its historical setting and with an interest in understanding all the influences and developments which affected it, then these lands should be regarded as forming an autonomous unit, and they should not be joined with Russian and Soviet studies. In this case, Greece and European Turkey would be included, but East Germany excluded from the list of nations covered.

If the latter approach is accepted, it is further agreed that these lands should be regarded as constituting three regions: Poland, East Central Europe, and the Balkans. The difficulties of finding a common definition for the limits of these areas is recognized. They should perhaps be determined by individual institutions. It was also believed that it would be preferable if an individual university chose to specialize in one of these regions. General courses should, of course, be given to cover the entire field of East Central and Southeast Europe, but individual professors and graduate students should concentrate their research and studies in one of the three categories named. It was considered less desirable for an institution to introduce a program with, for example, specialists in Greek folklore, Yugoslav geography, Czech sociology, Polish history, Hungarian anthropology, etc.

C. There was general agreement that the area certificate, which at one time served a purpose, should now be abandoned. Its present limited value does not justify the delay it involves in the training of graduate students.

D. The training of the M.A. and Ph.D. should be in the discipline. In view of the linguistic requirements of the area, a student should expect to spend one or two years longer in the completion of his degree. With this additional time, and using electives, he should have course and/or seminar work in at least four disciplines, in addition to his major field. The most important fact here must be the emphasis on flexibility in the selection of electives. Those interested in the contemporary period should obviously choose some combination of economics, political science, philosophy, sociology, law, history, and literature. Those who wish to study the area in depth and to understand the influences which conditioned it would perhaps prefer a selection from anthropology, folklore, geography, history, literature, musicology, and political science. The program chosen would also depend on whether the student is interested in East Central or Southeastern Europe. It is essential, however, that in this area, with its diversity, conflicting influences, and strong tradition, every student should become familiar with the contributions of the disciplines relevant to his interests.

F. Each student should have a reading knowledge of two major languages — French, German, or Russian — and two languages from the area. Ideally, the beginning graduate student should have an effective reading knowledge of his two major languages. If he has not had the opportunity to study a language of the area as an undergraduate, he should begin this immediately and continue it through a summer area language institute. Not later than his third year of graduate work, he should begin his second language, perhaps in a summer institute.

Since French and German are the international languages of the area, oral command of one of these is essential in order that the student may move freely throughout these countries.

SUMMER LANGUAGE INSTITUTES

A. *In the United States.* To meet the needs of the field, a NDEA summer language institute should be held every year for Polish and Serbo-Croatian, and every other year for Albanian, Bulgarian, Czech, Greek, Hungarian, and Romanian. This program should be continued for at least ten years and should be rotated regionally — East, Midwest, and Far West — among interested universities.

In these, as in regular language programs, the needs of two different types of students should be met: first, those who are linguists and who wish to improve their knowledge of a language or to add another, and, second, those who need a language as a *tool* to complement a more thorough knowledge of others.

B. *Abroad.* Funds should be made available so that advanced graduate students and faculty, especially those who have recently completed their doctorates, can improve and expand their language competence by attending a summer language institute for foreigners in East Central and Southeastern Europe.

SUMMER AREA INSTITUTES

A. Eight-week summer institutes for each of the three areas — Poland, East Central Europe, and the Balkans — should be held in rotation over a period of nine years. Five disciplines should be represented at these, with at least one or two professors from abroad. The program should include lecture courses and a carefully planned interdisciplinary seminar. The attendance should be limited to twenty students and young faculty members. Those attending should be selected in the fall semester. In the spring semester they would read extensively from a list of books prepared by the organizers of the institute.

B. In view of the fact that the study of Bulgaria, Greece, and Romania has been neglected in comparison with that of the other states, it is proposed that one special intensive summer institute be held for each. Courses on history, literature, religion, politics, geography, and economics should be included. The purpose of these institutes is to encourage study in the weaker sections of the field and to strengthen the knowledge of specialists in Balkan affairs.

COOPERATIVE AMERICAN-EAST EUROPEAN ACTIVITIES

A. *Translations.* A major effort should be made to translate into English standard works in literature, basic source materials, and other recommended works. This should be a cooperative project between American and European scholars. The translations can usually be done in Europe, but they must be checked for accuracy, style, and idiomatic English usage by an American scholar. These books would not only be of value to the specialist, but their existence would allow the expansion of general university courses to include material on the East European field. For example, translations of modern novels could be read in courses on comparative literature; other books could be used in Western civilization surveys and those on contemporary politics.

B. *Bibliographies.* As a supplement to our currently planned two-volume annotated bibliographic guide, we should also issue individual volumes for each country, including the social sciences and the humanities. In other words, there should be a volume prepared for each country similar to those now available for Bulgaria, Czechoslovakia, and Romania, which were prepared under the auspices of the Slavic Division of the Library of Congress.[12]

C. *Exchange or visiting professorships.* Attempts should be made to bring English-speaking scholars to American universities to teach courses in fields such as literature, where there is a shortage in this country. They should spend a year in America with perhaps a semester at two institutions. In fields where there are specialists, a joint course or seminar might be taught. If possible, an exchange arrangement on some basis with East European universities or institutes might prove possible.

LIBRARY NEEDS

A. *Guide to East European holdings in American libraries.* A systematic survey, financed by the Office of Education, should be made of the twenty American libraries with substantial East European collections. In

---

12. Marin V. Pundeff, *Bulgaria: A Bibliographic Guide* (Washington, D.C.: Library of Congress, 1965); Stephen A. Fischer-Galati, *Rumania: A Bibliographic Guide* (Washington, D.C.: Library of Congress, 1963); and Rudolf Sturm, *Czechoslovakia: A Bibliographic Guide* (Washington, D.C.: Library of Congress, 1967). A similar volume on Yugoslavia has been commissioned.

particular, information on source materials, collected works, journals, newspapers, and unique collections should be gathered. The results should then be published as a reference guide. Subsequently, arrangements should be made so that a journal will periodically publish information concerning new additions in the field.

B. *Training of librarians.* Three-month summer fellowships should be provided to enable Slavic librarians to gain competence in one or two of the non-Slavic languages, or for non-Slavic librarians to learn one or more Slavic languages. Without qualified personnel, it will not be possible to expand and develop library collections.

C. *Library purchases.* The interested universities should pool their efforts and employ a qualified person in each of the East European countries who would recommend, select, and order current publications and also locate out-of-print books.

EXCHANGES AND TRAVEL

A. The present IUCTG arrangements for Bulgaria, Czechoslovakia, and Hungary should be duplicated in Poland and Romania. Every encouragement should be given to any programs in the future which assist in the promotion of the increased exchange of scholars and students, whether on an institutional or private basis.

B. The feasibility of similar scholarly exchanges with Greece should be explored.

C. Fifty six-week summer travel grants, as opposed to research grants, should be made available to young postdoctoral scholars which would be similar to those introduced for the Soviet Union in 1956–58. The purpose would be to enable scholars teaching in the field to become familiar with the entire area and not only with their region or nation of specialization.

CONFERENCES

A. In view of the past close association of East European with Russian and Soviet studies to the neglect of the proper appreciation of Western influences in this area, there is an urgent need for an interdisciplinary conference on this aspect of political, economic, religious, and cultural relations. Specialists from America and West and East Europe should be included. It would perhaps be preferable to hold two conferences, one dealing with the Balkans, the other with Poland and East Central Europe.

B. American institutions are in a particularly advantageous position to sponsor a conference on intra-East Central and Southeast European problems because they are not under the political pressures which make these themes difficult to deal with in Eastern Europe. A conference which would consider the factors which divide or unite these people would be valuable.

FELLOWSHIPS

The most serious impediment to the expansion of research in this field is the lack of fellowships, particularly for young scholars. The present pooling of funds for the Russian and East European areas should be abandoned; each should have its own allotment. Because Russian studies are now so much further developed than those concerning East Europe, it is difficult for a beginning scholar to compete where his application is judged against those of senior scholars in the Russian area who have often several books and fifteen years of teaching experience. Moreover, many of these men are at smaller institutions which lack adequate library facilities, which do not give summer grants, and where sometimes sabbatical leaves are not available. These scholars should be given the opportunity to obtain support for summer, semester, or year research projects.

The following specific recommendations for fellowships are made:

A. *Graduate students and young scholars*

1. For individual graduate students to enable them to complete their language and discipline training.
2. Dissertation fellowships particularly for those who need to complete their research in East Europe. The difficulties of producing an acceptable thesis on the basis of material available within the United States has been commented upon.
3. Summer language fellowships to be used either in the United States or in one of the East European countries that has a language institute for foreigners.
4. Postdoctoral grants to enable young scholars to revise their dissertations for publication or to expand their professional competence by the study of a region or country outside of their specialization.

B. *Senior scholars*

1. Additional research fellowships for research in the region or country of major interest. The senior scholar is as hampered as the student by the fact that the principal material for his research is in Europe.

2. Grants for attendance at conferences in the United States and Europe organized by specialists for the study of a limited subject. Assistance so far has tended to be given to those who wish to participate at the large congresses, which may, in fact, not be of as great a value to the scholar as a more limited gathering.
3. Summer grants to attend area and language institutes outside of their country or region of specialization.

APPENDIX

Tables: 1–12

TABLE 1
DEGREES IN EASTERN EUROPEAN STUDIES BY DISCIPLINE, 1946–65
MASTER OF ARTS

	1946–55						1956–60				1961–65							Totals
	Chicago	Columbia	Illinois	Indiana	Stanford	Wisconsin	Chicago	Columbia	Illinois	Indiana	Chicago	Columbia	Illinois	Indiana	Stanford	Washington	Wisconsin	
Anthropology	0	1	0	0	0	0	0	0	0	0	0	0	0	0	0	0	0	1
Economics	5	11	0	1	1	0	2	11	0	1	3	5	0	0	0	0	0	40
Ethnomusicology	0	1	0	0	0	0	0	1	0	0	0	0	0	0	0	0	0	2
Folklore	0	0	0	0	0	0	0	0	0	0	0	1	0	0	0	0	0	1
Geography	0	0	0	0	0	1	1	0	0	0	0	0	0	0	0	0	0	1
History	4	31	0	0	0	0	2	23	0	1	1	19	0	18	2	2	0	104
International Relations	4	49	0	0	0	0	2	31	0	0	1	16	0	0	0	0	0	103
Law	0	1	0	0	0	0	0	0	0	0	0	6	0	0	0	0	0	7
Linguistics	2	7	0	0	0	0	2	3	0	0	3	11	0	3	0	0	0	31
Literature	2	9	0	0	0	0	0	6	0	0	1	5	0	8	0	0	1	32
Musicology	0	1	0	0	0	0	0	0	0	0	0	0	0	0	0	0	0	1
Philosophy	0	0	0	0	0	0	0	0	0	0	0	0	0	0	0	0	0	0
Political Science	2	12	4	0	0	0	1	4	1	1	3	4	1	7	1	0	1	42
Sociology	0	3	0	0	0	0	0	2	2	0	0	1	0	0	0	0	0	8
Other	0	1	0	0	0	0	0	0	0	0	0	0	0	1	0	0	0	2
Totals	19	127	4	1	1	1	10	81	3	3	12	68	1	37	3	2	2	375

TABLE 2
DEGREES IN EASTERN EUROPEAN STUDIES BY DISCIPLINE, 1946–65
DOCTOR OF PHILOSOPHY

Part I: 1946–60

	1946–55										1956–60										
	Chicago	Columbia	Cornell	Harvard	Illinois	Indiana	Michigan	Princeton	Stanford	Yale	Chicago	Columbia	Cornell	Harvard	Illinois	Indiana	Michigan	Notre Dame	Pennsylvania	Princeton	Wisconsin
Anthropology	0	1	0	0	0	0	0	0	0	0	1	0	0	0	0	0	0	0	0	0	0
Economics	1	2	0	0	0	0	0	0	0	0	2	5	0	1	0	2	1	0	0	0	0
Ethnomusicology	0	0	0	0	0	0	0	0	0	0	0	0	0	0	0	0	0	0	0	0	0
Folklore	0	0	0	0	0	0	0	0	0	0	0	0	0	0	0	0	0	0	0	0	0
Geography	1	0	0	0	0	0	0	0	1	0	0	0	0	0	0	0	0	0	0	0	0
History	2	2	0	0	0	0	0	0	0	0	3	6	0	2	3	0	3	0	0	3	1
International Relations	2	3	0	0	0	0	0	0	0	0	0	4	0	0	0	0	0	0	0	0	0
Law	0	0	0	0	0	0	0	0	0	0	0	1	0	0	0	0	0	0	0	0	0
Linguistics	0	1	2	1	1	1	0	0	0	2	0	2	1	1	0	0	1	0	3	0	0
Literature	0	2	0	0	0	0	0	3	0	0	0	2	0	0	0	0	0	0	0	0	0
Musicology	0	0	0	0	0	0	0	0	0	0	0	0	0	0	0	0	0	0	0	0	0
Philosophy	0	0	0	0	0	0	0	0	0	0	0	0	0	0	0	0	0	0	0	0	0
Political Science	0	2	0	0	0	0	1	0	0	0	0	3	0	0	1	0	2	3	0	4	0
Sociology	0	3	0	0	0	0	0	0	0	0	0	2	0	0	0	0	0	0	0	0	0
Other	0	1	0	0	0	0	2	0	0	0	0	0	0	0	0	0	0	0	0	0	0
Totals	6	17	2	1	1	1	3	3	1	2	6	25	1	4	4	2	7	3	3	7	1

TABLE 2 (continued)

Part II: 1961-65

	1961-65											Totals (1946-65)
	Berkeley	Chicago	Columbia	Harvard	Illinois	Indiana	Michigan	Notre Dame	Princeton	Stanford	Wisconsin	
Anthropology	0	0	0	0	0	0	0	0	0	0	0	2
Economics	0	0	7	0	1	1	0	0	0	0	0	23
Ethnomusicology	0	0	0	0	0	0	0	0	0	0	0	0
Folklore	0	0	0	0	0	0	0	0	0	0	0	0
Geography	0	0	0	0	0	0	0	0	0	0	0	1
History	0	4	9	4	4	4	0	1	1	3	0	53
International Relations	0	0	4	0	0	0	0	0	0	0	0	16
Law	0	0	4	0	0	0	0	0	0	0	0	5
Linguistics	1	1	1	6	0	7	3	0	0	0	0	38
Literature	0	0	3	0	0	0	0	0	0	2	2	11
Musicology	0	0	0	0	0	0	0	0	0	0	0	0
Philosophy	0	0	0	0	0	0	0	0	0	0	0	0
Political Science	0	0	2	0	0	3	1	0	1	0	1	24
Sociology	0	0	2	0	0	0	0	0	0	0	0	7
Other	0	0	0	0	0	0	0	0	1	0	0	4
Totals	1	5	32	10	5	15	4	1	3	5	3	184

TABLE 3
DEGREES IN EAST EUROPEAN STUDIES BY COUNTRY OF SPECIALIZATION
(M.A.'s AND PH.D.'s)

1946–65

	Albania	Bulgaria	Czecho-slovakia	Greece	Hungary	Yugoslavia	Poland	Romania	East Germany	Totals
Anthropology	0	0	0	0	0	1	0	0	0	1
Economics	0	0	13	11	5	15	13	1	4	62
Ethnomusicology	0	0	0	1	0	0	1	0	0	2
Folklore	0	0	0	0	0	0	0	0	0	0
Geography	0	0	6	0	0	0	2	0	0	8
History	2	4	14	9	22	18	27	4	3	103
International Relations	3	5	8	10	3	27	24	3	12	95
Law	0	1	5	0	0	2	0	0	0	8
Linguistics	6	2	4	10	7	8	7	2	0	46
Literature	1	1	4	0	7	7	17	0	0	37
Musicology	0	0	0	0	0	0	0	0	0	0
Philosophy	0	0	0	0	0	0	0	0	0	0
Political Science	1	2	6	5	10	8	10	1	2	45
Sociology	0	0	1	3	6	3	4	0	0	17
Other	0	0	0	1	0	0	2	0	0	3
Totals	13	15	61	50	60	89	107	11	21	427*

* The discrepancy which is apparent between these figures and if one adds the M.A.'s (375) and Ph.D.'s (184), or a total of 559, is explained by the fact that from the information provided it was not possible to determine in many cases which was the country, if any, of specialization.

TABLE 4
NDFL FELLOWSHIPS: GRADUATE AWARDS IN EAST EUROPEAN LANGUAGES
1959–66

	1959	1960	1961	1962	1963	1964	1965	1966	Total	Percentages
Albanian	0	0	1	1	4	4	3	1	14	0.9
Bulgarian	0	0	2	2	1	0	0	0	5	0.3
Czech	0	0	3	5	9	9	11	9	46	3.1
Greek	0	0	2	2	2	2	0	0	8	0.5
Hungarian	0	3	6	8	8	8	16	12	61	4.1
Polish	0	2	7	9	10	6	20	12	66	4.4
Romanian	0	0	1	6	2	2	1	1	13	0.9
Serbo-Croatian	0	0	8	9	9	9	11	10	56	3.7
Russian	69	132	190	175	135	125	202	200	1228	82.0
Totals	69	137	220	217	180	165	264	245	1497	99.9

TABLE 5
NDFL Fellows in Eastern Studies, 1963–67
by Discipline

	Albanian	Bulgarian	Czech	Greek	Hungarian	Polish	Romanian	Serbo-Croatian	Total
Anthropology	0	0	0	2	1	0	0	0	3
Area Studies	0	0	1	0	12	2	0	3	18
Economics	0	0	1	0	0	0	0	0	1
Geography	0	0	0	0	0	0	0	0	0
History	0	0	13	0	6	14	1	3	37
International Relations	0	0	1	0	1	2	0	0	4
Language and Literature	3	1	21	2	12	27	4	27	97
Linguistics	9	0	1	0	8	1	1	6	26
Political Science	0	1	0	0	3	3	0	0	7
Sociology	0	0	0	0	0	0	0	0	0
Total									193

TABLE 6
National Fellowship Awards and Grants for Training and Research in
East European Studies, 1946–65

	1946–50 SSRC Stud. Fac.	1951–55 FAFP Stud. Fac.		SSRC Stud. Fac.
Anthropology	2	0	0	1
Economics	4	3	1	1
Geography	0	0	0	1
History	3	10	2	0
International Relations	1	3	0	0
Law	0	1	1	0
Linguistics	0	0	0	0
Literature	0	5	1	0
Musicology	0	0	0	0
Philosophy	0	0	0	0
Political Science	4	3	0	1
Sociology	1	0	0	0
Other	0	1	0	0
Totals	15	26	5	4

TABLE 6 (continued)

| | 1956–60 | | | | | | |
| | FAFP | | SSRC | | ACLS (1958) | IIE | |
	Stud.	Fac.	Stud.	Fac.	only Fac.	Stud.	Fac.
Anthropology	7	0	2		0	0	
Economics	7	0	6		1	0	
Geography	3	0	3		0	0	
History	10	1	20		9	1	
International Relations	4	0	1		0	0	
Law	0	0	0		0	0	
Linguistics	0	1	3		1	0	
Literature	1	0	1		1	1	
Musicology	0	0	0		0	1	
Philosophy	0	0	0		0	0	
Political Science	6	0	3		1	1	
Sociology	1	0	5		1	0	
Other	0	0	0		0	1	
Totals	39	2	44		14	5	

TABLE 6 (continued)

| | 1961–65 | | | | | | |
| | FAFP | | ACLS-SSRC | IIE | | IUCTG | |
	Stud.	Fac.	Fac.	Stud.	Fac.	Stud.	Fac.
Anthropology	1	0	1	0		0	0
Economics	2	0	6	1		0	4
Geography	0	0	1	0		0	1
History	9	0	12	10		10	6
International Relations	0	0	0	0		0	0
Law	0	0	0	0		0	1
Linguistics	1	0	6	16		2	4
Literature	1	0	2	4		0	4
Musicology	0	0	0	2		0	0
Philosophy	0	0	0	1		0	0
Political Science	4	0	4	1		0	2
Sociology	1	0	0	2		0	0
Other	0	0	0	15		1	4
Totals	19	0	32	52		13	26

TABLE 7

PLACEMENT OF EASTERN EUROPEAN AREA STUDENTS, 1946–65

	Area Certificates		Master of Arts			Ph.D.					Totals
	Columbia	Indiana	Columbia	Indiana	Stanford	Columbia	Illinois	Indiana	Stanford	Foreign Area Fellows 1954–65	
Teaching	25	3	48	5	1	21	4	13	3	43	166
Research, academic	1	0	0	0	0	0	0	0	0	3	4
Government employment	3	1	6	5	2	0	0	0	0	7	24
Business	0	0	1	1	0	0	0	0	0	1	3
Journalism and radio	1	1	2	1	0	0	0	0	0	2	7
Other	2	2	4	10	0	0	0	0	0	13	31

TABLE 8

STUDENT RESPONSES TO THE QUESTION: Is your graduate program more closely associated with Russian-Soviet studies, the German-Habsburg area, Western Europe, the Ottoman-Byzantine field, or is the East Central and Southeast European program organized as an autonomous unit at your university?

	Russian-Soviet	German-Habsburg	Autonomous	Within Department
Economics	1			
Geography	3		1	
History	17	2	7	1
Language and Literature	1			
Political Science	1		5	
Totals	23	2	13	1

TABLE 9

STUDENT RESPONSES TO THE QUESTION: What do you regard as the major weakness of your own graduate training?

Response	Number
Inadequate library facilities	20
Too few courses offered	16
Unsatisfactory language training	11
Insufficient financial support	10
Eastern European area studies overshadowed by Russian-Soviet studies	7
Ph.D. programs require too many courses outside Eastern European field	7
Lack of competent faculty	5
Inadequate materials on area in English, including basic works on area	5
Excessive amount of time required to complete the Ph.D.	2
Lack of competent guidance from faculty	2
Need for stricter language requirements for admittance to Ph.D. program in Eastern European field	2
Lack of summer programs for study of language or area courses	2
Too much emphasis on discipline training	2
Too little emphasis on training in discipline	2
Lack of opportunity to travel and study in Eastern Europe	1

TABLE 10

STUDENT RESPONSES TO THE QUESTION: What do you think should be done too strengthen and improve graduate training and research in the field?

Response	Number
Better language training	17
Better selection of courses	15
Increase and improve library holdings and facilities	12
Provide more opportunities for travel and research in Eastern Europe	4
End connection with Russian-Soviet Studies	3
More financial support, especially long-term rather than one-year fellowships	3
More financial support for language study	2
More courses on Eastern Europe for undergradates	2
More competent faculty	2
Exchanges of Eastern European and American scholars	2
Other reasons	8

TABLE 11

FACULTY RESPONSES TO THE QUESTION: If increased financial support became available for this field, how do you believe it could best be allocated?

Response	Number
Research projects	13
Travel funds	11
Basic publications for teaching and research	8
Summer language and area institutes	7
Language training	6
More faculty and courses	5
More funds for advanced graduate students and new Ph.D.'s	5
Scholarships for East Europeans	4
Library development	4
Support for graduate students	4
Funds for graduate study abroad	4
Expand training in field to new institutions	2
Expand training opportunities in already existing programs	2
Subsidies for publications in the field	2
Translations	2
Bibliographic tools	2
Exchanges of faculty and students with East Europe	2
Recruit and support only the best graduate students	2

TABLE 12

FACULTY RESPONSES TO THE QUESTION: What kind of financial assistance would you personally be most interested in obtaining for your own research and study needs?

Response	Number
Travel funds	24
Research funds	23
Funds for research and graduate assistants	7
Funds for language study	5
Publication subsidies and expenses	5
Funds for secretarial help	4
Funds to develop library resources	2
Others reasons	6

2/ UNDERGRADUATE INSTRUCTION

Lyman H. Legters

University of Washington

This survey of East European studies would not have been proposed by the American Council of Learned Societies, or supported by the U.S. Office of Education, or carried out by the investigators if those concerned had not believed Eastern Europe to be a region of importance. The premise was that the region has been neglected, relatively speaking, in the postwar wave of academic attention to foreign areas. The survey was designed to discover more precisely the dimensions of that neglect. But it was also intended as stimulus and perhaps even guide to the process of overcoming the area's underprivileged status among academic programs.

Where scholarship and specialized graduate training are concerned, the presuppositions lead in quite a straightforward manner to the heart of the problem. There is no doubt that improvement, both qualitatively and quantitatively, is needed if the study of Eastern Europe is to emerge from the shadow of the Soviet Union or of sheer indifference. The central questions are thus: how much? how fast? by what devices? and the like.

But in the realm of undergraduate education the issue is more complicated and, in a sense, more controversial. Higher education is a continuum, not a set of compartments. And if an increase in knowledge and understanding of Eastern Europe is a proper educational goal, then it would be foolhardy to omit the undergraduate level from consideration. What happens at that level must, in the nature of our educational organization, have implications for anything attempted at the graduate level. So it is at least useful to know what aspects of existing undergraduate instruction relate to the overall need to improve our understanding of Eastern Europe.

As soon as undergraduate education is considered in its own terms, however, a dualism of purpose complicates matters. Are we concerned with undergraduate instruction solely as an avenue to graduate specialization? Or must we also consider it as terminal education for a substantial segment of the American population? Whichever emphasis prevails, one can find an enormous range of disagreement among East European specialists as to just what ought to be encouraged in undergraduate education. Unlike the graduate level, where we find essential unanimity at least that Eastern Europe deserves much greater attention, the undergraduate level of consideration produces such polar reactions as, on the one hand, the advocacy of full-scale language and area study programs and, on the other, the assertion that a student should not concern himself with the region at all until he commences graduate study.

The question really reduces to a weighing of Eastern Europe's importance. If we argue that subject matter from the area has no place in undergraduate study, this suggests that our society has no great stake in Eastern Europe as a part of the international environment in which we live. The argument for increased attention and support at loftier academic levels is then weakened accordingly. But if we contend that every undergraduate needs full exposure to East European subject matter, we run the risk that the whole argument will be dismissed as parochial and narrow-minded. To put it another way, few of us would be prone to place Eastern Europe on a plane with China or India or Russia as a world region to which all or most undergraduates should be introduced. Even to an educator convinced of the importance of educational attention to foreign societies and civilizations, we would not be likely to advocate large numbers of new specialized programs on Eastern Europe or to insist that every undergraduate must have courses on that region. (We might, on the other hand, propose that our region, like any other, offers the educational advantage of confrontation with alien modes of thought and behavior.) Yet we would hardly classify Eastern Europe on a par with Eskimo or Tibetan society either, that is, as a subject which repays scholarly investigation but scarcely cries out for systematic attention by undergraduates.

The field thus appears to offer something to and demand something of undergraduate education. But this still leaves completely open the question of the exact form in which the undergraduate curriculum ought to reflect our concern with Eastern Europe. This phase of the investigation has endeavored to find out what range of choice is available to undergraduates in the several types of higher educational institutions at which they study and, so far as possible, to ascertain how these institutions assess their own efforts in the East European field.

In addition, numerous East European specialists have been consulted as to the approaches that seem most appropriate and promising, and also as to the trends in the field which may present new demands and new opportunities for undergraduate education in the next decade or so.

Coming to the task from a recent period of employment in the U.S. Office of Education, where I presided over the expansion of the National Defense Education Act (NDEA) Language and Area Centers program to include members of undergraduate programs, my information-gathering was somewhat simplified. Since the vast majority of the institutions — those which ignore Eastern Europe — had no particular relevance to the task, I addressed a general inquiry to a selection of institutions of all types known to include some work on the area in their undergraduate curriculum. All but two or three of the institutions queried responded with information, on the basis of which I chose a few places to visit in person. The visits were made in order to supplement or update my experience from the NDEA Centers program, and also to provide opportunity to test my preliminary conclusions against other professional opinion.

The resulting report attempts to show something of what is currently being done about Eastern Europe in undergraduate curricula. These examples, plus several suggestions for further development of the field at that level, are intended for those institutions already persuaded that the area deserves more attention. While the report includes references to arguments on both sides of the question whether Eastern Europe is an appropriate undergraduate concentration, there is too much professional disagreement about this to warrant any clear-cut partisan stance. My own conviction is that much more can and should be done to permit undergraduates greater exposure to this neglected region without distorting the character or purpose of liberal education. Persons of like mind will, I hope, find useful suggestions in what follows. But I have tried to write this report with sufficient deference toward those of different persuasion that their opinions will not simply be ignored. I have had excellent cooperation from colleagues who were chosen as targets of my inquiries and from others associated with me in this survey, but I am solely to blame for defects in this report.

THE UNDERGRADUATE APPROACH TO EASTERN EUROPE

Concerted and systematic efforts to overcome the neglect suffered by so-called non-Western cultures in American higher education are essentially a postwar phenomenon. World War II dramatized the weakness of our academic grasp of world regions outside our own immediate tradition. Since then the college and university curriculum has undergone steady expansion to include neglected subject matter from Asia, Africa, Latin America, and Eastern Europe.

The device typically employed wherever the effort was undertaken deliberately was the program, center, or institute — a gathering of all the elements of the curriculum bearing on a particular world region, usually reinforced by extracurricular activity of one sort or another. In the process, the academic community slid somewhat unconsciously into general acceptance of a set of areas which blanketed the globe while reflecting prevailing scholarly preoccupations. East Asia, Southeast Asia, South Asia, the Middle East (including North Africa), Sub-Saharan Africa, Latin America, and Eastern Europe became, with minor quarrels and permutations at the edges, standard regional categories of study. And for most of these areas, programs appeared and proliferated throughout the 1950s as part of an educational trend that has by no means run its course.

At the outset it was hard to discern any sharp differentiation in these multiplying area programs between graduate and undergraduate levels of study and specialization. Indeed, when Robert B. Hall surveyed the state of area studies in 1946–47, he found more undergraduate than graduate programs. But he correctly perceived "that the undergraduate program in many places is but a forerunner of further and similar area development at the graduate level." [1] By 1950, when Wendell C. Bennett again surveyed the fields of area study, it was already clear that such programs were chiefly aimed at the training of specialists at the graduate level and at improvements in research and scholarship.[2] For most of the ensuing decade the literature concerned with area studies focused on graduate study and research, obviously a response to the most pressing needs of society and of higher education itself.

Despite occasional protests that undergraduate education should not be ignored in this transformation of the higher educational curriculum, the graduate focus prevailed on the campus and with the foundations and the government, which were the prime sources of outside support. By the end of the fifties, by which time many graduate programs had achieved a considerable development, some tentative but symptomatic steps were being taken for the benefit of undergraduates. The foundations were beginning to explore the difficult question of applying curricular lessons learned at the graduate level to the different needs of

1. *Area Studies: With Special Reference to Their Implications for Research in the Social Sciences* (New York: Social Science Research Council, 1947), p. 5.

2. *Area Studies in American Universities* (New York: Social Science Research Council, 1951).

undergraduate education. And the Language and Area Centers program established under Title VI of 1958 provided support, on an experimental basis, to four undergraduate programs among the forty-six centers designated in the first two years of NDEA. As an Office of Education memorandum stated the case, "It must be recognized that advanced language and area work in graduate centers cannot attain optimum effectiveness unless there are opportunities for prospective students to be recruited and given preliminary training at the undergraduate level." [3]

This attitude gained in strength during the early 1960s as the undergraduate NDEA Centers and numerous colleges with foundation support demonstrated the viability of regional studies for undergraduates. The experience of that period showed that undergraduates could and would learn the uncommon languages, that the resources of colleges could sometimes be combined effectively to strengthen the curriculum of each participating institution, and that university programs constituted a resource available in several ways to nearby colleges. Above all, the growing body of statistics on programs of regional study revealed that undergraduates were utilizing the offerings of centers and institutes in a major way. The educational literature concerning area studies came, in this period, to be dominated by an absorption in the problem of adapting such instruction to undergraduate needs.

The most conspicuous single development was undoubtedly the expansion of the NDEA Centers program to include a significant number of undergraduate programs. Thirty of the forty-four new centers designated in 1964–65 were undergraduate programs of language and area study.[4] And much of the increased support to the older centers went in that year to strengthen the undergraduate component of the larger graduate centers.

But it was also clear by this time that full-scale programs represented only one of several ways in which the undergraduate curriculum could give due recognition to non-Western cultures and peoples. Noteworthy efforts had been made to buttress faculty competence and to produce needed text materials so that pertinent individual courses in many disciplines could include appropriate accretions of subject matter from societies hitherto neglected. Although the wording of NDEA made the availability of language instruction a prerequisite for support, many

3. Reprinted in Donald N. Bigelow and Lyman H. Legters, *NDEA Language and Area Centers* (Washington: Office of Education, 1964), p. 75.
4. Lyman H. Legters, "NDEA Support for Undergraduate Language and Area Studies," *Liberal Education*, vol. 51, no. 2 (May, 1965): 278–83.

colleges elected to eschew the introduction of new languages while systematically infusing Asian, African, Latin American, and East European subject matter into conventional courses in history, art, literature, religion, political science, and other disciplines. And numerous new courses were developed for undergraduates at both colleges and universities on one or another of the non-Western civilizations. Another kind of recognition was given by still other colleges, not yet ready for curricular change, in their extracurricular emphasis on a global range of subjects. The Commission on International Understanding of the Association of American Colleges depicted the full variety and intensity of this process of change in undergraduate education in its report on *Non-Western Studies in the Liberal Arts College.*[5] The reports on eighteen individual programs contained therein provide the best summary to date of what the liberal arts college is doing about hitherto neglected subject areas.

Another dimension of undergraduate education, by no means so conveniently documented, is the extensive utilization by undergraduates of elements of full-scale university programs. Most of the languages offered in these programs, and many of the courses in the social sciences and humanities, are open to undergraduates. And in many cases, universities asked NDEA for support precisely for the development of undergraduate work in fields where graduate-level instruction was already well developed. Thus, several of the NDEA-supported undergraduate centers are located at universities, and for the simple reason that the NDEA program was designed to reach undergraduates irrespective of the type of institution at which they study.

With the foregoing sketch as background, it is time to narrow attention to Eastern Europe. Immediately after the war the heaviest emphasis was placed on Russia and the Soviet Union and remained there. The rest of Eastern Europe was largely overlooked, but when it received attention at all it was sometimes treated as a separate region, sometimes as an appendage of Europe. Only the initiation of other Slavic languages and literatures in Slavic departments linked East Central Europe and the Balkans with Russia at this stage. When Soviet hegemony was extended over all of Eastern Europe, academic fashion followed suit and the belt of countries from Poland to Greece became an appendage of Soviet studies. And, given the superficial assumptions about political uniformity in the Soviet bloc, this afforded little stimulus to concentrated study of anything but the Soviet Union. Linguists were

5. (Washington: Association of American Colleges, 1964).

naturally interested in the languages, and historians had to take account of the several strands of independent history in the region; but, with one or two exceptions, the area as a whole enjoyed none of the advantages of the limelight provided by full-scale integrated programs.

Thus, when the countries of Eastern Europe (taken from this point on to mean the Balkans and East Central Europe but excluding Russia) began to display a more differentiated pattern, they called attention to the fact that our academic programs had been treating them as incidental features of Soviet and Russian studies. This development coincided roughly with the attainment of maturity by such Russian programs, with the result that they were ready to enlarge their purview to include the rest of the region. When additional outside support became available in the 1960s, our Russian and East European programs were quite ready to give more forthright attention to Eastern Europe. And from that point onward, East European studies began to enjoy consideration in their own right, albeit largely within a Russian-dominated framework.

Yet this shift in perspective had few discernible effects at the undergraduate level. To be sure, the increase in language offerings opened up some possibilities for undergraduates at the large universities with comprehensive Russian and East European programs (see the next section for details); and some of the augmented coursework in other fields was also open to undergraduates. But the situation in the colleges was approximately analogous to the position of Russian studies for undergraduates described in the Black-Thompson survey of 1957–58.[6] The typical college curriculum reflected almost none of the growing interest in Eastern Europe — and with the added disadvantage that increasing graduate study of Eastern Europe was much less likely to be translated, as the trend in Russian studies had been a decade earlier, into augmentation of the college curriculum. This less hopeful outlook is illustrated by an example from the NDEA Language and Area Centers program. When proposals for undergraduate centers were first entertained on a large scale in 1964–65, nearly a hundred proposals were submitted and fully a quarter of these dealt with Russia and/or Eastern Europe. The great majority of these focused on Russia exclusively. And of the six such proposals receiving favorable consideration, only half included significant East European components. One of these, from Portland State College, was the only proposal submitted that had

6. Cyril E. Black and John M. Thompson, eds., *American Teaching about Russia* (Bloomington: Indiana University Press, 1959).

treated Eastern Europe (minus Russia) as a separate area appropriate for undergraduate concentration.

The record strongly suggests, then, that this region is not likely to find a prominent place in the undergraduate curriculum, certainly not at the smaller institutions. In this it seems to resemble Southeast Asia and, to a lesser extent, Africa. These too are commonly regarded as areas too fragmented, politically and linguistically, and above all too lacking in powerful discrete civilizations of major cultural import, to make them attractive as global additions to liberal education.

This being so, and I am inclined to think that it is valid, we have to look elsewhere for signs that Eastern Europe will receive due attention in undergraduate education. Except for the few universities with such elaborate offerings on the area that several courses are likely to attract some undergraduates, the evolution of regional studies programs, or language and area centers, holds little promise of redressing neglect of Eastern Europe at the undergraduate level. (This observation is not meant to suggest that the Portland State program is inappropriate. On the contrary, I think it is an experiment that we should be watching carefully for results that may modify some of the pessimism expressed above.)

There remain two, possibly three, more hopeful aspects of undergraduate education. The first of these relates to the strengthening of existing courses in the social sciences and humanities by making them more global. Sometimes called infusion, the technique presupposes an effort by instructors, backed by their institutions, to acquire whatever additional competence is needed to "de-parochialize" their courses, to make them germane to as much as possible of diverse human experience. International relations courses afford the best example of offerings that have necessarily widened their coverage to take in the entire international political arena.[7] Courses in world history, religion, literature, economic systems, social organization, and philosophy can presumably do no less if they purport to be as genuinely liberal as is implied by the banner of liberal education. The suspicion persists, and is borne out by cursory examination of standard textbooks, that remoter areas are handled significantly less well, wherever such courses have been given a global perspective, than is subject matter closer to our own experience. It will of course take a good deal of time before we have the teaching materials and the teaching competence to change this state of affairs. But Eastern Europe surely provides an appropriate

7. But for the limitations of this development, see Percy W. Bidwell, *Undergraduate Education in Foreign Affairs* (New York: King's Crown Press, 1962).

body of subject matter for any course that expands its coverage, and its closer ties with Western civilization make it susceptible of more satisfactory treatment at present than, say, Africa or South Asia. Certainly those courses that aim at furthering understanding of world politics or international communism cannot go on pretending that coverage of the Soviet Union is sufficient.

The second aspect relates primarily to European history courses, but also to any offering that purports to deal with Europe. Again, examination of texts now widely used displays the radical tipping of the European continent toward the Atlantic. The farther east one looks, the less attention is provided in textbooks and, presumably, also in courses. It is probably true, in defiance of the historical record, that Eastern Europe receives more attention in Russian history courses than in those devoted to Europe in general. Yet one of the commonest complaints among East European specialists is that their area is distorted by an undue orientation to Russia. On the credit side, we do now have texts which treat Europe as a whole. And one of the greatest benefits that could be conferred on East European studies would come with the corresponding improvement in the teaching of European history to undergraduates.

The two aspects just mentioned have as much bearing on the citizenship-training factor in terminal undergraduate education as they have on recruitment of graduate-level specialists. The third aspect — the growth of programs of study in the area — is certainly not negligible as an element of terminal education, but its primary justification lies in the attraction of undergraduates to the East European field for graduate work. Because parts of Eastern Europe have grown more accessible of late, particularly as compared with the Soviet Union, several institutions have launched programs of study and/or travel in the region. Despite all the skepticism that can be applied to such activity for undergraduates, so long as it exists it is a means of interesting undergraduates in the area. It may also create a demand for corresponding curricular development at home. Foolhardiness alone would permit us to ignore this recent development, for if it is to use public resources and provide genuine academic gains, it must be protected against degeneration into glorified tourism.

By way of summary, the main currents of educational change in the direction of global scope and coverage contain but little tangible evidence and only a few hopeful signs that Eastern Europe may attain a more prominent place in undergraduate education. The next two sections will indicate more precisely what is happening on the undergraduate level now.

THE PROBLEM OF LANGUAGE

Instruction in modern foreign languages has made enough progress in American higher education in the last decade that it is probably no longer difficult to secure a consensus of support for the language component of the curriculum. For several years the number of students enrolled in some modern foreign language class has hovered just under 20 percent. But there has been a steady climb in the number of languages offered and in the number of institutions offering one or more foreign languages. Higher education's commitment to language, this suggests, has grown stronger during the 1950s and 1960s. While many would still lament the sight of mature young adults undergoing an exercise they could have performed as well in childhood, few would question the importance of increasing American proficiency in languages.

In fall 1959, fewer than half a million students were enrolled in language classes in just over a thousand institutions. In fall 1965, 1,933 institutions reported over a million language enrollments. French, Spanish, and German accounted for the bulk of these, with Russian and Italian far behind. These five commonly taught languages accounted for all but a handful of language enrollments. The remaining 2.2 percent of all foreign language enrollments were spread over about eighty additional languages, including all of those indigenous to Eastern Europe.[8]

It would thus seem that Eastern Europe has scarcely shared in the heralded postwar renascence of language learning. As will be shown presently, this is not strictly true. But it does raise the question of what role these languages properly have in undergraduate education. Is it a matter of concern that few undergraduates have the opportunity to study Polish or Serbo-Croatian? Or is this as it should be? Is it important to work toward an increase in undergraduate enrollments in these languages? Or is the undergraduate level the place to stress other things?

It seems appropriate to exclude at the outset those undergraduates for whom the baccalaureate degree is terminal. Few of us are so enthu-

---

8. These figures, and the statistics that follow, have been obtained from the files and publications of the Modern Language Association. Like any statistical operation, the MLA compilations have doubtless undergone refinement from year to year. For this reason, and because of vagaries in the institutional reports on which MLA must rely, detailed comparisons are inadvisable. But general trends are clear, thanks to the regular publications on language enrollments. The richest single source for purposes of this report has been *Manpower in the Neglected Languages, 1963–64* (New York: Modern Language Association of America, 1965). For the period up to the enactment of NDEA in 1958, MLA files contain some valuable material, as does William Riley Parker, *The National Interest and Foreign Languages*, 3d ed. (Washington: Department of State, 1961). I am especially grateful to Mrs. Jean Martin of the MLA staff for help in gathering the data used herein.

siastic about the unique educational advantages offered by Eastern Europe that we would advocate Czech or Romanian as a replacement for French or German as the sole language of study forming a part of general education or "education for citizenship." Russian has by now graduated to the point that it can be considered a legitimate sole language, but this will probably never be true of any other language of Eastern Europe. But most students who elect a language or fulfill a language requirement stop short of functional proficiency, and reforming zeal in this realm should then have a reasonable command of French or German as its aim. Polish and Hungarian, although providing perfectly authentic language-learning experiences, hardly figure so prominently in our cultural tradition as to merit particular missionary emphasis.

This leaves out of account those undergraduates who, registered perhaps at a university or possibly at a college oriented to a particular ethnic tradition, elect an East European language for reasons of ethnic identification or family tradition. This form of reinforcement of ethnic tradition in American life is hardly to be deplored, but it also has little to do with the encouragement of East European studies. Only if such a student plans on graduate work with emphasis on Eastern Europe does his choice bear on our concern here.

Every professor who trains graduate students in, say, East European history has a vision of the ideally equipped beginning graduate student. With minor variations, the dream runs as follows: he will have acquired mastery of French and German by the time he graduates from high school (possibly also Latin in case he wants to work in medieval history) and will have begun the study of Russian. As an undergraduate he will complete his work in Russian and add either another Slavic language or Ottoman, depending on the field that interests him. Then he can learn the other Slavic languages as needed, while spending enough summers in intensive language programs to acquire a reading knowledge of Hungarian and Romanian. This may be something of an oversimplification of the language-learning problem; it certainly is a strained depiction of educational reality. Such students almost never occur.

What happens more typically is that an undergraduate who may sense early in his academic career that he wants to work on Eastern Europe, learns some French or German and gets a start in Russian by the time he commences graduate work. Or, by no means a rarity, he concentrates on Russian to the exclusion of West European languages. Such cases are not hopeless, but they necessitate untold waste of time in language study during the graduate years — waste in the sense that this time ought to be spent in other ways.

Such examples indicate the complexity of any attempt to ascertain what language work an undergraduate ought to choose if he plans a graduate specialization on Eastern Europe. (How much worse the case of a student who reaches this decision after spending three years on Spanish!) They also show why the language problem of Eastern Europe has been likened to that of Southeast Asia or even Africa. In fact the situation is not that forbidding. Russian, if properly learned, is a good starting point from which to acquire at least a reading knowledge of the other Slavic languages with minimal expenditure of time. And German unlocks an astonishing amount of the scholarly literature in several disciplines. Nevertheless, the problem is serious and admits of no easy solutions. The point is not to devise the perfect blueprint, but rather to examine the existing conditions and see what steps will improve them.

The periodic compilations of language enrollments by the Modern Language Association provide the best evidence not only of what language instruction is available but also of how our national capabilities have increased in recent years. Table 1 shows all enrollments, graduate and undergraduate plus some service school numbers, for the years from 1958 through 1963.

In 1962–63, the last year for which such full data are available, offerings somewhere in the country included one level of Albanian, two of Czech, modern Greek, Romanian and Serbo-Croatian, and three of Bulgarian, Hungarian, and Polish. Literature offerings were reported for Czech, modern Greek, Hungarian, Polish, Romanian, and Serbo-Croatian.

Table 2 shows undergraduate enrollments only for the fall of 1965 and the number of institutions offering the languages. (Some of the

TABLE 1
ALL ENROLLMENTS IN LANGUAGE COURSES

Language	1958	1959	1960	1961	1962	1963
Albanian	1	—	8	5	4	9
Bulgarian	9	—	23	34	32	50
Czech	42	49	95	192	171	160
Modern Greek	128	159	139	293	113	88
Hungarian	18	8	69	78	92	128
Polish	309	347	539	628	733	712
Romanian	—	1	23	26	36	46
Serbo-Croatian	36	47	149	145	102	133
Slovak	1	2	26	74	68	34
Slovene	—	—	4	5	5	12

vagaries of the figures, especially between the two tables, are accounted for by omission of service school enrollments in table 2 and by the fact that some language offerings are either not open to or not elected by undergraduates. And, as one might suppose, a sizable portion of enrollments in these languages has been made up of graduate students anyway. It might be added that Romanian and Slovene have since reappeared, with Romanian at least recording a handful of undergraduate enrollments; and Macedonian and Lusatian are both available.

TABLE 2

UNDERGRADUATE ENROLLMENTS IN LANGUAGE COURSES

Language	Institutions	Undergraduate Enrollments
Albanian	1	—
Bulgarian	3	7
Czech	11	137
Modern Greek	8	138
Hungarian	5	48
Polish	31	481
Romanian	—	—
Serbo-Croatian	16	76
Slovak	3	16
Slovene	—	—

The statistics given in tables 1 and 2 may be more meaningful in comparison with other more popular languages: Russian, for example, counted over 30,000 undergraduate enrollments in 1965, and German recorded over 200,000 in that same year.)

The pattern that emerges most clearly is that these languages are taught at two kinds of institutions: at large universities and at small colleges with an ethnic or religious identification. All but one of the Slovak enrollments, for example, appear to have no relation to other academic work on Eastern Europe; and well over half of the Polish enrollments are recorded at sectarian institutions. There are partly unexplained islands of enrollments — 65 in Czech at Nebraska, 22 in Polish at Wayne State, 9 in Hungarian at Western Reserve — that may not be entirely an ethnic phenomenon.[9] And, in general, the modern Greek

9. Such unusual figures as the one for Nebraska are sometimes explained by the existence of special programs, often ones undertaken for a government agency. Wayne State University was, however, one of the institutions I visited, and the Polish enrollment there is apparently indicative of general popularity won during many years of offerings, not — as I was assured by faculty there — of ethnic interest from communities in Detroit. Polish names are said to be rare among students electing the language.

offerings are not associated with East European programs. Perhaps the outstanding single example of uniformly high enrollments at an undergraduate institution is Portland State College with 18 in Czech, 24 in Polish, and 23 in Serbo-Croatian.

Since we are concerned only with undergraduates here, the most suggestive conclusions from the available data are that only Polish, modern Greek, Czech, and Serbo-Croatian appear to have significance in the numbers of undergraduates reached, and none of the East European languages has enjoyed the same rate of increase that is characteristic of such languages as Chinese, Japanese, Arabic, Russian, and Portuguese, all identified with a major country or culture of wider import. It can hardly be expected that even the East European languages studied by significant numbers of students will become mainstays of the undergraduate curriculum, and there is little reason at this point to advocate expansion in the number of institutions offering these languages.

On the contrary, the pressing problem now is to maintain the availability of instruction at the few institutions, chiefly large universities, which have developed such offerings in conjunction with ambitious programs on Eastern Europe. Even they have trouble enough, given the small and fluctuating clientele, to keep the offerings on a regular basis. But they are the best recruiting grounds for graduate specialization. And when present language courses have attracted enough enrollments to make them fairly economical, the next step will be to encourage additional levels of advanced instruction and the inclusion of work in literature and linguistics. Only when this has been accomplished at the few universities pioneering in the field will it make sense to talk of a national need for more widespread offerings in these languages.

Meanwhile, of course, it is always pertinent to improve instruction. The suspicion persists that isolated college offerings in the East European languages do not adhere to high qualitative standards. Where they do, or can be made to do so, the resulting language skills constitute a potential reservoir of graduate students specializing in the field. And, even in those places where the language is unaccompanied by any other work on Eastern Europe, the undergraduates may be attracted into an underpopulated specialization if they proceed to graduate school.

At these undergraduate colleges and at the universities alike, improved language instruction is the most important goal that can now be adopted. This necessitates employment of instructors who know not only the language in question but also how to teach it. It requires the development of better instructional materials — texts, tapes, and reference material — for most of the East European languages. And, so long as we are talking not about majors in Polish or Czech language and literature but rather about would-be historians and political scientists who need to acquire particular skills quickly, it also suggests the desirability of imaginative design of courses to meet these specific needs. We may have overdone the notion that only a two-year sequence in spoken language suffices to prepare a student for his task. Tasks differ, and some students may be better served if they can spend the same amount of time acquiring rudimentary reading familiarity with two or three languages.[10]

None of the foregoing is intended to deter a college from introducing an East European language that has justification in that particular curriculum. A Conference on Critical Languages in Liberal Arts Colleges [11] was held at the University of Washington in April, 1965, to provide encouragement and advice for colleges wishing to inaugurate instruction in one or more of the uncommon languages. Although it was addressed to the question of introducing languages having first priority in the scale of presumed national need (Russian, Chinese, Japanese, Arabic, Hindi-Urdu, and Portuguese), the conclusions apply also to other languages if a college is convinced that they belong in its curriculum. And a number of colleges are demonstrating that Polish or Serbo-Croatian can be taught to significant numbers of undergraduates. The conference recognized the financial problems facing most colleges and advised accordingly that full use be made of possibilities for sharing burdens. Instructors can be shared by neighboring institutions; several universities have adopted the Princeton scheme of admitting undergraduates from other colleges for a year of work in an uncommon language; and each summer several programs offer intensive instruction in, among others, the East European languages.

The summer intensive language program is probably the most fruitful device currently in use to counter the intrinsic problems of maintaining offerings for small bodies of students. Systematic exploitation of summer programs would make it possible for colleges to augment their offerings and for universities to reduce outlays for several levels of several languages, all of them probably underpatronized. Financial support for

10. This conclusion may not be popular among language teachers and linguists, and it is decidedly at variance with the recommendations of the conference report cited just below.

11. (Washington: Association of American Colleges, 1965). The term "critical" as used here refers to those languages of first-priority significance listed in the parenthesis; "neglected" and "uncommon" or "uncommonly taught" are more or less synonymous terms that exclude only French, German, Italian, peninsular Spanish, and Russian.

these programs, and fellowship support for students (including under-graduates), form one of the most valuable features of aid to language and area studies under Title VI of the National Defense Education Act. In the past, these supported programs have usually included two or three offering Polish and one or two offering Serbo-Croatian, or another Slavic language. In the summer of 1967, offerings included Polish in three programs and Czech, Serbo-Croatian, and Lusatian in one program. In summer 1968, all three Slavic programs offered Serbo-Croatian; two, Polish; and Czech, Romanian, and Macedonian were each available in one program. Nothing would serve current needs in the East European language field more directly than the assurance that federal support would make possible regular instruction in all the major languages each summer, preferably at two different locations and at as many levels as the traffic would bear. Subvention is all the more justified because enrollments might fluctuate or even disappear; and the NDEA amendment permitting up to 100 percent support for special programs would be especially pertinent as a means of keeping instruction in these important languages alive until they establish themselves more firmly.

There is a final feature of the undergraduate language curriculum that bears directly on the state of East European studies. This is the high degree of relevance, for purposes of graduate specialization, of good preparation in German and French. German especially has marked advantages in the study of all of Eastern Europe, for a vast body of literature is accessible only in that language. And this marks out a task that is unambiguously a part of the liberal arts curriculum. The under-graduate college is likely to do most for East European studies by pre-paring its graduates well in German and/or French. And the many institutions now teaching Russian can make a similar contribution by readying their graduates for work on other Slavic languages. Many pro-fessors participating in the training of graduate specialists of Eastern Europe would, if they had to choose, prefer a student to arrive with thorough command of either German or Russian than with mastery of any indigenous language of the region, if the latter has been acquired at the expense of work in German or Russian. Here is a challenge that poses no curricular problems for the college, only the demand that lan-guage be well taught.

At this point the interests of terminal undergraduate education and of preparation for graduate work coincide. The East European field has benefited enormously from the general improvements of the past decade in language training. If it cannot be hoped that Bulgarian will ever attract thousands of students, the study of the Balkans or East Central Europe has been made incomparably easier by the overall rise in language study and in pedagogical proficiency. The best hope for the field resides in a continuing trend of improvement in language teaching, particularly at the undergraduate level and below, coupled with the maintenance, in the summer and academic year, of varied language offerings at a few centers of regional specialization.

PATTERNS OF UNDERGRADUATE INSTRUCTION

The prevailing modes of providing instruction on Eastern Euope for undergraduates can be divided up into several rough categories. The subheadings of this section represent such a crude classification. A few examples can be found of full-scale university programs open to undergraduates; and one example of a college program is at hand. Then there is a wide variety of university offerings, and sets of offerings, several of which, it could be argued, form as ambitious programs as those chosen to illustrate the first category. College offerings, on the other hand, tend to be exceedingly modest, often almost fortuitous, in character. Finally, two overseas summer study ventures have been chosen to show another means of exposing undergraduates to Eastern Europe.

Once again it must be emphasized that all of the institutions mentioned in this chapter constitute a minuscule minority in American higher education. This is, as it were, the elite of East European studies in the sense that most curricula ignore the region altogether. There is of course no simple way to ascertain the extent to which the area is treated incidentally in such high-enrollment college courses as international relations, European diplomatic history, economic systems, world literature, and the like. I think no one would argue that coverage of Eastern Europe reaches impressive proportions in offerings of this sort. At any rate, it is indisputable that few undergraduates enjoy significant exposure to Eastern Europe. It is important, most East European specialists would agree, to utilize such general undergraduate courses to increase civic awareness of a region playing an increasingly influential role in the contemporary world. But it is less clear that this type of course bears very directly on the problem of attracting potential graduate students and utilizing the undergraduate years for appropriate forms of preparation for specialization.

The emphasis of this section rests, accordingly, on the varieties of undergraduate work most germane to the flowering of graduate work and, ultimately, of scholarship on the countries of Eastern Europe.

UNIVERSITY PROGRAMS

University programs are illustrated here, at their fullest state of development to date, by a more or less amalgamated description of offerings at three universities: Indiana, Michigan, and Washington. The choice may be somewhat arbitrary, but the three programs are certainly among the strongest in the country and all have substantial undergraduate components. Moreover, they have enough in common that a single description with periodic mention of variations and comparisons will suffice.

All three East European programs grew initially, and at a relatively early date, out of substantial concentrations on Russian and Soviet studies. They developed around vigorous departments of Slavic language and literature, but also with strong representation of the related disciplines of the social sciences and humanities. They all had NDEA Center support from the Office of Education, along with other kinds of outside subvention, which was applied to the development of East European offerings, including course work for undergraduates.

The three programs have all achieved good coverage of the area languages in recent years. Michigan limits its language offerings to the Slavic field, but maintains regular two-year sequences in Polish and Serbo-Croatian, supplemented by course work in Slavic linguistics, Polish literature in English, and South Slavic literature. Czech and Bulgarian are scheduled for early inauguration. Indiana, with the resources of its Uralic-Altaic program supplementing work on Slavic Eastern Europe, covers the language field more completely. The Slavic center lists two-year sequences in Czech, Polish, Serbo-Croatian, modern Greek, Romanian, and Bulgarian. Lusatian and Slovenian have also been introduced. The Uralic-Altaic program offers sequences in Hungarian and Finnish. Perhaps the most noteworthy advance in literature has occurred at Indiana, where serious efforts are being made to provide offerings in the several literatures of Eastern Europe. Washington falls somewhere between the other two in structure, combining Slavic and non-Slavic languages and literature under the single roof of its Russian and East European program. Two-year language sequences are available in Polish, Czech, Romanian, Hungarian, and Serbo-Croatian. Bulgarian has also been taught and would be reintroduced if student demand warranted. Washington also offers work in Slavic linguistics and the literatures of Eastern Europe. All three programs suffer in varying degree, Indiana evidently least of the three, from low or unpredictable enrollments in most of the languages named. But all have recorded some undergraduate enrollments in most of the languages named.

In the social sciences and humanities, all three programs list impressive disciplinary spread. Michigan's East European offerings include, besides the usual history, political science, and economics, courses in philosophy, education, and law. Indiana lists offerings for undergraduates in history, political science, economics, sociology, geography, and folklore. And the Washington program involves not only history, political science, and economics, but also noteworthy strength in geography and a potential for work in law.

Although the preponderant position of Russian studies is evident in all three programs, it is also clear that an undergraduate can choose from a substantial body of coursework on Eastern Europe in several departments. It is perhaps understandable that an East European specialist should feel disadvantaged at times in the face of the concentration of resources on Russia, yet it is also hard to believe that our region would now be receiving as much attention as it is but for the strength of the parent Russian programs. Where flexibility obtains in the choices a student can make within a program, the connection with Russian studies can hardly be called a liability. It becomes that only if Eastern Europe is viewed anachronistically as a pale reflection of Russia. And the swift pace of expansion of these three programs into Eastern Europe suggests, to the contrary, that the region will attain its proper level of attention first at those institutions where Russian studies are already strong, not least because the better attended Russian offerings can sustain the newer concentration on Eastern Europe until it wins a stable clientele.

General University Offerings

There is probably no way to survey East European studies at many universities under the heading of general university offerings without fashioning a rather dull catalog of repetitive information. To minimize this, the following review will concentrate on what is distinctive in a number of institutions. The review makes no claim to exhaustiveness, partly just because replies were not received from several institutions known to have significant offerings on East Europe (notably UCLA, Harvard, and Pennsylvania State University). But the samples offered here also run the gamut from programs approaching parity with the ones described in the previous section to isolated offerings resembling the college situation described below, so there is no intention to place the ensuing examples on a par with each other.

Three traditional centers of strength on Eastern Europe are Columbia, Berkeley, and Pennsylvania. But for their predominantly graduate orientation, the first two would certainly have had to be included in the previous section. Columbia, like Indiana, joins a Uralic program with its East European program to secure full coverage. Three levels each of Hungarian and Finnish are offered in the Uralic program. And in conjunction with the program of the Institute on East Central Europe, three levels each of Polish and Serbo-Croatian are offered, along with two of Czech. Greek, Bulgarian, and Romanian are available, and plans are afoot for introducing Slovenian. These are amply buttressed by work in literature and linguistics. The Institute lists several well-attended undergraduate courses in politics and history, but the bulk of Institute offerings are designed for graduate students.

Berkeley has doubtless the only Slavic program in the country offering a B.A. in Polish, Serbo-Croatian, and Czech language and literature. As this suggests, offerings at Berkeley are built on a strong Slavic department with extensive offerings (including Hungarian). Coursework is also available for undergraduates in economics, history, and politics.

Pennsylvania's Slavic program has long been oriented toward Russia and the Baltic. But it also offers two years each of Polish and Serbo-Croatian and several courses on Polish and Serbo-Croatian literature, all of which are open to undergraduates.

Another set of institutions — Colorado, Yale, and Fordham — also has a long-standing identification with Eastern Europe but with more of a focus on undergraduate study. Colorado's East European program developed under the direction of Professor S. Harrison Thomson and was for some time the only NDEA Center in the country concentrating chiefly on Eastern Europe. His retirement occasioned a refashioning of the program, a process resulting in a greater emphasis on Russia but with Eastern Europe also well covered. The program is strong in linguistics, with two levels of Polish and Czech available and with Bulgarian being introduced. The program is notable for its high undergraduate enrollments in history and politics.

Fordham, which had one of the first NDEA Centers in the Slavic field, has long sought to enlarge its coverage of Eastern Europe. Polish and Czech have been introduced, but low enrollments have kept them from becoming regular parts of the curriculum. Present plans, however, call for the establishment of two levels of each language and the introduction of Serbo-Croatian. Work in history and the social sciences has focused largely on Russia, especially after Professor O. Halecki's retirement, but a few undergraduates are registered in courses touching on Eastern Europe.

The Yale program in Russian and East European studies well exemplifies the tendency to augment the East European side of such programs. With instruction available in Polish, Czech, Serbo-Croatian, and Bulgarian, and with a strong faculty of specialists on Eastern Europe as well as Russia, the program has shifted substantially from its original Russian focus. The program is also one of the few with resources for offerings in Slavic music.

Three programs of more modest scope may be mentioned here for their distinguishing features. Notre Dame's program of Soviet and East European studies includes no language other than Russian, but it has an outstanding range of offerings for undergraduates in both the political science of Eastern Europe and the prevailing contemporary philosophy of the region. Vanderbilt, on the other hand, shows relatively little growth in the social sciences or history of Eastern Europe but a considerable strength in the Slavic languages and linguistics of the area. Wayne State University has moved on both fronts at once, with the development of offerings in history and geography and a continuing high level of enrollment in Polish. This institution has also enjoyed marked success with undergraduate survey courses in Slavic and in Polish culture.

In the past two or three years, five large Midwestern universities have provided compelling evidence that Eastern Europe commands significant academic attention. The most striking new development in many ways was the decision taken at the University of Chicago to establish a program focusing directly on the Balkans. Built around a strong staff in linguistics and literature, the program features a remarkable coverage of Balkan languages. But apart from the national languages offered (Greek, Polish, Czech, Romanian, Bulgarian, and Serbo-Croatian), the linguistic emphasis on Albanian, Slovene, and Macedonian has little immediate relevance to undergraduate programs. Indeed the whole program has determinedly focused on graduate work. Yet the long-range implications for undergraduate study, given the coverage of languages and literatures and the determination to fill gaps in history and the social sciences, are profound.

The Kansas program, which was designated an NDEA graduate center along with Chicago in 1965, joins Eastern Europe with Russian studies. But a distinct program on East Central Europe includes instruction in Serbo-Croatian and Polish, as well as offerings in history, linguistics, literature, political science, and geography. In 1965–66, sixty-five undergraduates were enrolled in these courses. Two exceptional features of the program are its attention to East European theater and its inclusion of East Germany.

In the Big Ten, Illinois, Wisconsin, and Ohio State have all taken steps to reinforce the East European component of their programs, and all are strengthening their language offerings to include more languages and more levels of each. Wisconsin has the incidental advantage of a Scandinavian program which offers Finnish and links up with existing faculty interest in the Baltic region. Thus, Wisconsin offers an undergraduate major in Polish and has at least one history course on Poland, along with courses of long standing on the Balkans. Illinois is another instance where a Russian program gathered substantial strength and offerings on Eastern Europe almost before it knew that this was happening. Polish, Czech, and Serbo-Croatian were added, and Bulgarian is anticipated. And the faculty, although not collected with a coherent East European program in mind, includes some unusual specialties such as agricultural economics, law, and sociology in addition to the usual courses in history.

Finally, passing mention must be made of several relatively new programs which contain interesting aspects. The Institute for Sino-Soviet Studies at George Washington University, for example, has found it advisable to move well beyond its name into the East European field. With the addition of Serbo-Croatian in 1968, plans were laid for Polish in 1969; and already they are considering Hungarian and Czech for the future. Related offerings in history and politics make this the only substantial program on Eastern Europe in the area of the national capital.

Stanford University has recently added to its faculty strength on Eastern Europe and, while elaborate program development is not foreseen, the prevailing emphasis on solid undergraduate instruction will be coupled with curricular expansion on the region, particularly in history. Rice University also presents a situation in which an ambitious program is probably not to be expected. But present faculty interest in Habsburg and Balkan history will possibly lead to some increase in language instruction and to supporting appointments in other fields.

The University of Texas has had an undergraduate program on Russia and Eastern Europe since 1954; more than thirty students have graduated under the direction of its Eastern European Committee. Instruction is available in Serbo-Croatian, Czech, Polish, Bulgarian, and Albanian, and each of six departments offers courses bearing on the area.

Two programs in the Boston area have recently emerged with significant new offerings for undergraduates. Boston University has combined Russia and Eastern Europe in a program leading to a B.A. in the regional field, and Polish is offered, along with courses in history and economics dealing with Eastern Europe. At Boston College, which may prove to be one of the more ambitious newer NDEA Centers at the undergraduate level, Polish, Romanian, and Serbo-Croatian have been introduced, as well as work in Balkan history.

Finally, two of the leading universities of the southeastern United States, Duke and North Carolina, have combined resources in a regional program with substantial course work on Eastern Europe. The two institutions may evolve a useful pattern of collaboration for others to follow in a field marked by scarcity of trained scholars, for their cumulative offerings form a most respectable beginning in history, political science, language, and literature.

COLLEGE PROGRAMS

The only college program that can be described as an integrated curriculum on Eastern Europe is the Central European Studies Center at Portland State College. This program was proposed to the Office of Education as a new undergraduate language and area center in 1964 and began operation with NDEA support in the fall of 1965. The rationale of this program is best shown by excerpts from the original proposal to the Office of Education:

> Portland State College is deeply committed to the area and language approach to international affairs. . . . Members of the faculty . . . , in cooperation with colleagues from neighboring institutions, have worked out an integrated program of studies in the languages and area of Central Europe. . . . Their present close association with the Soviet Union notwithstanding, it is safe to assume that they [the countries of Eastern Europe] will eventually gravitate again toward their neighbor to the west — Germany. The real problem of Central Europe is posed by the complex relationships — linguistic, historical, political and economic — between the Germanic peoples (Germany and Austria) and the Western and Southern Slavs (Poland, Czechoslovakia, Yugoslavia). We propose to subject it to an intensive course of studies. . . . Planned as a four-year sequence the program will make suitable adaptation of the college's regular B.A. requirements with the aim to concentrate attention to the languages and area of Central Europe. To qualify for a certificate, students must have fluency in two languages: German and Polish, or Czech, or Hungarian, or Serbo-Croat. In addition, they must have taken courses in the geography, history, politics, and economics of this area. Students who successfully complete this course of studies

will be encouraged to spend the summer following their graduation travelling and studying in Central Euope.

During its first year of operation, this center moved strongly toward its objectives. Polish, Czech, and Serbo-Croatian were offered, along with German of course, and Hungarian was slated for early inauguration. Courses were added in the history of Eastern Europe, the geography of Central Europe, and political, economic, and social trends in Central Europe. Both the faculty and the library were strengthened in support of the program. The newly introduced languages recorded substantial beginning enrollments: 13 in Czech, 20 in Polish, and 23 in Serbo-Croatian. Comparable numbers elected the history, geography, and economics offerings.

It will be some time before this program graduates its first generation of students, by which time it seems likely that the college will have added a masters' program in the field and possibly a research component as well. By then it will be possible to answer such conspicuous questions as: Does this program offer a genuinely liberal education? What sacrifices must a student make in order to fulfill the center's requirements? How good is the center's instruction as preparation for more advanced work? For the present, it is certainly warranted to observe that the Portland State College program merits close attention as a singular experiment in treating Central Europe as a focal point of liberal education. One is doubtless entitled to wonder what students will do with this kind of concentration if they do not pursue it into graduate school. But one may wonder the same thing about many undergraduate concentrations. The certificate program is superimposed on regular departmental majors, so it is not a matter of substituting an area for a discipline. Therefore, perhaps the key question should be phrased as follows: Why is Central Europe less suitable than any other regional concentration — Indian, Chinese, Western European, or North American — as a companion to departmental work for the baccalaureate degree?

COLLEGE OFFERINGS

Among more general types of college offerings on Eastern Europe, far and away the most numerous courses are in history. Some of these are straightforward treatments, ranging from a term to a year in duration, of modern Eastern Europe. In other cases, Eastern Europe gets passing attention in courses oriented chiefly to Russia, the Ottoman empire, or the Habsburg dynasty. Also fairly numerous are courses in political science or international relations which include Eastern Europe in treatments of Soviet foreign policy, the cold war, or the Communist world. The region is occasionally dealt with in economics courses which compare systems or touch on the problems of economic planning.

Bearing in mind that inquiries were sent in the first place only to institutions thought to have some interest in the region, some of the replies form the best available index to the position of Eastern Europe in numbers of college and university curricula.

Professor Ernst Helmreich of Bowdoin College mentioned his own semester course in the history of East Central Europe, offered since 1945 and now alternating with his year-long course on Europe since 1848 in which half the time is spent on Russia and Eastern Europe. Otherwise, he reported, no one else deals with the area at Bowdoin.

At Oregon State University, according to Professor George B. Carson, an undergraduate major has just been established in Russian studies but, apart from occasional interest in offering Polish, resources will not permit enlargement of the program to include Eastern Europe. Moreover,

> since there is no graduate work in the departments of the School of Humanities and Social Sciences, the recruiting of faculty for more specialized programs is quite difficult. When people cannot be offered much opportunity to teach in their specialties, the adding of qualified staff for East Central European or Balkan studies, whether in History or Modern Languages, is often a very frustrating business.

Professor Edgar Anderson replied from San Jose State College that it had proved impossible to introduce courses there on Eastern Europe apart from Russia, but that he had used his upper-division colloquia to cover topics of particular interest to him and his students on the area.

Professor Marin Pundeff of San Fernando State College reports three history courses on the area that have had good student response. He rightly emphasizes the importance of undergraduate courses to awaken student interest in the region.

From the University of Denver, Professor George Barany wrote of his one-quarter survey of East Central European history which attracts typically a dozen students, and of his occasional seminars for three to five students on Austro-Hungarian history.

Several common features unite these modest but far from negligible efforts to impart understanding of Eastern Europe to undergraduates. One is that the offerings are not usually buttressed by courses in other disciplines or by language instruction. Another is that if the particular professor were to disappear, the course probably would too; the presence of instructor and course often appears to be a fortuitous matter, not the result of a decision to teach about Eastern Europe. Finally, the maintenance of even the one course may at times seem doubtful in view of multiple demands on institutions and their curricula; Eastern Europe, even including Russia, is not yet regarded in many institutions as a subject that has to be covered. As noted before, history is the strongest contributor of courses in the field, and if that discipline has not yet fully acknowledged Eastern Europe, the situation is incomparably worse in other departments.

Loneliness has sometimes been mentioned as an acute problem for regional specialists who teach at smaller universities and colleges. The Middle Eastern specialist has, for example, been depicted as desperate for someone to talk with and for greater opportunity to exercise his training on the typical college campus. Happily, this does not seem to be an equally sore affliction for the East European specialist. Perhaps because his subject matter is more closely related to that of his colleagues, perhaps because he is readier to teach a broad range of subject matter, the historian or political scientist trained to deal with our area is not necessarily unhappy in the college. And it is surely salutary that this should be so, for the field would lose significantly if all specialists were to gather at a handful of large centers. The work done by the isolated East European instructor on a college or small university campus is vital to the health of the field, not least because it helps to demonstrate its relation to other more popular fields of study. It is to be hoped that our graduate training programs will continue to graduate young scholars willing and even eager to give up the narrow specialization of large university programs in favor of the necessarily greater scope of teaching in the college.

Overseas Study Programs for Undergraduates

The vexed question of overseas study programs for undergraduates has entered the East European field as a result of growing accessibility of the area and the availability of support through counterpart funds. Drawing on blocked currency accounts in Yugoslavia and operating under the authority of Section 102(b)(6) of the Fulbright-Hays Act, the Office of Education funded two undergraduate programs in the summer of 1966. These will suffice as examples of the kind of activity possible in this realm.

Louisiana State University staged one such program under the aegis of its NDEA-supported Russian studies center. The students were selected from among undergraduates majoring in Slavic studies, lower-division students with an interest in such a major, and others of high academic attainment. They spent six weeks in Belgrade in formal study and then traveled across Yugoslavia. Throughout their stay they mingled as much as possible with Yugoslavs.

All participants took two courses during the six-week period and received six hours of credit for successful completion. One course was in Serbo-Croatian meeting two hours a day, five days a week, under the tutelage of a native Yugoslav instructor. The other was in Yugoslav history, taught by Professor Jadran Ferluga of the University in Belgrade, consisting of fifteen two-hour lectures.

Louisiana State hopes to repeat the program, and reports meanwhile two significant developments on the campus that relate to the summer study program. Serbo-Croatian has been introduced into the home curriculum and is being taken by several students who went to Yugoslavia. And a number of the participants have, by their elective choices and, in some cases, by shifting fields, demonstrated the impact which the summer had on them. Both developments on the home campus illustrate the beneficial effects of such summer study and travel programs.

The other illustration comes from a college that is strictly oriented to the liberal arts, Iowa Wesleyan College. In this instance, there was no curricular program in Russian or East European studies to provide a springboard, but rather an incipient but singularly ambitious international program involving most major world regions. The International Center at Iowa Wesleyan resulted from a faculty committee's recommendations for comprehensive coverage of the non-Western world, both in the home curriculum and in programs of travel and study for undergraduates. One of its regional units is the East European Institute, which has been active mainly in extracurricular activity and in implementing the overseas study program.

The 1966 program consisted of a five-week stay in Belgrade punctuated by field trips to other parts of the country. Fifteen students spent two hours each morning, five days a week, in a course transplanted from the home campus, Comparative Economic Systems, taught by the director of the Institute. The course, for which three hours of credit were granted, was supplemented by lectures by Yugoslav and U.S. officials.

The 1966 experience was rewarding enough that Iowa Wesleyan plans to repeat it along the same lines and to add a similarly designed overseas program focusing on Polish and Swedish art and involving an eighteen-day sojourn in Poland.

The resulting impact on the Iowa Wesleyan campus appears to be less tangible than was the case at Louisiana State, although it is doubtless much too early to measure the effect on development of one of the more ambitious non-Western programs in American colleges. The summer program in Yugoslavia omitted any attention to language work, but the introduction of Russian instruction in the regular curriculum may well be related to a burgeoning interest in Eastern Europe fostered by the summer study.

There is little doubt that these summer programs, and others like them, serve as valuable stimulus, both to the participating students and the sponsoring institutions. The institutions in question can be credited with initiative and imagination in introducing these supplements to the undergraduate curriculum. Accordingly, the doubts raised by this type of program do not in any sense reflect on the institutions. But it is difficult to believe that this is the best conceivable use of public resources in the interest of academic development in the East European field. If public programs were not involved, or if resources were unlimited, one could of course only endorse this way of turning the summer months to good account. Yet at this stage, when numbers of scholars and advanced students could so well use the opportunity to visit their area of specialization, it would be hard to maintain that the Fulbright-Hays program is operating so as to maximize academic opportunity. Perhaps this has something to do with a dogma about international understanding and the proper way to bring it to pass. But if one is concerned with academic development, as the wording of Section 102(b)(6) of the Fulbright-Hays act suggests that it is, then the imagination of public officials and the wit of East European specialists should not be unequal to the development of more important ways to apply limited funds to the improvement of East European studies. Again, it would be splendid if we could stimulate undergraduates in these ways as well, and the institutions mentioned above can only be commended for undertaking such ventures. But the field as a whole has much more pressing needs.

One is driven to conclude from all of the foregoing that, while many improvements are desirable at the undergraduate level, graduate training must remain our central concern. In the very broadest sense, anything that improves liberal arts education, whether in regard to disciplinary training, language skills, or mental stimulation of undergraduates, may redound to the benefit of East European studies. Narrowing the perspective a bit, one can think of many rather less inchoate steps that would be advantageous: earlier acquisition of languages such as German and Russian, more opportunities for summer language study by undergraduates, greater awareness — on the part of instructors in the social sciences, especially — of Eastern Europe as a zone of contemporary ferment and change; a better understanding in history departments of the bonds between the western and eastern segments of Europe, and perhaps even more experiments of the Portland State type.

Nevertheless, the field appears to be at a stage where further refinement and definition of objectives at the graduate level will have to precede any consensus as to the place of Eastern Europe in liberal arts education. The major graduate programs are the ones providing fullest opportunity for undergraduates at this point, and considerably enhanced strength at these few places will not only do the most for undergraduates at the moment but will also contribute most to the evolution of a proper role for the liberal arts in the continuum of study with which we are concerned. Above all, only the graduate program can produce the more numerous body of specialists needed at this stage to give the region its proper place in higher education on all levels.

Meanwhile, however, assuming a due regard for maximizing return from limited resources, it is appropriate to welcome any improvement in undergraduate treatment of our region. If it lies on the borderline between what we conventionally study as Western civilization and what we are wont to call the non-Western world, so much the better. The subject then offers a double incentive for serious attention by undergraduates.

By no means the least of developments to be welcomed is the newer facet of the institutes program under Title XI of NDEA. With the addition of authority to deal with history, geography, civics, and such subjects of the secondary-school curriculum, a number of intriguing programs have been conducted on Russia and Eastern Europe, on the Communist world, and on European diplomacy. Assuming that secondary-school teachers must have more influence on their students than we have on ours, the added awareness fostered by such institutes' programs is an important net gain, not only among the teacher participants but in the sponsoring institutions of higher education.

The history of foreign area studies in the United States strongly suggests that the patterns delineated above — notable strength at a few large institutions, mostly random offerings at a few other places, and virtual neglect in almost all undergraduate curricula — represent an early stage in the emergence of a regional field of specialization. In the final analysis, Eastern Europe may in fact more closely resemble Southeast Asia or Africa as an undergraduate subject than it does Russia or the Far East. Yet it seems doubtful that the curriculum can stand still in its present neglect of an area so vital in the contemporary world. A genuine understanding of world communism and of international affairs in general is now clearly dependent on greatly increased attention to Eastern Europe. If the undergraduate level is not yet the place for concentration of resources, the time will come as it has in other regional fields when this level becomes as important to the health of the field as graduate study is now.

CONCLUSIONS

The findings of this undergraduate phase of the survey of East European studies are presented here in the form of recommendations designed to improve the situation over what has been described above. Underlying these recommendations, but unstated otherwise, is the belief that East European studies do not lend themselves to major expansion at the undergraduate level in the way that Russian studies have been developed. Our goals in this respect should be more modest. On the other hand, as the following propositions indicate, our field stands to gain, more directly than others perhaps, from general improvements in the caliber of liberal education, especially in the teaching of European history and in earlier mastery of key European languages.

1. *Support for outstanding programs.* At this stage the most significant gains in the field can be registered among undergraduates with access to the university programs that are already most developed. Neither government nor foundations should apologize for using their support to build on existing strength. Newly introduced languages are in particular need of outside assistance until they establish stronger student patronage. Undue emphasis on fostering new programs at this stage could only be pernicious, for with specialists so scarce that would only fragment our efforts.

2. *Treating Eastern Europe in different contexts.* Since the region falls so far short of being a unified area, there is no single framework that is best for instruction. In some cases the area will be handled separately, in others as an appendage of Russia or of Central Europe. In many undergraduate situations, the region will be touched only as an adjunct of Habsburg or Ottoman or German history. Such diversity of treatment should be deliberately encouraged, although always with due regard for Eastern Europe in its own terms.

3. *Injecting East European subject matter into existing courses.* Most colleges and some universities are unlikely to be able to offer their undergraduates a complete program or even significant numbers of highly specialized courses. Therefore, it is particularly important that existing courses in several academic disciplines include a measure of attention to Eastern Europe. This requires opportunities for instructors

to acquaint themselves with the subject matter and refined guidance on library development for undergraduates. Programs enabling college teachers to visit the area would be among the more useful ways to strengthen the field; and Eastern Europe should be among the area fields for which Title VI, NDEA, postdoctoral awards could be granted for advanced study at NDEA Centers.

4. *Development of teaching materials.* Many kinds of text materials are already badly needed: language texts, grammars, tapes, and student dictionaries; basic textbooks on the region and on individual countries in several disciplines, but especially in history since history courses are the most common means of introducing undergraduates to Eastern Europe; collections of readings and case studies; and reliable reference materials. The need can only grow more desperate as work in the field expands.

5. *Support for summer programs.* The complexities of the East European language situation and the high cost of most presently available academic-year instruction both point to summer intensive language programs as the best palliative. Students (and their advisers) should be able to plan on the availability each summer of offerings in all the major languages of the area, preferably at two or three well-separated locations. And the new authority for support up to 100 percent contained in amendments to NDEA passed with the International Education Act should be utilized as quickly as possible in this realm of great need.

6. *Coverage of Eastern Europe in general European history courses.* One of the best ways to acquaint significant numbers of undergraduates with the area would be to give Eastern Europe its rightful measure of attention in European history courses and textbooks, especially on subjects other than diplomatic history only.

7. *Development of diverse approaches to language teaching.* With such small likelihood of undergraduate concentration on Eastern Europe within language and literature, most undergraduates who do reach the stage of electing these languages will have quite varied needs, depending on their discipline or intended field of specialization. This suggests the desirability of greater flexibility in the style or technique of language instruction. Efforts should be made, for example, to develop reading courses that would provide limited proficiency and self-confidence in relatively short time; these might be available in summer or in the academic year or both.

8. *Rigorous standards in study/travel programs.* Although one can argue that public resources should not be used to send undergraduates to the area, it seems likely that programs of study and/or travel will continue — with or without public support. It is therefore worth emphasiz-

ing that such ventures can become farcical as educational undertakings. It is important to the students involved and to the field as a whole that a high level of academic performance be maintained as a condition of participation, for enthusiasm without achievement is of negligible value.

9. *Improved language instruction.* It would probably be doubtful wisdom to advocate more widespread college offerings in East European languages. But with scholarly work in the field so heavily dependent on proficiency in German, French, Latin, and Russian, most college curricula already have an important hidden resource for the field. Early and effective learning of these languages is vital.

3/ HISTORY

Charles and Barbara Jelavich
Indiana University

Although American interest in East Central and Southeastern European affairs was strongly evident at certain earlier periods, as, for example, during the Greek revolution of the 1820s and the Hungarian revolt of 1848–49, serious scholarly historical research commenced only at the beginning of this century. Then, under the leadership of Archibald Cary Coolidge at Harvard University, the first graduate students specializing in East European history were trained. Two of these, Robert J. Kerner and R. H. Lord, subsequently wrote standard studies in their respective fields of specialization. In addition, Kerner edited the first general bibliographical study published in the United States on Eastern Europe, entitled *Slavic Europe*.[1] During World War I, Kerner, Lord, and others of Coolidge's students served as experts on the various commissions responsible for the drafting of the peace settlement involving the former Habsburg and Ottoman empires. By 1918 a base for the study of Eastern European history had thus been created.

In the interwar years, research and training in this field continued at Harvard, where William L. Langer wrote on European diplomatic problems, including those of Eastern Europe, and directed students in this field; at Columbia, where Carlton J. H. Hayes and Philip Mosely were particularly interested in problems of nationalism and the Eastern Question; and at the University of California, where Robert J. Kerner

In the preparation of this report we are very grateful for the assistance of five scholars who provided us with the information on the countries of their specialization: Professor Piotr Wandycz — Poland; Professor Joseph Zacek — Czechoslovakia; Professor Peter Sugar — Hungary; Professor Keith Hitchins — Romania; and Professor Theofanis Stavrou — Greece.

1. *Slavic Europe: Selected Bibliography in the Western European Languages, Comprising History, Languages and Literatures* (Cambridge: Harvard University Press, 1918).

and his colleague in Slavic Languages and Literatures, George R. Noyes, placed particular emphasis on the study of the language and history of the entire area. At this time also S. Harrison Thomson of the University of Colorado, a keen student of Slavic affairs, especially Czechoslovak and Polish, gave great stimulus to research through the publication of the *Journal of Central European Affairs*. After World War II, the study of this area, like that of the Soviet Union, expanded rapidly. New centers — for example, at Chicago, Colorado, Florida State, Illinois, Indiana, Kansas, Michigan, Ohio State, Stanford, UCLA, Washington, Wisconsin, and Yale — joined the established institutions in providing training in the field. Today they are over fifty American historians engaged in research and teaching in some aspect of East Central and Southeast European history.

At first three problems in particular attracted the interest of American scholars — the Eastern Question, the nationality problem of the Habsburg Empire, and the fate of Poland. Inseparable from these was, of course, the nationality issue in the entire area. Influenced by Gladstonian and Wilsonian liberalism and disturbed by the real and alleged injustices prevalent in these lands, some Americans became both scholars and crusaders. They were thus sympathetic to the views expressed in the writings of contemporary French and English scholars, notably R. W. Seton-Watson, Henry Wickham Steed, Harold Temperley, E. Denis, Alfred Mousset, and Emile Haumant. The first American writing was, as a result, highly critical of Ottoman, Habsburg, Magyar, German, or Russian rule over other national groups. Moreover, the Poles, Czechs, and Yugoslavs, who were more articulate in the expression of their national resentments, received considerably more attention than did the Romanians, Magyars, Bulgarians, Greeks, and Albanians. This emphasis was naturally reflected in library acquisitions. As a result, the best library collections in the United States today are those on Poland, Yugoslavia, and Czechoslovakia.

PUBLICATIONS IN HISTORY

In general, American publications on Eastern Europe fall into two categories. The first includes those concerning the area as a whole, certain distinct portions of it, or problems which transcend national boundaries. The second group deals with the history of the individual countries or their subdivisions. In this report, we will first examine the general works in the field, and then proceed to an examination of national and local histories. A discussion of the periods and subjects which have not received adequate study will be included in each section concerning the individual states and at the end of the chapter. Some of the more important standard works by English historians have been included in this survey because of their obvious accessibility to American readers. Books in other languages which should be translated have also been mentioned throughout.

Because of the number of countries involved, the diversity of languages, and the great quantity of books, monographs, and articles published in the Eastern European countries, it would be extremely difficult for a single scholar to write a general, interpretive history of the entire area. It is also a question, as is discussed elsewhere, if this field is indeed historically unified to an extent that would make such a treatment possible or advisable. Consequently, few attempts have been made. The most successful is Oscar Halecki, *The Borderlands of Western Civilization*,[2] which, nevertheless, is illustrative of the difficulties involved in such an endeavor. The author is better in dealing with the Habsburg lands and Poland than with the Balkan states. Perhaps more effective, but limited to the Slavic peoples, is Francis Dvornik, *The Slavs in European History and Civilization*.[3] This work is the first successful attempt in any language to study the significance of the Slavs for Europe. The same author's *The Making of Central and Eastern Europe*[4] and *The Slavs, Their Early History and Civilization*[5] are also important. Equally valuable is Roger Portal's *Les Slaves: peuples et nations* in which the author's basic thesis is the movement of the Slavs during the last thousand years from a common Slavic civilization to a large number of national civilizations.[6] Other books covering the area in general, or a major portion of it, are few in number. William H. McNeill's *Europe's Steppe Frontier, 1500–1800*[7] is the best study available on the shifting borderlands of Eastern Europe. Doreen Warriner, ed. *Contrasts in Emerging Societies*,[8] is an extremely useful selection of readings, usually written by travelers, on social and economic conditions in nineteenth-century Hungary, Romania, Bulgaria, and the lands comprising present-day Yugoslavia.

By far the best synthesis of a part of the area is L. S. Stavrianos, *The Balkans since 1453*.[9] Combining a topical and a chronological approach, and revealing a real feeling for the subject, the author has produced a

2. (New York: Ronald Press, 1952).
3. (New Brunswick, N.J.: Rutgers University Press, 1962).
4. (London: Polish Research Center, 1949).
5. (Boston: American Academy of Arts and Sciences, 1956).
6. Paris: Armand Colin, 1965).
7. (Chicago: University of Chicago Press, 1964).
8. (Bloomington: Indiana University Press, 1965).
9. (New York: Holt, Rinehart and Winston, 1958).

work indispensable for the scholar and the graduate student. The book shows also the author's keen interest in the interdisciplinary approach to history. Highly provocative and stimulating is Traian Stoianovich's *A Study in Balkan Civilization*.[10] By making extensive use of anthropological, ethnographical, economic, historical, and sociological studies, the author has produced a work which is unique in any language. In 1960 a conference of American specialists on Balkan affairs, together with some European colleagues, considered certain problems of Southeastern Europe primarily in the period from the eighteenth century to 1945. The reports are published in Charles and Barbara Jelavich, eds., *The Balkans in Transition*.[11] The contributors looked for common denominators in Balkan history. Their aim was to stress the unity, and not the diversity of the area. The war and postwar period is covered in the thorough study of Robert Lee Wolff, *The Balkans in Our Time*,[12] which, however, omits Greece. Two short surveys, L. S. Stavrianos, *The Balkans, 1815–1914*[13] and Charles and Barbara Jelavich, *The Balkans*,[14] are available too. Problems involving the Balkan countries in general are also discussed in L. S. Stavrianos, *Balkan Federation: A History of the Movement toward Balkan Unity in Modern Times*.[15] Problems of economic history are discussed in Nicolas Spulber, *The State and Economic Development in Eastern Europe*,[16] and the two articles dealing with economic history by Traian Stoianovich, "Land Tenure and Related Sectors of the Balkan Economy, 1600–1800"[17] and "The Conquering Balkan Orthodox Merchant,"[18] both in the *Journal of Economic History*.

Unfortunately, no book similar to that by Stavrianos exists for the history of the Habsburg Empire for the entire period from either the thirteenth (the reign of Rudolph) or the sixteenth (Charles V) centuries to the present. Excellent studies are, however, to be found concerning the national problem and the conditions within the monarchy in the last period of its existence. Indispensable for the study of the area are thus Robert A Kann, *The Multinational Empire*,[19] Arthur J.

10. (New York: Knopf, 1967).
11. (Berkeley: University of California Press, 1963).
12. (Cambridge: Harvard University Press, 1956).
13. (New York: Holt, Rinehart and Winston, 1963).
14. (Englewood Cliffs, N.J.: Prentice-Hall, 1965).
15. (Northampton, Mass.: Department of History of Smith College, 1944; Hamden, Conn.: Archon Books, 1964).
16. (New York: Random House, 1966).
17. *Journal of Economic History*, 13, no. 4 (1953): 398–411.
18. *Journal of Economic History*, 20 (June, 1960): 234–313.
19. *The Multinational Empire: Nationalism and National Reform in the Habs-*

May, *The Hapsburg Monarchy, 1867–1914*[20] and *The Passing of the Hapsburg Monarchy, 1914–1918*,[21] and Victor Mamatey, *The United States and East Central Europe, 1914–1918*.[22] Kann emphasizes the political and legal aspects of the problem; May covers the entire history of the empire, including social and economic conditions; Mamatey presents an outstanding analysis of wartime diplomacy. These studies on World War I should be supplemented by the excellent works published in England by Harry Hanak, *Great Britain and Austria-Hungary during the First World War*, and Z. A. B. Zeman, *The Breakup of the Habsburg Empire*.[23] In addition, the pioneering work by Oscar Jaszi, *The Dissolution of the Habsburg Monarchy*,[24] although poorly translated, is indispensable for the social and economic questions. A provocative English study is A. J. P. Taylor, *The Habsburg Monarchy, 1809–1918*,[25] which should be balanced by R. A. Kann, *The Habsburg Empire: A Study in Integration and Disintegration*.[26]

In addition to these books which have already appeared, a number of other works covering the area in general, or a wide portion of it, are either being prepared or are in the process of publication. Of major significance for the student of the area is the ten-volume series being prepared by the University of Washington Press under the editorship of Professors Peter Sugar and Donald Treadgold, *The History of East Central Europe*.[27] In April, 1966, a conference on "The Nationality Problem in the Habsburg Empire: A Critical Reappraisal" was held at Indiana University. These papers were published in the third

burg Monarchy, 2 vols. (New York: Columbia University Press, 1950; New York: Octagon Books, 1964).

20. (Cambridge: Harvard University Press, 1951).

21. 2 vols. (Philadelphia: University of Pennsylvania Press, 1966).

22. (Princeton: Princeton University Press, 1957).

23. Hanak (London: Oxford University Press, 1962); Zeman (London: Oxford University Press, 1961).

24. (Chicago: University of Chicago Press, 1929, 1961).

25. (London: H. Hamilton, 1948; New York: Harper and Row, 1965).

26. (New York: Praeger, 1957).

27. Peter F. Sugar and Donald W. Treadgold, eds., *The History of East-Central Europe*. I. Omeljan Pritsak and Maria Gimbutas, *The Beginnings of History in East-Central Europe (to A.D. 1000)*; II. Spyros Vryonis, *Byzantium and the Balkans in the Middle Ages (to 1453)*; III. Imre Boba, *Northeastern Central Europe in the High Middle Ages (Bohemia, Moravia, Hungary, Croatia, 1000–1530)*; IV. Oswald P. Backus, *The Polish-Lithuanian Commonwealth (1000–1795)*; V. Peter F. Sugar, *Southeastern Europe under Ottoman Rule (1389–1804)*; VI. Robert A. Kann, *The Habsburg Empire (1526–1918)*; VII. Piotr S. Wandycz, *The Lands of Partitioned Poland (1772–1920)*; VIII. Barbara and Charles Jelavich, *Nationalism in the Balkans (1804–1918)*; IX. Joseph Rothschild, *Independent East-Central Europe (1918–1939)*; X. Wayne S. Vucinich, *East-Central Europe since 1939*; XI. Sugar and Treadgold, *Historical Atlas, Cumulative Bibliography, Cumulative Index*.

volume of the *Austrian History Yearbook* in three parts.[28] Three other surveys, Peter F. Sugar, ed., *Fascism in Eastern Europe in the Interwar Period*, Ivo J. Lederer and Peter F. Sugar, eds., *The History of Nationalism in East Central Europe* and Barbara Jelavich, *The Habsburg Empire in European Affairs, 1814–1918* will appear in 1969.

Of the more limited topics, the most thoroughly and successfully studied aspect of East Central and Southeastern European history is certainly the diplomatic rivalry in the nineteenth century. This emphasis is largely due to the prime importance of the Eastern Question in general European affairs from the end of the eighteenth century to the beginning of World War I. The subject has the added advantage that it can be studied on the basis of the foreign ministry archives of western and eastern European governments, which are open, and there is adequate published documentary material. There are two general treatments of this question both by Englishmen: J. A. R. Marriott, *The Eastern Question: An Historical Study in European Diplomacy*,[29] and M. S. Anderson, *The Eastern Question 1774–1923: A Study in International Relations*.[30] Anderson's work, which makes use of the basic published writings, including the more important Russian ones, was published in 1966 and supersedes Marriott's well-known study of 1917. However, Anderson's volume is not as lucid as Marriott's, although it does have an up-to-date bibliography. The only scholars in America who have attempted a similar survey are James T. Shotwell and F. Deak, *Turkey at the Straits: A Short History*,[31] where the emphasis is on the legal aspects of the problem.

For the first half of the nineteenth century, the four books of Vernon J. Puryear should be consulted. *Napoleon and the Dardanelles*[32] discusses the Straits problem in one period, while *France and the Levant*[33] and *International Economics and Diplomacy in the Near East*[34] cover economic aspects of the diplomatic problems. In *England, Russia and the Straits Question, 1844–1856*,[35] Puryear is critical of British policy, particularly of the activities of Stratford Canning. On the other hand, the great work by the British historian H. W. V. Temperley,

28. (Houston, Texas: Rice University, 1967).
29. (Oxford: Clarendon Press, 1917; 4th ed., 1958).
30. (London: Macmillan, 1966).
31. (New York: Macmillan, 1940).
32. (Berkeley: University of California Press, 1951).
33. *France and the Levant from the Bourbon Restoration to the Peace of Kutiah* (Berkeley: University of California Press, 1941).
34. (Stanford: Stanford University Press, 1935).
35. (Berkeley: University of California Press, 1931).

England and the Near East: The Crimea, is more sympathetic to Canning and Britain's goals.[36]

Two other books concerned with this period are P. E. Mosely, *Russian Diplomacy and the Opening of the Eastern Question, 1838–1839,*[37] and F. E. Bailey, *British Policy and the Turkish Reform Movement.*[38] Mosely's study, based upon Russian archival material, sets the background for the eastern crisis of 1839–41 and the internationalization of the Straits. Bailey has written the first scholarly study of the conflict between the reforming and the traditional elements in Ottoman society. He stresses also the political objectives of Britain, which sought Turkish reform in order that the sultan might better resist Russian influence. However, Bailey did not use Ottoman archival sources.

The next period, centering on the crisis of 1875–78, has attracted more attention in the United States and Europe than any other problem with the exception of the origins of World War I. William L. Langer's *European Alliances and Alignments* [39] and *The Diplomacy of Imperialism, 1890–1902,*[40] although concerned with a wider field and a more extended period, also covers the Eastern Question and the rise of Balkan nationalism. Specifically devoted to the Balkan crisis are two works by David Harris, *A Diplomatic History of the Balkan Crisis of 1875–1878: The First Year* [41] and *Britain and the Bulgarian Horrors of 1876.*[42] The first is a detailed study of this complex problem; the second shows how Britain reacted toward the atrocities in the Balkans, and how this sentiment was used politically. G. H. Rupp, *A Wavering Friendship,*[43] Walter G. Wirthwein, *Britain and the Balkan Crisis, 1875–1878,*[44] and David MacKenzie, *The Serbs and Russian Pan-Slavism, 1875–1878,*[45] complete the American contributions to this topic. They should, of course, be supplemented by the reading of the English historians B. H. Sumner, *Russia and the Balkans, 1870–1880* [46] and W. N. Medlicott, *The Congress of Berlin and After.*[47] Russia's attitude toward Bulgaria

36. (London: Longmans, Green & Co., 1936).
37. (Cambridge: Harvard University Press, 1934).
38. (Cambridge: Harvard University Press, 1942).
39. (New York: Knopf, 1931, 1962).
40. (New York: Knopf, 1935, 1960).
41. (Stanford: Stanford University Press, 1936).
42. (Chicago: University of Chicago Press, 1939).
43. *A Wavering Friendship: Russia and Austria, 1876–1878.* (Cambridge: Harvard University Press, 1941).
44. (New York: Columbia University Press, 1935).
45. (Ithaca: Cornell University Press, 1967).
46. (Oxford: Clarendon Press, 1937; Hamden, Conn.: Archon Books, 1962).
47. (London: Methuen & Co., 1938; Hamden, Conn.: Archon Books, 1963).

and Serbia in the years after the Congress of Berlin is discussed in Charles Jelavich, *Tsarist Russia and Balkan Nationalism.*[48]

The intricate diplomacy preceding the outbreak of World War I has produced a similar series of scholarly studies. Wayne S. Vucinich, *Serbia between East and West,*[49] sets the background for the Austro-Russian conflict. B. E. Schmitt, *The Annexation of Bosnia, 1908–1909,*[50] develops this theme and is particularly critical of Austrian and German diplomacy. The Balkan Wars are discussed in E. C. Helmreich, *The Diplomacy of the Balkan Wars, 1912–1913*[51] and in Edward C. Thaden, *Russia and the Balkan Alliance of 1912.*[52] Both books rely heavily on the published documentary collections, with Thaden's study making effective use of Russian materials. Two major works on the background of the war are S. B. Fay, *The Origins of the World War,*[53] and B. E. Schmitt, *The Coming of the War, 1914.*[54] Both books emphasize the general European background and not only the immediate events. This aspect is presented in *Sarajevo* by Joachim Remak.[55] The author believes that the assassination was planned in Belgrade by the head of the Serbian intelligence service. This thesis is disputed in the recent volume by the Yugoslav politician-publicist Vladimir Dedijer in *The Road to Sarajevo.*[56] In addition there is the monumental three-volume work by Luigi Albertini, *The Origins of the War of 1914*, which is translated from Italian.[57]

The Eastern Question in its traditional aspect reached a solution with the collapse of the Ottoman Empire. Two scholars have examined this phase of the problem. Harry N. Howard, *The Partition of Turkey: A Diplomatic History, 1913–1923,*[58] traces the fluctuations of European diplomacy. A more recent book by Laurence Evans, *The United States and the Partition of Turkey,*[59] makes extensive use of American documents which were not available to Howard. The same general period is discussed in C. J. Smith, *The Russian Struggle for Power, 1914–1917,*[60] which covers in detail Russian relations with the Balkan states

48. (Berkeley: University of California Press, 1958).
49. *Serbia between East and West, 1903–1908.* (Stanford: Stanford University Press, 1954).
50. (Cambridge, England: Cambridge University Press, 1937).
51. (Cambridge: Harvard University Press, 1938).
52. (University Park: Pennsylvania State University Press, 1965).
53. (New York: Macmillan, 1928; 2d ed. rev., 1948).
54. (New York: C. Scribner's Sons, 1930).
55. *Sarajevo: the Story of a Political Murder* (New York: Criterion Books, 1959).
56. (New York: Simon and Schuster, 1966).
57. 3 vols. (London: Oxford University Press, 1952–57).
58. (Norman: University of Oklahoma Press, 1931; New York: H. Fertig, 1966).
59. (Baltimore: Johns Hopkins Press, 1965).
60. (New York: Philosophical Library, 1956).

during the war. Different aspects of Balkan problems during the war are analyzed by a group of scholars in the essays found in Alexander Dallin, *et al.*, *Russian Diplomacy and Eastern Europe 1914–1917*.[61] Postwar diplomatic controversies are discussed in R. J. Kerner and H. N. Howard, *The Balkan Conferences and the Balkan Entente, 1930–1935*.[62]

Related to the Eastern Question are the works which have recently appeared concerning Ottoman history. In fact, among the most important and most welcome contributions to East European studies in the recent period have been the numerous books dealing with Ottoman affairs. Although most of the American contributions were written in the last two decades, the pioneering venture in Ottoman history of A. H. Lybyer, *The Government of the Ottoman Empire in the Time of Suleiman the Magnificent*,[63] appeared before World War I. Thirty years later R. B. Merriman, a distinguished scholar of Spanish imperial history, produced a well-written work, *Suleiman the Magnificent*.[64] Both were pioneering efforts, but neither used Turkish sources. Shortly after the appearance of Lybyer's book, H. A. Gibbons' *The Foundation of the Ottoman Empire* [65] was published, also based primarily on non-Turkish sources. All three books are now out of date. These works were followed by the two volumes of Barnette Miller, *Beyond the Sublime Porte: The Grand Seraglio of Stambul* [66] and *The Palace School of Mohammed the Conqueror*.[67] These studies represented the extent of American contributions until the appearance in 1947 of S. N. Fisher, *The Foreign Relations of Turkey, 1481–1512*,[68] a well-documented and revealing study of Ottoman diplomacy. Since then a series of excellent books have appeared which are of the highest value for students of Balkan history. Of first importance is H. A. R. Gibb and H. Bowen, *Islamic Society and the West*.[69] Both authors are British, but Professor Gibb was the director of the Center for Middle East Studies at Harvard for more than a decade. This two-volume work care-

61. (New York: King's Crown Press, 1963).
62. (Berkeley: University of California, 1936).
63. (Cambridge: Harvard University Press, 1913).
64. *Suleiman the Magnificent, 1520–1566* (Cambridge: Harvard University Press, 1944).
65. (Oxford: Clarendon Press, 1916).
66. (London: H. Milford, Oxford University Press, 1931).
67. (Cambridge: Harvard University Press, 1941).
68. (Urbana: University of Illinois Press, 1948).
69. *Islamic Society and the West: A Study of the Impact of Western Civilization on Moslem Culture in the Near East*, 1 vol. in 2 parts (London: Oxford University Press, 1950–1960; 2d ed., 1963–65).

fully examines the institutions and structure of the empire and it is based upon a wide use of Ottoman and Western sources.

Two Turkish scholars who received part of their training in the United States have also recently published important studies. In *The Development of Secularism in Turkey*,[70] Niyazi Berkes presents a study of the gradual introduction of the concept of secularism in Turkish thought. Şerif Mardin's *The Genesis of Young Ottoman Thought*[71] is written by a political scientist, but it is as much historical as political in nature. It is a study of the intellectual manifestations and expressions of nineteenth-century Ottoman reform. The examination of the Turkish reform movement, first considered by Bailey, is continued in the books of Roderic H. Davison and Robert Devereux, both using Ottoman as well as Western sources. Davison's *Reform in the Ottoman Empire, 1856–1876*[72] is a study of some of the principal aspects of Ottoman reform and the resulting institutions in the twenty years following the Crimean War. Devereux, *The First Ottoman Constitutional Period*,[73] continues an examination of the question through 1876–77. The background of the Young Turk revolution is presented in Ernest Ramsauer, Jr., *The Young Turks*.[74] The author discusses the ideological differences between those who wished to strengthen the central government and those who advocated some accommodation with the subject nationalities. On more recent history, the works of two scholars — one Israeli, the other British — Uriel Heyd, *Foundations of Turkish Nationalism*[75] and Bernard Lewis, *The Emergence of Modern Turkey*,[76] are primarily concerned with the developments of the nineteenth and twentieth centuries. Valuable also is Wayne S. Vucinich, *The Ottoman Empire: Its Record and Legacy*.[77] As a result of these new publications, which are based on Turkish materials as well as those of western Europe and of the former subject nationalities, the previous strong anti-Ottoman bias of much American writing has been balanced.

Although, as we have now seen, there have been attempts to consider the history of the entire area of Eastern Europe, or large sections of it, particularly in connection with Habsburg and Ottoman rule and

70. (Montreal: McGill University Press, 1964).
71. (Princeton: Princeton University Press, 1962).
72. (Princeton: Princeton University Press, 1963).
73. *The First Ottoman Constitutional Period: A Study of the Midhat Constitution and Parliament* (Baltimore: Johns Hopkins Press, 1963).
74. *The Young Turks: Prelude to the Revolution of 1908* (Princeton: Princeton University Press, 1957).
75. (London: Luzac, 1950).
76. (London and New York: Oxford University Press, 1961).
77. (New York: Van Nostrand, 1965).

international relations, the greater part of American writing in this field has been concerned with the individual nations and their development. These books will therefore be discussed in this form, commencing with Poland in the north and proceeding southward toward Greece. There is no separate section on Albania because American contributions here are limited. Most important is Stavro Skendi, *The Albanian National Awakening 1878–1912*,[78] which covers the origins of the modern state. He is also the editor of *Albania*,[79] a collection of essays. A third book is Fan S. Noli, *George Castrioti, Scanderbeg*,[80] concerning the life of the Albanian national hero. On contemporary affairs, Harry Hamm, *Albania — China's Beachhead in Europe*,[81] and William Griffith, *Albania and the Sino-Soviet Rift*,[82] are valuable works.

POLAND

Despite the fact that Polish history in comparison with that of other countries of this area has been the subject of much interest in American and English scholarship, no adequate, up-to-date general history has been written. The *Cambridge History of Poland*[83] has no index or bibliography and is a little uneven. Shorter histories by Halecki,[84] Rose,[85] Wojciechowski,[86] Dyboski,[87] Slocombe,[88] and Sharp[89] do not fill this need. Although there are no good surveys on economic, religious, or constitutional history, cultural history is in better shape with Manfred Kridl, *A Survey of Polish Literature and Culture*,[90] and Waclaw Lednicki, *Life and Culture of Poland*.[91] Works in English on foreign affairs

78. (Princeton: Princeton University Press, 1967).
79. (New York: Praeger, for Mid-European Studies Center of the Free Europe Committee, 1956).
80. *George Castrioti, Scanderbeg (1405–1468)* (New York: International Universities Press, 1947).
81. Trans. from the German by Victor Andersen (New York: Praeger, 1963).
82. (Cambridge: M.I.T. Press, 1963).
83. William F. Reddaway, *et al.*, eds., *The Cambridge History of Poland*, 2 vols. (Cambridge, England: The University Press, 1941–51).
84. Oscar Halecki, *A History of Poland* (New York: Roy, 1943).
85. William J. Rose, *Poland, Old and New* (London: G. Bell, 1948).
86. Zygmunt Wojciechowski, ed., *Poland's Place in Europe*, trans. B. W. A. Massey (Poznań: Instytut Zachodni, 1947).
87. Roman Dyboski, *Poland* (New York: C. Scribner's Sons, 1933).
88. George E. Slocombe, *A History of Poland* (London, New York: T. Nelson and Sons, 1939).
89. Samuel L. Sharp, *Poland, White Eagle on a Red Field* (Cambridge: Harvard University Press, 1953).
90. Trans. Olga Scherer-Virski (New York: Columbia University Press, 1956).
91. *Life and Culture of Poland as Reflected in Polish Literature* (New York: Roy Publishers, 1944).

are similarly lacking. Except for Roman Dyboski's brilliant lectures on Poland in *Poland in World Civilization*,[92] there are few studies on Poland and Germany, Poland and Russia, Poland and France, Poland and Bohemia, etc. Shorter studies, such as, S. Konovalov, *Russo-Polish Relations: An Historical Survey*,[93] or F. Heymann, *Poland and Czechoslovakia*,[94] are quite useful, although the latter is superior to the former. A. Zoltowski, *Border of Europe: A Study of the Polish Eastern Provinces*,[95] is quite valuable for Russo-Polish relations, but not adequate for a general study of Poland and the east.

As for the history of the main periods in Polish history, very little has been done in the United States on the prehistory and origins of the nation, although this subject has received much attention in postwar Poland. For the Middle Ages there is also hardly anything. Feudalism is the subject of one article by P. Skwarczyński, "The Problem of Feudalism in Poland up to the Beginning of the 16th Century," [96] in the *Slavonic and East European Review*. Problems of serfdom are touched upon in Jerome Blum, "The Rise of Serfdom in Eastern Europe," [97] in the *American Historical Review*. For the early modern period there is practically nothing on the Renaissance; the reader must turn to such a general work as Dvornik's previously mentioned book, *The Slavs in European History and Civilization*. The translation of S. Lorenz, *The Renaissance in Poland*,[98] is mainly an album of photographs. The Reformation is treated in an outdated book by Paul Fox, *The Reformation in Poland: Some Social and Economic Aspects*.[99] Relations between the Catholic and Orthodox churches are discussed by O. Halecki in *From Florence to Brest*.[100] The latter also contributed *The Crusade of Varna*.[101] Problems of the Polish-Lithuanian Union are not adequately dealt with in English, as is witnessed in the discussion in the *Slavic Review*.[102] Only *Jadwiga, Poland's Great Queen* [103] by C. H. Kellogg represents a contribution in the realm of biographies for this period.

92. Ludwik Krzyzanowski, ed. (New York: J. M. Barrett, 1950).
93. (Princeton: Princeton University Press, 1945).
94. (Englewood Cliffs, N.J.: Prentice-Hall, 1966).
95. (London: Hollis and Carter, 1950).
96. *Slavonic and East European Review*, 34 (January, 1956): 292–310.
97. *American Historical Review*, 62 (July, 1957): 807–36.
98. (Warsaw: "Prasa," 1955).
99. (Baltimore: Johns Hopkins Press, 1924).
100. *From Florence to Brest (1439–1596)* (New York: Fordham University Press, 1958).
101. (New York: Polish Institute of Arts and Sciences in America, 1943).
102. Oswald P. Backus, "The Problem of Unity in the Polish-Lithuanian State," *Slavic Review*, 22 (September, 1963): 411–55.
103. (New York: Macmillan, 1931).

For the seventeenth and eighteenth centuries, there is a marked improvement in output, if not always in quality. There are American studies by W. Kirchner, *The Rise of the Baltic Question*,[104] and Karol Marcinkowski, *The Crisis of the Polish-Swedish War, 1655–1660*,[105] on the Baltic question and the Polish-Swedish war, though there is no study of the entire crucial period of the mid-seventeenth–century collapse — military, economic, and constitutional. W. Konopczyński's great work on the "liberum veto," *Le liberum veto: Etude sur le développement du principe majoritaire*,[106] has never been translated from French. G. Vernadsky has a somewhat popular volume on Khmelnitsky, *Bohdan, Hetman of the Ukraine*,[107] and there is a recent study by C. B. O'Brien, *Muscovy and the Ukraine*,[108] on the seventeenth century. The eighteenth century has been dealt with more thoroughly. There is an excellent book by H. Kaplan, *The First Partition of Poland*,[109] and the classic by Robert Lord, *The Second Partition of Poland*.[110] The third has found no historian in the English-speaking world. Biographies on the whole are weak. There is one on Sobieski by J. B. Morton[111] and on Kościuszko by W. Haiman.[112] Educational changes are only treated in articles. A worthy attempt to integrate Poland at the turn of the eighteenth and nineteenth centuries into the mainstream of European history has been made by R. R. Palmer, *The Age of the Democratic Revolution*.[113]

The coverage for the nineteenth and twentieth centuries is quite extensive, although a large proportion of the books in English are written by British historians. Political history dominates over economic, social, intellectual, and constitutional. There is a real need to translate W. Feldman's work on Polish political doctrines, *Dzieje polskiej myśli politycznej w okresie porozbiorowym* (History of Polish Political Thought in the Post-Partition Period),[114] and Bohdan Winiarski on constitutional questions.[115] Polish-Russian problems centering around the 1830 and

104. (Newark: University of Delaware Press, 1954).
105. (Wilberforce, Ohio: Ohio University Press, 1952).
106. 2 vols. (Paris: Champion, 1930).
107. (New Haven: Yale University Press, 1941).
108. *Muscovy and the Ukraine: From the Pereiaslavl Agreement to the Truce of Andrusovo, 1654–1667* (Berkeley: University of California Press, 1963).
109. (New York: Columbia University Press, 1962).
110. *The Second Partition of Poland: A Study in Diplomatic History* (Cambridge: Harvard University Press, 1915).
111. *Sobieski, King of Poland* (London: Eyre and Spottiswoode, 1932).
112. *Kościuszko, Leader and Exile* (New York: Polish Institute of Arts and Sciences in America, 1946).
113. 2 vols. (Princeton: Princeton University Press, 1959–64).
114. 3 vols. (Kraków: Spółka Nakładowa "Książka," 1913–20).
115. *Les institutions politiques en Pologne au XIXᵉ siècle* (Paris: Picart, 1921).

1863 revolutions are treated in the classic by S. Askenazy (old *Cambridge Modern History*, vol. X) [116] and in two volumes by R. F. Leslie, *Polish Politics and the Revolution of November 1830* [117] and *Reform and Insurrection in Russian Poland, 1856–1865.*[118] The latter have a strong pro-Russian orientation. Polish-Prussian issues are discussed by R. W. Tims, *Germanizing Prussian Poland.*[119] The first treatment of Poles in Galicia in English is by H. Wereszycki and P. Wandycz in the *Austrian History Yearbook.*[120]

The twentieth century has probably received more attention than any other. While there are no adequate and recent biographies of Piłsudski, Paderewski, Dmowski, and others (the works by Reddaway,[121] Philip,[122] and other historians are dated), much has been written concerning the emergence of the Polish state after the First World War and the interwar period. A general history by Hans Roos, *A History of Modern Poland,*[123] has been translated from German, and it supersedes such American studies as those of R. L. Buell,[124] R. Machray,[125] or the volume edited by B. E. Schmitt.[126] T. Komarnicki's large book, *Rebirth of the Polish Republic,*[127] treats extensively the rebirth of the Polish state. Russian policy toward Poland during the First World War is brilliantly discussed in a chapter by Dallin, in his above-mentioned *Russian Diplomacy and Eastern Europe, 1914–1917.* Domestic affairs in the interwar period are less extensively covered than foreign relations. A recent volume by J. Rothschild on the coup d'état of 1926, *Piłsudski's Coup d'Etat,*[128] is a welcome exception. Major political parties await their historians. M. K. Dziewanowski's *The Communist Party of Poland* [129] is the only history of the Communist party in English, although

116. Simon Askenazy, "Russia, Poland and the Polish Revolution," in *Cambridge Modern History* (Cambridge, England: The University Press, 1907), 10:413–74.
117. (London: University of London, Athlone Press, 1956).
118. (London: Athlone Press, 1963).
119. (New York: Columbia University Press, 1941, 1961).
120. Vol. 3, pt. 2 (1967), pp. 261–313.
121. William F. Reddaway, *Marshal Pilsudski* (London: G. Routledge, 1939).
122. Charles Philip, *Paderewski* (New York: Macmillan, 1934).
123. Trans. J. R. Foster (New York: Knopf, 1966).
124. Raymond L. Buell, *Poland: Key to Europe* (New York and London: Knopf, 1939).
125. Robert Machray, *The Poland of Pilsudski* (London: G. Allen and Unwin, 1936).
126. Bernadotte E. Schmitt, ed., *Poland* (Berkeley: University of California Press, 1945).
127. *Rebirth of the Polish Republic: A Study in the Diplomatic History of Europe, 1914–1920* (London: W. Heinemann, 1957).
128. (New York: Columbia University Press, 1966).
129. (Cambridge: Harvard University Press, 1959).

in an outline form. There are a few works on economic affairs, notably by J. Taylor, *The Economic Development of Poland, 1919–1950*,[130] and F. Zweig, *Poland between Two Wars: A Critical Study of Social and Economic Changes*,[131] and the study on Upper Silesia by William Rose, *The Drama of Upper Silesia: A Regional Study*.[132] The survey of Polish foreign policy by R. Debicki, *Foreign Policy of Poland, 1919–1939*,[133] serves as a useful introduction to more detailed monographs and articles by Budorowycz,[134] Gasiorowski,[135] Korbel,[136] Wandycz,[137] Cienciala,[138] Smogorzewski,[139] and others. A translation of the short volume by A. Rosé, *La politique polonaise entre les deus guerres*,[140] would be a most welcome addition for the students.

World War II and its aftermath are mainly treated from the point of view of international relations and the Communist takeover. Apart from a few memoirs and semi-political works, there are several studies of wartime diplomacy by Rozek,[141] Wandycz,[142] and others. The Katyn massacre is ably discussed by J. Zawodny, *Death in the Forest: The Story of the Katyn Forest Massacre*;[143] the Oder-Neisse issue, by E. Wiskemann, *Germany's Eastern Neighbors*.[144] The postwar develop-

130. (Ithaca, N.Y.: Cornell University Press, 1952).

131. (London: Secker and Warburg, 1944).

132. (London: Williams and Norgate, 1936).

133. *Foreign Policy of Poland, 1919–39: From the Rebirth of the Polish Republic to World War II* (New York: Praeger, 1962).

134. Bohdan Budurowycz, *Polish-Soviet Relations 1932–1939* (New York: Columbia University Press, 1963).

135. Z. J. Gasiorowski, "Polish-Czechoslovak Relations 1918–1922," *Slavonic and East European Review*, 35 (December, 1956): 172–93; "Polish Czechoslovak Relations, 1922–1926," *Slavonic and East European Review*, 35 (June, 1957): 473–504; "Streseman and Poland before Locarno," *Journal of Central European Affairs*, 18 (April, 1958): 25–47; "Streseman and Poland after Locarno," *Journal of Central European Affairs*, 18 (October, 1958): 292–317.

136. Josef Korbel, *Poland between East and West: Soviet and German Diplomacy toward Poland, 1919–1933* (Princeton: Princeton University Press, 1963).

137. Piotr S. Wandycz, *France and Her Eastern Allies, 1919–1925* (Minneapolis: University of Minnesota Press, 1962), and *Soviet Russia and Poland, 1917–1921* (Cambridge: Harvard University Press, 1969).

138. Anna M. Cienciala, *Polish-German Relations 1938–1939* (Toronto: University of Toronto Press, 1968).

139. Casimir Smogorzewski, *Poland's Access to the Baltic* (London: 1934).

140. (Neuchâtel: Editions de la Baconnière, 1945).

141. Edward J. Rozek, *Allied Wartime Diplomacy: A Pattern in Poland* (New York: Wiley, 1958).

142. Piotr S. Wandycz, *Czechoslovak-Polish Confederation and the Great Powers, 1940–1943* (Bloomington: Indiana University Publications, 1956).

143. (Notre Dame, Ind.: University of Notre Dame Press, 1962).

144. *Germany's Eastern Neighbors: Problems Relating to the Oder-Neisse Line* (London and New York: Oxford University Press, 1956).

ments in Poland have become on the whole the domain of political scientists, economists, and journalists.

Recommendations for the needs for future study have been indicated. There is first the lack of a basic, scholarly history of the country. An economic history in English is also needed. Failing the preparation of one, works by Rutkowski [145] and the recent, Marxist-oriented, *Dzieje gospodarcze Polski* (Economic History of Poland) [146] by B. Zientara, A. Mączak, I. Ihnatowicz, and Z. Landau could be translated. On constitutional history, the classic by S. Kutrzeba, *Historja ustroju Polski w zarysie* (An Outline of the History of the Polish Government),[147] should also be considered for translation. On Polish relations with other countries, there are works in German, Polish, Czech, and French which should be made available in English. As has been indicated, the early and medieval field has been almost entirely neglected, and there do not seem to be many historians working in it. Modern history up to the eighteenth century fares little better. The eighteenth century shows more vitality and does attract more people, but there are serious gaps here too. The real concentration occurs in the nineteenth and twentieth centuries. This development can partly be explained by the research possibilities, and partly by the interests of faculty and graduate students. With the opening of the Polish archives, conditions exist for the fruitful study of the earlier periods. At the same time, there is a real need for the launching of a program of translation, publication of sources, bibliographies, atlases, etc.

CZECHOSLOVAKIA

Like Poland, the history of Bohemia and Czechoslovakia has been covered in several short surveys, long considered standard and trustworthy, but now seriously outdated.[148] These have been replaced by R. W. Seton-Watson, *A History of the Czechs and Slovaks*,[149] which is the only modern detailed treatment, S. Harrison Thomson, *Czechoslovakia in European History*,[150] which deals with basic themes and

145. Jan Rutkowski, *Historie économique de la Pologne avant les partages* (Paris: Champion, 1927).
146. *Dzieje gospodarcze Polski do 1939 r.* (Economic History of Poland to 1939) (Warsaw: Wiedza powszechna, 1965).
147. 4 vols. (Lwów: B. Poloniecki, 1920–21).
148. For example, Francis Lützow, *Bohemia: An Historical Sketch*, rev. ed. (London: J. M. Dent, 1939); and Kamil Krofta, *A Short History of Czechoslovakia* (New York: R. M. McBride, 1935).
149. (London: Hutchinson, 1943; Hamden, Conn.: Archon Books, 1965).
150. 2d ed. (Princeton: Princeton University Press, 1953).

problems, and Frederick G. Heymann, *Poland and Czechoslovakia*,[151] the most concise, current, and objective of the newer treatments. The only comprehensive and scholarly history of the Slovaks in any Western language is in German, and its publication is still in progress: Ludwig von Gogolák, *Beiträge zur Geschichte des slowakischen Volkes*, Vol. 1,[152] covering 1526–1790. Joseph M. Kirschbaum, *Slovakia: Nation at the Crossroads of Central Europe*,[153] and Joseph A. Mikuš, *Slovakia: A Political History, 1918–1950*,[154] reflect the extreme bias of refugees from the defunct Slovak republic. A unique pro-Czechoslovak orientation is presented in Jozef Lettrich, *A History of Modern Slovakia*.[155]

There are several multi-author, encyclopedic surveys of Czech and Slovak civilization in the Communist and pre-Communist periods: Robert J. Kerner, ed., *Czechoslovakia*;[156] R. W. Seton-Watson, ed., *Slovakia, Then and Now*;[157] Jan Hajda, ed., *A Study of Contemporary Czechoslovakia*;[158] Vratislav Bušek and Nicolas Spulber, eds., *Czechoslovakia*;[159] and Miloslav Rechcigl, ed., *The Czechoslovak Contribution to World Culture*.[160]

Sketchy surveys of Czech and Slovak historiography are given by Joseph S. Rouček, "Czechoslovakia," in *The Development of Historiography*,[161] George A. Waskovich, "Historiography: Czechoslovakia," in *Slavonic Encyclopedia*,[162] and Count Francis Lützow, *Lectures on the Historians of Bohemia*.[163]

For prehistory (anthropology, archaeology) Evžen and Jiří Neustupný, *Czechoslovakia: Before the Slavs*,[164] should be consulted. Harriet Wanklyn's *Czechoslovakia*[165] is a rare historico-geographical study.

151. (Englewood Cliffs, N.J.: Prentice-Hall, 1966).
152. *Beiträge zur Geschichte des slowakischen Volkes*, I: *1526–1790* (Munich: R. Oldenbourg, 1963).
153. (New York: R. Speller, 1960).
154. (Milwaukee, Wis.: Marquette University Press, 1963).
155. (New York: Praeger, 1955).
156. (Berkeley: University of California Press, 1940).
157. (London: Allen and Unwin, 1931).
158. (Chicago: University of Chicago Press for the Human Relations Area Files, 1955).
159. (New York: Praeger, for the Mid-European Studies Center of the Free Europe Committee, 1957).
160. (The Hague: Mouton, 1964).
161. In Matthew A. Fitzsimons *et al.*, eds., *The Development of Historiography* (Harrisburg, Pa.: Stackpole, 1954), pp. 301–11.
162. In Joseph S. Roucek, ed., *Slavonic Encyclopedia* (New York: Philosophical Library, 1949), pp. 423–28.
163. (London and New York: Henry Frowde, 1905).
164. (New York: F. A. Praeger, 1961).
165. (London: G. Philip, 1954).

Otakar Odložilík's *The Caroline University, 1348–1948*[166] is a unique survey of this central Czech institution.

The next epoch, the Hussite period (ca. 1415–1620) is unusually rich in recent American works of very high scholarship. (The studies and source editions of E. Denis,[167] F. Lützow,[168] D. S. Schaff,[169] J. Herben,[170] and H. B. Workman[171] are largely outdated.) Hus himself and his religious ideas have been competently covered in Matthew Spinka, *John Hus and the Czech Reform*,[172] and Spinka's translation of *John Hus at the Council of Constance* by Peter of Mladoňovice.[173] Important also are S. Harrison Thomson's two source editions: *Magistri Joannis Hus Tractatus Responsivus*[174] and *Magistri Joannis Hus Tractatus de Ecclesia*.[175] On the Hussite movement, there are two works of the highest scholarship: F. G. Heymann, *John Žižka and the Hussite Revolution* and Howard Kaminsky, *A History of the Hussite Revolution*.[176] Heymann's work is a more traditional, religion-oriented treatment, whereas Kaminsky considers nonreligious factors as well and attempts to place the movement in general European history. The crucial reign of the last native king of Bohemia is the subject of two recent and exhaustive analyses: F. G. Heymann, *George of Bohemia: King of Heretics*,[177] and Otakar Odložilík, *The Hussite King: Bohemia in European Affairs, 1440–1471*.[178] The most important Hussite successors are covered in Peter Brock, *The Political and Social Doctrines of the Unity of Czech Brethren in the 15th and Early 16th Centuries*.[179] Research on the period of the seventeenth century is limited and concentrates on the exiles after White Mountain, as, for example, Ernest Sommer, *Into Exile: The History of the Counter-Reformation in Bo-*

---

166. (Prague: Orbis, 1948).
167. E. Denis, *Huss et la guerre des Hussites* (Paris: E. Leroux, 1878), and *La fin de l'indépendance bohême*, 2 vols. (Paris: A. Colin, 1890).
168. Francis Lützow, *The Hussite Wars* (New York: E. P. Dutton, 1914), and *The Life and Times of Master John Hus* (New York: E. P. Dutton, 1909).
169. Jan Huss, *De Ecclesia*, Trans. with notes and introduction by David S. Schaff (New York: C. Scribner's Sons, 1915).
170. *Hus and His Followers* (London: G. Bles, 1926).
171. *The Letters of John Hus* (London: Hodden and Stoughton, 1904).
172. (Chicago: University of Chicago Press, 1941).
173. Peter of Mladoňovice, *John Hus at the Council of Constance*, trans. Matthew Spinka (New York: Columbia University Press, 1966).
174. (Princeton: Princeton University Press, 1927).
175. (Boulder, Col.: University of Colorado, 1956).
176. Heymann (Princeton: Princeton University Press, 1965) and Kaminsky (Berkeley: University of California Press, 1967).
177. (Princeton: Princeton University Press, 1965).
178. (New Brunswick, N.J.: Rutgers University Press, 1965).
179. (The Hague: Mouton & Co., 1957).

hemia, 1620–1650,[180] and M. Spinka's brief *John Amos Comenius, That Incomparable Moravian.*[181] Eighteenth-century studies are also few. R. J. Kerner, *Bohemia in the 18th Century,*[182] places its emphasis on the brief reign of Leopold II. It is reinforced by two recent and careful economic monographs: Herman Freudenberger, *The Waldstein Woolen Mill: Noble Entrepreneurship in 18th Century Bohemia,*[183] and William E. Wright, *Serf, Seigneur, and Sovereign: Agrarian Reform in 18th Century Bohemia.*[184]

Bohemia's great century, the nineteenth, is much studied by American scholars, though few books (but many periodical articles) have resulted. The only survey treatment of the Czech National Revival in a Western language is still Louis Léger's old *La Renaissance tchèque au XIX*[e] *siècle.*[185] An important institution of this revival is the subject of Stanley B. Kimball's detailed, statistical monograph, *Czech Nationalism: A Study of the National Theatre Movement.*[186]

On the period of World War I and the origins, especially diplomatic, of the new Czechoslovak state, Thomas G. Masaryk's translated accounts, *The New Europe*[187] and *The Making of a State,*[188] and Eduard Beneš, *My War Memoirs,*[189] are available. Dagmar H. Perman's *The Shaping of the Czechoslovak State, 1914–1920*[190] is a basic contribution to the history of the peace conference. There are many popular biographies of Masaryk, both British and American, the most recent being Edward W. Newman's *Masaryk,*[191] and the best, Paul Selver's *Masaryk: A Biography.*[192] Karel Čapek, *President Masaryk Tells His Story,*[193] is a valuable autobiography. There are several adequate biographies of Beneš: Pierre Crabites, *Beneš, Statesman of Central Europe,*[194] Edward B. Hitchcock, *I Built a Temple for Peace: The Life of*

180. Trans. Victor Grove (London: New Europe Publishing Co., 1943).
181. (Chicago: University of Chicago Press, 1943).
182. (New York: Macmillan, 1932).
183. (Boston: Harvard Graduate School of Business, 1963).
184. (Minneapolis: University of Minnesota Press, 1966).
185. (Paris: F. Alcan, 1911).
186. *Czech Nationalism: A Study of the National Theater Movement, 1845–1883* (Urbana: University of Illinois Press, 1964).
187. (London: Eyre and Spottiswoode, 1918).
188. (London: Allen and Unwin, 1927).
189. (Boston: Houghton Mifflin, 1928).
190. (Leiden: E. J. Brill, 1962).
191. (London: Campion Press, 1960).
192. (London: M. Joseph, 1940).
193. (New York: G. P. Putnam, 1935).
194. (New York: Coward-McCann, 1936).

Edward Beneš,[195] and Compton Mackenzie, *Dr. Beneš*.[196] The important and involved Czechoslovak diplomacy of the interwar period is covered by Felix J. Vondráček's *The Foreign Policy of Czechoslovakia, 1918–1935*,[197] which is based on the published documents, and by P. S. Wandycz's prize-winning *France and Her Eastern Allies, 1919–1925*.[198] Growing Czech-German tensions are surveyed against a historical background by Elizabeth Wiskemann, *Czechs and Germans*,[199] and extended to the postwar period by Radomír Luža, *The Transfer of the Sudeten Germans: A Study of Czech-German Relations, 1933–1962*.[200] Of the vast amount of writing on Munich, the best all-round study is still John W. Wheeler-Bennett, *Munich: Prologue to Tragedy*.[201] The definitive Czech view is Boris Čelovský, *Das Münchener Abkommen von 1938*.[202] Also authoritative is Hubert Ripka, *Munich: Before and After*. [203]

On World War II, Beneš' new memoir, *From Munich to New War and New Victory*,[204] and P. S. Wandycz's monograph, *Czechoslovak-Polish Confederation and the Great Powers, 1940–1943*,[205] are important.

The Communist coup and Marxist Czechoslovakia have been well covered by American political scientists, and some former Czech officials with a firsthand knowledge of the events described, as, for example, Josef Korbel, *The Communist Subversion of Czechoslovakia, 1938–1948*,[206] Hubert Ripka, *Czechoslovakia Enslaved: The Story of the Communist Coup d'Etat*,[207] Paul E. Zinner, *Communist Strategy and Tactics in Czechoslovakia, 1918–1948*,[208] and Edward Taborsky, *Communism in Czechoslovakia, 1948–1960*.[209]

Since the pioneer works of the Czech immigrant Thomas Čapek,[210] there have been many small studies of the Czech and Slovak immi-

195. (New York: Harper and Brothers, 1940).
196. (London: G. G. Harrap, 1946).
197. (New York: Columbia University Press, 1937).
198. (Minneapolis: University of Minnesota Press, 1962).
199. (London and New York: Oxford University Press, 1938).
200. (New York: New York University Press, 1964).
201. 2d ed. (New York: Duell, Sloan and Pearce, 1962).
202. (Stuttgart: Deutsche Verlags-Anstalt, 1958).
203. (London: Gollancz, 1939).
204. *Memoirs: From Munich to New War and New Victory*, trans. Godfrey Lias (Boston: Houghton Mifflin, 1954).
205. (Bloomington: Indiana University Press, 1956).
206. (Princeton: Princeton University Press, 1959).
207. (London: Gollancz, 1950).
208. (New York: Praeger, 1963).
209. (Princeton: Princeton University Press, 1961).
210. See, for example, Thomas Čapek, *The Czechs (Bohemians) in America* (Boston: Houghton Mifflin, 1920).

grants in the United States, but only one general (and outdated) survey: Kenneth D. Miller, *The Czecho-Slovaks in America*.[211] Currently the Czechoslovak National Council of America is sponsoring a publication project entitled *Panorama*, a historical-biographical account of Americans of Czech descent which is to appear in 1969.

In the pre-Communist period, Czechoslovak historians occasionally made contributions to English-language publications — for example, Kamil Krofta's chapters in the *Cambridge Medieval History*.[212] The current regime also encourages English translations of selected works, though these necessarily reflect strong Marxist orientation in topic and treatment — for example, František Kavka's *Outline of Czechoslovak History*.[213] Occasionally, English-language publications appear written by Sudeten German expellee-historians. Their pronounced anti-Czech bias is codified in Kurt Glaser, *Czechoslovakia: A Critical History*.[214]

From the above titles, together with the topics of doctoral dissertations in progress and completed, research reported in progress, and numerous articles in periodicals (often of great value), the following generalizations about American research on Czech and Slovak history seem clear. There is first and foremost no comprehensive, scholarly, and up-to-date history of the Czechs and Slovaks. There is a pressing need, also, for a comprehensive guide to research in Czech and Slovak history, something even the Czechoslovaks themselves do not possess. It should include a detailed bibliography, information on archival holdings, an overview of major historical issues and viewpoints, and a history of Czech and Slovak historical writing. Advanced teaching requires a printed collection of selected sources for Czech and Slovak history in English translation. A translation of the recent multivolume collection, *Naše národní minulost v dokumentech* (Our National Past in Documents),[215] might be advisable, as well as a series of translations of the selected papers and writings of important individuals. In the monographic coverage of historical events, there is noticeable unevenness. The periods stressed are the fifteenth century and the nineteenth century to the present; the topics emphasized are Hus and the Hussite movement, the nineteenth-century Czech National Revival, World War I diplomacy, Masaryk himself, the Sudeten German problem, interwar Czechoslovak foreign relations and Munich, and the Communist

211. (New York: George H. Doran, 1922).
212. Kamil Krofta, "John Hus — Bohemia in the Fifteenth Century," in H. M. Gwatkin, ed., *Cambridge Medieval History* (Cambridge: The University Press, 1911), 3:45–64.
213. 2d rev. ed. (Prague: Orbis, 1963).
214. (Caldwell, Idaho: Caxton Printers, 1961).
215. Václav Husa, ed. (Prague: Nakl. Československé akademie věd, 1954), vol. 1.

takeover of the country. There is a preference for religious and political, especially diplomatic, history. The important topics which are neglected are the period of Charles IV (fourteenth century), the Thirty Years' War in Bohemia, the Bohemian Enlightenment (eighteenth century), as well as social, economic, and cultural-intellectual aspects in general. Consideration should be given to the translating of Kamil Krofta, *Nesmrtelný národ: Od Bílé Hory k Palackému* (Immortal Nation: From White Mountain to Palacký),[216] to fill the large gap of the seventeenth–eighteenth centuries, and of Hermann Münch, *Böhmische Tragödie*,[217] a detailed and sympathetic treatment of the nineteenth–century Czech-German conflict. George of Poděbrady alone is the subject of a modern, thorough, scholarly biography. Other major figures (e.g., Hus, Comenius, Masaryk, Beneš, Štúr) have received only basic coverage, and some (e.g., Charles IV, Chelčický, Palacký, Havlíček, Rieger, Kramář, Bernolák, Hlinka, Kollár, Šafařík) are not treated at all in English and the other Western languages. Throughout, the Czechs have received far more scholarly attention than the Slovaks, and a special effort should be made to spur research on the latter. Specialized studies on Slovak history are almost completely unlisted here because, though of a considerable number, they have seldom been written by professional historians or published through scholarly channels. Authored chiefly by refugees from the clerico-fascist Slovak Republic and Communist Czechoslovakia, they are generally warped by an extreme Slovak nationalistic bias. The Slovak Institute in Rome is currently compiling a bibliography of such works entitled *Slovak Bibliography Abroad, 1945–1965.*

HUNGARY

In recent historical literature in the English language concerning Hungary, the name of the British historian C. A. Macartney stands out. He has devoted most of his writing to Hungarian history: *Magyars in the Ninth Century*,[218] *Hungary*,[219] *Hungary and Her Successors*,[220] *Studies on the Earliest Hungarian Historical Sources*,[221] *October Fifteenth*,[222]

---

216. (V Praze: J. Laichter, 1940).
217. *Böhmische Tragödie: das Schicksal Mitteleuropas im Lichte der tschechischen Frage* (Brunswick: G. Westermann, 1949).
218. (Cambridge, England: Cambridge University Press, 1930).
219. (London: E. Benn, 1934).
220. (London: Oxford University Press, 1937).
221. In the series entitled *Etudes sur l'Europe centrale orientale* (Budapest: Sarkany, 1938–40), vols. 18, 21, 21c.
222. 2 vols. (Edinburgh: The University Press, 1956).

and *Hungary: A Short History*.[223] Professor Macartney's other works, *National States and National Minorities*,[224] *Problems of the Danube Basin*,[225] and the volume co-authored with A. W. Palmer, *Independent Eastern Europe*,[226] also contain useful information concerning Hungary. His works are not free from bias (conservative in his earlier and somewhat leftist in his later books), and they lean toward political and administrative interpretations, but they are basically sound and very valuable scholarly ventures. No American historian comes near to what Professor Macartney has done in writing about Hungarian history.

Besides Macartney's *Hungary: A Short History*, mentioned above, approximately twelve other histories of Hungary are available in English: György Balányi, *History of Hungary*;[227] Ferenc Eckhart, *A Short History of the Hungarian People*;[228] L. Felbermann, *Hungary and Its People*;[229] Leon Kellner, *Austria of the Austrians and Hungary of the Hungarians*;[230] C. M. Knatchbull-Hugassen, *The Political Evolution of the Hungarian Nation*;[231] Dominic Kosáry, *History of Hungary*;[232] Louis Léger, *Austria-Hungary from the Earliest Time to the Year 1889*[233] and *Austria-Hungary*;[234] Emil Lengyel, *1000 Years of Hungary*;[235] Imre Lukinich, *History of Hungary*;[236] Denis Sinor, *History of Hungary*;[237] Count Pál Teleki, *Evolution of Hungary and Its Place in European History*;[238] Armin Vámbéry, *Hungary in Ancient, Medieval and Modern Times* and *The Story of Hungary*.[239]

Although the length of this list is impressive, it offers little to the modern American scholar. The Knatchbull-Hugassen and Léger volumes are scholarly, still useful, but they are outdated, hard to obtain, and deal almost exclusively with old-fashioned political history. The works of Balányi, Eckhart, and Lukinich are also basically old-fashioned political histories, and reflect, in addition, the irredentist approach of inter-

223. (Chicago: Aldine, 1962).
224. (London: Oxford University Press, H. Milford, 1934).
225. (Cambridge, England: Cambridge University Press, 1942).
226. (London: Macmillan, 1962).
227. (Budapest: Szent István Társulat, 1933).
228. (London: Grant Richards, 1931).
229. (London: Griffith, Farran & Co., 1892).
230. (London: Sir Issac Pitman & Sons, 1914).
231. (London: National Review Office, 1908).
232. (Cleveland and New York: Benjamin Franklin Bibliophile Society, 1941).
233. Trans. Mrs. A. S. Hill (London: Rivingtons, 1889).
234. (New York: 1913).
235. (New York: J. Day, 1958).
236. (London: Simkin Marshall, 1937).
237. (London: Allen and Unwin; New York: Praeger, 1959).
238. (New York: Macmillan, 1923).
239. *Hungary in Ancient, Medieval and Modern Times* (London: T. F. Unwin, 1887); *The Story of Hungary* (New York: G. P. Putnam, 1886).

war Hungarian historiography. Teleki's volume was clearly written with "Justice for Hungary" in mind, while the Vámbéry volumes suffer heavily from the fact that their author, while a great scholar, was not a historian. The Kellner and Felbermann volumes are not well known. This leaves, especially for university use, the Macartney, Lengyel, Kosáry, and Sinor volumes.

All four of the last-mentioned works are rather slender volumes and contain little besides the major outlines of the events in Hungarian history. Lengyel's volume is nationalistic, and contains several grave errors. Kosáry's is the most detailed study of the four, and although scholarly and factually reliable, it suffers from the biases that characterized the Horthy period. It is also out of print, hard to obtain, not up to date, and concentrates mainly on political history. Macartney's history is his latest and unfortunately not his strongest effort. It is not very detailed and emphasizes social history much too heavily, Sinor's work has the merits of being the least biased of the four studies and of being factually correct, but it is too slender for anyone who really wants to study Hungarian history.

Of the historical periods, the English language literature is the most satisfactory in the period of the Austro-Hungarian Monarchy. Here we have a great number of memoirs and biographies (mainly of Francis Joseph), with works like Gyula Szekfü's *Three Generations*[240] and the well-known books of: R. W. Seton-Watson, *Corruption and Reform in Hungary*,[241] *German, Slav, Magyar*,[242] *Racial Problems in Hungary*;[243] Oscar Jászi, *Danubia: Old and New*,[244] *The Dissolution of the Habsburg Monarchy*;[245] Robert A. Kann, *The Multinational Empire*;[246] Hans Kohn, *The Habsburg Empire, 1804–1918*;[247] Arthur J. May, *The Hapsburg Monarchy, 1867–1914*,[248] *The Passing of the Hapsburg Monarchy, 1914–1918*;[249] A. J. P. Taylor, *The Habsburg Monarchy*;[250] H. W. Steed, *The Habsburg Monarchy*,[251] and several others

240. (Budapest: M. K. Egyetemi Nyomda, 1922).
241. *Corruption and Reform in Hungary: A Study of Electoral Practice* (London: Constable, 1911).
242. (London: Williams and Norgate, 1916).
243. (London: Constable, 1908).
244. (Philadelphia: American Philosophical Society Proceedings, 1949), 93:1.
245. (Chicago: University of Chicago Press, 1929, 1961).
246. 2 vols. (New York: Columbia Press, 1950; New York: Octagon Books, 1964).
247. (Princeton, N.J.: Van Nostrand, Anvil, 1961).
248. (Cambridge: Harvard University Press, 1951).
249. 2 vols. (Philadelphia: University of Pennsylvania Press, 1966).
250. *The Habsburg Monarchy 1809–1918* (London: H. Hamilton, 1948; New York: Harper and Row, 1965).
251. (London: Constable, 1914).

which permit the interested American to acquire much more than simply a superficial acquaintance with this period.

On the interwar years, with the exception of the already mentioned *October Fifteenth* by Macartney, there is very little available. There are some memoirs, such as Horthy's,[252] which are of dubious value, and a few studies, including the above-mentioned Macartney-Palmer volume, which give fairly detailed information concerning these years. Among these, Hugh Seton-Watson, *Eastern Europe, 1918–1941* [253] and John A. Lukacs, *The Great Powers and Eastern Europe*,[254] are the most satisfactory from the point of view of Hungarian history. There are no social or economic histories dealing with this period. Fascism in Hungary is represented by seven pages in Eugene Weber's short *Varieties of Fascism* [255] and by István Deák's chapter, "Hungary" in Hans Rogger and Eugen Weber, eds., *The European Right*.[256]

The Communist period is better covered. Next to the years of the Austro-Hungarian Monarchy, the literature dealing with the last twenty years is the most satisfactory. The works which should be mentioned are: Francis Fejtö, *Behind the Rape of Hungary*; [257] "Through the Up-heaval; The Hungarian Intelligentsia" in *Survey*; [258] "Hungarian Communism" in W. Griffith, ed., *Communism in Europe*, Vol. 1; [259] Ferenc A. Váli, *Rift and Revolt in Hungary*; [260] Paul Zinner, *National Communism and Popular Revolt in Eastern Europe*; [261] Melvin J. Lasky, ed., *The Hungarian Revolution*; [262] R. F. Delany, ed., *This Is Communist Hungary*; [263] Ernst Helmreich, ed., *Hungary*; [264] Béla A. Balassa, *The Hungarian Experience in Economic Planning*; [265] United Nations General Assembly, ed., *Report of the Special Committee on the Problem*

252. Miklos Horthy, *Memoirs* (New York: R. Speller, 1957).
253. *Eastern Europe between the Wars, 1918–41* (Cambridge, England: Cambridge University Press, 1945; Hamden, Conn.: Archon Books, 1962).
254. (New York: H. Regnery, 1953).
255. (Princeton, N.J.: Van Nostrand, Anvil, 1964).
256. (Berkeley: University of California Press, 1965), pp. 364–407.
257. (New York: D. MacKay, 1957).
258. Survey, no. 31 (January–March, 1960), pp. 88–94.
259. (Cambridge: M.I.T. Press, 1964), 1: 177–300.
260. *Rift and Revolt in Hungary: Nationalism versus Communism* (Cambridge: Harvard University Press, 1961).
261. *National Communism and Popular Revolt in Eastern Europe: A Selection of Documents on Events in Poland and Hungary, February–November, 1956* (New York: Columbia University Press, 1956).
262. *The Hungarian Revolution: A White Book* (New York: Praeger, for Congress of Cultural Freedom, 1957).
263. (Chicago: H. Regnery, 1958).
264. (New York: Praeger, for Mid-European Studies Center of the Free Europe Committee, 1957).
265. (New Haven: Yale University Press, 1959).

of Hungary;[266] Congress for Cultural Freedom, *The Truth about the Nagy Affair*;[267] Paul Kecskeméti, *The Unexpected Revolution*;[268] Imre Kovács, ed., *Facts about Hungary*.[269] A great many memoirs, such as: Miklós Kállay, *Hungarian Premier*;[270] Imre Nagy, *On Communism*;[271] Ferenc Nagy, *The Struggle behind the Iron Curtain*;[272] László Beke, *A Student's Diary*;[273] Tibor Méray, *Thirteen Days That Shook the Kremlin*;[274] Tamás Aczél and Tibor Méray, *The Revolt of the Mind*,[275] and many others are also available. It would be relatively easy to produce a fairly impressive bibliography on the Communist period, but most of these books fall into the category of political science.

For all other subjects, we draw almost total blanks. There is no study comparable to Ivo Lederer, *Yugoslavia at the Paris Peace Conference*,[276] or Sherman Spector, *Romania at the Paris Peace Conference*,[277] on the critical years 1918–20. There is Alfred D. Low, *The Soviet Republic and the Paris Peace Conference*,[278] dealing with the diplomacy of some four months, and vol. 1 (1919–20) of the document collection, *Papers and Documents Relating to the Foreign Relations of Hungary* by Francis Deak and Dezso Ujvary,[279] but we have no comprehensive study of these years. Nor does any work exist discussing the peace treaty at the end of World War II. Here and there in other periods there is a volume of value, but never enough to permit

266. (New York: United Nations Official Records, 11th sess., supplement no. 18, 1957).

267. *The Truth about the Nagy Affair: Facts, Documents, Comments* (New York: Praeger, 1959).

268. *The Unexpected Revolution: Social Forces in the Hungarian Uprising* (Stanford: Stanford University Press, 1961).

269. (New York: Hungarian Committee, 1958).

270. *Hungarian Premier: A Personal Account of a Nation's Struggle in the Second War* (New York: Columbia University Press, 1954).

271. *On Communism, in Defense of the New Course* (New York: Praeger, 1957).

272. Trans. from the Hungarian by Stephen K. Swift (New York: Macmillan, 1948).

273. László Beke, pseud., *A Student's Diary: Budapest, October 16–November 1, 1956*, ed. and trans. Leon Kossar and Ralph M. Zoltan (New York: Viking Press, 1957).

274. Trans. Howard L. Katzander (New York: Praeger, 1959). Ministry for Foreign Affairs, 1939).

275. *The Revolt of the Mind: A Case History of Intellectual Resistance behind the Iron Curtain* (New York: Praeger, 1959).

276. (New Haven: Yale University Press, 1963).

277. *Rumania at the Paris Peace Conference: A Study of the Diplomacy of Ioan I. C. Bratianu* (New York: Bookman, 1962).

278. (Philadelphia: American Philosophical Society, 1963).

279. *Papers and Documents Relating to the Foreign Relations of Hungary, I. 1919–1920* (Budapest: Royal Hungarian University Press, for Royal Hungarian Ministry for Foreign Affairs, 1939).

the study of a period or issue in any fashion that could be called, if not comprehensive, then at least satisfactory. Occasionally we find books like Henrik Marczali, *Hungary in the Eighteenth Century*,[280] Stephen Kertesz, *Diplomacy in a Whirlpool*,[281] C. Proxton, *Palmerston and the Hungarian Revolution*,[282] the two memoirs of Count Michael Károlyi,[283] Alajos Kovács, *The Development of the Population of Hungary since the Cessation of Turkish Rule*,[284] and A. B. Yolland, *The Hungarian Diet of 1905*,[285] which are worth reading, but in general the selection is very meager.

What becomes evident from this partial and summary survey is that most of the available material is dated, and focuses either on political history, or on very specific issues which cannot be introduced profitably into a basic bibliography, given the present state of Hungarian historical studies in general. The field for writing on Hungarian history is thus wide open. What is needed first is a good one-volume history of Hungary with about equal attention paid to the different historical periods. The Historical Institute of the Hungarian Academy of Sciences will soon publish in English a one-volume Hungarian history. It was written for the English-speaking market by good historians, including Ránki, Hanák, Makkai, and Katus. Although it will be quite useful, it will undoubtedly reflect a heavy orientation toward economic history, economic determinism, and the last two-and-a-half centuries. American scholars should thus produce their own volume in the United States. As far as other studies in Hungarian history are concerned, some of the needs have already been indicated. Studies are needed of all major periods, of all important events, movements, etc. There is nothing on the medieval period, the days of the Hunyadis, the years of Turkish occupation, the "Great Reform Age," and many other topics. There are no books on the peasantry, the aristocracy, constitutional history, nationalism, industrialization, cultural history, economic history, etc. In these circumstances, it would be perhaps better to concentrate first on general works dealing with these large issues rather than more detailed monographs. We need several volumes which, together, would offer a comprehensive view of the various periods and aspects of Hungarian history in somewhat more detail than even the best one-volume national history can offer.

280. (Cambridge, England: The University Press, 1910).
281. (Notre Dame, Ind.: University of Notre Dame Press, 1953).
282. (London, 1919).
283. Mihaly Károlyi, *Memoirs of Michael Karolyi: Faith without Illusion*, trans. from the Hungarian by Catherine Karòlyi (London: J. Cape, 1956).
284. (Budapest: Pesti Könyvnyomda R.T., 1920).
285. (Budapest: Franklin Society, 1906).

ROMANIA

American historians began to display a serious interest in Romania only after the end of World War I. The first general history of Romania by an American was *Greater Roumania*, published in 1922 by Charles Upson Clark.[286] In it he gave considerable attention to Romania's diplomatic and military efforts during World War I, apparently in order to justify her acquisition of Transylvania, Bessarabia, and southern Dobrudja. In addition, he attempted to write a general survey of Romanian political, economic, and cultural development. A useful handbook when it appeared, and in a way a pioneer work, it is now obsolete. The same may be said of his *United Roumania*,[287] which deals with postwar Romania and is based in part upon his earlier work. Another description of the political, economic, and social conditions in Romania between the wars was attempted by Joseph S. Rouček in *Contemporary Roumania and Her Problems: A Study in Modern Nationalism*.[288] It is, however, little more than a chronicle. One of the most significant American works on Romania is Henry L. Roberts, *Rumania: Political Problems of an Agrarian State*.[289] Based upon an extensive use of published primary and secondary sources, it presents a detailed analysis of the political and economic development of Romania from the end of World War I to the early years of the Communist regime.

Besides these studies of a more general nature, American scholars have produced works dealing with Romania's international relations, the nationality problem, the functioning of the Communist system, and Romanian emigration to the United States. Outstanding among those in the first group is T. W. Riker's *The Making of Roumania: A Study of an International Problem (1856–1866)*.[290] Based upon exhaustive research in the English, French, and German archives, it deals primarily with the diplomatic negotiations of the great powers that led to their acquiescence in Romania's *de facto* independence. It gives comparatively little attention to developments within the Romanian principalities themselves. A companion work to Riker's study is Barbara Jelavich, *Russia and the Rumanian National Cause, 1858–1859*.[291] It uses the papers of Nikolai Karlovich Giers, Russian consul-general in Bucharest at the time of the union of the principalities, as a basis for an assessment of Russian policy. Diplomatic questions, particularly the role of British

286. (New York: Dodd, Mead, 1922).
287. (New York: Dodd, Mead, 1932).
288. (Stanford: Stanford University Press, 1932).
289. (New Haven: Yale University Press, 1951).
290. (London: Oxford University Press, 1931).
291. (Bloomington: Indiana University Publication, 1959).

and Russian diplomacy in the principalities is also discussed in Radu Florescu, *The Struggle against Russia in the Roumanian Principalities, 1821–1854.*[292] Sherman David Spector in *Rumania at the Paris Peace Conference: A Study of the Diplomacy of Ioan I. C. Bratianu*[293] has written a careful, well-documented study of Romanian diplomacy during the peace negotiations in 1919.

The nationality question in Transylvania after World War I has been the subject of two short books by L. C. Cornish, *Transylvania in 1922*[294] and *The Religious Minorities in Transylvania.*[295] The author, biased in favor of the Protestant communities, was not a historian and shows little understanding of the political and cultural background of nationalism in Romania. Charles Upson Clark deals with the political history of a dispute of longstanding in *Bessarabia: Russia and Roumania on the Black Sea.*[296] Like his other writings, it is pro-Romanian.

A number of general works concerning the Communist regimes in Eastern Europe contain sections on Romania. Three books which deal specifically with the latter are: Reuben H. Markham, *Rumania under the Soviet Yoke,*[297] which displays extensive firsthand knowledge of the subject but suffers somewhat from intense personal bias; *Romania,* edited by Stephen Fischer-Galati[298] for the series *East-Central Europe under the Communists,* a cooperative work containing individual essays on all aspects of the Communist experiment in Romania; and Michael J. Rura, *Reinterpretation of History as a Method of Furthering Communism in Rumania,*[299] an analysis of the methods and objectives of Communist historiography based upon a very limited number of historical works published during the early years of the regime.

Only one scholarly work has been published on the adjustment of Romanian immigrants to the American way of life: Christine Avghi Galitzi, *A Study of Assimilation among the Roumanians in the United States.*[300] The author has used a great variety of sources, including personal interviews, and emphasizes economic and religious questions.

As far as American research on and study of Romania is concerned, almost everything remains to be done. There is no worthwhile general

292. (Monachii: Societas academica Dacoromana, 1962).
293. (New York: Bookman, 1962).
294. (Boston, Beacon Press, 1925).
295. (Boston: Beacon Press, 1925).
296. (New York: Dodd, Mead, 1927).
297. (Boston: Meador, 1949).
298. (New York: Praeger, for Mid-European Studies Center of the Free Europe Committee, 1957).
299. (Washington: Georgetown University Press, 1961).
300. (New York: Columbia University Press, 1929).

history of Romania from ancient times to the present by an English-speaking historian except that of the English historian Robert W. Seton-Watson, *A History of the Roumanians from Roman Times to the Completion of Unity*,[301] published in 1934 and in some respects now out of date. The ancient and medieval history of Romania have been totally neglected. No scholarly studies of the nationality problem in Transylvania or of the Bessarabian question have been published. There are no monographic studies in English of the modern Romanian political parties and their leaders or, with the exception of two works by English writers David Mitrany, *The Land and the Peasant in Rumania: the War and Agrarian Reform, 1917–1921*,[302] a comprehensive treatment, and Ifor L. Evans, *The Agrarian Revolution in Roumania*,[303] on the central problem of Romanian agriculture and the peasantry.

Besides filling in these broad gaps, American scholars can make original contributions to the study of Romania's history and culture in many fields. The liberal, fascist, conservative, socialist, and communist movements and ideologies still await full and objective treatment as do the nationality problem in Transylvania and the delicate question of Romanian-Hungarian relations in the nineteenth and twentieth centuries, the contributions of the Orthodox and Uniate churches to the development of Romanian political and economic life, the history of Protestantism in Moldavia and Wallachia, the Phanariot regime of the eighteenth and early nineteenth centuries, the history of Romanian agriculture and the peasant, the development of capitalism and the growth of foreign investments, Romanian immigration to the United States, and the Jewish question. American scholars would also find the influence of the Renaissance, the Reformation, and the Enlightenment in Romania a rich area for study and research.

YUGOSLAVIA

Of the states of southeastern Europe, Yugoslavia has received perhaps the most attention in the modern period. The library holdings for Yugoslavia in the United States are more complete and more widely dispersed than those for any other Balkan state. Nevertheless, American research on the South Slav peoples is meager and limited largely to the history of the last one hundred years. There is not, for example, a single general history of Yugoslavia written by an American. Although there are several published in England, they serve primarily as outlines

301. (Cambridge, England: The University Press, 1934).
302. (London–New Haven: Yale University Press, 1930).
303. (Cambridge, England: The University Press, 1924).

or introductory textbooks, and they do not satisfy the needs of the graduate student or scholar. The single book on any of the South Slav peoples in the medieval period is the volume by Francis R. Preveden, *A History of the Croatian People: Prehistory to 1397*,[304] which, however, suffers from an overly nationalistic approach. There is nothing on the Ottoman period, nor for that matter on the decisive events of the first half of the nineteenth century.

The only works on the seventeenth, eighteenth, and nineteenth centuries are the two volumes on the Croatian military frontier by Gunther Rothenberg. *The Austrian Military Border in Croatia, 1522–1747*[305] and *The Military Border in Croatia, 1740–1881*.[306] Although they cover the relevant Croatian internal affairs very well, these books are more concerned with Habsburg institutions than with Croatian history as such. They are nevertheless indispensable for both Serbian and Croatian history. In many respects, these two volumes are the best in any language on the subject.

The only four books of a general nature about Yugoslavia are Robert J. Kerner, ed., *Yugoslavia*,[307] Robert F. Byrnes, ed., *Yugoslavia*,[308] Stephen Clissold, ed., *A Short History of Yugoslavia, from Early Times to 1966*,[309] and Jozo Tomasevich, *Peasants, Politics and Economic Change in Yugoslavia*.[310] The first two are collections of essays on different aspects of South Slav history. Their purpose is to explain recent events in Yugoslavia. The third is a collection of essays, edited and revised by Clissold, originally published by the Naval Intelligence Division of the British Admiralty as a handbook on Yugoslavia. Tomasevich's volume is a model study on economic history and is the best general survey we have, although naturally it lacks an intensive treatment of cultural, diplomatic, and religious affairs.

For the second half of the nineteenth century, two outstanding publications have appeared. Woodford D. McClellan, *Svetozar Marković and the Origins of Balkan Socialism*,[311] is an excellent study of a Serbian intellectual who tried to apply socialist principles to an agrarian state. Peter Sugar, *The Industrialization of Bosnia-Hercegovina, 1878–1918*,[312]

304. 2 vols. (New York: Philosophical Library, 1955–62).
305. (Urbana: University of Illinois Press, 1960).
306. *The Military Border in Croatia, 1740–1881: A Study of an Imperial Institution* (Chicago: University of Chicago Press, 1966).
307. (Berkeley: University of California Press, 1949).
308. (New York: Praeger, for Mid-European Studies Center of the Free Europe Committee, 1957).
309. (Cambridge, England: The University Press, 1966).
310. (Stanford: Stanford University Press, 1955).
311. (Princeton: Princeton University Press, 1964).
312. (Seattle: University of Washington Press, 1963).

admirably discusses the attempt of the Habsburg administration to make these provinces economically productive.

For the period of World War I and its origins, the volumes by Vucinich and Remak, cited previously in connection with the Eastern Question, discuss prewar Serbian problems. John C. Adams, *Flight in Winter*,[313] is a sympathetic account of the retreat of the Serbian army to Corfu after its defeat in 1915. Ivo Lederer, *Yugoslavia at the Paris Peace Conference*,[314] is an analysis of the international problems facing the state during the first year of its existence and the internal struggles between the Serbs and Croats over the organization of the new state.

In the interwar period, two volumes have appeared concerning internal affairs. Charles A. Beard and G. Radin, *The Balkan Pivot: Yugoslavia*,[315] is an attempt to explore the problem of centralism vs. federalism; Stephen Graham, *Alexander of Yugoslavia*,[316] is a sympathetic biography of the monarch assassinated at Marseilles in 1934. The complex problems preceding Yugoslavia's entrance into World War II are discussed in two books, one by an American, the other by a former Serbian officer now a resident of the United States. J. B. Hoptner, *Yugoslavia in Crisis, 1934–1941*[317] makes use of much unpublished private material to present an able account of the background of the coup d'état of 1941. Whereas Hoptner's work is in some respects critical of developments in Yugoslavia, Dragisha N. Ristić, *Yugoslavia's Revolution of 1941*,[318] is a very sympathetic account of General Simović's role in the event written by his aide-de-camp. These two publications supplement each other and should be read together.

For understandable reasons, the postwar period, especially the developments associated with Tito, has attracted considerable interest. Research on this phase of Yugoslav history has been, however, primarily by political scientists and economists, and these are discussed in other sections.

Of the individual national groups, only the Slovenes and Croats have been the subject of historical accounts. Thomas Barker[319] and F. Arnez[320] have produced brief surveys of aspects of Slovene history.

313. (Princeton: Princeton University Press, 1942).
314. (New Haven: Yale University Press, 1963).
315. (New York: Macmillan, 1929).
316. (New Haven: Yale University Press, 1939).
317. (New York: Columbia University Press, 1962).
318. (Stanford: Stanford University Press, 1966).
319. *The Slovenes of Carinthia: A National Minority Problem* (New York: League of CSA, 1960).
320. *Slovenia in European Affairs: Reflections on Slovenian Political History* (New York: League of CSA, 1958).

F. H. Eterovich, ed., *Croatia: Land, People, Culture*,[321] is a collection of essays, some of which are scholarly, others overly nationalistic in tone. There is no history of the Montenegrins, Macedonians, or Serbs by an American. The distinguished English historian, H. W. V. Temperley's *History of Servia*,[322] although outdated in certain respects, is still useful. Similarly, R. W. Seton-Watson, *The South Slav Question*,[323] also somewhat old, has valuable information on nineteenth-century Croatian history.

The needs in South Slav history are great. First, and most important, is the basic requirement of a comprehensive history of Yugoslavia. Moreover, since this state is composed of a number of nations, all of whom had individual and unique histories, some for over a thousand years, the past of each of these must be adequately covered. A separate history of each of these people would be desirable. The lack of general histories is not only characteristic of American writing, but also of that of Yugoslavia. In the interwar period, only one scholarly history of Yugoslavia, that written by Vladimir Ćorović, *Istorija Jugoslavije* (History of Yugoslavia),[324] appeared. At present, Yugoslav historians are preparing a collective history, and the two volumes that have been published bring the account up to 1800.[325]

Although the political and diplomatic aspects of Yugoslav history have been comparatively well studied, there is still need for further research in certain fields. In international affairs, a careful study of intra-Balkan relations and the ties between the national movements of the entire East European area would be most valuable. In political history, the influence of the army and military considerations on national life have not been explored, although its importance is great in internal politics and international relations. The national ideas of the individual peoples of Yugoslavia and their influence upon each other, in particular that of the greater Serbian and greater Croatian movements, have also not been considered. In this connection, a scholarly treatment of the Macedonian problem in the modern period is urgently needed. Most serious is the lack of emphasis on religious history. The Yugoslav lands, with their competing Orthodox, Catholic, and Moslem churches, are particularly interesting in this respect. In this question, the works

321. (Toronto: University of Toronto Press, 1964).
322. (London: G. Bell, 1917).
323. *The Southern Slav Question and the Habsburg Monarchy* (London: Constable, 1911).
324. (Belgrade: Narodno delo, 1933).
325. Bogo Grafenauer *et al.*, eds. *Historija naroda Jugoslavije* (History of the Peoples of Yugoslavia) 2 vols. (Zagreb, Školska knjiga, 1953–59).

hitherto published in Yugoslavia have been overly nationalistic and emotional. It is a field in which American scholars can make real contributions.

As far as the individual historical periods are concerned, the medieval and Ottoman eras, which left such an indelible mark upon these lands, have been virtually untouched by Western scholars. Yugoslav historians have made great contributions here, and a synthesis of these by an American writer is needed. Certain subjects in this period have not been adequately studied in any language. In particular, a careful analysis of Croat-Magyar relations in the twelfth, sixteenth, and eighteenth centuries is long overdue. The demographic changes in Croatia in the sixteenth and seventeenth centuries, the settlement of the Albanians in the Kosmet after its evacuation by the Serbs, and Dalmatia's role in the Renaissance and in South Slav history are other topics which might be explored.

Most serious is the lack of acceptable biographies in any Western language of the men who shaped Yugoslav history in the nineteenth and twentieth centuries. It is not possible to understand Yugoslav history without a knowledge of the career and ideas of such leaders as Karadjordje, Miloš Obrenović, Ilija Garašanin, Metropolitan Mihailo, Jovan Ristić, Nikola Pašić, Count Janko Drašković, Baron Josip Jelačić, Bishop Josip Juraj Strossmayer, Canon Franjo Rački, Ante Radić, and many others. Because of the intense controversy which surrounds the lives of some of these, their biographies can perhaps best be written by scholars who are not Yugoslav.

BULGARIA

Aside from Albania, the Balkan state which is least studied in America is Bulgaria. There is no history of Bulgaria by an American, not even a survey, although there are three recent histories in the English language. Two of these are by English writers, Stanley Evans, *A Short History of Bulgaria*,[326] and Mercia Macdermott, *A History of Bulgaria*,[327] and one is a translation from the Bulgarian, D. Kosev, H. Hristov, and D. Angelov, *A Short History of Bulgaria*.[328] None of these, however, meets the requirements of scholars or graduate students.

As far as the historical periods are concerned, there is nothing in

326. (London: Lawrence and Wishart, 1960).
327. (New York: Praeger, 1962).
328. (Sofia: Foreign Languages Press, 1963). Translated by Marguerite Alexieva and Nicolai Koledarov.

English on the medieval or Ottoman periods aside from the excellent work by the English historian Stevan Runciman, *The First Bulgarian Empire*.[329] The years before 1878 have been the subject of several interpretive articles by James F. Clarke.[330] A specialized work, covering the pre- and post-liberation eras is William W. Hall, *Puritans in the Balkans*,[331] which discusses American missionary activity in Bulgaria. The two most detailed studies which deal exclusively with Bulgarian history are C. E. Black, *The Establishment of Constitutional Government in Bulgaria*,[332] and Joseph Rothschild, *The Communist Party of Bulgaria: Origin and Development, 1883–1936*.[333] Black's book is an excellent analysis of Bulgarian developments from 1879 to 1884. It is based on material from the Austrian and British archives as well as on all published materials. Rothschild's study, although centering on the life of Dimitur Blagoev, covers much Bulgarian domestic history.

Of course, the books by Langer, Harris, Sumner, Jelavich, Helmreich, and Thaden, cited previously, deal directly with Bulgarian foreign affairs, but as a part of larger problems and issues. Aside from the volume *Bulgaria* edited by L. A. D. Dellin,[334] which is a collection of essays dealing with the recent postwar era, there are no other important historical works on Bulgarian history.

The needs in Bulgarian history parallel those of Yugoslavia. There is, first of all, a similar need of a satisfactory national history, stressing the economic, social, and religious developments as well as the political and diplomatic events. Second, a careful analysis of the effects of Ottoman rule in all its aspects should be made. The land system and commercial development within the empire are particularly important. The religious question, especially in respect to the formation of the Exarchate and the question of Greek control over the ecclesiastical organization of Bulgaria should be further studied. Again, as in the case of Yugoslavia, the Macedonian controversy should be dispassionately considered from its Bulgarian aspects. Biographies are also needed of the leading political figures such as Father Paisii, Karavelov, Botev, Stambulov, Stamboliskii, and others.

329. (London: G. Bell, 1930).
330. "Serbia and the Bulgarian Revival (1762–1872)," *American Slavic and East European Review*, 4 (December, 1945): 141–62; "Father Paisi and Bulgarian History," in H. Stuart Hughes, ed., *Essays in Honor of Lawrence B. Packard* (Ithaca, N.Y.: Cornell University Press, 1954), pp. 258–83.
331. (Sofia: 1938).
332. (Princeton: Princeton University Press, 1943).
333. (New York: Columbia University Press, 1959).
334. (New York: Praeger, for Mid-European Studies Center of the Free Europe Committee, 1957).

GREECE

The general neglect of modern Greek studies in the United States is largely the result of Greece's political evolution after World War II. The simple fact that Greece escaped the political fate of the other Balkan countries placed it outside the area of immediate concern to Western scholars as a whole. Greece and its islands became instead an attraction for tourists and artists, inspiring numerous literary and travel accounts ranging from Lawrence Durrell's novels to Robert Payne's exciting descriptions. Major American scholarly interest continued to limit itself to the field of classical studies and to making, simultaneously, progress or inroads in the study of Byzantine history and culture. The latter development was logical because of its chronological and thematic connections with classical civilization. On the other hand, the growing popularity of Byzantine studies was probably again determined by political considerations, namely the increasing interest in the cultural heritage of the Slavic peoples, especially the Russians.

The development of modern Greece has been the subject of a number of surveys, largely by Englishmen. Of chief interest are: Edward S. Forster, *A Short History of Modern Greece*; [335] William Miller, *A History of the Greek People, 1821–1921*; [336] *A Short History of Greece* by W. A. Heurtley *et al.*;[337] and N. Svoronos *Histoire de la Grèce moderne.*[338] From a chronological viewpoint, Greek history is characterized by the unevenness of its treatment by scholars. There is little in English on the period prior to or after the Turkish conquest and the occupation of Greece. The British historian William Miller has written two studies: *The Latins in the Levant, 1204–1566*[339] and *The Turkish Restoration of Greece, 1718–1797.*[340] James Morton Paton has edited *The Venetians in Athens, 1687–1688, from the Istoria of Christoforo Ivanovich.*[341] The era of the Turkish conquest is, in fact, the most neglected subject in general Greek historical studies.

Interest becomes somewhat livelier with the Greek War of Independence and its immediate background. S. C. Chaconas' biography of *Adamantios Korais: A Study in Greek Nationalism* [342] has been con-

335. Revised and enlarged by Douglas Dakin (London: Methuen, 1958).
336. (New York: E. P. Dutton, 1922).
337. *A Short History of Greece: From Early Times to 1964* (Cambridge, England: The University Press, 1965).
338. (Paris: Presses universitaires de France, 1953).
339. (London: J. Murray, 1908; New York: Barnes and Noble, 1964).
340. Helps for Students of History, no. 38 (London, 1921).
341. (Cambridge: Harvard University Press, 1940).
342. (New York: Columbia University Press, 1942).

sidered the standard work, but, in fact, it is only a prologue to a significant and complicated subject. Fortunately, it has been followed by serious studies, as well as by editions of Korais' works by Greek scholars such as G. Valetas and K. Dēmaras.[343] However, the intellectual origins of the Greek War of Independence have not been dealt with satisfactorily, although Raphael Demos, "The Neo-Hellenic Enlightenment (1750–1821)"[344] in the *Journal of the History of Ideas*, provides a general survey of the subject.

On the Greek War of Independence, the main event of modern Greek history, there are quite a few books in English, the majority by British historians. C. W. Crawley, *The Question of Greek Independence*,[345] and C. M. Woodhouse, *The Greek War of Independence*,[346] are surveys of the political and diplomatic aspects. More specialized topics are treated in C. M. Woodhouse, *The Battle of Navarino*,[347] and in the Greek historian Domna Dontas' *The Last Phase of the War of Independence in Western Greece, 1827–1829*.[348] The European interest in the Greek revolution is witnessed by the number of studies on Philhellenism, as, for example, the British study by T. Spencer, *Fair Greece! Sad Relic!*[349] American Philhellenism is discussed in Stephen A. Larrabee, *Hellas Observed: The American Experience of Greece, 1775–1863*,[350] and Douglas Dakin, *British and American Philhellenes during the War of Independence*.[351] The important memoirs of Makriyannis have recently been edited and translated by H. A. Lidderdale, *Makriyannis: The Memoirs of General Makriyannis, 1797–1864*.[352] G. G. Arnakis has been interested in the collection and publication of the records and lives of Americans who participated in the war. Thus far two have appeared under the general title *Americans in the Greek Revolution: George Jarvis*, edited by Arnakis and E. Demetrakopou-

343. G. Valetas, *Koraēs, Hapanta to prōtotypa erga* (Collected Original Works) vol. 1 in 2 parts (Athens: Dhorikos, 1964); K. Th. Dēmaras, *Adamantios Koraēs Allelografia* (The Correspondence of Adamantios Koraēs), vol. 1 (1774–1798), vol. 2 (1799–1809), (Athens: Hestia, 1964–66).

344. *Journal of the History of Ideas*, 19 (October, 1958): 523–41.

345. *The Question of Greek Independence: A Study of British Policy in the Near East, 1821–1833* (Cambridge, England: The University Press, 1930).

346. *The Greek War of Independence: Its Historical Setting* (London: Hutchinson's University Library, 1952).

347. (London: Hodder and Stoughton, 1965).

348. (Thessalonika: Institute for Balkan Studies, 1966).

349. *Fair Greece! Sad Relic: Literary Phihellenism from Shakespeare to Byron* (London: Weidenfeld and Nicolson, 1954).

350. (New York: New York University Press, 1957).

351. *British and American Phihellenes during the War of Independence, 1821–1833* (Thessaloniki: Institute for Balkan Studies, 1955).

352. (London: Oxford University Press, 1966).

lou,[353] and Samuel G. Howe, *An Historical Sketch of the Greek Revolution.*[354]

The establishment of the modern Greek state has been largely neglected. William P. Kaldis, *John Capodistrias and the Modern Greek State*[355] is too brief a study to do justice to so complex a personality as that of Greece's short-lived president. One aspect of the reign of Othon is covered in Barbara Jelavich's *Russia and Greece during the Reign of King Othon, 1831–1835: Russian Documents on the First Years of Greek Independence*[356] and *Russia and the Greek Revolution of 1843,*[357] both based primarily on documents from the Bavarian archives. Needless to say, similar studies are needed to cover Greek relations with other countries. The rest of the century receives little or almost no attention. There is some information in works such as L. S. Stavrianos, *Balkan Federation: A History of the Movement toward Balkan Unity in Modern Times,*[358] and William Langer, *European Alliances and Alignments.*[359] Pursuing his interests in the American Philhellenes, G. Arnakis has published *American Consul in a Cretan War, William Stillman,*[360] which is a revised edition of Stillman's *The Cretan Insurrection.*[361] A. J. May also discussed briefly American attitudes during this crisis in his "Crete and the United States, 1866–1869"[362] in the *Journal of Modern History.* There also are two works in English by Greek scholars which deserve attention: the first is by E. Prevelakis, *British Policy towards the Change of Dynasty in Greece, 1862–1863,*[363] the second by Domna Dontas, *Greece and the Great Powers, 1863–1875.*[364] In connection with Crete, one should also note the study by E. Prevelakis, *Hē Megalē Krētikē Epanastasē* (The Great Cretan Revolution).[365]

The twentieth century has also not attracted the attention it deserves.

---

353. *George Jarvis — His Journal and Related Documents* (Thessaloniki: Institute for Balkan Studies, 1965).

354. Pt. 1; ed. with an introduction and notes by George G. Arnakis (Austin, Tex.: Center for Neo-Hellenic Studies, 1966).

355. (Madison: State Historical Society of Wisconsin for Department of History, University of Wisconsin, 1963).

356. (Thessaloniki: Institute for Balkan Studies, 1962).

357. (Munich: R. Oldenbourg, 1966).

358. (Northampton, Mass.: Department of History of Smith College, 1944; Hamden, Conn.: Archon Books, 1964).

359. (New York: Knopf, 1931, 1956, 1962).

360. (Austin, Tex.: Center for Neo-Hellenic Studies, 1966).

361. *The Cretan Insurrection 1866–1868* (New York: H. Holt & Co., 1874).

362. *Journal of Modern History,* 16 (December, 1944): 286–93.

363. (Athens: Gertrude Christou & Sons, 1955).

364. (Thessaloniki: Institute for Balkan Studies, 1966).

365. (Athens: 1966).

There is as yet no satisfactory work in English on Greece and World War I, or Greece at the Paris peace conference. There is, to be sure, G. F. Abbott's *Greece and Allies 1914–1922*,[366] and the subject is also discussed in various works dealing with the diplomatic aspects of the war, such as E. Driault's *Histoire diplomatique de la Grèce*, Vol. 5,[367] and European scholars have dealt with the subject in the context of the Constantine-Venizelos controversy. Representative works of this sort are S. Phocas-Cosmetatos, *The Tragedy of Greece*,[368] and A. Frangoulis, *La Grèce et la crise mondiale*,[369] both of which are pro-Constantine, and the most important sympathetic biographies of Venizelos: D. Alastos, *Venizelos*,[370] and W. H. Crawfurd Price, *Venizelos and the War*.[371] But as yet there has been no serious attempt at scholarly synthe- sis of the various views and issues whose repercussions are still felt in the "Greek world." Alan Palmer, *The Gardeners of Salonika*,[372] dis- cusses principally the preparations for the allied Balkan campaign. For the interwar years, A. A. Pallis, *Anatolian Venture*,[373] covers the ill-fated campaign in Turkey. A. J. Toynbee, *The Western Question in Greece and Turkey*,[374] is also important. In the modern period, two topics in particular have attracted considerable attention — the exchange of minorities between Greece and her neighbors, and World War II and its aftermath. For the first, there is the standard work of S. P. Ladas, *The Exchange of Minorities: Bulgaria, Greece, and Turkey*.[375] The prob- lem is also discussed in H. Morgenthau, *I Was Sent to Athens*;[376] the author was the first chairman of the Greek Refugee Settlement Com- mission. The social and economic implications are partly covered in E. G. Mears, *Greece Today: The Aftermath of the Refugee Im- pact*.[377]

World War II and the civil war which followed have been of interest to American scholars at least partly because of American interest in and aid to Greece. This interest of the Western world in general is reflected

366. (London: Methuen, 1922).
367. *Histoire diplomatique de la Grèce de 1821 à nos jours*, 5 vols. (Paris: Les Presses universitaires de France, 1925–26).
368. Trans. E. W. and A. Dickes (New York: Brentano's, 1928).
369. (Paris: 1926).
370. *Venizelos, Patriot, Statesman, Revolutionary* (London: P. Lund, Humphries & Co., 1942).
371. (London, 1917).
372. (New York: Simon and Schuster, 1965).
373. *Greece's Anatolian Venture — and After* (London: Methuen, 1937).
374. (London: Constable, 1922).
375. (New York: Macmillan, 1932).
376. (Garden City, N.Y.: Doubleday, Doran, 1929).
377. (Stanford: Stanford University Press, 1929).

in, among other things, the translation of Field Marshal Alexander Papagos', *The Battle of Greece, 1940–1941,*[378] and in Philip P. Argentis' specialized study, *The Occupation of Chios by the Germans.*[379] The works of D. Kousoulas, *The Price of Freedom: Greece in World Affairs, 1939–1953,*[380] and L. S. Stavrianos, *Greece: American Dilemma and Opportunity,*[381] represent opposite views. The first praises both Greek and allied efforts, the second criticizes the irresponsible domestic policy of the Greek government as well as the acts of the United States leading to the Truman Doctrine. An admirably detailed, balanced, and almost definitive account of the preliminaries to the Truman Doctrine is Stephen G. Xydis, *Greece and the Great Powers, 1944–1947: Prelude to the Truman Doctrine.*[382] D. Kousoulas' views were expressed with more sophistication again in his *Revolution and Defeat: The Story of the Greek Communist Party,*[383] in which the author stresses the importance of the divisions among the Communists as factors contributing to their defeat. W. H. McNeill, *The Greek Dilemma: The War and Aftermath,*[384] is the most objective account done by an American scholar on the subject. Kousoulas' and McNeill's accounts compare favorably with the two English monographs by C. M. Woodhouse, *Apple of Discord,*[385] and Edgar O'Balance, *The Greek Civil War, 1944–1949.*[386] B. Sweet-Escott, *Greece: A Political and Economic Survey, 1939–1953,*[387] is a sober, careful study. American aid to Greece is discussed in W. H. McNeill, *Greece: American Aid in Action 1947–1956: Report on the Greeks,*[388] C. A. Munkman, *American Aid to Greece: A Report on the First Ten Years,*[389] and Theodore A. Couloumbis' *Greek Political Reaction to American and NATO Influences.*[390]

This brief chronological outline thus far suggests the scarcity of work done by American scholars on Greece, although British historians have contributed more. A brief topical survey of the entire field will reconfirm this conclusion. For a real understanding of Balkan history in

378. Trans. Pat. Eliascos (Athens: J. M. Scazikis "Alpha" Editions, 1949).
379. (London: Cambridge University Press, 1966).
380. (Syracuse, N.Y.: Syracuse University Press, 1953).
381. (Chicago: H. Regnery, 1952).
382. (Thessaloniki: Institute for Balkan Studies, 1963).
383. (London and New York: Oxford University Press, 1965).
384. (Philadelphia: J. B. Lippincott, 1947).
385. *Apple of Discord: A Survey of Recent Greek Politics in Their International Setting* (London and New York: Hutchinson, 1948).
386. (New York: Praeger, 1966).
387. (London and New York: Royal Institute of International Affairs, 1954).
388. (New York: Twentieth Century Fund, 1957).
389. (New York: Praeger, 1958).
390. (New Haven: Yale University Press, 1966).

general and Greece in particular, the study of the Orthodox Church is imperative. Yet this is one of the most neglected areas. More studies are needed similar to the Cypriote scholar Theodore Papadopoulos' *Studies and Documents Relating to the History of the Greek Church and People under Turkish Domination* [391] and the British historian Timothy Ware's *Eustratios Argenti: A Study of the Greek Church under Turkish Rule*,[392] and the two articles by G. Arnakis "The Greek Church of Constantinople and the Ottoman Empire" [393] in the *Journal of Modern History* and the same author's "The Role of Religion in the Development of Balkan Nationalism" [394] in *The Balkans in Transition*. The best account of the Greek Church in our time is Peter Hammond, *The Waters of Marah*.[395] Raymond Etteldorf's *The Soul of Greece* [396] is written from a Catholic point of view. S. M. Sophocles' *The Religion of Modern Greece* [397] is too sketchy. There is, in particular, a great need for a solid work on the role of the Greek Church in the rise of Greek nationalism. Histories of individual churches, the relations among the various patriarchates and aspects of the Church — such as Orthodox monasticism — require proper attention. There are no works on Mount Athos, for example, similar to Donald M. Nicol's *The Meteora*.[398] Constantine Cavarnos' *Anchored in God* [399] is merely an attempt at a sophisticated travel account. Greek scholars are doing a considerable amount of work in this field, even though many questions will remain unanswered until access to Turkish archives is made possible. Also in the field of religious history is the relatively unexplored question of American missionary activity in Greece.

Very closely related to church history and equally neglected is intellectual history. Neither Paideia under Tourkokratia nor the so-called neo-hellenic enlightenment have received their proper attention. Professor K. Th. Dēmaras' admirable study, *Historia tes neoellēnikes logotechnias* (History of Modern Greek Literature),[400] if translated could serve both as a model for the writing of intellectual history and as a

391. (Brussels: Bibliotheca Graeca Aevi Posterisris, 1952).
392. (Oxford: Clarendon Press, 1964).
393. *Journal of Modern History*, 24 (September, 1952): 235–50.
394. In Charles and Barbara Jelavich, ed., *The Balkans in Transition* (Berkeley: University of California Press, 1963), pp. 115–44.
395. *The Waters of Marah: The Present State of the Greek Church* (London: Rockliff, 1956).
396. (Westminster: Newman Press, 1963).
397. (Thessaloniki: Institute for Balkan Studies, 1961).
398. (London: Chapman and Hall, 1963).
399. *Anchored in God: An Inside Account of Life, Art, and Thought on the Holy Mountain of Athos* (Athens: Astir, 1959).
400. 2 vols. (Athens: Ikaros Press, 1948–49).

guide to areas where research for monographic studies is badly needed. Chiefly under the leadership of Dēmaras, there is a growing interest in Greek intellectual history among Greek historians. Also in this connection, Greco-Slavic relations, cultural as well as political, should be further emphasized. These topics are difficult for a Greek historian to handle, partly because of problems of nationalism and partly because of the lack of linguistic training. In this area American scholars can render a great service. An effort in this direction has been made by Theofanis G. Stavrou in his *Russian Interests in Palestine, 1882–1914*,[401] where he tries to suggest the interrelation between cultural and political rivalries between Hellenism and Slavism. There is not as yet a satisfactory account of the impact of the Bulgarian Exarchate on the relations of the Balkan states. The Greeks shared certain efforts and experiences in their struggles for national independence with other Balkan nations, and this cooperation or collaboration could make a fascinating study. Professor Lascaris' monograph *Hellēnes kai Serboi kata tous Apeleutherōtikous tōn agōnas, 1804–1830* (Greeks and Serbs during Their Wars of Liberation, 1804–1830)[402] should find more imitators, as should the various monographs of K. Amantos treating Greece's relations with its northern neighbors.[403]

In the field of foreign affairs, there is a need not only for specialized studies but for a new general evaluation of the imperatives of Greek foreign policy from 1821 to the present. In other words, E. Driault's and M. Lhéritier's five-volume *Histoire diplomatique de la Grèce*[404] needs to be brought up to date, and E. Driault's *La grande idée, la renaissance de l'Hellénisme*[405] reconsidered and expanded upon.

Constitutional, administrative, political, and economic history is literally virgin territory. The standard works of N. Kaltchas, *Introduction to the Constitutional History of Modern Greece*,[406] and J. A. Levandis, *The Greek Foreign Debt and the Great Powers, 1821–1898*,[407] need to be supplemented by more specialized works. N. G. Svoronos, *Le commerce de Salonique au XVIII* *siècle*,[408] should serve as a model for such studies. Professor Paul P. Vouras has written *The Changing Econ-*

---

401. *Russian Interests in Palestine, 1882–1914: A Study of Religious and Educational Enterprise* (Thessaloniki: Institute for Balkan Studies, 1963).
402. (Athens, 1936).
403.   *Hoi Boreioi gheitones tēs Hellados* (The Northern Neighbors of Greece) (Athens: Eleutheroudaki, 1923).
404. 5 vols. (Paris: Les presses universitaires de France, 1925–26).
405. (Paris: F. Alcan, 1920).
406. (New York: Columbia University Press, 1940).
407. (New York: Columbia University Press, 1944).
408. (Athens: Publications of the French Institute of Athens, 1954).

omy of Northern Greece since World War II,[409] which examines the whole problem from the geographer's point of view.

There is also a need for local histories or histories of the Islands, whose records are often more exciting and whose contributions are more significant than those of the mainland. The four-volume *History of Cyprus* by Sir George Hill [410] is an example of scholarship one wishes to see applied in the writing of the other islands' histories. Equally lacking are good biographies of national leaders — political, ecclesiastical, or intellectual. Even Eleftherios Venizelos, Greece's most notable statesman in modern times, is in need of a new biography utilizing the Venizelos papers which are gradually being made available. The existing accounts such as the one by Alastos, whatever their merits, are dated. The writing of good biographies can, in fact, be the most direct way to bridge the vast gaps which exist in our knowledge of modern Greek history.

Finally, there is another area that could be further investigated: the impact of the Greeks of the diaspora on the mother country. Theodore Saloutos has written on this subject, *They Remember America*,[411] but he concentrates on the social problems of reassimilation which the repatriated Greeks faced. The story of the economic contributions of the Greek immigrants to their own communities is yet to be written. Saloutos' *The Greeks in the United States* [412] deals to a limited extent with the background of the economic conditions in Greece which caused the wave of emigrants to come to the New World. Equally exciting would be the study of Greek commercial and cultural groups residing outside Greece proper in Constantinople and the Principalities, such as the Phanariotes, or in Russia, especially the Odessa area.

In summary, the need for monographs in modern Greek history is great. Most important is the lack of a good general history of modern Greece which would go far deeper than the surveys now available. The essential questions of Orthodoxy and the Orthodox Church in Greek history remain to be studied, despite their major role in Greek development. In the field of foreign relations, a new study of Greece's international role must be undertaken to replace the outdated work of Driault and Lhéritier. Of particular significance is the further study of Greek-Slavic relations in their cultural and social as well as their diplomatic aspects. Here, some of the contributions of the Greek scholar

---

409. (Thessaloniki: Institute for Balkan Studies, 1962).
410. 4 vols. (Cambridge, England: The University Press, 1940–52).
411. *They Remember America: The Story of the Repatriated Greek-Americans* (Berkeley: University of California Press, 1956).
412. (Cambridge: Harvard University Press, 1964).

Emile-Antoine Tahiaos should be translated. As regards the historical periods, all subjects remain open in the Ottoman period. The translation of two Greek works, D. A. Zakythinos, *Hē Tourkokratia: Eisagōgē eis tēn neōteran historia tou Hellēnismou* (Tourkokratia: An Introduction to Modern Greek History) [413] and A. E. Vacalopoulos, *Historia tou neou Hellēnismou* (History of Modern Hellenism; 3 vols.),[414] is to be recommended. In the modern period, a definitive history of the Greek revolution remains to be written. Further studies of the economic, political, and social evolution of the country are also needed.

GRADUATE TRAINING IN HISTORY

Among the historians in the field who were consulted in connection with this survey, it was the almost unanimous feeling that a specialist in East European history must be trained in the discipline. At the same time, however, it was agreed that the student should be strongly encouraged to take seminars or courses in other subjects — in particular, in literature, economics, political science (political theory and government), geography, anthropology, and sociology — to give him a broad interdisciplinary background. The choice of these secondary fields should be made dependent on his special interest within the East European field. It would be most advisable for a historian to take courses or seminars in literature, political science, and geography. Beyond this, a specialist in Poland and Czechoslovakia might find philosophy and economics a valuable preparation, whereas a Balkan specialist might find folklore and ethnomusicology more pertinent to his work. Area certificates, while useful for those not interested in a doctorate, are not believed of sufficient value to warrant the extra year of study which is normally necessary. The same result can be achieved with a wise choice of elective courses outside of history. Obviously, the preparation of students is dependent upon the courses offered in his university.

Perhaps the most serious defect in the training of historians in the East European area has been the over-emphasis on the Russian, particularly on the Soviet Russian, approach to the detriment of adequate preparation in general European history. In a number of instances doctoral candidates have succeeded in divorcing in their own mind the events of Eastern Europe from the great European movements of the time. In general, two groups of students are particularly susceptible to

413. (Athens, 1957).
414. 3 vols. (Thessaloniki, 1961–68).

this failing. The first are those who become interested in the area as undergraduates and direct most of their work to it. The second is the student, not an undergraduate history major, who in his senior year decides to shift his field and enters graduate school with a poor background in European history. In graduate school he takes primarily area courses or history courses directed to East European studies. It should thus be emphasized that before a student enters this field as a graduate, he should have a sound background in general European history.

In addition, proper undergraduate preparation for graduate study should include a reading knowledge of two foreign languages, chosen from French, German, Russian, or — in certain circumstances — Latin. A reading knowledge of French, German, and Russian would be ideal. The student should understand from the beginning of this period of study that this field is more demanding than certain others because of the absolute necessity of wide linguistic competence. In fact, this requirement may prolong his period of study a year or more. With the knowledge of two languages already acquired, the student should immediately upon entering graduate school commence the study of one language of the area. In his third year, he should begin another. After he becomes a member of a history faculty, he should add a non-Slavic language if his other two were Slavic. It should be impressed upon the student that research cannot be carried on in this area without command of at least four languages.

Another characteristic of this field for which the student must be prepared is, as a survey of those trained in it shows, that although they can continue their research along the lines of their choosing, only a minority have been able to teach exclusively in the East European area. The majority are obligated to teach general survey courses in European history, or to offer East European history in combination with German or Russian history. In rare instances a course in Ottoman history may be combined with one in this area. Typical combinations, for instance, are Polish and Russian history, German history and East Central Europe, the Habsburg empire and the Balkans, and Russia and the Balkans or Russia and Eastern Europe. The specialist in this field thus must be aware that he should be qualified also to teach either Central European and German history or Russian history.

Finally, as an essential part of his graduate study, each student should be given the opportunity to visit the country of his major interest, preferably in connection with the writing of his dissertation. A year would be best, but a summer should also be considered. In view of the reasonable group excursion rates now available and the effective summer language institutes for foreigners in Poland, Czechoslovakia, Hungary, Romania and Yugoslavia, a study and language tour could be combined. Every support should also be given to the expansion of exchanges with Eastern Europe either under the Fulbright program, the International Research and Exchanges Board (IREX), or by any other means which facilitates study in the East European countries.

In conclusion, it is advised that graduate training proceed within the discipline, that strong emphasis be placed on language training, and that the student be made aware that he will probably not be able to teach exclusively in his field of interest. Those already established in the field should use their influence to widen exchange programs and to obtain further sources of financing so that the young scholar has the opportunity to work in the libraries and archives of Eastern Europe. It is indeed most difficult to write or teach about a country without direct personal experience in living there.

COURSE OFFERINGS

An examination of the courses in the catalogs of the universities which have an interest in this area reveals the different possibilities available for the division of the area. There is no generally accepted progression or division such as that of medieval, Renaissance, Reformation, early modern and modern in European history. Usually the courses offered reflect the interests and emphasis of the instructor. Nevertheless, they may be divided into five groups: (1) general surveys of Eastern Europe, (2) the Balkans, (3) East Central Europe, or the Habsburg Empire (the term used varies), (4) Byzantium, (5) special offerings.

Only three universities — Columbia, Indiana, and Washington — attempt to present a coverage in depth of the entire field. Columbia has a particularly strong program in Ottoman history and in East Central Europe. There are three courses on the Ottoman Empire: a general survey, the cultural relations between the Ottoman Turks and the peoples of the Danubian Empire, and Ottoman Turkish historiography. In addition, there is a one-semester course on Balkan Peoples and Cultures. A special course is also given on the diplomatic history of Eastern Europe from 1848 to 1939. Three seminars are offered: Byzantium, the modern history of East Central Europe, and the Soviet Union and Eastern Europe. At Indiana, there is a two-semester survey course of the area from the medieval period to the present. In addition, there is an emphasis on the Balkans and the Habsburg lands, but also a particularly strong program on Hungary in connection with the Uralic-

Altaic department. Two courses of two semesters each are given on the Balkans and the Habsburg lands from the eighteenth century to the present. Byzantium is covered in a year course. The Ottoman Empire and the Orthodox Church are given for one semester each. Hungarian history from its origins to the present is covered in two semesters. There are seminars and colloquia to correspond to these subjects.

The University of Washington, although concentrating on the nineteenth and twentieth centuries, has the strongest program for the medieval period. There is thus a five-hour course on the origins of the East European states, followed by another on Central Europe in the Middle Ages, which covers Austria, Bohemia and Poland. Byzantine history is also given. Unlike other universities, Washington has both graduate and undergraduate courses in the field which cover the years 1772 to the present. Russian and East European bibliography is also offered. There are, of course, seminars to correspond with most of the courses, including one in Ottoman history.

The program at Yale also is most effective. Courses in East European history both on the undergraduate and graduate level are offered. The undergraduate course is a two-semester survey since 1500, plus a one-semester undergraduate seminar. Graduate students find rich offerings in a course on Byzantium and the Slavs, another on the Western Slavs in the nineteenth and twentieth centuries, and two more specialized courses — one on the diplomatic history of Eastern Europe since 1914 and the other on the Orthodox Church in the sixteenth century. In addition, there are two research seminars.

Other universities have courses on Eastern Europe, but not such an extensive selection. General surveys, covering different time periods, but all emphasizing the nineteenth and twentieth centuries, are given at Duquesne, Florida State, George Washington, Michigan, North Carolina, Virginia, UCLA, and Wayne State. Specialized courses on the Balkans are taught at California (both Berkeley and Los Angeles), Cincinnati, Colorado, Harvard, Kansas, Michigan, Minnesota, San Fernando State College, Stanford, and Wisconsin. The course at Harvard is associated with Ottoman history. At Wisconsin it commences with the origins of the Balkan peoples, at Michigan with the fall of Constantinople. The East Central European, or Habsburg, area is studied in particular at Berkeley, Colorado, Duquesne, Kansas, Minnesota, Pennsylvania, Rice, and UCLA. The most complete survey is given at Minnesota, where the course begins with the sixth century. In addition to the Byzantine offerings at Columbia, Indiana, and Washington, courses and seminars in this subject are given at Cincinnati, Chicago, Colorado, Harvard, Michigan, Stanford, Texas, UCLA, Wayne State, and Wisconsin. Among the special courses given, Columbia offers the political and institutional development of modern Greece; Illinois has a course on Habsburg-Russian relations; New York University has a unique course on Germany and Eastern Europe. Ohio State University teaches a survey of Polish history. UCLA has a special course on the history of the Turks.

Important for historians concentrating on the Slavic countries are the courses on Slavic civilization offered by a number of institutions within the department of Slavic languages and literatures. These courses generally combine information on art, folklore, history, literature, music, etc.

An analysis of the courses offered shows the reluctance of most historians to attempt a general survey of the entire field except in the nineteenth and twentieth centuries where the rise of nationalism serves as a common unifying consideration. There is also the difficulty of the lack of printed material in Western languages which could be used as reading for students in the medieval and early modern period. The volumes to be edited by Peter Sugar and Donald Treadgold will be of great assistance here, but national histories are still needed. Although it has been demonstrated that a general survey course can be effectively presented, it can be expected that the emphasis will continue to remain divided into the areas previously mentioned.

RECOMMENDATIONS FOR HISTORY

From a reading of this report on history it can be seen that the history of every country in every period, with the possible exception of the recent years, is in need of further investigation. The medieval and early modern periods have been especially neglected. Although scholarly interest increases with the eighteenth century, and particularly with the period from the end of the nineteenth century until the outbreak of World War I, it has been concerned primarily with the international problems or the development of the national state. There are thus books on the Polish partitions, the individual national revolutions, the Eastern Question, the origins of the war and the peace settlements, but — with certain limited exceptions — there is a lack of general studies of the great historical issues of the area. The student and specialist can find few adequate studies on a wide basis on such topics as the peasantry, the aristocracy and the commercial classes, or on constitutional, economic, intellectual, cultural, religious, and military history. Basic economic questions in the historical context, such as industrialization, demographic change, and land tenure, have received little attention. There are indeed excellent articles concerning many of these problems, but they are usually concerned with a limited time or area. The most serious deficiency in historical writing in the East European field has thus been the failure to produce studies essential to interdisciplinary interpretations. In particular, economic, intellectual, and cultural history has been neglected in favor of political and diplomatic studies organized usually on a strictly national basis.

The specific recommendations for history concern this problem as well as the obviously neglected areas in the traditional approach. The recommendations are as follows:

First, in regard to the training of graduate students, it is recommended that the emphasis be placed on the discipline, but that courses in history should be supplemented by electives chosen in other departments. It is also believed that the student should be given maximum flexibility to determine in consultation with his major professor the courses which he should take depending upon his specific interests and upon whether he intends to direct his research toward Russia, Central Europe or the Ottoman Empire. Thus a program including courses in the Renaissance, the Reformation, Romanticism and Realism, German history, intellectual history, geography, and economics might best fit the program of a student concentrating on Poland, Bohemia, Hungary, and Croatia, whereas courses on the Soviet Union, world communism and twentieth-century economic development would interest those specializing, for instance, in contemporary Bulgaria. Flexibility in choice rather than insistence upon attendance at certain fixed courses should thus be emphasized.

Second, in regard to the fields where scholarly writing is particularly necessary, first priority is given without exception by those consulted to the need for new, interdisciplinary histories of each country with which we are concerned. Where surveys exist, they are either too short, outdated, or popular. The projected ten-volume history of East Central and Southeastern Europe, edited by Peter Sugar and Donald Treadgold, will fill an urgent need for a survey of the entire area, but it will not present a continuous history of each national group. These studies are needed not only by the history student, but by those specializing in related disciplines who now lack a basic guide to the development of their area or country of interest.

After the completion of standard national histories, next in importance is the writing of general studies covering either the whole field (or a portion of it) of questions which are not limited by national boundaries. For instance, in economic history, comparative studies of systems of land tenure and agricultural production, of trade and commerce, and of industrial production within the area would be most useful. In religion, histories of the national churches are needed, but a wider discussion of the interaction of the Orthodox, Catholic, Protestant, Moslem, and Jewish faiths in Eastern Europe would be of great interest to all historians. In political history, monographs on subjects such as the growth of the national monarchies viewed on a comparative basis, the political parties in the states, and the influence of the army on the making of political decisions would be of great value. For cultural history, studies are needed of the life and thought of the peasant (using ethnographic materials), as well as of the upper classes. Common patterns in life, cultural development, and civilization in the area have yet to be described adequately outside of their national setting.

In addition, within the sections on national history, certain problems have been pointed out which deserve particular emphasis. Some of these are especially significant for American historians, since they can best be studied by a scholar from outside of the area.

Finally, a collective volume on the historiography of Eastern Europe, in which the writings of the leading historians in each of the East European countries were analyzed, would be a major contribution to our field. This book could be used in the general course on historiography which is taught in the department of history of almost every college and university. It could, in fact, be a very effective method of introducing the undergraduate student to East European history.

4/ INTERNATIONAL RELATIONS

John C. Campbell
Council on Foreign Relations

This paper covers some of the same ground as those on the principal social sciences, especially that of Paul E. Zinner on political science. Roughly the same background considerations exist, and similar conclusions may be drawn. Because Eastern Europe is made up of a number of small countries and has been close to the center of great-power politics, international relations play a major role in its history and deserve heavy emphasis as a field of study.

THE ORIGINS

American scholarly interest in international relations in East Central and Southeastern Europe dates from the time of World War I. The following three main currents have contributed to it and largely determined its nature:

1. *The involvement of the United States in the First World War and the peace settlement which followed it.* American scholars (Archibald Cary Coolidge, Robert H. Lord, Charles Seymour, Isaiah Bowman, and others) took part in preparations for that settlement and in the work of the American delegation at Paris. Although the United States repudiated the peace treaties and withdrew into isolation, the work of these men sparked a growing interest in Eastern Europe and its complex problems, especially as the area seemed to be a breeding ground of wars which could involve the entire world. Scholars in the interwar period devoted particular attention to the origins of the war of 1914–18, leaving largely to journalists the analysis of the many unsolved problems which seemed to presage the outbreak of another one.

2. *The coming to the United States, and especially to its institutions of learning, of many teachers, scholars, writers, and journalists of Central and Eastern European origin.* They added greatly to the skills and knowledge of the American scholarly community and stimulated interest in this field, although they generally differed from their American colleagues in background and training and often continued to hold strongly nationalistic points of view brought from their countries of origin.

3. *World War II and the Soviet Conquest of Eastern Europe.* The role of that area in the war (first the subject of a partition arranged by Germany and Russia, later subjected to German control, and then — except for Greece and Turkey — destined to fall into the Soviet theater of war in the final campaigns against Hitler and thus into a Soviet sphere of predominant influence) convinced many Americans of its importance in the relations of the great powers and for the hopes of an enduring peace. Again, American scholars had entered the government during wartime to work on problems of Eastern Europe, but the postwar settlement was dictated by military events, by geography, by wartime decisions based on military strategy, and by the balance of power, rather than by the recommendations of scholars or by the negotiations of statesmen at a formal peace conference. For the United States, the problems of international relations in an area which was falling or had fallen under Soviet domination became a part of the bigger problem of how to cope with the Soviet Union.

WHAT ARE THE MAJOR GAPS?

Thus, American interest and American accomplishment have been uneven, spotty, and often one-dimensional. A brief survey of American and other Western works in the field of international relations, over the period from the end of World War I will reveal the gaps as well as the accomplishments, thus indicating where scholarly effort may best be directed.

We already have a number of generally good books on the settlements which followed World War I, notably studies on frontiers and other problems of individual countries. Among them are those of Ivo J. Lederer on Yugoslavia,[1] Sherman D. Spector on Romania,[2] Francis

1. *Yugoslavia at the Paris Peace Conference: A Study in Frontiermaking* (New Haven and London: Yale University Press, 1963).
2. *Rumania at the Paris Peace Conference: A Study of the Diplomacy of Ioan I. C. Brătianu* (New York: Bookman Associates, 1962).

Deak on Hungary (now out of date),[3] T. Komarnicki on Poland,[4] and D. Perman on Czechoslovakia.[5] They build on Harold Temperley's six-volume history of the Paris Peace Conference [6] and on documents which have later become available, although the archives of most Eastern European foreign ministries remain closed.

By contrast, the international relations of the inter-war period represent a semi-desert as far as good works by Western scholars are concerned. They are touched on in general books such as Hugh Seton-Watson's *Eastern Europe between the Wars* [7] and the C. A. Macartney and A. W. Palmer survey, *Independent Eastern Europe*; [8] also in Stephen Borsody's work which concentrates on the central Danubian area and covers the period through World War II.[9] Macartney has also dealt at some length with international questions concerning Hungary in his *October Fifteenth: A History of Modern Hungary*.[10] Three monographs of good quality should be mentioned, notably Josef Korbel's work on Poland in Soviet-German relations,[11] Piotr S. Wandycz' study of French policy,[12] and Jacob B. Hoptner's account of Yugoslavia in the 1930s.[13] Other than those, there is very little. Works on Polish foreign policy are inadequate, although the study by Adam Rosé is a useful summary.[14] The book of Vondráček, now out of date, is the only good one on Czechoslovakia.[15] The foreign policies of Romania, Bulgaria,

3. *Hungary at the Paris Peace Conference: The Diplomatic History of the Treaty of Trianon* (New York: Columbia University Press, 1942).
4. *The Rebirth of the Polish Republic: A Study in the Diplomatic History of Europe, 1914–1920* (London: Heinemann, 1957).
5. *The Shaping of the Czechoslovak State: Diplomatic History of the Boundaries of Czechoslovakia, 1914–1921* (Leiden: Brill, 1962).
6. H. W. V. Temperley, ed., *A History of the Peace Conference of Paris* (London: Henry Frowde and Hodder & Stoughton, vols. 1, 2, 3, 1920; vols. 4 and 5, 1921; vol. 6, 1924).
7. *Eastern Europe between the Wars, 1918–1941* (Cambridge, England: The University Press; New York: Macmillan, 1945).
8. *Independent Eastern Europe: A History* (New York: St. Martin's Press, 1962).
9. *The Triumph of Tyranny* (New York: Macmillan, 1960).
10. C. A. Macartney, *October Fifteenth: A History of Modern Hungary*, 2 vols. (Edinburgh: Edinburgh University Press, 1956).
11. *Poland between East and West: Soviet and German Diplomacy toward Poland, 1919–1933* (Princeton: Princeton University Press, 1963).
12. *France and Her Eastern Allies, 1919–1925* (Minneapolis: University of Minnesota Press, 1962).
13. *Yugoslavia in Crisis, 1934–1941* (New York: Columbia University Press, 1962).
14. *La politique polonaise entre les deux guerres* (Neuchâtel: La Baconnière, 1944).
15. *The Foreign Policy of Czechoslovakia, 1918–1935* (New York: Columbia Press, 1937).

Greece, and Turkey have scarcely been touched. There is nothing on the Little Entente and the Balkan Entente other than works written in the 1930s on the basis of inadequate material,[16] although the Balkan federation movement has been fairly well covered.[17]

Even the familiar territorial disputes over such areas as Macedonia, Transylvania, and the Polish-German borderlands, while they have produced hundreds of polemical writings, have not been objectively and thoroughly studied as problems in international relations. Alfred Senn's study of the Vilna dispute is an exception.[18] Such studies, besides being valuable in themselves, would provide essential background for consideration of those same disputes in their later phases. Another open field for research is the period from 1938 to 1941, the death agony of the interwar system in East Central and Southeastern Europe. Books have been written on the Munich crisis, notably those of J. W. Wheeler-Bennett[19] and Boris Čelovský,[20] and on the Hitler-Stalin pact of 1939.[21] But the whole tangled skein of the policies of the small states of the area and of the great powers in that period invites further study.

The same considerations are largely true of the period of World War II. Herbert Feis, W. H. McNeill, and others have examined the diplomacy of the major powers with respect to Eastern Europe as a part of the broader picture of their overall relations. The conferences of Teheran, Yalta, and Potsdam have had their investigators, generally with a thesis to prove. John Lukacs' *The Great Powers and Eastern Europe*[22] is useful. Edward Rozek, using the Mikolajczyk papers, has written of great-power diplomacy as it affected Poland.[23] But again, much remains to be done. There are massive quantities of German material to draw upon, important for the story of German policy in the occupied and satellite states.

16. Mention should be made of a Columbian dissertation by Robert Rothstein (1961) on the Little Entente as a case study in maintenance of an alliance.

17. See L. S. Stavrianos, *Balkan Federation: A History of the Movement toward Balkan Unity in Modern Times* (Northampton: Smith College, 1944); Theodore I. Geshkoff, *Balkan Union* (New York: Columbia University Press, 1940); and Robert Joseph Kerner and Harry N. Howard, *The Balkan Conferences and the Balkan Entente, 1930–1935* (Berkeley: University of California Press, 1936).

18. *The Great Powers, Lithuania and the Vilna Question* (Leiden: E. J. Brill, 1966).

19. *Munich: Prologue to Tragedy* (New York: Duell, 1948).

20. *Das Münchener Abkommen, 1938* (Stuttgart: Deutsche Verlags-Anstalt, 1958).

21. For example, Gerhard L. Weinberg, *Germany and the Soviet Union, 1939–1941* (Leiden: E. J. Brill, 1954); Grigore Gafencu, *Prelude to the Russian Campaign* (London: Frederick Muller, 1945).

22. *The Great Powers and Eastern Europe* (New York: American Book, 1953).

23. *Allied Wartime Diplomacy: A Pattern in Poland* (New York: Wiley, 1958)

Andreas Hillgruber's work on German-Romanian relations is first-rate; [24] Stephen Kertesz' account of Hungary's plight is of unique value,[25] and C. M. Woodhouse has done a fine study on Greece.[26] But nothing comparable has been done for others. Yugoslavia's problems, those involving the government-in-exile as well as the conflicts within the country, still need thorough study, as do those of Poland and Czechoslovakia, although Polish-Czechoslovak relations on the question of confederation are considered in a monograph by P. S. Wandycz.[27] Even puppet states like Slovakia, Croatia, and the rump Serbian state under Milan Nedić, as they affected international relations, are worth consideration. Another good subject concerns the efforts of Romania, Hungary, and Bulgaria to leave the war and the negotiation of armistice agreements and peace treaties with those countries. The whole wartime period still involves delicate questions such as "collaboration." All the more need for objective studies of it. Only one book in English deals comprehensively with the treaties following World War II.[28]

Most important of all is further investigation of the postwar years and the contemporary scene. The specialists on the Soviet Union and on communism have produced our best books on the subject. Zbigniew Brzezinski's *The Soviet Bloc: Unity and Conflict*,[29] and the volumes on *European Communism* edited by William E. Griffith,[30] a mixture of scholarship and journalism, are of generally high quality. For reasons already stated, the great need is for work which will combine the factors specifically characteristic of Communist relationships with those which flow from all other influences bearing on the conduct of Eastern European states, the interaction of internal and international policies, and relations with states of the West and of the third world. R. V. Burks's book on Communist "dynamics" and J. F. Brown's *The New Eastern Europe* are good, but rather lonely, examples.[31] The period

24. *Hitler, König Carol and Marschall Antonescu: Die Deutsch-Rumänischen Beziehungen 1938–1944* (Wiesbaden: Steiner, 1954).
25. *Diplomacy in a Whirlpool: Hungary between Nazi Germany and Soviet-Russia* (Notre Dame, Ind.: University of Notre Dame Press, 1953).
26. *Apple of Discord* (London: Hutchinson, 1948).
27. *Czechoslovak-Polish Confederation and the Great Powers, 1940–1943* (Bloomington: Indiana University Press, 1956).
28. Amelia Leiss and Raymond Dennett, *European Peace Treaties after World War II* (Boston: World Peace Foundation, 1954).
29. *The Soviet Bloc: Unity and Conflict*, 3d rev. ed. (Cambridge: Harvard University Press, 1967).
30. *Communism in Europe: Continuity, Change, and the Sino-Soviet Dispute*, 2 vols. (Cambridge, Mass., and London: M.I.T. Press, 1964, 1966).
31. R. V. Burks, *The Dynamics of Communism in Eastern Europe* (Princeton:

and process of Communist "takeover" has been carefully studied only in a few instances, as in the books of Josef Korbel and Paul Zinner on Czechoslovakia.[32] Elizabeth Wiskemann's *Germany's Eastern Neighbours*,[33] on Poland and Czechoslovakia, is valuable. For the other Communist states, we have little more than the personal memoirs of Eastern European exiled leaders and Western diplomats. Greece in the early postwar period, however, is well covered in the works of W. H. McNeill, Stephen Xydis, D. Kousoulas, and L. S. Stavrianos.[34]

The evolution of international relations under conditions of the loosening of the Communist bloc has been considered in a general way, mainly in symposia,[35] but not thoroughly. Policies of individual outside powers have not received the attention they deserve, although two recent works deal specifically with American policy.[36] So far as individual Eastern European countries are concerned, Adam Bromke has made an excellent analysis in *Poland's Politics: Idealism vs. Realism*; [37] the book of Stephen Fischer-Galati performs a somewhat similar service for Romania, though largely limited to the Soviet-Romanian relationship.[38] *Yugoslavia: The New Communism*,[39] by George Hoffman and Fred Neal, deals only peripherally with international policy. The Soviet-Yugoslav dispute has received considerable attention because it was

Princeton University Press, 1961); J. F. Brown, *The New Eastern Europe* (New York: Praeger, 1966).

32. Josef Korbel, *The Communist Subversion of Czechoslovakia, 1938–1948* (Princeton: Princeton University Press, 1959); Paul E. Zinner, *Communist Strategy and Tactics in Czechoslovakia, 1918–48* (New York: Praeger, 1963).

33. Elizabeth Wiskemann, *Germany's Eastern Neighbours: Problems Relating to the Oder-Neisse Line and the Czech Frontier Regions* (New York: Oxford University Press, 1956).

34. W. H. McNeill, *The Greek Dilemma: The War and Aftermath* (Philadelphia: Lippincott, 1947); Stephen G. Xydis, *Greece and the Great Powers, 1944–1947: Prelude to the Truman Doctrine* (Saloniki: Institute for Balkan Studies, 1963); D. Kousoulas, *The Price of Freedom: Greece in World Affairs, 1939–1953* (Syracuse: Syracuse University Press, 1953); L. S. Stavrianos, *Greece: American Dilemma and Opportunity* (Chicago: Regnery, 1952).

35. William E. Griffith, *Communism in Europe*; Adam Bromke, ed., *The Communist States at the Crossroads between Moscow and Peking* (New York: Praeger, 1965), and Kurt London, ed., *Eastern Europe in Transition* (Baltimore: Johns Hopkins Press, 1966).

36. Zbigniew Brzezinski, *Alternative to Partition* (New York: McGraw Hill, 1965); John C. Campbell, *American Policy Toward Communist Eastern Europe* (Minneapolis: University of Minnesota Press, 1965).

37. *Poland's Politics: Idealism vs. Realism* (Cambridge, Harvard University Press, 1967).

38. *The New Rumania: From People's Democracy to Socialist Republic* (Cambridge, Mass.: M.I.T. Press, 1967).

39. *Yugoslavia: The New Communism* (New York: Twentieth Century Fund, 1962).

both spectacular and significant. Works by Adam Ulam [40] and Hamilton Fish Armstrong [41] did much to illuminate it. John Campbell has dealt with Yugoslav-American relations. [42] These above-mentioned works are but a beginning. There is a great lack of scholarly monographs.

Further attention to international relations in Eastern Europe, both the policies of these states and the policies of outside powers toward them, is necessary and desirable at a stage when the whole question of the future shape of Europe and Eastern Europe's place in it is being posed, a stage which is now upon us and will be with us for some time. Here the study of international relations is tied to many questions of politics, economics, and social development; it involves such concepts as sovereignty, federation, integration, nationalism, and varying degrees of collaboration across frontiers. It provides great opportunities for the political scientists and the economists to practice new methods. The essential point, however, is an understanding of Eastern European societies and of all factors which bear on their relations with other societies. Talent for such complex investigations is not easily found or trained in a short time. It requires a combination of training in a discipline, knowledge of related disciplines, and intensive language study. It is therefore necessary to assess where we stand, in relation to these needs, with respect to graduate training, language study, centers for area study, and the attraction of good students to the field.

We are now entering a period in which great scope exists for study and research by American scholars, both on the past and on the present. Records on the interwar period are now becoming available. Some are being published by the present governments; some are being used by their scholars in their own published work; some may become accessible to American students of international relations. At any rate, the latter can now go to the Eastern European countries. Even though there are political and other limitations on what source material scholars actually can find in Eastern Europe and on carrying out their work there, the opportunities for research both in the field and at home are widening and should be seized. Analysis of contemporary developments will be of the greatest importance in the coming years, especially in view of the rapid pace of change, the basic issues involved, and the relative openness of the region.

40. *Titoism and the Cominform* (Cambridge: Harvard University Press, 1952).
41. *Tito and Goliath* (New York: Macmillan, 1951).
42. *Tito's Separate Road: America and Yugoslavia in World Politics* (New York: Harper and Row, 1967).

Better training for scholars and greater understanding of international relations involving the nations of Eastern Europe are desirable ends in themselves. In expanding the frontiers of knowledge of this part of the world, American universities will be true to their own traditions and will perform a service for the world. At the same time they can serve as a training ground for experts needed by the U.S. government, by foundations, and by private organizations interested in research and discussion of international affairs. In both public and private institutions there is a great need for specialists which the universities are not now adequately filling.

EASTERN EUROPE AS A SPECIAL FIELD

Soviet dominance and the rule of Communist parties in most of East Central and Southeastern Europe after World War II set the pattern not only for governmental policies and popular attitudes but also for teaching and research in American higher education over the next two decades. This was a natural development. The satellite states had hardly any political and economic policies or international relations that were not determined by the decision, or by the example, of the Soviet Union. They could not be understood except by those who themselves understood how the Soviet system and Communist party relationships worked. It was not surprising that such subjects as the techniques of Communist takeover of national societies and the use of satellite states in the service of Soviet global strategy took precedence over others.

Nor was it surprising that Eastern European studies in American universities and research institutions tended to be swallowed up by Russian and Soviet studies. In the postwar years a major move was made by foundations and universities to build up Soviet studies, a very natural development in view of the limited prewar effort, the lessons of the wartime experience, and the enlarged role of the Soviet Union in world affairs. No such move was made for Eastern European studies, perhaps largely because that area seemed to be playing no role except as an appendage of the Soviet empire. At best, such studies had a similar satellite status, if any at all, in our Soviet and Russian institutes.

As one consequence, while some first-rate work on current developments in Eastern Europe was done by the specialists in Soviet affairs and in international communism, the whole field of international relations in Eastern Europe prior to 1945 tended to be neglected. Moreover, the methods of Sovietology, although not wholly suited to the interpretation of Eastern European developments in the period after Stalin's death, and especially after 1956, continued to dominate the field. In a situation of increasing diversity and independence of policy, new dimensions appeared in relations of the so-called satellites with each other, with East European states already independent such as Greece and Yugoslavia, and with the great powers. Perhaps one cannot properly say that the Soviet security system in Eastern Europe has broken up, but it certainly has undergone, and is undergoing, major changes. Many factors such as national interests, local political and economic pressures, and the desire for new relationships with the West have entered into the calculations of Eastern European governments. The Communist parties have shown that they are subject to change. Complex new relationships are growing within and between various East European countries.

Eastern Europe is definitely worthy of recognition and status as a special field of study and research. Experience has shown that when it is dealt with only as a minor segment of Russian or other studies, or as a subject of studies in comparative communism, it is not adequately covered or given the attention it deserves. It has its patterns of history and development which, while anything but uniform, are different from those of Russia or of any other outside area. It is no doubt a relevant and significant fact that the area has been a part of the "Communist world" during the period since World War II. But it is also a part of Europe. In another sense, it is a part of the less-developed world.

It is true that as the nature of communism and of the Communist world changes in practice, studies of comparative Communist systems, including those of Eastern Europe, are wholly justified. Such studies, however, which are now gaining momentum at several American universities, are not the full answer to the inadequate coverage of Eastern Europe in centers for Russian studies. Many give short shrift to that area. Eastern Europe is not explainable only in terms of communism and differing Communist systems. The international relations of its nations are not mere variations on the theme of international communism. It is a complex area with its own history, its own kinds of politics, its own societies. It should be studied for its own importance: for the history, culture, and politics of its several nations and its more than 100 million people, for the political and strategic significance of its territory, and for the relations of its nations to each other and to the outside world. The real problem is one of coexistence, without sacrificing the essential requirements either of the Eastern European or of the broader field.

PROBLEMS OF ORGANIZATION

Only one university (Columbia) has a separate institute on the East Central Europe area as such. Whether separate centers or institutes are created at other universities may not be so important. To have at least one, or the equivalent in the form of a strong Eastern European program within a larger center, in each of three major regions (East, Middle West, and Pacific Coast) seems warranted. It is desirable in any case to establish new programs, and at the very least to increase the emphasis on Eastern Europe in the various programs covering the Soviet Union, the Communist world, comparative Communist systems, or the whole of Europe. The important thing is that the field be given recognition and resources, and that specialists in the international relations of the area, as in its politics and economics, be encouraged and assisted. The leading universities will have to provide a firm understanding of the importance of the field and a continuing commitment to it.

The Eastern European field is so diverse and complex that it makes no sense, when considering the future, to have large numbers of specialized programs scattered over many educational institutions. Only by concentrating skills and resources at a limited number of centers at big universities can the necessary institutional support be given to the development of scholars in the field. This is particularly true of the study of international relations. Young scholars have to have strong centers to which they can go for guidance in advanced work, for continuing contact with stimulating scholars in the same or related fields, and for adequate resources to support their own research. These centers need not be limited solely to Eastern European studies, but must give that area strong emphasis.

One of the current phenomena is the lone expert on Eastern Europe existing in isolation at a college or university which cannot develop the field further. He does not have the chance to train students and even finds difficulty in advancing his own research. Obviously one cannot expect that all these scholars will be uprooted and transplanted to other institutions where there are centers for Eastern European studies, although perhaps some may make that shift. A partial substitute can be found in the form of cooperative arrangements whereby certain institutions can divide the field by having each specialize in one or more individual countries of Eastern Europe, and by making available documentation and library resources to each other. Universities in a given part of the country can work together among themselves and with undergraduate institutions in the region on such matters as fellowship and exchange programs, invitations to scholars from Eastern Europe, and cooperative research with Eastern European universities or institutes.

THE DISCIPLINE OF INTERNATIONAL RELATIONS

The field of international relations is not generally recognized as a discipline in American universities. Often associated with political science or with history, there is no compelling reason why it should have a separate status. Nevertheless, formal discipline or not, the field of international relations does require disciplined study related to its own needs. Actually it calls for an interdisciplinary approach, since it must draw on history, politics, and economics, as well as on other less traditional disciplines. Above all, it is a field for empirical research not falling into any set pattern. To take one example, the study of the process of discussion and decision on matters of foreign policy in these countries is infinitely complex, little known in the West, and lends itself to useful analysis only by a wide variety of flexible methods. The subject must be studied in two contexts: that of the entire contemporary scene in Eastern Europe itself, and that of international relations in worldwide scope.

There is some danger that international relations will be slighted or lost sight of as political science follows its present trend toward theory and model-building. Comparative political studies also may tend to squeeze out specialization in international relations. Comparative studies (e.g., of Eastern European states with other Communist states, with non-Communist developing states, with Western European states, or with each other) are all very useful if they can be done in depth. The magnitude of such undertakings by individual scholars is evident from the basic requirements in languages and in disciplines necessary for Eastern Europe alone. Perhaps the most valuable studies within practical reach will be comparisons of individual Eastern European states with others in the same area. It is likely that the results would be more meaningful than the results, say, of comparisons between Yugoslavia and China, or Romania and Peru.

Finally, the contribution which the study of international relations in Eastern Europe may make to the theory of international relations, a shadowy but nonetheless important subject, should not be overlooked. Both historically and on the contemporary scene, the actualities of Eastern Europe provide a laboratory for theories of international politics.

BUILDING A NEW GENERATION OF SCHOLARS

It is apparent from a survey of graduate teaching in our universities that not enough young scholars are being trained in Eastern European affairs. In one university after another it turns out that there is only a course or two for undergraduates, that little is being done for graduate research, that there is a lack of academic rigor, and that even where Eastern European studies are recognized and encouraged, the fields of political science, economics, and international relations receive little stress. This is partly the result of difficult language requirements, complexity of subject matter, and lack of assurance about future jobs for those who enter the field. Also, however, it is partly the result of insufficient attention and commitment on the part of universities to build strong traditions of graduate teaching in the field. We need not only scholars but great teachers to inspire younger scholars with an interest in Eastern Europe and to develop their talents. This is another argument for concentrating interests in a few large universities, or for tying the work of small universities and colleges in with that of institutions with larger resources. In some cases the initiative, spirit, and accomplishments of the smaller institutions have been admirable, and such gains should be preserved and built upon in any new arrangements that are made.

In American universities, graduate training in the Eastern European field has been spotty and generally inadequate. The conclusions emerging from surveys of graduate programs in history, economics, and especially political science (see pp. 147–49, below) apply also to the field of international relations. The unsatisfactory situation stems from several causes, including the complexity and diversity of the area, the possibility of overspecialization in a field where opportunities for employment are limited, and the fact that the field has not been "fashionable" in the sense that the Soviet Union, the underdeveloped countries, and other areas have been.

Graduate courses in the international relations of Eastern European states are almost nonexistent. Columbia and Indiana offer fairly broad coverage in Eastern European studies, including international relations. Yale, George Washington (by itself and in cooperation with four other universities in the Washington area), Illinois, Kansas, Colorado, Oregon, Stanford, California (Berkeley), and UCLA offer coverage which varies from considerable to something more than incidental. Many of our large universities have no programs, not even a specialist in Eastern European studies. Some less prominent ones (e.g., Western Michigan), on the other hand, have taken the initiative to build up specialized programs, including arrangements for travel and study in Eastern European countries.

Looking at the nationwide picture, the precise number and structure of programs or courses offered here or there is not so important as that there be (*a*) an irreducible minimum of adequately staffed programs in each of the main sectors of the country, (*b*) students specializing in one of the recognized social science disciplines in the Eastern European field, with the opportunity or obligation to study recent or contemporary international relations, and (*c*) a continuing number of graduate students, encouraged or induced to specialize in that subject and given expert guidance in pursuing it.

Proficiency in languages is essential to such specialization, but it should be emphasized that the main tools are three of the principal European languages: French, German, and Russian. One or more of the Eastern European languages should be acquired in the course of graduate work and later research. The language problem makes this area more difficult and demanding than some others. Some degree of persuasion or inspiration may be required to induce promising scholars to go into it. It is therefore especially important that language training be planned at an early stage of graduate work to fit into the student's course work and research, and that adequate facilities for instruction — either at the same university, at another American university, or abroad — be available. The language problem should not be an obstacle if its dimensions are recognized.

There is some danger that graduate training in international relations will suffer in the future, as it has in the past, by the tendency of historians, political scientists, and other scholars interested in Eastern Europe to neglect it in favor of other aspects of their respective disciplines. The way to counteract such a tendency is for a university to make sure, in planning its graduate program, that appropriate courses, seminars, and research projects are provided, and for scholars already in the field to see to it that the sources of supply of future scholars are replenished.

It is sometimes said that area studies, having performed a good purpose in building up expertise in fields like the Soviet Union, East Asia, the Middle East, and Latin America, have shown weaknesses and are not really meeting the needs of scholarship in present circumstances. One of the weaknesses, presumably, is that area studies tend to water down the established disciplines and to divert scholars from the new methodology in political science, economics, and the behavioral sciences. The conflict between discipline and area studies seems to be an endemic and unending one. But it need not be. Experience shows that the best area specialist is precisely the one who has made his mark in an established discipline. There has to be some compromise if the values of both are to be retained. The field of international relations, because it crosses and combines various disciplines, is particularly suited to area studies and has benefited from the existence of regional institutes and centers.

One does not have to be a fanatic for area studies to argue that the Eastern European field must be built up. The important thing is that expert knowledge of Eastern Europe be developed and not diluted or lost from view in more general studies. We need experts devoted to that area and its problems. Without them we shall not get good comparative studies or general works. Scholars in this field will have to devote years to language training and have frequent periods of residence in Eastern Europe. Such training is not antithetic to new methods and new horizons of comparative politics, but the first thing to be done is to establish the capabilities to deal with Eastern Europe in a thorough and well-informed way.

COOPERATION WITH EASTERN EUROPE TODAY

The field of international relations, especially for World War II and the postwar period, is one where diplomatic records are generally closed, in Eastern Europe as they are elsewhere. Also, because the subject involves relations with the Soviet Union, it is difficult for many Eastern European scholars to write about it, and even more difficult for them to collaborate with Western scholars. Nevertheless, there is much to be gained by the use of current published materials, by interviews with those who have been or still are active in local political life, discussions with Eastern European scholars, and consultation with them on sources and on the results of their work, and by the experience of working in those countries. All these considerations point up the need for student exchanges and visits, for the sending of visiting professors in both directions, and for joint seminars and research projects were possible.

It may be objected that it is silly to expect real cooperation from Communist regimes on subjects that are politically sensitive. The answer to that objection is that there is something to be gained by proceeding as far as we can in present circumstances. It will be some time before we have a sufficiency of trained scholars in this field, and meanwhile events will not stand still in Eastern Europe. Already Yugoslav institutions have agreed to several exchange arrangements and joint projects with American universities, and signs of the same trend can be seen in other Eastern European countries.

This kind of cooperation is possible without American scholars somehow being used, corrupted, or taken in. If they are themselves mature and well trained, there need be no compromise of integrity merely by the fact of working in a Communist country or with the scholars of that country.

CONCLUSIONS AND RECOMMENDATIONS

1. *That a major effort be made to increase the competence of the American academic community in the Eastern European field, and in particular the field of international relations.* The effort should encompass a number of disciplines and should emphasize combinations of disciplines, intensive language training, and increased understanding of Eastern European societies and cultures. Despite the obvious progress already made, there remains a shortage of specialists that must be overcome, both to strengthen scholarship and teaching and to fill positions in government and private institutions. Measures should be taken to stimulate student interest, to improve the quality of teaching and research, and to provide greater material support. A positive effort should be made to break out of the present stultifying combination of inadequate instruction and difficulties of recruitment.

2. *That international relations, in graduate teaching and research on Eastern Europe, should be given a place adequate to its importance.* This is not a plea for recognition of international relations as a special discipline but a statement of conviction that enough historians, political scientists, economists, and others concerned with Eastern Europe must devote attention to the significant international questions, whether they are confined within the bounds of a traditional discipline or not, if we are to maintain and raise the level of scholarship in the field.

3. *That impetus should be given to studies in two major areas in which yawning gaps now exist.* The first is the interwar period, where most of the work done at the time was superficial and not much has been done since. New material now has become or will become available on the basis of which scholars can go to work in the way that American and English historians have done for the diplomatic history of the nineteenth century in this area. The second is the period of World War II and after, where approaches can be broader, and investigations deeper than they have been and where research may create a new understanding of the recent past.

4. *That it is necessary, above all, to focus attention on the problems of*

the present and future in international relations. It is now possible to do so in ways not previously open, such as personal visits, interviews, and more intensive exploration of published and other material. The need for sound analysis of current developments in Eastern Europe is great, not just for the general purpose of widening the frontiers of knowledge but also for the practical tasks of foreign policy.

5. *That the direction needed for studies on Eastern Europe can best be provided and the work accomplished if centers of study are located in a few large universities with highly trained faculty, interdisciplinary collaboration, and rich library resources.* This is not to say that well-conceived specialized programs should not go forward at other institutions or that individual scholars cannot make significant contributions in books and articles wherever their home base may be; but multiplication of programs and understaffed centers of area study in a wide variety of institutions will only mean disperson of effort unless they are tied together in cooperative enterprises. A rational division of labor among institutions, involving specialization in different countries, languages, and disciplines, would be desirable.

6. *That care be taken to avoid having the field of international relations in Eastern Europe swallowed up by Communist studies.* For obvious reasons most studies of the past twenty years have generally been dealt with under the Soviet-Communist rubric. It is true that the best of the published work in international relations has been done by the Sovietologists and specialists on communism. Some countries of Eastern Europe, however, did not come under Soviet control, and others have in some degree escaped from it. In both East Central Europe and the Balkans it is important to look at international relations not merely from the viewpoint of participation in the Soviet system or of the strengthening or weakening of the bloc. There is much room for research on the nature and motives of foreign policy — on factors of continuity not limited to the Communist period — in all the states of Eastern Europe: in their relations among themselves, with the Soviet Union, and with the rest of the world.

7. *That contacts and cooperation be developed by American universities with centers of study on Eastern Europe existing in the area itself and elsewhere in the Western world.* Such cooperation should be fostered by regular exchange programs involving both students and advanced scholars, as well as by promotion and support of lectures, study, and research on the part of individuals, in both directions, on an ad hoc basis.

5 / POLITICAL SCIENCE

Paul E. Zinner
University of California

EASTERN EUROPE A NEGLECTED AREA OF STUDY

Reviewing the "state of the art" in government and politics in East Central and Southeast European Studies — that is, the existing body of literature and the current status of graduate training and research — one arrives at the general conclusion that against the background of a dismal past the present shows some improvement, although it still leaves a great deal to be desired, and that the future looks uncertain, but not entirely bleak.

East European political studies have been beset by endemic problems which need not be recited in detail, but can be recapitulated briefly. They reflect peculiarities of the area itself and of the conditions of American scholarship. East European political studies have been neglected both because the path of scholarship has been strewn with unusually great obstacles and because the reward for scholarly attainment has been extraordinarily meager.

Knowledge of the entire area has been beyond the reach of most scholars. Hardly a person lives who has traveled extensively throughout the entire region and knows the history, the culture, the economics, the social structure, and, perhaps above all, the language of every one of the national states crowded into Eastern Europe. Yet even specialization in the entire area has been looked at askance in the scholarly community, both by academic administrators and by practitioners of the discipline of political science. Expertise in individual East European countries has offered an even lesser incentive to scholars interested in serious topical studies.

It is a task to become really acquainted with even one country. Able students who have been trained in a given discipline and have demonstrated a capability for doing creditable work in it have not as a rule chosen to immerse themselves in the intricate and obscure problems of an Eastern European country. Thus, almost by default, the perusal of Eastern European societies has devolved mainly on those who by accident of birth have possessed the necessary language requirements and some knowledge of the social and cultural milieu and the history of the particular country. Unfortunately, such people frequently have lacked other scholarly qualifications, notably a thorough grounding in a discipline and objectivity. Their works have tended to give East European scholarship a bad reputation as a field of study that fails to measure up to expected standards.

The turbulent recent history of the countries in question, beginning with the dismemberment of the Austro-Hungarian Monarchy — if not earlier with the nationality struggles of the nineteenth century — and ending with the installation of Communist regimes in the 1940s — if not later, say, with the Polish October or the Hungarian Revolution of 1956 — has tended to impede dispassionate investigation and functional analysis in many ways. Studies were produced in the heat of momentary excitement, in the wake of catastrophic happenings, in an emotionally surcharged atmosphere. Topics crucial to a real understanding of the political process were frequently eschewed in favor of special pleading for one or another national cause.

The unavailability of reliable documentary sources and archival materials and the difficulty, if not the impossibility, of conducting research on the spot also had a deleterious effect on East European political studies. For approximately a decade and a half from 1948 to the early 1960s, Communist Eastern Europe was — with minor exceptions — entirely inaccessible to Western scholars. Even before the onset of Communist domination, the local regimes had been less than openly hospitable to probes by objective scholars in search of facts and truth.

The remedy, had it been within reach at all, would have required extraordinary foresight and courage backed up by a willingness to commit formidable resources to the promotion of extensive studies of Eastern Europe. The American scholarly community has lacked this foresight and courage to brave adverse trends and has not commanded the necessary resources. It is no slur on our academic establishment to say that the arrows of its endeavors have seldom been pointed to the distant and obscure frontiers of knowledge and understanding. Scholarship has tended to follow the flag, and only when national consciousness has been permanently aroused, not to say alarmed, has the effort of scholars been mobilized to fill grave gaps in our knowledge. Only at such times, belatedly but not ineffectually has money flowed from the coffers of foundations, and lately of the federal government as well, to finance crash programs of graduate training and research at a forced pace in order to make up for past omissions. The phenomenal proliferation of Soviet and Chinese studies, and more recently of studies of developing nations, attests to what can be achieved at least quantitatively when the pump is properly primed to cause institutions of higher learning to acquire a sustained vested interest in the pursuit of certain lines of scholarship.

Eastern Europe, for reasons that are neither entirely clear nor altogether inexplicable, has not managed to command the necessary attention to benefit from this bonanza. Despite professed concern for the "fate" of the countries in the area, they never really were regarded as having intrinsic importance, but rather as adjuncts of one or another great power. University administrators have been loath to underwrite long-range institutional programs of East European studies, and department heads have been reluctant to free ladder positions on their faculties for persons identified primarily as East European specialists. As a result, systematic study of government and politics in Eastern Europe, both on the undergraduate and graduate levels, has had little chance of developing in major centers of learning. This neglect has had an adverse effect on the flow of scholarly publications about Eastern Europe, although there is no complete correlation between graduate training and scholarly publication. A number of scholars scattered throughout the country and not primarily engaged in instruction about Eastern Europe have nevertheless written on the area.

GRADUATE STUDIES IN EAST EUROPEAN AFFAIRS

A comprehensive and reasonably accurate picture of the current state of graduate training and research emerges from information supplied by individual contributors to this survey and from other sources, such as the publication *Language and Area Study Programs in American Universities* put out by the External Research Branch of the Department of State. The picture is hardly encouraging, although it is not one of unrelieved gloom.

Generally, East European studies are adjuncts of Soviet or Russian studies and, as such, receive catalog listing but very little else. Of twenty-eight major institutions that offer area programs on the Soviet Union and Eastern Europe, only sixteen claim that Eastern Europe constitutes a regional focus of study along with the U.S.S.R. Closer examination reveals that among a majority of the sixteen, East European studies run a poor second to Soviet studies in terms of the number of professors engaged in teaching specialized courses, the number and variety of courses, the number of students enrolled, and the amount of financial support for research.

Area programs leading to a special certificate in regional studies, however, appear to be losing their appeal, and many institutions now favor granting degrees in the student's chosen discipline with the possibility of concentration on a cluster of courses and seminars under the general heading of comparative communist studies. Without examining the content of these offerings it would be difficult to say whether Eastern Europe is given serious or perfunctory attention. Properly done, the study of East European political systems in a broader comparative context can be extremely meaningful.

Among institutions with area programs, Columbia University stands out. Even there, however, the coverage of East European political systems can hardly be called complete. Other centers in which East European political studies receive serious attention include the University of Kansas, which has a surprisingly broad interest in East European affairs, as has the University of Oregon and Portland State College which has a newly created Central European Studies Center with a certificate program. At Stanford University, East European Communist systems are studied in the context of a mammoth behavioral project under the auspices of the Institute of Political Studies. At the University of California, Berkeley, the Center for Slavic and East European Studies does not offer courses of instruction, and there is no degree program for students desiring to concentrate in East European studies. The Center serves mainly as a "holding corporation" for promoting faculty research. It also provides limited opportunities for scholars from Eastern Europe — Yugoslavia, Poland, Czechoslovakia — to pursue their work in the United States. So far, there have been no political scientists among them. Their numbers, however, have included persons who could be appropriately classified as political sociologists.

The Berkeley Center's program of exchange with Yugoslavia points to one currently available means of furthering graduate study and research, and Berkeley is by no means alone in availing itself of this opportunity. Several institutions have initiated exchanges and cooperative programs with Yugoslavia, including field research in the country by joint Yugoslav-American teams. Projects underway seem for the most part well thought out and potentially significant. They do raise a question, however, about the advisability of coordinating efforts, lest Yugoslavia become surfeited with programs that unnecessarily duplicate each other.

The training and research in political science underway in several centers, for example, at the University of Oregon, constitute a tribute to the imagination and persistence of the faculty, and no doubt the receptivity of an enlightened administration as well. This contrasts with an utter neglect of East European offerings at prestigious institutions such as Harvard, Princeton, and the University of Michigan, which have, as far as it has been possible to ascertain, no special course or seminar dealing with politics in Eastern Europe and no plans for the hiring of personnel capable of giving graduate instruction in this area. Similarly Wisconsin, Notre Dame, and Vanderbilt have no East European offering. It is obvious that if East European studies continue to be ignored in the leading political science departments, the future of this particular field of scholarship is not likely to be very bright. Indeed, a survey of dissertations in progress and completed during the past ten years reveals glaring inadequacies in graduate training.

In all American institutions of higher learning, only sixty-eight doctoral dissertations dealing with Eastern Europe were *initiated* in the years 1956–66. Not all of them have been completed. This accounts for the discrepancy between the figures cited here and those listed in the chapter "Graduate Training and Research Needs," (p. 16). (The figures relate specifically to topics in government and politics. International relations in Eastern Europe were the subject of an additional thirty-six dissertations.) Among the sixty-eight, seven deal with Greece and four with Austria, leaving fifty-seven for the eight Communist countries.

The distribution of dissertations by country shows great unevenness. Yugoslavia was the subject of fourteen studies, East Germany and Hungary of nine each, Czechoslovakia of eight, Poland of seven, Albania of one, Bulgaria, and Romania of none. (Nine dissertations did not clearly focus on any one country.)

By topic, twenty-three dissertations dealt with political parties and organizations, sixteen with national politics, eight each with nationality problems and political institutions, five with theory, four with religion, three with legal systems and one with political aspects of economics. (These figures include dissertations dealing with Austria and Greece.) These data show that the sponsorship of dissertations does not necessarily require a formal program of instruction in the subject area. Completion of dissertations under such auspices, of course, places very great burdens on the student, who is likely to proceed with minimal guidance.

SCHOLARLY LITERATURE ON EASTERN EUROPE

The literature in the field of political studies to a large degree reflects the absence of serious, sustained research in most of the major centers of learning. The number of books on Eastern Europe by faculty members and graduates of leading universities is scandalously small. Great gaps in coverage exist and are only partly closed by incidental publications of the works of individual scholars with East European expertise who pursue their studies and researches in isolation, at their particular places of employment, usually under conditions of considerable hardship, far removed from library resources and other research aids.

The chronological pattern of publications and the topical distribution of East European studies clearly reflects the spasmodic nature of interest in the area nurtured by peaks of emotional distress. Systematic studies of political institutions and processes in the interwar period (1918–39) and the war years (1939–45) are very few.[1] Since 1945, more has been published. Catastrophic events such as the completion of Communist power seizure in 1947–48, and the internal upheavals in Poland and Hungary (resulting in the latter case in external intervention) were followed by a spate of publications. At other times, however, the flow of book-length publications has dwindled to a trickle.

Two series of handbook-type publications are available to the student of East European politics. In the late 1930s and early 1940s Professor Robert Kerner edited a series of studies centering on individual countries that eventually included Czechoslovakia, Poland, and Yugoslavia.[2] In the 1950s the Mid-European Studies Center sponsored studies of Communist-dominated countries. The volumes in this series, under the general editorship of Professor Robert F. Byrnes, cover all East European Communist systems except the East German.[3] They provide useful, basic information for the beginning student or the uninitiated layman. But their heavily propagandistic orientation limits their usefulness for the scholar. Besides, they are dated. There are thus no up-to-date basic

1. Among early texts on Eastern Europe, M. Graham, *New Governments of Central Europe* (New York: Holt, 1924) and *New Governments of Eastern Europe* (New York: Holt, 1927) deserve mention. They are the only serious attempts in the 1920s to portray the political institutions and practices of the successor states of the Habsburg Monarchy. Although they are obsolete and deficient by current standards of scholarship, they are essential reading for the student of East European politics.

2. R. J. Kerner, ed., *Czechoslovakia* (Berkeley: University of California Press, 1940); B. E. Schmitt, ed., *Poland* (Berkeley: University of California Press, 1945); R. J. Kerner, ed., *Yugoslavia* (Berkeley: University of California Press, 1949).

3. R. F. Byrnes, general editor, "East-Central Europe under the Communists." Country studies include: S. Skendi, ed., *Albania* (New York: Praeger, 1956); L. A. D. Dellin, ed., *Bulgaria* (New York: Praeger, 1957); V. Bušek, ed., *Czechoslovakia* (New York: Praeger, 1957); E. C. Helmreich, ed., *Hungary* (New York: Praeger, 1957); O. Halecki, ed., *Poland* (New York: Praeger, 1957); S. Fischer-Galati, ed., *Rumania* (New York: Praeger, 1957); R. F. Byrnes, ed. *Yugoslavia* (New York: Praeger, 1957).

studies that describe the political institutions and analyze the political processes of each East European country from 1918 to the present.

The absence of adequate basic texts by country is matched by the lack of serviceable general surveys of government and politics in the entire East European area. Not that general texts are altogether missing. Some cover even the earlier (1918–45) period.[4] But they are on the whole undistinguished. Others deal with only a part of the entire area. Professor Robert Lee Wolff's massive study of the Balkans traces the political, economic, cultural, and international developments of Yugoslavia, Romania, Bulgaria, and Albania through the ages.[5] It has a wealth of detailed information indispensable to an understanding of the complex realities of the area. Although it is a meritorious work of diligent scholarship, it is descriptive rather than analytical and is at best good political history. It deals with events, not with institutions and processes.

Two studies by the British historian Hugh Seton-Watson cover respectively the regimes of the interwar period [6] and the immediate postwar era up to and including completion of power seizure by the Communists.[7] Broad in scope (they encompass most of East Central and Southeastern Europe from Poland to Greece!), lucid in exposition, they are standards in the discipline. Yet perceptive as they are, they, too, fail to meet the test of rigorous political analysis. They are superficial, more journalistic than scholarly, inaccurate in many details, uneven in their analysis and, some might say, opinionated. There is a manifest need for a single, massive volume treating the political evolution of Eastern Europe from 1918 to the present from the vantage of a modern, American political scientist.

Various studies exist that seek to encompass the entire area but in a limited time span (the period of Communist power seizure, the post-Stalin thaw, the Khrushchev era and after). They are for the most part the work of collaborative scholarship and cover a plethora of other subjects beside politics.[8]

4. A. György, *Governments of Danubian Europe* (New York: Rinehart, 1949); J. S. Rouček, *The Politics of the Balkans* (New York: McGraw-Hill, 1939); R. R. Betts, *Central and Southeast Europe* (London: Royal Institute of International Affairs, 1950).

5. *The Balkans in Our Time* (Cambridge: Harvard University Press, 1956).

6. *Eastern Europe between the Wars 1918–1941* (Cambridge: The University Press, 1945).

7. *The East European Revolution* (New York: Praeger, 1956).

8. S. Kertész, ed., *The Fate of East Central Europe: Hopes and Failures of American Foreign Policy* (Notre Dame, Ind.: Notre Dame University Press, 1956), and *East Central Europe and the World, Developments in the Post-Stalin Era* (Notre Dame, Ind.: Notre Dame University Press, 1962); H. L. Roberts, ed., "The

Two individual works, by J. F. Brown [9] and H. Gordon Skilling,[10] respectively, come closer to satisfying scholarly expectations, although the former is not primarily a study of government and politics (much of it is devoted to foreign relations), and the latter is a conventional text. Both attempt to generalize, however, in meaningful conceptual categories, and both are structured around major organizing ideas. Skilling's book in particular represents a new departure in that it treats the systems as transitional, relating changing patterns of government to entrenched traditions and to newly arising issues. It is likely to be a landmark in East European political studies, for Skilling is the first in print to transcend the self-imposed blinkers of political scientists who have seen Eastern Europe only as an extension of a static, totalitarian system developed in Russia.

Moving from general surveys to monographic works, one does not encounter a more cheering scene. Among country-oriented studies, Poland and Yugoslavia have attracted most attention. Poland, for some reason, has traditionally been the subject of a greater number of studies than any other country, particularly in the interwar period.[11] Yugoslavia, in turn, became more fashionable in the postwar era, particularly after 1948.[12] Bulgaria, Romania, Albania, and East Germany have been almost entirely neglected. That there is no good political study of Albania is quite understandable. Few scholars have competence in Albanian studies and they have had meager documentary sources at their disposal. The scarcity of studies about Bulgaria, Romania, and particularly East Germany is baffling.

Satellites in Eastern Europe," *Annals of the American Academy of Political and Social Science*, vol. 317 (May 1958); J. Rouček, ed., "Moscow's European Satellites," *Annals of the American Academy of Political and Social Science*, vol. 271 (September, 1950); S. Fischer-Galati, ed., *Eastern Europe in the Sixties* (New York: Praeger, 1963) K. L. London, ed., *Eastern Europe in Transition* (Baltimore: Johns Hopkins Press, 1966), and others.

9. *The New Eastern Europe* (New York: Praeger, 1965).

10. *The Governments of Communist Eastern Europe* (New York: Crowell, 1966).

11. See, e.g., R. L. Buell, *Poland, Key to Europe* (New York: Knopf, 1939); R. Dyboski, *Poland* (New York: Scribners, 1933); R. Machray, *The Poland of Pilsudski* (London: G. Allen and Unwin, 1936), and by the same author, *Poland, 1914–1931* (London: G. Allen and Unwin, 1932); W. J. Rose, *The Rise of Polish Democracy* (London: G. Bell and Sons, 1944), and others. Postwar works on Poland range from S. L. Sharp, *Poland, White Eagle on a Red Field* (Cambridge: Harvard University Press, 1953) to A. Bromke, *Poland's Politics: Idealism vs. Realism* (Cambridge: Harvard University Press, 1967).

12. For example, A. N. Dragnich, *Tito's Promised Land — Yugoslavia* (New Brunswick: Rutgers University Press, 1954); G. W. Hoffman, and F. W. Neal, *Yugoslavia and the New Communism* (New York: Twentieth Century Fund, 1962); 1962); C. P. McVicker, *Titoism, Pattern for International Communism* (New York: St. Martin's Press, 1957).

Romania appears to have been abandoned entirely to Ghita Ionescu in England.[13] Henry L. Roberts' pioneering work, *Rumania: Political Problems of an Agrarian State* [14] is political history at its best, written by a politically minded historian. Its narrative stops in the late 1940s, and it has no sequel. Bulgaria has been the subject of an early (pre–World War II) study of its constitutional beginnings [15] (by a historian) and a Communist party history (by a historically oriented political scientist).[16] On East Germany, no product of American scholarship exists in print. There is an English language biography of Ulbricht by the German author Carola Stern. She has also contributed a brief study of the East German Unity (Communist) Party.[17] For the rest, one has to turn to German scholarship for information, despite nine Ph.D. dissertations about East Germany undertaken in American universities.

One of the reasons for the astonishing gap in writings on East Germany unquestionably is the political attitude prevailing in the United States. It appears that as long as we do not officially take cognizance of the existence of East Germany as a juridical entity in its own right, we cannot really study it as if it had the attributes of a political system. Equally baffling is the paucity of books about Czechoslovakia,[18] especially in the interwar period, and Hungary [19] at all times since 1918.

13. Gh. Ionescu, *Communism in Rumania, 1944–1962* (London: Oxford University Press, 1964). But there is also S. Fischer-Galati, *The New Rumania: From People's Democracy to Socialist Republic* (Cambridge: M.I.T. Press, 1967).
14. (New Haven: Yale University Press, 1951).
15. C. E. Black, *The Establishment of Constitutional Government in Bulgaria* (Princeton: Princeton University Press, 1943).
16. J. Rothschild, *The Communist Party of Bulgaria: Origin and Development, 1883–1936* (New York: Columbia University Press, 1959).
17. C. Stern, *Ulbricht: A Political Biography* (New York: Praeger, 1965) and her "History and Politics of the Socialist Unity Party of Germany (SED), 1945–1965," in W. E. Griffith, ed., *Communism in Europe* (Cambridge: M.I.T. Press, 1966), vol. 2.
18. On the interwar period, one must rely on J. Chmelař, *Political Parties in Czechoslovakia* (Prague: Orbis, 1926); R. W. Seton-Watson, *The New Slovakia* (Prague: Borovy, 1924) and his *Slovakia Then and Now* (London: G. Allen and Unwin, 1931); E. Táborský, *Czechoslovak Democracy at Work* (London: G. Allen and Unwin, 1945). None are works of American scholarship, although Edward Táborský eventually made his domicile in the United States. For the postwar period, there are O. Friedmann, *The Break-up of Czech Democracy* (London: Gollancz, 1950); I. Gadourek, *The Political Control of Czechoslovakia* (Leiden: Stenfert, 1953); J. Korbel, *The Communist Subversion of Czechoslovakia, 1938–1948* (Princeton: Princeton University Press, 1959); E. Táborský, *Communism in Czechoslovakia, 1948–1960* (Princeton: Princeton University Press, 1961).
19. For Hungarian politics in the interwar period, one is almost entirely limited to the works of the British historian C. A. Macartney. These include *Hungary* (London: E. Benn, 1934); *Hungary and Her Successors* (London: Oxford University Press, 1937); *October Fifteenth*, 2 vols. (Edinburgh: The University Press, 1956). Other studies by the same author touch on Hungary and related problems of na-

As for Greece, there is virtually nothing available in the English language.

Examining the literature by topic rather than country, one finds occasional bright spots, although no subject of importance has been treated adequately in all countries and many have been ignored altogether. Even the Communist parties have not been exhaustively studied. With the exception of several perceptive articles on Communist elites and the social composition of party membership, the literature is lacking in sound functional analyses. There are no complete political histories of any party (Joseph Rothschild's study of the Bulgarian Communist Party ends with 1936). Some important parties, like the Hungarian and Czechoslovak, although they have been written about in a broader context, have not been treated independently in book-length studies.[20]

A study of the Greek Communist party by George Kousoulas [21] stands by itself as a monument of scholarship, although other "party histories" also exist.[22] But these do not begin to exhaust the subject. They are methodologically deficient and rely on straight narrative rather than analytical evaluation of internal trends (changes in elite structure, social composition of membership, ideological commitment) and patterns of interaction between the parties and their respective social environments.

The Communist parties of East Germany, Czechoslovakia, Hungary, Poland, and Yugoslavia are expertly analyzed in short, chapter-length essays in the context of a broader study of communism in Europe under the general editorship of Professor William E. Griffith.[23] However, none of the contributors is an American scholar. Professor Griffith has reached across the ocean for talent to consummate his ambitious and worthwhile enterprise.

Communist political strategy and tactics during the process of power

tional minorities. These include *National States and National Minorities* (London: Oxford University Press, 1934); and *Problems of the Danube Basin* (Cambridge, England: The University Press, 1942). Studies of postwar politics include P. Kecskeméti, *The Unexpected Revolution: Social Forces in the Hungarian Uprising* (Stanford: Stanford University Press, 1961), and F. Váli, *Rift and Revolt in Hungary* (Cambridge: Harvard University Press, 1961).

20. My own work on *Communist Strategy and Tactics in Czechoslovakia, 1918–1948* (New York: Praeger, 1963) does not purport to be a party history. It is a case study of power seizure. Similarly, the analytical scope of my essay *Revolution in Hungary* (New York: Columbia University Press, 1962) transcends the party.

21. *Revolution and Defeat: The Story of the Greek Communist Party* (New York: Oxford University Press, 1965).

22. I. Avakumović, *History of the Communist Party of Yugoslavia* (Aberdeen: Aberdeen University Press, 1964); M. K. Dziewanowski, *The Communist Party of Poland* (Cambridge: Harvard University Press, 1959).

23. *Communism in Europe*, 2 vols. (Cambridge: M.I.T. Press, 1964, 1966).

seizure and after the consolidation of power remain to be systematically analyzed. Many works about the seizure of power were authored by refugee politicians and are one-sidedly anti-Communist.[24]

Questions of ideology and of the theoretical and legal foundations of the East European "people's democratic" systems have been sparsely explored. Professor Brzezinski's monumental inquiry on how ideology and power have interacted in the development of relations among Communist states and within them is as much a study of international as of internal politics.[25] It is surely a pathbreaking synthesis that has yet to be followed by tomes of equal scope and depth. Similarly, an early study by Professor Adam Ulam of ideological and organizational adjustments between the Communist parties of Eastern Europe and the Soviet "mother" party remains the only serious effort at appraising the phenomenon of Titoism and its political consequences.[26]

Constitutional developments have not been touched upon except by Professor Samuel Sharp in a pamphlet published in 1950.[27]

The role of the military under Communism is an almost entirely neglected subject of study,[28] as is the role of national fronts (whatever their specific name, such as fatherland front, independence front, and however artificial their makeup) and major mass organizations, especially the trade unions.

Problems attendant upon social mobilization at times of frenetic industrial expansion, social mobility, elite recruitment, policies of taxation and social welfare, control of education, restriction and diffusion of cultural opportunities have also eluded the attention of students of East European affairs.

Given the scarcity of solid monographs, one can hardly evince surprise at the absence of comparative studies. Exceptions such as R. V. Burks's *The Dynamics of Communism in Eastern Europe* [29] show that it is possible to begin at the top, so to speak, by writing a comparative study without the support of monographic building blocks. However, sensitive and insightful as this work is, it, too, is uneven. The parts

24. For example S. Mikolajczyk, *The Rape of Poland* (New York: Whittlesey House, 1948); F. Nagy, *The Struggle behind the Iron Curtain* (New York: Macmillan, 1948); H. Ripka, *Czechoslovakia Enslaved* (London: Gollancz, 1950).
25. *The Soviet Bloc: Unity and Conflict*, 3d rev. ed. (Cambridge: Harvard University Press, 1967).
26. *Titoism and the Cominform* (Cambridge: Harvard University Press, 1952).
27. *New Constitutions in the Soviet Sphere* (Washington: Foundation for Foreign Affairs, 1950).
28. I. de Sola Pool, ed. *Satellite Generals* (Stanford: Stanford University Press, 1955).
29. (Princeton: Princeton University Press, 1961).

dealing with the Greek guerrillas are substantially stronger than other portions, revealing quite clearly a greater intimacy of knowledge acquired by the author in the process of extensive field research.

A LOOK TO THE FUTURE

The vistas of the current status of graduate training and the present state of the art of East European studies in government and politics need not necessarily augur for a bleak future. Even now the literature contains samples of excellence, and the training of graduates proceeds with vigor and dedication in some institutions. More encouraging is the evidence of renewed public interest in the area. This time public interest appears to be reviving without the stimulus of catastrophic events. On the contrary, it seems to be predicated on mildly optimistic expectations of evolutionary change in the Communist systems. Public attitudes toward the Communist regimes are less colored by blind emotionalism than before. Varieties of communism are discerned, and by the same token, the individuality of countries is recognized. Jointly and severally the East European states seem to be coming into sharper focus as entities in their own right, not as derivations or adjuncts of a foreign power. It may not be too much to hope that interest in the fate of Eastern Europe will not rise capriciously to spectacular heights only to tumble into the great abyss of apathy again, but will be sustained with sophistication at a respectable level conducive to more extensive and intensive scholarly research about the area. The currently enunciated national policy of "bridge building" with Eastern Europe may well serve to keep attention riveted on the area and contribute significantly to greater "inputs" of scholarship as well. It would not take much to vitalize the study of East European affairs. The current national survey of which this report is a part represents an unprecedented, auspicious beginning.

Opportunities for expanding the scope and improving the quality of studies in government and politics exist. There is no longer a serious dearth of documentary sources. The publication policies of East European regimes have allowed the appearance in print of many, varied works of immediate and direct relevance to political studies of a contemporary as well as a historical orientation. Some richly annotated encyclopedias have been issued and valuable documentary collections have been disseminated (e.g., in Hungary on the 1919 revolution, on the workers' movement in the interwar period, etc.).

Of special interest are studies of social and economic developments in the interwar period. These, of course, are strongly tendentious in that they show the oppressive class character of the interwar regimes and the rampant social inequalities that marked their existence. But they also reveal new and important data. In a different vein, literature crit- cal of various phases and aspects of Communist rule has also been published. Hungary and Poland have produced extraordinarily frank appraisals of the Stalinist era; Czechoslovakia has yielded richly docu- mented evaluations of the strategy of power seizure and amazingly forthright accounts of the abortive Slovak revolution of 1944. A group of sociologists and legal theorists appears to be seriously engaged in explorations of the constitutional foundations of people's democracy as a social-political system *sui generis* and of the relationship between the individual and the state under socialism. Romanian officials have per- mitted the publication of statements by them sharply critical of the Soviet Union. Yugoslavia and Hungary have condoned searching analy- ses of the need for reform in the system of voting and popular repre- sentation. Poland, Czechoslovakia, and Hungary have revealed the results of crude sociological surveys that shed significant light on popu- lar attitudes. Thus, the problem today is no longer that documentary sources are unavailable, but that they are too plentiful to purchase with limited budgetary allocations and to assimilate in the time available to most scholars for research.

In addition to the alleviation of the problem of sources, the impedi- ment to scholarship posed by the inaccessibility of the area is also being lifted. It is now possible to travel and even to study on a limited scale. The complexities attendant upon exchanges are too well known to be re- hearsed here. Nevertheless, in the past few years extensive, if not always satisfactory, relations with Yugoslavia have been worked out and field research by American scholars has become a reality in that country. Else- where, too, one might be able to break through the timidity of adminis- trators and obscurantism of dogmatists. The opportunity to travel in the area is essential for young scholars. They surpass many of their elders in the field of East European studies by the thoroughness of their grounding in the discipline of political science, but their knowledge of the area, unlike that of most of their elders, is based wholly on book learning and tends to be unrealistic.

Progress in the field of political studies is likely to be made primarily through the efforts of well-trained, imaginative young people. Some established scholars are too set in their ways to adapt to changing re- quirements. Others with East European expertise have abandoned the field for greener pastures and are reluctant to return. The absence of large numbers of senior scholars should be regarded by younger men and women as an opportunity to make their mark more rapidly and rise to prominence in this field more easily than in some others.

The opportunity to gain first-hand knowledge of Eastern Europe should not be regarded as a one-way proposition benefiting only American scholars. East European scholarship, particularly in the delicate, ideologically rooted realm of political studies, is in need of "enlightenment." Contacts with representatives from the United States and opportunities to visit in the United States might well broaden the horizons of East European academicians and give them methodological tools with which they are as yet unfamiliar. There is, thus, a real chance to make a contribution to the advancement of serious academic work in Eastern Europe as well.

This listing of opportunities does not indicate that all major difficulties have been eradicated from the field of East European studies. The language problem, for one, remains. It constitutes a barrier to independent research in more than one or two countries. There are other obstacles as well, not the least being the persistent threat of political intervention by East European regimes. But the basic requisites of scholarship which have for so long been lacking are now at the disposal of enterprising scholars who care to make use of them. The very backwardness of East European political studies beckons to those with scholarly ambition. Almost any topic in any period since 1918 is open to investigation. Significant contributions to the body of existing knowledge can readily be made.

NEEDS OF THE FIELD

The needs in the field of East European political studies are almost too numerous to catalog. First priority undoubtedly belongs to the promotion of conceptually and methodologically sound studies of contemporary political processes in the general context of comparative analyses of Communist systems and comparisons between Communist systems and others. The East European area is particularly susceptible to comparative studies and thus fits well into the mainstream of current interests in the discipline of political science. But the attractiveness of Eastern Europe is not limited to contemporary studies with a comparative focus. The area has been, since 1918, a veritable laboratory of political and social experimentation. It has been in almost uninterrupted transition and has experienced in rapid succession various "types" of governmental systems (democratic, authoritarian, totalitarian). There are striking parallels between the political problems of

Eastern Europe (past and present) and those of the so-called developing nations.

Although the main thrust of scholarly effort in the immediate future might well be in the direction of comparative analyses, there is considerable room for other types of studies. Scholars of any conceptual orientation and methodological preference can easily be accommodated. It would be desirable to survey the recent political history of East European countries (that is, the interwar and wartime periods) with a view to social and economic determinants of national politics. But biographic studies of political leaders, histories of political parties (not just of the Communist party), analytical studies of the functioning of parliamentary institutions (however imperfect they might have been) are all in order.[30]

The impact of World War II on the East European political systems needs careful and dispassionate evaluation; and, in this context, special attention might be devoted to an objective assessment of the role of governments and movements in exile. The form and intensity of resistance to the occupying power should be subjected to close scrutiny, and the guerrilla experiences of various countries should be compared with one another.

Postwar reconstruction, which, of course, coincided with the graduated power seizure by Communists needs to be reexamined in the light of new evidence and from the perspective of greater emotional distance. Topics in need of study, or restudy as the case might be, include the evolution of the Communist parties themselves, the organization and exercise of power (the scope and intensity of coercion, the use of methods of persuasion, the efficacy of material incentives), and others which were indicated in the preceding survey of the "state of the art."

Obviously not all needs can be serviced at once; nor is it necessary that this be attempted. The development of the field of East European political studies can be guided at a modest pace commensurate with the allocation of resources for this purpose and the availability of trained personnel to undertake high-level research. The breadth and depth of needs should not prompt a crash program that would seek to fill gaps in our knowledge in one fell swoop. Barring unanticipated turns of events, there should be ample time to fill these gaps gradually, and it would serve the cause of East European scholarship better to move ahead with all deliberate speed. The field can absorb a substantial

---

30. The kind of retrospective work that can be accomplished is demonstrated by J. Rothschild, *Pilsudski's Coup d'Etat* (New York: Columbia University Press, 1966), and R. L. Tökés, *Béla Kún and the Hungarian Soviet Republic* (New York: Praeger, 1967).

number of trained people, but it cannot accommodate a deluge of careerists. It would be regrettable if entering the field of East European studies were to become a "fad." Sustained interest is what is needed on the part of all concerned: granting foundations, university administrators, and toilers in the field.

With outside support, the study of government and politics in Eastern Europe could easily be elevated to a level of permanent respectability in the profession. Should such support be forthcoming, it would be up to the existing hard core of scholars with interest in and knowledge about the area to make certain that future graduate training and research is conducted in accordance with the standards of the discipline, integrating empirical expertise and analytic rigor. This task should not be insuperable.

In the light of the foregoing evaluation, a few tentative recommendations are offered that would assist in developing East European political studies.

RECOMMENDATIONS

1. Instruction and research in government and politics should be fostered in conjunction with work in other disciplines including languages and literature. Isolation of political scientists should be avoided. This does not imply the creation of area institutes or even of certificate programs, the value of which is highly questionable. It does suggest, however, either the clustering of scholarly activity about the East European area in major regional centers of learning, or the dispersing of such activity in accordance with a rational plan among several minor centers that are close enough to one another to formulate mutually supportive cooperative schemes for a comprehensive coverage of East European studies.

2. Establishment of endowed chairs of distinguished professorships in political science would probably attract reputable scholars to guide programs of instruction and research. Allocation of adequate funds for predoctoral and postdoctoral fellowships would help to avoid attrition among graduate students embarking on East European studies.

3. The structural and functional framework of instruction and research might well be redesigned as follows: (a) giving greater emphasis to undergraduate instruction in order to stimulate interest in East European studies and provide background for high-level graduate work; (b) developing courses, seminars, and research projects with a focus on comparative analyses of the political process (in place of country-centered descriptions of institutions); (c) fostering field research

by faculty and students stressing particularly the employment of modern survey techniques.

4. The most rewarding endeavor of political scientists would be the contemporary study of Eastern Europe in the context of comparative analyses of Communist systems and the somewhat more historically oriented study of this area in the still broader context of "politics of developing nations."

5. American scholarship should be more closely attuned to research conducted abroad in Western and Eastern Europe. Systematic exchange arrangements should be worked out between our universities and centers of learning in the Federal Republic of Germany. Similar arrangements should be sought among East European scientific institutions for the purpose of exchanges of persons, the promotion of joint research enterprises, and the acquisition of raw data.

6. To avoid costly and wasteful duplication in the acquisition of data that frequently tend to be both ephemeral and esoteric, there should be close coordination among regional centers.

7. Equipping major regional data centers or "banks" would facilitate quick and efficient servicing of the research needs of many scholars, not only those in institutions that support systematic East European studies but those in other universities and colleges as well. Information processing and retrieval is a crucial problem that has to be solved.

6/ ECONOMICS

Nicolas Spulber

Indiana University

The concept of an East European "area," with common characteristics and common interests distinct from those of its big neighbors, is relatively new. Before World War I, the economic life of the larger part of this area was viewed as forming an integral part of the life and history of the great powers which dominated the region. Western economic historians, as Doreen Warriner once pointed out,[1] usually ignored that part of Europe or showed only a marginal interest in its development during the decisive formative decades of the latter part of the nineteenth and the beginning of the twentieth centuries.

The reshaping of the map of Europe after World War I gave rise in the East Central and Southeast part of the continent to new states which grouped themselves politically and, up to a point, economically according to their positions on the peace treaties. In a sense, two Eastern Europes emerged in the aftermath of World War I; a pro-Western one and a pro–Central European one, which were tied politically, diplomatically, and partially economically to Paris and Berlin, respectively. The rise of Nazi Germany and the reaffirmation of its *Drang nach Osten* gave, finally, a paradoxical "unity" to the area as a whole by absorbing it into the German economic zone of influence and by submitting it to the dictates of German foreign economic policy. The history — and hence the economic history — of East Europe in the last part

I am particularly indebted to Professors John M. Montias of Yale University and Benjamin Ward of the University of California, Berkeley, whose preliminary draft reports and recommendations on this subject (made some time ago) were invaluable for the drafting of the present report. I am also grateful to the International Development Research Center of Indiana University for the help extended to me in the preparation of this paper.

1. "Some Controversial Issues in the History of Agrarian Europe," *Slavonic and East European Review*, 33 (December, 1953): 168–86.

of the 1930s was thus closely knit together and strongly tied to changes and developments in one center, Berlin.

After World War II, the vast penetration of the Soviet Union into the region and the rise of socialist states patterned on the Soviet model gave to Eastern Europe a renewed semblance of "unity." "Communist" or socialist Eastern Europe — the larger part of the area including a slice of Germany but excluding Greece and Turkey — became, for a while, entirely dependent on the Soviet Union's interests and patterns of development. However, in the late 1950s, the increasing search for different methods of planning and management and the obvious reinforcement of centrifugal tendencies with respect to the U.S.S.R. revealed, even to the non-initiated, the deep and almost insuperable cleavages that exist in the area.

Indeed, in addition to certain common characteristics and some common historic interests, the area exhibits deep differences in economic structure, patterns of growth, and levels of development. Two of the countries of what is now called East Central Europe are what might be called highly industrialized countries: East Germany and Czechoslovakia. All the Southeastern European countries (Bulgaria, Yugoslavia, Romania, Albania, Greece, and Turkey) are, on the other hand, in large measure agricultural countries. Finally, Hungary and Poland occupy an intermediate position between the less-developed and the fully industrialized countries of the region.

Precisely because of this sharp diversity not only as "between" countries but also as "between" regions within each country, the area presents a unique testing ground for the study of the nature and impact of policies of deliberate industrialization of agricultural countries and of the problems raised in the spreading of modern economic growth into a hinterland which contains various stages of development. Furthermore, because of widespread experimentation with centralized planning of the Soviet model, socialist Eastern Europe presents also an extremely interesting area for the study of economic planning and management.

Certain socialist practices of planning and management may work with different effectiveness at *different* levels of development. Furthermore, unlike the U.S.S.R. or China, socialist Eastern Europe is comprised of *small* countries that must face problems common to other small nations. For instance, they, unlike the Russians, *must* participate intensively in foreign trade. In fact, what has been going on in these countries under socialist management and planning may be even more interesting to some underdeveloped countries than what has occurred in the Soviet Union itself. The study of the socialist phase in Eastern Europe is indeed indispensable for understanding not only how Communism spreads but also what its stresses and strains are — and how, ultimately, these pressures are bound to change it. Finally, the study of the diverse economic changes and of the experimentation with alternative forms of economic organization which have taken place there adds new dimensions to the understanding of the processes of growth and development, of planning and management, and also to the study of comparative systems as well.

I

An important body of data awaits the economist who is interested in studying the pace, scope, and direction of modern economic growth from the early formative years throughout the interwar years. Primary data on population censuses, on agricultural outputs, budget receipts and expenditures, imports and exports, and similar items were indeed published by the Central and East European countries since the middle of the last quarter of the nineteenth century, when all of them had established central statistics offices. (Much of this data has been reprinted in the international sections of the Austrian, German, or French statistical yearbooks of the time and are largely accessible.) A vast body of both descriptive and qualitative information on the legal, fiscal, and banking aspects of the early processes of modernization and industrialization became available during the interwar years on many of these countries; and much more comprehensive data on the industrial revolutions, capital formation, technology, and manpower in the formative years have started to be systematically collected, collated, and published in each of these countries, notably since the middle of the 1950s. While many of the studies based on this data now published in socialist Eastern Europe remain tendentious in orientation and biased in many of their interpretations, they do provide unique sources for new integrated area syntheses. The process of development of the modern industrial sectors, of the growth of the supporting banking, transportation, and related services in each country and in each region of the area may thus be increasingly followed through both older and recent studies — many, if not all, of which are unfortunately still only national in scope and available only in East European languages.[2]

2. For Czechoslovakia: Jaroslav Purš, *Průmyslová revoluce v českých zemích* (The Industrial Revolution in the Czech Lands) (Prague: Statní Naklad. technické lit., 1960); for Poland: Julius Lukasiewicz, *Przewrót techniczny w przemysle Królestwa Polskiego 1852–1886* (The Technical Revolution in the Industry of the Polish Kingdom, 1852–1886) (Warsaw: Państwowe Wydaw. Naukowe, 1963); for Hungary: Sándor Vilmos, *Nagyipari fejlödés Magyarországon 1867–1900* (The Development of Large-Scale Industry in Hungary, 1867–1900) (Budapest: Szikra, 1964); for Romania: Olga Constantinescu and N. N. Constantinescu, *Cu privire*

Vast and important data on strategies, instruments, and achievements in economic development during the interwar years; on the policies of industrializing agricultural countries in the 1930s; on capital requirements; on labor productivity; and so on are available and not yet fully explored.[3] Finally, the scope and intensity of the post–World War II industrialization and modernization efforts through the 1950s and 1960s can now be followed through a wealth of official statistics and publications for all countries of the area. After being withheld a long time until the late 1940s and early 1950s, data on almost all aspects of economic life — on investment patterns, capital formation, outputs, productivity, labor force, and so on — are now being released in almost overwhelming quantities.[4] The margin of error of the data released is decreasing, and the continuing processes of updating and improving this stream is evident — though an upward bias in national income, industrial output, and other aggregate statistics remains evident.

Thus, from the early formative years of economic modernization, through the interwar years, and through the socialist era, the data generated by the East Europe countries compares favorably with that of many — if not all — other less-developed areas of the world and presents a unique and challenging source of information for the study both of growth and development and of economic planning.

II

A relatively limited amount of noteworthy books and articles on the economics of the area were published in the Western languages during the interwar years. Most of the books published at the time were socio-

la problema revoluţiei industriale în România (Concerning the problem of the Industrial Revolution in Romania) (Bucharest: Editura ştiinţifică, 1957); for Bulgaria: Zhak Natan, *Stopanska istoriia na Bulgariia* (The Economic History of Bulgaria) (Sofia: Nauka i Izkustvo 1957); For Yugoslavia: Mijo Mirković, *Ekonomska historija Jugoslavije* (Economic History of Yugoslavia) (Zagreb: Ekonomski Pregled, 1958); and others.

3. New sources of interest in East European languages on the period available now include: for Czechoslovakia: R. Olšovský *et al.*, *Přehled hospodářského vývoje Československa v letech 1918–1945* (Survey of the Economic Development of Czechoslovakia during the Years 1918–1945) (Prague: S.N.P.L., 1961); for Poland: Zbigniew Landau and Jerzy Tomaszewski, *Zarys historii gospodarczej Polski 1918–1939* (Outline of the History of Poland's Economy, 1918–1939) (Warsaw: Książki i Wiedza, 1960); for Yugoslavia: Mijo Mirković *Ekonomska struktura Jugoslavije 1918–1941* (The Economic Structure of Yugoslavia, 1918–1941) (Zagreb: Školska Knjiga, 1952); and others.

4. Besides statistical yearbooks published regularly since the mid-1950s — after an elapse of some ten years — numerous specialized journals and books, as well as statistical compendiums, covering the last two decades since the war and concerning the economy as a whole and each of its main sectors, are now available.

economic or geoeconomic surveys, theses, or pamphlets on the agrarian question, or descriptive studies of industry, banking, and foreign trade.[5] By subject, the most significant among them were:

1. Studies on the economic consequence of the war: notably books in various series published in the 1930s (either in English or French) for the Carnegie Endowment for International Peace, such as George T. Danaillow, *Les effets de la querre en Bulgarie*;[6] David Mitrany, *The Effects of the War in Southeastern Europe*;[7] and others.

2. Studies on the new land reforms and on their impact on peasant problems: David Mitrany, *The Land and the Peasant in Romania: The War and the Agrarian Reform*;[8] O. S. Morgan, ed., *Agricultural Systems of Modern Europe*;[9] D. Warriner, *Economics of Peasant Farming*;[10] *The European Conference on Rural Life*;[11] and so on.

3. Studies on the rising economic nationalism (typical for all of these states in the later 1920s and mid-1930s): Leo Pasvolsky, *Economic Nationalism of the Danubian States*;[12] and Leo Pasvolsky, *Bulgaria's Economic Position*.[13]

4. Studies on the connections between industrialization efforts and the changing patterns of international trade: H. Liepmann, *Tariff Levels and the Economic Unity of Europe: An Examination of Tariff Policy, Exports Movements, and the Economic Integration of Europe, 1913–31*,[14] which was translated from German.

Some notable contributions were made during the war years. Among these may be recalled: Howard Ellis, *Exchange Control in Central Eu-*

---

5. For detailed listing of these books, see notably: *International Bibliography of Historical Sciences*, published for the International Committee for Historical Sciences, vols. 1–14 (Paris and Zurich, 1926–39); *The Balkans: A Selected List of References*, 5 vols., vol. 1, *General*; vol. 2, *Albania*; vol. 3, *Bulgaria*; vol. 4, *Romania*; vol. 5, *Yugoslavia* (Washington, D.C.: Library of Congress, 1945); William L. Langer and Hamilton Fish Armstrong, eds., *Foreign Affairs Bibliography, 1919–1932: A Selected and Annotated List of Books on International Relations, 1919–1932* (New York: Harper, for Council on Foreign Relations, 1933); Robert Gale Woolbert, ed., *Foreign Affairs Bibliography, 1932–1942: A Selected and Annotated List of Books on International Relations, 1932–1942* (New York: Harper, for the Council on Foreign Relations, 1945); and Leon Savadjian, ed., *Bibliographie balkanique, 1920–1938*, 8 vols. (Paris: Société générale d'imprimerie et d'édition, 1931–39).
6. (Paris: Presses universitaires de Frances, 1932).
7. (New Haven: Yale University Press, 1936).
8. (New Haven: Yale University Press, also for the Carnegie Endowment for International Peace, 1930).
9. (New York: Macmillan, 1938).
10. (New York: Oxford University Press, 1939).
11. 6 vols. (Geneva: International Institute of Agriculture, 1939).
12. (Washington, D.C.: Brookings Institution, 1928).
13. (Washington, D.C.: Brookings Institution, 1930).
14. (London: Allen and Unwin, 1938).

TABLE 1
PUBLICATIONS ON THE ECONOMICS OF SOCIALIST EASTERN EUROPE*: 1945–65

	Total	E.E. (as a whole)	Alb.	Bul.	Cze.	Hun.	Pol.	Rom.	Yug.
Articles[a]	583	127	20	32	84	62	140	38	80
Books incl. monographs	76	30	1	1	4	14	14	2	10
Short documents	119	20	5	14	11	14	18	20	17

* Excluding East Germany.
[a] Excluding minor articles.
SOURCES: Robert F. Byrnes, *Bibliography of American Publications on East Central Europe, 1945–57*, Indiana University Publications, Slavic and East European Series, vol. 11 (Bloomington, 1958); the yearly *American Bibliography of Russian and East European Studies*, 1957 through 1965 (various editors), Indiana University Publications, Slavic, then Russian and East European Series, vols. 10, 18, 21, 26, 27, 29, 32, 34, and 37.

rope; [15] Antonin Basch, *The Danube Basin and the German Economic Sphere*; [16] and the celebrated study by Paul N. Rosenstein-Rodan, "Problems of Industrialization of Eastern and Southeastern Europe." [17] This work inspired similar studies on area development, notably the remarkable contribution to growth and planning, written in 1943 and 1944, by K. Mandelbaum. His book, *The Industrialization of Backward Areas*,[18] used prewar Southeastern Europe as the background for a trial program in development for the postwar years.

III

In the last two decades since World War II (1945–65), a vast increase in books, monographs, and articles, particularly on socialist Eastern Europe, was registered. According to the entries in the *American Bibliography of Slavic and Eastern Europe Studies* issued by Indiana University, a total of 583 articles were published on the economics of socialist Eastern Europe (excluding East Germany) during those two decades. Regionally, the largest amount of this output focused first on the area as a whole, then on Poland, and then on Czechoslovakia

15. (Cambridge: Harvard University Press, 1941).
16. (New York: Columbia University Press, 1943).
17. *The Economic Journal*, vol. 53 (1943).
18. Oxford Institute of Statistics, Monograph 2 (London: Blackwell and Mott, 1945).

and Yugoslavia; topically, the largest amount was concerned with general economics, then agriculture, manpower problems, and finally industry (see tables 1 and 2). The articles, books and monographs covered by these statistics were not all the work of professional economists. Professionally, the economist is, of course, not directly interested in area studies as such. He is interested in the latter in as much as they expand his understanding of, say,

TABLE 2

ARTICLES ON THE ECONOMICS OF SOCIALIST EASTERN EUROPE° BY TOPICS: 1945–65

	Total	E.E. (as a whole)	Alb.	Bul.	Cze.	Hun.	Pol.	Rom.	Yug.
Gen. Econ.	170	38	6	10	28	15	38	13	22
Growth & dev't.	18	7	0	2	0	0	5	3	1
Agriculture	96	21	4	3	14	11	20	4	19
Industry	76	14	4	5	11	5	21	7	9
Manpower	92	14	3	4	10	12	27	6	16
Trade & for. rel.	61	22	2	4	9	7	10	3	4
Consumption	23	3	1	1	4	2	6	1	5
Value & prices	7	1	0	0	0	3	3	0	0
Planning	40	7	0	3	8	7	10	1	4
Total	583	127	20	32	84	62	140	38	80

° Excluding East Germany.
SOURCES: *Bibliography of American Publications on East Central Europe 1945–57* and *American Bibliographies of Russian and East European Studies 1957–65*.

the functioning of various economic systems — capitalist or socialist — or his understanding of the processes of formulation, implementation, and control of execution of various economic policies in different settings at different levels of economic development. When choosing his illustrative examples, he is hence not necessarily keen on limiting his studies to one area. The professional economic journals focus for their part on their main interest of analytical problems, which may be tenuously related to specific area examples. On the contrary, the area-oriented interdisciplinary programs and journals are, of course, keenly interested in area-oriented economic expertise. The results of these conflicting tendencies are reflected clearly in the publication outlets used for the studies dealing with the economics of the area during the last two decades. Of the 583 articles published between 1945 and 1965, only 16 were published in highly professional economic journals (such as the *American Economic Review*, the *Quarterly Journal of Economics*, or others).

The sharp intensification of interest in the economics of socialist Eastern Europe which has occurred since the late 1950s has scarcely changed the underlying conflicting tendencies concerning publication interest and the resulting publication pattern. Of the 514 economic articles dealing with socialist Eastern Europe published from 1957 to 1965, only 13 were published in the highly recognized professional economic journals. This does not compare very favorably with 982 articles dealing with the economic problems of the Soviet Union published by the same sources during the same period, and of which 55 were published in the typical journals of the economist. A significant amount of the rest was published in the excellent, highly reputable, interdiscipline, area-oriented journals (such as the *Slavic Review, Soviet Studies, Survey,* and so on), which have a totally different clientele.

According to the Indiana bibliographies, some 76 books and monographs were published in English, on the economics of the area from 1945 to 1965. (Many other books and monographs have appeared since then.) These publications had the following foci:

1. *Long-term economic growth and development.* Works in this field usually consider specifically either the area or Europe as a whole — but with great attention to the area's characteristics. Among these works are: Ingvar Svennilson, *Growth and Stagnation in the European Economy,*[19] which examines the patterns of Europe's industrialization and urbanization along with those of the area of our concern, and Nicolas Spulber, *The State and Economic Development in Eastern Europe,*[20] which discusses in a number of essays the role of the state in the modernization and industrialization of the area from 1860 to 1960.

Among studies focusing on long-term developments in one country only is the study by Jozo Tomasevich, *Peasants, Politics, and Economic Change in Yugoslavia.*[21] Studies concerned with long-term growth and development in a specific region are still rare. Of particular note are the works of Peter F. Sugar, *Industrialization of Bosnia-Hercegovina, 1878–1918,*[22] and of Toussaint Hočevar, *The Structure of the Slovenian Economy 1848–1963.*[23]

2. *Patterns of planning, management, and growth under socialism.* General analytical studies of this area concerning the alternative patterns of planning and management under socialism, the recurrent reforms taking place in the economies, and on their changing operating princi-

19. (Geneva: U.N. Economic Commission for Europe, 1954).
20. (New York: Random House, 1966).
21. (Stanford, Calif.: Stanford University Press, 1955).
22. (Seattle: University of Washington Press, 1963).
23. (New York: Studia Slovenica, 1965).

ples are relatively rare. Most of the studies focus on the Soviet experience and only incidentally on the East European experience. Broader syntheses, like Peter Wiles's *Political Economy of Communism* [24] and Benjamin Ward's *The Socialist Economy: A Study of Organizational Alternatives*,[25] set up ideal organizational models which admittedly provide only limited clues to the wide variety of alternatives which could be implemented in Eastern Europe and even in some underdeveloped countries.

Focused on the first decade of socialist transformation in the area is the work by Nicolas Spulber, *The Economics of Communist Eastern Europe*,[26] a synthesis, paralleled in scope and range of interest, by the French study by Jan Marczewski, *Planification et croissance économique des démocraties populaires*.[27] A general discussion concerning capital and labor inputs and growth of output in the economy as a whole and in its main sectors throughout the 1950s, in both the planned economies of Eastern Europe and the Soviet Union and in the market economies, may be found in "Some Factors in Economic Growth in Europe during the 1950's," published as Part 2 of the *Economic Survey of Europe in 1961*.[28] A discussion of various strategies of both pre- and postwar industrialization and of the progresses achieved in a number of countries of the area is presented by Alfred Zauberman in *Industrial Progress in Poland, Czechoslovakia, and East Germany, 1937–1962*.[29]

Focusing on planning models and experience within a country of the area but with wider implications are two outstanding works by the Hungarian economist, Janos Kornai (available in English translation), *Overcentralization in Economic Administration: A Critical Analysis Based on Experience in Hungarian Light Industry* [30] — which discusses the shortcomings, inefficiencies, and disastrous consequences of "excessive centralization"; and *Mathematical Planning of Structural Decisions* [31] — which presents a brilliant composite of the author's experience in operations research, his theoretical analysis of socialist planning problems, and his survey of actual long-term planning practice in Hungary. Also useful and important are the books of Bela A.

24. (Cambridge: Harvard University Press, 1962).
25. (New York: Random House, 1967).
26. (New York: Technology Press of M.I.T. and John Wiley, 1957).
27. (Paris: Presses universitaires de France, 1956).
28. (Geneva: United Nations Secretariat of the Economic Commission for Europe, 1964).
29. (London: Oxford University Press, for the Royal Institute of International Affairs, 1964).
30. (London: Oxford University Press, 1959).
31. (Amsterdam: North-Holland Publishing Co., 1967).

Balassa, *The Hungarian Experience in Economic Planning*[32] and John Michael Montias, *Central Planning in Poland*,[33] which examine the broad problems of planning theory and practice and analyze the changing patterns of economic management against the background of economic change in these countries throughout the 1950s. Somewhat narrower in scope but equally interesting for the study of the economic experience of the other area countries are: John M. Montias, *Economic Development in Communist Rumania*;[34] Jan M. Michal, *Central Planning in Czechoslovakia*;[35] Stanislaw Wellisz, *The Economies of the Soviet Bloc*,[36] which centers on the Polish experience; and, three books on Yugoslavia: Albert Waterston, *Planning in Yugoslavia*;[37] George Macesich, *Yugoslavia: The Theory and Practice of Development Planning*;[38] Svetozar Pejovich, *The Market-Planned Economy of Yugoslavia*[39] and a collection of articles by Yugoslav economists on a variety of interesting topics, "Yugoslav Economists on Problems of a Socialist Economy," issued as a special number of *Eastern European Economics* edited by Radmila Stojanović.[40] Not available in English are a number of books deserving a wider audience: notably on East Germany, Peter Dietrich Propp, *Zur Transformation einer Zentralverwaltungswirtschaft sowjetischen Typs in eine Marktwirtschaft*;[41] and, on a lesser plane, Guy Roustand, *Development économique de l'Allemagne Orientale*;[42] on Hungary, Peter Kende, *Logique de l'économie centralisée, un exemple: la Hongrie*;[43] and on Yugoslavia, Harry Schleicher, *Das System der betrieblichen Selbstverwaltung in Yugoslavien*.[44]

Of particular interest among the analytical books focused on economic policies and on growth and development in nonsocialist countries are the Research Monograph Series on Greece published by the Athens Center of Economic Research led by Professor Andreas G. Papandreou until 1967. Among these monographs may be noted: Andreas G. Papandreou, *A Strategy for Greek Economic Development*

32. (New Haven: Yale University Press, 1959).
33. (New Haven: Yale University Press, 1962).
34. (Cambridge: M.I.T. Press, 1967).
35. (Stanford, Calif.: Stanford University Press, 1960).
36. (New York: McGraw-Hill, 1946).
37. (Baltimore: Johns Hopkins Press, 1962).
38. (Charlottesville: University Press of Virginia, 1964).
39. (Minneapolis: University of Minnesota Press, 1966).
40. (New York: International Arts and Sciences Press, 1963–64), vol. 2, no. 1–2.
41. (Berlin: Duncker & Humblot, for Osteuropa Institut, 1964).
42. (Paris: SEDES, 1963).
43. (Paris: SEDES, 1964).
44. (Berlin: Duncker & Humblot, 1961).

(1962); Benjamin Ward, *Greek Regional Development* (1963); Daniel Suits, *An Econometric Model of the Greek Economy* (1964); and a number of sectorial studies to which I will refer below. Also worthy of note is the study of P. Pavlopoulos, *A Statistical Model for the Greek Economy, 1949–1959.*[45] The model provides an excellent insight into the workings of the Greek economy both in and outside the sample period.

Very detailed current survey types of studies have been published by the United Nations — in its *Economic Bulletin(s) for Europe* and in its yearly *Economic Survey of Europe* published by the Organization for Economic Co-operation and Development (OECD), particularly on Greece, Yugoslavia, and Turkey — and by various U.S. congressional committees. Among the latter's publications are a number of studies on the "Soviet economies," including various papers on the economies of Eastern Europe.

3. *Sectorial studies.* A variety of notable sectorial studies have been published, particularly on agriculture, industry, and foreign trade. On agriculture, of special interest are: Jerzy Karcz, ed., *Soviet and East European Agriculture,*[46] which contains, *inter alia,* studies on peasant agriculture in Yugoslavia, Poland, and Czechoslovakia; "Some Problems of Agricultural Development in Europe and the Soviet Union," *Economic Survey of Europe 1960,*[47] especially chapter 4; and the older and still useful symposium on collectivization edited by Irwin T. Sanders, *Collectivization of Agriculture in Eastern Europe.*[48] Various other studies of interest are scattered in a number of United Nations publications. Also of interest are a number of monographs published by the already mentioned Center of Economic Research of Athens, Greece, particularly: Adam A. Pepelasis and Pan A. Yotopoulos, *Surplus Labor in Greek Agriculture, 1953–1960* (1962) and Kenneth Thompson, *Farm Fragmentation in Greece* (1962).

On industry, a number of "occasional papers" have been released by the Research Project on National Income in East Central Europe of Columbia University, directed by Thad P. Alton. A detailed study of industrial progress in Poland, Czechoslovakia, and East Germany is to be found in the previously mentioned book of Alfred Zauberman. Industrial progress and problems of industrialization in Greece are examined in a number of monographs of descriptive or analytical interest

45. (Amsterdam: North Holland Publishing Co., 1966).
46. (Berkeley: University of California Press, 1967).
47. (Geneva: United Nations, 1961).
48. (Lexington: University of Kentucky Press, 1958).

published by the Athens Center, notably: George Coutzoumaris, *The Morphology of Greek Industry*[49] and Howard Ellis, *Industrial Capital in Greek Development*,[50] which is a case study in financing economic development.

A number of books are available on foreign trade — particularly on intersocialist cooperation and on intersocialist economic planning coordination. Of particular significance are F. Pryor, *The Communist Foreign Trade System*[51] and Michael Kaser, *Comecon, Integration Problems of the Planned Economies*.[52] Interesting discussions on the same questions may also be found in Istvan Agoston, *Le Marché Commun Communiste, principes et pratique du COMECON*,[53] and in Théofil I. Kis, *Les Pays de l'Europe de l'Est, leurs rapports mutuels et le problème de leur intégration dans l'orbite de l'URSS*.[54] These subjects are treated also in some German books, such as Karl Ernest Schenk's *Arbeitsteilung im Rat für Gegenseitige Wirtschaftshilfe*.[55] In the same field a number of studies on the economic relations between East and West are available, such as Philip E. Uren, ed., *East-West Trade*,[56] which contains some substantive papers on the subject, and various reports by U.S. congressional committees, for example, *East-West Trade*, issued by the Committee on Foreign Relations,[57] which discusses national policies and practices in this field. Finally, a number of books focus on the specific economic relations of one East European country with the rest of COMECON or with other countries. Such books include Laszlo Zsoldos, *Economic Integration of Hungary into the Soviet Bloc*[58] and Heinz Kohler, *Economic Integration in the Soviet Bloc, with an East German Case Study*.[59]

4. *Population, manpower, labor-force planning.* A systematic stream of high-quality monographs on population and manpower for the area as a whole and for each of these countries has been produced since the 1950s by the U.S. Department of Commerce, Bureau of the Census. Of

49. 1963.
50. 1964.
51. (Cambridge: M.I.T. Press, 1963).
52. (London: Oxford University Press, for Royal Institute of International Affairs, 1965).
53. (Geneva: Droz, 1964).
54. (Louvain: Nauwelaerts, 1964).
55. (Berlin: Duncker & Humblot, for Osteuropa Institut, 1964).
56. (Toronto: Canadian Institute of International Affairs, 1966).
57. (Washington, D.C.: U.S. Government Printing Office, 1964), 88th Cong., 2d sess.
58. (Columbus, Ohio: Ohio State University, Bureau of Business Research, 1963).
59. (New York: Praeger, 1965).

particular note are various monographs by Andrew Elias, *Industrial Manpower in Eastern-Europe, 1948–1960* [60] and *Agricultural Manpower in Eastern-Europe, 1948–1962*,[61] and various studies on "The Labor Force" of each of these countries by Andrew Elias, James N. Ypsilantis, Samuel Baum, Zora Prochazka, and Jerry W. Combs, Jr.[62] Useful monographs on labor-force planning now available in English are: Janos Timar (chief of Hungary's manpower planning), *Planning the Labor Force in Hungary*,[63] and S. Cohen, *Planning of Educational Requirements for Economic Development as Applied to Yugoslavia*.[64]

5. *National accounting and structural interdependence.* The study of the structural changes in the economies of some of these countries and their intersectorial relations have been analyzed in a number of books, among which must be noted the pioneering work of W. G. Stolper, *The Structure of the East German Economy*;[65] The Research Project on National Income in East Central Europe, working under the direction of Thad P. Alton, has, for its part, produced a number of national income and product studies, notably for the mid-1950s, all published by Columbia University Press: Thad Alton, Vaclav Holesovsky, Gregor Lazarcik, Paul D. Sivak, and Alexej Wynnyczuk, *Czechoslovak National Income and Product, 1947–48 and 1955–56* (1962); Thad Alton, Laszlo Czirjak, George Pall, and Leon Smolinski, *Hungarian National Income and Product in 1955* (1963); and Thad Alton, Andrej Korbonski, Bogdan Mieczkowski, and Leon Smolinski, *Polish National Income and Product in 1954, 1955, and 1956* (1965).

All in all, notwithstanding the rather special professional strictures under which the economist who tends to circumscribe his analysis to a given area is bound to operate, the contribution of the American economic scholar to the study of Eastern Europe compares favorably with the post–World War II contributions of his French or German colleagues. Major contributions have indeed been made here, for instance, in the study of planning and management under socialism (viz., the works of Balassa and Montias); in the study of growth and structural interdependence (viz., the books by Stolper and of Alton and associates); in the study of comparative and "Soviet economics" in general (e.g.,

60. 1962.
61. 1936.
62. U.S. Department of Commerce, Bureau of the Census, International Population Statistics Reports, Series P-190, nos. 11, 13, 14, 16, 18, 20, 22, issued between 1959 and 1965.
63. Translated from the Hungarian (White Plains, N.Y.: IASP, 1966).
64. (Rotterdam: Netherlands Economic Institute, 1966).
65. (Cambridge: Technology Press of M.I.T., 1960).

by Benjamin Ward and others). Research in the economics of development and growth under centralized planning and management, with emphasis on East Europe's experience, continues now in the United States on what may be called a modest scale but on a high professional level, with a solid promise of fruition. The increasing professional interest in the study of economic development, planning patterns, and quantitative economic policy, and the diversification in planning and management patterns in Eastern Europe, should further increase the interest of the economist in the planning experience and the growth and development of the area. How to surmount, in these circumstances, the language barrier in order to increase economic research on the area, how to combine the systematic and, at times, exclusive interest of the area specialist with the transient interest of the economist in a given problem of the area are questions of importance not only for Eastern Europe, but also for any area-oriented study. We shall try to return to these problems later.

IV

Nine major universities have developed what could be called *integrated* programs in East European studies, including some form of graduate training in "socialist" economics — and have made contributions to research and publication in this field: California (Berkeley, Davis, Los Angeles, and various subcenters), Chicago, Columbia, Cornell, Indiana, Michigan, Washington, Wisconsin, and Yale. Five institutions have, during the last decade, played the key role in research, training, and degrees awarded in the field at either the M.A. or Ph.D. level: California (Berkeley), Columbia, Harvard, Indiana, and Yale. Contributions of note have come also from other institutions with a long-established interest in the study of Eastern Europe, such as Colorado, Florida State, Illinois, Kansas, Princeton, Stanford, Syracuse, Texas, and others.[66] Other contributions to research in the field have been made by scholars working in various governmental departments who have made known some of the results of their work through reports published

66. Roughly three Ph.D.'s per year were awarded in the United States during the past decade to candidates who had successfully completed their dissertations on some aspect of the economic development of Eastern Europe. In the typical fields of planning, development, economic history, and national economics, Eastern Europe attracted far less student research than almost any other less-developed area (e.g., Latin America, Africa, Southeast Asia, or the Middle East). (For a detailed listing see the September issues of the *American Economic Review.*) Few of these dissertations were of special significance; hardly any one of them crowned integrated area studies; more often than not, they were only marginally related to area programs.

either directly by their departments or by various congressional committees.

Some thirty-five active (publishing) U.S. scholars may be identified who have demonstrated a major — if not always a continuous — interest in the area and who have published books, monographs, or major studies from the mid-1950s to the mid-1960s on East European economic problems. Roughly a dozen of these scholars work in large universities and in their subcenters, where they may eventually supervise graduate research in the field. Roughly another dozen work in smaller colleges and universities. The balance works in government institutions. A number of scholars previously active in the East European field have branched out into Soviet economics and into planning in general. Perhaps a dozen have completely left work in the area and may be classified as "formerly active" (e.g., Antonin Basch and P. Rosenstein-Rodan). Of the economic scholars now active in the field, the majority has been U.S. trained. Few scholars who completed their education in European universities have made a mark on this study in the United States, though many have done brilliant work in other economic fields (e.g., W. Fellner, T. Scitovsky, N. Georgescu-Rogen, P. Rosenstein-Rodan, and others).

Courses focused exclusively on the economics of Eastern Europe are only rarely offered in American colleges and universities. Materials on economic development or on the planning experience of at least somê country of the area — particularly Yugoslavia — are, on the other hand, often included in textbooks or in readings in comparative economics, soviet economics, economic development, or planning.[67] The latter types of courses are themselves not well integrated into the curricula and, judging by textbooks or readings available, the materials used are often

67. See, for instance, in comparative systems the texts of Gregory Grossman, *Economic Systems* (Englewood Cliffs, N.J.: Prentice-Hall, 1967); Alan G. Gruchy, *Comparative Economic Systems* (Boston: Houghton Mifflin, 1966); William N. Loucks, *Comparative Economics*, 6th ed. (New York: Harper & Bros., 1961); Carl Landauer, *Contemporary Economic Systems* (Philadelphia and New York: J. B. Lippincott Co., 1964) — which all contain a chapter on the Yugoslav type of socialist economy. See also the reader by Marshall I. Goldman, *Comparative Economic Systems, Models and Cases* (Homewood, Ill.: R. D. Irwin, 1965), which contains a number of papers on the Yugoslav economic system. Yugoslav planning is also examined in a number of economic development or general planning studies, such as Max F. Millikan, ed., *National Economic Planning* (New York: Columbia University, for the National Bureau of Economic Research, 1967); Everett E. Hagen, *Planning Economic Development* (Homewood, Ill.: R. D. Irwin, 1963); Joan Mitchell, *Groundwork to Economic Planning* (London: Secker and Warburg, 1966). The experience of the other East European countries is, however, rarely discussed, since many assume that it simply "duplicates" the discussion on the Soviet experience.

overlapping. A major effort of coordination is now underway in this respect in a number of universities. Advances in the theory of economic policy in the West—particularly systematization of the relations between economic theory and quantitative data concerning the structure and performance of economic subsystems—convergence in the use of a number of planning and programming techniques in different economic systems, and continuous experimentation in development planning and economic management everywhere, make it both possible and imperative to provide a unifying focus to the economic studies in these fields. The unifying focus of economic theory and of the empirical data concerning structure and performance of subsystems is provided by the increasing literature on quantitative economic policy. The study of the latter is considered at Indiana University, for instance, to provide the capstone of two fields of graduate studies in economics: economic development, on the one hand, and planning (including special sequences on Soviet economics with materials on Eastern Europe), on the other. (The student in "planning" who wishes to focus on the Soviet planning experience may or may not feel the necessity of relating this particular focus with various area-oriented courses administered by other departments and integrated into a number of requirements for a special certificate in Russian or East European studies. The latter route, as all of us know, lengthens graduate studies without always providing the necessary professional incentives.)

Also at Indiana, at the undergraduate level, separate courses on development provide a broad view of the contemporary world: Analysis of Development—the Western Developed Areas; Analysis of Development—the Socialist Economies; Analysis of Development—the Underdeveloped Areas. The second of these focuses on the increasing heterogeneity in management and planning practices in the socialist world, and contains, as needed, materials on Eastern Europe's economic growth and change.

Given the strictures placed by the profession on area expertise, the limited opportunities open to the area-oriented expert, the formidable barriers presented by the languages of the area, and the lengthening of graduate studies which the certificate entails, only basic changes in a number of directions could spur training and research on the economics of Eastern Europe. Changes notably in opportunities, expectation of security, support over a number of years, data accessibility—along with new and better combinations of part-time and full-time scholarly work in the field—could alone significantly increase the quality and the scope of the studies in the economics of the area. We shall return to these points later.

V

An enormous amount of useful and illuminating research on industrialization of backward areas and on planning and management could, and should, indeed be done on the basis of the vast and complex East European experiences. The work could be carried on in a number of directions:

1. *Background Studies.* In particular, general economic histories of countries and subregions are now virtually non-existent. Synthetic studies of this kind, carried out by competently trained economic historians, are hence a major need.

2. *Recent period surveys in depth.* Notably, research on performance, accounts of evolving economic policies, and descriptions of changes in organization setups are in short supply, with Poland having perhaps the best coverage at the moment and with limited work available on Yugoslavia, Hungary, and Czechoslovakia. Integration of these three types of research is still rare and remains of great interest.

3. *Annals of current developments, assessments of problems and forecasting.* Current survey type work is partly covered by UN, OECD, various U.S. government publications, and occasional articles. What would be useful is to extend this work to all the countries of the region (the OECD limits its annual country studies to Yugoslavia, Greece, and Turkey only). Attempts at forecasting performance under planning would also be extremely useful.

4. *Analytical studies.* Major research opportunities exist with respect to data generation, analysis of existing data, and model building. (Yugoslavia and Greece still offer the best opportunities for data generation, but prospects are improving for various types of studies in some of the other countries as well.) Finally, comparative studies involving both intersocialist experience and the socialist versus the nonsocialist experience could usefully serve for broader-based intersystems comparisons.

According to reports available from scholars working in the field, a significant amount of long-term research work is currently underway — particularly in some of the directions defined above under 2, 3, and 4. Here is a sample of the major studies in progress:

— Economic Growth in East Central Europe (Dr. Thad P. Alton, Columbia University)

— Price reforms in Eastern Europe (Professor Morris Bornstein, University of Michigan)

— Inflation in Eastern Europe (Professor Andrezj Brzeski, University of California, Davis)

— Labor markets in Eastern Europe (Professor Walter Galenson, Cornell University)

— Agricultural policies in Eastern Europe (Professor J. F. Karcz, University of California, Davis)

— Agricultural organization and performance in East Central Europe (Dr. Gregor Lazarcik, Columbia University)

— Public budgetary expenditures in East and West (Professor Frederic Pryor, Swarthmore College)

— Structure and determinants of value added in Yugoslavia (Charles Rockwell, Yale University)

— Planning and management under socialism (Professor Nicolas Spulber, Indiana University)

— Decentralized socialist economies, with a special focus on Yugoslavia (Professor Jaroslav Venek and George Staller, Cornell University)

— Comparative production organization and control — East and West (Professor Benjamin Ward, University of California, Berkeley)

— Forecast for futuribles — forecasts concerning performance of heavy and light industries, agriculture, consumption, and so on (a collective effort under the direction of Professor Peter Wiles, London University, with participation of a number of American scholars)

— Economic growth and economic reforms in Eastern Europe (a collective effort of a number of U.S. scholars, under the aegis of the International Development Research Center of Indiana University)

The research effort is thus varied and designed to further our knowledge on economic development, growth, and planning, and to integrate usefully the area-oriented studies.

VI

In order to expand and deepen research in the field and to attract fresh talent toward it, a way must be found to surmount a major dilemma typical, in fact, of all area-oriented studies: namely, that the linguistic and background-knowledge requirements for the full-time researcher in this area conflict with the professional requirements of the practicing economist. This dilemma is reinforced by the variety of potential users of the researcher's products, and by the existence of many useful economic research projects in other areas which can be carried out with substantially less preparation.

The dilemma suggests a dichotomizing of researchers into types, full-timers and part-timers. For the former, support should be aimed at providing some form of security and stable incentives. The latter, on the other hand, are economists who acquire an interest either in bringing some aspect of East European experience into a broad study or in making a one-shot study of some aspect of East European economies. Many such studies could be successfully completed within, say, a year (appropriate support for such work and encouragement for efforts of this kind seem evidently highly desirable). The following list offers a few tentative suggestions for implementing a program of this kind:

1. *Centers in the United States.* Two to three centers for East European studies located in the United States would certainly be useful as organizing foci for both full-time and part-time scholars. They would provide easily visible pools of both formal and informal contacts, expertise, and sponsorship for continuing programs of training and research. However, in a field which is almost certain to be scholar-poor for some time, over-administration is a serious risk; two to three centers are hence an upper limit.

2. *Chairs.* Chairs in a few locations which are also major data centers would be a stimulus to research. They would provide some increased expectation of security also; chairs in the social sciences would be very useful even if not occupied by economists. (There is precedent for this kind of support for particular areas.)

3. *Facilities in Eastern Europe.* The widely acknowledged success of the Center for Economic Research in Athens (led by Professor Andreas Papandreou) stemmed in part from its ability to provide support for the part-time scholar who spends only a year — at times even less — in Greece. A much more limited version of the Center is presently operating in Yugoslavia and is not beyond the realm of possibility for some other countries.

4. *A data census of materials.* This would be a partial substitute for a center abroad. Essentially the census should provide a clear and easily accessible picture for the non-area specialist as to what kinds of economic studies are feasible with existing data, what research results are available, and perhaps what the prospects are for generating data for various kinds of studies.

5. *Research funding.* A national committee (in which economists dominate, but the nonacademic economists-noneconomists clientele is adequately represented) is perhaps the best organizational form for allocation of research funds. Competent people are not going to be coming into the field or making proposals at a rate which can reasonably be supported by a fixed or steadily growing budget. It should be expected that grants will be made irregularly and that on occasion very substantial grants will be desirable. For the full-timers, not only training in the area but also training in economics should be carried out at intervals

throughout a scholar's career and be supported. For part-timers, access to the language will probably not go beyond acquiring a reading knowledge in most cases, but support for this should be assured. Grants covering several years should be possible; for example, an established scholar willing to commit himself to a major synthetic study may well require five years of assured support.

Without systematic and generous support, without the ability of drawing to it fresh talent, without the possibility of imaginatively combining part-time and full-time economic research, the area-focused economic investigations will remain limited in range, and probably also in scope, to the detriment of both area studies and the knowledge of the processes of growth and development in general.

7 / DEMOGRAPHY

Paul Demeny

University of Michigan

I

Demography as a discipline has some apparent common characteristics with the area called East Central and Southeastern Europe which may not appear convincing to a logician but seem real enough to one surveying contributions to the "demography" of that "area": fuzzy boundaries, absence of well-defined contents, and lack of an identity recognized by insiders and outsiders alike. But problems of precisely delineating disciplines are notoriously insoluble, hence perhaps should not be bothered with excessively. Concerning the notion of an area, the problems of definition for practical purposes are simple since a delineation is usually imposed by current political boundaries and groupings, much to the chagrin of those of us who could think of more imaginative arrangements. Certainly if one would attempt to define Eastern Europe — to use that label for the sake of brevity even if at the further expense of precision — in demographic terms, the demographic boundaries would not coincide with the political ones. But this is merely the conventional complaint of the purist. In a more positive vain, one might add that neither would they differ too much. J. Hajnal in a recent essay [1] suggests that to separate East from West one may draw a straight line between Trieste and Leningrad: a solution as good as any, and a great deal simpler than most. At first look the straight line does not seem to coincide very well with the political boundaries, but actually Hajnal's

I am indebted to a number of professional colleagues, in particular to Dr. James W. Brackett of the Agency for International Development, Department of State, and to Dr. Karol Krótki of the Dominion Bureau of Statistics, for their valuable comments on an earlier version of this paper.

1. "European Marriage Patterns in Historical Perspective," in D. V. Glass and D. E. C. Eversley, eds., *Population in History* (Chicago: Aldine, 1965).

criterion is more flexible than the ruler. It is to follow the deep dividing line that separates geographically the Western European pattern of nuptiality — a historically unique pattern characterized by late and far from universal marriage — from the non-Western one in which marriage is early and quasi-universal. If the borders between East and West would be so drawn, apart from minor qualifications, only the Slovenes and the Czechs would fall outside the present political definition, and of course the East Germans.

It is worth pausing for a moment at the above example of a possible demographic definition of what constitutes East. If the example suggests that political Eastern Europe constitutes a fairly meaningful grouping in nonpolitical terms as well, it drives home other lessons too. It cautions against circumscribing too narrowly what demography should be about and illustrates the point that students of other disciplines can remain uninformed about demographic measurement techniques often only at their own peril. How to measure whether marriage at any given place is "early" or "late" sounds like a rather simple matter, but appearances are deceptive. Also, differential behavior with respect to nuptiality could be only too easily overlooked since such a difference is no longer strikingly manifest: Western Europe has abandoned much of its peculiar behavior in the last two decades or so. But past differences might not be less relevant: for example, with respect to marriage, an East-West cleavage has existed for centuries and the imprints of such a long-lasting difference in the fundamental conditions of people's lives are likely to be with us for a long time to come. As Hajnal speculates, a great deal more may be involved than the fact that with the Western pattern went much lower death and birth rates than those experienced in the East. Other connections may be less obvious but nevertheless just as real. What are the implications of the fact that a Western European peasant spent, say, an average of five more years in early adulthood free from the responsibility to support a family than did his Eastern counterpart? For instance, how did it affect skill development, innovation, aspiration levels? How did it affect saving behavior and what did it imply on the level of demand for goods other than basic necessities? A student of differences in East-West patterns of economic development could hardly ignore such questions and neither should demographers.

Nevertheless, to broaden this survey sufficiently so as to encompass writings on all questions that have an obvious connection with demographic phenomena would encroach too much upon fields that others would consider the proper domain of economics, history, sociology, or some other discipline. A restriction on the definition of demography is, after all, called for. In a narrow interpretation, demography is simply the study of quantitative aspects of human populations, or, more specifically, it is a discipline limited to the description and analysis of the state and evolution of human aggregates in terms of their size, territorial distribution, and composition as shaped by such factors as mortality, fertility, and migration. Such is the definition which will restrict the scope of the literature to be surveyed in this paper.

It should be observed that our definition does not imply that the focus of demography is necessarily on the population of some particular geographical area as such: in fact much of the work carried out by demographers is in the field of formal demography, which aims at establishing mathematical formulations of the relations among general demographic processes. Thus, for example, the outstanding early American contribution to demography, that of Lotka, was a highly abstract and general theory of self-renewing aggregates. Even purely descriptive demographic work is more often oriented toward problems than concerned with geographic areas, although the necessity to work with data that relate to specific populations makes this distinction somewhat blurred. It may be noted, finally, that area research in demography always had an extremely strong gravitation toward the home territory, since it is in most instances natural that production and analysis of data be merely different stages of the same operation, carried out under the same agencies, and often by the same persons.

The foregoing remarks, quite apart from the fact that only a very small number of scholars were working in demography before World War II, would go far to explain the paucity of early American work on Eastern European populations. Nevertheless, two important contributions date from the period prior to 1941 — contributions that remain required readings for a student of Eastern European demography. One is the monumental two-volume work on international migration edited by Walter Wilcox[2] which constitutes a still unsurpassed compilation and analysis of national statistics of immigration and emigration up to the mid-1920s. The other is R. R. Kuczynski's famous study on the levels and trends of fertility and reproduction in Europe. The second volume of this work[3] is largely devoted to the Eastern part of the Continent and contains a wealth of material from early statistical sources

2. *International Migrations*, vol. 1, *Statistics*, with Introduction and Notes by Imre Ferenczi; vol. 2, *Interpretations* (New York: National Bureau of Economic Research, 1929, 1931). Of special relevance to Eastern Europe are the contributions to volume 2 by Gustav Thirring, V. V. Obolensky-Ossinsky, Liebman Hersch, and Felix Klezl.

3. *The Balance of Births and Deaths*, vol. 2, *Eastern and Southern Europe* (Washington, D.C.: Brookings Institution, 1931).

many of them obtained from previously unpublished materials. Despite its technical details, Kuczynski's book has become the work on demography which was perhaps the most widely known to laymen before World War II and has done much to arouse general interest in population problems, particularly in the decline of fertility and its presumed long-run implications in Europe.

It is interesting to note that these early contributions were made possible by factors that in later years were to explain a significant part of the rapid and successful development and international impact of American demographic research. First, there was the support of a foundation, in Kuczynski's case the Brookings Institution, which recognized the value of a work on an inadequately charted field. Second, with the migration study, there was the cooperation of independent scholars with an international agency (the International Labour Office) as well as the concerted contribution by a variety of experts backed by a large American research organization (the National Bureau of Economic Research). Third, both projects cut across national boundaries, thus avoiding the narrow national focus that characterizes an even larger part of the research output in demography than is the case in other disciplines.

All these three factors were present in the genesis of the four important volumes commissioned by the League of Nations and written under the aegis of the Office of Population Research [4] at Princeton University during the early 1940s. Two of these volumes are studies of some topics in the demography of the whole of Europe, including much emphasis on the Eastern European area. The better part of another volume is entirely on Eastern Europe, while a fourth, by Frank Lorimer, is on the population of the Soviet Union. The appearance of the last two volumes in this series in the year following the end of the war (still as publications of the League) makes 1946 a natural dividing line between the classic and the contemporary periods in American demography. Completed during the war, the effort of the first study,[5] which sought to extrapolate past trends into the future, could not have been successful as a prediction but represented important methodologi-

4. The office of Population Research, jointly with the Population Association of America, publishes *Population Index*, a bibliographical quarterly with exhaustive international coverage on scholarly writings and official publications in the field of demography. Its thorough geographical indexes offer the easiest approach for a survey of works concerning the demography of Eastern Europe, or of any particular country of that area, published in the last three decades. It includes works written in the local languages.

5. Frank W. Notestein, Irene B. Taeuber, Dudley Kirk, Ansley J. Coale, and Louise K. Kiser, *The Future Population of Europe and the Soviet Union* (Geneva: League of Nations, 1944).

cal advances. Wilbert Moore's well-known study on the economic demography of Eastern Europe[6] was also overtaken by events but remains indispensable reading for an understanding of the background of debates on agrarian overpopulation in Eastern Europe. The picture in Dudley Kirk's book[7] on the comparative demographic patterns in interwar Europe has also rapidly faded into history in the wake of the war, partly because the reversal of the fertility decline in the West and its qualified continuation in the East has changed the relative balances of births and deaths, and partly because there were heavy losses of population, massive population transfers, and much redrawing of frontiers in the East. However, the book remains the standard work of reference on Europe's population in the interwar years in general, and the only systematic comparative treatment of the demography of Eastern Europe in particular.

II

To describe and analyze the cataclysmic effects of World War II and its aftermath on the demography of Eastern Europe was an obvious prime task of demographic research in the postwar years. Widely conflicting estimates on the size of war losses that gained quick currency had to be checked and evaluated. From diverse sources of uneven quality, demographic changes of vast long-run historical, political, and cultural consequences had to be recorded and painstakingly analyzed. The German expansion toward the East that has sent successive waves of migrants to Eastern Europe since the eleventh century has been nullified within the fraction of a decade by the huge westward refugee movement in the last years of the war and then by mass expulsions during the years following. There was a tragic decline in the size of the Jewish population of Eastern Europe. There was a vast Slavic migration toward the West as Poland gained or regained territories previously German and as Poles withdrew from former eastern provinces to be replaced by Russians and Ukrainians. Other unilateral transfers or exchanges of population, mostly forced, have greatly accelerated and in some instances completed the earlier historical trends toward ethnic homogeneity within the countries of Eastern Europe.

The documentation of such events with objectivity shortly after their occurrence is not an easy task, particularly for researchers in close

---

6. Wilbert E. Moore, *Economic Demography of Eastern and Southern Europe* (Geneva: League of Nations, 1945). For an earlier and briefer formulation, see *idem*, "Agricultural Population and Rural Economy in Eastern and Southern Europe," in *Demographic Studies of Selected Areas of Rapid Growth* (New York: Milbank Memorial Fund, 1944).

7. *Europe's Population in the Interwar Years* (Geneva: League of Nations, 1946).

geographic proximity. American research, including European scholarly work made possible by American research facilities or outlets for publication, had an obvious advantage in this field which is well reflected in the existing literature on the subject. The most ambitious work on the demographic effects of the war and on the related migratory movements is Eugene Kulischer's. His main contribution [8] presents an analysis of the effects of World War I and of the migrations in the interwar years, as well as the more recent events. The coverage extends to the whole Continent, although the focus is on East and Central Europe. A book-length study by Gregory Frumkin [9] is of purely statistical character, aimed solely at estimating war-induced changes in terms of population sizes and balances. Other works concentrate on particular countries of Eastern Europe, or treat some specific aspects of the demographic consequences of the war, while some studies, even though not written by professional demographers, include voluminous demographic materials.[10] Discussion of war losses, refugee movements, and related matters are of course usually included in lesser or greater detail in most general works (to be referred to in subsequent paragraphs) that discuss demographic evolution in Eastern Europe or in its constituting lands.

Demography, in the original sense of "description of people," has a core area well recognized by anyone who has ever looked up more than one general report put out by a statistical agency or research organization on some "population," be that the population of the Grand Duchy of Luxembourg or of the Canadians living in the United States. Chapter follows chapter in orderly succession on size, distribution, age-sex structure, religious composition, and on a host of similar topics, all generously interspersed with statistical tables and lengthy technical foot-

8. *Europe on the Move: War and Population Changes, 1914–47* (New York: Columbia University Press, 1948). See also *idem*, "Population Changes behind the Iron Curtain," *Annals of the American Academy of Political and Social Science*, vol. 271 (September, 1950): 100–111.

9. *Population Changes in Europe since 1939* (New York: Augustus M. Kelley, 1951).

10. Stefan Szulc, "Demographic Changes in Poland: War and Postwar," *Population Index*, vol. 13 (January, 1947); Leszek Kosinski, "Demographic Problems of the Polish Western and Northern Territories," in Norman J. G. Pounds, ed., *Geographical Essays on Eastern Europe*, Indiana University Publications, Russian and East European Series, vol. 24 (Bloomington, 1961), pp. 28–53; J. A. Steers, "The Middle People: Resettlement in Czechoslovakia," *Geographical Journal*, vol. 112 (January, 1949); Radomír Luža, *The Transfer of the Sudeten Germans* (New York: New York University Press, 1964); Joseph B. Schechtman, *European Population Transfers, 1939–1945* (New York: Oxford University Press, 1946); *idem*, *Postwar Population Transfers in Europe* (Philadelphia: University of Pennsylvania Press, 1962); Malcolm J. Proudfoot, *European Refugees, 1939–52: A Study in Forced Population Movement* (Evanston, Ill.: Northwestern University Press, 1956).

notes explaining why the figures in those tables show something else than what they are supposed to show. Inevitably, the casual reader will be tempted to see in some of the topics covered not much more than another example of the proverbial curiosity of statisticians. The fact remains, however, that there is a steadily growing demand for all kinds of demographic information by all kinds of people, and chances are that our reader himself will have picked up the report in search for some specific information—only to find that the data he is seeking are not available.

As a by-product of the postwar political transformation, a grotesquely strict policy of statistical secrecy has been adopted by the new regimes of Eastern Europe, including secrecy on demographic information. Censuses were still taken, vital statistics collected and analyzed, but the results were not for the public and much less for foreign consumption. Since the steady flow of data dried out precisely when interest in those data outside Eastern Europe suddenly increased (not exactly as a coincidence, to be sure), it was inevitable that Western researchers should try to fill the statistical void. Projects seeking to put together a mosaic from the fragments of miscellaneous new information available were set up to study the demography of various Eastern European states. Statistical pronouncements dropped by political potentates in holiday speeches (almost invariably in percentage form only) and figures that somehow got published in popular weeklies for women came under equally close scrutiny. Effective work with sources of this sort requires the expenditure of a large amount of energy, skill, and analytical talent, superior research facilities, and a sizable organization.

By the mid-1950s a commanding lead in research on the Eastern European area in this special field was taken by the U.S. Bureau of the Census, in particular by its Foreign Demographic Analysis Division (formerly Foreign Manpower Research Office). The results of the research efforts undertaken by this organization can be classified into three groups. The first and most important among these from the point of interest of this summary review are the four monographs written on the population of Czechoslovakia,[11] Poland,[12] Yugoslavia,[13] and Hungary.[14] As work on

11. U.S. Bureau of the Census, *The Population of Czechoslovakia*, by Waller Wynne, Jr., International Population Statistics Reports, Series P-90, no. 3 (Washington: Government Printing Office, 1953).
12. U.S. Bureau of the Census, *The Population of Poland*, by W. Parker Mauldin and Donald S. Akers, International Population Statistics Reports, Series P-90, no. 4 (Washington: Government Printing Office, 1954).
13. U.S. Bureau of the Census, *The Population of Yugoslavia*, by Paul F. Myers and Arthur A. Campbell, International Population Statistics Reports, Series P-90, no. 5 (Washington: Government Printing Office, 1954).
14. U.S. Bureau of the Census, *The Population of Hungary*, by Jacob S. Siegel,

these projects progressed, official secrecy on statistics was gradually relaxed in Eastern Europe and it was possible to build into these studies more "solid" material than could be envisaged at the outset. By and large, however, these monographs, particularly those for Czechoslovakia and Poland, are monuments to statistical ingenuity that achieved very good results from very little material, as was proven in the late 1950s when data were again freely available from official Eastern European sources. They remain important reference works for students of the countries concerned.

A second and more recent set of monographs is the result of projects on the labor force of Czechoslovakia, Romania, Bulgaria, and Hungary. The primary orientation of these projects was economic, but each monograph contains much demographic information and analysis of a general interest.[15]

Finally, a third line of research carried out at the Bureau of the Census has concentrated on the preparation of population projections for individual countries of Communist Eastern Europe. The earlier projections were recently updated and brought together in a single report.[16] Unpublished computer printouts in great detail (e.g., single-year age distributions up to 1990 for each country under various assumptions concerning future fertility and mortality) are available to interested researchers at the Bureau of the Census.

Apart from the monographs referred to in the preceding paragraphs, several shorter American studies on various aspects of Eastern European demography may be cited from recent years. A lucid summary of demographic changes in Eastern Europe in the postwar period by Jerry Combs draws on the work carried out at the U.S. Bureau of the Cen-

International Population Statistics Reports, Series P-90, no. 9 (Washington: Government Printing Office, 1958).

15. U.S. Bureau of the Census, *The Labor Force of the Soviet Zone of Germany and the Soviet Sector of Berlin,* by Samuel Baum and Jerry W. Combs, Jr., International Population Statistics Reports, Series P-90, no. 11 (Washington: Government Printing Office, 1959). Other reports in the same series: *The Labor Force of Czechoslovakia,* by James N. Ypsilantis (no. 13, 1960); *The Labor Force of Rumania,* by Samuel Baum (no. 14, 1961); *The Labor Force of Bulgaria,* by Zora Prochazka (no. 16, 1962); and *The Labor Force of Hungary,* by Samuel Baum (No. 18, 1962).

16. U.S. Bureau of the Census, *Projections of the Population of the Communist Countries of Eastern Europe, by Age and Sex: 1965–1985,* by James L. Scott, International Population Reports, Series P-91, no. 14 (Washington: Government Printing Office, 1965). The earlier reports published in the same series were for Poland (no. 6, 1958); for Hungary (no. 7, 1958); for Bulgaria (no. 8, 1959); for Czechoslovakia (no. 9, 1959); for Romania (no. 10, 1960); and for East Germany (no. 11, 1960). The report first quoted (no. 14) includes projections also for Albania and Yugoslavia.

sus.[17] A discussion of population and related labor force problems is offered in a book by Wolfgang Stolper.[18] A paper by Gwendolyn Johnson affords useful comparisons of fertility in Eastern and Western Europe.[19] Dorothy Good's study places recent fertility trends in Hungary into historical perspective.[20] However, some countries of Eastern Europe, notably Albania, Greece, and European Turkey, are not adequately covered, and those who seek up-to-date general information and data on special topics must usually be referred to non-American studies.[21] Specialized literature on recent international migration of the classical variety is also scanty, but this reflects the relatively minor importance of this factor in all countries of Eastern Europe, with the notable exception of Greece.[22]

The demographic picture that emerges from contemporary studies of Europe is often in striking contrast to historic patterns. In no other

17. "Demographic Changes in Eastern Europe," in *Population Trends in Eastern Europe, the USSR, and Mainland China* (New York: Milbank Memorial Fund, 1960).

18. *The Structure of the East German Economy* (Cambridge: Harvard University Press, 1960), especially chap. 1.

19. "Differential Fertility in European Countries," in Universities–National Bureau Committee for Economic Research, *Demographic and Economic Change in Developed Countries* (Princeton: Princeton University Press, 1960).

20. "Some Aspects of Fertility Change in Hungary," *Population Index*, vol. 30 (April, 1964): 137–71.

21. For a discussion of the demographic situation in Albania, see Jaho Dibra and Pasko Vako, "La population de l'Albanie d'après les rescensements de 1955 à 1960," *Population* (Paris), 20 (March–April, 1965): 253–64. An overview of demographic trends in Greece is contained in Vasilos G. Valaoras, "Population Profiles as a Means for Reconstructing Demographic Histories" in *International Population Conference Wien 1959* (Vienna: Union internationale pour l'étude scientifique de la population, 1959), pp. 62–72. A marked East-West fertility differential was found to exist in Turkey, fertility in European Turkey occupying an intermediate position between Greece (or Bulgaria) and Anatolia, in Paul Demeny and Frederic C. Shorter, *Estimating Turkish Mortality, Fertility and Age Structure: Application of Some New Techniques* (Istanbul: Institute of Statistics, Faculty of Economics, University of Istanbul, 1968). An excellent and up-to-date comparative study on the demography of Eastern Europe (excluding Greece) can be found in two articles published under the title "La population des pays socialistes européens," in *Population* (Paris), 21 (September–October, 1966): 939–1012; The articles are: Egon Szabady, Kálmán Tekse, and Roland Pressat, "La fécondité" (pp. 941–70); and Chantal Blayo, "Autres aspects de l'évolution démographique" (pp. 971–1012).

22. Cf. Dudley Kirk, "A Survey of Recent Overseas Migration in Relation to Population Pressure in Europe," in *Proceedings of the World Population Conference, 1954*, vol. 2 (New York: United Nations, 1955), pp. 93–104. Notable recent studies on external migration affecting Greece that are readily accessible to American readers are Bernard Kayser, "Nouvelles données sur l'émigration grecque" *Population* (Paris), 19 (August–September, 1964): 707–26; and Xenophon Zolatas, *International Labor Migration and Economic Development* (Athens: Bank of Greece, 1966), especially pt. 2.

respect is the change sharper than in levels of fertility. Few readers of Kuczynski's tables would have anticipated that in the early and mid-1960s the gross reproduction rate would be far above unity in France and below unity in Romania, for instance. Kirk's fertility maps for inter-war Europe, with the shades darkening as one's eyes move from left to right, would look very different if redrawn today. Not surprisingly, in recent years special attention was given to the factors that might provide an explanation of postwar fertility trends in Eastern Europe. Thus, population policies of the various governments were examined at some length and their objectives were discussed.[23] A main instrument of policy were controls over abortions — now made strict and now re-laxed in sometimes puzzling reversals. In the past decade or so, abor-tions were legal in all Communist Eastern Europe with the exception of Albania and East Germany (although substantial changes in such a policy are likely to materialize once again, as is confirmed by recent moves on this matter in several countries, most notably in Romania). Accordingly, the number of abortions was very high in much of Eastern Europe; particularly so in Hungary, where since 1957 their number has exceeded the number of births each year; in some years by more than 50 percent.[24] The decisive role of simple legal-administrative-medical measures in setting the level of fertility, however, may be ques-tioned. It is to be expected, for instance, that even in the absence of a change in population policy, birth rates will stabilize at a somewhat higher level than registered in recent years in the low-fertility regions of the area. Conversely, the longer-run effects of introducing new and stringent restrictions on abortion are likely to be minor. The latter prop-osition, however, may not hold true with respect to a policy aimed at stimulating fertility by economic means. But much further research is needed before more satisfactory answers to these questions can be ar-rived at. Such research, above all, requires the gathering of more basic statistical facts, a task that can be carried out only by the demographers

23. On this subject, see especially: W. Parker Mauldin, "Fertility Control in Communist Countries: Policy and Practice," in *Population Trends in Eastern Eu-rope, the USSR and Mainland China*, pp. 179–215; *idem*, "Population Policies in the Sino-Soviet Bloc," *Law and Contemporary Problems*, 25 (Summer, 1960): 490–507; and James W. Brackett and Earl E. Huyck, "The Objective of Govern-ment Policies on Fertility Control in Eastern Europe," *Population Studies*, 16 (November, 1962): 134–46.

24. Cf. Christopher Tietze and Hans Lehfeldt, "Legal Abortion in Eastern Europe," *Journal of the American Medical Association*, 175 (April, 1961): 1149–54; Christopher Tietze, "The Demographic Significance of Legal Abortions in Eastern Europe," *Demography*, 1 (1964): 119–25; and Andras Klinger, "Abortion Pro-grams," in Bernard Berelson *et al.*, eds., *Family Planning and Population Programs* (Chicago: University of Chicago Press, 1966), pp. 465–76.

of the countries concerned. For instance, until recently practically no quantitative information has existed in any of the European countries on knowledge and attitudes about birth control methods, or on plans and preferences concerning family size. Moves to introduce new data-gathering techniques in demography — in particular, sample surveys — were pioneered and perfected largely by American researchers. Such techniques have now been adopted in Eastern Europe and, in some countries, important advances were made. They will provide a much more solid basis for the analysis of demographic behavior than was available through the traditional methods of observation.[25]

As for the far past, that is so remote that it can no longer be recovered from human memory; obviously no new data will be forthcoming. But the time when exploitation of the already existing data on the demographic history of Eastern European populations will yield sharply diminishing returns is still far away. Even the nineteenth century is uncharted territory for much of the area, although for that period there exists a wealth of material, such as parish registers, that await utilization. In this field, too, much first-rate work has been done already, most notably in Hungary. It is to be hoped that larger resources will be devoted to it in the coming years.[26]

III

Concerning problems related to graduate training, research facilities, and professional exchanges, it appears that the current situation

25. See D. V. Glass, "Family Limitation in Europe: A Survey of Recent Studies," in Clyde V. Kiser, ed., *Research in Family Planning* (Princeton: Princeton University Press, 1962), pp. 231–61. A large collection of papers, mostly by Eastern European demographers, contains several that are relevant in this context. See Egon Szabady, ed., *Studies on Fertility and Social Mobility* (Budapest: Akadémiai Kiadó, 1964). Results of a sample survey on fertility carried out in Greece are reported in V. G. Valaoras, Antonia Polychronopoulou, and Dimitri Trichopoulos, "Control of Family Size in Greece," *Population Studies*, 18 (March, 1965): 265–78.

26. Success in historical research in Eastern European demography largely depends on adoption of research methods already developed, but naturally each area raises new problems for which imaginative new solutions will have to be found. The leading work on utilization of parish registers is French, British, and Canadian. To the analysis of more conventional sources (such as early censuses), technical advances that originated from efforts to correct faults in statistics of contemporary underdeveloped countries are more relevant. On this the American literature is large and cannot be reviewed here. For two works at least partly based on research on Eastern European data, see Vasilos G. Valaoras, "A Reconstruction of the Demographic History of Modern Greece," *Milbank Memorial Fund Quarterly*, vol. 38 (April, 1960); and Ansley J. Coale and Paul Demeny, *Regional Model Life Tables and Stable Populations* (Princeton: Princeton University Press, 1966). In the latter work, a historical mortality pattern is identified that is distinctly East Central European.

is generally satisfactory. This summary will be therefore limited to a few observations on these subjects.

1. A conclusion that emerges from the above survey of past American research in the demography of Eastern Europe is that those who had made notable contributions were invariably demographers in the first place, rather than area specialists. The development of demography as an independent discipline requiring more and more specialized training makes it unlikely that on this score the finding of a similar survey conducted perhaps twenty years from now could be different. In other words, the new achievement on which a future reviewer will be able to report are primarily a function of the quality and scope of current and future training and research in demography in general. There are now some twelve American universities with substantial graduate programs in population studies. Although only a few of these, notably Cornell, Michigan, and Princeton, are now conducting research on Eastern European demography, conditions exist in most other demographic centers as well for expansion into that field. Such an expansion naturally requires that funds to support worthy research proposals become available as such proposals will be forthcoming. While it is to be expected that graduate training in demography will be adequately supported from general sources, area-oriented research in demography in most instances requires funding from agencies interested in the given area, rather than in the discipline per se. It may be noted here that the nature of demographic research is such that although knowledge of the local languages is most valuable in area studies, it is not in general a necessary condition for the ability to make a first-rate contribution.

2. It would be most desirable to expose students specializing in various related disciplines, particularly in economics, history, sociology, and geography, to at least some formal training in demographic analysis. In view of the demographic peculiarities of Eastern Europe, this general point appears to be particularly well taken with respect to researchers, or prospective researchers, on Eastern European problems. Such training need not be, indeed should not be, focused on the demography of Eastern Europe; rather it should aim at developing a "feel" for the field; a sense for orders of magnitude and orders of importance; an awareness of the nature of the basic demographic processes and of the availability and general nature of various analytical techniques and possibilities. In short, it should provide a background which would enable the non-demographer specialist to recognize the presence of problems that call for cooperation with demographers and to take the initiative in establishing such cooperation.

3. As far as teaching programs in population studies are concerned,

there is no need for courses, either graduate or undergraduate, specialized in the demography of Eastern Europe. The best preparation for outstanding work and substantive contributions in that field is provided by intensive training emphasizing formal demography, quantitative analysis, and applied statistics, in combination with thorough general training in a related discipline (economics, history, etc.). Specialization in the Eastern European area in this field should come at the doctoral dissertation level or, and preferably, at an even later point in the professional career. Even then, specialization should remain non-exclusive and/or temporary.

4. Holdings of libraries in basic demographic documents need strengthening throughout the United States. For instance, all important research libraries should acquire full sets of European census for the nineteenth and twentieth centuries as such censuses become available in microfilm or microfiche editions. Acquisition of basic publications in demography, particularly publications containing tabulations of unanalyzed data, should be given adequate support and carried out routinely at all universities with active population programs, even when no immediate demand exists for them on the part of the faculty or staff.

5. It would be desirable to secure financial support that would enable distinguished East European scholars to do postdoctoral work in the field of demography at leading U.S. research institutions and universities.

IV

What should be the main directions of future work in this country on Eastern European population studies? As a general proposition, research in the United States concerning the demography of Eastern Europe should emphasize problem areas in which American scholars enjoy a comparative advantage over their colleagues in the countries concerned. To observe this rule would not only prevent wasteful duplication of effort but in most instances, if not necessarily all, would also serve as the best basis for mutually satisfying cooperation with the expanding number of scientific workers and research institutions in this field in Eastern Europe. It follows from these observations that much of the future American research output on this subject should fit one or more of the categories outlined below.

1. Cross-national studies, that is, studies not limited to a particular country in Eastern Europe. Demographic research, owing to its continued strong dependence on government agencies whose basic function

is the generation and gathering of primary data, is still strongly compartmentalized in Eastern Europe by national boundaries.

2. Interdisciplinary studies, using the skills of experts in various related fields outside the narrowly defined bounds of demography, particularly studies involving cooperation between demographers, on the one hand, and economists, sociologists, and historians, on the other, thus breaking the compartmentalization of research by discipline, still strong in Eastern Europe.

3. Studies applying analytical techniques developed in research not related to Eastern Europe and not yet adequately known there. For instance, advances in demographic estimating techniques based on limited (scanty and/or biased) data have been rapid during the past ten years or so and have opened up a rich new field of application, particularly in historical research.

4. Studies utilizing research skills and tools that are in comparatively abundant supply at American universities and research institutions, notably studies utilizing computer technology and experience with the organization and analysis of large masses of heterogeneous data, for example, by multivariate techniques.

5. Studies that utilize Eastern Europe as a demographic laboratory but whose primary focus is outside that area. For instance, research in the history of Eastern European populations appears to offer the best, and in some respects the only, available testing ground for the validity of various theories of demographic transition on the basis of which future population trends are predicted and population policies are formulated for developing countries of Asia or Latin America.[27]

On a more specific level, the following research areas seem to hold potentially the greatest rewards:

1. Extensive descriptive work, in the narrowest sense of "demography," aimed at establishing long time-series of various population characteristics on a comparable basis — in particular, series that are unaffected by boundary changes. Such statistics would be of great use in various disciplines, in particular in research in the economic history of Eastern Europe.

2. Research in the history of demographic transition (i.e., of the secular decline of fertility and mortality) in Eastern Europe on an area-wide basis. A clarification and a systematic presentation of intercountry differences within the area in the origin, diffusion, timing, speed, and pattern

27. Some of the potentials of historical analysis in this respect are illustrated in Paul Demeny, "Early Fertility Decline in Austria-Hungary: A Lesson in Demographic Transition," *Daedalus*, (Spring, 1968), pp. 502–22.

of these changes would constitute a fundamental contribution to our understanding of Eastern European societies. A second important aspect of such research would be a comparison between Eastern and Western Europe as a whole. Our current knowledge on these topics is spotty and poorly documented, and there are strong indications that in many respects it is also plainly wrong or misleading.

3. A systematic application of new advances in evaluating the quality of demographic statistics, and of the techniques recently developed for adjusting and correcting basic statistical information to demographic data available for Eastern Europe, often uncritically used as valid, would be a worthwhile undertaking.

4. Related to, yet distinct from, the topic just outlined is research in various specific aspects of secular changes in the demographic behavior of Eastern European populations. Thus, for instance, a study of the pattern and of the various social, economic, and cultural correlates of the adoption of family limitation by the Eastern European peasantry could make a contribution to a more rational formulation of population policies in underdeveloped areas. It may be relevant to note in this context that in a number of instances the onset of fertility decline in Croatian, Hungarian, or Romanian peasant populations appears to have preceded the onset of decline in industrializing Western Europe.

5. Either one-country or area-wide studies of the successful solution or of the persistence of the economic problems of rural overpopulation in Eastern Europe could constitute an important contribution to our understanding of fundamental effects of population pressure in agrarian economies. These problems have been studied more extensively with reference to pre–World War II Eastern Europe than is the case for any other area. Despite the growing analogous interest in the economies of underdeveloped countries, little work has been done to evaluate the implications of the recent Eastern European experience. Such evaluation is exceedingly difficult because of the disturbing influence of the simultaneous political transformation in the area, but the task should nevertheless be a rewarding one.

6. Eastern Europe also offers ideal opportunities in research on the economics of population also in a wider sense, since it presents demographic extremes in the world in several important ways — for example, with respect to the lowest level of fertility attained in any country (Hungary); with respect to extremely distorted age and sex distribution (East Germany); with respect to an unusual combination of very low fertility with high rates of emigration (Greece); with respect to lagging decline of fertility in Europe (Albania, Poland); etc.

7. Eastern Europe represents a uniquely extreme case within Europe

of achieving very low levels of fertility through legalized abortion. Further studies on sociological and public health aspects of this phenomenon would be most desirable.

8. A definitive study of population policies adopted in postwar Eastern Europe, in particular a study of the frequent changes of these policies in relation to the underlying ideological and socioeconomic factors that explain the changes, would make an illuminating chapter in the recent political and intellectual history of the area.

8/ GEOGRAPHY

George W. Hoffman

University of Texas

INTRODUCTION

Perhaps it will be useful in the introduction briefly to define in geographic terms the area under consideration as well as the use of the various names given to this area. Geographers have always hesitated to link the studies of the Soviet landscape with those of the region variously called Eastern Europe, East Central Europe or Mid-Europe, and the Balkans or Southeast Europe. It must be said, however, that since World War II — for university administrative reasons — the study of the Soviet Union and the countries of East Central and Southeast Europe have been combined in teaching more often than they have been separated.

The area between Central Europe and the Soviet Union,[1] bordered by three seas, includes seven countries (Poland, Czechoslovakia, Hungary, Romania, Yugoslavia, Bulgaria, and Albania) and is usually arbitrarily grouped because of its location in relation to other areas within Europe. (For the purpose of this study, East Germany, Greece, and European Turkey are included.) To geographers the specific character

Appreciation is extended to Professors Chauncy D. Harris, H. Louis Kostanick, and Robert Taaffe for critically reviewing my preliminary report. The final product is a greatly improved version largely due to their effort. Jack C. Fisher of Wayne State University and Jack L. Romanovsky of the University of Washington, Seattle, have provided me with certain basic background material. With due regard to the many colleagues who provided me with important source material or who critically reviewed my preliminary report, I take full responsibility for the final product which, it is hoped, presents to the profession as well as to all other interested colleagues, foundations, and government agencies a picture of increased geographic work in the area, as well as the problems and needs.

1. Parts of this discussion are taken from George W. Hoffman, "Eastern Europe," in *A Geography of Europe*, George W. Hoffman, ed., 3d ed. (New York: Ronald Press Co., 1969).

199

of this area has often been underlined. Sir Halford Mackinder spoke of the importance of the "tier of independent states between Germany and Russia." [2] Moodie referred to the fact that this 500-mile–wide thoroughfare has been essential for the "movements of peoples, goods and ideas between the Russian realm, on the one hand, and Central and Western Europe, on the other." [3] Hoffman stressed that "location is paramount in any explanation of the importance of this region. . . . Eastern Europe is an area of transition, instability, and diversification and this is clearly expressed in its physical as well as its cultural-political characteristics." [4]

Geographers, like other scholars, have used many different names for this area and the exact grouping of countries included also has varied in the standard textbooks in the English language and in monographic publications. [5] Professor Charles Jelavich, in his report, "Graduate Training and Research Needs," presents some thoughts about the unity of the area after consulting with many scholars (see pp. 3–7). The conclusions he derived after an exhausting study can apply to geographers only with some modifications. East Central Europe, a term which is being used more and more often, would include Poland and Czechoslovakia

2. *Democratic Ideals and Reality* (New York: Henry Holt & Co., 1919, 1942), pp. 158 ff.
3. Arthur E. Moodie, *The Changing World* (Yonkers, N.Y.: World Book Co., 1956), p. 111.
4. Hoffman, "Eastern Europe," p. 432.
5. Pierre Deffontaines, ed., *Larousse Encyclopedia of Geography — Europe* (New York: Prometheus, 1961): *Central Europe*: Czechoslovakia, Poland, Hungary, Romania, Bulgaria and the Alps, Switzerland, Liechtenstein, Austria and Germany; *Mediterranean Europe*: Yugoslavia, Albania, Greece and the other Mediterranean countries; Jean Gottmann, *A Geography of Europe*, 3d ed. (New York: Henry Holt & Co., 1962): *Central Europe*: Poland, Czechoslovakia, Hungary and Romania and Finland, Germany, Austria; *Mediterranean Europe*: Yugoslavia, Albania, Greece, European Turkey and the other Mediterranean countries; *Eastern Europe*: Soviet Union; George W. Hoffman, ed. *A Geography of Europe*, 3d ed. (New York: Ronald Press Co., 1969): *Eastern Europe*: Poland, Czechoslovakia, Hungary, Romania, Bulgaria, Yugoslavia and Albania, *Southern Europe*: Greece, and the other countries of Southern Europe; Norman J. G. Pounds, *Europe and the Soviet Union*, 2d ed. (New York: McGraw-Hill Book Co., 1966): *Central Europe*: Poland, Czechoslovakia, Germany, Austria and Switzerland; *Southeastern Europe*: Hungary, Romania, Yugoslavia, Bulgaria, Albania; *Mediterranean Europe*: Greece and the other countries of Mediterranean Europe; Margaret R. Shackleton (W. Gordon East, rev.), *Europe: A Regional Geography* (New York: F. A. Praeger, 1966): *Central Europe*: Poland, Czechoslovakia and Germany, Switzerland, Austria; *South-Central Europe*: Romania, Yugoslavia, Albania, Bulgaria, Turkey in Europe, and Northern Greece (Macedonia and Thrace). As far as *books on the area* are concerned, only a few have appeared thus far: Alice F. A. Mutton, *Central Europe* (London: Longmans, Green, 1961). Includes Czechoslovakia. R. H. Osborne, *East-Central Europe* (New York: F. A. Praeger, 1967). Includes all seven countries, excluding Greece and Turkey-in-Europe.

(it may also include Germany, Austria, and Switzerland) and a good case can also be made for including Hungary or to allocate it to Southeastern Europe — but not Southern Europe. The latter would include Greece and European Turkey. The term "Balkan" is unacceptable to geographers.[6] The division suggested by Professor Jelavich of the "Habsburg Lands" is largely a historical one and has little meaning for geographers.

All this points to the problem of assigning one or even more names, and the countries to be included in this transitional and diverse area. One fact stands out in these interdisciplinary discussions. The definition of this area inevitably raises questions concerning the specific emphasis with which individual scholars and universities approach the problems.

MAIN CURRENTS OF EAST EUROPEAN GEOGRAPHIC WORK

The "state of the art" of geography in East Central and Southeast Europe studies leaves a great deal to be desired, as can be seen from the following discussion. Work in Eastern European studies is carried on by few American geographers, though it can be stated that the number is slowly increasing. The reasons for such a long-term neglect of the field lie in the peculiarities of the area itself and the few rewards resulting from scholarly attainment.

Thorough knowledge of the whole area by an individual is literally beyond the realm of possibility. Knowledge even of one country presupposes not only training as a geographer but also a thorough understanding of the history, the economics, the social structure, the political organization and, above all, the languages of the individual country (in many cases more than one), including one or two of the most common European languages (German, French, or Russian). A geographer familiar with several countries is expected to have a proficiency in several languages and must have traveled extensively throughout the entire region. Another problem results from the difficulty in obtaining sufficient documentary sources, including statistical material reliable enough for work concerning administrative subregions. Until recently, thorough field research was impossible with the exception perhaps of Greece, Yugoslavia, and, to a lesser extent, Poland.

Encouragement by foundations, government agencies, and university administrators in terms of commitment to long-range programs of Eastern European studies is needed in view of the extraordinary difficulties

---

6. George W. Hoffman, *The Balkans in Transition*, Searchlight book no. 20 (Princeton: D. Van Nostrand Co., 1963), pp. 11–12.

of scholarship in this area. Hardly any departments of geography employ persons who are primarily East European specialists. The postwar tie between Soviet and East European studies has been most detrimental to specialization by undergraduate and graduate students and younger instructors in one of the countries or a combination of countries within the region's subdivisions (East Central and Southeast). This is a complex area and must be studied as a special unit. As a result of these difficulties, the study of the area on the undergraduate and graduate level has been largely neglected and the number of students specializing in the area is dismayingly small.

Scholarly output is confined to a few American geographers, though with increased opportunities for fieldwork and the increased availability of travel funds provided by foundations and government agencies the picture has improved. Geographic work in the area has been strengthened by a close association with interdisciplinary programs, and it is here that geographers thoroughly trained as regional specialists can make the most important contribution. A recent working paper prepared by W. A. Hance and G. G. Weigend for the Commission on College Geography, Panel on Interdisciplinary Cooperation, stresses this important relationship and makes some very significant observations:

> Most regional institutes are not interested in hiring geographers simply to have geography represented in their interdisciplinary program; some are even poorly informed regarding the contribution which geography can make. They are interested, however, in aggregating a group of qualified and recognized specialists from a variety of fields including geography. Geography's failure to be more widely represented in these programs reflects on us more than on the lack of understanding of persons from other disciplines. We must encourage geographers to become real experts in the various foreign areas, which probably means that we must ary in the past. We need greater sophistication in geographic permit them to concentrate on fewer areas than has been customstudies, greater emphasis upon the dynamic rather than the static, a focus upon analysis rather than description.

SCHOLARLY PUBLICATIONS BY AMERICAN GEOGRAPHERS

From the above introduction it is obvious that the total number of geographers writing on Eastern Europe is small indeed when compared with geographic contributions in other key areas of the world. Poland, Yugoslavia, and Greece are the only countries where, until recently, extensive fieldwork was possible. More than three-fourths of the articles and books published by American geographers (or those permanently teaching at American universities) are contributions from four scholars — Jack C. Fisher, George W. Hoffman, H. Louis Kostanick, and Norman J. G. Pounds — only two of whom wrote a dissertation on the area. It must immediately be added that this proportion will be changed in the near future as fieldwork opportunities and financial aid for research increasingly become available. A few of the prewar generation of American geographers have written on problems of the area, largely concentrating their research on Poland, but their work was less as regional specialists than for comparative purposes. While at the present time American geographic publications on East Central and Southeast Europe are confined to an all too small group of members of the profession, an increasing number of publications are added to the geographic literature by regional specialists and those using the problems of the region for comparative purposes.

Perhaps it would be useful to discuss the major scholarly publications by American geographers, presenting a picture of regional spread and topical interests.

Among the earliest contributions by American geographers were the studies in the 1930s by the dean of political geography, Richard Hartshorne, dealing with the political and industrial geography of Upper Silesia,[7] and by Eugene Van Cleef on "Danzig and Gdynia."[8] On the margin between academic scholarship and travel account are the two contributions by Louis A. Boyd on Poland, published in the mid-1930s by the American Geographical Society.[9]

General regional discussions, usually chapters in regionally oriented textbooks primarily designed for college use, for the most part are descriptive and are organized in the traditional manner.[10] Gottmann devotes 86 pages to the geography of the individual East European countries; Hoffman contains the most detailed discussions of any college textbook in English, devoting nearly 100 pages to the region; Pounds' discussion contains 68 pages. H. Louis Kostanick's chapter on "Geo-

7. "The Polish Corridor," *Journal of Geography*, 36 (May, 1937): 161–76; "The Upper Silesian Industrial District," *Geographical Review*, 24 (1934): 423–38, and "Geographic and Political Boundaries in Upper Silesia," *Annals of the Association of American Geographers*, 23 (December, 1933): 195–228.

8. "Danzig and Gdynia," *Geographical Review*, 23 (January, 1933): 101–7.

9. *Polish Countryside*, photographs and narrative, with a contribution by Stanislaw Gordzuchowski, American Geographical Society, Special Publication no. 20 (New York, 1937), and "The Marshes of Pinski," *Geographical Review*, 26 (1936): 376–95.

10. Gottmann, *A Geography of Europe*; Hoffman, *A Geography of Europe*; and Pounds, *Europe and the Soviet Union*.

politics of the Balkans"[11] contains a problem-oriented survey as an introduction to the book edited by Charles and Barbara Jelavich, *The Balkans in Transition.*

A number of recent substantial scholarly contributions have added to the otherwise scant bibliography of the area. A unique contribution is Jacques May's [12] on *The Ecology of Malnutrition in Five Countries of Eastern and Central Europe,* studies in a series on Medical Geography, and George W. Hoffman and Fred Warner Neal, *Yugoslavia and the New Communism.*[13] In the latter, a geographer and a political scientist collaborated to analyze the political and economic changes in Yugoslavia since World War II.

The number and quality of scholarly articles on the area by American geographers has been increasing slowly during the last ten years. Here again Poland and Yugoslavia receive by far the greatest attention. *Geographical Essays on Eastern Europe,* edited by Norman Pounds,[14] is the only exclusive publication in the English language devoted to a series of geographical problems of Eastern Europe. It was published as an outgrowth of a symposium on Eastern Europe, organized by George W. Hoffman and held at the annual meeting of the Association of American Geographers in Dallas in 1960. The monograph contains papers by four European geographers and Pounds on the land use on the Hungarian Plain and by Hoffman on the changes in agriculture in Yugoslavia.

Norman Pounds, besides co-editing a book on Eastern Europe, authoring a political geography on Poland, a regional study in Upper Silesia, and a forthcoming book on Eastern Europe, has four contribu-

11. In *The Balkans in Transition,* Charles and Barbara Jelavich, eds. (Berkeley and Los Angeles: University of California Press, 1963).

12. (New York and London: Hafner Publishing Co., 1963.) Also, their *The Ecology of Malnutrition in Central and Southeastern Europe,* "Studies in Medical Geography," vol. 6 (New York: Hafner Publishing Co., 1966).

13. George W. Hoffman and Fred Warner Neal, *Yugoslavia and the New Communism* (New York: Twentieth Century Fund, 1962).

14. Norman J. G. Pounds, ed., *Geographical Essays on Eastern Europe,* Indiana University Publications, Russian and East European Series, vol. 24 (Bloomington, 1961); Norman J. G. Pounds and Nicolas Spulber, eds., *Resources and Planning in Eastern Europe,* Indiana University Publications, Slavic and East European Series, vol. 4 (Bloomington, 1957); Norman J. G. Pounds, *Poland between East and West,* Searchlight book no. 22 (Princeton: D. Van Nostrand Co., 1964); *The Upper Silesian Industrial Region,* Indiana University Publications, Slavic and East European Series, vol. 11 (Bloomington, 1962); *Eastern Europe* (London: Longmans, Green, 1968); "The Industrial Geography of Modern Poland," *Economic Geography,* 36 (1960): 24–40; "Planning in the Upper Silesian Industrial Region," *Journal of Central European Affairs,* 18 (1958–59): 409–22; "Nowa Huta: A New Polish Iron and Steel Works," *Geography,* 43 (1958): 54–61; "The Spread of Mining in the Coal Basin of Upper Silesia and Northern Moravia," *Annals of the Association of American Geographers,* 48 (1958): 149–63.

tions on aspects of the changing industrial geography of Poland (see footnote 14). Hoffman, in addition to contributions on Eastern Europe as a whole, concentrates his research on the countries of Southeast Europe.[15] His main concern has been with Yugoslavia as a country and with the impact of its various socioeconomic changes. Recently he expanded his work to include studies on comparative socioeconomic developments in Southeast Europe.[16] Kostanick published a study in depth of the "Resettlement of Bulgarian Turks in Turkey" in the early postwar period, but most of his recent studies deal with various effects of the political geography on individual countries in Eastern Europe.[17] Of the more recently trained geographers, work by Jack C. Fisher on the analysis of spatial planning in Eastern Europe and the contributions of geography to planning in Eastern Europe should be cited. Fisher's dissertation dealt with historical urban geography of selected Yugoslav cities and the impact that planning in the postwar period had on traditional urban patterns. Subsequent to the completion of his dis-

15. *On Eastern Europe as a whole*: George W. Hoffman, "Eastern Europe," in *A Geography of Europe* (see note 1, above); "The Political Geographic Bases of the Austrian Nationality Problem," *Austrian History Yearbook*, 3 (1967): 120–46; "Eastern Europe: A Study in Political Geography," *Texas Quarterly*, 2 (Autumn, 1959): 57–88; "The Shatter-Belt in Relation to the East-West Conflict," *Journal of Geography*, 51 (October, 1952): 266–75; *On Southeast Europe*: George W. Hoffman, "Die Unwandlung der landwirtschaftlichen Siedlungen und der Landwirtschaft in Bulgarien," *Geographische Rundschau*, 17 (September, 1965): 352–61; "Problems of Agricultural Change in Southeast Europe," *Geographical Review*, 55 (July, 1965), notes, pp. 428–31; "Transformation of Rural Settlement in Bulgaria," *Geographical Review*, 54 (January, 1964): 45–64; "Die Agrarentwicklung der Vojvodina seit 1945," *Wissenschaftlicher Dienst Südosteuropa*, 12 (1963): 123–30; "The Changes in the Agricultural Geography of Yugoslavia," *Geographical Essays on Eastern Europe*, Norman J. G. Pounds, ed., Indiana University Publications, Russia and East European Series, vol. 24 (Bloomington, 1961): 101–40; "Yugoslavia: Changing Character of Rural Life and Rural Economy," *American Slavic and East European Review*, 18 (December, 1959): 555–78; "Yugoslavia in Transition: Industrial Expansion and Resource Base," *Economic Geography*, 33 (October, 1956): 294–315.

16. "The Problem of the Underdeveloped Regions in Southeast Europe: A Comparative Analysis of Romania, Yugoslavia and Greece," *Annals of the Association of American Geographers*, 57 (December, 1967): 637–66 and, "Thessaloniki, The Impact of a Changing Hinterland," *East European Quarterly*, 2 (March, 1968): 1–28.

17. "The Resettlement of Bulgarian Turks in Turkey, 1950–53," *University of California Publications in Geography*, 8 (1957): 65–164; "Poland: Geography for Disaster," *Current History*, 36 (April, 1959): 205–9; "Eastern Europe – Retrospect and Prospect," *Yearbook of the Association of Pacific Coast Geographers*, 19 (1957): 5–12; "Postwar Population Shifts in Poland," *Bulletin of the California Council of Geography Teachers*, 5 (1957–58): 2–6; "American Aid in East-Central Europe," *Current History*, 33 (July, 1957): 1–6. Mention should also be made of Kostanick's "Macedonia: A Study in Political Geography" (Ph.D. diss., Clark University, Worcester, Mass., 1947).

sertation, the City Planning Commission of Zagreb published an atlas of the historical geography of the city which had been collected and compiled by Fisher. A more detailed urban analysis on Zagreb was published in the *Annals of the Association of American Geographers*.[18] In other studies, Fisher analyzes the role of political decisions on agricultural change, the ideology and political motivation on East European postwar urban development (with major examples from Yugoslavia), and the changing role of the basic Yugoslav territorial unit — the commune — from the early days of Yugoslavia's postwar development to the 1963 Constitution. In 1966 Fisher published a book in which he is concerned with an evaluation of the impact of interrelationship between administrative policy and organization on regional and urban developments. This theme was discussed in a detailed quantitative analysis of Yugoslav cities and communes in *Yugoslavia: A Multinational State.* Finally, in 1966 he edited the first in a projected series of books on comparative planning, *City and Regional Planning in Poland*.[19] Mention should also be made of Earl Brown's work on economic regionalization of Poland and Barbara Zakrzewska's study on small towns in Poland.[20]

Albania is still largely *terra incognita* for American geographers. Edward Ackerman published a brief study before the war, and Richard Harrington in 1967.[21] No studies have been published on East Germany by American geographers. Hoffman wrote a detailed study about rural settlements in Bulgaria (see footnote 15), and Kostanick's study on the resettlement of the Bulgarian Turks was cited earlier (see footnote 17). The increasing exchange between Hungarian and American geogra-

18. Jack C. Fisher, "The Continuity of Urban Patterns under Socialism: The Yugoslav Experience" (Ph.D. diss., Syracuse University, 1961); Department of City Planning, Zagreb, *Stari Planovi Zagreba* (The Old Plans of Zagreb) (Zagreb, 1961); "Urban Analysis: A Case Study of Zagreb, Yugoslavia," *Annals of the Association of American Geographers*, 53 (September, 1963): 266–84.

19. Jack C. Fisher, "Political Decision: A Factor in the Changing Agricultural Geography of Yugoslavia," *Journal of Geography*, 58 (November, 1959): 399–406; "Planning the City of Socialist Man," *Journal, American Institute of Planners*, 28 (November, 1962): 251–65; "The Yugoslav Commune," *World Politics*, 16 (April, 1964): 418–41; *Yugoslavia A Multinational State. Regional Difference and Administrative Response* (San Francisco: Chandler Publishing Co., 1966); Jack C. Fisher, ed., *City and Regional Planning in Poland* (Ithaca: Cornell University Press, 1966). Polish geographers were major contributors in this last volume.

20. S. Earl Brown and Charles E. Trott, "Grouping Tendencies in an Economic Regionalization of Poland," *Annals of the Association of American Geographers*, 58 (June, 1968): 327–42; Barbara Zakrzewska, "The Changing Face of Small Towns in Poland: Problem of Growth or Problems of Adjustment to Socialized Economy," *Polish Institute of Arts and Sciences in America*.

21. Edward A. Ackerman, "Albania — a Balkan Switzerland," *Journal of Geography*, 37 (1938): 253–62, and Richard Harrington, "Albania, Europe's Least Known Country," *Canadian Geographical Journal*, 74 (April, 1967): 133–43.

phers, it is to be hoped, will establish much needed contact, and result in scholarly contributions. Fred Dohrs' study on agriculture in Hungary is the only American contribution thus far.[22] William Horbaly, who spent a year as an exchange student at Charles University in Prague shortly after World War II, wrote his doctoral dissertation at the University of Chicago on geographic aspects of agricultural conditions in Czechoslovakia.[23] It was apparently the first postwar field research by an American geographer in East Central Europe. Ronald Helin's contribution of the administrative map of Romania [24] is, it is hoped, the beginning of increased interest by American geographers on this country. Hoffman's comparative study, mentioned earlier, also concerns itself with developments in Romania (see footnote 16). Theodore Myers contributed a chapter on the Danube [25] and Andrew Burghardt's study on the Burgenland [26] with its Magyar, Slovene, and Croatian minorities needs also to be included in our analysis.

Descriptive studies by Paul Vouras, *The Changing Economy of Northern Greece since World War II*, John Baxevanis on the *Port of Thessaloniki* and "Population, Internal Migration and Urbanization in Greece," [27] and the excellent dissertation by Roger Kasperson on the Dodecanese exploring the effects of selected economic, social, and political experiences upon political diversity and unity [28] are important contributions on that country. K. Thompson has collaborated with B. Kayser on a Greek national atlas and has published on Greek agricultural development, including his valuable monograph, *Farm Fragmentation in Greece*.[29] G. W. Hoffman wrote a lengthy study on the

22. "Incentives in Communist Agriculture: The Hungarian Models," *Slavic Review*, 27 (March, 1968): 23–38.

23. William Horbaly, *Agricultural Conditions in Czechoslovakia, 1950*, mimeographed, University of Chicago, Department of Geography, Research Paper no. 18 (1951).

24. Ronald A. Helin, "The Volatile Administrative Map of Romania," *Annals of the Association of American Geographers*, 57 (September, 1967): 481–502.

25. Theodore C. Myers, "The Danube," in *International Rivers: Some Case Studies*, Norman J. G. Pounds, ed., Indiana University, Department of Geography, Occasional Paper no. 1 (1965).

26. Andrew F. Burghardt, *A Historical and Geographical Study of Burgenland, Austria — Burgenland* (Madison: University of Wisconsin Press, 1962).

27. Paul P. Vouras, *The Changing Economy of Northern Greece since World War II* (Thessaloniki: Institute for Balkan Studies, 1962); John J. Baxevanis, *The Port of Thessaloniki* (Thessaloniki: Institute for Balkan Studies, 1963), and by the same author "Population, Internal Migration and Urbanization in Greece," *Balkan Studies*, 6 (1965): 83–98.

28. Roger E. Kasperson, *The Dodecanese: Diversity and Unity in Island Politics*, University of Chicago, Department of Geography, Research Paper no. 108 (1966).

29. Kenneth Thompson, *Farm Fragmentation in Greece* (Athens: Center of Economic Research, 1962), and his valuable summary on "Recent Greek Emigration,"

historical geography of "Thessaloniki and its relationship with the Hinterland" (see footnote 16).

No scholarly works remain unpublished for lack of publication outlets. Numerous geographic and nongeographic journals, university presses, and commercial publishers, many established in Canada and the United Kingdom, are most anxious to publish scholarly material on Eastern Europe by geographers.

In appraising and evaluating research on East European geographic topics published in the postwar era, it can be said that the number of scholarly contributions is slowly increasing and, generally speaking, their quality is comparable to other studies published by the geography profession. In trying to draw a summary of the sixty or so scholarly publications in the postwar period by American geographers, it can be said that geographers give special attention to studies dealing with political geographic problems, for example, boundary problems; population transfers and their impact on the economic viability of individual regions or the country as a whole; the problems of nationalities and ethnic minorities; various aspects of economic geography such as raw materials as a basis for industrial production; agricultural production, including the impact of political changes on the social adjustment of the rural population; studies in historical geography; and, more recently, studies of urban and transportation problems. Studies on individual East Central and Southeast European countries, with the exception of Pounds' study on Poland and Hoffman-Neal on Yugoslavia, do not exist, though a number of general studies on the area as a whole have been published in textbooks. Forthcoming publications on the regional geography of the whole area by Pounds and a cultural geography on Southeast Europe by Hoffman have been announced. The complexity and diversity of the area make the publication of regional studies, including several countries, a very difficult and risky assignment indeed. Methodological studies and those using quantitative techniques are still extremely rare. The more recent studies concentrate on more sophisticated geographical topics, comparing developments in several regions, analyzing regional differences, studying the impact of the technological changes, and on questions of planning; a few apply newly developed quantitative meth-

Geographical Review, 57 (October, 1967): 560–62; with Bernard Kayser and in collaboration with Roger Vaternella and others, *Economic and Social Atlas of Greece* (Athens: National Statistical Service of Greece, 1964) (350 pp., 132 maps, 64 diagrams, 172 tables).

ods. Microgeographic studies have, on the whole, been left to local geographers.

ACADEMIC RELATIONS BETWEEN AMERICAN AND EAST EUROPEAN
GEOGRAPHERS

Contacts between American and East European geographers are of recent date. Work by American geographers in East Central and Southeast Europe can greatly benefit by a careful study of published material by East European scholars. Increasingly it is available in English abstracts, full-length reproduction, special journals in the English language, and abstracts of scientific literature usually combined for geology and geography. Considerable material is also available in German and French. Work can also benefit by personal contacts between American and East European geographers. These contacts benefit regional specialists but are also invaluable to the profession as a whole. The recent visits by East European geographers in American universities (from Poland, Yugoslavia, and Hungary), largely as a part of the Ford Foundation program, have brought benefits to both sides. They made American geographers aware of some of the first-rate work by their East European colleagues, and, in reverse, left an important impact on many East European geographers which is expressed in their better understanding of the American geographic past and their present methodology.

The purpose here is to discuss the results of mutually beneficial contacts between American and East European geographers, the men involved in these contacts, and the important literature in English available to American geographers interested in this area. East European geographers are well aware of the importance of establishing contacts with their American colleagues, and one indication of this interest is the increased number of publications by East European geographers in English, with translated or abstracted articles from the original publications. Ever since the seventeenth International Geographical Congress (IGU) in Washington in 1952, and more particularly the eighteenth Congress in Rio de Janeiro in 1956, a small number of American geographers have become interested in establishing contacts with their East European colleagues. (Chauncy D. Harris should here be given special credit.) An ever increasing number of American geographers attend meetings in Eastern Europe and these are usually followed by well-planned field trips (either those sponsored by individual commissions of the IGU or by individual East European geographical institutes). This certainly does not mean that these American geographers either intend to or have become East European regional specialists, but it goes without saying that these contacts have brought about an exchange of ideas and understanding of each other's work which is expressed in the literature of both countries.

Here again Poland stands far in the forefront with United States contacts. A number of American geographers, besides regional specialists, have been traveling in Poland (such as the tour of American geographers in Poland in 1964), and literally the cream of the Polish geographic community has been in the United States for extended studies. As a result of these contacts, Polish geographers refer widely to the writings of their American colleagues and the American colleagues and the American profession are well aware of the work by Polish geographers. The Geographical Institute of the Polish Academy of Sciences is now publishing a geographical journal in English — *Geographia Polonica* — and many of its works are published in English, making available to American geographers a good cross-section of Polish geographic work. The work by many Polish geographers is well known to American geographers. To cite only a few: S. Leszczycki, director of the Institute of Geography of the Polish Academy of Sciences and also chairman of the Department of Geography of the University of Warsaw in general economic geography; B. Winid in regional geography; J. Kostrowicki in settlement, land use, and agricultural geography; K. Dziewoński (chairman of the IGU Commission on Methods of Economic Regionalization) in city planning and settlement geography; A. Kuklinski in regional planning and industrial locations; L. Kosinski in population problems; A. Wrobel in problems of economic regionalization. A number of Polish geographers have published in English in both American and European geographic journals. The libraries of the various geographical institutes of Polish institutions are well stocked with American publications, and Polish geographers are well aware of the work and trends in American geography. B. J. L. Berry, J. C. Fisher, C. D. Harris, G. W. Hoffman, D. Jackson, H. L. Kostanick, and N. J. G. Pounds, to mention only a few, have extensive contacts among Polish geographers.

Yugoslavia is certainly next in contacts with American geographers. Starting with the visit by Chauncy Harris at the Second Congress of Yugoslav geographers in 1951 and the attendance of the four senior Yugoslav geographers (S. Ilešić, A. Melik, B. Ž. Milojević, and J. Roglić) at the 1952 International Geographical Congress in Washington, D.C., a continuous flow of visits has been kept up between scholars of the two countries. Hoffman made a total of ten visits to Yugoslavia between 1952 and 1967; J. C. Fisher, H. L. Kostanick, N. J. G. Pounds, T. M. Poulson, and others have established close contacts with Yugoslav geographers and other social scientists and brought the work of Yugoslav geographers to the attention of their American colleagues. During the last few years a number of Yugoslav geographers have visited, studied, or taught in American universities, for example, J. Roglić, S. Zuljić, V. Rogić, V. Kokole and they now make extensive use in their work of American geographic literature. Several Yugoslav geographers also have published in English and other West European languages in American as well as West European journals. Mention can only be made of a very small number of those who have published: W. B. Johnston and I. Crkvenčić, J. Roglić, M. Vasović, J. Petrović, V. Klemenčić, and S. Ilešić.[30] The dean of Yugoslav geographers, B. Ž. Milojević wrote several studies in English and French besides compiling a bibliographic guide for the Library of Congress.[31] He followed in the footsteps of the founder of Serbian geography, Jovan Cvijić. The libraries of the two most important Yugoslav geographical institutes, Ljubljana and Zagreb, have available most of the important American geographical literature.

Brief mention should also be made of the first American–East European cooperative research project (Cornell and now Wayne State–Yugoslav Urban and Regional Planning Project in Ljubljana) under the direction of J. C. Fisher and V. Musić. American social scientists, among them geographers, are working in cooperation with their Yugoslav

30. W. B. Johnston and I. Crkvenčić, "Changing Peasant Agriculture in NW Hrvatsko Primorje, Yugoslavia," *Geographical Review*, 44 (July, 1954): 352–72, and "Examples of Changing Peasant Agriculture in Croatia, Yugoslavia," *Economic Geography*, 33 (January, 1957): 50–71; Josip Roglić, "Die wirtschaftsgeographischen Beziehungen des jugoslawischen Küstenlandes mit den östlichen Bundesländern Österreichs," *Österreichische Osthefte*, 4 (March, 1962): 111–22, "The Geographical Setting of Medieval Dubrovnik," in *Geographical Essays on Eastern Europe*, Norman J. G. Pounds, ed., and "The Yugoslav Littoral," in J. M. Houston, *The Western Mediterranean World* (London: Longmans, Green, 1964). Also M. Vasović and I. Petrović, "Aspects Regionaux du Montenegro," *Méditerranée*, July–September, 1963, pp. 3–29; Svetozar Ilešić, "Die Flurformen Sloweniens im Lichte der europäischen Flurforschung," *Münchner Geographische Hefte* 16 (Kallmünz/Regensburg: Verlag Michael Lassleben, 1959) (German ed. of study published earlier in Solvenian); Vladimir Klemenčić, "Some Elements of Urbanization and Regional Development of Slovenia," in *Aspects of the Study of Regional Geographical Structure*, Acta Geologica et Geographica, Universitatis Comenianae, no. 6 (Bratislava, 1966), pp. 145–74.

31. Among the many contributions in West European languages by Professor B. Ž. Milojević, the following are perhaps more easily available: *Geography of Yugoslavia: A Selective Bibliography* (Washington: Library of Congress, Reference Department, Slavic and East European Division, 1955), p. 79; *Yugoslavia: Geographical Survey* (Belgrade: Committee for Cultural Relations with Foreign Countries, 1958); "Les Vallées principales de la Yougoslavie," *Mémoires de la Société Serbe de Géographie*, vol. 9 (Belgrade, 1958). Also Jovan Cvijić's best-known work, *La Peninsula Balkanique* (Paris: Librairie Armand Colin, 1918).

212   *George W. Hoffman*

counterparts on interdisciplinary problems concerned with the measurement of spatial changes and possible implications for local and regional territorial units.

Hungarian geographers have established during the past few years valuable relations with the United States. Several studied and lectured at American universities and their work has become better known to American geographers through their publications and abstracts in the English language. The irregularly published *Studies* by the Geographical Institute of the Hungarian Academy of Sciences is translated mostly into English, and an excellent *Geography of Hungary* by Márton Pécsi and Béla Sárfalvi has brought that country closer to the understanding of American geographers.[32] Hungary, Bulgaria, Czechoslovakia, and Romania have published a regional and topical study of their country in English and/or German.[33] The Hungarian geographer G. Enyedi recently published an article in the *Geographical Review*.[34]

Increased contacts exist with Bulgarian geographers, though no Bulgarian geographer has as yet been in the United States. G. W. Hoffman, H. L. Kostanick, and R. N. Taaffe are familiar with Bulgarian geographic work, have traveled in Bulgaria, and have published on it; others have established valuable contacts. Bulgarian geographers have not published in English, though a number of contributions are available in German,[35] and a few have abstracts in foreign languages (mostly German). Valuable contributions are available in Bulgarian with brief abstracts in German and here H. Marinov's detailed methodological

32. Márton Pécsi and Béla Sárfalvi, *Geography of Hungary* (London and Budapest: Collet and Corvina Press, 1964); Márton Pécsi, *Ten Years of Physiographic Research in Hungary* (Budapest: Hungarian Academy of Sciences, 1964), and Béla Sárfalvi and Márton Pécsi, eds., *Applied Geography in Hungary* (Budapest: Hungarian Academy of Sciences, 1964). Also Gyorgy Enyedi has abstracts in English for many of his publications on Hungarian agricultural developments.

33. A. S. Beškov, *Volksrepublik Bulgarien: Natur und Wirtschaft* (Berlin: Verlag der Wirtschaft, 1959); Miroslav Blažek, *Ökonomische Geographie der Tschechoslowakischen Republik* (Berlin: Verlag der Wirtschaft, 1961); Jaromir Demek and associates, *Geography of Czechoslovakia* (Prague: Publishing House of the Czechoslovak Academy of Sciences, 1968); Sándor Rádo, ed., *Ökonomische Geographie der ungarischen Volksrepublik* (Berlin: Verlag der Wirtschaft, 1962), and Tiberiu Morariu, Vasile Cucu, and Ion Velcea, *The Geography of Romania* (Bucharest: Meridiane, 1966).

34. Gyorgy Enyedi, "The Changing Face of Agriculture in Eastern Europe," *Geographical Review*, 57 (July, 1967): 358–72.

35. Beškov, *Volksrepublik Bulgarien: Natur und Wirtschaft*; also, Ljubimir Dinev's contribution in Nikolai Todorov, Ljubomir Dinev, Ljuben Melnischki, *Historisch-geographischer Überblick* (Sofia: Fremdensprachenverlag, 1965): "Bulgarien auf der Landkarte"; Ignat Penkoff, "Die Siedlungen Bulgariens, ihre Entwicklung, Veränderungen und Klassifizierung," *Geographische Berichte*, 5 (1960): 211–27.

studies on economic regions must receive special mention.[36] A very detailed regional study of the country, unfortunately only in Bulgarian, is also available.[37]

Field research in Romania by American geographers has only been possible in the last few years. Hoffman, Matley, Pounds, and Poulson know the country well. A number of Romanian contributions appear now in English, French, or German, and the earlier cited general geography of Romania in the English language by Morariu, Cucu, and Velcea is a most useful reference volume. The recent report on the development of Romanian geography in the *Professional Geographer* [38] is the only article which has appeared in an American publication by Romanian geographers. The journal *Revue roumaine de géologie, géophysique et géographie* (*Série de géographie*), issued semiannually, publishes articles from various Romanian geographic journals in French, English, or German. It is carefully edited and a most valuable reference source on the Romanian geographical literature. The basic reference book on Romanian geography is, like its Bulgarian counterpart, unfortunately, published in Romanian only.[39]

Several American geographers recently have attended international meetings and field trips in different parts of Czechoslovakia. Miroslav Blažek's economic geography of Czechoslovakia, a standard descriptive study, was published some years ago in German. A new geography in the English language is in preparation by Jaromir Demek and his staff (see footnote 33). K. Ivanička's study on the East Slovakian iron works in Košice has an English abstract and was distributed during the twentieth International Geographical Congress in London in 1964. The work by Czechoslovak geographers is slowly becoming better

36. Hristo Marinov, *Ikonomichesko o Raionirane na NR. Bulgariia* (Economic Regionalization of Bulgaria) (Sofia: Bulgarian Academy of Sciences, 1963), and *Osnovni Vuprosi Geografskoto Razpredelenie na Proizvodstvoto i Ikonomicheskoto Raionirane* (Distribution of Production and Economic Regionalization). (Varna: Durzhavno Izdatelstvo, 1963), and *Sotsialisticheski Mezhunarodnoi Kompleksi i Raioni* (Socialist International Complexes and Regions) (Varna: D'rzhavno Idatelstvo, 1965).

37. I. P. Gerasimov and Zh.S. Galabov, *Geografiia na Bulgariia: Fizicheska Geografiia* (Geography of Bulgaria: Physical Geography) (Sofia: Bulgarskata Akademiia na Naukite, 1966), vol. 1, and A. S. Beshkov and E. S. Valev, *Geografiia na Bulgariia: Ikonomicheska geografiia* (Geography of Bulgaria: Economic Geography) (Sofia: Bulgarskata Akademiia na Naukite, 1961), vol. 2.

38. Ion Sandru and Vasile Cucu, "Some Considerations on the Development of Geography in the Socialist Republic of Romania," *Professional Geographer*, 18 (July, 1966): 219–23 (editorial work and bibliographical compilations by G. W. Hoffman).

39. Various authors, *Monografia Geografica a Republicii Populare Romine* (Geographic Monograph of the People's Republic of Romania), 2 vols. text and 2 vols. maps (Bucharest: Academiei Republicii Populare Romine, 1960).

known in the United States, and some of the Czech and Slovak geographical journals now publish abstracts or even whole contributions
in English, French, or German.[40]

Brief mention should be made of the major geographical writing in
East Germany, though no American geographer has engaged in field research in this area since World War II. *Petermanns geographische Mitteilungen*, world renowned for its scholarship, has published English
abstracts since 1961 and a special English issue in connection with the
1964 International Geographical Congress is "must" reading for every
serious student of geography. *Geographische Berichte*, the official journal of the East German Geographical Society, has also published English abstracts since 1960. The quality of their contributions generally is
considered of high caliber.

Turkish geographers of the Geographical Institute of the University
of Istanbul publish *Review* (international edition and published irregularly). It contains translations in French and English of their major
scholarly contributions. E. Tümertekin of Istanbul studied in the United
States in the early 1950s, but few contacts exist between Turkish and
American geographers.

Geography is not a university subject in Greece. Economists teach
courses and write on economic geography. A. N. Damaskenides, D. J.
Delivanis and his wife, Maria Negroponti, from the University of Thessaloniki write extensively on rural problems, economic development,
etc. No real scholarly work in geography has appeared in Greece. Interestingly enough, an active geographical society in Athens published
an occasional volume. As noted earlier, only a few American geographers have worked in Greece.

No contacts exist between American geographers and their Albanian
colleagues, but a number of West European scholars have published
about Albania.

Finally, it should be pointed out that several excellent publications,

40. Koloman Ivanička, ed., *Geografia Rajonu Východoslovenských Zeleziarní*
(The Geography of the Region of the East-Slovakian Iron Works), Acta Geologica
et Geographica, Universitatis Comenianae, no. 4 (Bratislava, 1964); K. Ivanička,
A. Zelenska, J. Mladek, "Functional Types of Country Settlements in Slovakia," in
Aspects of the Study of Regional Geographical Structure, Acta Geologica et Geographica, Universitatis Comenianae, no. 6 (Bratislava, 1966), pp. 51–92; Vlatislav
Haeufler, "Changes in the Geographical Distribution of Population in Czechoslovakia," *Transactions of CSAV, Mathematical and Natural Science Series*, 76,
no. 8 (Prague: Publishing House of the Czechoslovakian Academy of Sciences,
1967); various contributions, *Economic Regionalization, Proceedings of the 4th
General Meeting of the Commission on "Methods of Economic Regionalization"*
of the International Geographical Union, September 7–12, 1965, Brno, Czechoslovakia.

including bibliographies, are published by the various East European institutes located in West Germany. The Osteuropa institutes at Munich, Berlin, and other cities, Südost-Institut (Munich), Johann Gottfried Herder — Forschungsrat (Marburg), and others issue many publications of interest to geographers.

WEST EUROPEAN CONTRIBUTIONS ON EAST CENTRAL AND SOUTHEASTERN EUROPE

West European scholars have always been much aware of and interested in developments of the eastern part of their continent. Many outstanding regional studies were published before World War II, but to list all these publications is simply not possible within the framework of this report. Therefore only a small selection of the more important and substantial works are mentioned.

Studies by French geographers are considered of special lasting merit, for example, those by J. Brunhes, C. Vallaux, E. de Martonne, Y. Chaitaigneau, and J. Sion, the last three in the famous *Géographie universelle*.[41] German and Austrian geographers have for a long time shown special interest in regional studies of East Central and Southeastern Europe. Best known are the studies by J. Gellert, N. Krebs, F. Machatschek, and O. Maull.[42] Studies in depth are by J. Gellert and H. Wilhelmy on Bulgaria,[43] H. Louis, E. Nowack, and M. Urban on Albania,[44]

41. Y. Chaitagneau and J. Sion, "Les Pays Balkanique," in P. Vidal de la Blache and L. Gallois, eds., *Géographie universelle*, vol. 7 (Paris: Armand Colin, 1934); E. de Martonne, "The Carpathians: Physiographic Features Controlling Human Geography," *Geographical Review*, 3 (June, 1917): 417–27, also his contributions to *Géographie universelle*.

42. Fritz Machatschek, "Länderkunde von Mitteleuropa" (includes most of today's Czechoslovakia and Romania and Hungary, as well as northern Yugoslavia), in *Enzyklopaedie der Erdkunde*, O. Kende, ed. (Leipzig and Vienna: Franz Deuticke, 1925); Otto Maull, "Länderkunde von Südeuropa: Die Südosteuropäische Halbinsel," in *Enzyklopaedie der Erdkunde*, O. Kende, ed. (Leipzig and Vienna: Franz Deuticke, 1929).

43. Johannes F. Gellert, "Mittelbulgarien," in *Das kulturgeographische Bild der Gegenwart* (Berlin: Junker & Dunnhaupt, 1937); Herbert Wilhelmy, "Hochbulgarien," vol. 1: *Die ländlichen Siedlungen und die bäuerliche Wirtschaft*; vol. 2: *Sofia, Wandlungen einer Grosstadt zwischen Orient und Okzident* (Kiel: Schriften des Geographischen Instituts der Universität Kiel, band 4, 1935–36), also "Völkische und Koloniale Siedlungsformen der Slawen," *Geographische Zeitschrift*, 42 (1936): 81–97.

44. Herbert Louis, "Albanien: Eine Landeskunde vornehmlich auf Grund eigener Reisen," *Penck's Geographische Abhandlungen*, vol. 2, no. 3 (1927); Martin Urban, "Die Siedlungen Südalbaniens," *Tübinger geographische und geologische Abhandlungen*, series 2, vol. 4 (1938), and E. Nowack, "Morphogenische Studien aus Albanien," *Zeitschrift der Gesellschaft für Erdkunde zu Berlin*, 1920, pp. 81–117.

H. Hassinger on Czechoslovakia,[45] K. Kayser, N. Krebs, L. Schultze on Yugoslavia, and J. Schulze on Greece.[46] British geographers made important contributions to prewar regional studies of the area. M. L. Newbigin, *Geographical Aspects of the Balkan Problem*, A. Oglivie's study on Macedonia, M. R. Shackleton's regional study on Europe with her excellent observations on the East European countries (now in its seventh edition), E. Wiskemann's thoughtful study on Czechs and Germans, the excellent geographical description of historical changes by V. Cornish in his "Bosnia, the Borderland of Serb and Croat," and H. G. Wanklyn's book *The Eastern Marchlands of Europe* are all considered outstanding contributions.[47]

The postwar period shows a decided growth of publications. This was made possible by increased interest in the problems of the area. British geographers have taken the lead, in both number and quality. Many have extensive field experience. Books were published by A. E. Moodie on the *Italo-Yugoslav Boundary*, H. R. Wilkinson on the political geography of Macedonia, *Maps and Politics*, H. G. Wanklyn on *Czechoslovakia*, E. Wiskemann on *Germany's Eastern Neighbors*, F. E. I. Hamilton on *Yugoslavia: Patterns of Economic Activity* and a recent descriptive introductory geography by R. H. Osborne, *East-Central Europe: A Geographical Introduction to Seven Socialist States*.[48]

45. Hugo Hassinger, *Die Tschechoslovakei: Ein geographisches, politisches und wirtschaftliches Handbuch* (Vienna, 1925).

46. Kurt Kayser, "Westmontenegro: Eine kulturgeographische Darstellung," *Geographische Abhandlungen*, 3–4 (1931); Norbert Krebs, *Beiträge zur Geographie Serbiens und Rasciens: Ergebnisse zweier Studienreisen im Auftrag der Wiener geographischen Gesellschaft und der Akademie der Wissenschaften* (Stuttgart: Engelhorn, 1922); Leonard Schultze, *Makedonien: Landschafts- und Kulturbilder* (Jena: Fischer, 1927); Joachim Schulze, "Neugriechenland: Eine Landeskunde Ostmakedonien und West Thrakiens mit besonderer Berücksichtigung der Geomorphologie, Kolonistensiedlung und Wirtschaftsgeographie," *Petermanns Geographische Mitteilungen, Ergänzungsheft*, no. 233 (1937).

47. Marion L. Newbigin, *Geographical Aspects of the Balkan Problem, in Their Relations to the Great European War* (London: Constable, 1915; New York: G. P. Putnam's Sons, 1915); Vaughn Cornish, "Bosnia, the Borderland of Serb and Croats," *Geography* 2 (December, 1933): 260–70; Margaret R. Shackleton, *Europe: A Regional Geography*, 1st ed. (section 5: South Central Europe) (London: Longmans, Green, 1934); Alan G. Oglivie, "A Contribution to the Geography of Macedonia," *Geographical Journal*, 55 (January, 1920): 1–34; Harriet G. Wanklyn, *The Eastern Marchlands of Europe* (London: George Philip & Co., 1941), and Elizabeth Wiskemann, *Czechs and Germans* (Oxford: University Press, 1938).

48. Arthur E. Moodie, *The Italo-Yugoslav Boundary: A Study in Political Geography* (London: George Philip & Co., 1945); H. R. Wilkinson, *Maps and Politics: A Review of the Ethnographic Cartography of Macedonia* (Liverpool: University Press, 1951); Harriet G. Wanklyn, *Czechoslovakia* (London: George Philip & Co., 1954); Elizabeth Wiskemann, *Germany's Eastern Neighbors* (London: Oxford University Press, 1956); F. E. I. Hamilton, *Yugoslavia: Patterns of Economic Activity* (New York: F. A. Praeger, 1968); R. H. Osborne, *East-Central Europe: An*

Articles covering a variety of topics reach several dozen and those by H. R. Wilkinson, F. E. I. Hamilton, S. H. Cousens, J. C. Creigh, and T. H. Elkins are among the most valuable.

Outstanding also is the work by French geographers. Though smaller in number than British publications, the traditional French emphasis on human geography makes their contributions most valuable. A. Blanc has probably done more work on Southeastern Europe than most other Western geographers. His first postwar book, *La Croatie Occidentale*, is based on most thorough fieldwork. He also is the author of *Géographie des Balkans, Yougoslavie*, and, with others, *Les Républiques socialistes d'Europe Centrale*. Besides these books he authored numerous articles dealing with such diverse problems as the urban problems of Romania, the regional geography of Hungary, Albania, and Yugoslavia, the rural habitat in Croatia, and agriculture in Albania.[49] B. Kayser wrote on Bulgaria and numerous excellent contributions on Greece, including his book, *Géographie humaine de la Grèce*[50] and, with the American K. Thompson, the previously mentioned *Economic and Social Atlas of Greece*. One of his students, P.-Yves Péchoux, has spent considerable time in Greece working on a series of small city-regional studies.[51] Other French contributions include a detailed study on the transformation of agriculture in Romania by J. Poncet, P. Birot's study on the Balkans in *Le Méditerranée orientale et le Moyen-Orient*, contributions by Jean Chardonnet, R. Ficheaux, and A. Fichelle on Poland, Romania, Czechoslovakia, and Bulgaria to *Larousse Encyclopedia of Geography — Europe* and G. Castellan's study *La République démocratique allemande*.[52]

German and Austrian geographers, after some interruption, are again contributing to the scholarly output on East Central and Southeastern

Introductory Geography (New York: F. A. Praeger, 1967) (published in London as *East-Central Europe: A Geographical Introduction to Seven Socialist States*, 1967).

49. André Blanc, *La Croatie Occidentale: Etude de géographie humaine* (Paris: Institute d'études slaves de l'Université de Paris, 1957); *Géographie des Balkans* (Paris: Presses universitaires de France, 1965); *Yougoslavie* (Paris: Librairie Armand Colin, 1967); André Blanc and others, *Les Républiques socialistes d'Europe Centrale* (Paris: Presses universitaires de France, 1967).

50. Bernard Kayser, *Géographie humaine de la Grèce: Eléments pour l'étude de l'urbanisation* (Paris: Presses universitaires de France, 1964).

51. Pierre-Yves Péchoux, "Les problèmes du travail et de l'emploi dans une ville de province en Grèce: l'exemple de Kavala," *Revue de géographie de Lyon*, 41 (1966): 339–65.

52. Jean Poncet, "Les transformations de l'agriculture roumaine," *Annales de Géographie*, 73 (September–October, 1964): 540–67; Pierre Birot, "Les Balkans," in Pierre Birot and Jean Dresch, eds., *La Méditerranée orientale et le Moyen-Orient* (Paris: Presses universitaires de France, 1956); Pierre Deffontaines and Mariel Jean-Brunhes Delamarre, eds., *Larousse Encyclopedia of Geography — Europe* (New York: Prometheus Press, 1961); Georges Castellan, *La République démocratique allemande* (Paris: Presses universitaires de France, 1961).

Europe. First mention must be made of the two basic studies by the late A. Philippson, Germany's foremost regional specialist on the Mediterranean: *Das Klima Griechenlands* and his four-volume study, *Die griechischen Landschaften*. Fieldwork for both these major studies was completed before World War II, but actual publication had to be delayed.[53] Monographic studies and books are relatively few. Three should be mentioned: A. Krager's historical geographic study on settlements in Western Slavonia (Yugoslavia), H. Guenther on urban problems in Yugoslavia, and E. Lichtenberger and H. Bobek on the cultural geography of Yugoslavia.[54] Articles are more numerous and cover all countries of the area, for example, H. Schwalm on Yugoslavia, J. Schultze on East Germany, A. Beuermann on Greece, and G. Schmidt and K. Nernheim on Albania.[55]

Two studies authored by Swiss scholars should be mentioned: Hans-Peter Kosack's excellent contribution on Epirus (Greece), and W. Kuendig-Steiner's regional study on Northern Dobrudja (Romania).[56] Obviously there are many other periodical contributions from the countries listed above, as well as other European countries, including the U.S.S.R., but within this restricted space they present a general picture of West European interests and contacts in the area.

53. Alfred Philippson, *Das Klima Griechenlands* (Bonn: Ferd. Duemmlers Verlag, 1948), and *Die Griechischen Landschaften: Eine Landeskunde*, 4 vols. (Frankfurt: V. Klostermann, 1950–59).

54. Adolf Krager, "Die Entwicklung der Siedlungen im westlichen Slawonien, Ein Beitrag zur Kulturgeographie des Save-Drau-Zwischenstromlandes," *Kölner Geographische Arbeiten*, vol. 15 (1963) (Wiesbaden, Steiner); Horst Guenther, *Die Verstädterung in Jugoslawien: Darstellung und Probleme*, Osteuropastudien der Hochschulen des Landes Hessen, series 1: Giessener Abhandlungen zur Agrar- und Wirtschaftsforschung des europäischen Ostens, no. 35 (Wiesbaden: Harrassowitz, 1966); Elisabeth Lichtenberger and Hans Bobek, "Zur kulturgeographischen Gliederung Jugoslawiens," *Geographischer Jahresbericht aus Österreich*, 26 (1955–56): 78–154.

55. Hans Schwalm, "Räumliche Grundlagen Jugoslawiens," in Werner Markert, ed., *Jugoslawien*, Osteuropa-Handbuch (Cologne-Graz: Boehlau Verlag, 1954), pp. 1–13; Joachim H. Schultze, *Die Naturbedingten Landschaften der Deutschen Demokratischen Republik* (Gotha: Geographisch-Kartographische Anstalt, 1955); Arnold Beuermann, "Studien zur griechischen Agrarlandschaft," *Verhandlungen des deutschen Geographentages* (Würzburg), 31 (1957): 456–64, and "Typen ländlicher Siedlungen in Griechenland," *Petermanns Geographische Mitteilungen*, 100, no. 4 (1956): 278–85; Gerhard Schmidt, "Albanien: Eine landeskundlicher Abriss unter Verwertung von Reiseeindrücken," *Geographische Rundschau*, 13 (October, 1961): 396–407, and Klaus Nernheim, "Albanien, eine Landes- und Wirtschaftskunde," *Zeitschrift für Wirtschaftskunde*, 10 (January, 1966): 10–17.

56. Werner Kuendig-Steiner, *Nord-Dobrudscha: Beiträge zur Frage der Beziehungen zwischen Natur und menschlicher Tätigkeit in einer Region der pontischen Waldsteppe und Küstengewässer (Donaudelta) während des 19. und 20. Jahrhunderts* (Zürich: Aschmann & Scheller, 1946); Hans-Peter Kosack, "Epirus," *Geographica Helvetica*, 4 (1949): 78–92.

DEFICIENCIES AND NEEDS FOR PH.D. TRAINING

With a very small number of geographers in America concentrating their work in East Central and Southeast Europe, it is only natural that course offerings or research opportunities among geography departments are greatly deficient. From the various sources available,[57] it is evident that only eleven departments listed nineteen East European content courses; four are graduate courses. In addition, nine departments list courses as East Europe and the Soviet Union (or a similar title). The small number of courses in the area taught is the obvious

57. The sources for these details are the following: *Language and Area Study Programs in American Universities* (Washington, D.C.: External Research Staff, Department of State, 1964); *Directory of College Geography of the United States, Academic Years 1966–67*, vol. 18 (April, 1967), and questionnaires answered by colleagues (total mailed during early 1967 — 34; answers — 31, including one answer from an American teaching in Canada).

Teaching — course offerings (incl. 1967–68 academic year): (1) Departments with courses specifically listed as Eastern Europe: 11; Undergraduate courses: 15 (Florida State, University of Nebraska, University of Cincinnati, Ohio State University, University of Washington, Beloit College, Michigan State, Indiana University, Wayne State, University of Pittsburgh, and University of Wisconsin [Milwaukee]; graduate courses (many taught irregularly): 4. (2) Departments with courses listed as Soviet Union and Eastern Europe: 9 (UCLA, USAF [Colorado], De Paul [Chicago], University of New Mexico, University of Texas, Michigan State University, Chipola Junior College [Marianna, Florida], University of Michigan [Kalamazoo], Rutgers University. (3) Fourteen colleagues reported undergraduate courses with some East European content; 11 colleagues reported graduate courses or seminars with East European content. Attention should be called to the fact that the *Directory* listed a total of 528 European content courses offered (exclusive of Soviet Union) during the same period.

Interdisciplinary institutes (based on the 1964 Department of State publications): Total number of programs in Russian and East European Studies (including Slavic) listed: 31 (Russian content only, 20; Russian and East European content, 8; East European content, 3). None of the three East European Institutes has a geographer specializing in the area. Three of the eight Russian and East European programs have a geographer with East European specialization.

Four colleagues reported the possibility of *expanding* East European programs — University of Washington, Portland State, University of Wisconsin [Milwaukee], and Wayne State. The University of Washington has the only Department of Geography with more than one staff member concentrating on East Central and Southeast Europe.

Geographers active in the administration of East European work: (1) Geographers during the last five years have headed (or were associate directors) three interdisciplinary programs. (2) The following geographers with special interest in East Europe served or still serve as members of committees of national foundations: Chauncy D. Harris, George W. Hoffman, and Robert N. Taaffe.

Ph.D.'s awarded with specialty in Eastern Europe: According to 29 questionnaires returned, 6 Ph.D.'s were awarded (incl. 1966–67) with East Central and Southeast European topics, none by a faculty member with East European specialization. To this figure, presumably, should be added a few additional dissertations completed under the supervision of faculty members not specializing in East Europe.

result of the small number of available area specialists. Training of area specialists is dependent upon six basic facts:

1. Early language training — for the East European area, this means proficiency in speaking and reading in a minimum of three foreign languages. All, ideally, should be acquired before entering graduate training.
2. Sufficient library facilities not only in geography but in all social sciences.
3. Field research opportunities — students should have an extended opportunity to pursue fieldwork in the country of their major specialization and in addition, a survey trip should be made possible to other East Central and/or Southeast European countries to get better acquainted with comparative area problems.
4. Sufficient time for training, which is closely related to adequate financial support — this is simply not available and handicaps the competitive advantages of students seeking to specialize in the East European area. Students in geography are here at a certain disadvantage because many are attracted to the field of geography only in their later college career or at the beginning of their graduate work. This results in insufficient background training — language and area work — at a time when advanced work should begin.
5. Interdisciplinary cooperation, joint seminars, lectures, etc., with geographers as part of the interdisciplinary setup at the appropriate educational institution.
6. Attracting superior senior area specialists as visiting professors, at the same time giving younger members of the profession financial and job opportunity encouragement to devote themselves to additional training needed to acquire proficiency in the area.

Certainly among the most important requirements to alleviate the serious lack of area interest and competence is encouragement for students by financially attractive scholarships to undertake the long and arduous road of language training and field competence. Cooperation among individuals and universities, such as regional training centers with faculty to be drawn from several institutions, would concentrate the meager resources for the benefit of training of students and faculty alike. As additional Ph.D.'s are trained in the area and obtain teaching positions, it is hoped that they will become the spearhead for additional course offerings and serve to encourage graduate students to choose the area of East Central and Southeastern Europe as their regional specialty. But this is neither a quick nor an easy solution to the problem.

Very much the same can be said to encourage greater research in the area. Here the offerings of work in other disciplines, including language and literature, is of great importance in broadening the knowledge of individuals. Scholarly exchanges among different disciplines is essential for the preparation of area specialists in geography and for continued attraction and training for those already in the field. This does not imply that graduate training should be interdisciplinary — the author has never thought very highly of area M.A.'s or even interdisciplinary Ph.D.'s. Interdisciplinary contacts are of great value, but certainly do not replace the rigors of disciplinary training. Basic area interests are obtained by well-organized and interesting offerings of undergraduate courses, interesting lectures presented by senior area specialists, and ample offerings in the languages and literature of the area. The geographic profession simply has an insufficient number of area specialists to perform such an assignment in many institutions. Regional cooperation between educational institutions and, even more important, between individuals, and long-term planned financial support are therefore some of the key remedies to the situation.

RECOMMENDATIONS

Based on the discussions with a group of geographers at the 1966 meeting of the Association of American Geographers and the comments received to my questionnaires, the following recommendations are offered. They affect geographers both directly and indirectly.

1. *Granting agencies should give special attention to underdeveloped disciplines such as geography with specialization on this area.* In this way they would encourage the addition of a geographer to the staff and subsequently the training of students in the discipline.

2. *Financial assistance to graduate students.* Graduate students find more attractive offers for money and fieldwork in the African, South American, and the Middle East areas, etc., at the moment. In spite of what we may wish, most of today's graduate students take a very pragmatic view of the opportunities offered and do not base their decisions on their love of the field. Competition is strong and the field of East European studies has little to offer in terms of long-term financial support, though financial aid is available for Eastern Europe area work. Funds should specifically be made available to graduate students for accompanying senior members of the profession on their overseas field trips.

3. One of our senior regional specialists suggested *a different way of encouraging student interest in the area.* His point was:

It is my considered opinion that if you really want to help Eastern European studies, give the few senior and mature regional scholars in our profession sizable grants for students (undergraduate as well as graduate, but even more important undergraduate) to work a few hours each week as research assistants under the guidance of the senior professor. This money should go directly to the senior professor and not to the departments, institutes, or the university. If money goes to institutes it gets siphoned off in the director's salary, office staff, assistance, etc., and all that gets accomplished is the next year's budget. Hence I think that grants to the specific individual would accomplish much more in direct relation to attracting students and to getting significant research done.

4. Earmark increased *library funds* to the underdeveloped fields, including geography. Teaching aids and library assistance, especially for smaller departments was urgently needed, according to some geographers.

5. The need for considerable *language training* seems to present the most important problem for adequate student interest in the area. Special language incentives for students including geography should be given, for example, summer institutes including actual area language training. The programs should primarily be designed to provide language competence when actually in the field.

6. *Centers and/or institutes should clearly define their specific regional interests,* and funds should be clearly earmarked for work in East Central and Southeastern Europe only. Inasmuch as a large part of research funds for students and faculty come directly from these centers, faculty interested in Eastern Europe would have greater incentive and perhaps would find it easier to apply for and receive funds. It should also be added that several geographers in their comments expressed themselves strongly against centers in the area, feeling that geographers were at a disadvantageous position in such centers. Money seems to go to those fields of study with the strongest university departments — for example, history and political science. It was strongly felt by those geographers that geography would have a better chance to seek direct support from foundations and not via a center organization. Other geographers suggested that centers should earmark specific funds for the underdeveloped fields, such as geography.

7. *Availability of small grants and financial support for short-term research needs for senior research specialists,* including funds for research assistants, especially at institutions without an area institute or

center. Funds should be earmarked for the senior specialist on an annual basis. It is time-consuming and not realistic to expect a senior man to write lengthy requests for relatively minor sums, and each time attach a long list of reasons and other background information.

8. *Increased funds for travel* to overseas meetings should be made available for area specialists. Special consideration should be given to national and special subject meetings.

9. *Evaluation committees (foundations, government agencies) should have competent area geographers on them,* or a geographer should at least be consulted. His name should be listed together with the other committee members. Geographers would be more likely to apply if they knew that a geographer would participate in the evaluation.

10. A program should be sponsored to provide training in the *East European Area without requiring extensive language competence* — perhaps German, French or Russian — for teachers who already have distinguished themselves as teachers in colleges, teachers colleges, and other professional colleges, to enable them to increase their knowledge of East Europe. This will permit them to introduce courses about the area or add information to existing courses in their institutions. With the increased importance of the East European area, this type of program could assume a major contribution to increasing knowledge in teachers colleges and other professional schools. It would also encourage the training of knowledgeable students, though not necessarily specialists.

11. Special attention should be given to the *establishment of seminars and in-service programs for high school teachers.* (The 1967 and 1968 programs offered by the Department of Geography of the University of Washington on Geographic Patterns of Soviet Development, and supported by NDEA, Title XI, is an excellent example).

12. Much more effort must be put into *scholarly collaboration,* both between American and East European geographers (funds for visiting scholars) and between American regional specialists in the form of annually sponsored area conferences, with ample time for papers and discussions.

9/ SOCIOLOGY

Irwin T. Sanders

Education and World Affairs

Sociologists in the United States have up to now shown little interest in the countries of Eastern Europe, though the situation is beginning to change. This report will first document the general neglect of these countries by describing the little that is actually being done and offering explanations for this neglect; second, it will offer personal evaluations by United States sociologists of East European studies in the United States, Western Europe, and Eastern Europe itself; third, it will present a country-by-country and regional review; and, finally, it will offer recommendations designed to increase activities by United States sociologists in East European studies.

GENERAL NEGLECT OF EAST EUROPEAN STUDIES

The "state of the art" can be shown by citing numbers of sociologists involved, noting the courses offered, and mentioning the research in progress.

Numbers Involved in Sociological Study of Eastern Europe

A letter sent to the chairmen of sociology departments offering graduate work in United States universities requested that they list on an enclosed postcard the names of any sociologists in their institution (a) who were teaching courses in which they used East European materials or (b) who were doing research on Eastern Europe. Letters went out to 127 departments, of which 101 returned the card. In 75 of the replies, the answer was simple: "No sociologists here working on Eastern Europe." The total number of names mentioned in the other replies was 50. Of these, 6 wrote back when questioned that they did not really

225

have any concern with Eastern Europe. Thus, we can conclude that out of the several thousand sociologists in the United States connected with universities, only 44, plus a few more who might have been missed in this roundup, are interested in Eastern Europe. What is just as clear is the fact that most of these do not consider themselves East European specialists but they do use comparative materials from Eastern Europe in their courses and their research. In the federal government, the foundations, and other nonacademic settings there are probably 10–12 sociologists with East European research interests. Frequently, these interests are secondary to the main duties for which they are employed. But even this small number of academic and nonacademic sociologists provides a nucleus for an occasional meeting to discuss problems of study by sociologists on East European societies. Those who work on Greece tend to think of it as Mediterranean rather than East European, though they readily recognized the logic of including Greece in any study which would include its neighbors of Albania, Yugoslavia, or Bulgaria.

Courses Offered

Thirteen sociologists out of the 31 whose replies were used offered one or more courses in which they dealt with East European materials. The only courses dealing specifically with a given country were taught by two of these replying — Modern Greek Social Institutions, Sociology of Modern Greek Life, and Greek Society in Process — but these were taught in Greece while these sociologists were visiting there. They have not been offered in the United States.

Courses which provide a coverage of the East European area are the following: (1) Problems of Marxism, (2) East European and Russian Social Political Movements, (3) Contemporary Communist Societies, and (4) Demography, Marxism, and Socialist Reality.

Most of the courses, however, were listed because the instructor used materials from East European countries in the course, but by no means exclusively so. Among those mentioned were courses on political sociology, international tension areas, comparative sociological analysis of political systems, totalitarian societies, political systems, sociology of industrial societies, industrial sociology, economic sociology, sociology of development, community decision-making, systems change, culture change, modern sociological theory, history of social theory, seminar on the family, comparative family sociology, family and society, and history of the family.

Courses on racial and cultural minorities do take up the adjustment of East European immigrants to United States society, with some attention to the type of societies from which they have come. One instructor in an undergraduate course in basic concepts of sociology encourages students to write papers on Greek culture. These courses, although not representing all of the courses where East European materials are used, do constitute a fair sample of what goes on in sociology departments today. It should be remembered that the survey reported on here dealt only with institutions offering graduate work in sociology. There may be several sociologists who teach in undergraduate colleges and offer courses in Eastern Europe there. But these scattered courses hardly provide a basis for consistent preparation of a specialist.

The state of the field is such that one would be hard put to it to advise any student where to go if he wanted to do graduate work in sociology and specialize in Eastern Europe. (See Walter Schenkel's letter in Appendix to this chapter.) The few East European studies centers across the country do not now have any sociologists working on Eastern Europe, though some at these institutions have done so in the past or may be shifting from concentration on the Soviet Union to other socialist countries. If the student went to work with those who taught the courses listed above, he would almost invariably be in an institution without the supporting work in Eastern Europe that would be required for sound area study training. Most probably, however, there is not apt to be a marriage between sociologists interested in Eastern Europe and the East European studies centers. As will be pointed out later, the Area Studies Center is not congenial to the sociological style.

Research in Progress

The research picture is somewhat brighter than the instructional one. From 20 to 25 professors of the 30 whose replies are relevant listed research which they had completed in the last five years or now had underway. The topics run the whole gamut of sociological inquiry and will be treated in more detail on a country-by-country basis in a later section. Whereas it is difficult (and sometimes considered inappropriate) for a sociologist to offer a course dealing with a specific country or a given region, there is no problem in his conducting research on a specific *locus*, particularly when he undertakes to relate this to the general body of sociological theory.

Why U.S. Sociologists Have Neglected East European Studies

1. Sociologists are reluctant to become area specialists, since they seek to draw up general principles about social phenomena irrespective of political boundaries. A sociologist specializing in a foreign area is

heading for a peripheral position in United States sociology; unless he develops an additional specialty, his chances for a sociological career are limited. Further, young sociologists are trained to be oriented predominantly toward the formation of theory. Area studies in the traditional sense have little relevance for theory formation.[1]

2. Eastern European studies have been disproportionately staffed by former Eastern Europeans who, much too often, have had particular (if from a value standpoint both understandable and admirable) axes to grind. The Communist-anti-Communist battle line has been an aspect of a great deal of the work and this may have detracted from the scholarly appeal of this field to American sociologists.

3. American sociologists are generally uninformed about (a) interesting theoretical problems waiting to be researched in Eastern Europe; (b) funding for research, available though inadequate; (c) current activities of fellow United States sociologists interested in Eastern Europe; (d) ways of gaining access to Western and Eastern European professional literature; and (e) how to develop contacts with East European sociologists.

4. Lack of knowledge of the wide variety of languages in Eastern Europe is especially pronounced among sociologists.

5. For those sociologists who have sought to work in Eastern Europe, there are serious research problems: (a) host colleagues have little financial support for research; (b) academic sociologists in these countries may be isolated from the research sociologists in the institutes; and (c) honest fieldwork may not be possible because of political considerations.

Despite this rather bleak assessment, two positive trends are worthy of note. First, comparative studies are becoming increasingly popular among the most prestigious United States sociologists and in the best-known universities. Certainly, the search for comparative data will draw increasing attention to Eastern Europe. Second, the current rehabilitation of sociology in some East European countries (e.g., Poland where it has had a long tradition) and its development in other countries (e.g., particularly in Yugoslavia but also in Bulgaria and Greece) is an exciting fact of life to American sociology. There is growing interest by Americans in sharing with sociologists in these countries whatever contribution United States sociology might make to the development of their discipline. Americans who do this find, in turn, that they have much to gain from the work abroad.

1. One temporary way out of the dilemma according to Professor Alexander Vucinich would be to give some sociological training to graduate students in East European history.

EVALUATION OF SOCIOLOGICAL STUDIES OF EAST EUROPE IN THE UNITED STATES, WESTERN EUROPE, AND EASTERN EUROPE

THE UNITED STATES

The points listed in the previous section reinforce the earlier claim that East European studies have been neglected by United States sociologists. Further support of this view comes from the comments made by the relatively few who are engaged in such studies and who are therefore in position to make a knowledgeable assessment. Direct quotations from letters received delineate the situation as follows:

I do not consider the state of sociological inquiry regarding East Europe very satisfactory, using as a criterion quality and quantity of research connected with comparable regions of the world. In part, our research effort — and often educational emphases —seems to run in fashions and fads, which is explainable in part by the relative flow of government and foundation funds.

My impression is that the state of sociological studies about Eastern Europe in the United States is at a low ebb [similar statement by at least four respondents].

I can comment only on demographic studies of Eastern Europe. On the American side, these are so few in number to be almost nonexistent today. [Professor Demeny, author of the report "Demography," observes that there is definitely more literature on demography than this statement seems to indicate.]

The state of sociological studies about Eastern Europe is quite primitive from a theoretical angle. What holds sociology back is not only its provincialism in terms of lack of interest in comparative studies, but also its miniscule efforts to deal theoretically with large-scale social changes. Theories of change such as those of Marx or Weber are characteristic of European but not American sociology.

Few United States sociologists are knowledgeable about Eastern Europe — either the nature of these societies or current developments and possibilities for social science research.

Only one respondent was in any way more favorably inclined, stating that there had been a great expansion since the first sputniks. It was clear, however, that he was not distinguishing between Soviet and East European studies.

WESTERN EUROPE

Sociological studies of Eastern Europe by West European sociologists reflect (1) the recency of acceptance of sociology and therefore less involvement in some countries, such as Great Britain, and (2) the offsetting fact of proximity to Eastern Europe. The following statements present evaluations by United States sociologists of the West European activity in East European studies.

A center of East European (Communist) studies is the Institut für Politische Wissenschaften at the Free University of Berlin, where West German sociologists analyze the various aspects of Communist society. Recently, the University of Frankfurt has acquired some excellent young sociologists with an extensive knowledge of the East German scene.

The Dutch publishers seem to be covering Eastern Europe.

There is a considerable amount of research being done in Eastern Europe by sociologists in West Germany (especially Dr. Erwin Scheuch, Institut für Vergleichende Sozialforschung, Köln.)

Work in Western Europe is generally no better or only slightly better than that being done in the United States. Several Europeans have been involved in various cross-national studies.

There are dangers in making comparisons when you consider the numbers of sociologists in Western Europe. In most European countries we tend to judge by one or two individuals, whereas in the United States we have thousands to draw from.

Germany has done some studies but not to any great depth.

On the basis of periodicals, I would judge that the West European studies about Eastern Europe are somehow superior to the studies done by us. Perhaps the immediacy of their problems as well as the vicinity of their contacts gives the West Europeans an advantage. But certainly with our financial advantages this should not be so.

West German studies of East Germany are on a medium level, partly because the sociological talent is too scarce there (as in other parts of Europe) to attract any overflow from central concerns of sociology into what must still be considered a marginal area.

Western Europeans are historically and theoretically well-equipped to study Eastern Europe and, in particular, the French and German work is of a high quality.

West Germany shows much more interest in Eastern Europe than the United States, but the quality of its sociological studies may not be at the same scholarly level as at least some of the studies produced in the United States.

The research of German sociologists on Eastern Europe is very complex. As you know, European social scientists still have the broad analytical approach which combines the areas of history and cultural anthropology, of political science and sociology, of literature and art, etc. The surveying and defining of their activities is therefore a job requiring much time.

In evaluating these and other comments about Western Europe, one should remember that no attempt is being made here to describe East European studies in general, but only those done by sociologists. That is why little mention is made of some of the European research institutes specializing in Eastern Europe but which use no sociologists on their staffs. (See Walter Schenkel's letter, Appendix.)

EASTERN EUROPE

Special comments about particular countries will be taken up in the country-by-country sections which follow. Here we note some general evaluations by United States sociologists of efforts by the East Europeans to study their own societies. These random comments should be compared with descriptions by East Europeans (and others) of the state of sociology in their respective countries.

Clearly, the Polish, Yugoslav and Hungarian situations are most encouraging. While the emphasis must be, for some time, on problems roughly in "industrial sociology" and problems applicable to governmental use, there is much fermentation. I expect that in five years or so, there will be no sacred cows barred from genuine research, even if interpretations of data will continue to be affected by considerations of dialectical/historical materialism in the appropriately orthodox fashion of the day.

East European countries which I know best are under the Communist system of rule. A number of sociologists in these countries find it still difficult to emancipate themselves sufficiently from the dominant ideology to produce high-quality research, particularly in the fields which touch upon subjects related directly or indirectly to politics.

In general the state of sociological studies *about* East Europe is pretty primitive in the *specific* specialty in which I happen to be interested, namely, the study of social organization of social science in East Europe. Part of the reason for this is that such studies must proceed from a larger theoretical analysis and from a comparative perspective on the historic origins of sociology in Western Europe and the United States. We must, in short, supplant the history of social theory by the sociology of sociology and we are only now, small bit by small bit, proceeding to do this. [This statement would apply to the United States, West European as well as the East European sociologists.]

The Poles, Hungarians, and Yugoslavs have, of course, done excellent work on their own societies.

In assessing the work by East European sociologists, a great deal depends on the basic mental outlook of the person who is reporting: optimistic vs. pessimistic. Balanced judgment is difficult, since the alleged changes are taking place *now*. The degree of liberalization from the Marxist dogma is not measurable under present circumstances. Perhaps the subfields in sociology furthest from the dogma, such as family, criminology, etc., have the greatest potentialities.

Formal demographic research is quite well developed in certain countries, particularly Hungary and to some extent Czechoslovakia. But what I can call sociological demography has only barely begun in these countries and very little is known about the demographic behavior of these peoples.

There is some pretty good demographic research going on in Eastern Europe. There is general and widespread interest among the demographers we have contacted in Yugoslavia, Hungary, Poland, and Czechoslovakia about the prospect of doing coordinated studies in Eastern European Demography.

My overall reaction was that none of the sociologists I met in Russia, Poland, and Yugoslavia had much intellectual independence; their positions are all a positive or negative reaction against one or another branch of American sociology. Being in Eastern Europe reminded me an awful lot of being in Latin America.

Two respondents referred to intellectual output in Eastern Europe as moralistic, descriptive, and reminiscent of the mid-nineteenth century. They thought that the individual scholars there did not lack intelligence or skills but asked unsophisticated questions and applied archaic skills.

In general, the United States sociologists, as the above comments show, tend to view the East European accomplishments in terms of their own subspecialty within sociology. As one would expect, most of these are still relatively undeveloped in these countries. Just which ones seem to be moving ahead can be seen in a closer inspection of what occurs on a country-by-country basis.

COUNTRY-BY-COUNTRY REVIEW

ALBANIA

Charles C. Moskos, Jr., of Northwestern University, has written on "From Monarch to Communism: The Social Transformation of the Albanian Elite."[2] As the title implies, the article compares the 1935 Monarchist elite with the 1955 Communist elite in respect to religion, education, and ethnicity. Professor Moskos' interests, however, lie more with Greece than with Albania.

Mehmet Bequirj, now with the Institut für Agrarpolitik, University of Bonn, Germany, did a thesis while a student at Cornell University on the general problem of social change in Albania (1945–60).

Albania would not therefore be said to hold much interest for American sociologists, particularly since travel there has been almost impossible and, once there, fieldwork would be out of the question. In addition, there is serious question about the value of any statistical series originating in Tirana, a fact which would further discourage any sociologists doing quantitative studies.

BULGARIA

Irwin T. Sanders, of Education and World Affairs, is the only American sociologist to have done fieldwork in Bulgaria. This was in the 1930s and resulted in a doctoral dissertation at Cornell which was rewritten for publication as *Balkan Village*.[3] Several journal articles both in Bulgaria and the United States grew out of this research, which was interrupted by World War II. Sanders is now including Bulgaria along

2. In Herbert R. Barringer, George I. Blanksten, and Raymond W. Mack, eds., *Social Change in Developing Areas: A Reinterpretation of Evolutionary Theory* (Cambridge, Mass.: Schenkman Publishing Co., 1965).
3. (Lexington: University of Kentucky Press, 1948).

with Greece and Yugoslavia in his comparative studies of social change in the Balkans.

In the replies being analyzed in this survey, not a single other sociologist mentioned Bulgaria as an area of interest or as one supplying comparative data for courses or research. As in the case of Albania, the reason is not far to seek. The postwar regime in Bulgaria has not until very recently encouraged scholarly exchange with the United States. Furthermore, the development of sociology in Bulgaria has proceeded at a very slow pace. The situation looks much more promising with the recent establishment of an Institute of Sociology in the Bulgarian Academy of Sciences.

CZECHOSLOVAKIA

Several Czech-born North American sociologists still maintain an interest in developments in Czechoslovakia, but one reports that he is turning more and more to Latin American studies, since it is easier to get research funds to study Brazil than to study East European countries.

Daniel Kubat, a visiting professor at the University of Florida, has written on social mobility, youth movements, the role of intellectuals, and political problems in Czechoslovakia in the 1960s. Jiri Kolaja, McMaster University, is organizing a study comparing Canadian and Czechoslovak student images of what the future has in store for them. Jiri Nehnevajsa, University of Pittsburgh, published a chapter entitled "Anticipated Futures of Czechoslovakia." [4] This deals with possible social transformation in that country. He hopes to work out comparative United States–Czechoslovak research with Czechoslovak sociologists. Jan Hajda, Portland State College, wrote a volume on Czechoslovak society, published by the Human Relations Area Files.[5]

Before World War II, Czechoslovakia shared in the European sociological tradition, but the rise of sociology since World War II has taken place only in the last two to three years. Most of the Czechoslovak sociologists are reformed economists in the Marxian philosophical mainstream; they feel far behind sociological developments in Poland and Hungary in particular. This sense of "having been left behind" gives them a strong desire "to catch up," which may mean faster, more vigorous progress there than would at first be expected.

4. In Miloslav Rechcigl, ed., *The Czechoslovak Contributions to World Culture* (Leiden: Mouton, 1964).
5. *A Study of Contemporary Czechoslovakia* (Chicago: University of Chicago Press, 1956).

EAST GERMANY

Mark van de Vall, State University of New York at Buffalo, was the first American sociologist (and perhaps still the only one) to do field-work in East Germany. For two months during the summer of 1966 he conducted social research on East German industrial relations, where he concentrated on the interrelation of state, trade union, party, and workers in the process of production. He paid special attention to the system of workers' participation in decision-making. The research is still in progress.

There is no satisfactory sociological publication in English on East Germany, although the German work by Peter Christian Ludz, *Soziologie der DDR*[6] is sound. Empirical sociology in East Germany started about three or four years ago. Its present level is still very low. It is mainly in the hands of economists, strongly ideological, and 80 percent applied. Knowledge of American sociology is almost non-existent, partly because of low familiarity with English. However, the East German sociologists are mostly young, enthusiastic, and hard-working. Knowledge of their own society is relatively poor. They have had to proceed cautiously, as sociology has until recently been a "suspected" discipline.

GREECE

Through the years there have been different United States sociologists writing on scattered topics about Greece, but without any sustained effort. At the present time, however, some beginnings of sound empirical research are well underway. Evan C. Vlachos, University of Colorado, served as chairman of the Department of Sociology at Pierce College (1964–66) in Athens and as the director of two projects in the Social Science Centre, Athens. The projects dealt with the problem of large emigration, especially toward Western Europe, and the consequences of rapid urbanization, especially of the Greater Athens Area. Five publications by Professor Vlachos have appeared or are soon to appear on these topics.[7] He is currently working on a book, combining bibliographical and research trends in modern Greece, with a tentative

6. (Cologne: Westdeutscher Verlag, 1964).
7. *An Annotated Bibliography on Greek Migration*, limited cyclostyled ed. (Athens: Social Science Centre, 1966); *The Socio-Economic Structure of Greek Cities*, limited cyclostyled ed. (Athens: Social Science Centre, 1966); *Greek Migration: Theoretical Perspective and Bibliographical Analysis* (in press); *Recent Greek Emigration: The Prospects for Returning Migrant Workers* (in press); *The Assimilation of Greeks in the United States* (in press).

title of "Materials for the Study of Modern Greek Society." Melvin Bobick, University of New Hampshire, spent the 1964–65 academic year at the American School of Classical Studies in Athens preparing a monograph on "Plato as a Sociologist." Panos D. Bardis, University of Toledo, has studied dating patterns as well as social distance, using Greek subjects as his informants. Constantine A. Yeracaris, State University of New York at Buffalo, has completed fieldwork in Greece on a study of the role of conflict in a specific agricultural innovation in a Macedonian village, and is now analyzing his data.

Constantina Safilios-Rothschild, the Merrill-Palmer Institute, during the summer of 1964 conducted a survey study on "Family, Social Class and Mental Illness in Urban Greece" and in a seven-month field study in 1966 followed up with an extensive survey on "Family and Fertility among Working and Non-Working Athenian Women." Five publications based on this study have already appeared.[8] She expects to replicate this study among rural women in the summer of 1968. Irwin T. Sanders is currently working on a study of "Greek Society in Transition" which updates the analysis in his book *Rainbow in the Rock: The People of Rural Greece*.[9] Michael N. Cutsumbis, Franklin and Marshall College, has recently completed a comparative study of self-reported anxiety in certain native Greek and Greek-American student populations.

Sociology as a scientific discipline is a very new development in Greece. The Athens Social Science Centre was established only in 1960 by UNESCO and most of the studies have been of an anthropological or demographic nature and only very recently have some clearly sociological studies been undertaken. There is still no chair of sociology at the University of Athens and graduate training in sociology is still not possible. Pierce College for Girls recently established a department of sociology (where sociology courses are taught by some Greek and some American sociologists) leading to a B.A. in sociology. Some other universities, such as the College of Business Adminis-

8. "Some Aspects of Fertility in Urban Greece," *Proceedings of the World Population Conference, 1965*, vol. 2 (New York: United Nations, 1967); "Class Position and Success Stereotypes in Greek and American Cultures," *Social Forces*, 45, no. 3 (March 1967): 374–83; "Marital Role Definitions by Urban Greek Spouses," paper read at the National Council for Family Relations Meetings, Toronto, Canada, October 21, 1965; "A Comparison of Power Structure and Marital Satisfaction in Urban Greek and French Families," *Journal of Marriage and the Family*, 29, no. 2 (May, 1967): 345–52; "Comparative Analysis of Family Power Structure: Problems of Measurement and Interpretation," paper read at the International Seminar for Family Research, Tokyo, Japan, September 1965 (prepared with Robert O. Blood, Jr., University of Michigan, Reuben Hill, University of Minnesota, Andrée Michel, Centre d'Etudes Sociologiques).

9. (Cambridge: Harvard University Press, 1962).

tration of Salonica and of Athens have a chair of sociology held by a social scientist with no training in sociology, while some trained sociologists are available but are not considered for academic chairs. There are no Greek sociology textbooks and the very few sociological, anthropological, and demographic studies have not been integrated. Thus, teaching about Greek social institutions is quite problematic. In 1966 a sociological journal was published for the first time, under the auspices of the Athens Social Science Centre. It is called *The Sociological Thought*. Further development of sociology in Greece will depend largely upon the opportunities offered to young people for graduate training in sociology in other countries, especially in the United States. A basic difficulty encountered by some sociologists working in Greece, whether Greek or American, is the location and training of interviewers or research assistants. Almost no young people in Greece have a career investment in being trained in sociological research and in obtaining research experience. Therefore, the work commitment is very low and the research help unpredictable and sporadic.

HUNGARY

Paul Hollander, Harvard University, who is originally from Hungary, published an article in the *American Sociological Review* entitled, "Models of Behavior in Stalinist Literature." [10] This was based on both Soviet and Hungarian data. Professor Hollander notes that the state of sociological studies about Eastern Europe in the United States is obviously undeveloped, while in Hungary, developments — though moderately promising — are still in their beginning stages. He indicates that Hungarian literary journals provide a great deal of sociological data for Hungary. John Kosa, Harvard Medical School, did a study of his former countrymen from Hungary who migrated to Canada, under the title *Land of Choice*,[11] but his primary concern in recent years has not been on East European problems.

POLAND

The relationships between United States and Polish sociologists both before World War II and since have been closer than that between the United States and any other East European country. In the first place, sociology was well developed in Poland before the war, and during the war some of the outstanding Polish sociologists came to the United

10. 31 (June, 1966): 352–64.
11. (Toronto: University of Toronto Press, 1957).

States, some temporarily and some permanently. Second, the Polish sociologists have tended to show an independence of spirit not usually
manifested by those in other East European countries, even to the point
of making an open break with the regime and suffering the consequences.
During the period of the Ford Foundation–financed exchange program with Poland from 1957 to 1962, approximately twenty sociologists
came to this country to familiarize themselves with American sociology.
This date was in advance of the Yugoslavs, who later came in similar
numbers under the same program, to be followed even later by one or
two Hungarian sociologists.

Despite this series of contacts, very few United States sociologists have
shown an interest in Polish problems. Feliks Gross, Brooklyn College of
the City University of New York, had a good start on a career in Poland
as a sociologist before he came to the United States. His best known
prewar publication was *The Polish Worker*, published in New York in
1945.[12] At the time, it was the only sociological monograph done in Eastern Europe on this subject. Professor Gross hopes to bring this up to
date. He is also working on a short study of "Changes in Social Structure
in Poland," basing it in part on his earlier writings. Jiri Kolaja, McMaster University, has published a sociological analysis entitled *A Polish
Factory: A Case Study of Workers' Participation in Decision-Making*.[13]

ROMANIA

From evidence gathered to date, it would appear that no United States
sociologist is pursuing any professional interest in Romania. This reflects,
as in the case of Bulgaria, the absence of scholarly interchange as well
as the undeveloped state of sociology in Romania. Before World War II,
the work of D. Gusti and his students in the sociological analysis of
rural communities was attracting the attention of Western sociologists,
but this type of research ended with the war.

YUGOSLAVIA

Within the past six or seven years, the interest of United States sociologists in Yugoslavia has grown greatly. Many Yugoslav sociologists have
spent a year of study in the United States and have formed contacts
which have led to productive visits by American colleagues to the
social science institutes which have been springing up dramatically in
Yugoslavia. Collaboration has been genuine between sociologists from

12. (New York: Roy Publishers, 1945).
13. (Lexington: University of Kentucky Press, 1960).

abroad and the Yugoslavs, and the level of discourse has avoided many of the ideological overtones that could impede sound empirical research. The international conferences staged in Yugoslavia, ranging from the World Population Congress to smaller meetings of specialists in many fields, introduces the outsider to Yugoslavia for the first time and modifies his preconceptions about a Communist society. This leads to lines of inquiry which sometime result in collaborative research.

Immediately after World War II, one of the most active researchers on Yugoslav matters was Dinko Tomasic, Indiana University, whose book *Culture and Personality in East European Politics* [14] compared the Dinaric mountain society with that of the plains in Yugoslavia. This continued the study which Professor Tomasic had carried out in Yugoslavia. Though controversial, it did call attention to some of the sociological aspects of Yugoslav life. In 1957 he published *National Communism and Soviet Strategy*.[15] Other Yugoslav-trained sociologists who have migrated to the United States do not seem to be working on Yugoslav problems. Some American-born sociologists of Yugoslav extraction, such as Arthur Vidich of the New School for Social Research, are carrying out small-scale studies on Yugoslav problems.

More recently, however, the wave of interest in Yugoslavia has involved those with neither ethnic background in the area nor with previous knowledge about the country. Such individuals become connected with some research project or a seminar worked out by a United States university with an institute, university, or agency in Yugoslavia. Most notably, this has included Indiana University and the University of California (Berkeley). The Yugoslav-American Colloquium, held in 1962 jointly by the University of Skopje and Indiana University and published as *Selected Problems of Social Sciences and Humanities*,[16] had two papers on sociology. Joze Goričar dealt with "Some Problems of Methodology in Yugoslav Empirical Sociology" and Irwin T. Sanders with "Aspects of Sociological Research in the United States." The University of California (Berkeley) project is directed in Belgrade by Bogdan Denitch, an American sociologist. Within the past year or two, Cornell has cooperated with Slovene authorities in the creation of an International Center for Regional Studies in Ljubljana. Two Cornell sociologists, George C. Myers and Robert McGinnis, are now associated with the demographic and labor mobility studies being undertaken by the Center.

Professor Myers' research in Yugoslavia, described in a letter,

14. (New York: George W. Stewart, 1948).
15. (Washington, D.C.: Public Affairs Press, 1957).
16. (Skopje: Universitetska pečatnica, 1963).

is devoted to analyses of migration differentials using registration data for Slovenia with the express intention of testing several mathematical models of migration. Using the rich data available for small areas on births, deaths, and migration, we also are preparing a series of projections of population for the next 25 years in Slovenia, Yugoslavia. These projects use matrix procedures and are being processed on computers located in Yugoslavia. The final research undertaking is a joint endeavor with the Sociological Institute at the University of Ljubljana. It is concerned with (1) a social area analysis of the Ljubljana Metropolitan area and (2) a subsequent study on the community power structure and the institutional mechanisms, both formal and informal, for carrying out local decisions regarding community development.

Professor McGinnis' research project is intended to bring stochastic process models to bear in an investigation of the recent development and contemporary mobility patterns of the Yugoslav labor force. This study might continue for a period of several years. The Boston University Department of Sociology and Anthropology had a cooperative arrangement with the University of Skopje to study residential mobility to and within this capital of Macedonia under the general supervision of Irwin T. Sanders, but with the field study being in charge of Bernard S. Phillips and Desenka Miljovska. The research conducted by Professor Phillips and Professor Miljovska centered on the process of personality transformation as the result of migration from rural to urban areas, based on a sample of approximately 275 individuals who had migrated to Skopje, Yugoslavia. Professor Phillips finds Yugoslav sociology — in its analysis of Yugoslav social structure — much superior to American or West European studies from the standpoint of content. He also sees in Yugoslavia a good opportunity to match theory and research. He writes:

> It is possible to conceive of a great deal of sociology as having to do with the problem posed by large organizations for the life of the individual in the organization. This topic reaches, in one way or another, into most fields of sociology; it has to do most centrally with the problems of alienation in the modern world. Yet very few sociologists realize that modern Yugoslavia represents perhaps the only attempt ever made on a national scale to meet head-on the problems posed by bureaucracy for the individual's autonomy. Granting that Yugoslavia is meeting much failure, we have no sociological research to tell us exactly what is going on.

William Beittel, a doctoral candidate in sociology at the University of Pittsburg, is currently working with Professor Evgeni Pušić at the University of Zagreb. He is doing a study of the Yugoslav commune especially from the standpoint of its changing role (increasing autonomy) vis-à-vis the federal government of that country. Jiri Kolaja, McMaster University, published a study, *Workers' Councils: The Yugoslav Experience* [17] which paralleled his factory study in Poland.

Yugoslav sociologists are also engaged in several multilateral research projects in which United States scholars are also involved. This is borne out in a brief look at some of the regionwide projects which are underway.

STUDIES WITH A REGIONAL FOCUS

There are a number of studies which cover several countries and cannot therefore be properly included in the country-by-country survey which is to follow. The works of J. S. Roucek, University of Bridgeport, including the *Slavonic Encyclopaedia* [18] and the issue of *The Annals* on "Moscow's European Satellites," [19] are illustrative. So is the volume *Collectivization of Agriculture in Eastern Europe*, edited by Irwin T. Sanders and containing a chapter on "East European Peasantry" by him. [20] This resulted from a conference which was held for the purpose of interesting American rural social scientists in the convulsive rural changes occurring on a gigantic scale with forced collectivization but which were not being followed systematically by United States rural sociologists. Apparently no converts were made, since United States rural sociologists have been quite oblivious to these revolutionary changes.

Demographic studies have been more numerous, beginning with that of Wilbert E. Moore, of Princeton University and the Russell Sage Foundation, *Economic Demography of Eastern and Southern Europe*. [21] Such studies have been continued by the International Division of the United States Bureau of the Census. George Myers, Cornell University, is preparing a paper entitled "Population Policies and International Migration in Poland, Hungary and Czechoslovakia."

Walter Shafer, University of Oregon, is making contacts with sociologists from Poland, East Germany, Bulgaria, Czechoslovakia, Soviet

17. (London: Tavistock Publications, 1965).
18. (New York: Philosophical Library, 1949).
19. American Academy of Political and Social Sciences (September, 1950).
20. (Lexington: University of Kentucky Press, 1958).
21. (Geneva: League of Nations, 1945).

Union, Yugoslavia, and Hungary on the general topic of "The Sociology of Sport and Leisure."

A study of the effect of social values upon local political decision-making has involved the cooperation of social scientists from the University of Pennsylvania. Two or three United States sociologists have collaborated, chiefly from the standpoint of strengthening the methodology of the study, while first-rate Polish and Yugoslav sociologists have served as principal investigators for their country. Terry N. Clark, University of Chicago, is American director of the decision-making section of the study.

Peter L. Berger, editor of *Social Research* published by the New School for Social Research, has been collecting material from almost all of the East European countries for a special issue on Marxist sociology. Norman Birnbaum, also of the New School for Social Research, is gathering materials on intellectuals in Eastern Europe, studying them as a social group and their relations to the larger group of technical intelligentsia. Dinko A. Tomasic, Indiana University, has for several years been studying communist elites in Eastern Europe as well as elsewhere.

Feliks Gross, mentioned earlier in connection with Poland, has published case studies on ethnic and political tensions in Eastern Europe as well as on the differences between interpersonal and intergroup relations in Central Eastern Europe. Two important contributions are his *World Politics and Tension Areas* and "Structure of Human Relations in Central Eastern Europe," *Human Relations*.[22] Alvin Gouldner, Washington University (St. Louis), has been studying the institutional conditions for the emergence in Eastern Europe of the Western type, academic-oriented sociology, especially in light of the new Soviet sociology.

Alexander Szalai, formerly professor of Sociology at the University of Budapest, now Principal Scientific Research Officer of the UNITAR, directed the Multinational Comparative Time Budget Research Project of the European Coordination Center for Research and Documentation in Social Sciences, the "Vienna Center" of the International Social Science Council. The pilot study of this project was carried out in 1965–66 with collaboration of social research institutes doing parallel surveys in about a dozen Eastern and Western countries and contributing their field data for common comparative evaluation. The institutes from Eastern Europe associated with the pilot study are: Scientific Research Group of the Trade Union Council, Sofia, Bulgaria; Sociological Research

22. (New York: New York University Press, 1966), and 9, no. 2 (Winter, 1961): 143–54.

Group of the Hungarian Academy of Sciences, Budapest; Central Statistical Office, Budapest; Institute of Philosophy and Sociology of the Polish Academy of Sciences, Warsaw; Labour Institute, Warsaw; Sociological Laboratory of the Prague Polytechnical Institute, Prague; Institute for Economy and Organization of Industrial Production of the USSR Academy of Sciences, Novosibirsk; Institute for Sociology, Belgrade; Institute for Philosophy and Sociology of the University of Ljubljana. Data from 30,000 individuals were collected as part of this overall study.

RECOMMENDATIONS

Against the background presented in the preceding pages, the following recommendations are offered:

1. The American Association for the Advancement of Slavic Studies should recognize sociology as a discipline with growing interest in Eastern Europe and provide for representation of sociologists in its committee structure.

2. The American Sociological Association, through its Committee on International Cooperation, should set up a subcommittee on Eastern Europe as a parallel group to its subcommittee dealing with Soviet sociologists. Such a group can explore the possibility of having a session at the annual meeting devoted to problems of sociological research and scholarly exchange with East Europeans. Such a group can serve as a clearinghouse for the dissemination of information about sociology in Eastern Europe, activities of United States sociologists in that area, recent publications, and current developments and problems regarding such matters as travel, language institutes, funding, and the like.

3. A national summer workshop or conference on sociological research in Eastern Europe would give visibility to this field and would add to the competence of those now working or expecting to work in this field. It should be of at least one month's duration, with stipends provided for those who attend. It could furnish some historical background on the region as well as a knowledge of Marxism and the history of Communist movements. This is in addition to a review of the state of sociology in the various countries.

4. Research grants designed especially for sociologists would be a distinct advantage. In competition with historians, political scientists, linguists, etc., sociologists are not in a very good position because of the different professional preparation and experience which they have had. A few grants annually to senior sociologists as well as at the graduate level would begin to attract greater attention to the field.

5. An increased effort to bring visiting lecturers and visiting profes-

sors in sociology from Eastern Europe to United States institutions is necessary. Parallel with this there needs to be a plan to inform the American Sociological Association, sociology departments, and individual sociologists what kind of contribution can be expected from such visitors. The guests should study English in the home country, at the expense of the program, before they depart for the United States.

6. There is a major need for a summer language institute, one which would serve several disciplines and not just sociology. The program would be primarily designed to provide language competence to American social scientists for use as a research tool, and would include ability to speak it. But the emphasis would be upon the needs of the mature scholar. The main activity, several hours each day, would be on language training, but there could also be some discussion of research libraries in Eastern Europe, programs of various research institutes there, and problems connected with doing studies in various fields. Such a language institute should perhaps be located abroad rather than in the United States, if financing permitted.

7. Preparation of a sociological reader on Eastern Europe is essential. Several sociologists say that they would introduce Eastern European materials in their courses on political sociology, comparative sociology, social stratification, etc., if they had suitable sociologically oriented teaching materials.

8. Acceleration of the few efforts now being made to train United States and East European graduate students for research on topics of mutual interest should be encouraged. Field experience is indispensable in such training, as is some language proficiency. Graduate students from the United States should be involved where possible in research being done by senior United States scholars on the area.

9. Much better stocked and staffed libraries and documentation centers specializing in East European materials, though few in number, would attract sociologists interested in comparative data. This in turn might lead to a much fuller investment of effort by such sociologists in Eastern Europe studies. Grants to such libraries and centers would be based on the actual use to which their materials are put.

10. Throughout all of the arrangements suggested above, there needs to be a stress on the nature of scholarly collaboration. Wherever possible, United States sociologists should establish a close working relationship with a local sociologist or institute. They (and this holds true for other disciplines) must develop the confidence of those with whom they work abroad, demonstrate a mutual respect, and patience with and an understanding of the difficulties under which such colleagues (including editors of social science journals) work. Lack of secretarial

services, graduate assistants, and library resources, as well as the need to hold down two or three positions are some of the limitations faced.

APPENDIX

In order to present Walter Schenkel's careful assessment in its entirety, his letter is reproduced here:

. . . I read your report with great interest and would like to take up some of the points. First, with respect to the teaching of sociology within East and Southeast European area programs I couldn't agree more with your statement that "there is not apt to be a marriage between sociologists interested in Eastern Europe and the East European Studies Centers." I had come to the same conclusion based on correspondence with faculty members at several universities that have relatively strong sociology departments as well as East and Southeast European area centers or programs (my aim had been to find out whether some universities offered possibilities of combining studies in sociology with area studies):

(a) *Columbia University*: Apparently no graduate student in sociology has so far been encouraged by the Institute on East Central Europe or by the Department of Sociology to combine studies in sociology with area studies. The Institute still offers no provisions for sociology (political science, however, is acceptable as a major subject), and the Department of Sociology is not encouraging its students to divert their energies into fields other than sociology (sources: talks with faculty members, both at the Institute and in the Department in 1966 and 1967).

(b) *University of California, Berkeley*: The Center for Slavic and East European Studies still offers an Area Certificate which can be taken by sociologists as well as other majors concurrently with an advanced degree in the major subject, but the Center actively discourages students from working for the Certificate, encouraging students to concentrate on their major subject only, at least on the pre-Master's level (source: talk with the secretary of the Center, summer 1966).

(c) *Indiana University*: The Russian and East European Institute officially recognizes sociology as a legitimate major subject which can be studied in conjunction with area courses, but unofficially sociologists studying concurrently at the Institute are discriminated against in that they have to take a heavier course load than other majors to fulfill the Institute requirements for the certificate (source: talk with Professor Tomasic, summer 1966).

(d) *University of Washington, Seattle*: The Far Eastern and Russian Institute started offering a two-year program leading to an interdisciplinary Master's degree in East European Studies in 1966. The students are, however, required to choose a major subject as the university expects them eventually to work for a Ph.D. degree. Political science is an acceptable major while sociology is not. [Professor Lyman Letgers writes that they can permit concentration only in history, geography, and literature, those being the fields in which they have sufficient faculty strength.] However, the Institute is in principle interested in appointing a sociologist knowledgeable in Eastern Europe, and if it finds such a rare bird it is willing to accept sociology as a major field (source: letters from Professor Sugar, Department of History, summer 1966).

(e) *University of North Carolina*: The North Carolina-Duke joint program in Slavic studies does not offer courses in either Soviet or East European sociology: ". . . work in Russian-East European areas studies would have to be accomplished outside of sociology. This is certainly feasible and may even have certain academic and intellectual (sic!) advantages . . ." (source: letter from the secretary of the Committee on Russian and East European Studies, November 1966).

Second, research on Eastern Europe among sociologists in the United States: your five reasons why sociologists have neglected East European studies certainly include all the sore points. The first of the two positive trends you outline — growing importance of cross-national studies — is beginning to appear at Columbia University: Professor William J. Goode is also interested in Greek and Yugoslav family studies within the framework of his interest in cross-national family research. Professors Terrence K. Hopkins and Immanuel Wallerstein mention Eastern Europe in their course on comparative cross-national research (in which, ironically, only few sociology majors enroll — most of the students are from the School of International Affairs). Although Professor George Fischer has only very little time for East and Southeast European sociology, he is willing to back actively any sociologist who develops an interest in the area.

With respect to research on Eastern Europe among Western European sociologists I might add the following information:

(a) *United Kingdom*: Miss Jennifer Platt, lecturer in industrial sociology at the University of Sussex, has a long-standing interest in the Yugoslav system of workers' self-management, and she is familiar with the Yugoslav literature on the subject.

(b) *France*: Dr. Albert Meister at the Ecole des Hautes Etudes is in a position similar to Miss Platt's; his book "Socialisme et autogestion — L'experience yougoslave" (Paris: Editions du Seuil, 1964), is much more extensive than Kolaja's study on the same subject. Professor Henri Mendras did a comparative study of six villages in the Epirus in Greece in 1958, but I don't think that he has done any more work in the area since. The only French sociologist I know of who has shown a sustained interest in comparative studies in the Mediterranean area (in the framework of which he includes Greece and Yugoslavia) is Dr. Jean Cuisenier of the Centre de Sociologie Européenne in Paris. Dr. Cuisenier has so far done at least two village studies in Greece and one in Yugoslavia, and he comes nearest to what could be considered a "Southeastern Europe area sociologist" who not only does research in the area but who also follows the development of sociology in the area. He organizes the annual "Colloque de Sociologie des Pays Méditerranéens" in which Greek and Yugoslav sociologists participate.

(c) *Germany*: Most of the German sociologists who consider themselves specialists in Eastern and Southeastern Europe are not sociologists proper, but rather traditional political scientists with a strong sociological interest. Professor H. Gross holds the Chair of "Wirtschaft und Gesellschaft Südosteuropas" at the University of Munich, but I gather from some correspondence with him that his sociological interest in Southeastern Europe is rather marginal. The same is true for Professor Raupach who holds the Chair of "Wirtschaft und Gesellschaft Osteuropas" at the same university. Professor F. Ronneberger, Director of the "Institut fur Politik- und Kommunikations-wissenschaft" at the University of Erlangen-Nürnberg, considers himself and is at this point considered by Professor Gross the only German sociologist truly knowledgeable of Southeastern Europe. Professor Ronnenberger's main sociological fields of interest are rural sociology and political sociology; presently he seems to be working on a major cross-national comparison of Southeast European societies, a study which should be completed this year. Professor Ronneberger is preparing another major project, namely a comparative study of social change in the Balkan village within the last few decades (source: "Mitteilungen der Südosteuropa-Gesellschaft," 6, 4 [October–December 1966]).

Third, with regard to your recommendations, I would wholeheartedly back them. May I add two comments? (1) I wonder whether there would be any possibility to publish a small duplicated news sheet which would circulate among sociologists who are specifically interested in one way or another in East and Southeast European sociology; these persons could possibly be encouraged to contribute whatever information they might like to share with other sociologists who are interested in the area. I feel that if young sociologists are to be attracted to studies in or about Eastern and Southeastern Europe such an information sheet might prove to be very valuable. (2) I refer to your recommendation no. 7 (sociological reader in Eastern Europe). The information sheet mentioned in my first proposal could at first serve this purpose, but there is another side which might be considered: relatively little is known in coherent form about sociology in the countries of Eastern and Southeastern Europe. It seems to me that one prerequisite for attracting more sociologists to study Southeastern and Eastern Europe would be to provide rather detailed information about the "state of the art" in sociology in each of the respective countries. Most of this information would have to be gathered in the countries themselves. A survey could include the following topics:

  (a) the teaching of sociology (information on personnel, curricula, and institutions),

  (b) social research (information on personnel, projects, institutions, and publications),

  (c) general information about published materials (periodical and non-periodical literature),

  (d) information about existing and possible cooperation between Southeast and East European sociological institutions and organizations and their counterparts in the United States.

As such a survey would require a considerable amount of time, one could conceive of two surveys done simultaneously, one in Southeastern Europe (Bulgaria, Greece, Romania, and Yugoslavia), and one in East Central Europe (Czechoslovakia, East Germany, Hungary, and Poland). I hope that this idea of a "state of the art" survey does not sound like too preposterous a proposal. I have been thinking the idea over for months and discussed it with a number of persons who are interested in the sociology of Eastern and Southeastern Europe, and the response was encouraging. . . .

10 / ANTHROPOLOGY

Conrad M. Arensberg
Columbia University

This survey will be a summary canvass of American anthropologists called upon to discuss their experiences of scholarly work in their field, and will deal with the anthropology, most broadly conceived, of the East European countries, with research in anthropology here and abroad, and with instruction in courses about it. The survey was not exhaustive or statistical. It was made by postcard to interested members of the professional associations in anthropology who listed the region — East Central and Southeast Europe — to be one of their geographic fields, and to chairmen of departments of anthropology listed in the *Guide to Graduate Departments of Anthropology, 1966–1967*, published by the American Anthropological Association. Letters which offered comments, related experiences, and made suggestions for professional work in, and which dealt with, East European countries were solicited and received from a total of thirty-eight anthropologists including archaeologists, linguists, and physical anthropologists (the usual subdivisions of the discipline in the United States).

The letters are summarized here for their content, for information about the field and about American anthropologist's involvement in it, and for the suggestions the letter writers have made. Their suggestions have been combined, as well, to provide recommendations which summarize their recommendations and experiences. The conclusions are not theirs, of course, but rather those of the author of this report, who evaluated them according to his own perception of the situation, its needs, and its possibilities.

The report, then, will be divided into seven parts, following the divisions of content of the letters of the canvass and of the subject matters of the recommedations:

1. American anthropological interest in the East European countries: its small size, growth, and subdivisions
2. The difficulty presented by the quite different organization of anthropology in Eastern European countries
3. Problems of liaison with East European scholarship
4. The question of a center for development of anthropological specialization on the East European countries
5. Political and administrative difficulties in such development and in the conduct of American anthropological research and scholarship in East Europe
6. The question of the restrictiveness of the designation of East Europe as an area of anthropological concern
7. Recommendations of this report

AMERICAN ANTHROPOLOGICAL INTEREST

This survey asked for self-reports of American activities in the East European field, that is, Poland, Czechoslovakia, Hungary, Romania, Bulgaria, Yugoslavia, Albania, and Greece. The questions were:

1. In the past three years have you taught any courses which feature Eastern Europe or which include much East European materials as part of the course content? If so, would you please give me a brief description of the courses, how often offered, whether at the undergraduate or graduate level, and approximate course enrollments?

2. Have you conducted any research dealing with Eastern Europe within the past five years? Could you give me a brief description of the project and whether or not the results have been published or whether the research is still in progress? In the event you have research projected but not started, could you give brief details concerning it?

3. In your opinion, what are the major difficulties faced by anthropologists who wish to do work in the East European field?

4. What steps need to be taken to: (*a*) support those U.S. anthropologists who would like to work in East European studies; (*b*) attract new students with high ability into the field?

To deal with the specific answers to these questions would not serve, in any way, as a statistical summary of courses, projects, persons, or other data about anthropologists dealing with East European countries, as no attempt was made at complete coverage, nor do we know how representative the answers were that came in. Nevertheless, in their rather personal nature, as letters, the broad nature of American anthropological interest in the region emerged quite clearly. By far the larger number of the interested anthropologists were archaeologists, and the courses they gave were most often courses on the prehistory of the region or the bearing of the prehistory of the region on European and Old World prehistory in general. But many of the anthropologists were, instead, cultural anthropologists and a few were physical anthropologists. American anthropology groups together, under the common rubric of their science, four main branches of scholarship. They are all parts of an anthropology conceived historically as an evolutionary, comparative, and analytic summation of the nature, history, and culture of all mankind, treating thus the social as well as the physical evolution and differentiation of man.

The four branches traditional to American anthropology are archaeology, physical anthropology (somatology), cultural and social anthropology (ethnology and ethnography), and anthropological linguistics, the last two sometimes overlapping with folklore and ethnomusicology. As we shall see, the European countries, including the Western ones but especially the Eastern ones, do not conceive anthropology in quite these terms and do not divide it so into comparable branches but instead group the named subjects in quite other ways. Suffice it to say as a first introduction to this problem of the different organization of the science that the letter writers represented sometimes archaeology and, rarely physical anthropology, but sometimes as well the growing interest of American cultural anthropology in the region.

The interest in East Europe of the American cultural anthropologists no longer reflects the older concerns with the cultures of primitive people or prehistorical survivals, either as these might have been once sought in the surviving peasant and transhumant (mountaineer-isolate) popular cultures of the East European countries or in the collections of artifacts, implements, costumes, folktales, folksongs, and other contents of the often thriving national museums of the various countries. Rather, the American interest reflects the newer concerns in American (and West European) cultural and social anthropology in matters of comparative human ecology, comparative social organization, peasant kinship and values, national character and ethos, and cultural and social change.

Interest in American cultural anthropology has moved away from collection and documentation of cultural materials to such matters as cultural classification, cultural process, and to efforts at interpretation and explanation of social, economic, and religious institutions in cultural and socio-psychological, but ethnologically comparative, terms. Its methods are now community study, village study, and analysis of interview, statistical, and behavioral materials, methods which bring the science closer than ever before to sociology, social psychology, and economics. As we shall see, the newer interests and techniques of the science are not always shared in East Europe or, if they are, they are oftener pursued in the other social sciences, not in the locally recognized "anthropology."

Nevertheless, it is just this growth of comparative interest in the transformation of peasant life through the modernization of traditional cultures, and the comparative analysis of different values, behaviors, and institutions in the worlds of the Mediterranean and Middle Eastern and European cultures, in terms serving as well for comparable phenomena from preliterate or other than European civilizations, that marks the usefulness of East Europe to anthropology today. Anthropology has moved strongly from the study of preliterates, tribal, small and "simple" peoples into the study of complex civilization. It has moved from the study of supposedly static cultures to that of changing ones, and it has long ago brought village and urbanizing peasants into its purview all around the world.

The current cultural anthropological interest in East Europe is thus reflective of the major trend within the science. It accounts for the frequent offering of courses in peasant cultures, in culture change, and in areal studies, now the chief elements in the graduate and undergraduate curricula of today reported in the survey. The same move marks the research of a cultural anthropological sort reported; for example, such topics as these are general:

1. Continuing "national character" studies, including older ones still in search of a publishing outlet
2. Village studies, treating the social organization and its psychological functions for peasant life, with such typical titles for resulting articles as "Quarrels in a Balkan Village" and "Kinship and Marriage and Residence Rules"
3. The acculturation of village emigrants in the cities; urbanization of peasants and peasantization of cities
4. Ritual kinship, friendship networks, and kindreds in social organization among peasants and among industrial workers
5. Roles of peasant women, and effects of education thereon
6. Peasant markets

The character of these inquiries, illustrating the trend mentioned above, raises problems for American anthropologists interested in East Europe which make the course of their work difficult both at home and abroad. We will turn to the difficulties faced abroad in the next section. The difficulties at home are that many of the profession, older and more conservative (not, of course, in archaeology but in cultural anthropology) tend to read Europe, indeed even the Middle East and sometimes India and the Far East, that is, all the areas of high civilization, as outside anthropology. They place these areas in the purview of the sociologists or the area specialists: Slavicists, Islamists, Sinologues, etc. Of course there are common subject matters in all civilizations, and indeed much of the new anthropological work is closer, at home and abroad, to that of sociologists than it is to older anthropological concerns. Yet the distinctions are now methodological and conceptual, no longer contentual and historical. Many of the American anthropologists who study East Europe complain that they fall between two stools. Sometimes they are counted out of anthropology because their region — one of a high and literate civilization — seems too modern for anthropology and, in addition, their colleagues, the universities, and even the foundations do not always recognize that social anthropology now works with these modern and literate cultures as well as in peasant and primitive ones. Or sometimes they find themselves counted out because the same colleagues, universities, and foundations assign their newer concerns, like those just enumerated, to disciplines other than anthropology. A concern with urbanization somehow seems unanthropological to those who still think of the anthropologist as a specialist in simple societies. Not all American anthropologists are ready to welcome either European studies or problems of complex modernity and current social change into the purview of their science.

ORGANIZATIONAL DIFFICULTIES

Apart from their facing the great difficulties of knowing the languages, establishing contact, and maintaining rapport with East European scholars and researchers, American anthropologists working in East Europe encounter organizational frustrations there. The quite different placement among disciplines and institutions of the parts, branches, and facilities of anthropology makes for obstacles to contact and obscures interchange of information and effectuation of collaboration. The unitary anthropology of American experience is not present, not even to the degree it exists in Britain and France. Archaeology and prehistory are normally parts of history or relegated to a museum or institute devoted to antiquities. "Anthropology" as a name for a science usually designates physical anthropology and human biology, *tout court.* Cultural and social anthropology are divided between ethnography and ethnology (descriptive and generalizing) and are often confined to museums and the study of preliterate peoples in the extra-European world, on the one hand, and, on the other, to the study of national ethnography, the inquiry into local culture history, variation, and identity, which, along with museums and archives of folk techniques, arts, costumes, legends, literature, and the survivals of folkways, rituals, and customary law of the national, explores the pasts of the countries in question. National ethnography is little cultivated by American anthropologists at home. Its development abroad, because of its sharply localized concern and its confinement to publication in the national languages, as well as because of its heavy concentration on material culture and on other technical interests of an older-day ethnography, is almost unknown to them. Likewise, human geography, village studies, and sociography — much developed in European sociology and geography — and local demography — a prime concern in European sociology, West and East — are not normally treated by Americans as anthropology (if they are known to them at all), even though they are sources of rich primary data and give exquisitely detailed information about the past and present ways of life of the nations in question.

Even in archaeology, however, local specialization is important and must be reckoned with. As an archaeologist of experience puts it:

> National fragmentation of the East European area and the nationalisms that have characterized the area for over a century have led to local archaeological traditions which are reflected in local archaeological reports in the languages of each country and the development of a terminology which is pertinent only to a particular locality. It is only recently that there has begun to develop some notion of a Pan-European archaeology, although the practice of issuing reports and journals in the local language still provides a formidable obstacle to effective communication. One major accomplishment would be to find some means by which the archaeological results would be published in a single language or the requirement that all such publications be accompanied by a precis in some one or two agreed upon languages. While I address myself to the archaeological picture, for it is only with that I have any familiarity, my impression is that other areas of anthropology are beset by similar difficulties.

> One other general difficulty that I found was the separation in the various institutes of the various branches of anthropological investigation. I was surprised, for instance, to find that the Institute for Archaeology is quite separate from the Institute of Ethnography and that there was little communication between the two. Furthermore, it would seem to me that there was a fair degree of separation between the institutes, which are the research centers, and the university, which is the teaching center.

Archaeology is, of course, much less sensitive politically than are other areas of anthropology, particularly ethnography and ethnology. Whether there are kinds or problems which cultural anthropologists would have difficulty in investigating, I do not know; but I had the feeling from my talk with those academics with whom I was associated that such difficulties could be overcome.

Outside archaeology more generally, the state of affairs can be best summarized by quoting at length from Dr. Bela C. Maday of the Behavioral Sciences Training Branch of the National Institutes of Health, who recently gave a paper, soon to be published, on the state of anthropological science in East Europe, at the Sixty-fifth Annual Meeting of the Anthropological Association:

When considering the contemporary scene, it has to be noted that research and higher education have been government responsibilities much before the present political system was introduced in Hungary. Thus, scientific organization has been handicapped in acquiring the necessary flexibility for timely adjustment to the steady growth of human knowledge, a situation not uncommon in other countries, but usually for quite different reasons. The results, however, seem to be identical. The bureaucratic and arbitrary separation of the various scientific activities which in the contemporary American concept of anthropology are intimately interrelated assists in maintaining a frame of reference that is not overly conducive to the development of anthropology as a synthetic discipline.

Anthropologically related work is presently carried out by (a) the Hungarian Academy of Science, (b) the universities, and (c) the museums. The organizational structure of all three institutions emphasizes traditional idiosyncrasies. Within the Academy, ethnography is part of the Department of Linguistics and Literary Sciences; physical anthropology is grouped under Biological and Medical Sciences; and archaeology under the Department of Social and Historical Sciences. In the universities, the departments of ethnography, ethnology, and archaeology are in the schools of philology, while departments of physical anthropology are in the organizational frame of medical schools. Physical anthropology is the concern of the Museum of Natural History, archaeology that of the Hungarian National Museum, while ethnography and ethnology are within the Hungarian Ethnographic Museum.

In general, the Hungarian Academy of Science is the supreme

authority on scientific affairs. It decides policy directives, arranges debates on theory and methodology, coordinates activities of scientific institutes and museums, sponsors laboratory and field work, arranges participation in scientific meetings abroad, and publishes a score of scientific journals and a large portion of all scholarly books.

Cultural and social anthropological activities are carried out under the labels of ethnography, ethnology and folklore. All three fields of study concern themselves with both material and social aspects of culture. A somewhat unusual deviation from the common European pattern is shown in the fact that the term "ethnography" implies also a geographical or ethnic limitation and is used in reference to the study of one's own culture or the subcultures of one's own society. When a study is comparative in character and involves other European cultures, it is referred to as being in the field of European or East European ethnology. The term "ethnology" without qualifying adjectives is used in reference to works on non-European primitive cultures.

The most active research in cultural anthropology is taking place within the framework of the Ethnographic Research Group of the Hungarian Academy of Science. The traditional centers of research are situated in the Ethnographic Museum and in the ethnographic departments of some forty-five regional museums. The entire field of cultural-social anthropology is under the guidance of the Ethnographic Committee of the Academy, which decides on the priority of long-range research and study programs, on selection and schedule of publications, and on budgetary matters including appropriations. In the various university departments and institutes, there are now some 100 professionals, of whom 94 are classified as ethnographers and 6 as ethnologists.

Methods applied depend mainly on the subject matter of research. In the study of material culture and economy, the historical method still predominates. There seems to be a growing interest in such economic topics as the various phases and forms of production, approached on a historical basis from primitive economics to modern mechanization. Although a considerable effort is still concentrated on the ethnography of orally transmitted peasant cultures, and the understanding of the Hungarian ethos, the general trend seems to point increasingly toward ethnological studies comparing Hungarian cultural elements with those found in neighboring cultures and with those of geographically removed but ethnically related cultures.

Perhaps the greatest proliferation of publications can be found in the field of ethnomusicology. A school has emerged in the wake of Béla Bartók and Zoltán Kodály which analyzes Hungarian folk music in its European, even Eurasian interconnections. Extensive work is being carried out and a good number of books and papers have been published on East European peasant cultures on a cross-cultural basis. A study on maize-growing patterns traces the diffusion of maize from its first appearance in East Central Europe to the present day. Another study concerns itself with cereal threshing practices and factors of technology affecting change. There are recent cross-cultural studies on hemp and tobacco cultivating methods and their correlation with the land tenure system. Some of the most significant studies published in recent years include an intensive survey of animal husbandry and pastoral life in Eastern Europe, a volume which complements similar works published in Poland and Romania. Community studies focus on structural and functional aspects of culture. Monographs, such as a study on Szentgal and another on the social institutions of Atany, a village in Heves County, are examples of recent efforts in this field. Other monographs include urban areas.

The long quotation gives the state of affairs for Hungary. It can be taken as representative, in that comparable but specifically complex organizations of anthropological activities mark the other countries' current efforts. Complex and idiosyncratic institutional organization of anthropology in each country makes access and liaison difficult to attain, and thus each suffers from unfamiliarity on both sides.

LIAISON

The East European anthropologists report that a poor state of communication exists between them and their American colleagues. They feel that not only older work, but also recent work of theirs escapes attention. Even their intensive ethnological work, for example, carried on in their home cultures by perhaps a score of anthropologists in Eastern and Southeastern European countries during recent years, seems to have escaped American attention. The American journal *Current Anthropology*, of course, has pioneered in offering international exchanges of correspondence and some clearance of concepts and results for East Europe along with other non-American regions. The Americans working in the region have done much, on a personal basis, to establish contact, but the contact is still largely individual. Difficulties, in general, in liaison seem to be (1) language difficulties, (2) the divergent disciplinary interests instanced above, (3) divergences in the classification of subdisciplines and their practitioners, as already reviewed, and (4) international political tensions.

Language difficulties are mutual. Few anthropologists speak the languages of the various small East Central European and Balkan countries, and, in turn, few articles of East European origin have been translated into English. There seems to be a tendency to translate articles into German and Russian, a fact that does not improve accessibility to American readers. No such series as those made available on Soviet anthropology in the *Anthropology of the North: Translations from Russian Sources*,[1] or Lawrence Krader's "Recent Trends in Soviet Anthropology,"[2] or in the quarterly publication *Soviet Archaeology and Anthropology*[3] exist in respect to the small East Central European and Balkan countries. And as far as can be ascertained, none is being planned.

Nevertheless, despite these difficulties, many of the American scholars reported, in the words of one, "the level of cooperation [in East Europe] was extremely high. I could not have asked for greater cordiality or finer hospitality on social and intellectual grounds." Administrative and official difficulties of liaison were another matter, but, as we shall see, once permissions were obtained and the administrative maze understood and penetrated, cooperation was nowhere reported as a major difficulty. Liaison seems to fail, then, over lack of commonality of interest and over mutual misunderstanding. One man speaks for the others in reporting the coordination of library facilities as being much needed, and he says it is "like pulling teeth to get journals out of the countries in question." Others report that the major lack abroad is access to American and foreign publications, which are not available to the East European scholars through lack of language facility, lack of money, and lack of understanding of the location of relevant materials. Thus, Professor Eugene Hammel of the University of California sums up (for Yugoslavia) a personal appraisal of the troubles of liaison. He tersely comments on the state of affairs:

> Anthropological knowledge about Eastern Europe in the U.S. is poor, but it is vastly better here than it is anywhere else except England. I am not speaking of ethnographic knowledge, in which the Jugoslavs themselves excel (in some areas of culture), but

1. Arctic Institute of North America (Toronto: University of Toronto Press, 1961).
2. Chap. 5 in *Biennial Review of Anthropology: 1959*, Bernard J. Siegel, ed. (Stanford: Stanford University Press, 1959).
3. (New York: International Arts and Sciences Press).

rather of theoretically oriented knowledge. Southeast Europe is a gold mine of theoretically relevant data on exchange, complementary filiation, fit and lack of fit between terminology and role structure, and the like. The Jugoslavs (with the exception of Professor Milenko Filipović) are not interested in those problems, and we do not have the access to the data here which would allow us to get the job done properly.

Several suggestions (which will appear later as recommendations of this report) recur in the letters of the American anthropologists to improve what liaison now exists. Professor Joel Halpern of the University of Massachusetts strongly urges close work with the sociologists of East Europe, who are active in many of the concerns treated by anthropologists here and who are, in addition, often active men of affairs. Professor Asen Balikci of Montreal University suggests it would be very useful indeed to send gifted North American students for a year's training period, after language instruction, to a local research institute in the country of their future field work. A period of residence at a local institution would enable the student to become acquainted with the general ethnography of the area and with the possibilities of locating common interests among the national scholars. Several individuals suggested that European scholars, both young and old, might be brought to this country, either to a single center of coordinated East European research or, better, perhaps, to many different places for research of their own in North America. They could be helped to publish their North American work both at home and in this country. All agree that what is needed is deeper contact and more continuous reading of one another's outputs.

CENTER FOR SPECIALIZATION

The establishment of a center for anthropological studies of East European countries was very frequently a theme of the letters. It was presented as one means of clearing publications and of providing liaison of the kinds mentioned in the preceding section. It was argued that it would not only centralize interest in this country in East Europe, but that it would present, for East Europeans, a continuing example of the integrated "science of man." This example might set in motion a continuing, historical interfertilization of the branches of anthropology. Thus archaeology and prehistory would keep pace as a cultural history of the region connected with the modern trends in comparative cultural anthropology (ethnology). The center could as well serve to bring back into touch the Slavicists and others interested in area studies and the local national cultures or the region in other than anthropological disciplines: history, economics, law, political science, sociology, and human geography. It could contribute greatly to interfertilizing the treatments of social and economic change, of peasant and industrializing national developments, and of comparative social organization and cultural evolution which these disciplines provide. It could serve as a model for integrated social science scholarship on other world areas and it could elevate concern with East Europe to some equality with American concern for other world areas.

Professor David Rodnick of Midwestern University expressed very well indeed, in his letter, the need for such a center and its ancillary support to the field:

> The steps which need to be taken to support U.S. anthropologists who would like to work in East European studies would require that the latter be put on an equal footing with those whose fields are the American Indian, Polynesia, linguistics, archaeology, and physical anthropology — all from the point of view of field support, publication funds, and positions on anthropology faculties. Thus far East European studies do not even occupy the position of stepchildren but rather that of slaveys in anthropology. More support is needed to develop interdisciplinary studies by anthropologists, sociologists, political scientists, and historians on the various aspects of East European life: urban, social, rural, familial, educational, political, etc.
>
> In my opinion there is no interest in the United States in studies dealing with Eastern Europe either on the part of anthropology faculty members or college administrators. With each passing year, the number of archaeologists, linguists, and physical anthropologists increases (along with American Indian specialists), but there is little support for studies of complex, urban, industrial civilizations — and yet these are the areas that will determine the directions of the future.

Organization and location of such a center was not suggested, and its financing was not discussed.

ADMINISTRATIVE AND POLITICAL DIFFICULTIES

The major difficulties faced by anthropologists in Eastern Europe, as reported in the survey, are much the same as those faced everywhere, heightened but not altered by the ideologies and political characters of the present governments. The writers of letters report no great difficulties if proper channels are followed, if permissions are obtained, if clearances with local police authorities for field work are obtained, and if some caution, openness as to affiliations and commitments — academic and institutional — is maintained. No financial support is to be expected from local authorities, or even institutes and museums, but the courtesy of help, provision of student assistants, even cooperative research, whether in archaeology or in cultural anthropology, seems forthcoming, provided interest is evoked and some personal contact and liaison with counterpart scholars is achieved. The experience of anthropologists in foreign countries of all political persuasions has been recently the subject of rather full committee exploration among members of the American Anthropological Association. A report on the subject covering in detail East European and Russian experience of Americans, as well as that in other world regions, as these are affected by governmental procedures and policies and by the vagaries of political relationships between the United States and the host countries, has recently been made under the committee leadership of Professor Ralph Beals for the American Anthropological Association.[4]

From that report, as well as from the letters, it can be said that the writers emphasize that difficulties have always been resolved; no outright closing down has occurred, though sensitive local concerns have had to be respected. There seems to be no restriction on publication other than the usual discretions of anthropologists in protection of persons, offices, and reputations. American political scientists publish regularly in many of the countries on far more sensitive subjects of national politics and policy than do anthropologists and sociologists. The situation has improved vastly over the conditions of the immediately postwar decade when modern social science did not exist and a better application of Marxism-Leninism seemed to be the sole official solution to social problems. The current empirical social science of the countries in question is a quite recent development. Research of an applied nature pertinent to U.S. policy interests could not be carried out, of course, but grants and fellowship support coming from governmental sources are understood, even expected — since, indeed, communist doctrine would deny the possibility of completely neutral scholarship. Universities, research institutes, museums, medical institutes, etc., may be severally appropriate to one kind of research or another and can and do offer useful possibilities of collaboration. While their jealousies (not unknown also in this country) may be trying, they are not unexpected or insurmountable.

4. Available in *Fellows News Letter* (October, 1967).

DEFINITION AND OVERLAP OF AREAS

Unresolved, and of interest to the writers of the letters, is the matter of the cogency of present areal divisions of scholarship in the regions of the earth and especially in the modern trend toward interest in changing societies and transforming cultures in anthropology. The present regions or areas, like the East European one under discussion, are largely historical and linguistic ones, or politico-geographic ones, not especially relevant to anthropology or even sociology, economics, and human geography and ecology, but reflect, instead, philological, literary, historical scholarship. Thus the cultures of East Europe are more often linked to Slavic studies, though not all the peoples are Slavs, nor are Slavs confined to the East European countries. There is not much reason to separate East Central Europe from Russia, or to put the Balkans and Greece, traditionally European, in East Europe rather than in the Mediterranean or the Middle East (if the last is conceived more broadly than Islam). The matter was raised in several letters and could well be a subject of discussion in foundations, learned societies, and American universities.

Suffice it to say, here, that the discussion of the appropriateness of the areal designation *Eastern European Countries* is raised in the section of recommendations which follows.

RECOMMENDATIONS

The tenor of the suggestions of the anthropologists reporting experience in scholarly work with and in Eastern European countries leads to the following recommendations:

1. The relevant learned societies, such as the American Association for the Advancement of Slavic Studies, might be urged to broaden their representation of disciplines to include sections on the social sciences not now represented, sociology, social psychology, and anthropology. In the case of anthropology, though the numbers are not great, representation might be solicited from the subdisciplines of American anthropology, physical and racial anthropology, primatology, and, especially for its active connection with museums and excavations in East Europe, archaeology and prehistory. American anthropology tries, in its professional association and in most of the established university graduate departments offering the Ph.D., to keep all these specialties together, grouping with them sometimes even folklore, aspects of human geography (village and community studies, ecological anthropology), and philosophical and psychological anthropology. In most of the East European countries, because they respond to other organizational

traditions, these disciplines are grouped quite otherwise, often in quite separate faculties of the universities and in separate professional associations. The recommendation here is that representation for American anthropology be provided and an allocation of liaisons with, review of, and communication with the otherwise organized and separated East European scholars be worked out through such anthropological representation.

2. It is recommended that the same task be undertaken by special East European subcommittees to be set up in the professional associations in their existing committees for liaison with foreign scholars.

3. In view of the very small effort now being put into anthropology of the East European countries, and the very limited contact, understanding, and scholarly cooperation existing between American and East European scholars, it is recommended that the following special efforts be undertaken to remedy this situation.

a) One major center be set up for East European studies with a full program of research, course instruction, language training, and exchange of scholars.

b) Provision be made to bring foreign anthropologists, including especially East European ones, to carry on research in the United States projected and undertaken by themselves, with and without the collaboration of American anthropologists, and with publication subsidies for their work both in English and in the language of their home countries. These scholars should be both visitors lecturing and studying at American universities and research scholars working on problems of their own interest on American materials and settings. They should be thus both young East Europeans brought for long periods of study and mature scholars helped to do research or criticism in this country, and they should be provided with facilities permitting them to take part in collaborative exchange with American professionals and to report in their own professional and organizational terms at home.

c) In view of the unfamiliarity of Americans with East European journals in the fields relevant to American anthropology, either because of the separateness of the materials or their small circulation in journals of non-English language publication, it is also recommended that a major effort at summarization and digesting of East European materials be undertaken by the Americans and that the East European scholars be provided with subscriptions to and abstracts of American publications. For reasons of poverty, differences of language, paucity of communication and contact, and differences of professional, disciplinary, and university organization already mentioned, it is often reported and much stressed that East European scholars do not know and read

American anthropology and often do not see the value or interest of American anthropological concerns, concepts, and researches. It is also often reported that Americans sometimes look down on the concerns, concepts, and research efforts of the East Eastern scholars because many of them seem to confine themselves to narrowly national audiences. It should be emphasized that summarization, digesting, and publication should open communication in both directions.

d) There seems to be no great difficulty, indeed much effective cooperation is reported, in research by Americans in East Europe, especially in Yugoslavia and Greece, where most anthropological work has been carried out. Lack of interest and communication, rather than usual and expectable political and administrative problems with field research, are reported, and it is to this condition that recommendations (*c*) and (*d*) above are addressed. It is recommended, however, for future American fieldwork in anthropology in East Europe, that two measures be adopted in this country:

i) The provision of summer language institutes in which graduate students preparing for fieldwork can be well grounded ahead of time in the local languages.

ii) The extension of research grants to include a year of local residence, language familiarization, and involvement in the scholarly background of parallel East European concerns to be followed by the usual year or more of field study in a problem matter or regional culture. Such a year of immersion, perhaps involving some attachment to a national institute, would assure a better grounding in the national culture and it would provide for future personal contact and collaborative effort between nationals and Americans.

e) It is recommended that the learned societies, foundations, granting institutions, and universities in the United States concerned with anthropology review the growing, if as yet small, real interest in European, Mediterranean, and Near Eastern cultures, that they recognize more explicitly in their procedures the large amount of anthropological work being done in these areas of high civilizations, and that they somewhat expand or otherwise standardize their geographical divisions of the countries and regions whose culture, archaeology, social change, national character, and racial composition are more and more standard and necessary parts of international and American anthropology. Thus work in Yugoslavia is now being reported under the following rubrics: European culture, Mediterranean culture, Near Eastern and Middle Eastern (Orthodox Christianity, etc.), and Slavic culture, all of which are legitimate inclusions. Many anthropologists working in Europe see no reason to separate the peoples of the great North European plain and do not see why East Europe does not include the Russophone peoples of the Soviet Union. Nor do they understand why Greece, the area of major anthropological research interest in recent years among the countries covered here, is classified by foundations and in scholarly meetings sometimes as being European and sometimes not, when, by any anthropological standard as employed in England and France, there is more to be learned by making Greece a part of a focus on the "Circum-Mediterranean" peoples. Similarly, there are other scholarly orphans: Finland, the Baltic Countries, the Caucasian ones. The matter is of course largely arbitrary and the divisions, in learned council and university practice, are either political or linguistic. In the social sciences, however — and especially in anthropology — scholarly interest is problem-centered, rather than geographical and literary. The present separation of countries into linguistic groupings or into Russian and satellite seems to compound the already difficult communications of a region where common problems of scholarly interest unite areas of diverse political structures and unrelated languages. It is recommended that some sort of review of geographical groupings imposed on Americans by their own scholarship and learned council procedures and organization be undertaken with a view to clarifying, loosening, and quickening our scholarly attention to the large and important area of the globe east of Germany and Italy and north of the Indian Ocean.

Lastly, in aid of American research in East Europe, it is felt that it would be wise to urge on universities, foundations, and learned societies in the United States that regular and frequent research semesters be provided their teaching anthropologists, with continuation of salary and provision of funds for travel and documentary acquisitions in support of research. It is urged also that funds be available on short notice to enable mature scholars to take advantage of short-term opportunities (conferences, visits, and the like) for liaison and collaboration. In the interest of long-term improvement of American anthropological research in East Europe, it is urged that good students can best be recruited into the field (for which there are as yet limited career prospects) by extending provision of career fellowship programs covering language and area training, fieldwork, and Ph.D. write-up, which is, of course, long-term support, but which is necessary to the preparation and the recruitment of good candidates.

BIBLIOGRAPHY

PARTIAL LIST OF WORKS ON EAST CENTRAL AND SOUTHEASTERN
EUROPE BY AMERICAN CULTURAL ANTHROPOLOGISTS

Andromedas, John. "The Maniats." Ph.D. dissertation, Columbia University, 1962.

Balikci, Asen. "Quarrels in a Balkan Village." *American Anthropologist*, 64 (1962): 328–39.

Friedl, Ernestine. *Vasilika*. New York: Holt, Rinehart & Winston, 1962.

Halpern, Joel. *Serbian Village*. New York: Columbia University Press, 1960.

———. "Yugoslav Peasant Society in Transition — Stability in Change." *Anthropological Quarterly*, 36:156–82.

Koenig, S. "Marriage and the Family among Galician Ukranians." In *Studies in the Science of Society*, edited by G. P. Murdock. New Haven: Yale University Press, 1937.

Krader, L. "Recent Trends in Soviet Ethnography." In *Biennial Review of Anthropology*, edited by B. Siegal. Stanford: Stanford University Press, 1959.

Sanders, Irwin T. *Balkan Village*. Lexington: University of Kentucky Press, 1949.

Shimkin, D. "National Forces and Ecological Adaptations in the Development of Russian Peasant Societies." In *Process and Pattern in Culture: Essays in Honor of Julian H. Steward*, edited by R. A. Manners. Chicago: Aldine, 1964.

Zborowski, Mark, and Herzog, Elizabeth. *Life Is with People*. New York: Schocken Books, 1952.

11 / LAW

Kazimierz Grzybowski
Duke University

ACTUALITY AND PROSPECT

At present the United States is a classical country in Soviet research.
We do more in this field than any other country and we set the pattern
for imitation. This is particularly true in the field of law. A number of
important American law schools offer courses in Soviet law and support
research in this field. The situation is quite different with respect to
other socialist countries. No courses dealing with legal systems of the
Eastern European people's democracies are offered, and research is
carried out sporadically by a few scholars only. In this area we are far
behind Germany, or even Holland.

There are at least two basic reasons for this. One is the absence among
American law professors of competent teachers with proper linguistic
qualifications. The other is a firm belief that the need to study socialist
legal systems is adequately met by teaching Soviet law. No thought is
being given to the question whether there would be a demand for a
course of instruction in socialist law other than Soviet. And yet on
two occasions this writer was able to offer a course in the legal systems
of the East European people's democracies and student response was
excellent.

It is clear, however, that neither student interest, nor teacher availability is decisive in this connection. The study of non-Soviet socialist
law deserves a place in law school curricula only if it offers a new opportunity to gauge the role of law in society, and reveals a different technique for social polity from that either of free societies or of the Soviet
Union. The study of non-Soviet socialist law deserves a place in law
school curricula if it would open the minds of young lawyers to a new
understanding of social and political processes.

The next question concerns method. Would not the proper procedure

267

be to enlarge the instruction of Soviet law by shifting the emphasis to comparative treatment of socialist law as such, deemphasizing Soviet legal institutions in the strict sense of the word? From a historical point of view it is true that legal systems of the socialist states in Eastern Europe are the result of a forced reception of Soviet legal institutions. However, the process of reception was different in each individual state and the degree of penetration of Soviet legal techniques into the fabric of national laws differed from country to country. Sometimes (in Yugoslavia, Bulgaria, and Albania) socialist legal order emerged as a result of the total repeal of pre-revolutionary laws. In a majority of the people's democracies in Eastern Europe, however, sovietization of their legal systems was a much more subtle process, involving a good deal of reform, adaptation, and evolving new processes and techniques of administration. Frequently, reform was the continuation of a process begun before the war, the realization of concepts and programs latent in the social mind and not connected with socialism or communism. In countries like Czechoslovakia, Poland, Hungary, and East Germany, where the tradition of legal order was well established, and where laws and codes reached a high degree of perfection, it was almost impossible to divorce the new system from the fundamental and traditional juristic thinking, which has remained a part of the new system. Specialized judicial bodies had to be created in order to meet the revolutionary situation, staffed by non-jurists, members of the Party, or even (as in Poland and Hungary) by members of the Soviet armed forces or of the Soviet judiciary.

Thus, even from the point of view of the technique of the reform, it seems hardly possible to integrate the treatment of the legal systems of the socialist countries of Eastern Europe into already existing courses in Soviet law. It is to be feared that this experiment would disrupt a pattern of instruction which has behind it a well-established tradition, and, by trying to combine disparate elements, distort also the vision of the legal evolution of Eastern European countries.

It is frequently overlooked that legal systems of socialism, including the Soviet legal order, are the result of an evolutionary process of considerable duration. The resultant modernization of social structures under the impact of new industrial technologies and scientific developments was a process which set in a long time before the October Revolution. Soviet scholars, in their effort to prove the uniqueness of Soviet experience and the general validity of the Soviet model of transition for other societies, claim that the legal system of the first land of socialism is exclusively the result of the socialist revolution and represents a higher type of law with no antecedents in earlier social and economic formulations. This claim is sometimes repeated uncritically by Western scholars who fail to see the present phase in the development of law in Eastern Europe in proper historical perspective.

Myopia of those scholars was valiantly aided by the fact that the present legal system in the Soviet Union, a legal system of the industrial society, is indeed entirely the work of the Soviet legislator, because at the moment of the revolution Imperial Russia had only the beginnings of modern laws. It is true nevertheless that some Soviet institutions have their roots in the past. The institution of procuracy, land tenure, institution of artel, principles of collegiality in public administration, all are purely Russian and prosper as truly national institutions under the Soviet regime. Other features of the Soviet order which seem to be characteristic of Soviet public life — factory regime, discipline of labor, certain aspects of criminal law and criminal policy, and regimentation of the press — were clearly the result of the struggle of the regime with the backwardness of the country, the need to regiment the population of a predominantly agricultural society to adapt itself to the tempo of work in the factories and life in the urban environment, and to create new social classes and new professions. But once this has been accomplished, these features of the Soviet legal system will be gradually, though slowly and cautiously, discarded. One day they will probably disappear altogether, and one may predict quite confidently that, at that moment, socialist law will differ only in form, but not in social function, from the law of the free societies.

This is clearly visible in the socialist countries of Eastern Europe, where socialism came at the moment when the foundations of the modern society were already in existence, where an industrial economy (in Czechoslovakia, Hungary, and to some extent Poland) was already either fully developed or partially in existence. While antecedents of a modern legal system were absent in Russia, they were present in other socialist countries in Eastern Europe. In Eastern Europe the communist legal system was superimposed on an existent legal order clearly Western European in form and tradition. It drew from a variety of sources, all of them part of the Western European tradition. It included Roman heritage, either directly or through the influence of French and Austrian civil law. It drew from Western European models of constitutionalism. In criminal law, reform was inspired by French philosophers, and particularly the ideas of Beccaria, and in their wake by the whole line of schools of criminology ending with the Italian *scuola positiva*. Public administration derived its patterns from the administrative laws of France, Prussia, and Austria.

At the moment of the arrival of socialism, fostered and imposed by the Soviet Union, Eastern Europe was in terms of legal development at least a generation ahead of Imperial Russia, which was fully conscious that its legal system was not adequate for a modern state. The Imperial government was highly conscious of the backwardness of Russian law, and maintained the civil codes of the Polish Kingdom, of the Baltic provinces, and of the legal system of Finland. Neither, in Russian opinion, was the Russian system of government fit to serve as a model for the government in other countries, and after the liberation of Bulgaria, when the constitution was being prepared, its Russian draft was that of a constitutional monarchy closely resembling the Belgian fundamental law.

It is clear now, at a time when society in the Soviet Union and in the majority of the socialist countries is moving into a period of relative maturity, that structural alterations in socialist societies with respect to the function of social groups in public life, to the status of the individual, and to social and moral ills of the socialist man, bear striking resemblances to the developments and problems on our side of the world. The study of the legal systems of the socialist countries in Eastern and Southeastern Europe could still be Soviet-oriented should their position as Soviet satellites have remained unchanged. However, since the death of Stalin, and the ensuing revolts in Hungary and Poland, former satellites have regained a relative independence which is singularly pronounced in the field of legislation and the administration of justice. Legal systems of people's democracies can no longer be analyzed in terms of the reception of Soviet legal patterns, but must be seen in terms of their social and political reality, which is a continuation of their presocialist past.

WHY STUDY EASTERN EUROPEAN SOCIALIST LEGAL SYSTEMS?

Of the Socialist Commonwealth of Nations, only the Soviet Union was without a modern legal system, as developed in the West, at the time of the Revolution. All other states were in this respect a part of the Western European tradition, and a part of the civil law area as it was developed under the influence of the French *Code Civil*. While this fact sets Eastern European countries apart, and calls for a separate approach, it is also of singular interest for legal research in free societies. As compared to the socialist revolution in Russia, socialism in the countries of the people's democracy in Eastern Europe was a phenomenon which occurred in a different social and cultural environment and represented, sociologically speaking, a different experience. Because of the historical retardation of Russia, the Russian experience could have little significance for advanced societies. By contrast, the evolution toward socialism in East European countries of the people's democracy permits one to examine meaningfully the impact of socialism in the Soviet form upon modern societies in general, particularly in regard to the functioning of legal institutions, the legal position of the individual, of social organizations, and the function of public authority.

Scholars of the free world may look upon the legal regimes of Eastern European countries as experiments which bear directly upon their own societies, regimes which have already experienced the characteristic features of the socialist public order (nationalization, governmental functions of social and professional organizations, government monopoly of industrial activity). Studies of Eastern European governments could be of great significance for the analysis of such phenomena as the institution of legal reform, bureaucracy, centralization and decentralization, correlation of administrative functions performed by political organizations, social bodies and agencies of local and central government, control of expediency and legality, and, finally, the operation of the credit system and the finances of the state.

One of the key problems of the situation of the individual in modern society is his identification with larger groups and his participation through them in performance of public functions. Where is the danger point at which his participation in collective processes and official functions so identify him with the public authority that there are only two positions open, either that of government functionary or that of the enemy of the public order? How to avoid total identification of the private right with the public function, and of the private law with the public law?

Another important problem is the question of the criminal and criminality in the modern industrial society. Socialism in its Soviet version sought independent solutions to these problems by affirming the basic connection between capitalism and the phenomenon of crime and the duty of work as the most important integrating force in the socialist system. Under socialism, it was alleged, alienation and collectivity-individual conflicts would disappear and crime problems would automatically be solved. These expectations were not fulfilled, and now a more sober attitude toward crime is demonstrated. Criminal statistics are again published and it is possible to measure the impact of the socialist regime upon the individual psyche in terms of criminal deformations. The interesting aspect of the criminological studies in people's democracies is in the fact that some of these countries (Poland, Yugoslavia) experimented in the interwar years with modern criminological techniques, and statistical data from that period are still available.

Thus studies of the legal developments in Eastern Europe may serve to open new vistas for the study of social sciences, instructive particularly for the problem of legal reform. They should be of interest both within the framework of law school curricula, and in the programs of other university departments. At the undergraduate level, particularly in the law schools, courses in the legal systems of the people's democracies in Eastern Europe may be used in order to broaden the horizon of the American law student in the same manner as the study of comparative or international law, of jurisprudence, Roman law, or legal history. It may have more meaning for the basic issue of the function of law within an international order in which systems of states are tending to replace sovereign nations as units of which the international community consists, and the degree of mutual accommodation of which socialist and free economy legal systems are able. Legal studies dealing with problems of legal commerce with Eastern Europe are still in their infancy and little has been done for the understanding of the nature of legal commerce in an ideologically divided world which will have to develop ever closer techniques of economic and cultural, if not political, cooperation.

While theoretical aspects of legal research in socialist law, as represented by the people's democracies of Eastern Europe, are of high interest, there are also important practical reasons which law school curricula and research programs ought to anticipate. After long years of stalemate in East-West economic cooperation, we seem to be moving in the direction of a steady and important expansion of trade, experience, and even capital investment. In the mind of the American public, all problems of this type are dominated by the presence of the Soviet Union and the basic conflict of interests between the two superpowers of the world. European governments and business circles are able to distinguish between the Soviet giant, never too anxious to develop trade relations with the outside world, and other socialist countries in Eastern Europe which were always a part of the European economic organism and are now in the process of gradual economic rapprochement with the West.

The problems of American participation in foreign trade with Eastern Europe is of a complex nature, and calls for overcoming obstacles of an emotional nature. And yet it is clear that the political meaning of economic cooperation in the field of electronics or plastics with Poland and Yugoslavia, or in making tires in Romania, is in terms of national security a problem of different magnitude from similar ventures in cooperation with the Soviet Union. It is interesting to note that some of the socialist countries (Poland, Yugoslavia, Romania) have modified their legal regimes to permit property rights for foreign business ventures, or have established techniques for permanent economic cooperation between the capitalist and socialist enterprises to produce for international markets, a situation not yet known in the Soviet Union. Each of these countries has also departed from the principle of monopoly of foreign trade.

Another development which is causing considerable reorientation of industrial development programs is the growing conviction among economic planners in the socialist countries of Eastern Europe that the socialist economic system, even within the circle of the entire Socialist Commonwealth of Nations stretching from the Far East to the gates of Western Europe, is unable to solve alone the problem of plant modernization. It must seek cooperation with the advanced industries of the United States and Western Europe. The technique of lifting patents and piracy of models is giving way to a policy of acquiring patents and plant equipment. This type of cooperation calls for the training of lawyers and foreign trade and patent experts able to serve American business in the same manner as the American lawyer is serving it in assisting trade and economic relations with free economy countries. While it is possible to use the services of foreign lawyers in foreign business relations, this is not practical in relations with a socialist state, as the legal profession there is under a bond of total loyalty to state interests.

THE STATE OF RESEARCH

The beginnings of a systematic study in this country of the socialist legal systems in Eastern Europe were made in 1949. A Mid-European Law Project financed by a leading American foundation was set up in the Library of Congress in order to expand, with the help of native lawyers, the collections of law books for their countries and to initiate legal studies of the laws of their respective countries. This research program laid solid foundations for the study of the legal systems of Eastern Europe, which at that time were under the full pressure of Stalinist sovietization.

The result of the project was a series of bibliographies of legal sources and of legal literature for Bulgaria, Czechoslovakia, Hungary, Poland, Romania, and Yugoslavia. For some of those countries, the bibliographies, including short descriptions of the history of legal systems and explanations of their legal sources, were the first works of this type.

In 1959, a major two-volume compendium appeared, *Government,*

Law and Courts in the Soviet Union and Eastern Europe.[1] This was a collective effort, with the members of the project systematically treating various questions relating to the emergence of the socialist legal systems in Eastern Europe.

In addition to this compendium, a number of minor studies were published in multilithed form, among them a study of economic treaties and agreements of the Soviet bloc countries.[2] Finally, the project published a monthly *Highlights of Current Legislation and Developments in Mid-Europe* which reported developments, trials, new laws, and administrative reforms. The project came to an end in 1960, and since that time no other center for a systematic study and research of Eastern European legal systems has been created.

At the present time, a few isolated scholars from time to time contribute articles to legal periodicals and review the legal literature from Eastern Europe. Under the leadership of Professor John Hazard of Columbia University, a number of researchers study the question of the spread of Soviet legal institutions in Eastern Europe. Professor W. Wagner of Indiana University Law School is the author of a number of articles dealing with the civil law in Poland, and an association of Polish lawyers in exile has published a volume of essays on Polish law in the initial period of the communist regime in Poland.[3]

In contrast with the present situation in this country, studies in Eastern European law are actively pursued in Germany, Holland, France, and Belgium. After the reestablishment of statehood in West Germany, a number of centers and institutes for the study of Soviet and Eastern European legal regimes were founded.

These institutes and research centers established a Study Group on Eastern European Law which includes both the Soviet Union and people's democracies in Eastern Europe. The Seminarabteilung für Ostrechtsforschung in Hamburg, under the leadership of Georg Geilke, is exclusively concerned with the legal systems of people's democracies in Eastern and Central Europe. These institutes and research centers contribute articles, notes, and monographic studies to specialized legal periodicals (*Ost-Europa Recht, Jahrbuch für Ostrecht, Recht in Ost*

---

1. Vladimir Gsovski and Kazimierz Grzybowski, eds., *Government, Law and Courts in the Soviet Union and Eastern Europe*, 2 vols. (London: Stevens & Sons; New York: F. Praeger, 1959).

2. Kazimierz Grzybowski, *Economic Treaties and Agreements of the Soviet Bloc in Eastern Europe* (Washington, D.C.: Library of Congress Law Library, 1952).

3. Zygmunt Nagorski, ed., *Legal Problems under Soviet Domination*, vol. 1 (New York: Studies of the Association of Polish Lawyers in Exile in the United States, 1956).

und West) and prepare translations of codes and laws which come out in regular serial publications devoted to familiarizing scholars with foreign legislation.

Important work is being done by the Osterreichisches Ost- und Süd-osteuropa Institut in Vienna, which publishes a series under the name *Dokumentation der Gesetze und Verordnungen Osteuropas.*

In Holland, the University of Leiden set up an Institute for Eastern European Law which occupies a leading position in Western Europe. Its publication series *Law in Eastern Europe* has devoted several volumes to translations and studies of Eastern European legal systems. The remarkable feature of the Leiden program is that it covers the entire world of socialist law, including China, and that it combines the work of domestic and foreign scholars. Its importance is further enhanced by its library, which was assembled with rare competence.

Important work is done by the Center for the Study of the U.S.S.R. and of the countries of the East at the University of Strasbourg in France. Its program is not limited exclusively to the study of law, but includes social, economic, and political developments, in line with the general approach to legal studies in France. The important feature of the research program of this center is that it was able to obtain active cooperation of the jurists from the socialist countries. It publishes a yearbook and a quarterly which gives a review of articles appearing in the periodical press in the Soviet Union. In addition, the center is responsible for the publication of a series of monographs, including translations from East European works.

Comparative legal science in Western Europe has elaborated a suitable legal terminology and frame of reference enabling Western scholars to analyze Eastern European legal institutions in the context of their socioeconomic reality. It has provided sufficient material to permit the examination of the theoretical bases, the history, and the codes of these legal systems. Considerable literature has been published in Western European languages; standard textbooks and codes of law have been translated and analyzed.

It must be realized that all these studies and research programs are financed from public funds and are organized as part of the public instruction program. The importance which is attached to these studies was underscored by the fact that the Council of Europe (Strasbourg) adopted Resolution 312 (Jan. 27, 1966) on the coordination of research concerning the legal systems of the countries of Central and Eastern Europe. In turn, the council convened an international conference of the directors of the institutes, associations, and law faculties in the member states of the Council of Europe carrying out research concerning the legal systems of the countries of Central and Eastern Europe, enabling them to gain an overall view of their work in order to coordinate their activities, to establish exchanges of information and documentation, and, possibly, to agree on a division of labor.

TEACHING — APPROACH AND MATERIALS

It is not the purpose of this section to prescribe how to organize a course of instruction in the socialist legal systems of Eastern Europe. The area includes eight countries, among them a federation (Yugoslavia). Governments and legal systems of these countries feature great contrasts and diversification in the degree of regimentation and liberalism, in the forms and institutions of the codes and legal processes. Their common feature is the ultimate purpose of their public policy, that is, the building of a communist society. Whether this goal is to be treated seriously is a matter which is outside the scope of this paper. Its importance lies in the fact that various legislative measures are enacted in order to achieve that purpose, a goal which in terms of official philosophy cannot be contested.

It is evident, however, that it would not be desirable, and only rarely possible, to give a course in which the laws of all eight people's democracies would be covered. In certain situations a cross-section study of selected legal problems of a number of countries would be useful. At times, a course concentrating on legal developments of a single country with occasional reference to similar developments elsewhere would be indicated. The choice of approach should depend upon the significance of a given country in a specific field of legislation. The study of industrial management and of industrial relations must include the legal systems of Yugoslavia, Poland, Hungary, and East Germany. Study of the criminal law would profit from inclusion of the laws of Poland, Bulgaria, and Yugoslavia, while the conflict of laws should deal at least with the situation in Hungary, Czechoslovakia, and possibly Poland again.

The only country in the free world which actively pursues independent studies of the legal systems of Eastern Europe is West Germany. Its experience is quite instructive. At the University of Göttingen a course called "Reception of Soviet Law in East Germany" is offered. In Hamburg a seminar on "Selected Problems of Eastern Law (Ostrecht)" was organized, and a parallel course on "Private Law of Czechoslovakia" is given. Another model for the type of course that can be offered is found in England. In the King's College Faculty of Laws (University of London), Professor Albert Kiralfy offers alternatively courses in Soviet law and in selected legal problems of people's democracies in Eastern Europe.

The effective organization of instruction in a field of comparative law is always a major enterprise. In this case it is complicated by the fact that the instructor must have a working knowledge of at least one language of the area. Consequently he must rely to a large degree on translations and treatises and textbooks.

The lists of literature on East Central and Southeast European law given below do not pretend to be complete. Their purpose is to orient those interested — not only teachers, but also those outside the profession — in the availability of material which could profitably be used for the purpose of instruction. Another limitation is that these lists are restricted to works and authors in English, German, French, and Russian, as well as to the standard reference tools — guides to the jurisprudence and legal materials of the Eastern European people's democracies. Neither does this list pretend to be presented in a form which is acceptable for bibliographical information. For some countries, this information is already found in existing bibliographies.

1. *Bibliographies*

The Mid-European Law Project in the Library of Congress prepared bibliographies of legal sources and jurisprudential writings, published by F. Praeger (New York) for the following countries: Bulgaria (1956), Hungary (1956), Czechoslovakia (1959), Poland, Romania, and Yugoslavia (1964).

For books and articles in English, *A Bibliography on Foreign Comparative Law: Books and Articles in English* by Charles Szladits (1955–62) should be consulted.

In 1958, *Bibliographie juridique polonaise 1944–1956*, prepared by the Institute of Juridical Science in Warsaw, was published.

2. *Periodicals*

Only Germany has a number of periodicals devoted to the law of Eastern European and Soviet socialist legal systems. They include important articles on the legal systems of Eastern European people's democracies and regularly carry information on legal developments there, as well as translations of important laws and decrees. *Ost-Europa Recht, Recht in Ost und West*, and *Jahrbuch für Ostrecht* are leading periodicals in this field.

In the United States, since *Highlights of Current Legislation and Developments in Mid-Europe* has ceased publication, there is no publication devoted mainly to Eastern European and Soviet legal problems. The main publication at present which covers the Soviet and East European area is the *American Journal of Comparative Law*. Otherwise articles and notes on Eastern European law are scattered in individual law school journals.

Materials and studies important for legal students of the area appear in *East Europe*, a monthly publication, *Slavic Review (American Slavic and East European Review)*, *Monthly Labor Review*, *Revue internationale du droit d'auteur*, *International Copyright Bulletin*, published by UNESCO, *International Digest of Health Legislation*, published by the World Health Organization, and similar bulletins published by the International Labor Office, Patent Union, International Postal Union, International Railway Organization, International Civil Aviation Organization, etc.

Scientific organizations, and lawyers' associations in several countries of the people's democracies in Eastern Europe publish periodicals and bulletins in Western European languages containing translations of laws and articles by leading specialists of those countries valuable for the understanding of underlying policy.

In Poland, the Institute of International Affairs in Warsaw issues, somewhat irregularly, a bulletin in English, French, German, and Russian under the title *Legislation of Poland (Legislation polonaise, Gesetzgebung des Polnischen Volksrepublik, Zakonodatel'stvo Polskoi Narodnoi Respubliki)*. Since 1963, a review, *Droit polonais contemporain*, has been published in Warsaw in French and English.

The Association of Hungarian Jurists issues a *Revue de la législation hongroise* devoted mainly to the publication of legislative texts and official documents, such as legislative reports of the Ministry of Justice.

Since 1950, when Yugoslavia turned away from the Stalinist form of government and legislation, the Association of Jurists has issued a quarterly *Bulletin on Law and Legislation in the Federal People's Republic of Yugoslavia*. The French title of this publication is *Nouveau droit yougoslave*.

In addition, Yugoslav lawyers publish in separate volumes *Collected Yugoslav Laws* dealing with specific fields: constitutional laws and government organization, nationality legislation, electoral laws, laws on associations, meetings and assemblies, laws concerning business enterprises, domestic relations, etc.

Finally, Czechoslovakia has published, since 1925, a most useful publication — *Bulletin of Czechoslovak Law* — containing texts of laws, government regulations, and studies by Czechoslovakian jurists.

3. Official collections of laws in Western languages

One of the most important sources of information regarding the provisions of laws in force in the Eastern European people's democracies is the Legislative Series published by the Secretariat of the United Nations, or by United Nations technical organizations. Of these, legislative series published by the International Labor Office, World Health Organization, World Food and Agriculture Organization, and Civil Aviation Organization are of great importance. For example, the United Nations Legislative Series includes, among others, the following titles: *Laws Concerning Nationality, Nationality of Married Women, Legislation on Merchant Marine Vessels*, etc.

Another United Nations publication which regularly contains legislation from Eastern Europe is the *Yearbook on Human Rights*. UNESCO publishes in its bulletins translations of copyright laws in Eastern Europe, comments of learned jurists, and notes on development in the socialist part of Europe. In 1961, UNESCO sponsored a publication of collected copyright legislation which also included copyright legislation of Eastern European people's democracies, *Copyright Laws and Treaties of the World*.

4. Private collections of laws

Only the most important collections are mentioned here:

a) Amos J. Peaslee, *Constitutions of Nations* (Concord, N.H.: Rumford Press, 1950).

b) Richard Flourney, and Manley O. Hudson, *A Collection of Nationality Laws of Various Countries as Contained in Constitutions, Statutes and Treaties* (New York: Oxford University Press, 1929).

c) Carl B. Hyatt, ed., *U.S. Immigration and Naturalization Service, Laws Applicable to Immigration and Nationality* (Washington, D.C.: G.P.O. 1954).

d) American Joint Distribution Committee, *European Legislation on Declaration of Death* (Paris: Joint, 1949).

e) Aleksander N. Makarov, *Quellen des Internationalen Privatrechts* (Berlin: Walter de Gruyter, 1953).

f) *Collection of Foreign Criminal Laws* — which appears in Germany (Berlin: Walter de Gruyter, 1888) — contains translations of several criminal codes from Eastern Europe; editor varies.

5. A special case: East Germany

Within the family of socialist states in Eastern Europe, East Germany possesses exceptional features calling for separate treatment. In the socialist commonwealth of nations, the German Democratic Republic alone is in the position where its legal sources and legal literature are available in a language which is one of the most important languages of the West. Not only is this position intimately linked with the German jurisprudential tradition, but even now it is a part of the legal system of Germany as a whole, which finds its reflection in the jurisprudential writings of German authors and in the decisions of German courts. Legal order of East Germany is frequently discussed in terms of deviation from the traditional institutions of the German polity, or in terms of the reception of foreign juristic concepts into the living law of Germany.

All these factors, including the fact that West German jurists are, for obvious reasons, greatly interested in the legal developments in East Germany, make East German law and legal literature one of the most fruitful areas of research.

Among the East German legal materials, attention must be drawn to a collection of the laws and regulations *Das geltende Recht*, published in 1965, which included the laws in force for the period of July 10, 1949, until the end of 1964. Prepared by the Bureau of the Council of Ministers, it is a most useful tool for research and study. It is also a handy item to start a working collection of East German legal materials.[4]

In regard to the history of the East German regime the works of Detlev Ahlhardt Travers[5] and of Siegfried Mampel[6] deserve attention. In regard to the basic principles of the East German legal order, a book by Siegfried Petzold[7] is recommended, while Wolf Preuss's study of the socialist legality[8] represents another aspect of the fundamentals of the legal order in East Germany. The list which follows includes works of German scholars for the following areas of East German legal order: administration and civil service, a book by Gustav Leissner;[9] civil law of the Democratic German Republic, a collective work by the experts of the Law Institute;[10] educational policy in the Soviet

4. *Das geltende Recht — chronologisch und systematisch geordnet. Verzeichnis der geltenden gesetzlichen Bestimmungen der Deutschen Demokratischen Republik vom 7.10. 1949 bis 31.12. 1964* (Berlin: Staatsverlag der Deutschen Demokratischen Republik, 1965).

5. *Entwicklung und ideologische Hintergründe der Verfassungsarbeiten in der sowjetischen Besatzungzone Deutschlands bis zur Gründung der "Deutschen Demokratischen Republik"* (Freiburg im Breisgau, 1962) (Dissertation).

6. *Die Entwicklung der Verfassungsordnung in der sowjetisch besetzen Zone Deutschlands von 1945 bis 1963* (Tübingen: J. C. B. Mohr, 1964); Sonderdruck aus *Jahrbuch des öffentlichen Rechts*, vol. 13:455–579; *Die Verfassung der sowjetischen Besatzungszone Deutschlands: Text und Kommentar*, 2d ed. (Frankfurt am Main: Alfred Metzger, 1966); *Der Sowjetsektor von Berlin* (Frankfurt am Main and Berlin: Alfred Metzger, 1963).

7. *Grundzuge der sozialistischen Gesetzbegung in der Deutschen Demokratischen Republic* (Berlin: VEB Deutscher Zentralverlag, 1962).

8. *Der Begriff der sozialistischen Gesetzlichkeit in der DDR und die Methoden Ihrer Verwirklichung als Herrschaftsinstrument der SED* (Munich: A. Schubert, 1963).

9. *Verwaltung und öffentlicher Dienst in der sowjetischen Besatzungszone Deutschlands: Eine kritische Würdigung aus gesamtdeutscher Sicht* (Stuttgart: W. Kohlhammer Verlag, 1961).

10. *Das Zivilrecht der Deutschen Demokratischen Republik* (Berlin: VEB

occupation zone of Germany, a study by Siegfried Baske and Martha Engelberth; [11] penal law and its enforcement, an essay by Hans-Heinrich Jeschek; [12] conflict and arbitration commissions in criminal cases, a study edited by Michael Benjamin and Harry Creuzburg; [13] labor code and labor regulations, a private edition; [14] collection of international treaties and agreements concluded by the German Democratic Republic, compiled by Lothar Kapsa (a multilithed edition).[15]

6. *General works, monographs, and authors*

Gsovski and Grzybowski, in *Government, Law and Courts in the Soviet Union and Eastern Europe*, cover the initial period of the developments of the legal systems of Eastern Europe until 1958, when the post-Stalinist legal reform was beginning to reshape them. Later events were partly described in two works by Kazimierz Grzybowski, *Soviet Legal Institutions*, which came out in 1962, and *The Socialist Commonwealth of Nations*, which appeared in 1964 and contains, among other things, a description of commercial arbitration (organization and procedure) in the European countries of the socialist system.

Another work covering all legal systems under review here is the study by Arpad Bogsch, *International Copyright*, Part I: *European Countries* (New York: R. R. Bowker Co., 1958). In 1964, *Private International Law in the European People's Democracies*, by Istvan Szaszy, was published in Budapest by the Hungarian Academy of Sciences.

Works, monographs, and articles dealing with individual countries are far more numerous, and it would be impossible to list them fully here. Only the names of the most important authors are mentioned.

Aleksander Rudzinski, W. J. Wagner, Zygmunt Jedryka, Zygmunt Nagorski, Bronislaw Helczynski, Georg Geilke, and Dominik Lasok are primarily interested in legal developments in Poland. Ivan Sipkov and Constantine Katsarov have written on Bulgarian law and on international agreements dealing with problems of the conflict of laws.

Deutscher Zentralverlag, 1955–56), vol. 1: *Allgemeiner Teil*; vol. 2: *Schulrecht, Besonderer Teil*; vol. 3: *Sachrenrecht*.

11. *Zwei Jahrzehnte Bildungspolitik in der Sowjetzone Deutschlands: Dokumente*, 2 vols. (Berlin, 1966).

12. *Penal Law and Its Application in the Soviet-Occupied Zone of Germany* (Tübingen: J. C. B. Mohr, 1965).

13. *Die Übergabe von Strafsachen an die Konflict und Schiedskommissionen*, 2d ed. (Berlin: Staatsverlag der Deutschen Demokratischen Republik, 1966).

14. *Gesetzbuch der Arbeit und eine Auswahl anderer Bestimmungen arbeitsrechtlichen Inhalts: Textausgabe mit Anmerkungen und Sachregister* (Berlin: Staatsverlag der Deutschen Demokratischen Republik, 1965).

15. *Zusammenstellung der von der "Deutschen Demokratischen Republik" seit deren Gründung (7.10. 1949) abgeschlossenen internationalen Verträge und Vereinbarungen*, 3d ed. (Bonn, 1962). (Als Manuscript vervielfältigt).

Branko Pešelj, Fran Gjupanović, Stojan Cigoj, and Borislav Blagojević specialize in the problems of Yugoslav law, in particular, in the governmental and administrative reforms which have set Yugoslavia apart as a classical country experimenting with the basic notions of socialist legality.

Two Hungarian jurists, Istvan Zaitay and Laszlo Reczei, deal with problems of Hungarian law, while among Czechoslovak jurists Ian Bistricky is mostly concerned with foreign trade and conflicts of law in the Czechoslovak legal order.

Among those who must be mentioned for having contributed shorter works of general importance for the study of socialist legal systems are Georges Langrod, Dietrich Loeber, Zygmunt Jedryka, and Friedrich Drobnig.

In addition, economists and political scientists have produced works which furnish background information about the fundamental institutions of the socialist economy in Eastern Europe. The works of Thad P. Alton, John M. Montias, Frederic L. Pryor, Henri Wronski, and Jack C. Fisher are important.

7. *Soviet publications and authors*

From the very beginning of the people's democracies in Eastern Europe, Soviet jurists paid close attention to legal developments there, and this interest continues unabated until the present day. Nearly every issue of the leading legal journal *Sovetskoe Gosudarstvo i Pravo* carries a column devoted to legal developments in Eastern Europe and frequently includes translations of important pieces of legislation or articles by leading Eastern European jurists.

In addition, monographs and collective works by Soviet and foreign authors deal with various important legal issues, and separate volumes contain translations of legislative acts in various important areas of legal regulation, following a definite pattern:

> Constitutional laws and organization of government
> Organization of local government and people's councils
> Agricultural reform and land tenure
> Organization of the administration of justice: courts and procuracy
> Nationalization of industrial establishments
> Monopoly of foreign trade
> Criminal legislation and criminal policy
> Criminal procedure
> Anti-state crimes

In addition to these areas, other scholars turned their attention to legal problems arising in trade and economic cooperation in relations between the Soviet Union and other socialist countries of Eastern Europe.

In addition, various departments of the Soviet government publish collections of legal texts, conventions, and agreements between administrations of shipping, railway, air companies, radio and television networks, providing important information on the operation of these various services and the technique of cooperation within the socialist commonwealth of nations.

RECOMMENDATIONS

To broaden the knowledge of Eastern European legal systems in this country, action is needed on three different levels:

1. A firm basis of research must be established. The value of foreign research is reflected in the perspective taken, and in the absence of emotional involvement. In the case of research on the socialist rule of law outside its immediate environment, the added ingredient is in the absence of the element of propaganda, which unfortunately mars a good deal of the legal research in the socialist countries. It is indeed impossible to rely exclusively on the works of the legal scholars working in the socialist environment, as only the exceptional among them may express opinions at variance with the general line of the Party. It is not surprising therefore that at times Western scholars have produced works far superior to those appearing in the Soviet Union and some, though fortunately not all, of the people's democracies of Eastern Europe. This type of activity, which has produced excellent results in research on Soviet law, ought to be organized also for the countries of the people's democracy.

The next question is a technical one. Should such a center be created by extending the scope of activities of a research center for the study of the Soviet Union? This would perhaps be the easiest solution, and at times may even be the only possible one. The danger is, and the writer speaks from experience, that research under such conditions may be deviated from an independent inquiry into a search for common features, frustrating the real purpose of scholarly investigation. It is to be feared that, unless there is firm delimitation of responsibilities, the result of the scientific inquiry would underemphasize those aspects of the socialist states of Eastern Europe which are at variance with the Soviet legal regime.

2. Courses of instruction in the legal systems of the people's democracies must be introduced. Their purpose would be to train legal schol-

ars, to teach and to conduct research, and also to prepare experts to serve the legal profession, federal government, foreign trade and banking interests. It is the responsibility of the leading law schools to formulate proposals in this direction and to obtain financing for such programs. The following courses are suggested:

a) Legal Institutions of Eastern European Socialist Countries
b) Socialist Commonwealth of Nations
c) Private International Law of the People's Democracies
d) Regime of Economic Relations with Eastern Europe (selected problems)
e) Socialist Jurisprudence (basic doctrines)
f) Socialist Countries in International Organizations

Courses should be optional for undergraduates, but should be obligatory for candidates for higher degrees in comparative law.

3. Institute of Comparative and International Law. The writer would like to draw attention to the long-discussed project to establish a Comparative Law Institute, or better still, an Institute of Comparative and International Law, as a cooperative effort of the American law schools, of the foundations, of the American Bar Association, and of foreign and international law societies and associations.

An institute of this type should be located in Washington, D.C., in proximity to the Library of Congress, with its great comparative law and international law collections permitting meaningful research in all areas of legal culture and all periods of the rule of law. Its organization should include a small group of permanently appointed scholars, with a number of American and foreign scholars on a visiting basis. It would serve as a research center, and as a graduate school for American and foreign students, preferably exclusively for doctoral candidates.

In due course, research and instructional programs of this institute should be organized to meet specialized demands such as (a) preparing international civil servants; (b) preparing foreign service officers in legal positions; and (c) preparing lawyers specializing in foreign trade. In all these programs, instruction and research in foreign law, including that of the Soviet Union and that of other socialist countries, should play an important role.

12/ PHILOSOPHY

George L. Kline
Bryn Mawr College

In East Central and Southeast Europe, philosophers were, until fairly recently, close adherents of one or another Western school of thought. Those few thinkers who made an independent name for themselves (e.g., Rudjer Bošković, Bernhard Bolzano) either lived abroad or published in Western languages, or both, and thus became effectively part of the world community of philosophers and men of learning.

In the period since World War II, Marxism-Leninism has been — in all the countries covered by this report except Greece and European Turkey — the official philosophy and ideology, exercising a virtual monopoly, until 1948 in Yugoslavia, until 1956 in Poland and Czechoslovakia, and until the early 1960s in Hungary, Romania, and East Germany, on institutional appointments in teaching and research, and on all forms of publication. Since the dates indicated, and especially since 1956, there has been some toleration of philosophers who do not profess Marxism-Leninism, or even Marxism. In Poland and Yugoslavia, non-Marxists have been able to teach and to publish in the field of philosophy. In Czechoslovakia, the teaching of philosophy by non-Marxists, discontinued in 1948–49, was not resumed until 1964.

Between the East European non-Marxists, most of whom are close to familiar schools of philosophy such as existentialism, phenomenology, positivism, and linguistic analysis, and the more or less orthodox Marxist-Leninists stand the philosophical revisionists of Marxism. This is not the place to discuss in detail the nature of philosophical revisionism or its relation to political revisionism.[1] Let me simply say that East

I am happy to acknowledge the expert assistance of the following special consultants: John P. Anton (Greece), Ervin Laszlo (Hungary), Nicholas Lobkowicz (Czechoslovakia), and Esen Ortaç Traub (European Turkey).
1. For details, see my article, "Leszek Kołakowski and the Revision of Marxism," *European Philosophy Today* (Chicago: Quadrangle Books, 1965), pp. 113–56.

European revisionists ignore or reject the main philosophical theses of Engels and Lenin, in particular the three pillars of contemporary dialectical materialism, namely, (a) philosophical materialism, (b) the epistemological "theory of reflection," and (c) the generalization of the Hegelian-Marxist dialectic to all of (non-human and non-historical) nature.

East European revisionists draw doctrinal support from the early writings of Marx and also from Kant, contemporary existentialists, or contemporary positivists and analytic philosophers. Their revisions are concentrated in ethics and the "philosophy of man," on the one hand, and in theory of knowledge and methodology, on the other. Those revisionists who work in the former field tend to ignore the latter, and vice versa.

Since the various forms of non-Marxist philosophy cultivated in East Central and Southeast Europe differ little from their West European (and American) originals, there would seem to be little point in mastering such difficult languages as modern Greek or Turkish, Hungarian or Czech, in order to study those forms.[2] An exception might be made for the specialist who wishes to carry out a comparative study of the influence of a given school in two or more countries — one in West Europe (or America) and one or more in East Central or Southeast Europe.[3]

For similar reasons, there would seem to be little point in learning difficult languages in order to study the orthodox East European Marxist-Leninists, since their writings are, for the most part, echoes of what appears in more accessible form in the works of Soviet philosophers. However, certain Czech, Polish, and, more recently, Bulgarian Marxist-Leninists have produced specialized studies which are doctrinally "orthodox" but marked by greater methodological scruple and analytical skill than most of those of their Soviet counterparts.

Within the general field of Marxist philosophy in East Central and Southeast Europe, it is the revisionist works which are most rewarding. But of course the scholarly historian of philosophy will find many minor figures in the period stretching back to the eighteenth century who will

2. In a country such as contemporary Albania, where Marxism-Leninism exercises a philosophical monopoly, the appearance of a quite orthodoxly Husserlian, Heideggerian, or Wittgensteinian work would be a significant intellectual event. To my knowledge, nothing of the sort has taken place.

3. Followers of a given Western thinker may make interesting and even important contributions to intellectual history. Jan Patočka, the Czech Husserlian, apparently does this in his highly original study of the concept of motion and the mathematicization of motion in Aristotle, his predecessors, and his successors, *Aristoteles: jeho předchůdci a dědicové* (Aristotle: His Predecessors and His Followers) (Prague: Nakladatelství Československé akademie věd, 1964).

repay careful study. Here, too, comparative studies would seem especially appropriate.

Up to the present time, all of the monographs and most of the journal articles devoted to philosophy in East Central and Southeast Europe have been written by émigrés. Studies by non-émigrés should be encouraged — despite the difficulty of the languages involved — among other reasons because non-émigrés still find it easier than do émigrés to spend prolonged periods of study and research in East Central and Southeast Europe. (Neither Zbigniew Jordan nor Nicholas Lobkowicz, each of whom has written a substantial study of philosophy in his native land, has made a return visit. On the other hand, both Ervin Laszlc and Milić Čapek have made recent visits to their native lands.)

The American or West European student of philosophy in East Central and Southeast Europe shares the advantages of the historian, literary critic, political scientist, or economist interested in the area — namely, real possibilities for long-term research and study "in the field."[4] In addition, there are now opportunities for meaningful dialogue with East European philosophers — both Marxist and non-Marxist — who pay one-year visits to the United States under Ford and other fellowships.[5]

In philosophy, as in economics (see Professor Spulber's recommendation, pp. 180–81), it would seem appropriate to encourage "less than full-time" specialization — by competent philosophers who have the linguistic equipment and interest to carry out a specific study or specific studies, but who do not wish to devote themselves entirely to East Central and Southeast European philosophy.

RECOMMENDATIONS

GRADUATE STUDY

The area student interested in philosophy, like the area student interested in history, political science, economics, or literature, should first of all be thoroughly trained in his discipline. His further studies would presumably include area work in two or three other disciplines, and at least one East Central or Southeast European language. He would also need a reading knowledge of French and German (and, for study of earlier periods, Latin). Even where translations exist, the specialist will

4. At least one American student has taken a Ph.D. in philosophy at Warsaw University (1965).
5. The Ford fellowship program for Poland was suspended in 1964 because of noncooperation by Polish authorities; it may be resumed in 1969. The Yugoslav program continues; other East European countries are being added — Romania and Bulgaria among them.

need to consult the original texts — just as serious students of Hegel, Heidegger, and Sartre now turn to the original texts, despite the availability of more or less adequate English versions.

RESEARCH

It would not seem worthwhile to undertake the writing of general histories of philosophy in the manner of Ueberweg[6] for most countries of this area, since such histories would inevitably include much non- or para-philosophical material. Greece may be an exception; it would appear to be appropriate to compile a history of modern Greek philosophy from the sixteenth to the twentieth century.

Partial or specialized studies would be desirable: for example, a reassessment of those earlier Hungarian thinkers classified by contemporary Marxist-Leninists as "materialistic" or "progressive" (I Martinovics, By. Bessenyei, M. Csokonai, J. Eötvös) and those intellectual historians classified as "reactionary" (B. Homan, Gy. Szekfü, J. Erdélyi, J. Kvacsala). There is a need for a survey of Czech aesthetic theory in the nineteenth and twentieth centuries, also for a special study of aesthetics in Greece, and of the impact of Marxism on such Greek political philosophers as D. Glynos, I. Kordatos, X. Theodorides, and I. Zeugos.

Concerning research on the contemporary period, a distinction must be made between the communist and non-communist countries. First, in studies of philosophy in the communist states emphasis should be on philosophical revisionism of the two main types mentioned above: (a) that which focuses on ethics and the philosophy of man, and is strongly influenced by Western existentialism, and (b) that which focuses on methodology and logic, and is chiefly influenced by Western positivism and linguistic analysis.

We need comparative studies of the revisions of Marxism in specific fields; for example, aesthetics in Poland and Hungary; ethics in Yugoslavia, Poland, and Hungary; philosophy of man in Yugoslavia and Czechoslovakia; methodology and philosophy of science in Poland, Czechoslovakia, and Yugoslavia; perhaps history of philosophy in Romania and East Germany; possibly philosophy of physics in Bulgaria and Poland. For all countries of the area except Albania, it would be helpful to study the impact of Western thought on Marxism-Leninism of the more orthodox type as well as upon the various kinds of Marxist revisionism.

6. Friedrich Ueberweg, ed., *Grundriss der Geschichte der Philosophie* (Berlin: E. S. Mittler & Sohn, 1928).

Also in the recent period, it would be of interest to study the works of the non-Marxist philosophers in this area, even though most of them are fairly close followers of one or another Western school. Thus, there might be comparative studies of existentialism in France and Poland (or Hungary), or analytic philosophy in Great Britain (or the United States) and Yugoslavia. There is also a need for a general survey of the development of Marxism-Leninism both as philosophy and ideology in East Germany.

For non-communist countries, that is, Greece and European Turkey, it would be desirable to study the impact of Western thought, including (where appropriate) Marxism, on such philosophers as Nermi Uygur (Istanbul) or I. Theodorakopoulous and E. Papanoutsos (Athens). One could envisage a comparative study of Husserlian phenomenology in West Germany and Greece. The influence of Continental existentialism, as well as positivism, linguistic analysis, and American pragmatism, might be explored.

In all of the East Central and Southeast European countries – but particularly in those with communist regimes – it would be interesting to study the place of philosophy in cultural and intellectual life generally. To what extent is philosophy as such, and not merely orthodox Marxism-Leninism, discredited? Do philosophers like Kołakowski, Kosík, Petrović, and Marković have an impact on younger intellectuals? Do they play any role in the shaping of public policy?

Finally, there is a pressing need for readable and accurate English – or French or German – versions of significant philosophical writings published in the several languages of the area. A few translations have already appeared; others are currently in preparation (see Bibliography, below).

Following is a list of philosophy texts which it would seem desirable to translate into English.

Works mainly historical

1. Panagiōtēs Kanellopoulos, *Historia tou Eurōpaïkou pneumatos*, 2 vols., rev. ed. (A History of the European Mind). Athens: J. D. Kollaros, 1966.
2. Leszek Kołakowski, *Jednostka i nieskończoność: wolność i antynomie wolności w filozofii Spinozy* (The Individual and the Infinite: Freedom and the Antinomies of Freedom in Spinoza's Philosophy). Warsaw: Państwowe Wydawnictwo Naukowe, 1958.
3. György Márkus and Zádor Tordai, *Irányzatok a mai polgári*

filozófiában: egzisztencializmus, katolikus filozófia, neopozitiviz-mus (Trends in Contemporary Bourgeois Philosophy: Existential-ism, Catholic Philosophy, Neopositivism). Budapest: Gondolat, 1964.

4. Jan Patočka, *Aristoteles: jeho předchůdci a dědicové* (Aristotle: His Predecessors and His Followers). Prague: Nakladatelství. Československé akademie věd, 1964.

Works mainly theoretical

1. August von Cieszkowski, *Prolegomena zur Historiosophie.* Berlin: Veit, 1838; reissue, Posen [Poznań]: J. Leitgeber & Co., 1908. (By a Polish neo-Hegelian).

2. Tamás Földesi, *Az akaratszabadság problémája* (The Problem of Freedom of the Will). Budapest: Gondolat, 1960.

3. Ágnes Heller, *A morál szociólogiája avagy a szociológia morálja* (The Sociology of Morals and the Morality – or "the Moral" – of Sociology). Budapest: Gondolat, 1964.

4. Miloslav Král, *Pojem hmoty v dialektickém materialismu* (The Concept of Matter in Dialectical Materialism). Prague: Na-kladatelství Československé akademie věd, 1960.

5. György Lukács, *Geschichte und Klassenbewusstsein.* Berlin: Malik, 1923. (Major work by a Hungarian Marxist. There is a French translation, but an English version is also needed.)

6. Panagiōtēs Michelēs, *Aisthētika theorēmata,* 2 vols. (Studies in Aesthetics). Athens, 1962, 1965.

7. Maria Ossowska, *Podstawy nauki o moralności* (Principles of the Science of Morals), 2d ed. Warsaw: Państwowe Wydawnictwo Naukowe, 1957.

8. E. P. Papanoutsos, *Philosophika problēmata* (Philosophical Prob-lems). Athens: Ikaros, 1964.

9. Iōannēs N. Theodōrakopoulous, *Systēma philosophikēs ēthikēs* (A System of Philosophical Ethics), vol. 1. Athens: P. D. Karabakos, 1952.

10. József Ujfalussy, *A valóság zenei képe: a zene müvészi jelenté-sének logikája* (The Musical Image of Reality: The Logic of the Aesthetic Meaning of Music). Budapest: Zenemükiadó Vállalat, 1962.

It would be useful to bring together in individual volumes collec-tions of the most interesting and representative articles published in the journals of each of the countries – except for Albania – competently translated into English. These should be drawn not only from the professional philosophy journals — *Cercetări filozofice* (Bucharest), *Deutsche Zeitschrift für Philosophie* (East Berlin), *Filosofický Časopis* (Prague), *Filosofska misúl* (Sofia), *Filosofija* (Belgrade), *Filozofia* (Bratislava), *Magyar Filozófiai Szemle* (Budapest), *Praxis* (Zagreb) and *Studia Filozoficzne* (Warsaw)[7] — but also from such journals of general culture as *Literární Noviny* (Prague), *Tvář* (Prague; suspended in 1966), *Twórczość* (Warsaw), and *Valóság* (Budapest), which often publish more interesting and original work in philosophy (Marxist, revisonist, and non-Marxist) than the professional philosophy journals. Articles of philosophical interest also appear in such journals of general culture as *Platon* and *Epoches* (Athens).

BIBLIOGRAPHY

Since the number of Western works devoted to philosophy in East Central and Southeastern Europe is still relatively small, the following list is intended to be substantially complete as of January 1968. Works are arranged by country to which they refer; countries are listed in alphabetical order.

BULGARIA

Articles

Telčarov, Paul. "Hegel bei den Bulgaren." In *Hegel bei den Slaven*, pp. 467–73. Reichenberg, 1934; reissue, Darmstadt: Wissenschaftliche Buchgesellschaft, 1961.

Tsanoff, Radoslav A. "Bulgarian Philosophy." In *Encyclopedia of Philosophy*, 1:423–24. Edited by P. Edwards. New York: Macmillan and Free Press, 1967.

CZECHOSLOVAKIA

Monographs

Král, Josef. *La Philosophie en Tchécoslovaquie*. Bibliothèque des problèmes sociaux no. 2. A l'occasion du VIIIe Congrès de Philosophie à Prague. Prague, 1934.

Lobkowicz, Nicholas. *Marxismus-Leninismus in der ČSR: Die tschechoslowakische Philosophie seit 1945*. Dordrecht: Reidel ("Sovietica"), 1961.

---

7. *Praxis* and *Studia Filozoficzne* publish polygot international editions (see Bibliography, p. 299).

Articles — General

Čapek, Milić. "Czechoslovak Philosophy." In *Encyclopedia of Philosophy*, 2:287–88.

Čyževski, Dymtryo. "Hegel bei den Slovaken." In *Hegel bei den Slaven*. Reichenberg, 1934; reissue, 1961.

Fajfr, F. "Hegel bei den Čechen." In *Hegel bei den Slaven*, pp. 413–59. Reichenberg, 1934; reissue, 1961.

Lobkowicz, Nicholas. "Die marxistisch-leninstiche Philosophie in der Tschechoslowakei." *Zeitschrift für Ostforschung*, 9 (1960): 386–96.

———. "Marxism-Leninism in Czechoslovakia." *Studies in Soviet Thought* (hereafter: *SST*) 1 (1961): 100–110.

———. "Philosophy in Czechoslovakia since 1960." *SST* 3 (1963): 11–32.

———. "Philosophical Revisionism in Post-War Czechoslovakia." *SST* 4 (1964): 89–101.

Patočka, Jan. "La Philosophie en Tchécoslovaquie et son orientation actuelle." *Etudes philosophiques* 3 (1948): 63–74.

Pelikán, Ferdinand. "Die tschechische Philosophie." In Friedrich Ueberweg, ed., *Grundriss der Geschichte der Philosophie*, 5:289–98. 12th ed. Berlin: E. S. Mittler & Sohn, 1928.

Articles — On individual thinkers

Bar-Hillel, Yehoshua. "Bernard Bolzano." In *Encyclopedia of Philosophy*, 1:337–38. (Note: Bolzano lived in Czechoslovakia — then Bohemia — but since he wrote all of his philosophical works in German there is some question whether he should be included among Czech philosophers. No further Western studies of Bolzano will be listed here; for bibliography, see the article just cited.)

Čyževski, Dmytro. "Comenius' *Labyrinth of the World*: Its Theses and their Sources." *Harvard Slavic Studies*, 1 (1953): 83–135.

Ulich, Robert. "Comenius." In *Encyclopedia of Philosophy*, 2:146–47. (Note: Comenius [or Komenský] was an educational theorist and theologian, rather than a philosopher in the strict sense. For further bibliography, see the article just cited.)

Wellek, René. "Tomáš Garrigue Masaryk." In *Encyclopedia of Philosophy*, 5:176–77.

EAST GERMANY

Articles — General

Croan, Melvin. "East German Revisionism: The Spectre and the Reality." In L. Labedz, ed., *Revisionism: Essays on the History of*

Marxist Ideas, pp. 239–56. London: Routledge & Kegan Paul; New York: Praeger, 1962.

Articles — On individual thinkers

Lombardi, Franco. "Ernst Bloch." In *Encyclopedia of Philosophy*, 1:321–23.

Rühle, Jürgen. "The Philosopher of Hope: Ernst Bloch." In Labedz, ed., *Revisionism*, pp. 166–78. (Note: Since Bloch left East Germany in 1961 and has since resided in West Germany, there is some question whether he should be included among East German philosophers. I shall not give further titles of works devoted to his thought; for a full bibliography see the article by Lombardi cited above.)

GREECE

(Note: Modern Greek is considered a "Western" language; therefore Greek-language studies of Greek philosophy are included, although Polish-language studies of Polish philosophy are not included under Poland, for example.)

Monographs — General

Apostolopoulos, Ntimēs. *Syntomē historia tēs Neoellēnikēs philosophias* (A Short History of Modern Greek Philosophy). Athens: Helēno-Gallikē Henōsis Neōn (Collection de l'Union Franco-hellénique des jeunes), 1950.

Kissabos, Maria I. *Philosophia en Helladi apo tēs anastaseōs tou ethnous* (Philosophy in Greece since the Rebirth of the Nation [i.e., 1827]. Athens, 1951.

Kontzias, N. *Historia tēs philosophias apo tōn archaiotatōn chronōn mechri tōn kath'hēmas* (A History of Philosophy from the Earliest Times to our own Day), 6 vols. Athens, 1875–84.

Loubaris, N. J. *Die Philosophie der Gegenwart in Griechenland.* Munich, n.d. (inaccessible: mentioned in Apostolopoulos and Kissabos).

Papanoutsos, Evangelos P., ed. *Neoellēnikē philosophia* (Modern Greek Philosophy). Athens: Aetos, Basikē Bibliothēkē, 1953, 1956. (An anthology in 2 vols., with introductions and notes.)

Monographs — On individual thinkers

Tsourkas, Cleobule. *Les Débuts de l'enseignement philosophique et de la libre pensée dans les Balkans: La Vie et l'oeuvre de Théophile Corydalée.* Bucharest, 1948.

Articles

Boreas, Theophilos. "Die neugriechische Philosophie." In Ueberweg, ed., *Grundriss* . . . , 5:363–68.

Demos, Raphael. "The Neo-Hellenic Enlightenment (1750–1821): A General Survey." *Journal of the History of Ideas,* 19 (1958): 523–41.

Spetsieris, Konstantin. "La Philosophie dans la Grèce contemporaine." *Sophia: Rivista internazionale di fonti e studi di storia della filosofia* 7 (1939): 198–202. (An annotated bibliography.)

HUNGARY

Monographs — General

Laszlo, Ervin. *The Communist Ideology in Hungary: Handbook for Basic Research.* Dordrecht: Reidel ("Sovietica"), 1966.

Tordai, Zádor. *Esquisse de l'histoire du cartésianisme en Hongrie.* Budapest: Akadémiai Kiadó, 1965.

Monographs — On individual thinkers

Zitta, Victor. *Georg Lukacs' Marxism: Alienation, Dialectics, Revolution — a Study in Utopia and Ideology.* The Hague: Nijhoff 1964. (Note: Many articles, and parts of several books, have been devoted to Lukács. No attempt is made to list all of them here. For bibliography, see Zitta's monograph, pp. 285–87; also the Lukács eightieth-birthday *Festschrift,* edited by Frank Benseler, which contains a bibliography of 886 items compiled by Jürgen Hartmann.)

Articles — General

Hanák, Tibor. "Hungary Five Years After: Philosophy under Kádár." *Survey,* no. 40 (1962): 140–48.

Kovesi, Julius. "Hungarian Philosophy." In *Encyclopedia of Philosophy,* 4:93–95.

Laszlo, Ervin. "A Concise Introduction to Hungarian Marxism-Leninism." *SST* 4 (1964): 20–32.

———. "Geistige Wandlungen eines ungarischen Individualisten." *Moderne Welt,* 1964/3, pp. 314–22.

———. "The Planification of Hungarian Marxism-Leninism." *SST* 5 (1965): 273–88.

———. "Sind Ideen Planbar? 'Planifikation' der staatlichen Ideologie in Ungarn." *Moderne Welt,* 1965/4, pp. 442–48.

———. "The Second Sovietology." *SST* 6 (1966): 274–90.

———. "Trends in East European Philosophy: A Case Study on Hungary." *SST* 7 (1967): 130–41.

Medveczky, Friedrich von. "Zur Geschichte der philosophischen Bestrebungen in Ungarn." *Ungarische Revue* 6 (1886): 257–76, 386–98, (covers period to early eighteenth century).

Meray, Tibor. "Existentialism in Hungary." *Hungarian Quarterly*, 2, no. 1 (1962): 32–39.

Rácz, Ludwig. "Die ungarische Philosophie." In Ueberweg, ed., *Grundriss* . . . , 5:348–57.

Szlavlik, Mátyás. "Zur Geschichte und Litteratur der Philosophie in Ungarn." *Zeitschrift für Philosophie und philosophische Kritik*, 107 (1895): 216–32.

Articles — On individual thinkers (concerning Lukács, see note following Zitta's monograph, above)

Bloch, Ernst. "Aktualität and Utopie" (on Lukács). *Der neue Merkur*, October 1923–March 1924, pp. 457–77.

McInnes, Neil. "Georg Lukács." In *Encyclopedia of Philosophy*, 5:102–4.

Rieser, Max. "Lukács' Critique of German Philosophy." *Journal of Philosophy* 55 (1958): 177–96.

Steiner, George. "Georg Lukács and His Devil's Pact." *Kenyon Review* 22 (1960): 1–18.

Watnick, Morris. "Relativism and Class Consciousness: G. Lukács." In Labedz, ed., *Revisionism*, pp. 142–65.

POLAND

Monographs

Jordan, Zbigniew A. *The Development of Mathematical Logic and of Logical Positivism in Poland between the Two Wars*. Oxford: Oxford University Press, 1945.

———. *Philosophy and Ideology: The Development of Philosophy and Marxism in Poland since the Second World War*. Dordrecht: Reidel ("Sovietica"), 1963.

Skolimowski, Henryk. *Polish Analytical Philosophy*. London: Routledge & Kegan Paul; New York: Humanities Press, 1967.

Tymieniecka, Anna-Teresa. *Essence et existence: Etude à propos de la philosophie de Roman Ingarden et Nicolai Hartmann*, Paris: Aubier, 1957.

Articles — General

Bocheński, J. M. "La Philosophie." In *Pologne 1919–1939*, 3:229–60. Neuchâtel, 1942.

Gromska, Daniela. "Philosophes polonais morts entre 1938 et 1945." *Studia Philosophica*, 3 (1948): 31–97.

Jordan, Zbigniew A. "The Development of Philosophy and Marxism-Leninism in Poland since the War." *SST* 1 (1961): 88–89.

———. "The Philosophical Background of Revisionism in Poland." *East Europe*, 11, no. 6 (1962): 11–17; 11, no. 7 (1962): 14–24.

Kline, George L. "Leszek Kołakowski and the Revision of Marxism." In G. L. Kline, ed., *European Philosophy Today*, pp. 113–56. Chicago: Quadrangle Books, 1965.

Kotarbiński, Tadeusz. "Grundlinien und Tendenzen der Philosophie in Polen." *Slavische Rundschau* 5 (1933): 218–29.

———. "La Philosophie dans la Pologne contemporaine." In R. Klibansky, ed., *Philosophy in the Mid-Century*, 4:224–35. Florence: La Nuova Italia, 1959.

Krzywicki-Herburt, George. "Polish Philosophy." In *Encyclopedia of Philosophy*, 6:363–70.

Kühne, Walter. "Die Polen und die Philosophie Hegels." In *Hegel bei den Slaven*, pp. 7–143.

Lutosławski, Wincenty and Puciata, Leon. "Die polnische Philosophie." In Ueberweg, ed., *Grundriss . . .* , 5:299–334.

Skolimowski, Henryk. "Analytical-Linguistic Marxism in Poland." *Journal of the History of Ideas* 26 (1965): 235–58.

Articles — On individual thinkers

Lejewski, Czesław. "On Leśniewski's Ontology." *Ratio*, 1 (1958): 150–76.

R. Rand, "Kotarbińskis Philosophie auf Grund seines Hauptwerkes: 'Elemente der Erkenntnistheorie, der Logik, und der Methodologie der Wissenschaften,'" *Erkenntnis* 7 (1937–38): 92–120.

ROMANIA

Articles — General

Eliade, Mircea. "Rumanian Philosophy." In *Encyclopedia of Philosophy*, 7:233–34.

Articles — On individual thinkers

Eliade, Mircea. "Nae Ionescu." In *Encyclopedia of Philosophy*, 4:212.

———. "Constantin Rădulescu-Motru." In *Encyclopedia of Philosophy*, 7:63–64.

Horia, Vintilă. "Introduction à la pensée de Lucian Blaga." *Acta Philosophica et Theologica* 2 (1964): 163–74.

Rus, G. "Il personalismo energetico di C. Rădulescu-Motru." *Acta Philosophica et Theologica* 2 (1964): 411–38.

YUGOSLAVIA

Monographs

Atanasijević, Ksenija. *Penseurs yougoslaves.* Belgrade: Bureau central de presse, 1937.

Nedeljković, Dušan. *Aperçus de la philosophie contemporaine en Yougoslavie.* Belgrade: Imprimerie de l'Etat, 1934.

Vrtačič, L. *Einführung in den jugoslawischen Marxismus-Leninismus.* Dordrecht: Reidel ("Sovietica"), 1963.

Zeremski, Sava Davidović. *Essays aus der südslawischen Philosophie* (includes chapters on Bošković, Knežević, and Petronievié). Novi Sad: Kommissionsverlag der Buchhandlung, 1939 (?).

Articles — General

Atanasijević, Ksenija. "Hegel bei den Yugoslawen." In *Hegel bei den Slaven.* pp. 461–66.

Marković, Mihailo. "La filosofia jugoslava contemporanea." *Il Protagora,* 2 (1960): 2–43.

——. "Yugoslav Philosophy." In *Encyclopedia of Philosophy,* 8:359–64.

Stojanovich (Stojanović), Svetozar. "Contemporary Yugoslavian Philosophy." *Ethics,* 76 (1966): 297–301.

Vrtačič, L. "Marxist-Leninist Literature in Jugoslavia (1945–1959)." *SST* 1 (1961): 111–19.

——. "Der jugoslawische philosophische Revisionismus im Lichte der sowjetischen Kritik." *SST* 2 (1962): 104–18.

Articles — On individual thinkers

Tomashevich, G. V. "Božidar Knežević: A Yugoslav Philosopher of History." *Slavonic and East European Review,* 35 (1957): 443–61.

(Note: There are a number of monographs and articles in Western languages on Rudjer Bošković — or Roger Boscovich — which discuss his contributions to both philosophy and physics. Although he was born in what is now Dubrovnik, Yugoslavia, Bošković spent most of his adult life in Italy and published his many works in Latin. For these reasons, I am not including him in this bibliography.)

Šešić, Bogdan. "Branislav Petronievič." In *Encyclopedia of Philosophy*, 6:128–29.
Stojković, Andrija. "Svetozar Marković." In *Encyclopedia of Philosophy*, 5:164–66.

GENERAL WORKS

Articles

Fetscher, Iring. "New Tendencies in Marxist Philosophy." *East Europe*, 16, no. 5 (May, 1967): 9–14.
Griffith, William. "What Happened to Revisionism?" *Problems of Communism*, 9, no. 2 (1960): 1–9.
Kline, George L. "Philosophic Revisions of Marxism." In *Proceedings of the Thirteenth International Congress of Philosophy*, 9:397–407. Mexico City, 1963; Mexico, D.F.: Universidad Nacional Autónoma de México, 1964.
A special issue of the journal *Inquiry* (vol. 9, no. 1, 1966), edited by Ervin Laszlo, was devoted to "Philosophy in Eastern Europe."

TRANSLATIONS

Existing translations made in the West:
Kołakowski, Leszek. *Der Mensch ohne Alternative*. Munich: Piper, 1960, 1964. (A collection of philosophical and political essays.) Certain of Kołakowski's essays have appeared in French in *Les Temps modernes* (Paris).
———. *Toward a Marxist Humanism: Essays on the Left Today*. Translated by Jane Zielonko Peel. New York: Grove Press, 1968.
———. *The Alienation of Reason: A History of Positivist Thought*. Translated by Norbert Guterman. New York: Doubleday, 1968.
Kosík, Karel. *Die Dialektik des Konkreten*. Frankfurt: Suhrkamp, 1967. (There are also Italian and Spanish translations.)
Papanoutsos, Evangelos P. *The Foundations of Knowledge*. Translated by Basil P. Coukis and John P. Anton. Albany: State University of New York Press, 1968.
Petrović, Gayo. *Marx in the Mid-Twentieth Century*. New York: Doubleday, 1967. (A collection of philosophical essays.)
Several books by the Polish Communist philosopher Adam Schaff have been translated into English, French, and German. An English translation of his most recent book, *Marxism and the Human Individual*, is forthcoming.
Translations by Max Rieser of philosophical essays by Tadeusz

Czezowski, Tadeusz Kotarbiński, Roman Ingarden, Wladyslaw Tatarkiewicz, Adam Schaff, and Maria Ossowska, appeared in the *Journal of Philosophy*, 57 (1960): 201–58.

Existing translations made in East Central and Southeast Europe:

Kotarbiński, Tadeusz. *Praxiology: An Introduction to the Science of Efficient Action*. Oxford, Warsaw, and Long Island City: Pergamon Press 1965.

———. *Gnosiology: The Scientific Approach to the Theory of Knowledge*. Warsaw, Oxford, and Long Island City: Pergamon Press, 1966.

Pfeiffer, A. *Dialogues on the Fundamental Questions of Science and Philosophy*. Long Island City: Pergamon Press, 1967. (Pfeiffer is a professor at Dresden University.)

Tordai, Zádor. *Existence et réalité*. Budapest, 1967. (A critique of Sartre's *L'Etre et le néant*.)

Most philosophy books published in the languages of the area include brief abstracts in French, German, or English. Some Hungarian titles are published in English, German, or French in the "Studia Philosophica" series of the Hungarian Academy of Sciences in Budapest.

The journal *Studia Filozoficzne* (Warsaw) publishes an international edition every two or three years, containing translations into English, French, German, and Russian of selected articles originally published in Polish.

A similar international edition of the Yugoslav journal *Praxis* (Zagreb) began to appear in 1965, but was suspended in 1968. It differed from the international edition of *Studia Filozoficzne* in two respects: (1) it did not include Russian translations, and (2) it appeared much more frequently (several times a year).

Translations in preparation in the West:

Additional works by Kołakowski are currently (1968) being prepared for publication in the United States.

Kosik's *Dialektika konkrétního*, Prague, 1963, 1965, the German translation of which was mentioned above, will appear in an English version by Karel Koecher edited by N. Lobkowicz and G. L. Kline.

JOURNALS

Studies in Soviet Thought (Fribourg, Switzerland: edited by J. M. Bocheński, editer of the "Sovietica" series of monographs). Publishes occasional articles and frequent reviews and notes on philosophy and ideology in East Central Europe. (It does not include Greece or European Turkey.)

East Europe (New York). Publishes occasional translations of East
European philosophical texts as well as interpretive articles.
Hungarian Quarterly
Slavic Review (New York). In recent years this journal has published
only reviews, not articles, in this field.
Journal of the History of Ideas (New York). Has published two or
three survey articles on recent Polish philosophy.
Journal of Philosophy (New York) Has published translations and
brief articles on Polish philosophy, Lukács, etc.

Note: Articles and reviews dealing with philosophy and philosophers
in East Central Europe appear regularly in the Polish émigré journal
Kultura and the Czech émigré journal *Svĕdectví*, both of which maintain high scholarly standards.

13 / LITERATURE

William E. Harkins
Columbia University

In the East Central and Southeast European area it was the Slavic languages and literatures which attracted Western attention earliest, and they have since maintained an almost unbeatable supremacy over the non-Slavic ones. Of the latter, only modern Greek studies attracted considerable attention in Western Europe, England, and the United States in the nineteenth century; but this early advantage has been largely lost by the present time. Revolutions in several of the Eastern European countries helped to win American sympathy and interest, particularly in Greece (1821–29), though little of this resultant concern was to be permanent. Other episodes have merely aroused sporadic interest in America in one or more of these literatures. The participation of Kościuszko in the American Revolution, the literary friendship of J. F. Cooper and A. Mickiewicz, the popularity of the Serbian epic songs here and in Western Europe, or of writers such as H. Sienkiewicz, Jaroslav Hašek, Karel Čapek, Ferenc Molnár, or Carmen Sylva — none of this has apparently created a deep or abiding interest in the serious study of the national literature as a whole. Nor have the numerous émigrés coming here from Eastern Europe or the literary and cultural societies which they founded here accomplished much. Occasionally these foster the publication of translations or literary histories, but the impact of this activity seems largely to have been contained among the émigré movements themselves, which, in a country

The following report was prepared with the kind and most helpful assistance of Professors Robert Austerlitz (Hungarian and Romanian), Harold B. Segel (Polish), Stavro Skendi (Albanian, Bulgarian, Serbo-Croatian), Rado L. Lenček, (Slovene), and Professor and Mrs. Peter Topping (modern Greek). Their cooperation is warmly acknowledged.

301

such as America, are in any event doomed to extinction through assimilation. The creation of independent states in Southeastern Europe in the nineteenth century, and in Eastern Europe following World War I, did arouse some interest. The chief beneficiary of this was the infant Czechoslovak state. Its first president, T. G. Masaryk, was well known as a democratic philosopher whose wife was American and who was himself interested in Anglo-American literature and philosophy. But even the especial popularity of Czechoslovakia here during the 1920s and 1930s hardly produced much literary echo, if we except translation of the works of Karel Čapek.

It is Russia which, of course, has largely been responsible for our interest in and concern with the other Slavic peoples and their languages and literatures. Nineteenth-century dilettantes in the West were committed to a romantic belief in the uniqueness of a "Slavic soul," which they conceived as uniting all the Slavic peoples in a close unity; this notion was inherited, apparently, from Pan-Slavists such as Kollár. The more sober scholarship of the present century has helped to correct this distortion, but at the price of a certain loss of interest in the non-Russian Slavic peoples; the real focus of American interest — cultural, political, educational, and even scholarly — remains Russia. Still, the creation of graduate departments of Slavic languages and of programs of area studies for Eastern Europe has greatly benefited the serious study of several of the other Slavic languages, in particular Polish, Czech, and Serbo-Croatian, and, to a much lesser extent, the non-Slavic languages of the area.

The nineteenth century approached the Slavs as a unit, and produced several compendia on the history of the Slavic literatures, the first ones in German, though these were mostly written by Slavs.[1] German primacy in the field helped to establish a dominance which has survived to some extent to this day, though the rise of Hitler and World War II caused a notable setback. The first book in English on the literature of

---

1. The first of these is P. J. Šafařík, *Geschichte der slawischen Sprache und Literatur nach allen Mundarten* (Ofen: Kön. ung. Universitätsschriften, 1926). Šafařík also left a more detailed history of the South Slavic literatures, *Geschichte der südslawischen Literatur*, ed. J. Jireček (Prague: Verlag Friedrich von Tempsky, 1864–65). Somewhat later there appeared a German translation of A. N. Pypin and V. D. Spasović, *Geschichte der slawischen Literaturen*, trans. T. Pech (Leipzig: F. A. Brockhaus, 1880–84) as well as a French version of the same work: *Histoire des littératures slaves*, trans. Ernest Denis (Paris: Leroux, 1881). Other later comparative Slavic treatments published in German include M. Murko, *Geschichte der älteren südslawischen Literaturen* (Leipzig: C. F. Amelang, 1908); A. Bezzenberger, A. Brückner, and A., *Die osteuropäischen Literaturen und die slawischen Sprachen* (Berlin and Leipzig: B. G. Teubner, 1908); etc. Murko's work on South Slavic literatures is still a classic in the field, and a reprint is expected to appear soon.

the Slavs was written by a German,[2] and only in this century have we succeeded in approaching the Slavic world independently of German sources. But already early in the nineteenth century Sir John Bowring had published selections from the poetry of the Poles, Czechs, and Serbo-Croats, with some commentary,[3] and a second, though also dilettantish, study of the history of Slavic literatures was to appear in England before the century's end.[4] Slavic studies in English have advanced to such a point that one can almost speak of English as the *lingua franca* of Slavic studies in this century (in the nineteenth century it was German which played this role). Besides British and Americans, a considerable amount of this scholarship in English has been produced by Dutch, Scandinavians, and the Slavs themselves, especially those who have emigrated. Slavic studies are also being developed in Canada, Australia, and New Zealand.

Serious graduate study of the Slavic languages and their literatures hardly reached this country until World War II and its aftermath, though attempts had been made somewhat earlier to broaden the scope of Russian studies by adding one or more other Slavic languages and their literatures.[5] At Harvard University Leo Weiner early in this century directed graduate study, at least on an informal basis, of Polish literature. His outstanding student, George Rapall Noyes, introduced a regular course in Polish literature in English translation, alternating with a similar course in "Bohemian" literature, at the University of California at Berkeley as early as 1904. At Columbia University regular graduate instruction in Polish literature was started in 1916, with courses in Czech and South Slavic literatures added within the next several years. The University of Texas has offered courses in Czech literature continuously since 1915.

The postwar years have seen the burgeoning and growth of one graduate department of Slavic languages and literatures after another in this country until it is possible to say that Slavic studies in America have reached a satisfactory level of seriousness and intensity. This is not to

2. Talvj (Therese Albertine Louise von Jacob), *Historical View of the Languages and Literatures of the Slavic Nations, with a Sketch of Their Popular Poetry* (New York: Putnam, 1850).

3. *Servian Popular Poetry* (London: privately printed, 1827); *Specimens of the Polish Poets, with Notes and Observations on the Literature of Poland* (London: privately printed, 1827); *Cheskian Anthology, Being a History of the Poetical Literature of Bohemia, with Translated Specimens* (London: A. Hunter, 1832).

4. W. R. Morfill, *Slavonic Literature* (London: Society for Promoting Christian Knowledge, 1883).

5. For more information on the development of Slavic studies in this country, see C. A. Manning, *A History of Slavic Studies in the United States* (Milwaukee: Marquette University Press, 1957).

say that all the individual languages and their literatures are taught to a sufficient extent: perhaps only Polish, beside Russian, has reached a satisfactory level of intensity of instruction at several of our universities. Of the others, only Czech,[6] Serbo-Croatian,[7] and Bulgarian[8] are competently taught by recognized specialists, while Slovenian and Macedonian literatures are not taught at all. But a framework of Slavic studies has been laid down which makes possible intensive study on the graduate level of most of the Slavic literatures, and library collections, though far from complete, are probably adequate for such study, at least at several of the greater universities.

This is not to say that Slavic studies as now practiced here have necessarily reached maturity. Americans still have difficulty in mastering the languages, a necessary prerequisite to study of the literatures on the graduate level. Grammars, bilingual or annotated readers, anthologies of literature, etc., are still totally unavailable or grossly inadequate. The pattern of Slavic studies laid down in almost all of our graduate departments is too rigid. Almost without exception a Germanic pattern, with heavy emphasis on linguistics and philology, has been adopted, though other useful models exist, for example, literature and history, or studies in comparative literature.

By comparison, there is little to say concerning the study of the non-Slavic literatures of the area. Serious graduate study of Hungarian literature began with the establishment of Uralic programs at Indiana University in 1945 under Thomas Sebeok, and at Columbia University in 1947 under John Lotz. The late Joseph Reményi had earlier taught Hungarian for many years at Western Reserve. No university at present offers a graduate program in Romanian literature, though several have programs in Romance philology which include Romanian. There is no graduate program in Albanian literature in this country.

Modern Greek literature is a special case, since English and American interest in it developed early in the nineteenth century,[9] when several professors of ancient Greek showed an interest in modern Greek as well. In 1860 a chair of ancient, Byzantine, and modern Greek was es-

6. Serious study of Czech literature in the United States began in 1946, when Roman Jakobson appeared at Columbia University.
7. The serious study of Serbo-Croatian literature in America began in 1939, when Albert Lord introduced the subject at Harvard University.
8. Albert Lord introduced a course in Bulgarian literature at Harvard in 1951. C. A. Manning taught the subject for many years at Columbia University, beginning in 1929.
9. A collection of modern Greek poets in English translation appeared as early as 1825, translated from French: C. B. Sheridan, trans., *The Songs of Greece* (London: Longman, Hurst, Rees, Orme, Brown and Green, 1825).

tablished at Harvard, though it was not to be permanent. In 1919 a chair of Byzantine and modern Greek language, history, and literature was established at the University of London; its first incumbent was Arnold Toynbee. There has been a lively interest in modern Greek literature recently, with the translation of such authors as Kazantzakis and Vassilikos into English. Yet, paradoxically, modern Greek studies at American universities are just beginning. The University of Chicago added a graduate course in modern Greek literature in 1967–68, and the University of Maryland offered one the following year.

STATE OF THE ART

GENERAL AND COMPARATIVE

Slavic literatures. Though the great bulk of Slavic studies in this country is devoted to Russian studies, or to Russian and one or two other Slavic languages, still the creation of departments of Slavic and the training of Slavic experts has helped to inspire the study of the other Slavic literatures, particularly Polish, Czech, and Serbo-Croatian, and there is a considerable volume of publication in these fields. Slovak, Slovene, Macedonian, and Bulgarian have benefited much less. Also, there is very little true study of Slavic literature (unlike linguistics) on a comparative basis. An exception is Čiževsky's recent survey of the Slavic literatures in English, which has many good qualities, including its emphasis on the study of period features (especially of the Baroque) and its stress on form and technique (at the expense of the more usual presentation of literature as a part of intellectual and cultural history).[10] But it is also necessarily uneven and at times misleading. Outstanding special works include a superbly documented Russian study of Italian Renaissance influences on the West and South Slavic literatures,[11] as well as a German study of Slavic art, literature, and thought in the Baroque period.[12] There is also a scholarly monograph on Slavic Romanticism,[13] as well as a study of nationalism in the South Slavic literatures.[14] Fascinating is Roman Jakobson's thesis that common fea-

10. Dmitry Čiževsky, *Outline of Comparative Slavic Literatures (Survey of Slavic Civilizations)*, vol. 1 (Boston: American Academy of Arts and Sciences, 1952).
11. I. N. Golenishchev-Kutuzov, *Ital'ianskoe vozrozhdenie i slavianskie literaturu xv–xvi vekov* (Moscow: Izdatel'stvo Akademii Nauk SSSR, 1963).
12. Andreas Angyal, *Die slavische Barokwelt* (Leipzig, E. A. Seeman, 1961).
13. Jiří Horák *et al.*, "Die Romantik in den slavischen Literaturen," *Slavische Rundschau*, 11 (1939): 125–260.
14. Albert B. Lord, "Nationalism and the Muses in Balkan Slavic Literature in the Modern Period," in Charles and Barbara Jelavich, eds., *The Balkans in Transition* (Berkeley: University of California Press, 1963), pp. 258–96.

tures in the Slavic languages themselves "poetize," though it probably suffers from exaggeration of the common Slavic element in the poetic traditions of the modern Slavic peoples.[15] Pan-Slavism is treated in Hans Kohn's book on the subject, which makes considerable use of literary materials, though it begins its treatment only with the nineteenth century.[16] Three individual Slavic literatures find excellent treatment in the volumes edited by Oskar Walzel, *Handbuch der Literaturwissenschaft*: Polish, Serbo-Croatian, and Czech.[17] The surveys, written by specialists, incline toward a cultural-historical approach. On the other hand, an encyclopedia of Slavic studies in English is so full of errors that it is unusable.[18]

Slavic and non-Slavic. "East Central Europe under the Communists," a series of handbooks prepared by the Mid-European Studies Center of the Free Europe Committee and published by Frederick A. Praeger in the late 1950s, treats all the countries in the area except Greece; each of these handbooks (except the one on Yugoslavia) contains a chapter on literature, but these chapters are at best sketchy, and most of them are uneven in value. Higher in caliber are the articles contained in several reference books on European and world literature, published in English, which treat all the literatures in the area.[19] Though brief, most of the articles in these compilations can be recommended. The forthcoming *Reader's Encyclopedia of World Drama*, edited by John Gassner and Edmund G. Quinn, will treat most if not all the countries of the area.

Striking is the almost complete absence of comparative monographs, either among the literatures of the area or between one of them and an outside literature (this is true especially of the non-Slavic literatures). It is almost as if these literatures existed each in a vacuum, at least insofar as scholarship in Western languages was concerned. The only note-

15. Roman Jakobson, "The Kernel of Comparative Slavic Literature," *Harvard Slavic Studies*, 1 (1953): 1–71.
16. Hans Kohn, *Pan-Slavism, Its History and Ideology* (Notre Dame: University of Notre Dame Press, 1953).
17. Julius Kleiner, "Die polnische Literatur," vol. 17; Gerhard Gesemann, "Die serbo-kroatische Literatur," vol. 18; Arne Novak, "Die tschechische Literatur," vol. 18 (Potsdam: Akademische Verlagsgesellschaft Athenaion, 1929–31).
18. Joseph S. Roucek, ed., *Slavonic Encyclopedia* (New York: Philosophical Library, 1949).
19. Horatio Smith, ed., *Columbia Dictionary of Modern European Literature* (New York: Columbia University Press, 1947); Stanley J. Kunitz and Vineta Colby, eds., *European Authors, 1000–1900* (New York: H. W. Wilson, 1967); Alex Preminger, ed., *Encyclopedia of Poetry and Poetics* (Princeton: Princeton University Press, 1965).

worthy exception I have found is a recently published monograph comparing modern Polish and Hungarian poetry;[20] there is also a brief article comparing Petöfi and Eminescu.[21]

Periodical publication. American journals which specialize in this area include the *Slavic Review*, the *Slavic and East European Journal*, as well as the new *East European Quarterly*, published at the University of Colorado under the editorship of Stephen Fischer-Galati. A new Canadian journal, *Canadian Slavic Studies*, started publication in 1967. The chief British journal is the *Slavonic and East European Review*; in French there is the *Revue des études slaves*; in German, the *Zeitschrift für slavische Philologie, Die Welt der Slaven*, and *Zeitschrift für Slawistik*; and in Italian, the *Ricerche slavistiche*. Most of these are too well known to need description. Also important is the *International Journal of Slavistics and Poetics*, with articles for the most part in English, as well as *Scando-slavica*, which has many articles in English. The American, British, and Canadian delegations to the International Congress of Slavicists (held at five-year intervals) produce important collections of articles; the Dutch and Scandinavian delegations also publish for the most part in English.

Other series in English include *Harvard Slavic Studies, Indiana Slavic Studies, California Slavic Studies, Canadian Slavonic Papers*, and *Oxford Slavonic Papers*.

Publication series. Twayne Publishers has announced ambitious lists of forthcoming monographs for some of the languages in the area, but little has appeared to date. Columbia University has a series of Slavic studies, though this is now partly moribund, as well as a series of East Central European studies. Mouton and Company, The Hague, have published and are publishing many monographs in the Slavic field, mostly in English.

Gaps in research. These are well-nigh ubiquitous. As noted above, almost no comparative study of the literatures in question exists outside the Slavic field. American scholars could play an especially useful role in investigating such sensitive comparative topics as the interrelations of Czech and Slovak literatures, or the literatures of Yugoslavia, or those of Transylvania (including writing in German, Hungarian, and Romanian), or those of Macedonia (Macedonian, Bulgarian, Serbo-Croatian, Greek).

---

20. George Gömöri, *Polish and Hungarian Poetry, 1945–1956* (Oxford: Oxford University Press, 1966).

21. László Gáldi, "Petöfi and Eminescu," *American Slavic and East European Review*, 7, no. 2 (April, 1948): 171–78.

POLISH

American interest in Poland dates back to the Revolutionary War, when Poles helped fight for American independence; American interest in Polish literature, to the friendship of the writers Cooper and Mickiewicz. An English collection of Polish poetry appeared in the 1820s.[22] But Polish literature was hardly introduced to the Anglo-Saxon world before the translation of many novels by Sienkiewicz in 1889–1906. By the 1920s a number of works, mostly popular and dilettantish in character, had appeared, including a mediocre history of Polish literature,[23] along with several works by Monica Gardner — a study of Polish culture with much information concerning literature, as well as three biographies of well-known Polish writers.[24]

The great expanse in American Polish studies comes after 1941. Today we possess good histories of Polish literature, one in English by Manfred Kridl,[25] as well as a German translation of Karel Krejčí's excellent survey,[26] and the older German version of Julius Kleiner's fine history.[27] There is also an indifferent history in French.[28] The Kridl history of Polish literature is capable of serving as a standard work except that, translated from the Polish, its style is uneven. Treatment of the Baroque period and the twentieth century is sketchier, less uniform, and less useful than that of the other periods.

There is a substantial number of books on Mickiewicz in English, to the actual detriment of other subjects. Outstanding is Wiktor Weintraub's study,[29] a sober, reliable analysis of Mickiewicz' major poetic works. Several fine volumes of essays and translations appeared in English around the centenary of the poet's death in 1955.[30] The first volume

22. Bowring, *Specimens of the Polish Poets.*
23. Roman Dyboski, *Periods of Polish Literary History* (London: Oxford University Press, 1923).
24. Monica Gardner, *Poland: A Study in National Idealism* (London: Burns and Oates, 1915); *Adam Mickiewicz, the National Poet of Poland* (London: J. M. Dent, 1911); *The Anonymous Poet of Poland, Zygmunt Krasiński* (Cambridge: Cambridge University Press, 1919); *The Patriot Novelist of Poland, Henryk Sienkiewicz* (London: J. M. Dent, 1926).
25. *A Survey of Polish Literature* (The Hague: Mouton; New York: Columbia University Press, 1956).
26. *Geschichte der polnischen Literatur* (Halle: Max Niemeyer Verlag, 1958).
27. "Die polnische Literatur."
28. M. Herman, *Histoire de la littérature polonaise des origines à 1961* (Paris: A. G. Nizet, 1963).
29. *The Poetry of Adam Mickiewicz* (The Hague: Mouton, 1954).
30. The most important of these are: Manfred Kridl, ed., *Adam Mickiewicz: Poet of Poland* (New York: Columbia University Press, 1951); Wacław Lednicki, ed., *Adam Mickiewicz in World Literature* (Berkeley: University of California Press, 1956); *Adam Mickiewicz, 1798–1855* (Paris: UNESCO, 1955).

of the projected Twayne series of studies on Polish authors has appeared and deals with Mickiewicz.[31] Like the Weintraub book, it deals only with Mickiewicz' major poetry, but factual errors and an almost complete disregard for highly pertinent historical and political considerations detract from its value. The interest in Mickiewicz is all very gratifying, though scholars have tended to confine their attention almost exclusively to his poetry; a more comprehensive study of his life and work, with greater emphasis on the period after *Pan Tadeusz*, is needed.

Krasiński has been treated in a monograph which unfortunately is now obsolete.[32] There is also an uneven but useful volume of essays on him in English.[33] A small but good introductory study of Słowacki has appeared as a translation from the Polish; there is also a large and impressive volume on Słowacki's early period in French, which, however, relies rather too much on Polish sources and opinions.[34] A short, rather impressionistic, and perhaps superficial study of Sienkiewicz' life and work is also available in English; it has some value as an introduction.[35] Also worth mention is an English translation of most of Sienkiewicz' letters from America.[36]

Victor Erlich's study, *The Double Image*, treats the figure of the poet in Polish as well as Russian poetry.[37]

A useful monograph by Olga Scherer-Virski concerns the Polish short story, its formal structure, and chronological evolution.[38] A small survey of Polish drama is available in German.[39]

A special word should be said concerning the writings of Arthur P. and Marian Moore Coleman. Popular in character and not always free from mistakes, the works of these two American scholars have none-

31. David Welsh, *Adam Mickiewicz* (New York: Twayne, 1967).

32. Gardner, *The Anonymous Poet of Poland*.

33. Wacław Lednicki, ed., *Zymunt Krasiński, Romantic Universalist* (New York: Polish Institute of Arts and Sciences in America, 1964).

34. Stefan Treugutt, *Juliusz Słowacki: Romantic Poet* (Warsaw: Polonia Publishing House, 1959); Jean Bourrilly, *La Jeunesse de Jules Słowacki (1809–1933)* (Paris: A. G. Nizet, 1959).

35. Wacław Lednicki, *Henryk Sienkiewicz: A Retrospective Synthesis* (The Hague: Mouton, 1960).

36. Henryk Sienkiewicz, *Letters from America (Portrait of America)* (New York: Columbia University Press, 1959).

37. Victor Erlich, *The Double Image: Concepts of the Poet in Slavic Literatures* (Baltimore: Johns Hopkins Press, 1964).

38. Olga Scherer-Virski, *The Modern Polish Short Story* (The Hague: Mouton, 1954).

39. Karl Hartmann, *Das polnische Theater nach dem Zweiten Weltkrieg* (Marburg: N. G. Elwert, 1964).

theless played a very considerable role in acquainting American students with Polish literature.[40]

Journals. The *Polish Review* is published by the Polish Institute of Arts and Sciences in America. Its standards are uneven, but it has published a considerable number of valuable articles.

Publication series. Twayne Publishers has announced a series of forthcoming volumes on a number of Polish authors, but only one work has appeared to date (see footnote 31), and the future of the series hardly seems promising. Not all the authors selected are real scholars or specialists.

Anthologies and scholarly translations. The voluminous *Anthology of Polish Literature* edited by Manfred Kridl has texts in Polish and annotations in English;[41] its selection leaves much to be desired. There are a number of volumes of Polish poetry and short stories in translation, but few have adequate introductions or other critical apparatus for the discerning student. Only one bilingual anthology is found, also almost without commentary.[42] Exceptions are the translations made by George Rapall Noyes at the University of California, which contain adequate and even model commentaries;[43] his translations include renderings of Mickiewicz' *Pan Tadeusz* (in prose) as well as selections of the poetry of Jan Kochanowski and Adam Mickiewicz and others. Two works forthcoming on the playwright Fredro by H. B. Segel will contain translations of the plays and memoirs as well as extensive introductions and annotation.

Gaps in research. Up-to-date monographs on such figures as Kochanowski, Norwid, Słowacki, Prus, Tuwim, etc., are clearly needed. More important than monographs on individual authors at this time are monographs on periods, such as Romanticism and its many aspects, or on genres, such as the drama. Historical studies of Old Polish literature

---

40. Of many publications by the Colemans, outstanding are M. M. Coleman, *The Young Mickiewicz* (Cambridge Springs, Pa.: Alliance College, 1956); and M. M. and A. P. Coleman, *Wanderers Twain* (Cheshire, Conn.: Cherry Hill Books, 1964), on the travels in California of Sienkiewicz and the Polish actress Helena Modrzejewska.

41. *Anthology of Polish Literature* (New York: Columbia University Press, 1957).

42. T. M. Filip and M. A. Michael, eds., *A Polish Anthology* (London: Duckworth, 1944).

43. *Pan Tadeusz* (London: Everyman's Library, 1917); *Poems by Jan Kochanowski* (Berkeley: University of California Press, 1928); *Poems by Adam Mickiewicz* (New York: Polish Institute of Arts and Sciences in America, 1944). Here also might be listed Noyes's versions of *Konrad Wallenrod and Other Writings of Adam Mickiewicz* (Berkeley: University of California Press, 1925); Zygmunt Krasiński's *Irydion* (trans. with Florence Noyes) (London: Oxford University Press, 1927); Juliusz Słowacki's *Anhelli* (Berkeley: University of California Press, 1930).

and Baroque literature would be welcome. Polish twentieth-century literature is scarcely touched. Scholarly or even merely adequate English translations of the same writers and periods are also badly needed, no less than studies. The gaps are endless.

Polish-Russian, Polish-German, Polish-French, Polish-Italian literary relations are potentially rich topics, well worth exploring in depth.

CZECH

Anglo-Saxon interest in Czech literature began, paradoxically, early in the nineteenth century with translations of the forged manuscripts of Králové Dvůr and Zelená Hora.[44] At the beginning of the twentieth century, Francis Lützow published the first history of Czech literature in English, a sketchy study now outdated.[45] Much better was the German work by Jakubec and Novák,[46] which gives more accurate and greater detail; indeed, it is still the finest history of Czech literature in one volume, and is not superseded even by Novák's later but brief treatment in German.[47] Hanuš Jelínek published a three-volume history in French, which gives valuable detail and includes plot summaries, though it is excessively sentimental in tone.[48] František Chudoba's short survey in English is good, but by now out of date and insufficient in scope.[49]

There are a number of special studies in English. Matthew Spinka's study of Comenius is excellent, though not confined to Comenius' activity as a poet and writer of fiction.[50] Čiževsky has an extremely important study of the sources and devices of Comenius' *Labyrinth of the World*.[51] Milada Součková has published a valuable book on the three Czech romantics, Mácha, Erben, and Němcová,[52] and she has also published a definitive monograph on the Parnassian poet Vrchlický,[53] as well as a political study of the development of Czech literature under the impact first of Marxist ideology and later of enforced Com-

44. E.g., Sir John Bowring's *Cheskian Anthology*.
45. Francis Lützow, *A History of Bohemian Literature* (London: Heinemann, 1907).
46. Jan Jakubec and Arne Novák, *Geschichte der čechischen Literatur* (Leipzig: C. F. Amelang, 1913). There is also a Russian translation of this work.
47. Novák, "Die tschechische Literatur."
48. *Histoire de la littérature tchèque* (Paris: Editions du Sagittaire, 1930–35).
49. *A Short Survey of Czech Literature* (London: K. Paul, Trench, Trubner, 1924).
50. *John Amos Comenius, That Incomparable Moravian* (Chicago: University of Chicago Press, 1943).
51. Dmitry Čiževsky, "Comenius' *Labyrinth of the World*: Its Theses and Their Sources," *Harvard Slavic Studies*, 1 (1953): 83–135.
52. *The Czech Romantics* (The Hague: Mouton, 1958).
53. *The Parnassian Jaroslav Vrchlický* (The Hague: Mouton, 1964).

munism.[54] Harkins has a study of the influence of the Russian folk epos in Czech literature,[55] as well as a monograph on the writer Karel Čapek.[56] A Dutch monograph on Čapek is briefer and concentrates mostly on his early period.[57] There is also a version in English of the fine monograph by the Slovak critic Alexander Matuška.[58] Also in English is a short monograph on the poet Březina by Paul Selver.[59] Czech theater in the early years of Czechoslovak independence is the subject of a special number of the Paris journal Choses de théâtre.[60] Besides this, there is an important monograph in French on the poet Mácha.[61]

The significant role played by René Wellek in promoting Czech studies in this country is unique. Of the greatest value are his essays on Czech literature, now collected in a single volume.[62] Wellek's important essay on Czech literature between 1918 and 1938 is supplemented by informative articles in English by Arne Novák and Egon Hostovský covering the same period.[63]

Scholarly texts and translations. A large and comprehensive volume of Old Czech texts published by H. Kunstmann is equipped with annotations in German.[64] There is also a German scholarly edition of the Old Czech Alexandreida, edited by Reinhold Trautmann.[65] An anthology of modern Czech literature, with introductions and notes, is edited by Harkins.[66] A small volume of translations of Czech poetry published to-

54. A Literature in Crisis: Czech Literature, 1938–1950 (New York: Mid-European Studies Center, National Committee for a Free Europe, 1954).
55. William E. Harkins, The Russian Folk Epos in Czech Literature, 1800–1900 (New York: King's Crown Press, 1951).
56. William E. Harkins, Karel Čapek (New York and London: Columbia University Press, 1962).
57. Aimé van Santen, Over Karel Čapek (Amsterdam: Jacob van Campen, 1949).
58. Karel Čapek: Man against Destruction (London: Allen and Unwin, 1966).
59. Otakar Březina (Oxford: Blackwell, 1921).
60. Choses de théâtre, vol. 2, numéro spécial (May, 1923).
61. Henri Granjard, Mácha et la renaissance nationale en Bohême (Paris: Institut d'études slaves, 1957).
62. Essays on Czech Literature (The Hague: Mouton, 1963). Important essays treat the period in literature between 1918 and 1938, Karel Čapek, and Mácha and English literature.
63. Arne Novák, "Czech Literature in and after the War," Slavonic and East European Review, 2, no. 4 (June, 1923): 114–32; Egon Hostovský, "The Czech Novel between Two World Wars," Slavonic and East European Review, 21 (November, 1943): 78–96.
64. Heinrich Kunstmann, ed., Denkmäler der alttschechischen Literatur von ihren Anfangen bis zur Hussitenbewegung (Berlin: VEB Deutscher Verlag der Wissenschaften, 1955).
65. Die alttschechische Alexandreis, mit Einleitung und Glossen (Heidelberg: Carl Winter, 1916).
66. Anthology of Czech Literature (New York: King's Crown Press, 1953).

gether with the originals by A. French is the only bilingual anthology.[67] Spinka's translation of Comenius' *Labyrinth of the World* is a definitive version, equipped with model annotation.[68]

Gaps. Czech fourteenth-century literature, the Czech revival in the late eighteenth and early nineteenth centuries, Czech Romanticism (in spite of the existence of Součková's study), and modern Czech literature (especially the period between the two world wars) are the periods which most demand study. Good artistic and scholarly translations and anthologies are also badly needed.

SLOVAK

Though American Slovak immigrants have been active in popularizing their language and literature in this country, it can hardly be said that any real interest for or understanding of Slovak literature has taken root here. The creation of a Czechoslovak state in 1918 hardly inspired much interest in Slovak either, though Masaryk himself was partly Slovak by background.

One reliable history of Slovak literature, that by Andrej Mráz (though it was published under Hitler), is available in German.[69] In addition, the reader in French will find a great deal of information concerning Slovak literature in Jelínek's history of Czech literature.[70] Brief but inadequate histories are likewise found in several English sources also dealing with Czech literature.[71]

Texts. One bilingual anthology is available, a short collection of lyric poems representing both folklore and written literature.[72]

Gaps. A good, comprehensive history of Slovak literature in English is imperative. Next in order of priority would be a suitable anthology

67. A. French, ed., *A Book of Czech Verse* (London: Macmillan, 1958). Professor French is currently preparing several more volumes of Czech poetry in English translation.

68. Jan Amos Comenius, *The Labyrinth of the World and the Paradise of the Heart*, trans. Matthew Spinka (Chicago: National Union of Czechoslovak Protestants in America, 1942).

69. *Die Literatur der Slowaken* (Berlin: Volk und Reich Verlag, 194?).

70. *Histoire de la littérature tchèque.*

71. William E. Harkins and Klement Šimončič, *Czech and Slovak Literature, with a Bibliography on Lusatian Literature by Clarence A. Manning* (New York: Columbia University, Department of Slavic Languages, 1950); Vladimir Nosek, *The Spirit of Bohemia: A Survey of Czechoslovak History, Music and Literature* (London: Allen and Unwin, 1926); Paul Selver, *Czechoslovak Literature: An Outline* (London: Allen and Unwin, 1942).

72. Ivan J. Kramoris, trans., *An Anthology of Slovak Poetry* (Scranton, Pa.: Obrana Press, 1947).

of annotated texts, or of annotated translations of Slovak poetry and prose.

HUNGARIAN

American-Hungarian contacts began after the Revolution of 1848, when Hungarian émigrés came to the United States. But one can scarcely point to any real systematic development of interest in Hungarian literature here; even the Revolution of 1956 has not inspired this.

Before 1920, several standard histories of Hungarian literature had already appeared, including one in English by Frederick Riedl which is unimaginative and places rather too much emphasis on the Romantic period.[73] Two German histories also appeared, cursory, uninspired efforts by Kont and by Katona.[74]

The best history of Hungarian literature seems to be the most recent, the work by Klaniczay, Szauder, and Szabolcsi, which gives a good, balanced, if somewhat superficial introduction for the Western student.[75] A short introduction by Joseph Reményi is too cursory and popular to be of much value.[76] The period since 1900 is specially surveyed by Antal Sivirsky, in a competent but somewhat hurried compilation.[77] A study by Julius von Farkas concentrates on Hungarian Romanticism, but suffers for the American reader from an overly Germanic conception of that literary period.[78] Otherwise, there are few monographs or special studies on Hungarian literature in Western languages; exceptions are a recently published volume in English on five Hungarian writers,[79] and an older German study of the poet Petöfi.[80]

Scholarly editions. There are several good selections of texts in Hungarian with notes for the English reader,[81] but no actual scholarly translations into English.

73. *A History of Hungarian Literature* (New York: Appleton, 1906); a German version appeared in 1908).
74. I. Kont, *Geschichte der ungarischen Literatur*, 2d ed. (Leipzig: Amelang, 1909; a French edition appeared in 1900); Ludwig Katona, *Geschichte der ungarischen Literatur* (Leipzig: Göschen, 1911).
75. Tibor Klaniczay, József Szauder and Miklós Szabolcsi, *History of Hungarian Literature* (London: Collet's, [1964]).
76. *Hungarian Literature* (Washington, D.C.: American-Hungarian Federation, [1946?]).
77. *Die ungarische Literatur der Gegenwart* (Berne: Francke, 1962).
78. *Die ungarische Romantik* (Berlin and Leipzig: de Gruyter, 1931).
79. D. Mervyn Jones, *Five Hungarian Writers: Zrinyi, Mikes, Vörösmarty, Eötvös, Petöfi* (London and New York: Oxford University Press, 1966).
80. A. Fischer, *Petöfi's Leben und Werke* (Leipzig: W. Friedrich, 1889).
81. G. Cushing, *Hungarian Prose and Verse: A Selection with an Introductory Essay* (London: Athlone Press, 1956); John Lotz, *Hungarian Reader: Folklore and*

Gaps in research. These are obvious; the whole field is one large gap. While studies of such world-renowned figures as Petöfi or Molnár [82] would be useful, monographs on periods and movements in Hungarian intellectual and literary history would be more important, for example, a study of Hungarian romanticism in political and social thought as well as in literature. Readers and scholarly translations are also urgently needed.

ROMANIAN

While the practice of the discipline of Romance philology in this country aroused some interest in the study of Romanian language, there has been almost no concern here for Romanian literature. In the present century there was some interest in the writer Carmen Sylva, abetted by a visit paid by her daughter-in-law, Queen Mary, to the United States in the 1930s.

Several histories of Romanian literature appeared in Western languages prior to 1941. The best is the one by Basil Munteanu, available in English, French, and German versions, comprehensive and covering modern Romanian literature since 1850 through the 1930s.[83] Less valuable is an older one in German by Alexici, which is uneven and unoriginal.[84] The period before 1941 also includes a monograph in English on Romanian poetry with a too eclectic and rather sentimental approach to the subject.[85] There is a monograph in French which traces the development of Romanian poetry since 1905; it is sensitive and scholarly, and treats both native and foreign influences, as well as problems of poetics.[86]

Since 1941, no additional histories or monographs of any importance have appeared in Western languages.

Journal. The University of Illinois plans to issue a *Journal of Rumanian Studies* the first number of which is planned for 1969. The

Literature, with Notes, Uralic and Altaic Series, vol. 11 (Bloomington: Indiana University Press, 1962).

82. The longest study in English of this once celebrated figure seems to be Louis Rittenberg's "Ferenc Molnár, a Portrait," in *The Plays of Ferenc Molnár* (New York: Vanguard, 1929), pp. xi–xxii.

83. *Modern Rumanian Literature,* trans. from the French by C. Sprietsma (Bucharest: Curentul, 1939). There is also a German edition.

84. Georg Alexici, *Geschichte der rumänischen Literatur* (Leipzig: Amelang, 1906).

85. Leon Feraru, *The Development of Roumanian Poetry* (New York: Columbia University, Institute of Roumanian Culture, 1929).

86. Mario Roques, *La poésie roumaine contemporaine* (Oxford: Clarendon, 1934).

editor is Keith Hitchins. Subjects treated will include archaeology, history, language, and literature.

Scholarly editions and translations. An old German volume of texts in Romanian edited by Karl Tagliavini remains of very great usefulness.[87] Besides accurate texts (stressing the older period and folklore), the work contains an excellent introduction to Romanian culture and literature approximately one hundred pages long; there are also helpful notes.

Two anthologies of Romanian literature in English are undistinguished, but do contain at least a minimum of useful introduction and annotation for the foreign reader.[88]

Gaps. Again, the whole field is a gap. A monograph on Eminescu would be a "natural," but more important would be studies of such important cultural and literary phenomena as Romania's Western orientation (Carmen Sylva), Romanian Romanticism, etc. Readers and scholarly translations are also critical needs.

SLOVENIAN

Poetry, and especially the poetry of the great Slovene poet Prešeren, has been readily available in English translation only since World War II, and it is still too early to say that there is any strong or permanent interest in Slovenian literature here.

An accurate, critical, comprehensive and up-to-date history of Slovenian literature by Anton Slodnjak is available in German.[89] A chapter on Slovenian literature is found in the English translation of the history of Yugoslav literature by Anton Barac.[90] There is a monograph in French on the poet Župančič.[91] Two volumes of Slovene poetry are available in good English translations, and their introductions have some scholarly value.[92]

---

87. *Rumänisches Lesebuch: Ausgewählte Proben rumänischer Schriftsteller mit deutschen Anmerkungen und einem Grundriss der rumänischen Literaturgeschichte* (Heidelberg: Groos, 1923).

88. Eric D. Tappe, *Rumanian Prose and Verse: A Selection with an Introductory Essay* (London: University of London Press, 1956); Jacob Steinberg, *Introduction to Rumanian Literature* (New York: Twayne, 1966).

89. *Geschichte der slovenischen Literatur*, Grundriss der slavischen Philologie und Kulturgeschichte, vol. 13 (Berlin: de Gruyter, 1958).

90. *A History of Yugoslav Literature* (Belgrade: Committee for Foreign Cultural Relations of Yugoslavia, 1955).

91. L. Tesnière, *Oton Joupantchitch, poète slovène: l'homme et l'oeuvre* (Paris: Les Belles-Lettres, 1931).

92. W. K. Matthews and A. Slodnjak, eds., *Poems by Francè Prešeren*, new enlarged ed. (London: John Calder, 1963); W. K. Matthews and A. Slodnjak, eds.,

SERBO-CROATIAN

Interest in Serbo-Croatian literature in English translation goes back to the discovery of the Serb epic songs, popularized all over Europe by Goethe and Mérimée. Sir John Bowring published an English version as early as 1827.[93] Njegoš' great poem *Gorski vijenac* has been available in English since 1930.[94] One scholarly history of Serbo-Croatian literature in German was available prior to 1941, that of Gerhard Gesemann, an excellent if brief survey.[95] Pavle Popovic's historical study in French stresses common elements in Yugoslav literature.[96]

Since World War II, two more fine histories of Serbo-Croatian literature have been written or translated into Western languages. The best in English is the work by Barac, translated from Serbo-Croatian.[97] It is comprehensive, and only slightly slanted politically. Another good history is Arturo Cronia's in Italian, also comprehensive, but sometimes rhetorical in style and inclined to strongly personal views.[98] The recently published booklets by Ante Kadić on contemporary Croatian and Serbian literature actually cover most of the twentieth century.[99]

Monographs on Serbo-Croatian literature in Western languages for the most part treat periods or movements rather than individual writers. Certain phases of the writing of the Ragusan republic and of Dalmatia have been well studied in several monographs.[100] Monographs cover the work of Marulić, Ilić, and Andrić,[101] the only Yugoslav to receive the

The Parnassus of a Small Nation: An Anthology of Slovene Lyrics (London: John Calder, 1957); a second, enlarged edition was edited by Janko Lavrin and A. Slodnjak and published in Ljubljana in 1965).

93. *Servian Popular Poetry* (London: the author, 1827).

94. Peter II P. Njegoš, *The Mountain Wreath*, trans. James W. Wiles, with an introduction by Vladeta Popović (London: Allen and Unwin, 1930).

95. "Die serbo-kroatische Literatur."

96. "La littérature Yougoslave," *Le Monde slave*, 7 (1930): 39–58, 161–85; 8 (1931): 289–320.

97. *A History of Yugoslav Literature.*

98. *Storia della letteratura serbocroata* (Milan: Nuova Accademia, 1956).

99. *Contemporary Croatian Literature* (The Hague: Mouton, 1960); *Contemporary Serbian Literature* (The Hague: Mouton, 1964).

100. Konstantin Jireček, "Beiträge zur ragusanischen Literaturgeschichte," *Archiv für slavische Philologie*, 21 (1899): 399–542; Josip Tobarina, *Italian Influence on the Poets of the Ragusan Republic* (London: Williams and Norgate, 1931); Edelgard Albrecht, *Das Türkenbild in der ragusanisch-dalmatischen Literatur des XVI. Jahrhunderts* (Munich: Otto Sagner, 1965); Arturo Cronia, *Il Settecento nella letteratura serbo-croata di Dalmazia* (Padua: Liviana, 1948).

101. Robert Felber, *Vojislav Ilić* (Munich: Otto Sagner, 1965); Mirko A. Usmiani, "Marko Marulić (1450–1525)," *Harvard Slavic Studies*, 3 (1957): 1–48; E. D. Goy, "The Work of Ivo Andrić," *Slavonic and East European Review*, 41, no. 97 (June, 1963): 301–26.

Nobel Prize for literature, while recent fiction has also been treated in English.[102] A monograph on the writer Njegoš has just appeared in English; it, however, emphasizes his activities as a political and cultural figure more than as a writer per se.[103]

Scholarly anthologies and translations. Noyes's annotated translation of the autobiography of Dositej Obradović can be recommended.[104] There is an excellent edition of Njegoš' *Gorski vijenac* in German; [105] the English version is less scholarly, but has a good introduction.[106] The English rendition of Njegoš' *Luča mikrokozma* is exceptionally well annotated.[107]

Gaps. Again, scholarly readers, translations, and well-edited anthologies are the most pressing needs. A more literary monograph on Njegoš than the recent one by Djilas, as well as a monograph on Gundulić, are obvious needs. More study should be made of twentieth-century Serbo-Croatian literature, and studies of Krleža and Andrić would be especially desirable.

MACEDONIAN

Little seems to be available in Western languages aside from the short monograph by Horace Lunt, which omits the recent period and pays almost as much attention to linguistic problems as to literary history as such.[108]

Both a literary history and a scholarly anthology in English are obvious needs; at present it would be idle to specify anything beyond these.

BULGARIAN

Ivan Vazov's masterpiece, *Under the Yoke*, was published in English translation as early as 1912. But it can hardly be said that any deep

102. E. D. Goy, "The Serbian and Croatian Novel since 1948," *Slavonic and East European Review*, 40, no. 94 (December, 1961): 54–84.

103. Milovan Djilas, *Njegoš: Poet, Prince, Bishop* (New York: Harcourt, Brace, 1966).

104. *The Life and Adventures of Dimitrije Obradović*, trans. George Rapall Noyes (Berkeley: University of California Press, 1953).

105. Petar II Petrović Njegoš, *Der Bergkranz: Einleitung, Übersetzung und Kommentar von A. Schmaus* (Munich: Otto Zagner, 1963).

106. *The Mountain Wreath*, trans. James W. Wiles.

107. Petar II Petrović Njegoš, "The Rays of the Microcosm," trans. with introduction by Anica Savić-Rebac, *Harvard Slavic Studies*, 3 (1957): 105–201.

108. "A Survey of Macedonian Literature," *Harvard Slavic Studies*, 1 (1953): 363–96.

or permanent interest in Bulgarian literature has developed in the Anglo-Saxon world, either through translations or scholarly investigation. There has been somewhat greater interest in France and Italy. The best, most comprehensive and most accurate of the older histories of Bulgarian literature in a foreign language was published in France, in 1937.[109] Slightly earlier, a sketch of the Bulgarian Renaissance had appeared in the same language.[110] Short histories also appeared in Italian and English during the 1930s.[111]

The war years brought the publication of a second history in Italian,[112] while the postwar years saw the production of a third history in that language, written by a scholar, comprehensive and accurate, extending up to World War II.[113] The same period has seen the production of a longer history in English, which extends from the beginnings to the Communist period but which suffers from some inaccuracy and unevenness, including overemphasis on Ukrainian-Bulgarian literary relations.[114]

Vazov has attracted most attention as a subject for monographs, with no less than three important ones in Western languages, including a study of his art.[115] The beginnings of modern Bulgarian literature have been described in two works of importance,[116] and there is also a study of foreign influences on Bulgarian literature in French.[117]

Scholarly anthologies and translations. There is a good annotated an-

109. G. Hateau, *Panorama de la littérature bulgare contemporaine* (Paris: Editions du Sagittaire, 1937).

110. Boian Penev, *La renaissance bulgare* (Sofia: La Bulgarie, 1933).

111. Luigi Salvini, *La letteratura bulgara della liberazione alla prima guerra balcanica (1878–1912)* (Rome: Istituto per l'Europa orientale, 1936); Dmitri Shishmanov, *A Survey of Bulgarian Literature*, trans. Clarence A. Manning (Williamsport, Pa.: Bayard Press, 1932).

112. E. Damiani, *Sommario di storia della letteratura bulgara dalla origina ad oggi* (Rome: Associazione italo-bulgara, 1942).

113. Lavinia Borriero Picchio, *Storia della letteratura bulgara, con un profilo della letteratura paleoslava* (Milan: Nuova Accademia, 1957).

114. Clarence A. Manning and Roman Smal-Stocki, *The History of Modern Bulgarian Literature* (New York: Bookman Associates, 1960).

115. P. Christophorov, *Ivan Vazov: la formation d'un écrivain bulgare* (Paris: Droz, 1938); E. Damiani, *Patria e umanità in Ivan Vazov* (Rome: 1942); Wolfgang Gesemann, *Die Romankunst Ivan Vazovs* (Munich: Otto Sagner, 1966).

116. E. Damiani, *Gli albori della letteratura e del riscatto nazionale in Bulgaria* (Rome: Anonima romana editoriale, 1928); Veselin Beshevliev, "Die Anfänge der bulgarischen Literatur," *International Journal of Slavic Linguistics and Poetics*, 4 (1961): 16–45.

117. Nicolai Donchev, *Influences étrangères dans la littérature bulgare* (Sofia: La Bulgarie, 1934).

118. E. Damiani, *Antologia della poesia bulgara contemporanea (testo bulgaro e interpretazione poetica italiana)* (Naples: Pironti, 1950).

thology of Bulgarian poetry in Italian,[118] also a volume in English which commands attention at least for its good introductory essay.[119]

Gaps. The whole field is a gap. A comprehensive history of Bulgarian literature is still an essential in English. (One is currently being prepared by Charles A. Moser.) Annotated anthologies of prose and poetry for students in English are also badly needed.

ALBANIAN

The political isolation of Albania has effectively prevented interest in Albanian literature from developing in the English-speaking world; to date there are almost no translations of Albanian literature available in English, though several short histories of the literature do exist. The earlier of these, that by Stuart Mann, is fragmentary and uneven,[120] while the second, a translation from Albanian, is slanted and partial, though it does have the merit of covering the contemporary period.[121] An Italian work by Pappas Petrotta on Albania includes a brief survey of the literature.[122] The history in Italian by Giuseppe Schirò is the most comprehensive and accurate in any foreign language; it also treats the writing of the Italo-Albanians in great detail.[123] Scholarly monographs on Albanian literature are few, and largely confined to treating older literature from the point of view of textual criticism.[124]

Scholarly anthologies and texts. There is a good anthology of Albanian poetry translated into Italian, with a fine introductory essay; it extends up to 1963.[125] A German bilingual reader in two volumes is also excellent,[126] and there is a scholarly translation of the poet Fishta's great epic work into German.[127]

119. Vivian de Sola Pinto, *Bulgarian Prose and Verse: A Selection with an Introductory Essay* (London: Athlone Press, 1957).
120. *Albanian Literature* (London: Bernard Quaritch, 1955).
121. Koco Bihiku, *An Outline of Albanian Literature*, trans. Ali Cungu (Tirana: "Naim Frashëri" State Publishing House, 1964).
122. *Svolgimento storico della cultura e della letteratura albanese* (Palermo: privately printed, 1950).
123. *Storia della letteratura albanese* (Milan: Nuova Accademia, 1957[?]).
124. Martin Camaj. *Il "Messale" di Gjon Buzuku*, (Rome: "Shejzat," 1960); Mario Louis Roques, *Recherches sur les anciens textes albanais* (Paris: P. Geuthner, 1932).
125. *Antologia della lirica albanese; versione e note a cura di Ernesto Koligi* (Milan: Vanni Scheiwiller, 1963).
126. Maximilian Lambertz, *Albanisches Lesebuch, mit Einführung in die albanische Sprache*, 2 vols. (Leipzig: Otto Harrassowitz, 1948).
127. Gjergj Fishta, *Die Laute des Hochlandes (Lahuta e Malcis), übersetzt, eingeleitet und mit Ahmerkungen versehen, von Max Lambertz* (Munich: R. Oldenburg, 1958).

Gaps. Again the whole field is a gap. English lacks an adequate survey of Albanian literature as well as an anthology of translated oral and written literature or bilingual reader. Translations of classical writers are also completely lacking.

MODERN GREEK

Though recently there has been a lively interest in modern Greek literature, and such authors as Kazantzakis, Vassilikos, and Seferis have been translated into English yet, paradoxically, modern Greek language and literature seem to be taught no more today in American universities than they were in earlier decades.

Nor is any history of modern Greek literature available today in English. There are, however, three solid studies in French, one a translation of a Dutch work;[128] a second one written in French by a Swedish scholar and covering modern Greek literature up to 1821;[129] and a third adapted from a Greek history of modern Greek literature.[130] English has fared somewhat better where special monograph studies are concerned. A study of the writer Solomos is excellent and could well serve as a model for other monographs in English.[131] A fine collection of essays on various modern Greek poets has been published by Philip Sherrard, who analyzes the problems and peculiar imaginative patterns of the Greek people and their poets.[132] One Greek monograph has also been translated into English, a study of Kazantzakis' *Odyssey*.[133] A volume of essays by George Seferis on Greek literature is also available in English translation.[134] A French collection of essays treats a number of modern Greek poets, but in insufficient depth.[135] A French monograph treats

128. D. C. Hesseling, *Histoire de la littérature grecque-moderne* (Paris: Université, Institut d'études byzantines et néo-helléniques, 1924).

129. Börje Knös, *L'Histoire de la littérature néo-grecque* (Uppsala: Acta Universitatis Upsaliensis, 1962).

130. C. Th. Dimaras, *Histoire de la littérature néo-hellénique* (Athens: Institut francais, 1965).

131. Romilly Jenkins, *Dionysius Solomos* (Cambridge: Cambridge University Press, 1940).

132. *The Marble Threshing Floor: Studies in Modern Greek Poetry* (London: Valentine, Mitchell, 1956). Includes essays on Solomos, Palamas, Cavafy, Sikelianos and Seferis.

133. Panteles Prevelakis, *Nikos Kazantzakis and His Odyssey*, trans. Philip Sherrard (New York: Simon and Schuster, 1961).

134. *On the Greek Style: Selected Essays in Poetry and Hellenism* (Boston: Little, Brown, 1966).

135. Samuel Baud-Bovy, *Poésie de la Grèce moderne* (Lausanne: Edition de la Concorde, 1946). Includes essays on Calvos, Solomos, Palamas, Cavafy, and Sikelianos.

the work of Seferis, the only Greek writer to receive a Nobel Prize;[136] there is also a monograph in Swedish on the same poet.[137]

Scholarly anthologies and translations. Trypanis' well-published anthology of poetic texts has a good introduction and notes in English.[138]

Journal. The Charioteer, a Quarterly Review of Modern Greek Culture (New York, 1960 to date) publishes many scholarly and critical articles on modern Greek literature.

Publication series. Twayne Publishers has announced a very ambitious list of monographs on Greek authors, including many who belong to the modern period, but apparently none has appeared so far.

GRADUATE STUDY

As stated before, the Slavic languages of the area, and in particular Polish, Czech, and Serbo-Croatian are far ahead of their non-Slavic brothers in the attention they receive in American graduate (and undergraduate) education.

GENERAL AND COMPARATIVE

Some American universities have programs in Slavic languages and literatures, or in comparative literatures which give opportunity for study of more than one of the literatures in the field. Most institutions which offer programs in West or South Slavic literatures on the graduate level permit their comparative study, though a given university may not always have the personnel required to sponsor any particular combination or topic. The University of California at Berkeley, Chicago, Columbia, Harvard, Indiana, Pennsylvania, and Wisconsin offer the largest number of Slavic literatures in this country (for details see below). A few schools offer survey courses in comparative Slavic literature, for example, California at Berkeley, NYU, University of Washington, and Wisconsin. Courses in Slavic civilization are fairly common at leading universities, but it is doubtful if these contain much if any literary content. Also common are reading courses or seminars in several or all Slavic literatures, but these seem to be created for reasons of economy in budget or assignment of teaching staff, and can scarcely be considered as truly comparative. The numerous courses in Czech and Slovak literature seem to have similar motivation.

136. André Mirambel, *Georges Séféris, Prix Nobel 1963* (Paris: 1964).
137. Sture Linner, *Giorgos Séferis, en entroduktion* (Stockholm: Bonnier, 1963).
138. C. A. Trypanis, ed., *Medieval and Modern Greek Poetry* (Oxford: Clarendon Press, 1951).

In principle, many programs in comparative literature could supervise graduate students in the East and Southeast European area, though the extent to which this is actually done is difficult to assess. The University of Maryland's comparative literature department does, for example, accept topics in modern Greek. No doubt certain courses, undergraduate and graduate, in comparative literature cover the dramas of the brothers Čapek or of Molnár, or the novels of Krleža and Andrić, or the novels and poetry of Kazantzakis. But for the most part, serious study for advanced degrees cannot and should not be supervised by the great majority of comparative literature departments in this country unless actual specialists in the nation or the area are available.

Many schools sponsor area course programs (e.g., Columbia, Chicago, Indiana), but these can hardly be said to favor the comparative study of several literatures in the area; rather they favor the combination of several disciplines focused on a single country.

The University of Chicago has a Center for Slavic and Balkan Studies, but does not offer any comparative courses or degrees in comparative literature studies in the field, though special degree programs can be worked out with the approval of faculty advisers. Chicago seems, however, to be the only university in the country with regularized administrative facilities for the comparative study of both the Slavic and non-Slavic literatures of the area. Columbia University gives what is perhaps a unique course in Balkan literatures (Yugoslav, Albanian, Greek, Bulgarian), but awards no degrees in the field.

POLISH

Polish no doubt enjoys a considerable advantage over the other non-Russian Slavic languages as the one most frequently studied. Serious training of graduate students in Polish literature began in this country with the coming of the late Manfred Kridl to Columbia University in 1949, and Wiktor Weintraub to Harvard in 1950. Previously, Leo Wiener at Harvard, George Rapall Noyes and Wacław Lednicki at Berkeley, and Arthur P. Coleman at Columbia had conducted courses, but sponsored few if any dissertations in the field (though it must be noted that Noyes was Wiener's student). Professors Kridl and Weintraub, along with Professor Weintraub's student, Professor H. B. Segel at Columbia, have trained the majority of American Ph.D. candidates in the field.

At present, M.A. and Ph.D. degrees in Polish literature are offered at the University of California at Berkeley, Chicago, Columbia, Harvard, Michigan, Pennsylvania, and Wisconsin. In at least three of these schools (Berkeley, Chicago, Columbia) no less than three-year sequences of courses are offered, though usually on an alternating basis. Graduate courses in Polish literature, but no degree, are offered in at least eight other universities, including several (e.g., Indiana, Wayne, UCLA) in which Polish literature is offered as part of a program of graduate interdisciplinary studies.

The quality of instruction is generally good, with several outstanding specialists in the field. About twelve Ph.D.'s have been granted in this country, principally at Columbia and Harvard, with several fine dissertations.

Library collections are excellent and adequate for graduate studies in the field, especially at Harvard, Columbia, Chicago, and Wisconsin.

CZECH

Serious study in this country began in 1946, when Roman Jakobson appeared at Columbia University. At present California at Berkeley, Chicago, Columbia, Harvard, and UCLA maintain graduate courses and offer M.A. and Ph.D. degrees in the field. Four or five Ph.D. degrees have been completed by American students.

The quality of instruction is reasonably high, though the number and variety of courses is limited. There are good library holdings at Columbia and Harvard, while Chicago and Cleveland possess excellent public library collections.

SLOVAK

All the institutions which offer Czech literature (California at Berkeley, Chicago, Columbia, Harvard, Indiana, and UCLA) include some Slovak literature in the same courses, though one suspects that this is largely lip service. There are no outstanding specialists in Slovak literature as such in the country, and no students seem to have completed Ph.D.'s in Slovak literature.

Columbia and Harvard have fair library collections.

HUNGARIAN

Serious graduate study began with the establishment of Uralic programs at Indiana University in 1945 under Thomas Sebeok, and at Columbia University in 1947 under John Lotz. These two universities remain the only institutions which offer M.A. and Ph.D. degrees in the field, though at least four other schools offer graduate courses.

One Ph.D. degree is known to have been granted so far, at Columbia University.

The quality of instruction is fair to good at the two schools giving graduate degrees, though both are stronger in linguistics than in literature. Course offerings in the latter subject are very limited. There is a good library collection at Columbia, supplemented by the New York City Public Library; a fair one at California at Berkeley.

ROMANIAN

No university at present offers graduate degrees in Romanian literature, though several universities give programs in Romance philology which include Romanian, and perhaps half a dozen schools teach Romanian language. Indiana has a graduate course in Romanian literature. No more than one or two Ph.D.'s for Romanian literature have been granted so far, apparently, in this country.

SLOVENIAN

Slovenian literature is not taught. (Courses in South Slavic literature at Chicago and Indiana presumably include Slovenian and Macedonian, as may the course in Yugoslav literature offered at UCLA, but little more than lip service seems to be paid to these literatures.) Columbia and Indiana (and no doubt others) will accept dissertations in the field.

SERBO-CROATIAN

Serbo-Croatian literature was first taught seriously in this country by Professor Albert Lord, who introduced the subject at Harvard University in 1939. Serbo-Croatian literature is taught on the graduate level at California at Berkeley, Columbia, Chicago, Harvard, UCLA, Pennsylvania, and Wisconsin, with M.A. and Ph.D. degrees offered at these institutions; Indiana, NYU, and Yale give graduate courses but no degrees. Course offerings are limited in scope, though several institutions (Chicago, Columbia, Harvard) offer folklore as well as literature. Quality of instruction varies from fair to good, and several teachers are outstanding specialists in folklore. There are good library collections at Columbia and Harvard.

MACEDONIAN

Macedonian literature is not taught (see remarks under Slovenian, above). Harvard University could presumably sponsor dissertations in the field.

BULGARIAN

Serious graduate study begins with the introduction of Bulgarian literature at Harvard University by Professor Albert Lord in 1951. Courses and graduate degrees are offered at Harvard and Wisconsin. At Columbia a graduate course was offered for many years by Professor C. A. Manning. Yale has been offering a course, but gives no degrees. Courses at Chicago and Indiana in South Slavic literatures presumably include Bulgarian, and Chicago apparently offers a graduate degree concentration in the field, but no course as such. Instruction is probably best at Harvard, which has a well-known specialist in the field. To date one or two Ph.D.'s have been completed in this country.

ALBANIAN

There are no graduate programs in Albanian literature in this country. A single course in Balkan literatures taught at Columbia University includes Albanian literature. Theses and dissertations in the field are accepted at the University of Chicago, which offers a graduate course in Albanian linguistics. Fair library collections are found at the Universities of Chicago, Columbia, and Harvard.

MODERN GREEK

The University of Chicago introduced a course in modern Greek literature in 1967–68. The single course in Balkan literature taught at Columbia includes modern Greek literature. The University of Maryland intends to introduce a course within the next several years. Theses and dissertations in the field are acceptable at the University of Cincinnati, Maryland, and presumably at Chicago and Princeton. The best library collections are found at the University of Cincinnati and at Harvard. I have been unable to find any record of dissertation completed in modern Greek literature in this country, but there are indications that a number are in progress.

RECOMMENDATIONS

GRADUATE STUDY

1. A teaching Institute of Balkan Studies, or Balkanology, should be established at some university in the United States. This institute should teach the languages and literatures of all the Balkan countries (Greece, Albania, Bulgaria, Yugoslavia, Romania, and perhaps Turkey in Eu-

rope), as well as their history, ethnography, folklore, linguistics, philology, and antiquities. Thus the institute would cover the principal humanistic disciplines as they concern the countries in question. The social sciences might be added, but the basic conception of such an institute should be centered around the humanistic disciplines.

In preparation for the establishment of such an institute, a conference should be convened by the American Council of Learned Societies to consider ways and means. Leading representatives of the disciplines mentioned having some knowledge of the countries in question should be invited, together with members of the committee responsible for the present survey representing the humanistic disciplines named above, representatives of the ACLS and the Office of Education, and, perhaps, representatives of the several universities listed just below.

The University of Chicago would seem to be the most logical choice of location for such an institute, since it offers the largest number of graduate courses in the field. Harvard, Columbia, the University of California at Berkeley, and Indiana also have some claim to consideration, and recently the University of Wisconsin has also entered the field of Balkan studies. Representatives of the administrations of these universities might be invited to attend the developmental conference.

This institute should grant M.A. and Ph.D. degrees in the disciplines mentioned, and, perhaps, certificates in area studies combining several disciplines. All certificate candidates should know the history of the country in question, whatever their specialized discipline. M.A. candidates should know one language in the area and have a reading knowledge of French or German; certificate candidates and Ph.D.'s should know at least two area languages, of which at least one should be a non-Slavic language. Ph.D. candidates should have a reading knowledge of both French and German.

2. Generally speaking, the Slavic literatures seem to be adequately represented and taught at American universities. Slovak, Slovene, and Macedonian literatures are poorly represented, if at all, but it is believed that students interested can find universities and faculty advisers competent to direct study of these literatures on a special basis. However, most of the Slavic graduate programs in this country are insufficiently flexible, and insist on a rigid program of studies with a heavy linguistic bias. While it is true that the study of the literature of one country is hardly a sufficient discipline for a graduate degree, certainly not a Ph.D., it is believed that literary studies can be joined to the study of history or of comparative literature with at least as much profit to the graduate student as he obtains from the present combination of literature and linguistics.

3. The non-Slavic languages of the East Central and Southeast European area are greatly neglected by comparison with the Slavic languages. The following recommendations are aimed at encouraging their teaching and study:

a) Institutions teaching the language and linguistics or philology of a given language should be encouraged to add more work in literature (some of them have none at present), and to offer at least a M.A. degree in that literature. Thus, Stanford and the University of Chicago should be advised to add Romanian literature, the University of Chicago to add Albanian literature, Columbia and Indiana to strengthen their present programs in Hungarian literature, etc.

b) Institutions offering graduate study of Byzantine literature should be advised to add courses in modern Greek literature (for example, UCLA).

c) In this, the principle should obtain that at least one university in the United States of high caliber should offer the language, literature, linguistics, and, if possible, history and folklore of a given country, with at least an M.A. and if possible a Ph.D. in the field of literature as such. An inter-university committee of these and possibly several other leading universities, joined with representatives of the ACLS and the Office of Education, should be formed to reach agreements among the universities in the field to avoid unnecessary duplication of teaching and library resources.

d) Institutions with NDEA summer institutes in the Slavic and non-Slavic languages of the East and Southeast European area should be encouraged to include literature, linguistics, and history in their programs.

RESEARCH AND PUBLICATION

1. In order to meet the many needs outlined in this survey, the subsidized preparation and publication of the following types of materials is recommended for each of the languages in the area:

a) A history of literature in English, specially written and aimed at the American graduate student, but giving titles of literary works, technical terms of literary history, etc., in the original language as well as in translation. The volume should cover the whole field of literary history, including folklore, to World War II, though not further. Treatment should be a compromise between a chronological survey and a survey by genres. Generous background material on cultural and intellectual history should be provided. Literary criticism and literary journals should be treated in some detail. Foreign literary influences should be covered. A bibliography and index should be appended. The length of such a history should vary from perhaps 200 pages in the case of Albania to about 1,000 pages in the case of Poland.

b) A two-volume bilingual anthology of poetry and prose, including stories, sketches, essays, and even occasionally outstanding critical articles, but avoiding excerpts from longer works (unless they can stand on their own feet as independent literary works), should be prepared. The first volume should give the texts selected in the original, and vary from perhaps 100–150 pages in the case of Albania to 800–1,000 pages in the case of Poland. Some folklore should be included in each case. The second volume should give English translations of the texts as well as notes and commentary directed specifically toward the American graduate student.

c) A companion to the study of the national language, literature, history, folklore, ethnography, etc., should be prepared for each country in the area. This study should have approximately the same length as the history of literature. It should treat the following topics:

(1) Geography and economics
- A. Geography
  - (*a*) Physical, economic, and political
  - (*b*) Demography
- B. Economics in general (historical aperçu)

(2) History
- A. Ethnogenesis and early migrations
- B. Earliest cultural contacts as revealed by sources
- C. Earliest political organization (incl. tribal)
- D. Western (or Byzantine) sources on the early period
- E. Middle Ages; Byzantine, Ottoman periods
- F. Transitional period; great-power interventions and alignments
- G. Nationalism; contacts with the West
- H. Formation of a national state (kingdom)
- I. History until 1918
- J. History 1918–30s

(3) Specific cultural segments
- A. Greek Orthodoxy vs. Western churches (vs. Islam) (or Catholicism vs. Protestantism)
- B. Pan-Slavism
- C. Romanticism, rise of nationalism
- D. Agrarianism
- E. Armenians, Greeks, Jews, Gypsies
- F. Nationals abroad (e.g., Greeks in Egypt; nationals in the U.S.)

(4) Intellectual culture
   A. Folklore
   B. Literature
   C. Theatre
   D. Music
   E. Other arts
   F. Miscellaneous: education, criticism, etc.
(5) Twentieth-century politics
   A. Inherited problems
   B. Solutions via alliances with (or against) neighbors
   C. Solutions imposed by Big Powers (end with World War II)
(6) Appraisal (sketches) of present-day
   A. Political
   B. Cultural
   C. Relations with the West
(7) Language (brief sketch for the layman only)
(8) Most important areas for research
   Bibliography for each chapter (Western vs. Russian vs. native sources)

The above works should each be prepared by a single scholar (except for the last one [c], which should be prepared by a committee of scholars working under a chairman). Manuscripts should then be submitted to a group of scholars in the fields of literature, history, folklore, linguistics, and philology for their criticisms and suggestions.

2. Gaps in research in literature in English, French, and German are enormous, but there seems to be no reason for any presumption that the whole history of the literature of any of the East or Southeast European countries should be covered completely in the Western European languages, except in outline form. More important than filling in gaps in research would be to encourage comparative studies within the area, or between countries in the area and other literatures, particularly Anglo-American. This is particularly important for the non-Slavic countries, since the study of comparative Slavic literature is already relatively well developed and is encouraged by the emphasis placed on comparative topics at the International Congresses of Slavicists.

As outsiders, American scholars should be encouraged to make objective studies of such peculiarly sensitive topics as the Czech-Slovak problem, the interrelations of the peoples of Yugoslavia, the Yugoslav-Albanian question, the literatures of Transylvania (German, Magyar, and Romanian) and their interrelations, Macedonian literature, etc. These problems of course also apply to disciplines other than literature and folklore.

While commercial publishers may be more willing to publish mono-graphs on single writers, still, studies of periods, genres, ideological questions, influences, etc., may be intellectually more stimulating and more imperatively needed in English. It would be presumptuous to suggest a full list of these, but suffice it to mention as examples Czech fourteenth-century literature, or the Polish Romantic drama, or Renais-sance literature in Eastern Europe. The influence of the Turks on the literature of the Balkan peoples is a significant topic, as is that of German literature on the literatures of East Central Europe, or a com-parative study of the process of "de-Stalinization" in Communist East Europe and the Soviet Union.

3. Outstanding doctoral dissertations completed in the field should be published. This is particularly true of Polish, for which several fine dissertations remain unprinted, including Bronisław de Laval Jezier-ski's study of Sienkiewicz' Russian reputation, and Harold B. Segel's dissertation on the Polish Baroque comedy and theater.

4. While many of the outstanding East European writers remain in-adequately treated in English (e.g., Krasiński, Mácha, Hviezdoslav, Petöfi, Eminescu, Njegoš, etc.), the most urgent needs of the field are adequate translations of classic works (edited for English-speaking stu-dents), anthologies equipped with introductions and notes for the for-eign reader, as well as annotated translations. While it is true that graduate specialists should not have to rely on translations, student interest in a given literature can hardly be stimulated unless attractively presented and intelligible translations are widely available in English or other Western languages.

14/ FOLKLORE AND ETHNOMUSICOLOGY

Albert B. Lord and David E. Bynum
Harvard University

The following report on the state of American ethnomusicological and folkloristic studies of East Central and Southeastern European cultures is based on a survey of books and monographs published in the United States, and of articles on these subjects published in the principal learned journals in this country. We have also reviewed the courses offered in American colleges and universities, unpublished collections of primary materials in this country, and the living scholars of our subjects in the United States, where these were known to us.[1]

In the field of ethnomusicology we have been helped considerably by consulting Frank Gillis and Alan P. Merriam, *Ethnomusicology and Folk Music: An International Bibliography of Dissertations and Theses.*[2]

GENERAL REMARKS

The material before World War II is generally scanty, uncritical, and not representative of the fields; there are a few notable exceptions in the nineteenth century which are now of historical interest, for example, Talvj (Robinson), *Historical View of the Languages and Literature of the Slavic Nations; with a Sketch of Their Popular Poetry.*[3] Until World War II, publications in this country present not only an inadequate but also often a distorted view of the folklore and folk music of central Europe and the Balkans. This kind of publication con-

---

1. The parts of this survey that deal with books and monographs, and ethnomusicology in American journals, were prepared by Albert Lord, and the parts on periodical writing on folklore, university courses, and personnel were written by David Bynum. The general remarks and recommendations are our joint conclusions.
2. (Middleton, Conn.: Wesleyan University Press, 1960).
3. (New York: George P. Putnam, 1850), pp. 315–404.

tinues after World War II, but it is joined then by a small number of scholarly works; these mark the real beginnings of American contributions to knowledge of our subjects. In some instances, the scholarly contributions to these fields made in the United States in this century have been unnaturalized derivatives of European scholarship, published here but intended for émigré readers or frankly for export to Europe, not for either the educated or learned American, and sometimes not even in English.

BOOKS AND MONOGRAPHS

ALBANIA

The earliest publication in the United States that we have found of Albanian folklore is Paul Fenimor Cooper's translation of tales in the Tosk dialect from the collections of Holger Pedersen of Copenhagen and August Dozon, *Tricks of Women and Other Albanian Tales.*[4]

The northern Albanian ballads and folksongs in the Harvard College Library collected by Milman Parry in 1934 and 1935 and by Albert Lord in 1937 have not yet been published; Dr. John S. Kolsti at the University of Texas (Austin) is presently preparing an edition of them with translations. Stavro Skendi's book, *Albanian and South Slavic Oral Epic Poetry*,[5] is the only scholarly work on Albanian folklore that has been published in English in the United States to the present. John S. Kolsti's doctoral dissertation on bilingual epic singing (Albanian and Serbo-Croatian) in the Archives of the Harvard College Library is, like Stavro Skendi's book, concerned with both Albanian and Yugoslav folklore.

Earlier than any of the publications in English is a work in Italian which contains some Albanian folklore texts: Antonio Scura, *Gli Albanesi in Italia e i loro canti tradizionali.*[6]

Our search has disclosed no ethnomusicological contributions for the Albanian field, outside of Albania itself, where the Folklore Institute in Tirana is very active under its president, Zihni Sako, in all branches of folklore research.

BULGARIA

A considerable unpublished collection of Bulgarian folklore texts made by Albert Lord in 1958 and 1959 is in the Harvard College Library.

4. (New York: William Morrow & Co., 1928).
5. Memoirs of the American Folklore Society no. 44, (Philadelphia, 1954).
6. (New York: F. Tocci, 1912).

Typical of the unscholarly current of activity are two anthologies containing "retold" folktales, which we would not cite here at all except to indicate the poverty in this country of bona fide collections and studies. They belong rather to a kind of marginal belles lettres than to scholarship: Parker Fillmore, *The Laughing Prince: A Book of Jugoslav Fairy Tales and Folk Tales*,[7] contains Bulgarian among other tales rewritten from South Slavic; Elena Borikova Craver, *Bulgarian Folk Tales*,[8] is the same kind of book forty years later, except that it contains stories remembered and collected from grandparents and friends.

The only published learned work in either of our two fields is that of Boris Kremenliev in ethnomusicology. This scholar is a regular contributor to Bulgarian ethnomusicology who publishes in the United States: Boris A. Kremenliev, *Bulgarian — Macedonian Folk Music*.[9]

An unpublished master's thesis on Bulgarian ethnomusicology speaks for itself, Mrs. Nadia Mihailovska Stevens' "Some Aspects of the Bulgarian Folk Music":[10]

> The study attempts to trace the origin of Bulgarian folk music with its lyric, and to show how it has kept its unifying qualities so as to remain uniquely Bulgarian. Topics include an historical sketch, lyrics, rhythm, dancing, instruments, intervals, harmony, and scales.

The Bulgars themselves have been very active in the folklore field since the middle of the last century when the collection of the Miladinov brothers first appeared (1861). The *Sbornik za narodni umotvorenia, nauka i knizhnina* (Collection for Folk Poetry. Science and Literature), begun by the Ministerstvo na narodnoto prosveshtenie (Ministry of Public Instruction) in 1889, and later continued by the Bulgarian Academy of Sciences under the title *Sbornik za narodni umotvorenia i narodopis* (Collection for Folk Poetry and Ethnography), has been and still is a major resource. Recently a twelve-volume collection of *Bŭlgarsko narodno tvorchestvo* (Bulgarian Folk Art) was published by the publishing house, Bŭlgarski pisatel (Bulgarian Author). The work of the Ethnographic Institute of the Bulgarian Academy and of such scholars as Petŭr Dinekov, Cvetana Romanska, Stefana G. Stoikova, of Stoian Diudiev in the field of music, and of Raina Katsarova in the dance is worthy of special mention.

7. (New York: Harcourt, Brace, 1921).
8. (New York: Vantage Press, 1964).
9. (Berkeley and Los Angeles: University of California Press, 1952).
10. No. 757, Gillis and Merriam, "Ethnomusicology and Folk Music," M.A. thesis, Boston University (music), 1937, music, texts.

CZECHOSLOVAKIA

As with the other nationalities, so for the Czechs there are at least two popular works of retold tales, one by the ubiquitous Parker Fillmore (1919) and the other by Dr. Josef Baudis of Prague (1917). The last is actually a British publication distributed in New York by Macmillan, but it has more scholarly authority than Fillmore's book.

Except for Talvj's publication noted earlier, the first work treating Czech folklore that we have found published in the United States is *Bohemian Legends and Other Poems* by Mrs. Flora Pauline Kopta (née Wilson).[11] A number of the poems were written by Mrs. Kopta herself. An earlier edition of some of the poems was printed in Schüttenhof in 1890 and confiscated by the Austrians.

During the last few years there have been four theses in ethnomusicology written in the United States on Czech subjects. Typical of one group of interests is the M.A. thesis by V. M. L. Litle, "A Study of the Significance of Three National Dance Groups in Los Angeles."[12] Two of the theses reflect the use of folk songs and dances in schools: A. A. Turecheck, "Problems Involved in Arranging a Selected Group of Czech Folk Songs for Educational Purposes,"[13] and Katherine Von Wenck, "A Critical Evaluation of Czechoslovakian Folk Dances for Use in American School Situations."[14] Of slightly more interest is Brownlee Waschek's "A Study of Czechoslovak Folk Music Transplanted to the Community of Masaryktown, Florida."[15]

Thus the state of Czechoslovak folklore and ethnomusicological studies in the United States is not at all encouraging. There is no outstanding publication in book or monograph form.

MODERN GREECE

Modern Greek folklore, like modern Greek studies in general, has been neglected in the United States, in spite of our large population of Greek descent, though the neglect is not so grave as in the case of some of the Slavic cultures. The earliest monograph we have found (it is in reality only a short article) is entitled *The Klephts in Modern Greek Poetry: An Inquiry into a Graeco-Turkish Cultural Conflict*, written by Gabriel Rombotis.[16]

11. (New York, 1894; 2d ed., 1896).
12. M.A. thesis, University of California, Los Angeles, 1943.
13. M.A. thesis, University of Iowa, 1945.
14. M.A. thesis, New York University, 1933.
15. M.A. thesis, Florida State University, 1959.
16. Part of a Ph.D. dissertation in the Department of Comparative Religion and Sociology at the University of Chicago, 1932.

The one thesis on ethnomusicology on a Greek subject written in this country is of the pedagogical variety, and is dated 1940: J. S. Huston, "Greek Folk Music for the Elementary and Junior High Schools." [17]

The situation improved in the 1950s because of the splendid collection of tape recordings and manuscripts made in Greece in 1952–53 by James Notopoulos of Trinity College, Hartford.[18] In 1956 some of his material appeared with commentary and texts in the Folkways Record Series.[19]

The 1960s have produced even more. In 1961 two works appeared in New York: T. Petrides, *Folk Dances of the Greeks*,[20] and R. S. Seth, *Fairy Tales of Greece*.[21] In 1964 Al. Oikonomides reissued J. C. Lawson's *Modern Greek Folklore and Ancient Greek Religion*,[22] and in 1966 he performed the same service for another older work, J. T. Bent's *Aegean Islands*.[23] In 1965 two quite different works appeared, one concerned with folk arts, M. Gentles, *Turkish and Greek Island Embroideries*, and an ethnomusicological monograph, nearer to the interests of this survey: Sotirios (Sam) Chianis' *Folk Songs of Mantineia, Greece*.[24]

Clearly Greece is better represented in folklore and ethnomusicological books and monographs than certain others of the eight nationalities, at least as far as material appearing in the United States is concerned.

HUNGARY

The oldest book we have found published in this country about Hungarian folklore is *Tales and Traditions of Hungary*, by Theresa Pulszky.[25] As in so many other cases, this book was first published in England (London, 1851) and was republished the following year in America, with a letter to George Bancroft, the historian. It is therefore not strictly an American product.

17. M.A. thesis, Ohio State University, 1940.
18. Died in October, 1967, during the preparation of this survey.
19. Folkways Records FE 4468 *Modern Greek Heroic Oral Poetry*, with an introduction, "Modern Greek Heroic Oral Poetry and Its Relevance to Homer, the Oral Poet" (New York, 1959).
20. (New York: Exposition Press, 1961).
21. (New York: Dutton, 1961).
22. (Hyde Park, N.Y.: University Books, 1964; originally published by Cambridge University Press, 1910).
23. (Chicago: Argonaut, 1966); first appeared in England in 1884.
24. University of California Folklore Studies 15 (Berkeley).
25. (Clinton Hall, N.Y.: Redfield, 1852).

Next in time is a thin volume, privately published, entitled *Volk-Songs* translated from the *Acta comparationis litterarum universum*, by Henry Phillips, Jr.[26] It contains twenty-one Hungarian folk songs and twenty songs of the "Transylvanian Zigeuner." Mr. Phillips also translated some of the poetry of Alexander Petöfi, of whose poems a few appear in Mrs. Pulszky's volume, cited above. Henry Phillips was a numismatist, historian, and antiquarian who wrote also on the folklore of Philadelphia.

The two works above belong in the amateur or "antiquarian" category, but were typical of their period. In contrast to them, Jeremiah Curtin's *Myths and Folk-Tales of the Russians, Western Slavs, and Magyars*[27] was a professional accomplishment of merit in its time, though it is now outmoded. In the field of folktales the latest publication is in the series Folktales of the World of which Richard W. Dorson is general editor: *Folktales of Hungary*, edited by Linda Dégh and translated by Judit Halasz.[28]

Hungary's greatest contributions to folklore studies have been in ethnomusicology. The works of Béla Bartók and Zoltán Kodály have been both pioneering and definitive and their influence has been very great. However, their work on Hungarian folk song and folk music was done in Hungary, or at least in Europe, and does not belong to the story of American scholarship in the field, though it has been a strong formative force on American ethnomusicology.

Theses written in the United States dealing with Hungarian folk music or dance are as follows: Elizabeth Charlotte Rearick, *Dances of the Hungarians: A Study of the Dances Found Today in Hungary, Together with a Description of Some of the Peasant Festivities*.[29] It deals with the "social significance of Hungarian folk dances, their origin and original purpose in folklore." I. K. Banyay wrote on "The History of the Hungarian Music."[30] It is "primarily a history of art and religious music. The thesis includes a chapter on Gypsy music and one on the instruments of the Magyars." A third thesis, that of Stephen Erdely, to judge from its title and description, is of particular interest. "An Essay on Methods and Principles of Hungarian Ethnomusicology"[31] is described as follows: "Kodály's four studies, *Strophic Structure*

26. (Philadelphia, 1885; printed for private circulation).
27. (Boston: Little, Brown, 1890).
28. (Chicago: University of Chicago Press, 1965).
29. Ph.D. dissertation, Columbia Teacher's College, 1939, published as no. 770 in the Columbia University Contributions to Education.
30. M.A. thesis, University of Southern California, 1942.
31. Ph.D. dissertation, Western Reserve University, 1962, bibliography, music, and tables.

of Hungarian Folksong, Pentatonism in Hungarian Folksong, Characteristic Melodic Structure in Cheremis Folksong, and *Folk Music of Hungary* are evaluated, critically compared, and extended by new research on the part of the writer." Erdely's thesis seems to be in the best tradition of Hungarian musicology, and may represent an important continuation of the work of the great master. We are happy to add that it was published in 1965 under the title *Methods and Principles of Hungarian Ethnomusicology.*[32]

POLAND

Only one publication is worthy of note, though it is actually not a product of American scholarship. In 1946 at the Naklad Dziennika Zwiazkowega in Chicago there was published in Polish *Polska piesn ludowa, wybor* (Polish Folksong, a Selection) by Jan St. Bystron, Professor at the University of Poznan.

Of the theses on ethnomusicology produced in the United States, only two deserve notice and they are both master's theses in music at Wayne State University. The first was in 1940: Harriet Pawlowska, "Polish Folk Songs Gathered in Detroit, with an Analysis of the Music by Grace L. Engel." [33] It is described as "a good collection of European material in an American urban tradition. Transcriptions are moderately reliable, analysis uses rather obsolete methods. Brief introduction on the cultural background of the informants is included. Exists only on microfilm." The other thesis was done in 1951: Helen Goranowski, "An Analysis of 65 Polish Folk-Songs; with Conclusions Based on This Analysis concerning the Relation between Language Rhythms and Music Rhythms; and concerning the Evolution and Transplantation of These Songs to America." [34] The description is as follows: "Background information on informants, introduction on folk music and Polish immigration to the United States; analysis of the music; comparison of Polish songs brought from Poland with others learned in the United States."

ROMANIA

The fairy tales written by Carmen Sylva, or Elizabeth, Queen of Romania, were the most popular, but were of course written by the queen "on the basis" of old stories and legends. They have appeared

---

32. Indiana University Publications, Uralic and Altaic Series, vol. 52 (Bloomington), music.
33. 41 songs with music and texts in Polish.
34. Maps, music, tables.

in popular editions in translation in both New York and Chicago in this century.

The oldest book published in the United States on Romanian folk-lore that we have found is *Roumanian Fairy Tales*, collected by Mite Kremnitz, adapted and arranged by J. M. Percival.[35] Some of the tales in it are from the collection of Petre Ispirescu, some from periodi-cal literature, and some were written by various authors. Ispirescu's collection is also the basis for another translation by Julia Collier Harris and Rea Ipcar, published under the title *The Founding Prince and Other Tales.*[36]

Two other volumes of about the same vintage, the first and second decade of this century, contain material collected by Helen Vacaresco. The first is called *The Bard of the Dimbovitza: Roumanian Folk-Songs*, collected from the peasants by Helene Vacaresco, translated by Carmen Sylva and Alma Strettell.[37] The second bears the title *Songs of the Val-iant Voivode* "and other strange folk-lore for the first time collected from Romanian peasants and set forth in English by Helene Vaca-resco." The publisher is the same, and the date is about 1905.

Another work is *Roumanian Folk Tales*,[38] retold from the originals by Jacob Bernard Segall. The tales are from Ispirescu's collection.

The most recent entry is *Folk Tales from Roumania*, translated by Mabel Nandris from the Romanian of Ion Creanga.[39]

As is the case with both Czechoslovakia and Poland, we know of no monographs or of significant work now being done in the United States in the folklore of Romania. We know of no theses in Romanian ethnomusicology done in the United States.

YUGOSLAVIA

The Yugoslavs have collected and studied their folklore and folk songs seriously since the beginning of the nineteenth century to the present day in an unbroken tradition. In Western Europe, the most significant work in this century has been done by Alois Schmaus in Munich, who collected material among the Moslems in Novi Pazar and also investigated and analyzed the Moslem epic of the old "Krajina."

Talvj's work mentioned at the beginning of this survey is the first (1850), we believe, to introduce Serbian or Croatian folklore to the

35. (New York: Henry Holt, 1835).
36. (Boston and New York: Houghton Mifflin, 1917).
37. (New York: Scribners, 1902?).
38. University of Maine Studies, vol. 26, no. 10 (June, 1925).
39. (New York: Roy Publishers, 1953).

United States. Probably the second work is Owen Meredith's *The National Songs of Servia*.[40] As most everyone knows, Owen Meredith was Robert Bulwer-Lytton's pseudonym. It is sad to note that the American edition of this work, which had first been published in London in 1861 with the title *Serbski Pesme, or National Songs of Servia*, makes no mention of the fact that Bulwer-Lytton had taken these songs from August Dozon's *Poésies populaires serbes traduites sur les originaux avec une introduction et des notes*.[41] There is little excuse for this, because in 1869 Lytton reprinted his "translations" in *Orval, or the Fool of Time; and other Imitations and Paraphrases* (pp. 359–431), providing them with a new preface in which he apologized for his misleading statements in the first preface. We believe that the American editor must have known of this second preface, since he printed on the title page the motto *Omne meum: nihil meum*, which appears only in the 1869 edition. Thus the second translations (Talvj's were first) of South Slavic epic to appear in the United States were not real translations, and were accompanied by a hoax, however polite. Lytton's poems are retellings in his own way of songs he had read in Dozon's French translations of some of the poems in Vuk Stefanović Karadžić's collection.

The next book in time is also a translation, or, more strictly, an anthology of translations: *An Anthology of Jugoslav Poetry: Serbian Lyrics*,[42] edited by Beatrice Stevenson Stanoyevich. This contains translations by Bowring, Bulwer-Lytton, Wiles, and the editor. In a preface Milivoy Stanoyevich says (p. 9) that the claims we make today on a translator are different from those in Bowring's time, but he says nothing of Owen Meredith.

In 1913, also in Boston, there appeared the first truly American product of scholarship in the field of South Slavic folklore. This is *Heroic Ballads of Servia*, translated into English verses by George Rapall Noyes and Leonard Bacon.[43]

In 1921, another of the usual popular fairy tale books appeared, *The Laughing Prince: Jugoslav Folk and Fairy Tales*, by Parker Fillmore.[44]

While selected material from Karadžić's classic collection was thus being made available in the United States in various forms of English translation, the publishing house of Dushan B. Popovich in Chicago

40. (Boston: James R. Osgood & Co., 1877).
41. (Paris: E. Dentu, 1859).
42. (Boston: Richard G. Badger, Gorham Press, 1920).
43. (Boston: Sherman, French & Co., 1913).
44. (New York: Harcourt, Brace & Co., 1921).

was printing songbooks in Serbo-Croatian containing both poems from Karadžić's collection and new poems written in the manner of the folk poetry (sometimes called *nove narodne pjesme*, "new folk songs") although not authentic oral traditional songs. Thus we have *Od Sinaja do Siona, Nove srpske narodne pjesme* (From Sinai to Zion, New Serbian Folk Songs), 1920. These are dedicated to the Serbian army, and the book has a preface dated 1917, but no author's name is given. Presumably the author was D. B. Popovich himself. There is a *Bosanska pjesmarica: Narodne junačke pjesme* (Bosnian Songbook: Heroic Folk Songs) that came out in 1924, and in the same year *Nova evropska pesmarica* (A New European Songbook); some of its songs have author's names. A list of other books of this sort was printed on the back cover of the last two works mentioned. Thus, as it were, a branch of the publishing activity in the new Yugoslavia was operating among the Serbian immigrants in the United States. Very probably a similar activity was to be found among the Croatian immigrants, but we do not have any information about it at hand.

Such was the situation when the American classicist Milman Parry began his collecting in the summer of 1933. His collection, made in Yugoslavia during that summer and in the fifteen months from June, 1934, to September, 1935, is now housed in Harvard's Widener Library. It has since been expanded by further collecting by Albert B. Lord and David E. Bynum, and by their microfilming of large parts of the collections of the Matica hrvatska in Zagreb and of the Serbian Academy of Arts and Sciences in Belgrade. Albanian and Bulgarian materials have also been added to this original collection, and it is a center not only for the study of Serbo-Croatian oral epic song but, more generally, of Balkan oral epic poetry.

Several publications have already come from this center at Harvard, and more are in manuscript and soon to appear. First was a study by Béla Bartók of the music of some of the so-called "women's" songs in the Parry Collection, with his transcriptions of the music from the phonograph records.[45] Then in 1953–54 came two volumes of text and translation of traditional epic song, with some transcriptions of its music by Béla Bartók, published jointly by the Harvard University Press and the Serbian Academy of Sciences in Belgrade.[46] Finally, in 1960 appeared a description of the techniques of oral epic composition and transmission, based on the texts of and experience with the

45. Albert B. Lord and Béla Bartók, *Serbo-Croatian Folk Songs* (New York: Columbia University Press, 1951).

46. Milman Parry and Albert Lord, *Serbocroatian Heroic Songs*, vol. 1 (1954) and vol. 2 (1953) (Cambridge and Belgrade).

Parry Collection, by Albert B. Lord, *The Singer of Tales*.[47] Further volumes of texts and translations and a study by David E. Bynum of the thematic composition and repertory of the Serbo-Croatian tradition are now being readied for the press.

EAST EUROPEAN ETHNOMUSICOLOGY IN AMERICAN JOURNALS

During forty years from 1915 to 1955 the *Musical Quarterly* carried some nine articles on folk music in Eastern Europe, and at least four of these were not by American scholars: in 1926, Anton Dobronić contributed "A Study of Jugoslav Music";[48] in 1933, Béla Bartók wrote "Hungarian Peasant Music"[49] and, in 1947, "Gypsy Music or Hungarian Music?";[50] in 1951, the distinguished Turkish musicologist, A. Adnan Saygun, wrote "Bartók in Turkey."[51] Three of the remaining five articles in the *Musical Quarterly* were about Hungarian folk music: Arthur Hartmann, "The Czimbalom, Hungary's National Instrument";[52] Edward Kilenyi, "The Theory of Hungarian Music";[53] and Helen Ware, "The American-Hungarian Folk Song."[54] The other two articles are by Rodney Gallop and cover "Folk Music of the Southern Slavs"[55] and "Folk-Songs of Modern Greece."[56]

The importance of Hungarian tradition in East European ethnomusicology as we know it in America is borne out also by a bibliography gleaned from the pages of *Ethnomusicology*. There are three items in it concerned with Hungary. Two of these are by Stephen Erdely in Cleveland, whose thesis was mentioned above in the review of books and monographs; they are: "classification of Hungarian Folksongs"[57] and "Folksinging of the American Hungarians in Cleveland."[58] The third concerns Béla Bartók and is by John Vinton: "The Folk Music Research of Béla Bartók, Part I."[59]

47. (Cambridge: Harvard University Press, 1960).
48. Vol. 12: 56–71.
49. Vol. 19: 267–287.
50. Vol. 33: 240–257.
51. Vol. 37: 5–9.
52. Vol. 2 (1916): 590–600.
53. Vol. 5 (1919): 20–39.
54. Vol. 2 (1916): 434–441.
55. Vol. 23 (1937): 516–531.
56. Vol. 21 (1935): 89–98.
57. *The Folklore and Folk Music Archivist*, 5 (3): (Fall, 1962): 1–2.
58. Ethnomusicology, 7, no. 1 (January, 1964): 14–27.
59. *Folk Music and Dance*. Newsletter of the U.S. National Committee IFMC no. 2 (June, 1963): 1–5.

Bulgaria is represented by two entries, both by Boris Kremenliev, whose work is also recorded elsewhere in this survey: "Balkans Revisited, 1962," [60] and "Extension and its Effect in Bulgarian Folksong." [61] The first of these is a very informative report on ethnomusicology in the Balkans in 1962; the second deals with a technical point in the study of Bulgarian song.

In the same series as the last-mentioned article is another technical one by Sam Chianis on "Aspects of Melodic Ornamentation in the Folk Music of Central Greece." [62] Chianis' monograph on the folk music of Mantinea has already been mentioned in this survey.

The Hungarian influence of Béla Bartók is seen once again in an article by George Herzog, "The Music of Yugoslav Heroic Epic Folk Poetry." [63]

The contributions of Yury Arbatsky to this discipline stand in a controversial class by themselves: "Communication on the Chromatic Balkan Scale," [64] "Beating the Tupan in the Central Balkans," [65] and "The Roga, a Balkan Bagpipe, and Its Medico-Magical Conjurations." [66] To these we add Walter G. Nau's "A Triptych from the Arbatsky Collection at the Newberry Library, Chicago, Illinois." [67]

A single Czech item has come to our attention in the article by Bruno Nettl and Ivo Moravcik, "Czech and Slovak Songs Collected in Detroit." [68]

Finally, we note that, although the contribution is not strictly American, Barbara Krader published in *Ethnomusicology* a "Memorial to Danica S. Yanković, 1898–1960," [69] the well-known collector and student of Yugoslav folk dance.

In summary, for the field of East European ethnomusicology in the United States, we find three living American scholars who have contributed both a serious book and one or more serious articles on the subject: Sam Chianis (Greece), Boris Kremenliev (Bulgaria), and

60. *Ethnomusicology*, 7, no. 3 (September, 1963): 248–51.
61. *Selected Reports* (Los Angeles: Institute of Ethnomusicology of the University of California), 1 (1966): 1–27, music.
62. *Selected Reports* (Los Angeles: Institute of Ethnomusicology of the University of California), 1 (1966): 89–119, music.
63. *Journal of International Folk Music Council*, 3 (1951): 62–64.
64. *Journal of the American Musicological Society*, 5 (1952): 150–51.
65 (Chicago: Newberry Library, 1953).
66. Paper read at meeting of the American Musicological Society at Chapel Hill, December, 1953, mimeographed.
67. (Chicago: Gertners, 1954), song collection.
68. *Midwest Folklore*, 5 (1955): 37–49; transcription and texts: 40–49.
69. *Ethnomusicology*, 5, no. 2 (May, 1961): 128–29.

Stephen Erdely (Hungary). Their work is a real contribution to musicological knowledge, not mere popularization.

PERIODICAL PUBLICATION ON THE FOLKLORE OF
EAST CENTRAL AND SOUTHEASTERN EUROPE

In contrast to the increased incorporation of our fields into university instruction and the slowly improving standards in the writing of monographs, periodical literature in the United States on the folklore of East Central and Southeastern Europe continues to languish in a condition essentially unchanged during the past fifty years. We are concerned here with articles on the folklore of any, some, or all of the eight European nationalities treated in this report when those articles were written by scholars domiciled principally in the United States and published in American journals. There have been no more than half a dozen such articles for any of the eight national groups in the past hundred years.

One of the more serious implications of this fact is its reflection on the quality of the courses of instruction that have appeared in the field of Eastern European folklore in some of our major universities during the last five years. When teaching in this field has been more than an adventure in curiosities, it has been fruitful in the periodical press either here or abroad. The fact of so few worthwhile articles published here would reflect even more gravely on our national competence in this field did not some of our scholars publish in pertinent European journals, several of which have a deservedly international reputation, society of contributors, and readership.

The bare bibliographic information that can be gathered in a review of the annual *Journal of American Folklore Supplement* or the *PMLA Bibliography* indicates only a sporadic pattern of effort in our fields between the turn of the century and World War II. After World War II, a still scanty but more regular production of articles reached its zenith in the 1950s, and then subsided again in the present decade. We should like to think that the abatement in the flow of articles in the 1960s marks a growth of discrimination in this country that can now better distinguish between sound and silly learning than it could during the scramble to learn about foreign cultures immediately after World War II. We hope that we may now expect an increase in both productivity and in the quality of our domestic periodical publication in this field.

A list of the titles of articles published after World War II gives an impression of some learning, but examination of the articles themselves discloses a general lack in this country of: (1) knowledge of the primary materials of folklore collected in Eastern Europe and published or housed in archives both in Europe and in America; (2) knowledge of relevant foreign scholarship; (3) competent familiarity with the general discipline of folklore as applied to any national culture. Our common knowledge has been only slightly better in regard to item (2) than to (1) or (3).

So it is that the sum of our national contribution of learning to the field of Eastern European folklore in our own periodicals does not alter the conclusion we drew from reviewing American monographic contribution and publication of translated texts: it is impossible to obtain an accurate conception of this discipline, whether in regard to its methods, materials, or significance, from what has been published about it in America by American scholars. To put it simply, there is at present still no tradition of learning in this field in the United States, but only a few scattered expert individuals working to create such a tradition.

Yet the persistence of at least some efforts in periodical publication over more than half a century past attests to the unabated attraction of East Central and Southeastern European folklore and folk music to educated and learned Americans alike. The pretensions to scholarship and the actual lack of it in that writing show a pathetically unrealized ambition not only to know but to understand these ancient and remarkably durable features of Eastern European cultures. The impulse has been correct and laudable.

But while a certain interest in this field has long existed in America, and although there have been some efforts to appeal to it and to satisfy it, that interest has remained so diffused that it has never offered any particular reward for accomplishment to native Americans. Since there has been little or no public or institutional encouragement to the folklorist, young or old, to learn and write well about Eastern European folklore, so our efforts have been only occasional and mostly unprofessional. Indeed, there have been, and there still exist certain serious discouragements. One of these is the absence of any journal in this country which is a natural forum for studies in the folklore of the Balkans and East Central Europe. But more gravely, there is beneath the three direct causes for the weakness of our periodical literature, which we have already indicated above, another more general prejudicial premise which will doom us to nothing but more of the same inadequacy if it remains uncorrected. This prejudicial circumstance is an old and deep-seated isolationism in the American tradition of folklore scholarship which is egregiously biased toward the folklore of

English-speaking and aboriginal cultures of the Western Hemisphere and Pacific Oceania. There is a strong tradition of folklore scholarship in America, and even a profession of sorts, but it has always known more of the Apaches or Eskimos than it has of Eastern Europe, and so it has in its own way developed an American counterpart to the nationalism and the restricted horizons of folklore scholarship in Eastern Europe itself. Of all Eastern Europe's folklore traditions, only classical Greek folklore and mythology have been a lasting intellectual concern to Americans, and even that was more widely known among our educated people fifty years ago than it is today.

So the progress in the United States of folklore studies devoted to Eastern Europe is resisted by an old inertia and narrowness that are surely less obstructive in such disciplines as history or sociology, which as they are practiced in America, traditionally have more catholic perspectives.

The *Journal of American Folklore* is the oldest and most prominent organ of folklore studies in this country. Contributions from our fields in Eastern Europe and the Balkans have always been welcome in its pages; in 1956 it devoted an entire number to papers on Slavic folklore, and it was in no way the fault of the editors that more was not contributed on the folklore of our eight nations. Yet no Eastern Europeanist or Balkanist would be likely to prefer publication in it if he had a choice, since the bulk of its readership would ignore him, and those who should read his work would not readily find it in a publication so remote from Eastern European learning. The same may be said for the only other leading journal of folklore in the United States. Neither publication has on its editorial board persons competent to judge the merit of articles which might be submitted to it on at least half of the eight nationalities we are here concerned with. The serious American scholar of Eastern European or Balkan folklore would at present be best advised to publish in London, Munich, Helsinki, or in one of the capitals and cultural centers of the respective Eastern European countries.

There are a few other highly respectable journals published in the United States which will entertain articles on Balkan and Eastern European folklore: *The Hungarian Quarterly*, *PMLA*, the *Slavic Review* and the *Slavic and East European Journal* are among them. Depending on the nature of an article submitted, the pages of many other journals would also certainly be open. It is unthinkable that a good article in our discipline could not be published in this country for want of a fine journal or an editor willing to take it; there are enough of both.

The question is whether any other Eastern Europeanist would ever see the article when it was published.

There has been a variety of other journals now defunct or merged which have carried articles from our discipline in the past. Among them were the *AATSEEL Bulletin*, the *Alliance Journal*, *Midwest Folklore*, and the *Southern Folklore Quarterly*.

Only one venture in periodical publication has been devoted entirely to our field, or to part of it; it is now defunct. Its inspiration, rise, and decline are instructive. *Polish Folklore: A Bulletin from Alliance College* was an amateur journal with higher aspirations born in the spring of 1956 and discontinued without heir in 1962. In its first number it declared:

> We have in mind to build up a center devoted to studies in the great middle area of Europe. Since, moreover, the college was founded by people coming from Poland, and receives support largely from gifts made by people of Polish origin, emphasis will be laid on studies in the Polish field.
>
> Naturally one of the branches to be cultivated in our Mid-Zone Area Program will be Folklore.
>
> This is no new thing for us. More than ten years ago, the editor of this publication, under the inspiration of Harold W. Thompson's mammoth compendium of New York State lore, *Body, Boots and Britches*, began collecting the lore of Poland as preserved and cherished in this country. . . .[70]

Its ambitious program ultimately came to no more than the small collection of reminiscences, fragments of immigrant folklore, and translated extracts from Polish books which one may find in the pages of *Polish Folklore*. At its best, the journal consisted of enthusiastic publicism; at its worst, it published quaint stories "adapted" and "abstracted" from old Polish collections and doggerel translations of Polish verse edited beyond recognition as folklore. During the seven years of its existence it published not a single text *in Polish*, despite its self-appointed role as a repository of Polish lore gathered in America. How did it stray so far from its mission to help "build up a center devoted to studies in the great middle area of Europe"?

It is plain from the experience of this and so many other journals and cultural undertakings connected with immigrant groups that the notion of service to the immigrant community is not a principle on which

70. Marion M. Coleman, ed. (Cambridge Springs, Pennsylvania), 1, no. 1 (March 15, 1956): 1.

lasting scholarly endeavors can be founded. If our disciplines have a future in the United States, it will be as branches of the sciences of folklore and ethnomusicology developed out of and applied to the *primary* materials of Eastern European and Balkan folklore and folk music collected in the Old World. The cultural histories of the immigrant peoples from Eastern Europe have been such that the survivals of their native traditions, which indeed have been and can still be found in the United States, can in no way be properly understood without prior expert knowledge of the traditions behind them in the Old World. Such expert knowledge is quite rare, both here in the United States, in Western Europe, and even in Eastern Europe itself.

Moreover, inasmuch as the eight nationalities are now and have long been linked to one another by a continuous spectrum of common cultural properties, the separate treatment of each national group is artificial, and when it delimits an enterprise such as a journal or an academic program, it is anachronous. The truth of that is tacitly but plainly recognized in the recent burgeoning of university courses in this country on the folklore and mythology of the Slavs, or of Eastern Europe, or of the Balkans — all regional approaches.

Lastly, the school of folklore scholarship which has arisen in the United States out of the labors of the antiquarians of our early European settlers' cultures and out of the anthropology of aboriginals in the Western Hemisphere is not the school to be emulated in our scholarship on Eastern European folklore and folk music. One could not possibly criticize the unfaltering loyalty of *Polish Folklore* to the model of Harold W. Thompson's "compendium" and the school it represents; it was simply not an appropriate school. But it is that school which has most influenced our periodical writing on the folklore of Eastern Europe to be the disoriented conglomerate of occasional efforts that it is, instead of a vigorous branch of the science of folklore such as the field of Eastern European history is to the parent discipline of history.

Scholarly writing on Eastern European and Balkan folklore for American periodicals falls into the following classes:

1. Articles on folkloristic features of immigrant cultures written by members of the respective immigrant groups.
2. Articles by members of immigrant groups concerning folklore in the Old World cultures from which the immigrants have come, based on (*a*) evidence collected in the new world; (*b*) foreign books. In the case of (*b*), the articles are usually summaries or compilations for the benefit of those who cannot, or can no longer, read the original languages.

3. Articles reporting work being done abroad.
4. Short articles describing minor genres or other small categories of material; for example, proverbs, or superstitions about preternatural beings.
5. Articles on elements of folklore in literary works.
6. Articles summarizing in English materials provided by foreign scholars.
7. A miniscule number of critical or interpretive articles.

Considering the plurality of articles presenting only primary materials, it is gratifying to note that we have found none in which the materials reported are drawn solely from the memories of the authors. That old malpractice of European romanticism seems never to have struck root in the United States.

A smattering of articles has been published in the United States by foreign scholars, for example, Alexander Schreiber of the Jewish Theological Seminary in Hungary on topics in Hungarian folklore. Since these authors are not Americans, we have not analyzed their articles for this survey.

ALBANIAN

Almost nothing has been produced. The only item known to us is by Stavro Skendi (note, too, his book listed above): "The South Slavic Decasyllable in Albanian Oral Epic Poetry." [71]

BULGARIAN

Boris Kremenliev has contributed most, and his work is among the best done by Americans on the folklore of any of the eight nationalities, although it is confined to Bulgarian. He has written on Bulgarian folksongs and proverbs, as well as on purely musical topics. Another contributor was Louis Petroff (Southern Illinois University at Carbondale) who wrote reminiscences of folklore recalled from his childhood in Bulgaria which he compared with (uncited) learned Bulgarian sources. [72]

CZECHOSLOVAK

Typical contributions were on Czech and Slovak songs in Detroit, with music, texts, and translations, published collaboratively by an

71. (Slavic) *Word*, December, 1953, pp. 339–48.
72. "Magical Beliefs and Practices in Old Bulgaria," *Midwest Folklore*, 7 (1957): 214–20.

émigré and Bruno Nettl.[73] Paul G. Brewster published an article on folk games in 1957; it consists of primary material provided by Olga Hrabalova of the Czechoslovak Academy in Brno, so that it hardly qualifies as an American contribution.[74] A recognized American folklorist and collector, Svatava Pírková-Jakobson, contributed an article in Czech on Czech cultural survivals in New York, entitled "Moje meno je Anna Sečený" (My name is Anna Sečený).[75]

GREEK

Dorothy Demetracopoulou-Lee (Vassar) has done most to increase the number of articles on modern Greek folklore, but once again the materials are those of émigré culture: *e.g.*, Greek anecdotes and folktales about priests and their wives, provided by informants in metropolitan Boston, are examples.[76] An American (with no Greek) collaborated with a Greek to write an article on Child Ballads 268 and 246 and their Greek parallels, while Richard Dorson (Indiana University) wrote on Greek-American folktales. Yet, except as noted below, one will search in vain for an American contribution to knowledge of Greek folklore *in Greece*. And he will discover with disappointment that even the articles on Greek émigré folklore are uncritical offerings of primary material without any gesture toward interpretation or evaluation. A notable exception, very special in its nature and significant in its wider implications in scholarship, is the writing of James A. Notopoulos in such articles as: "The Song of Daskaloyiannes" (dictated to a scribe in a sung version by the oral bard Barba Pantzelyo in 1786) [77] and "The Genesis of an Oral Heroic Poem."[78]

HUNGARIAN

Thomas Sebeok (Indiana University) is the one American who has contributed. This writer, whose main interests lie further east than our regions, has to his credit an article of somewhat more ethnographic

73. Bruno Nettl and Ivo Moravcik, "Czech and Slovak Songs Collected in Detroit," *Midwest Folklore*, 5 (1955): 37–49.
74. *Southern Folklore Quarterly*, 1957, pp. 165–76.
75. " 'Moje meno je Sečený'; venkovské obrazy newyorského života' " (My name is Anna Sečený; Rural Forms of Life in New York), in Ladislav Matejka, ed., *Kulturní sborník Rok* (New York: Moravian Library, 1957), pp. 137–56.
76. *Journal of American Folklore*, 1942, 1947, 1951.
77. *American Journal of Philology*, 73 (1950): 225–50.
78. *Greek, Roman, and Byzantine Studies*, 3 (1960): 135–44. See also "The Influence of the Klephtic Ballads on the Heroic Oral Songs of Crete" (in Greek) *Kritika Chronika* 15 (1963): 78–92.

than folkloristic import consisting of data about nakedness and related traits in Hungary (with a map of distribution). The significance of the data compiled in the article is left to the reader's conjecture.

POLISH

American contributions to Polish folkloristics have been somewhat more numerous than those on the other nationalities, but everywhere among them one feels the unquestioned omniscience of the spirit that moved *Polish Folklore*, discussed above. Polish riddles from Michigan appeared in the *Journal of American Folklore* in 1949, Polish tales from Albany, New York, in the *New York Folklore Quarterly* in 1954, and *Western Virginia Folklore* once carried a folktale remembered by a Pole in West Virginia.[79] Here are materials enough, but one can hardly speak of authors for these articles, since the raw data are served up without a word of criticism or an idea to suggest what they might mean.

But another current can also be detected trickling through American awareness of Polish folklore. In 1902, Alexander F. Chamberlain, then editor of the *Journal of American Folklore*, reported in an editorial note a European scholar's paper read at a congress of folklorists in Paris and dealing with folklore elements in the works of Mickiewicz. That kind of literary interest in folklore, long a feature of European scholarship, finally bore fruit in American Polish studies in 1957 in an article on elements of folklore in a play by Stanisław Wyspiański.

ROMANIAN

The last-mentioned form of Polish folklore studies is the only one known to us in American periodical writing on Romanian folklore. There was a solitary essay on elements of folklore in the literary work of Mihail Sebastian, published in 1956. Otherwise, studies of Romanian folklore are almost unknown in learned journals in the United States.

YUGOSLAV

Albert Lord's well-known studies of Yugoslav oral epic tradition are the chief contributions here. Otherwise, the kind of inexpert articles familiar from the other nationalities appear here, too: mere lists of fact (or alleged fact) about fortune-telling and superstitions in Dal-

79. Vol. 3 (1953): 45–59.

matia, or a collaborative piece by an American and a Yugoslav scholar on Yugoslav folk games in which the materials are the contribution of the Yugoslav and the American's part seems to be an editorial service to his foreign colleague.[80]

The impression left by the numbers of articles published in this country by our learned citizens would indicate Greek and Polish folklore as the most studied. But in fact, except for James Notopoulos' excellent writing, they have been triflingly studied. The two South Slavic folklores, Bulgarian and Yugoslav, are the only others among the eight national traditions that have been treated seriously in our periodical press.

UNIVERSITY OFFERINGS AND PERSONNEL IN THE UNITED STATES

Serious learning in the folklore of East Central and Southeastern Europe has been nurtured in the United States only in the academic community. Teaching of the subject supported by that learning has been confined to only a few of our universities.

To the best of our knowledge there are at present six recognized professional folklorists and two ethnomusicologists in the United States engaged in teaching the East Central and Southeastern European materials of their disciplines. All of them have been formally trained in their disciplines and their competence is proven. One of these folklorists is at Columbia University, two are at Indiana University, three are at Harvard University; one of the ethnomusicologists is at UCLA, one at the University of Illinois at Urbana.

There are at present seven American universities which offer courses in the folklore of one or more of the eight nationalities under consideration. Where it is treated at all, the ethnomusicology of these countries is touched upon in general courses in the subject; only the University of California at Los Angeles offers a course (Kremenliev) specifically on the music of the Balkans.

The courses offered in our universities are intended principally for graduate students and advanced undergraduates.

At the University of California at Berkeley, Arshi Pipa (assistant professor of Italian) has offered a graduate seminar in Albanian language, literature, and folklore when enrollment has been large enough.

80. Paul G. Brewster and Jelena Milojković-Djurić, in *Southern Folklore Quarterly*, 20, no. 3 (September, 1956): 183–91.

This is the only course we know of offered anywhere in this country which names Albanian folklore as a subject.

At the University of California at Los Angeles, the Department of Dance (offices in the Women's Gymnasium) has an especially remarkable offering of courses. There are two general courses given by its staff, one of lower and one of upper level, which include the dance of Greece and the dance of Yugoslavia simultaneously with those of Bali, Ghana, Hawaii, Israel, Japan, Scotland, etc. These are "performing courses." The same department offers another upper-level course on dance in the Balkans, with the following description:

> An introduction to the dance of the Balkans, including factors influencing development and social functions, and consideration of the relationship of dance to other art forms. Concurrent enrollment in a performing group.

The same university has an Introduction to Baltic and Slavic Folklore and Mythology, but offered by an archaeologist, not a folklorist. This university also offers an Introduction to Hungarian Folklore and Mythology, taught by its lecturer in Hungarian.

The University of Chicago lists courses on Slavic folklore and South Slavic epic tradition, and its course on Slavic peoples and languages considers "early Slavic mythology."

Columbia University has in Stavro Skendi a scholar of literature known for his work in folklore who offers two courses (at different levels) on South Slavic oral literature, and who is, moreover, competent in Albanian folklore.

Harvard University offers courses in general Slavic folklore, Balkan oral epic tradition, and Slavic folklore in America, taught by trained folklorists. It also houses the Milman Parry Collection, a large collection of various folklore from Yugoslavia, Bulgaria, Albania, Greece, and Romania.

Indiana University offers courses on the folklore of the Southern and Western Slavs and a survey of East European folklore. It has a collection of recorded music which includes some East Central and Southeastern European folk music.

The University of Pennsylvania offers a course on South Slavic folklore.

ACTIVE SCHOLARS

David Bynum, Harvard University
Sotirios Chianis, Wesleyan
Linda Dégh, Indiana University

Stephen Erdely, Member, Cleveland Symphony Orchestra
William Harkins, Columbia University
John Kolsti, University of Texas
Barbara Krader, International Folk Music Council
Boris Kremenliev, University of California at Los Angeles
Albert Lord, Harvard University
Bruno Nettl, University of Illinois
Felix Oinas, Indiana University
Svatava Pírková-Jakobson, University of Texas
Stavro Skendi, Columbia University

GENERAL OBSERVATIONS

Certain general observations may be made on the state of our disciplines in Western Europe and in the countries of our eight nationalities themselves.

In all of Western Europe, only the Germans are seriously aware of the folklore of Eastern Europe. Their outstanding general contribution to learning in this field was their provision of the impulse to all the nationalities of Eastern Europe to take scholarly interest in their own folklore traditions. However, since making that contribution in the nineteenth century, with the exception of some individuals, they have rather followed developments in Eastern European learning than tried to participate in it themselves.

For various reasons, the cultures of Eastern Europe have retained living traditions of certain forms of folklore long after the disappearance of their historically attested counterparts in Western Europe. In the nineteenth century, the Germans made their Eastern European neighbors keenly aware of that fact, and in response a vigorous collecting activity arose throughout Eastern Europe. That activity, which is still productive, has laid up in each country of Eastern Europe and the Balkans a wealth of published and unpublished resources to benefit not only those nationalities' understanding of themselves, but also the disciplines of folklore and ethnomusicology at large, as the two examples of Hungarian ethnomusicology and American research on Yugoslav oral epic tradition have demonstrated.

The preoccupation with collecting primary material has dominated the scholarship in our fields of all eight of the nationalities we are treating here. After World War II, most of these national groups experienced a weakening of nonpolitical social and humanistic learning, and folklore scholarship particularly underwent a period of official disfavor as an atavistic science dedicated to perpetuating the memory of national "backwardness," hence useful only for the promotion of tourism. Partly because of its old devotion to collecting activity, or fieldwork, folklore scholarship in Eastern Europe had no strong, forward-looking theoretical tradition to resort to for proofs of other usefulness, either domestically or to the international learned community. In such an uncongenial climate of official opinion, Eastern European folklorists have tended to represent the now outdated aims and methods of their nineteenth-century predecessors' ethnography as a national tradition of learning in itself worthy of national reverence and protection. If this tactic has helped to save both the discipline and its rich collections from abandonment in a time of adversity, it has also left the discipline in a state of some antiquation in the 1960s in regard to its theoretical equipment, for both that tactic of retrospection and the political climate that fostered it have worked together to make Eastern European folklorists neglectful of insights gained by anyone working with other than their national materials and irrationally suspicious of all scholars other than their own nationals.

Confronted with this situation in Eastern European scholarship in our disciplines, we in the United States are under a special obligation to maintain an open and varied market of ideas, in the knowledge that progress in understanding Eastern European cultural traditions will depend on applying to them the very best thinking we can, no matter when or with whom such thinking originates. Our success in this can be of the greatest value both to our disciplines and to our Eastern European colleagues, who even now are still collecting, but turning more and more to sorting the rich store of their collections and to discovering its unsuspected informative properties.

RECOMMENDATIONS

We think that finding means for the enlargement and perpetuation of an American profession of folklorists of Eastern and Southeast Central Europe is of first concern. Responsibility for accomplishing this rests finally with the present members of the profession, but they need the awareness, good will, and greater financial support of the learned community in order to train and establish permanently a small, self-renewing cadre for this discipline. We feel strongly that while the interest and help of émigré groups are of value, well-established American universities, both public and private, must be our direct sponsors, and particularly those universities which already have some commitment to, hence familiarity with, our effort. Financial help will be needed from sources outside the already hard-pressed universities, but that help should be directed to the universities, where the only seed of our future development now is.

Further, we think that it would be uneconomical and stultifying to attempt to concentrate the development of Central European folklore studies at one or two locations in this country. The present pattern of our association with established departments of our universities as an ancillary discipline is in principle a good one, both for our own discipline which is thereby required to contribute meaningfully to a larger design of cultural studies, and, we believe, good also for those departments.

We need new manuals or monographic textbooks written by American scholars on the folklore of each of the eight nationalities. In addition, we need a more general manual of Slavic folklore treated as a whole; for want of a polymathic folklorist to prepare all of such a work, it might be fashioned on an encyclopedic model such as Funk and Wagnall's *Standard Dictionary of Folklore, Mythology and Legend*.[81] Manuals of the ethnomusicology of the region based on such groupings of national traditions as musicologists might find useful would also be desirable, if somewhat less in demand. Funds for grants-in-aid to support the writing of these manuals will be needed. Such funds must, however, be restricted to support of *new writing*, not translation projects, since there are no foreign works of the kind required which might be translated, and no foreseeable prospect of their appearance abroad, for the reasons stated earlier in this report.

If it could be sustained chiefly by contributions from American scholars in other disciplines than ours, an *American Journal of Central European Studies* would be a useful market for research on the folklore (or ethnology) of central Europe and the Balkans. We think that the ethnomusicology of the region, in view of that discipline's special nature, is best served by existing journals, or journals devoted specifically to musicology.

If an *American Journal of Central European Studies* were to be launched, we believe it would be indispensable to make clear from the beginning its commitment to articles on literature and folklore, and that one, or if necessary two, of the members of its editorial board should always be a scholar trained and active in each of these two related disciplines. Only in this way can we foresee avoidance of problems in editorial policy and judgment of contributions in literature and folklore. The early years of the (American) *Slavic Review*'s career showed how intractable such problems can be for learned journals

81. (New York: Funk and Wagnalls Co., 1950), vols. 1 and 2.

that represent several disciplines when their editorial boards are not equally broad. Genuine catholicity would be the only acceptable policy for any such new journal in America.

However, we feel some uncertainty that a new journal of Central European studies would attract a large number of contributions in folklore even when there is an established professional cadre in this country working in the Eastern European field, as we hope there will be within the next decade or two. We do not anticipate that the total national complement of professional folklorists whose primary interests are in Eastern Europe will ever be or should be so great that existing journals here and abroad will be unable to accommodate all they may produce. Because their number will be small, and because, like economists or historians, they will find their natural audience among others in their discipline of folklore or literature, or in Slavic, Hellenic, or Balkan studies, etc., American folklorists of Eastern Europe may prefer, and even feel compelled, to publish in journals more narrowly concerned with either their disciplines or the nationalities they treat.

15 / MUSICOLOGY

MILOŠ VELIMIROVIĆ
University of Wisconsin

The term "musicology" is defined as "the systematic study of musical composition and its history."[1] It has become customary, however, to use this term as a synonym for studies in the *history of music*, recognizing at the same time the wider implications of the term itself. Consequently, within this report on the "state of the art" the emphasis shall be on an examination of the involvement of American musicology and of American musicologists in the study of the history of music in the East European countries.

Comparatively speaking, musicology is a relatively recent newcomer in the world of scholarship. In the United States, musicology became recognized as an independent branch of the humanities only in 1930 when the first professorship in musicology was established at Cornell University. Since that time American musicology has achieved remarkable growth, both in quantity and quality, so that it may be stated without any danger of exaggeration that some of the most advanced research work in musicology, as well as some of the best training for such studies, is now found in this country. Whereas much of the work of European scholars in this area was, and to a certain extent still is, used for chauvinistic purposes, one of the basic characteristics of the best of the American musicological studies has been a detachment from the pettiness of nationalistic interpretations and a broader view of the development of various musical styles in the course of the general history of music. One of the consequences of this approach has been the tendency to concentrate the teaching and research on specific periods, on stylistic traits which transcend national and political boundaries and, especially in recent years, on investigation of the con-

1. J. A. Westrup, and F. Ll. Harrison, *The New College Encyclopedia of Music* (New York: W. W. Norton & Co., 1960), p. 445.

tributions to the evolution of musical styles by specific individuals, besides the reverse approach of studying the influence of the prevalent musical styles on the formation of individual composers and their idioms.[2]

In juxtaposition to linguistics, for example, the study of the music of the East Central and Southeast European countries has not yet achieved a similar standing in the profession and there are, as of the time of this writing, no traditions of any sort in this respect in the United States. It must immediately be stressed that owing to historical circumstances the most significant developments in the history of music did take place in Western Europe. American musicological research work, quite naturally, has been concentrated primarily if not exclusively on the study of the history of music in Western European countries. At present, there is also a growing trend toward a study of the music in the Americas. As for the study of music of the non-European population of the world, it is usually conducted in a rather heterogeneous branch of studies under the common name of "Ethnomusicology," which, interestingly enough, does embrace the study of folk music and folk dances in Europe and the Americas besides the rest of the world. This approach leaves the East European area and its artistic music at the periphery of general musicological studies. The area has been, and remains, of unquestionable interest for ethnomusicologists. Professional historians of music usually have a very limited knowledge of the artistic attainments of the area under consideration, an area which cannot totally be ignored if for no other reason than for the important achievements of individual composers, more specifically Russians.[3] It is interesting to observe that if one excludes the works of "native" scholars from the non-Russian East European area, the only serious contributions of some consequence about the musical achievements of these peoples have been by German scholars, for some of whom this area

2. Cf. F. Ll. Harrison, Mantle Hood, and Claude V. Palisca, *Musicology*, Humanistic Scholarship in America, Princeton Studies, (Englewood Cliffs, N.J., 1963).

3. As an example of this attitude, see, for instance, the otherwise comprehensive and quite informative volume by William W. Austin, *Music in the 20th Century* (New York: W. W. Norton & Co., 1966). Under the heading "Contemporaries in Slavic Lands" (pp. 67–84), one-half of the chapter is devoted to Russian composers, then a quite unusual five-page section deals with Janaček. However, the more modern Czech composers after Janaček are dismissed in two paragraphs. Polish music receives barely a page and a half. Hungarian composers (with the always venerable exception of Bartók) is summed up on half a page. Yugoslav composers are disposed of by listing four names on less than a quarter of a page, and Bulgarian music is summed up in one sentence containing the names of two Bulgarians. To be sure, however, some of the more prominent musicians are treated individually, yet not in the context of their countries but either as creators or as epigones of a prominent stylistic trend.

represents the "borderlands" of Germanic influences and thus a natural domain of their interests. On the opposite side, the studies of Russian scholars dealing with this area are far from systematic and can best be scrutinized in a separate survey of the status of musicological studies in the U.S.S.R.

In the light of the preceding remarks, it is no surprise then to learn that with the exception of a few irregularly offered courses on the history of Russian music (and even these could literally be listed on the fingers of one hand!), there has been at no time a scheduled course on the history of music of any of the East European countries at any of the recognized colleges and universities in the United States. The reasons for such a state of affairs are quite understandable: (a) lack of trained and qualified scholars and teachers, and (b) usually inadequate resources in the standard type of music libraries in this country. Furthermore, one of the frequently encountered clichés in educational circles is that the artistic level of composers in East European countries is so low that it is not worthwhile studying, not even in specialized seminars for graduate students. The prevalent tendency in the teaching of music on the undergraduate level in most American colleges and universities is to concentrate on the most important points in the general history of music and musical styles. In the graduate studies, and very rightly so, the basic stress is on the methodology of research work which, however, is usually restricted to a reexamination of some vital points in the rich heritage of the Western European music.

It may be granted that on the whole the creative attainments and pacesetting of composers in Eastern Europe has not matched either in significance or in sophistication the standards of the art of music in Western Europe. Yet in almost every one of these countries there have been individuals who achieved high artistic levels and whose compositions have transcended the narrow national boundaries and become part of the accepted musical repertory all over the world. One has only to mention the names of Chopin, Liszt, Dvořák, and Bartók, to realize that the non-Russian East European countries are by no means barren in significance for the development of musical styles both in the past and in the present, when two Polish composers of our time, Lutosławski and Penderecki, are currently viewed as probably the most creative composers in all of Europe. American musicology and the professional establishment of practicing musicians have not ignored such composers, who, as a rule, were first recognized as significant musicians within the German-speaking orbit. Yet a study about Chopin and his compositions does not necessarily represent a study in depth on the history of Polish music, although some sort of lip service will be rendered to it even in the most superficial accounts of Chopin. For the purposes of this survey, such studies which deal with the well-established "names" in the general history of music will be ignored, even though they may provide, to a limited extent, some glimpses into the actual historical development of the musical art in a given country.

GRADUATE DISSERTATIONS

If doctoral dissertations submitted to American universities may serve as a yardstick in measuring the degree of interest of American musicologists in the non-Russian East European area, then the picture obtained is one of almost total neglect. According to data available as of the fall of 1966,[4] there were approximately 1,300 doctoral dissertations registered with the American Musicological Society. Most of these were completed, but a number of them are still in progress. This accounting does not embrace the theses written as a requirement for the attainment of the M.A. degree, since for these there is no reliable guide or any comprehensive listing available at present. Of the roughly 1,300 dissertation topics, there are *only two* which without any qualifications are pertinent for this survey:[5]

(No. 338) John Glowacki, "The History of Polish Opera," Boston University, 1952

(No. 520) Jerzy Golos, "Organ Music in Poland before 1750," New York University (in progress)

On the periphery of this area are two more dissertations:

(No. 1076) Charles Hirt, "Graeco-Slavonic Chant Traditions Evident in the Part-Writing of the Russian Orthodox Church," University of Southern California, 1946

4. The following data are obtained from *Doctoral Dissertations in Musicology*, comp. Helen Hewitt, 4th ed. (Philadelphia: American Musicological Society, 1965), listing 1,204 doctoral dissertations. Added to this are the data from the "Supplement (1966) to Doctoral Dissertations in Musicology," *Journal of the American Musicological Society*, 19 (Fall, 1966): 383–97, listing approximately 100 dissertation topics. The 1967 supplement, published in the same periodical, 20 (1967): 450–68, lists 120 additional dissertations now in progress. Of these one could be included in this survey only because it deals with a musician born in Bohemia, but his career was associated with West European countries. This is a dissertation being prepared by Earl A. Saunders, "A Stylistic Study of Selected Symphonies of Adalbert Gyrowetz," at Indiana University.

5. The numbers preceding each title are those in Hewitt's listing. See the preceding note.

(No. 19) Miloš Velimirović, "Byzantine Elements in Early Slavic Chant," Harvard University, 1957

Definitely dealing with this geographical area, yet at the same time much more difficult to classify in the light of the roles of individual composers in the musical life of their own and the neighboring countries, are the following dissertations:

(No. 156) W. M. Insko, "The Cracow Tablature," Indiana University, 1964

(No. 696) G. K. Wolf, "The Symphonies of Johann Stamitz," New York University (in progress)

(No. 717) V. Thompson, "Wenzel Johann Tomaschek, His Predecessors, His Life, His Piano Works," University of Rochester, 1955

(No. 722) H. A. Craw, "A Biography and Thematic Catalogue of the Works of J. L. Dussek (1760–1812)," University of Southern California, 1964

(No. 793) F. Mitchell, "Piano Concertos of Johann Nepomuk Hummel," Northwestern University, 1957

(No. 1024) G. Zack, "The Music Dramas of Manolis Kalomiris," Florida State University (in progress)

Relevant, yet at the same time questionable for listing here is the dissertation:

(No. 763) M. R. Aborn, "The Influence on American Culture of Dvořak's Sojourn in America," Indiana University, 1965 (Ph.D. in Music Education)

Of all these dissertations, only those on the Cracow tablature, on Tomaschek, and on Kalomiris may be accepted as genuine contributions toward the history of music in Eastern Europe. The activities of Stamitz, Dussek, and Hummel belong much more to the Western European orbit than to East Europe. These three composers have already been thoroughly studied by Germans because of the roles they played in the development of musical life in German-speaking lands in the past. One might also argue that since some German composers lived and worked in the East European area (e.g., Johann Joachim Quantz [1697–1773], Karl Ditters von Dittersdorf [1739–99], Johann Friedrich Reichardt [1752–1814], and others), a study of their works could also represent a contribution to the knowledge of musical developments in Eastern Europe. Yet even this approach, although undoubtedly useful, still remains a far cry from a systematic study of documents and a comprehensive examination of the evolution of the art of music in the respective countries. This listing of doctoral dissertations may be slightly expanded with a few theses written for the M.A. degree, that have been brought to our attention:

> Jerzy Golos, "Polish Baroque Music," Columbia University, M.A., 1958
>
> Mary Ann Lisewsky, "Music in Poland," Northwestern University, M. Mus., 1944
>
> I. K. Banyay, "The History of the Hungarian Music," University of Southern California, M. Mus., 1942 (893 pp.) [6]

Even with these additional listings, the fact remains that *less than 1 percent of American musicological research work deals with Eastern Europe* and it may be added that the figure would not change significantly even if dissertations on Russian music were to be included in this survey.

PUBLICATIONS OF AMERICAN SCHOLARS

If the picture of doctoral dissertations of the American musicological research work dealing with East Europe is bleak, that of book-length publications on a scholarly level is a total blank.[7] According to the best available information at the time of this writing, there is not a single book from the pen of an American musicologist giving a comprehensive view of the history of music in any of the East European countries, Russia being excepted, of course. The only books available in English containing histories of music in some of the countries are either translations of solid studies by native scholars, as is the case with Benze Szabolcsi's *A Concise History of Hungarian Music*,[8] or pam-

6. The titles of the last two theses are cited from *Ethnomusicology and Folk Music: An International Bibliography of Dissertations and Theses*, compiled and annotated by Frank Gillis and Alan P. Meriam, Special Series in Ethnomusicology, no. 1 (Middletown, Conn.: Wesleyan University, 1966).

7. We are excluding from consideration numerous monographs and articles on Chopin, Liszt, and other well-known names. One of the outstanding achievements dealing with famous composers is, e.g., Halsey Stevens' remarkable volume on Bartók *Life and Music of Béla Bartók*, 2d ed. (New York: Oxford University Press, 1964). The amount of nearsightedness and even misinformation about the music in East European countries is especially conspicuous in "concise" articles for encyclopedias and dictionaries, e.g., the respective entries by countries in the *Harvard Dictionary of Music* by Willi Apel (Cambridge, Mass.: Harvard University Press, 1944).

8. (London: Barrie and Rockliff, 1964).

phlets written either by benevolent foreigners, such as Rosa New-march's *The Music of Czechoslovakia*[9] and L. Cassini's *Music in Rumania*,[10] or as a propaganda tool sponsored by the respective governments, as is the case with the otherwise informative pamphlet *Yugoslav Music*.[11]

Slightly brighter is the picture of articles published in scholarly or nonscholarly journals. The fact that these studies are so scattered and that there is no complete bibliography of such articles at present points out the need for at least an annual cumulative index of such studies. The *American Bibliography of Russian and East European Studies*, published by Indiana University, contains in its classification a category for music in Russia, but not for other countries, and it is not always as complete as may be desired. That it already fulfills the function of a central register represents an admirable achievement, and it is to be desired that it begin including bibliographies for the countries not yet included, specifically Greece and Turkey insofar as the subject matter has significance for the East European area.

GRADUATE TRAINING

Although modern musical notation knows no national boundaries and anyone who learns it can play, perform, and enjoy musical compositions regardless of the country of origin of the composer, musicological studies of the music in East European countries are nevertheless greatly hampered by some obstacles (such as lack of linguistic or historical background), none of which is insurmountable. It should be stated at the outset that the basic type of training in the techniques of musicological work, such as is presently to be found in most of the music departments at American universities offering graduate studies in musicology, must be considered a prerequisite for anyone desiring to become a musicologist, and that no immediate change in the substance of these techniques is contemplated. However, depending on the teacher and on the availability of library resources at any given university, there can be a different degree of emphasis on topics dealing with the history of music in East European countries. Topics cen-

9. (London: Oxford University Press, 1952).
10. (London: Fore Publications, 1954).
11. Josip Andreis and Slavko Zlatić, eds. (Belgrade: Edition Jugoslavija, 1959). At the occasion of the Tenth Congress of the International Musicological Society, held in Ljubljana in September, 1967, a number of pamphlets were also issued, as was a special issue of the periodical ZVUK containing articles on Yugoslav music in foreign languages. Needless to say, some of them bordered on the pathetic.

tering on this area could quite usefully be incorporated into the process of studies about the methodology of research work, on either an elementary or advanced level of learning. This is especially true of instrumental music.

For one particular aspect of music, that is, for songs, choral works, and operas, not to mention the actual study involving archival documents about sources of instrumental music, one of the basic problems is the mastery of languages. Thus at the outset the "language barrier" eliminates a substantial number of prospective candidates for research from dealing with the music of this area. The result has been that whatever information has been conveyed to students of musicology about the music in these countries was and is dependent in part on a teacher's own knowledge and/or commitment to the study of music in these countries, or on the availability of secondhand literature on this subject in one of the Western European languages. Among the students who display an interest in the music of this area, some may come from immigrant families in which the practice of using the language of the "old country" has been maintained. In such instances, even with the greatest desire on the part of the student to study the music of an Eastern European country, he may not necessarily receive expert advice, and may find that the library resources are inadequate for such a study. In the light of such situations the following recommendations are suggested:

1. In an analogy to centers for study of Latin American music, the creation of a center for musicological studies dealing with East European countries is to be encouraged. A possible alternative to the creation of a center for study of East European music would be to examine the present state of available resources in the already existing libraries at American universities. Those which contain the basic tools for teaching and research and/or qualified faculty members should be encouraged to broaden their present course offerings by instituting, at least periodically, courses on the music of East European countries. Once such institutions are recognized as appropriate places for this type of musicological studies, qualified students should be advised to attend them. If a student prefers to study at another school, he should be allowed access to resources of well-equipped libraries, especially material that is not being used.

2. Students who are already enrolled and proficient in any of the East European languages should be encouraged to concentrate on topics dealing with these countries rather than to belabor problems in Western European music.

3. The preparation of basic textbooks on the history of music in

each of the individual countries of East Europe should be encouraged and even sponsored. Besides these, for certain areas and within certain historical periods, a regional approach may prove to be more satisfactory than a piecemeal study by countries. In the Middle Ages, for example, Byzantine music influenced church repertory all over the Balkans and beyond.

4. Translation into English of the most competent studies by European scholars dealing with this topic should be encouraged. In this respect, a careful screening of texts should precede the actual commitment to translation, and a committee of American and East European scholars could perform valuable services in selecting appropriate texts for consideration.

5. Exchanges of scholars from East European countries should be promoted. Scholars from these countries may also be entrusted with special courses on the music of this area, but with the active participation of American scholars in the planning and execution of such courses.

Even if the language problem were eliminated, one is faced with the problem of library resources for musicological studies at American universities. Owing to the variety of interests of faculty members at institutions of higher learning, there is at present not a single place in this country which could be considered fully supplied for studies of this area. Materials are unevenly distributed and some cooperation among the libraries is necessary in order to consolidate holdings and make them useful for this purpose. With modern duplication processes (microfilming and Xerox), any sufficiently interested and committed library may be able to acquire the basic minimum of already obtainable literature (editions of music and monographs) and start servicing those endeavoring to study the music of this area. By these duplication techniques, many of the older publications which are currently out of print can again become accessible. Furthermore, during the last fifteen years especially, there has been a true "publication explosion" in the field of musicology in most of these countries. Thus the main problem today appears to be how to keep up to date, rather than how to recover publications from the past.

The most significant musical publications of a musicological nature appearing in these countries are periodically recorded in at least one of the two most frequently consulted bibliographies available to American scholars — in the *Musical Quarterly* and in the *Notes of the Music Library Association*. As far as it is possible to determine at present, it would seem that the bibliographers are doing an excellent job in trying to keep track of the musicological publications in these countries. This has been especially the case in recent years with a relatively new reference tool, the *Music Index* (an equivalent to *Readers' Guide to Periodical Literature*), which started publication in 1949 and has greatly expanded its coverage since 1959 to include listings from the periodicals of several East European countries. The most significant of these publications have been listed and critically annotated in the two-volume bibliographical guide edited by Paul Horecky in connection with this survey.

It should also be added at this point that the East European countries, with few exceptions, eagerly participate in the UNESCO-sponsored project, *Répertoire international des sources musicales* (known as RISM). The aim of this enterprise is to make available the fullest possible listing of both manuscript and printed sources of the music of the past. While the degree of participation varies from country to country, the first results as well as progress reports (listed in the quarterly *Fontes artes musicae* [FAM]) [12] have been most encouraging. Similar to this international endeavor is the newly initiated *Répertoire international de littérature musicale* (RILM), with the central clearinghouse located at Queens College in Flushing, New York. The stated aim of RILM is to computerize all musicological publications and index them. Furthermore, a quarterly entitled *RILM Abstracts of Music Literature* will make easily accessible summaries of all significant studies from 1967 onward. In order to be effective, RILM will depend on a large network of contributors who will abstract articles and books on specially prepared forms and send them to the central clearinghouse. With the exception of Albania, all East European countries have responded most enthusiastically to this project, so that it is to be hoped that many earlier bibliographical problems may be wiped out in the future.

In order to gain some perspective both about the traditions as well as the present intensity of musicological studies in Eastern Europe, it may be useful to review briefly here, even if incompletely, these activities by countries.

POLAND

Musicological studies in Poland have a tradition which goes back to the period preceding World War I. There are two main centers in which these studies are fostered, Warsaw and Krakow. At the moment, the Warsaw group, led by the able and ambitious Zofia Lissa, is

12. (Kassel: Bärenreiter Verlag).

one of the most active musicological groups in Europe, outside of Germany. Polish scholars have actively participated in international meetings and enterprises and the exchange of information and of publications has grown especially since the last meeting of the International Association of Music Libraries, held in Warsaw in September, 1966. Polish scholars appear to be among the most prolific writers in Eastern Europe. An incomplete survey of East European musicological periodicals prepared several years ago by James Coover and published in *Fontes artes musicae* indicates that in Poland alone 105 periodicals dealing with music *were* or *are* published.[13]

CZECHOSLOVAKIA

Musicological studies have truly deep roots in this country. Almost a century ago some of the leading musicologists of Austria-Hungary were Czechs. Between the two world wars an especially prominent center for musicological studies was established in Brno, which, to this day, has not lost its significance for scholarship. The relatively small group in Bratislava counts among its members some very fine individuals, yet this center appears to lack the cohesiveness and organizational ability which characterize the much more numerous and therefore more conspicuous group in Prague, which produces a great number of publications (many in foreign languages) and long-playing records. There is a distinct need for updating Coover's data listing some 105 musical periodicals in that country.[14]

HUNGARY

As in the case of Czechoslovakia, musicological activities in Hungary date from the period of Austria-Hungary. Much of the work has been spurred by the fact that this relatively small country produced some outstanding composers (Liszt, Bartók, Kodály), and that its geographic position played an important role in the past, attracting musicians to make at least temporary stopovers in Hungary. Although the number of scholars at present is rather small, a few of them have acquired international reputation and there is a very intense publishing activity, including publications in foreign languages to offset the problems involved in mastering Hungarian. In the light of historical circumstances, and the closeness of Vienna especially, it is not sur-

13. FAM, 7 (1960): 16–21.
14. FAM, 4 (1957): 97–102.

prising that Coover was able to list 114 periodicals devoted to music and musical problems in Hungary.[15]

ROMANIA

While a few Romanians achieved international renown working outside of Romania (specifically Eusebius Mandyczewski [1857–1929]), musicological studies inside this country have only recently achieved the kind of recognition they deserve. Small in numbers, yet highly ambitious, this group may be expected to become more significant in the future. Comparatively speaking, the number of publications is unusually small for a country of this size and Coover found only 15 periodicals for his bibliography.[16]

YUGOSLAVIA

Perhaps in no other country can one find the distinct division of scholarly centers so influenced by historical factors as is the case in Yugoslavia. The most prominent center for musicological studies is located in Ljubljana, which is also the main center for musical publications. Next in importance is Zagreb, followed by Belgrade and, in recent years especially, Sarajevo and Skopje. The number of thoroughly trained and expert scholars is very small, the quality of publications is very uneven, ranging from first-rate to pamphleteering. The diversity of cultural backgrounds still feeds the centrifugal forces in scholarship, making it exceedingly difficult to undertake a comprehensive and unified approach for a history of music of this country as a whole. In the circumstances, it is somewhat surprising to find that Coover in his incomplete listing found 36 periodicals on this territory.[17]

BULGARIA

Musicological studies in Bulgaria are truly only in their first stages. Yet compared to the neighboring countries, Bulgaria appears to have taken some of the most advanced steps to "catch up" with them. An institute for music at the Bulgarian Academy of Sciences has highly ambitious plans. Musicological publications of the last ten years seem to indicate that there is a great potential for further development in

15. FAM, 5 (1958): 93–99.
16. FAM, 7 (1960): 69–70.
17. FAM, 9 (1962): 78–80.

Bulgaria for historical studies dealing with music, as may also be inferred from the fact that for a relatively small country Coover found 57 periodicals published there.[18]

GREECE

Musicological studies have yet to become established in Greece. Most earlier works are either compilative in nature or, if original, highly uncritical and valueless for scholarship. The work of the few Greeks who achieved recognition as scholars (e.g., Minos E. Dounias) dealt with Western European subjects rather than Greek music. There is at present no institution in Greece fostering musicological studies, which, in some instances, are treated rather as a hobby than a profession. On the basis of this writer's experience inside Greece, there is barely a handful of scholars or students who show some promise for developing into scholars. There are no known regular publications and there is a total lack of any musical bibliography.

ALBANIA

Albania is an unknown quantity. A more or less "regular" musical life in Albania appears to have started only within the last two or three decades and data about music and studies about music are nearly nonexistent.

On the basis of this survey of musicological studies in these countries, together with the previous remarks about American interest in this area, it is rather curious to observe that the degree of American involvement in studies about the music of these peoples appears to correspond in a proportionate way to the degree of the development of musicological studies in each. Also, in the light of the publication explosion and the availability of these publications on the international market, it appears that there should now be no lack of resources for a study of music in East European countries, provided that at least one American university's music library makes an effort to keep up to date with the flourishing publishing activities now in progress.

In connection with the recommendation for the establishment of a center for musicological studies dealing with the music of East Europe, it is of no small interest to mention that the Germans have again devoted their efforts in recent years to a most systematic study of the

18. FAM, 3 (1956): 223–26.

music of their eastern neighbors. Some six years ago a special *Johann-Gottfried-Herder-Forschungsstelle für Musikgeschichte* was established in Kiel. Attached to this research institute is a library consisting mostly of photostats of unavailable books and a collection of reproductions of musical manuscripts. Since 1962 this research center has been issuing an annual (appearing irregularly) publication, *Musik des Ostens* (printed and distributed by the ablest German music-publishing house, Bärenreiter, in Kassel and with distribution outlets in Basel, Paris, London, and New York), containing studies dealing with the history of music in exactly the area covered by this report. It should be added, however, that just as in the United States the German musicologists have been publishing studies in a number of other periodicals and not exclusively in this one. American musicologists have a number of outlets in which to publish their studies about the music of East Europe, whether specialized area journals, or professional journals. At present, at least, there is no urgent need for another journal devoted exclusively to history of music of this area. What is actually needed much more than a new journal is a more active collaboration and communication among individual scholars.

PERSPECTIVES

The main emphasis of this report has been on the studies of music of past centuries, that is, on historical musicology. So far, the accomplishments of American musicology have been minimal in this area. In conclusion, however, it is heartening to observe that some steps in the right direction have been made insofar as the music of the present is concerned. On the occasion of the celebration of fifty years of its publication, the renowned musical periodical, *Musical Quarterly*,[19] produced a special issue in January, 1965, containing reports and surveys of the present state of musical composition in almost all of the European countries, including the countries of Eastern Europe. It is to be hoped that from a desire to keep informed about the present, an interest in the past may also develop, and that from an initially limited curiosity about some detail, a much more intensive flow of information may follow. This should also lead to exchanges of scholars to the benefit of scholarship in the countries of Eastern Europe and to the advantage of American musicology.

Yet it cannot be stated strongly enough that even with the best equipped music library in this country, with complete sets of musical

19. (New York: G. Schirmer).

publications from East European countries and with volumes of musicological studies by American musicologists devoted to the music of this area, there is going to be little use for fostering these studies unless the music itself can be heard, either in live performances or on recordings. In this respect it appears that some snobbishness exists in some musical circles. This is the attitude, much too frequently encountered to be easily ignored, which considers that a piece of music which has not been heard or performed for several decades or centuries, especially if it originated in Eastern Europe, is ipso facto inferior and unworthy of present-day performance. It is exactly for this reason that the following recommendation is submitted for consideration.

Performing artists (individuals as well as groups — choral and instrumental — and opera companies) should be sponsored and encouraged to visit the United States in order to give American musical audiences an opportunity to hear authentic renditions of works never before accessible. Only by making the "sound of music" echo in American concert halls and classrooms may one count on a possible awakening of interest in the neglected music of the various East European countries. Even then there will remain the problem of how to get beyond the one or two "popular" musical compositions which could so easily be overplayed (a case in point, for example, is, Enesco's *First Rumanian Rhapsody* for orchestra) to the degree that audiences become accustomed to listening to a single piece rather than a diversified musical repertory. It is exactly in this need for offering a variety of possibilities from the musical output by composers of Eastern Europe that the musicologists could play an important role. They can pave the way to new musical experiences and can prepare audiences by lecturing and writing about the musical pieces yet to be heard.

Graduate students studying about Mozart, for instance, encounter numerous references to Mozart's contemporaries who were gifted musicians in their day, and a good many of them came from Bohemia (Jan Křtitel [Johann Baptist] Vanhal [1739–1813], Josef Mysliveček [1737–81], Leopold Koželuh [1747–1818], etc.). Yet their works are available in only some American music libraries and they have seldom been performed publicly in this country. Although their musical activities were centered in Vienna, they have also contributed to the spread of the musical art among the Czechs. A study of their works, for example, as well as a performance of the artistically and culturally important works of these and other European composers would represent an enriching experience in American musical life as well as in American musicological studies.

16 / LINGUISTICS

EDWARD STANKIEWICZ
University of Chicago

I

The study of the East Central and Southeast European languages in the United States is a direct outgrowth of the development of Slavic and East European studies, which dates back to the immediate postwar period. While this country has an excellent tradition in Indo-European linguistics and in the study of modern European languages, American linguists did not concern themselves before World War II with the Eastern European countries. At best they were students of Russian (like Leonard Bloomfield), or of Common Slavic (like Carl Darling Buck), for whom these subjects were a sideline or a subsidiary pursuit within the framework of other interests and not their main fields of specialization. In the prewar period there were already several centers of Slavic studies (notably Harvard, Berkeley, Wisconsin, and Columbia). These centers fostered the study of Slavic philology in the broad sense, emphasizing in particular the study of Slavic literatures and of Russian and, to a lesser extent, of Polish and Serbo-Croatian. American linguistic journals of that period contain few articles devoted to the languages of East Central and Southeastern Europe, while only one linguistic dissertation was written on Serbo-Croatian and one on the history of Greek.

The uninterrupted immigration of Eastern Europeans into this coun-

The present report deals only with linguistic research and graduate instruction in the East Central and Southeast European languages in the United States published by American linguists and by foreign scholars permanently residing in the United States. The works of the latter published prior to their arrival in America are not normally cited. Scholarship which is on the periphery of linguistic or which does not deal specifically with East Central or Southeast European languages has been ignored in this survey. Works on Old Church Slavonic, which is considered a common Slavic literary language, have been omitted.

try, the existence of compact Slavic or Greek centers, and the ethnic
and cultural cohesion of some ethnic groups had no perceptible influence on the development and cultivation of East European scholarship in America before World War II. The linguistic activity of these
immigrant groups hardly ever went beyond the production of textbooks and dictionaries of individual languages which were intended
for practical purposes. The work produced in this country by visiting
professors (such as Witold Doroszewski's *Język polski w Stanach Zjed-
noczonych*[1]) likewise remains outside the mainstream of American
linguistics. This situation began to change at the end of World War II
with the emergence of new centers of Slavic and East European studies.

The development of American descriptive linguistics, with its interest in languages of most diverse structures, and the national needs
of the war period, which prompted the preparation of various language manuals, have contributed to a heightened awareness of the importance of the East Central and Southeast European languages. The
chief advance in the study and instruction of these languages was,
however, the work of European linguists who were transplanted by
the war to the United States, and whose specialties lay specifically
in the area of Eastern Europe. They included such outstanding scholars as Roman Jakobson and John Lotz, who had established their
reputations in Slavic and Hungarian linguistics, respectively, before
their arrival in this country. Roman Jakobson, especially, deserves
credit for his work in educating a new generation of American Slavists who have turned their efforts not only to Russian and comparative
Slavic linguistics, but also to the South and West Slavic languages.
Among the earliest studies produced by Jakobson's students were such
works as Herbert Rubenstein's *Comparative Study of Morphophonemic
Alternations in Serbocroatian, Czech, and Russian*[2] and Horace
Lunt's *Grammar of Literary Macedonian*.[3] The rapid advances made
by American Slavic linguists became quite apparent at the Fourth
International Congress of Slavists in Moscow (1958), where Slavic lin-
guistics was outstandingly represented by the American delegation
and where two American papers were specifically devoted to West and
South Slavic languages. The main achievements of Slavic linguists
in the first postwar decade were to remain within the field of Russian.
This fact is apparent from the report on Slavic linguistics in America
delivered by Jakobson at the International Meeting of Slavists in Bel-

1. (The Polish language in the United States, Prace Towarzystwa Naukowego
Warszawskiego, vol. 1, no. 15 (1938).
2. (Ann Arbor: 1950). Xerox of dissertation.
3. (Skopje: Državno Kn-vo, 1952).

grade in 1955.[4] This report mentions only about ten studies in the fields of both South and West Slavic linguistics! Among these is also Carlton T. Hodge's Serbo-Croatian textbook,[5] which is one of a series of manuals produced in connection with the war effort.

The rapid advance of Slavic and East European linguistics in America came only in the late fifties, and it was largely connected with the launching of the Russian sputnik. Universities which had until then ignored Slavic and East European studies, or which had embryonic Slavic departments, became in a short time major centers of Slavic instruction and research, and some began work in other East European languages. Graduate courses in one or more of the East Central and Southeast European languages are presently taught in about thirty institutions, with some of them (Chicago, Indiana, Columbia) offering instruction in all or almost all of these languages.

The sixties could be characterized as a period of further expansion and consolidation in the East Central and Southeast European area. Among the major achievements of this period are to be noted a larger number of dissertations coming from midwestern institutions, the addition of South and/or West Slavic courses to most Slavic graduate programs, an increase of the number of active linguists (including some well-known European scholars who have accepted American positions), and an increase of books and articles devoted to the East Central and Southeast European languages. Also to be noted is the establishment of solid Hungarian programs at Indiana and Columbia, the beginning of serious work in Romanian, Albanian, and modern Greek, and the establishment of a Center for Slavic and Balkan Studies at the University of Chicago.

The scholarly production of American scholars in East European linguistics is concentrated in several closely related areas, which include original research, reviews, textbooks, and doctoral dissertations. In this survey we shall take up in turn American contributions to the study of the Slavic languages, of Albanian, Romanian, Greek, Hungarian,[6]

---

4. "Izuchenie slavianskikh iazykov i sravnitel'noe slavianovedenie v Soedinennykh Shtatakh Ameriki za poslevoenoe desiatiletie" (The Study of Slavic Languages and Comparative Slavic in the United States in the Postwar Decade), *Beogradski medjunarodni Slavistički Sastanak* (Belgrade: 1957), pp. 415–25.

5. *Spoken Serbo-Croatian*, 2 vols. (New York: H. Holt, 1945/46).

6. The material for Albanian, Romanian, and Greek was furnished by Kostas Kazazis (University of Chicago) and that for Hungarian by Thomas A. Sebeok (Indiana University). Except for minor stylistic changes, I have closely adhered to the prose of their submitted reports. Robert Austerlitz (Columbia) has also furnished useful information for Romanian and Hungarian. It is regrettable that I could not find any scholar to review the "stateless" languages of the area, such as Gypsy and Judeo-Spanish. The omission of Yiddish is also regrettable.

and of the so-called "Balkan linguistic league." We shall complete this report with a survey of graduate instruction, and a list of recommendations.

II

The Polish language has been at the center of West Slavic linguistic research. Almost all levels (such as phonology, morphology, syntax, vocabulary) have been explored in books and in numerous articles. Polish phonology was treated before the war by George L. Trager [7] from a purely distributionalist viewpoint. The Polish phonemes have also been discussed by Zbigniew Folejewski,[8] a Polish-trained linguist who has also taught in Sweden. A distinctive-feature interpretation of the Polish phonemes was given by Edward Stankiewicz in an article devoted primarily to Polish dialectology.[9] Phonemic and morphophonemic problems are combined in Charles Bidwell's study, "The Morphophonemics of Polish." [10] Special problems of Polish sounds are taken up by Maria Zagórska-Brooks in an acoustic study [11] and by Henrik Birnbaum, who deals with the historical development of some Polish clusters.[12] Both studies fall into areas which have been insufficiently explored in this country. Birnbaum and James Ferrell have also been active in the field of Old Polish philology.[13] The largest study of Polish morphology is that by Alexander Schenker,[14] in which the author gives a descriptive analysis of the nominal declension with special emphasis on its case system. The various functions of the Polish

7. "La systématique des phonèmes du polonais," *Acta Linguistica* (Copenhagen) 1 (1939): 179–88.

8. "The Problem of Polish Phonemes," *Scando-Slavica* (hereafter cited as SS), 2 (1956): 37–92.

9. "The Phonemic Patterns of the Polish Dialects," *For Roman Jakobson: Essays on the Occasion of His Sixtieth Birthday,* 11 October 1956 (The Hague: Mouton, 1956), 511–30.

10. *General Linguistics* (hereafter cited as GL), 2 (1957): 71–99.

11. "On Polish Affricates," *Word,* 20, no. 2 (1964): 207–10; "Nasal vowels in Contemporary Standard Polish," *International Journal of Slavic Linguistics and Poetics* (hereafter cited as IJSLP), 8 (1964): 102–9.

12. "Zum sekundären implosiven *j* im Polnishen," in *Lingua viget. Comentationes Slavicae in honorem V. Kiparsky* (Helsinki, 1965).

13. H. Birnbaum, "Zu den Anfängen der Hymnographie bei den Westslaven," in *Orbis Scriptus: Dmitrij Tschizewski zum 70 Geburtstag* (Munich: Wilhelm Fink, 1966); "Zu den Anfängen der Hymnographie bei den Westslaven," SS, 11 (1965): 69–92; J. Ferrell, "The Nominative Singular Masculine of the Present Participle Active in the *Kazania Swiętokrzyskie,*" *Rocznik Slawistyczny* (hereafter cited as RS), 28, no. 1 (1967): 69–78.

14. *Polish Declension: A Descriptive Analysis* (London: Mouton, 1964) (Slavistic printings and reprintings, no. 39).

nominal endings have also been analyzed by E. Stankiewicz.[15] The Polish verb has been treated in the studies of Schenker,[16] Frank Gladney,[17] and Charles Bidwell.[18] The first two studies, which are based on Jakobson's analysis of the Russian verb, have also influenced the work of some Polish linguists. Another article by Schenker on Polish conjugation was published in Poland.[19] Polish derivation received its first, albeit superficial treatment, in an article by Philip Scherer.[20] Questions of nominal derivation have been discussed by Stankiewicz.[21] Polish dialectology was treated from a structural viewpoint in Stankiewicz' previously mentioned article and in a monograph by Folejewski[22] which attempts to establish a bridge between linguistic and literary analysis. While Polish scholarship on Kashubian has in the last decade made significant progress, this area has been almost completely neglected in the United States, which has several compact centers of Kashubs. The impact of English on Kashubian has nevertheless attracted the interest of Jan L. Perkowski, who has written a doctoral dissertation on the subject,[23] and a (non-linguistic) article on the emigration of the Kashubs to America.[24] The impact of English on American Polish was studied by a young Polish scholar, Franciszek Lyra, who was trained at Indiana University and who summarized his findings in the *Polish Review*.[25]

The linguistic activity of American Slavists includes also the evaluation of foreign scholarship. Reviews of Polish linguistic works cover

15. "The Distribution of the Morphemic Variants in the Declension of Polish Substantives," *Word*, 11 (1956): 554–74.
16. "Polish Conjugation," *Word*, 10 (1954): 469–81.
17. "Próba ekonomicznego opisu morfologii czasowników w języku polskim" (A Tentative Economical Description of Polish Verb Morphology), *Biuletyn Polskiego Towarzystwa Językoznawczego* (hereafter cited as *BPTJ*), 22 (1963): 55–61,
18. "The Polish Verb," *GL*, 4 (1960): 77–142.
19. "Kilka uwag o koniugacji w języku polskim" (A Few Remarks about Conjugation in Polish), *BPTJ*, 24 (1966): 225–29.
20. "Derivation in Polish," *Language*, 24 (1948): 294–97.
21. "Expressive Derivation of Substantives in Contemporary Russian and Polish," *Word*, 10 (1954): 457–68; "The expressive formant -x- in Polish and in other Slavic Languages," *Zbornik za filologiju i lingvistiku* (hereafter cited as *ZborFilLingv*), 4/5 (1961–62): 313–18.
22. *La fonction des éléments dialecteaux dans les oeuvres littéraires: recherches stylistiques fondées sur la prose de W. Orkan*, Publications de l'Institut slave d'Upsal, no. 1 (Uppsala: Almqvist & Wiksell, 1949).
23. *A Kashubian Idiolect in the United States, International Journal of American Linguistics* (Bloomington, Ind.) (hereafter cited as *IJAL*), vol. 33 (1967).
24. "The Origins of the Kashubs and Their Emigration to America," *Polish American Studies*, vol. 23 (1966), no. 1.
25. "The Polish Language in the United States: Some Problems and Findings," *Polish Review*, 7, no. 2 (1962): 81–96.

a wide array of problems and are singularly useful in that they stimulate diachronic research, which is far less emphasized in this country
than in Eastern Europe. Reviews on the history of Polish include Stieber's *Phonological History of Polish* by Stankiewicz and Folejewski,
respectively,[26] and Nieminen's *Beiträge zur altpolnischen Syntax*
by Scherer;[27] the edition of the Gnezno Sermons by Schenker,[28] and
Sławski's Polish etymological dictionary by Stankiewicz.[29] Studies pertaining to Polish dialectology have been analyzed by Uriel Weinreich,[30] Z. Folejewski,[31] George Shevelov,[32] and L. Solano.[33] Morris
Halle reviewed the acoustic study of Koneczna and Zawadowski,[34]
and several reviews have been published on S. Westfal's *Study in Polish Morphology*.[35]

Recent years have also witnessed an interest in Sorbian or Lusatian,
the two closely related Slavic languages which are still spoken
in Eastern Germany, and in the defunct Western Slavic language,
Polabian. American work on Lusatian is reflected in a doctoral disserta-
tion by James Sehnert, in a doctoral dissertation and a review by J.
Cheek of Schroeder's Upper Sorbian dialect study,[36] and a note on
Germanisms in the Upper Sorbian literary language by John W.
Raede.[37] Sehnert is the only American Slavist working on Polabian.
In addition to a note on some Polabian forms,[38] he and the Polish lin-

26. "Stieber, Z., Rozwój fonologiczny języka polskiego," *Word*, 11 (1955):
630–37; 13, no. 1 (1957): 193–95.
27. *Language*, 27 (1951): 384–87.
28. "Vrtel-Wierczyński (ed.), Kazania gnieźnieńskie" (Gnezno Sermons), *Language*, 31 (1955): 124:27.
29. "Sławski, F., Słownik etymologiczny języka polskiego" (Polish Etymological
Dictionary), *Word*, 9 (1953): 627–30.
30. "Dejna, K., Polsko-laskie pogranicze językowe na terenie Polski" (Polish-
Lach Linguistic Border on Polish Territory), *Language*, 31 (1955): 292–95.
31. "Sobierajski, Z., Gwary Kujawskie" (The Kujav Dialects), *Word*, 13, no. 1
(1957): 195–96.
32. "Bąk, S., Gwary ludowe no Dolnym Śląsku" (Folk Dialects in Lower Silesia),
Word, 13, no. 1 (1957): 189–92.
33. "Wodarz, H., Satzphonetik des Westlachischen," *Slavic Review* (hereafter
cited as *SR*), 24, no. 1 (1965): 156–57.
34. "Koneczna, H. and Zawadowski, W. Przekroje rentgenograficzne głosek
polskich" (Spectograms of Polish sounds), *Word*, 9, no. 4 (1953): 394–96.
35. A. Schenker, "Westfal, S., A Study in Polish Morphology: The Genitive
Singular Masculine," *Language*, 33 (1957): 456–60; U. Weinreich, *Word*, 14,
no. 2/3 (1958): 412–18; Z. Folejewski, *Slavic and East European Journal* (hereafter cited as *SEEJ*), 1 (15) (1957): 70–71.
36. "Schroeder, A., Die Laute des wendischen (sorbischen) Dialekts von Schleife
in der Oberlausitz," *IJSLP*, 5 (1962): 146–50.
37. "De-Germanization of the Upper Lusatian Language," *SEEJ*, 11 (1967):
185–90.
38. J. Sehnert, "Polabian *tvorzaiků*," *RS*, 24 (1965): 109–10.

guist, K. Polański, have prepared the first Polabian-English dictionary [39] which includes texts and words in phonemic transcription along
with meanings, Common Slavic forms, a section on Polabian phrase-
ology, and a reverse dictionary.

Several American scholars have contributed to the study of Czech
in monographs and research papers. One of the earliest papers in this
field was Paul Garvin's "Standard Average European and Czech," [40]
which draws some parallelisms between Czech and other European
languages. A new and many-sided description of the sound system
of Czech was given by Henry Kučera in his book, *The Phonology of
Czech*.[41] The modern sound system is here examined from the viewpoint of its coexisting systems and of the syllabic structure and relative
frequency of phonemes. Kučera's book was reviewed by Zdenek
Salzman, Lawrence Thomas, and Ladislav Matejka.[42] Statistical problems of Czech phonology were taken up by Kučera in two other studies: "Entropy, Redundancy, and Functional Load in Russian and
Czech" [43] and "Mechanical Transcription and Phoneme Frequency
Count of Czech." [44] The question of the Czech literary, spoken, and
colloquial varieties was considered by the same author in an article in
Word [45] and (within a comparative framework) in his contribution
to the Fourth International Congress of Slavists.[46] Czech morphophonemics was treated in detail in Herbert Rubenstein's previously
mentioned dissertation. Basing his work on Jakobson's Russian verb
analysis, Rubenstein also described the Czech conjugation [47] in an
article to which Kučera subsequently added some substantive corrections.[48] The Czech linguist Komárek's phonemic analysis of Old Czech
vowels was restated by Eric Hamp.[49]

Several reviews by American scholars have dealt with works on Czech

39. K. Polański and J. Sehnert, *Polabian-English Dictionary* (The Hague:
Mouton, 1967).
40. *Studia Linguistica*, 3 (1949): 65–85.
41. (The Hague: Mouton, 1961).
42. *Word*, 20 (1964): 246–53; *Language*, 38 (1962): 195–96; *SEEJ*, 7 (1963):
209–11.
43. In *American Contributions to the V. International Congress of Slavists*,
Sofia (hereafter cited as *Am. Contr. V*) (The Hague: Mouton, 1963).
44. *IJSLP*, 6 (1963): 46–50.
45. "Phonemic Variations of Spoken Czech," *Word*, 11, no. 4 (1955): 575–602.
46. "Inquiry into coexistent phonemic systems in Slavic languages," in *American Contributions to the IV International Congress of Slavicists, Moscow* (hereafter cited as *Am. Contr. IV*) (The Hague: Mouton, 1958).
47. "The Czech Conjugation," *Word*, 7 (1951): 144–54.
48. "Notes on the Czech Conjugation," *Word*, 8 (1952): 378–86.
49. "Der Vokalismus im 'älteren Tschechisch,'" *Zeitschrift für Slawistik*, 5
(1960): 462–64.

published in Europe. E. Stankiewicz has reviewed the historical grammar of Czech by Lehr-Spławiński and Stieber.[50] Stankiewicz also wrote a review of Mann's *Czech Historical Grammar*.[51] G. Shevelov reviewed the Czech grammar of Havránek and Jedlička.[52] Svěrák's study on the Karlovice dialects was examined by Kučera,[53] while H. Rubenstein reviewed G. Bech's syntactic study.[54] Daneš' intonational-syntactic study was reviewed by Paul Garvin, Henry Kučera, and Cornelius van Schooneveld.[55]

Slovak is the only Slavic language which has been almost totally neglected by American Slavists. The popular papers by C. Potoček[56] and J. Kirschbaum[57] are contributions of Canadian Slavists. Bidwell's article on the language of the Bačka Ruthenians[58] deals with a mixed Ukrainian-Slovak dialect whose identity is not clearly defined by the author. Shevelov has reviewed Stanislav's *History of the Slovak Language*[59] and Lunt has written on Blanár's *Slovak Bibliography* and on Štolc's dialect study.[60] An older review is that by Scherer on Pauliny's *Štruktúra slovenského slovesa*.[61]

One of the lesser South Slavic languages, Slovenian, has attracted far wider attention. The vowel system of the modern literary language was discussed by Stankiewicz[62] and, from an acoustic point of view

50. "T. Lehr-Spławiński and Z. Stieber, Grammatyka historyczna języka czeskiego" (Historical Grammar of Czech), *IJSLP*, 3 (1960): 162–65.
51. "Mann, S., Czech Historical Grammar," *IJSLP*, 3 (1960): 165–67.
52. "B. Havránek and A. Jedlička, Česká mluvnice" (Czech Grammar), *SR*, 20, no. 4 (1961): 727–28.
53. "Svěrák, F., Karlovické nářečí" (The Karlovice Dialects), *Word*, 15, no. 3 (1959): 521–23.
54. "Bech, G., Zur Syntax des tschechischen Konjunktivs mit einem Anhang über den russischen Konjunktiv," *Word*, 9 (1953): 399.
55. "Daneš, F., Intonace a věta ve spisovné češtině" (Intonation and the Sentence in Literary Czech), *Language*, 34 (1958): 121–22; *SR*, 17 (1958): 3, 380–81; *IJSLP*, 1/2 (1959): 290–92.
56. "The First Written Slovak Language," *Slovak Review*, 1 (1947): 5–8.
57. "Contemporary Tendencies in Slovak Philology," *Etudes slaves et esteuropéennes*, 4 (1960): 163–75.
58. "The Language of the Bačka-Ruthenians in Yugoslavia," *SEEJ*, 10 (1966): 32–46.
59. "Stanislav, J., Dejiny slovenského jazyka. I Úvod a hláskoslovie" (History of Slovak. I. Introduction and Phonetics), *SR*, 16, no. 4 (1957): 580–82.
60. "Blanár, V., Bibliografia jazykovedy na Slovensku v rokoch 1939–1947" (Bibliography of Linguistics in Slovakia in 1939–1947); "Štolc, J., Nárečie troch slovenských ostrovov v Mad'arsku" (The Dialect of Three Slovak Islands in Hungary), *Language*, 27 (1951): 178–80.
61. "Pauliny, E., Štruktúra slovenského slovesa" (Structure of the Slovak Verb), *Language*, 25, no. 3 (1949): 308–11.
62. "The Vocalic Systems of Modern Standard Slovenian," *IJSLP*, 1/2 (1959): 70–76.

by Ilse Lehiste.[63] Stankiewicz has also analyzed the morphophonemic alternations of the Slovenian nominal declension,[64] while Rado L. Lenček has published a completely revised version of his Ph.D. thesis on the Slovenian conjugation.[65] H. Lunt has contributed some remarks on the syntax of Opčine, a Western Slovenian dialect [66] and a generative description of the Slovene verb.[67] The phonology of Slovenian dialects is briefly sketched by Stankiewicz (in his phonemic typology of the Slavic languages),[68] who also wrote on the loss of the neuter gender in the dialects,[69] and on the historical development of the Slovenian accents.[70] Joseph Paternost has recently published a Slovene-English glossary of linguistic terms.[71]

Gunnar Svane's Slovene grammar was reviewed by Lunt and by Stankiewicz;[72] Magner reviewed Bezlaj's book on Slovenian hydronymics.[73]

Serbo-Croatian has been one of the important subjects of American Slavistic research. As far back as 1940, George Trager gave a lucid description of Serbo-Croatian quantity and accent,[74] and Rajko Ružić wrote a doctoral dissertation, *The Aspects of the Verb in Serbo-Croatian* published in 1943.[75] The Serbo-Croatian suprasegmentals were taken up by C. T. Hodge [76] and by C. Bidwell,[77] whose restate-

63. "The Phonemes of Slovene," *IJSLP*, 4 (1961): 48–66.
64. "Accent and Vowel Alternations in the Substantive Declension of Modern Standard Slovenian," *SEEJ*, 3 (17) (1959): 144–59.
65. *The Conjugational Pattern of Contemporary Standard Slovene* (Wiesbaden: Harrassowitz, 1966).
66. "A Note on Slovenian Dialect Syntax," *IJSLP*, 7 (1963): 14–17.
67. "Attempt at a Generative Description of the Slovene Verb," in R. I. Lenček, *Conjugational Pattern*, pp. 138–87.
68. "Towards a Phonemic Typology of the Slavic Languages," *Am. Contr. IV*, 301–19.
69. "Neutralizacja rodzaju nijakiego w dialektach słoweńskich" (The Neutralization of the Neuter Gender in Slovenian Dialects), *Studia z filologii polskiej i słowiańskiej*, 5 (1965): 179–87.
70. "The Common Slavic Prosodic Pattern and Its Evolution in Slovenian," *SEEJ*, 10 (1966): 29–39.
71. *Slovenian-English Glossary of Linguistic Terms* (University Park: Department of Slavic Languages, Pennsylvania State University, 1966).
72. "Svane, G., Die Grammatik der slowenischen Schriftsprache" (Copenhagen, 1958); *Word*, 15 (1959): 511–17; *SEEJ*, 17, no. 4 (1959): 408–9.
73. "Bezlaj, F., Slovenska vodna imena" (Slovene Water Names), *Language*, 34 (1958): 303–6.
74. "Serbo-Croatian Accents and Quantities," *Language*, 16 (1940): 29–32.
75. University of California Publications in Modern Philology, vol. 25, no. 2 (Berkeley and Los Angeles, 1943).
76. "Serbo-Croatian Stress and Pitch," *GL*, 3 (1958): 43–54.
77. "The Phonemics and Morphophonemics of Serbo-Croatian Stress," *SEEJ*, 7 (1963): 160–65.

ments lack the sense of realism which marked Trager's earlier study. Hodge's description of the Serbo-Croatian phonemes [78] is valuable in that it gives an exhaustive list of the Serbo-Croatian consonant clusters. The acoustic values of the Serbo-Croatian accents have been studied by Ilse Lehiste in collaboration with the Yugoslav linguist, Pavle Ivić. Their findings were published in *Michigan Slavic Materials* and continued in *Zbornik za filologiju i lingvistiku*.[79] The acoustic properties of the Serbo-Croatian accents were discussed earlier by Lehiste in another study.[80] The conjugation in Serbo-Croatian was analyzed by Bidwell [81] and by C. H. van Schooneveld.[82] The latter study introduces a number of new formulations which considerably simplify the analysis of the verbal system, especially of its accentual alternations. The aspects of Serbo-Croatian were compared with those of Russian by T. F. Magner.[83] The relation of the tenses and reported speech in Serbo-Croatian were discussed in a brief but excellent article by Michael Samilov [84] (presently at the University of London). A summary of Serbo-Croatian syntax is given by Bidwell [85] who has also analyzed the Serbo-Croatian comparative.[86] Among the few American works on West or South Slavic lexicology is the study by E. Hammel on Serbo-Croatian kinship terminology.[87] Historical problems of Serbo-Croatian have been treated by G. Shevelov, who investigated the fate of the *jers*,[88] and by Stankiewicz, who studied the development of Serbo-Croatian palatals compared with their development in Polish.[89]

78. "Serbo-Croatian Phonemes," *Language*, 22 (1946): 112–21.

79. I. Lehiste and P. Ivić, *Accent in Serbo-Croatian: An Experimental Study*, Michigan Slavic Materials, no. 4 (Ann Arbor, 1963). I. Lehiste and P. Ivić, "Prilozi ispitivanju fonetske i fonološke prirode akcenata u savremenom srpskohrvatskom jeziku" (Contributions to the Study of the Phonetic and Phonemic Properties of the Accents in Contemporary Serbo-Croatian), *ZborFilLingv*, 6 (1963): 33–73; 8 (1965): 75–117; 10 (1967).

80. "Some Acoustic Correlates of Accent in Serbo-Croatian," *Phonetica*, 7 (1961): 114–47.

81. "The Serbo-Croatian Verb," *Language*, 40 (1964): 532–50.

82. "Serbo-Croatian Conjugation," *IJSLP*, no. 1/2 (1959): 55–69.

83. "Aspectual Variations in Russian and Serbo-Croatian," *Language*, 39 (1963): 621–30.

84. "The Witnessed Past in Serbo-Croatian," *Canadian Slavonic Papers*, 2 (1957): 98–105.

85. "Serbo-Croatian Syntax," *Language*, 41 (1965): 238–59.

86. "The Serbo-Croatian Comparative," *Language*, 35 (1959): 259–63.

87. "Serbo-Croatian Kinship Terminology," *Kroeber Anthropological Society Papers*, 167 (1957): 45–75.

88. "Weak *jers* in Serbo-Croatian and South Slavic: Developments in the Word Initial Syllable," *ZborFilLingv*, 7 (1964): 23–43.

89. "Polish mazurzenie and the Serbo-Croatian palatals," in *Studi in onore di Ettore lo Gatto e Giovanni Maver* (Florence and Rome: Sansoni, 1962).

The neglected problem of the urban varieties of Serbo-Croatian was tackled in T. F. Magner's A Zagreb Kajkavian Dialect.[90] Although the book is essentially a collection of loanwords, it contains useful information on the phonology and grammar of this urban dialect. A classification of Serbo-Croatian dialects, based on morphophonemic criteria was proposed by Kenneth Naylor,[91] who has also written on the nominal declension.[92]

The reviews pertaining to Serbo-Croatian deal primarily with its history and dialectology. The historical monographs of Ivan Popović were criticized by Lunt,[93] whereas the dialect works of P. Ivić have received acclaim in the reviews of Samilov, Harold L. Klagstad, L. Thomas, and Stankiewicz.[94] The book by C. van den Berk on the Čakavian substratum in Dubrovnik was discussed by Samilov,[95] who also examined the onomastic work of Schutz.[96] Bidwell has reviewed the loanword studies of Edmund Schneeweiss and Hildegard Striedter-Temps.[97] The book of Rudolf Filipović on the English loanwords in Croatian was reviewed by Klagstad, Kučera, and Einar Haugen.[98]

The youngest Slavic literary language, Macedonian, received its first scholarly treatment in Lunt's grammar,[99] which prepared the ground for the subsequent descriptive grammars and studies of Macedonian. A review of the book was written by Gordon H. Fairbanks.[100] Lunt

90. Pennsylvania State University Studies, no. 18 (University Park, 1966).
91. "The Classification of the Serbo-Croatian Dialects," SEEJ, 10 (1966): 453–57.
92. "A Comparison of the Nominal Declension of the Čakavian Dialects, Literary Serbo-Croatian, and Russian," ZborFilLingv, 9 (1966): 67–72.
93. "Popović, I., Istorija srpskohrvatskog jezika, Novi Sad, 1955," Word, 11 (1955): 623–26; "Popović, I., Geschichte der serbokroatischen Sprache, Wiesbaden, 1960," Language, 37 (1961): 224–34.
94. "Ivić, P., Die Serbokroatischen Dialekte: Ihre Struktur und Entwicklung, vol. 1," SEEJ, 3 (17) (1959), 405–6, 407–8; Language, 36 (1960): 146–52; Word, 15 (1959): 367–76. "Ivić, P., Dialektologija srpskohrvatskog jezika: Uvod. 1 Štokavsko narečje" (Dialectology of Serbocroatian: Introduction. 1. Štokavian), SEEJ, 3 (17) (1959): 405–6, 407–8.
95. "Berk, C. van den, Y a-t-il un substrat čakavien dans le dialecte de Dubrovnik? Contribution à l'histoire de la langue serbo-croate," IJSLP, 3 (1960): 158–60.
96. "Schutz, J., Die geographische Terminologie des Serbokroatischen," SR, 17 (1958): 380–81.
97. "Schneeweiss, E., Die deutschen Lehnwörter im Serbokratischen in kulturgeschichtlicher Sicht"; "Striedter-Temps, H., Deutsche Lehnwörter im Serbokroatischen," Word, 18 (1962): 367–76.
98. "Filipović, R., The Phonemic Analysis of English Loanwords in Croatian," SEEJ, 5 (19) (1961): 167–69; SR, 20 (1961): 728–30; Language, 36 (1960): 548–51.
99. Grammar of the Macedonian Literary Language (Skopje: Državno knigoizdatelstvo, 1952).
100. "Lunt, H. G., A Grammar of the Macedonian Literary Language," Language, 30 (1954): 124–28.

has also provided a morphological analysis of the Macedonian verb,[101] along the lines of Jakobson's analysis of the Russian conjugation, and an outline of the formation of the Macedonian literary language.[102] A number of structural studies dealing mainly with the Macedonian verb and syntax, and with the position of Macedonian within the Balkan league were written by Zbigniew Gołąb (who arrived in the United States in 1961). These studies cover the Macedonian perfect,[103] the etymology of the Macedonian *baram* and *sakam*,[104] Arumanian-Macedonian isogrammatism,[105] syntactic redundance in Macedonian,[106] Macedonian dialectology,[107] the influence of Turkish on Macedonian dialects,[108] and the Balkan type of conditional in Macedonian.[109] Gołąb also summarized the history of literary Macedonian.[110] Among the reviews dedicated to Macedonian we find the critical analyses of Kepeski's grammar, written by Lunt and by Bidwell,[111] and Klagstad's review of the new Macedonian dictionary.[112] The problem of the Yugoslav literary languages and dialects was examined by Bidwell.[113]

Bulgarian has been receiving more scholarly attention in recent

101. "Morfologijata na makedonskiot glagol" (The Morphology of the Macedonian Verb), *Makedonski Jazik* (hereafter cited as *MJ*), 2 (1951): 123–31.

102. "The Creation of Standard Macedonian. Some Facts and Attitudes," *Anthropological Linguistics*, 1 (1959): 19–26.

103. "Nowomacedoński typ perfektum ze słowem *imam//sum*" (The Neo-Macedonian Type of Perfect with the Word *imam//sum*), *Zeszyty Uniwersytetu Warszawskiego. Filologia*, 8 (1961): 321–25.

104. "Macedońskie *baram* 'żądam, szukam' i *sakam* 'chcę, lubię, kocham'" (Macedonian *baram* "I desire, seek', and *sakam*, 'I want, I love') in *Studia linguistica in honorem T. Lehr-Spławiński* (Warsaw: Państwowe wydawnictwo naukowe, 1963).

105. "Some Arumanian-Macedonian Isogrammatisms and the Social Background of Their Development," *Word*, 15 (1959): 415–35.

106. "Syntactic Redundance," *SEEJ*, 8 (1964): 37–41.

107. "Dva Makedonski govora (na Suho i Visoka vo Solunsko), Razdel 3, Imenki" (Two Macedonian Dialects [Sukho and Visoka in the Salonika Area], Part 3, Nouns), *MJ*, 13/14 (1962–63): 173–276.

108. "The Influence of Turkish upon the Macedonian Slavonic Dialects," *Folia Orientalia*, 1 (1959): 26–45.

109. *Conditionalis typu bałkańskiego w językach południowo-słowiańskich ze szczególnym uwzględnieniem macedońskiego* (The Balkan Type of Conditional in South Slavic with Special Consideration of Macedonian), Prace Komisji Językoznawczej Polskiej Akademii Nauk, vol. 2 (Wrocław: 1964).

110. "Uwagi nad historią języka macedońskiego" (Remarks on the History of Macedonian), *Sprawozdania Akademii Umiejetnosci* (1961), pp. 138–39.

111. "Kepeski, K., Makedonska gramatika" (Macedonian Grammar), *Language*, 27 (1951): 180–87; *Studies in Linguistics* (hereafter cited as *SIL*), 13 (1958): 91–94.

112. "Rechnik na makedonskiot jazik so srpskohrvatski tolkuvanja" (Dictionary of Macedonian with Serbocroatian Definitions), *SEEJ*, 6 (1962): 274–76.

113. "Language, Dialect and Nationality in Yugoslavia," *Journal of Human Relations*, 15 (1962): 217–26.

years. The phonology of Bulgarian has been treated in detail by H. L. Klagstad,[114] and in an article by Joseph van Campen and Jacob Ornstein which refutes the traditional interpretation of the Bulgarian palatized consonants.[115] The phonemic systems of Bulgarian dialects were presented for the first time in a study by Klagstad,[116] which was favorably received in Bulgaria. The vowel/zero alternations and the system of genders were discussed by Howard Aronson,[117] who also wrote (with Stankiewicz) on the accentual system of the Bulgarian declension.[118] A generative approach to Bulgarian morphophonemics was presented by J. A. van Campen.[119] The phonemic system of a Bulgarian dialect in the Banat was analyzed by Bidwell.[120]

American reviews have dealt with some major works of Bulgarian linguists: Samilov discussed the historical grammar by Mirchev,[121] Garvin the descriptive grammar by Andreichin, et al,[122] and van Campen the dictionary of the Bulgarian Academy.[123]

A useful contribution to Slavistic scholarship is the production of linguistic bibliographies and surveys of the history of Slavic linguistics, which include the South and West Slavic languages. The largest bibliographical tool is the *Selective Bibliography of Slavic Linguistics* by Stankiewicz and Dean S. Worth,[124] which is supposed to encompass all Slavic languages. The South Slavic languages are contained in the first volume, and the West Slavic languages in the second (in press). A shorter bibliography was published by Ladislav Matejka in the *Michi-*

114. "The Phonemic System of Colloquial Standard Bulgarian," *SEEJ*, 2 (1958): 42–54.

115. "Alternative Analyses of the Bulgarian Nonsyllabic Phonemes," *Language*, 35 (1959): 264–70.

116. "A Phonemic Analysis of Some Bulgarian Dialects," *Am. Contr. IV*, pp. 157–68.

117. "Vowel/Zero Alternations in the Bulgarian Inflection," *SEEJ*, 6 1962): 34–38; "The Gender System of the Bulgarian Noun," *IJSLP*, 8 (1964): 87–101.

118. "Accentual Alternations in the Bulgarian Declension," *Indiana Slavic Studies*, 3 (1963): 130–39.

119. "Alternative Solutions to a Problem in Bulgarian Morphology," *SEEJ*, 6 (1962): 143–47.

120. "Neke beleške o bugarskom narečju banatskog sela Belo Blato" (Some Remarks on the Bulgarian Dialect of the Banat Village Belo Blato), *ZborFilLingv*, 4–5 (1961): 2, 29–33.

121. "Mirchev, K., Istoricheska gramatika na bulgarskiia ezik" (Historical Grammar of Bulgarian), *IJSLP*, 3 (1960): 167–68.

122. "Andreichin, L., Kostov, N., and Nikolov, E., Bulgarsko gramatichno obuchenie v gimnazite" (Bulgarian Grammar Instruction in the Secondary Schools), *Word*, 8 (1952): 401–3.

123. "Romanski, S. (ed.), Rechnik na suvremeniia bulgarski knizhoven ezik" (Dictionary of the Contemporary Bulgarian Literary Language), *IJSLP*, 9 (1965): 180–84.

124. (The Hague: Mouton, 1966).

388   *Edward Stankiewicz*

gan *Slavic Materials*.[125] A survey of Slavic studies in America was presented in Jakobson's previously mentioned article at the Belgrade International Meeting (1955). Also useful are the annual bibliographies of Slavic linguistics given in the *PMLA* and in *The American Bibliography of Slavic and East European Studies* published by Indiana University.

The linguistic achievements of the postwar period in Bulgaria, Czechoslovakia, Poland, and Yugoslavia were analyzed respectively by Gołąb, Garvin, Stankiewicz, and Lunt in a collective volume surveying the state of linguistics in the Soviet Union and in Eastern Europe.[126] The state of postwar linguistics in Yugoslavia was sketched by Schenker,[127] and Naylor compiled a bibliography of Yugoslav linguistics for 1958–62.[128] Kučera outlined Czech contributions to modern linguistics[129] and Jakobson analyzed contributions of Polish linguists to modern phonology and linguistic theory.[130]

The growth of Slavic linguistic scholarship in this country has gone hand in hand with graduate instruction in the languages. The success of the latter has been possible only in conjunction with new teaching materials. The following is a list of textbooks and dictionaries for West and South Slavic languages prepared by American scholars:

Polish

Sigmund Birkenmayer and Zbigniew Folejewski, *Introduction to the Polish Language*, 2 vols. (New York: Kościuszko Foundation, 1965).

Alexander Schenker, *Beginning Polish* (New Haven and London: Yale University Press, 1966).

Czech

William Harkins, *A Modern Czech Grammar* (New York: King's Crown Press, 1953). (Reviews: C. T. Hodge, *SIL*, 12 [1954]: 32; H. Kučera, *Word*, 9 [1953]: 396–98.)

125. *Introductory Bibliography of Slavic Philology* (Ann Arbor: Department of Slavic Languages and Literatures, University of Michigan, 1965).
126. T. Sebeok, P. Garvin, H. Hunt, and E. Stankiewicz, eds., *Current Trends in Linguistics*, vol. 1, *Soviet and East European Linguistics* (The Hague: Mouton, 1964).
127. "Slavic Linguistics in Today's Yugoslavia," *SEEJ*, 1 (15) (1947): 272–79.
128. K. Naylor and J. Kašić, "Prilozi bibliografiji jugoslovenske lingvistike na strani (za period od 1958–1962 godine)" (Contributions to the Bibliography of Yugoslav Linguistics Abroad [for 1958–1962]), *ZborFilLingv*, 6 (1963): 191–208.
129. "Czech Contributions to Modern Linguistics," in *The Czechoslovak Contribution to World Culture* (The Hague: Mouton, 1964).
130. "Kazańska szkola polskiej lingwistyki i jej miejsce w światowyn rozwoju fonologii," *BPTJ*, 19 (1960): 3–34.

Serbo-Croatian

Carlton T. Hodge, *Spoken Serbo-Croatian*, 2 vols. (New York: H. Holt, 1945–46).

Carlton T. Hodge (with J. Jankovic and E. Ivanovich), *Serbo-Croatian: Basic Course* (Washington, D.C.: Foreign Service Institute, 1965).

Albert Bates Lord, *Beginning Serbo-Croatian* (The Hague: Mouton, 1958). (Review: T. Magner, *SEEJ*, 3 [17] [1959]: 80–81.)

Thomas F. Magner, *Introduction to the Serbo-Croatian Language* (Minneapolis, 1956; 2d ed., Pennsylvania State University, 1962). (Reviews: A. Lord, *SEEJ*, 1 [15] [1957], 73–74; M. Samilov, *SEEJ*, 7 [1963]: 216–17; C. E. Bidwell, *Modern Language Journal*, 45 [1961]: 231–32).

Bulgarian

Carlton T. Hodge and Associates, *Bulgarian: Basic Course*, 2 vols. (Washington, D.C.: Foreign Service Institute, 1961). (Review: H. I. Aronson, *SEEJ*, 7 [1963]: 73–75.)

Albert Bates Lord, *Beginning Bulgarian* (The Hague: Mouton, 1962). (Reviews: C. T. Hodge, *SEEJ*, 7 [1963]: 217–18; H. I. Aronson, *IJSLP*, 8 [1964]: 133–35.)

Special mention should be made of Schenker's Polish textbook, a work prepared under the auspices of the Office of Education. Although primarily a pedagogical tool, it provides a fresh approach to some problems, clear explanatory tables, and abundant exercises based on conversational, everyday Polish.

The only valuable bilingual dictionary is the English-Polish and Polish-English dictionary by Kazimierz Bulas and Francis J. Whitfield (the second volume in collaboration with Lawrence L. Thomas).[131] Particularly successful is the first (English-Polish) volume.

The above survey would not be complete without mentioning the contributions of American Slavists to general Slavic linguistics, and specifically to the exploration of historical and typological problems. Although not directly concerned with specific Slavic languages, books and papers in these areas have in one way or another advanced our knowledge of the South and West Slavic languages as well. We shall list only the principal areas of research and the names of the main contributors. Questions of historical phonology have been treated by R. Jakobson, G. Shevelov, M. Samilov, H. Birnbaum, H. Lunt, C. Bidwell, E. Stankiewicz; Slavic morphophonemics has been explored by

131. *The Kościuszko Foundation Dictionary*, 2 vols. (The Hague: Mouton, 1959–61).

M. Halle, D. Worth, and E. Stankiewicz; the study of Slavic versification and poetics has attained a singularly high level thanks to the works of R. Jakobson and K. Taranovski (the latter's work in the field of Serbo-Croatian metrics should be especially noted); questions of Slavic typology have been dealt with in studies by E. Stankiewicz, J. Ferrell, H. Birnbaum, and H. Kučera; Slavic syntax has been revitalized through the work of D. Worth and Z. Gołąb; historical lexicology and the history of the Slavic literary languages have been examined by Gerta Worth and G. Shevelov.

Lest one be tempted to self-congratulation, let us now assess the general nature and direction of American linguistic research in the West and South Slavic areas.

One of the main achievements of American Slavic linguistics in the last decade is the recognition of the importance of the "minor" Slavic languages and the awareness that all Slavic languages deserve equal attention independently of extraneous expediencies and considerations. The study of all or most Slavic languages also holds the promise of a further enrichment of comparative Slavic and general linguistics.

Research in the South and West Slavic languages has so far been restricted mostly to synchronic problems. This situation is slowly changing, as more and more Slavists turn their attention to diachronic problems. But so far there has been little interest in a number of fields, such as lexicology, semantics, syntax, poetics, the formation of Slavic literary languages, and bilingualism. Particularly neglected are the questions of linguistic diffusion, for which the American landscape, with its multilingual Slavic centers, provides a natural basis for exploration and for far-reaching generalizations. In other areas (such as lexicography), American Slavists lack the equivalent of East European research centers and institutes, which are indispensable for long-range research projects. The absence of organized teamwork is, however, offset by the freedom of individual research, which tends to yield works of more limited size but of greater depth and variety.

American research of the last two decades has not produced enough monographic works on individual West and South Slavic languages to match the linguistic output of Eastern Europe. Nor can it compare in scope and size with the books and monographs on the South and West Slavic languages produced in the prewar period by Western European scholars. No American works are equivalent to the many-sided explorations of Macedonian and Serbo-Croatian by A. Mazon and A. Vaillant, to the monographs on Slovenian by L. Tesnière, to the dialectal studies of Serbo-Croatian by O. Broch, or to the pioneering works of F. Lorentz on Kashubian, not to speak of the classical works produced by such outstanding nineteenth-century Slavists as A. Schleicher or A. Leskien. American Slavic linguistics has, on the other hand, been in the forefront of structural linguistics at a time when a structural approach to language was proscribed in Eastern Europe and ignored in Western Europe. American Slavists were thus able to formulate new theoretical approaches or to follow lines of research which have subsequently been accepted also in Europe. The political "thaw" and resumption of scholarly contacts between American and East European Slavists promises, in turn, to enrich Slavic linguistic scholarship on both sides of the ocean. The initial leadership of American Slavists in comparative Slavic and in linguistic theory must not obscure the fact that many of the above-listed studies were of mediocre quality and limited scope. The quest for novelty and the flair for "structural restatements" was in some cases but a surrogate for solid knowledge or interesting ideas. The quality of Slavic scholarship is, however, improving as more and more researchers in the South and West Slavic languages come to these fields with a training in Slavic linguistics, rather than in American Indian or in Uzbek, as was the case one or two decades ago. Still, American linguists are not trained just in one or two of the modern Slavic languages, but in Slavic linguistics with a minor in one of the three major Slavic areas. This type of training seems to be most suited to American conditions, and it is fair to assume that the increased interest in the South and West Slavic languages will not in this country supersede the primary concern with Russian.

III

American contributions to the field of Albanian are not very numerous. Only two American linguists, Eric Hamp and Leonard Newmark, have shown more than a passing interest in that language. Of these two, Newmark has written exclusively on the present-day language, while Hamp's contributions are both synchronic and diachronic, but with a greater emphasis on the latter.

The only full-scale description of an Albanian dialect by an American scholar is Newmark's first-class *Structural Grammar of Albanian*.[132] The variety of Albanian described here is a north-central Tosk dialect of the city of Berat.

Hamp's contributions include articles on Albanian phonology [133] and

132. *Structural Grammar of Albanian* (IJAL, 23, 4 (1957): pt. 2).
133. "Palatal before Resonant in Albanian," *Zeitschrift für vergleichende Sprachforschung*, 76 (1960): 264–80; "Mythical Prothetic Vowels in Albanian," *Annali Istituto Universitario Orientale*, Napoli, Sezione Linguistica, 2 (1960): 185–90.

morphology.[134] The possible genetic relationship between Albanian and Illyro-Messapic was examined by him in "Albanian and Messapic,"[135] while the place of Albanian in the Indo-European language family was the subject of "The Position of Albanian."[136] Of related interest is his assessment of the Albanian reflexes of the Indo-European laryngeals.[137] The dialect of an isolated Albanian enclave in northern Greece is studied by Hamp in "The Albanian Dialect of Mandres,"[138] and the Albanian dialects of Attica and the Megarid are discussed in notes to a study by P. A. Furikis.[139] Hamp has also been the author of a number of Albanian lexical and etymological notes, most of them published in the *Zeitschrift für vergleichende Sprachforschung*.[140] Gordon M. Messing has attempted to establish a connection between Albanian *triskë* and Greek *trik*.[141] In "An Albanian Case System,"[142] Newmark shows how two alternative accounts of Berat Tosk might treat the case system of that variety of Albanian. Stavro Skendi studied the history of the Albanian alphabet as a test case of cultural-political relations.[143]

G. Messing has reviewed Stuart S. Mann's *An Historical Albanian-English Dictionary and An English-Albanian Dictionary*.[144] The latter

134. "Gender Shift in Albanian Plurals," *Romance Philology*, 12 (1959): 147–55.

135. "Albanian and Messapic," in *Studies Presented to Joshua Whatmough on His Sixtieth Birthday* (The Hague: Mouton, 1957).

136. "The Position of Albanian," in *Ancient Indo-European Dialects*, H. Birnbaum and J. Puhvel, eds. (Berkeley and Los Angeles: University of California Press, 1966).

137. "Evidence in Albanian," in *Evidence for Laryngeals*, W. Winter, ed. (The Hague: Mouton, 1965).

138. "The Albanian Dialect of Mandres," *Die Sprache*, 11 (1965): 137–54.

139. E. Hamp, "On the Arvanitika Dialects of Attica and the Megarid," *Balkansko Ezikoznanie*, 3, no. 2 (1961): 101–6; P. A. Furikis, "Hē en Attikē hellēnalbanike dialektos" (The Albanian Dialect in Attica), *Athēna*, 44 (1933): 28–76; 45 (1933): 49–181.

140. "Albanian arë," 75 (1958): 237–38; "Albanian *be,- besë* 'oath'," 77 (1961): 252–53; "Albanian *natë* 'night'," 77 (1961): 254–56; "Albanian *pas, mbas* behind, after'," 75 (1958): 23; "Albanian *pishk* 'fish'," 77 (1961): 256–57; "Albanian *pres* 'I wait'," 76 (1960): 135; "IE. *bhendh-* in Albanian," 77 (1961): 253–54; "O. Pruss. *soye* 'rain'," 74 (1956): 127–28 (correspondences between Baltic and Albanian). Also: "Albanian *dimën, dimër*," *Indogermanische Forschungen*, 66 (1961): 52–55; "An Albanian Alphabet of Demetrio Camarda" and "An Irregular-Regularized Albanian Alphabet of Demetrio Camarda" and "An Irregular-Regularized Albanian Noun," *Annali Istituto Universitario Orientale*, Napoli, Sezione Linguistica, 3 (1961): 105–8, and 5 (1963): 61–62; "Two Notes on Albanian: 1. Albanian *plak* and *IE. */a/*. 2. Suppletion Exploited.", *Language*, 33 (1957): 530–32.

141. "Modern Greek *trik* and Albanian *triskë*: Problems in Derivation," *Language*, 31 (1955): 232–35.

142. "An Albanian Case System," *Lingua*, 11 (1962): 313–21.

143. "The History of the Albanian Alphabet: A Case of Complex Cultural and Political Development," *Südost Forschungen*, 19 (1962): 263–84.

144. *Language*, 26 (1950): 240–422, and 34 (1958): 530–33.

was also reviewed by Newmark.[145] Newmark's own *Structural Grammar of Albanian* was reviewed by Werner Winter.[146] Hamp's review of *Le dialecte de Dushmani* by Wacław Cimochowski[147] is particularly interesting because of the reviewer's structural restatement of a number of points. One might also mention here Hamp's corrections of Pokorny's etymological dictionary.[148] An audio-lingual textbook of Albanian is Newmark's *Spoken Albanian.*[149]

IV

Modern Greek linguistics in the United States looks rather promising at the present moment. For a long time there had been a handful of American linguists interested in the language, as well as an even smaller number of Greek scholars living in this country. The promise resides in the fact that, although there has been no spectacular increase in the number of American neo-Hellenists, linguistics seems to have finally caught the fancy of native Greek young men and women studying in America and intending to remain here. We are still dealing, of course, with a small number of people, about a dozen or so. For a minor language, however, this is not a particularly poor show. It should be noted that most of the young linguists who constitute our "promising" future either have not yet received their degrees or else have done so very recently. That is why the present report does not reflect their presence as decisively as the above optimistic remarks would normally warrant. There has certainly been to date no avalanche of fresh scholarly activity in modern Greek linguistics.

There has been only one more or less full description of the language published in the United States, namely the *Reference Grammar of Literary Dhimotiki*, by Fred W. Householder, Kostas Kazazis, and Andreas Koutsoudas.[150] Although not entirely an original scholarly contribution, this grammar not only filled a gap sorely felt but also made some of the principles formulated in Triantaphyllides' modern Greek grammar[151] available to people whose mastery of Greek did not enable them to consult the latter work.

145. *SEEJ*, 2 (16) (1958): 173–74.
146. *Language*, 34 (1958): 533–40.
147. *Language*, 29 (1953): 500–12.
148. "Albanian Corrigenda to Pokorny's Indogermanisches Etmologisches Wörterbuch," *Indogermanische Forschungen*, 57 (1962): 142–50.
149. *Spoken Albanian* (Bloomington, Ind., 1954; 2d ed., 1959). (Out of print, but new edition being prepared by K. Kazazis, at the University of Chicago.)
150. (Bloomington, Ind., and The Hague: Mouton, 1964).
151. M. A. Triantaphyllidēs, *Neoellenikē grammatike (tes demotikes)* (Modern Greek Grammar [of the Popular Language]) (Athens, 1938).

In the field of phonology and morphophonemics, we find various articles, some dealing with the standard language, and others with different modern Greek dialects. Ralph L. Ward discusses permissible final consonants in ancient and modern Greek,[152] F. Householder analyzes some earlier claims of Greek phonemicists,[153] Henry and Renée Kahane have studied modern Greek external sandhi, accent, and how the two combine.[154] Of related interest is the rigorous and phonetically sophisticated study of modern Greek suprasegmentals by A. Barton Jones, Jr.[155] Andreas and Olympia Koutsoudas have performed a pedagogically very useful task in their contrastive analysis of Greek and English phonemes.[156] Hamp analyzed gemination in the Greek island dialects of Kos, Nisyros, and Rhodes.[157] Bidwell had the good fortune of locating and describing the speech of a second-generation Sarakatsan (or Karakatšan) speaker in Bulgaria.[158] A. Koutsoudas treats mostly morphophonemic phenomena of modern Greek in an article of a more general linguistic nature.[159]

Very little work has been done in this country on modern Greek syntax. In the area of modern Greek morphology, contributions have been few but of high quality. An article by H. and R. Kahane contains, among other things, an interesting analysis of markedness vs. unmarkedness in the Greek tense-aspect system.[160] A. Koutsoudas has written the only American book-length study of the modern Greek verb,[161] a neat, rigorously post-Bloomfieldian treatment of the subject, which has been reviewed by Swanson.[162] Hamp has a shorter study on the same subject.[163]

Turning now to lexicography and related areas, we find again a

152. "The Loss of Final Consonants in Greek," *Language*, 22 (1946): 102–8.
153. "Three Dreams of Modern Greek Phonology," in *Papers in Memory of George C. Pappageotes* (hereafter cited as *Papers in Memory of Pappageotes*), Special Publications no. 5, Issued as a Supplement to *Word*, 20, no. 3 (1964): 17–27.
154. "Syntactical Juncture in Modern Greek," *Language*, 21 (1945): 92–95.
155. "Stress and Intonation in Modern Greek," *Glotta*, 44 (1966) 254–62.
156. "A Contrastive Analysis of the Segmental Phonemes of Greek and English," *Language Learning*, 12 (1960): 211–30.
157. "On So-Called Gemination in Greek," *Glotta*, 39 (1960): 265–68.
158. "On Karakatšan Phonology," *Papers in Memory of Pappageotes*, pp. 7–16.
159. "The Handling of Morphophonemic Processes in Transformational Grammars," *Papers in Memory of Pappageotes*, pp. 28–42.
160. "The Tense System of Modern Greek," in *Omagiu lui Iorgu Iordan* (Bucharest: Editura Academiei Republicii Populare Romine, 1958), pp. 453–74.
161. "Verb Morphology of Modern Greek," *IJAL*, vol. 28, no. 4, pt. 2 (Bloomington, Ind., 1962).
162. *Language*, 40 (1964): 273–75.
163. "To rēma en tē sēmerinē homiloumenē hellēnikē glōssē" (The Verb in Contemporary Spoken Greek], *Athēna*, 65 (1961): 101–28.

significant contribution by H. and R. Kahane.[164] A lexicographic achievement worthy of special mention is Swanson's *Vocabulary of Modern Spoken Greek*,[165] reviewed by Messing.[166] This "vocabulary" is, despite its shortness, easily the most serious effort toward a dictionary of contemporary spoken Greek hitherto published in the United States. Swanson has also studied the phonological and morphological features of English loanwords in Greek,[167] which include English words that entered Greek through French and Italian intermediaries. Demetrius J. Georgacas had been the author of many etymological and toponymic studies long before he came to this country. Since settling here, he has contributed various studies in the same areas.[168] Messing has attempted to trace the origin of one Greek term for "so-and-so,"[169] and a problem of Greek-Albanian lexical interference.[170] John Andromedas' letter to the editor[171] is important in that it corrects some inaccuracies in Munro S. Edmonson's study of kinship terms, were *katharevousa* terms had been presented as being *the* modern kinship terms. Fortunately, such instances of confusion between the vernacular and puristic varieties of modern Greek have nowadays become rather infrequent. This very problem of modern Greek diglossia is the subject of a paper by George C. Pappageotes and James Macris.[172]

Some reviews have already been mentioned in conjunction with the works discussed. Here we shall list some other reviews of books dealing with modern Greek. Georgacas' thorough review of Pring's *Grammar of Modern Greek*[173] shows that several of Pring's statements apply to the dialects rather than to the standard language which his gram-

---

164. "Problems in Modern Greek Lexicography," in *Problems in Lexicography*, F. W. Householder and S. Saporta, eds. (*IJAL*, 28, no. 2 [1962], pt. 4).

165. (Minneapolis: University of Minnesota Press, 1959).

166. *Language*, 36 (1960): 143–46.

167. "English Loanwords in Modern Greek," *Word*, 14 (1958): 26–46.

168. "The Post-Classical Names Designating the Peninsula of the Peloponnesus," *IV. Kongress für Namenforschung* II (1961): 302–7; "Medieval and Modern Greek Place Names," *Beiträge zur Namenforschung*, 14 (1963): 283–99; "The River Systems of Messenia and Laconia," *Beiträge zur Namenforschung*, 16 (1965): 70–95; "A Contribution to the Study of Modern Greek Toponymy. I," *Names*, 7 (1969): 65–83.

169. "The Etymology of Greek he he tò deîna," *Language*, 23 (1947): 207–11.

170. "Modern Greek *trík* and Albanian *triskë*: Problems in Derivation," *Language*, 31 (1955): 232–35.

171. "Greek Kinship Terms in Everyday Use," *American Anthropologist*, 59 (1957): 1086–88.

172. "The Language Question in Modern Greece," *Papers in Memory of Pappageotes*, pp. 53–59.

173. "Remarks and Corrections on Pring's *A Grammar of Modern Greek*," *Orbis*, 7 (1958): 536–58.

mar purports to be describing. On the other hand, one or two of Georgacas' own statements have less general an application than he himself claims: for example, /l/ and /n/ are *not* palatalized before /i/ in the speech of all Greeks. Georgacas' book on the origin of the Sarakatsans was reviewed by G. Messing,[174] who also reviewed Gerard Blanken's *Les grecs de Cargèse* (Corse).[175] The same work was also reviewed by the late George Pappageotes.[176] Pappageotes was also the author of a review of Emile Missir's French-Greek dictionary.[177] Finally, two of the most important books on modern Greek written since the end of World War II were reviewed respectively by H. and R. Kahane[178] and by D. Swanson.[179]

There are two useful textbooks of modern Greek; one by H. and R. Kahane and R. Ward,[180] and the other, less well organized but based on excellent spoken Greek, by Ann Arpajolu, an instructor at the Defense Language Institute in Monterey.[181]

V

Research in Romanian in the United States is conspicuous mostly by its scarcity. The only book-length American contribution to Romanian scholarship is Frederick B. Agard's *Structural Sketch of Rumanian.*[182] A refreshing feature of Agard's *Sketch* is the extensive treatment of Romanian syntax at a time and age when syntax was generally relegated to a subordinate position in treatments of whole languages.

Agard has also written a neatly organized "Noun Morphology in Rumanian."[183] The origin of some Romanian verb tenses, with remarks

174. "D. S. Georgacas, *Peri tēs katagōgēs tōn Sarakatsanaiōn kai tou onomatos autōn*" (On the Origin of the Sarakatsans and of Their Name), *Language*, 28 (1952): 388–90.

175. "G. Blanken, Les grecs de Cargèse (Corse), vol. 1, Partie linguistique, Leyde: Sijthoff, 1951," *Language*, 30 (1954): 278–81.

176. *Word*, 9 (1953): 70–73.

177. "E. Missir, Dictionnaire français-roméique. A-J, 2nd edition, Paris: Klincksieck," *Word*, 10 (1954): 86–87.

178. "H. Seiler, L'aspect et le temps dans le verbe néo-grec (Paris: 'Les Belles Lettres', 1952)," *Language*, 30 (1954): 115–23; "A Mirambel, La langue grecque moderne: description et analyse, Paris: Klincksieck, 1959," *Language*, 38 (1962): 191–96.

179. *Language*, 38 (1962): 191–96.

180. *Spoken Greek* (New York: H. Holt, 1946).

181. *Modern Spoken Greek for English-Speaking Students* (Thessaloniki, 1961; New York: Hadrian, 1964).

182. Language Monograph no. 26 (Baltimore: Waverly Press for Linguistic Society of America, 1958).

183. *Language*, 29 (1953): 134–42.

of a comparative Romance interest, was studied by Karl G. Bottke.[184] Problems of Romanian historical phonetics were treated in an article by L. F. Solano[185] which also contains some interesting comparisons with Italian and Sardinian.

Tatiana Fotitch enriched the study of Romanian historical lexicology with some studies on its religious terminology.[186] Gołąb's "Outline of the Dialect of the Macedonian Arumanians"[187] belongs to the few studies which are devoted to the second most important group of Romanian dialects, namely, Arumanian (alias Macedo-Romanian or Vlach), and to its relationship with other Balkan languages. Gołąb shows that the extension to Macedonian of some restricted Balkanisms is due to the influence of Arumanian, which is spoken in Yugoslav Macedonia by a numerically weak but prestigious group of people.

Among the reviews of works on Romanian, we find Agard's review of Alain Guillermou, *Manuel de langue roumaine*,[188] Agard and G. Fairbank's review of Emil Petrovici, *Kann das Phonemsystem einer Sprache durch fremden Einfluss umgestaltet werden?*[189] Sol Saporta's review of A. Rosetti, ed., *Recherches sur les diphthongues roumaines*,[190] as well as a number of reviews by Messing.[191]

184. "Rumanian Imperfect, Perfect and Pluperfect Indicative," *Orbis*, 9 (1960): 116–18.
185. "The History of Diphthongization and Metaphony in Rumanian," in *Mediaeval Studies in Honor of J. D. M. Ford*, (U. T. Holmes, Jr., and A. J. Denomy, eds.) (Cambridge, Mass., 1948).
186. "Abstract Terminology in the Rumanian Version of the Liturgy of Saint John Chrysostomos," *Orbis*, 6 (1957): 168–76; "Rumanian Ecclesiastical Terminology of Byzantine Origin. IV: The Appellations for Ecclesiastical Offices," *Orbis*, 9 (1960): 119–27, "The Development of Religious Terminology in Rumanian," *Acta Philologica* (Rome, Societas Academica Dacoromana), 3 (1960): 137–46; "The Semantic Ramifications of Rumanian *Popa*: A Study in Balkan 'Words and Things'," *Premier Congrés International de Dialectologie Générale, Communications et rapports*, 3 (1964): 210–18; "Rumanian Ecclesiastical Terminology of Byzantine Origin: The Cult and Its Objects," *Orbis*, 2 (1953): 423–38.
187. Z. Gołąb, "Szkic dialektu Arumunów macedońskieh" (An Outline of the Dialect of the Macedonian Arumanians), *Zeszyty Naukowe Uniwersytetu Jagiellońskiego. Seria Nauk Spolecznych, Filologia. Prace Językoznawcze*, 37, no. 4 (1961): 175–200.
188. *Language*, 30 (1954): 153–59.
189. *Language*, 34 (1958): 297–303.
190. *Romance Philology*, 19 (1966): 84–86.
191. "Alejandro Cioranescu, Diccionario etimológico rumano, Fas. 1–2", *Language*, 39 (1963): 120–25; "Sextil Puşcariu, Die rumänische Sprache, ihr Wesen und ihre völkliche Prägung," *Language*, 24 (1948): 226–31; "Nicolae Draganu, Elemente de sintaxa a limbii romîne (Elements of Rumanian Syntax) and Istoria sintaxei (The History of Syntax)," *Language*, 23 (1947): 287–94; "H. Mihăescu, Limba latină în Provinciile Dunărene ale Imperiului Roman" (Latin in the Danube Provinces of the Roman Empire), *Language*, 39 (1963): 673–77; "Omagiu lui Iorgu

No scholarly textbook of Romanian has been produced in the United States.

VI

Significant work in Hungarian linguistics in America began during World War II. Its theoretical orientation during the war and for about ten years thereafter may fairly be characterized by the term "structuralist." It is significant that at this time there was practically no structural work being done in Hungary itself. The American achievements of this time stimulated some linguists in Hungary and eventually led to a synthesis of domestic and foreign views of Hungarian phonology and grammar along structuralist lines. Recently, as young Hungarian linguists came to adopt structuralist attitudes and methods and as their work became readily accessible to us, Hungarian linguistics in America seemed to decline proportionately. Most of the American contributors turned either to general linguistic problems, or applications in other Uralic languages, or both.

The earliest work applying structuralist methods to Hungarian phonology and morphology was that of Robert A. Hall, Jr.[192] Thomas A. Sebeok was very active in Hungarian linguistics in the 1940s, with several major publications[193] which include a textbook[194] and an analysis of the Hungarian and Finnish case systems.[195] The latter is a portion of his dissertation, in which he applied methods developed by R. Jakobson for the analysis of the Russian case system. Paul Garvin also contributed an article on the Hungarian suffixes and postpositions.[196] In 1947 John Lotz was invited by Columbia University to occupy the first American chair in Hungarian (in 1949 transformed into a chair in general linguistics). In contrast to other American scholars who occasionally contributed to Hungarian linguistics, Lotz was primarily a specialist in Hungarian, and most American M.A. theses

Iordan, cu prilejul împlinirii a 70 de ani" (In Honor of Iorgu Iordan, on the Occasion of his 70th Birthday), *Language*, 38 (1962): 417–26.

192. *An Analytical Grammar of the Hungarian Language*, Linguistic Society of America, Language Monograph 21 (Baltimore, 1938; 2d ed., new title, 1944).

193. "Analysis of the Vocalic System of a Given Language Illustrated by Hungarian," *Quarterly Journal of Speech*, 28 (1942): 449–52; "Notes on Hungarian Vowel Phonemes," *Language*, 19 (1943): 162–64; "The Phoneme /h/ in Hungarian," *SIL*, 1 (1943), 22 pp.; "Vowel Morphophonemics of Hungarian Suffixes," *SIL*, 2 (1943): 47–50; "Equational Sentence in Hungarian," *Language*, 20 (1944): 320–27.

194. *Spoken Hungarian* (New York: H. Holt, 1945).

195. *Finnish and Hungarian Case Systems; Their Form and Function*, Acta Instituti Hungarici Universitatis Holmiensis, series B, Linguistica, 3 (1946).

196. "Pure-Relational Suffixes and Postpositions in Hungarian," *Language*, 21 (1945): 250–55.

and Ph.D. dissertations in the field have been produced under his direction (cf. below under the lists of dissertations). Lotz's work deals with such diverse aspects of the Hungarian language as phonology,[197] morphology,[198] semantics,[199] and contrastive grammar (with English).[200] In addition to his own work, special mention should be made of the studies done along the same lines by Lotz and his students and associates.[201]

Among the reviews are Lotz's discussion of L. Országh's English-Hungarian and Hungarian-English dictionaries,[202] and Sebeok's review of the English-Hungarian dictionary [203] and of Sauvageot's grammar.[204]

A few individuals in scattered institutions have applied principles of generative grammar to Hungarian problems. Zeno Wendel worked on "The Interrogative Sentence in Hungarian" in Z. S. Harris' group at Pennsylvania. M. Breuer worked "On Hungarian Morphology for Mathematical Linguistics" in V. Yngve's former group at MIT. Marianne Esztergár is preparing a generative phonology of Hungarian at the University of California at San Diego, and Szilard Szabó is working on an automated procedure for Hungarian syntax and for a phrase structure grammar at the Rand Corporation.

Finally, Lotz has reported on the impact of the National Defense Education Act on Hungarian language background and research projects in a publication which should be consulted for a more detailed study than we have space for here.[205]

197. "Vowel Frequency in Hungarian," *Word*, 8 (1952): 227–35.
198. "The Imperative in Hungarian," *American Studies in Uralic Linguistics*, Indiana University Publications, Uralic and Altaic Series, vol. 1 (1959), pp. 83–92; "Semantic Analysis of the Tenses in Hungarian," *Lingua*, 11 (1962): 356–62; "The Place of the Implicative (-LAK) Form in the Conjugational Pattern of Hungarian," *Mémoires de la Société Finno-Ougrienne*, 125 (1962): 317–27.
199. "The Semantic Analysis of the Nominal Bases in Hungarian," *Travaux du Cercle Linguistique de Copenhague*, 5 (1949): 185–97.
200. "Contrastive Study of the Morphophonemics of Obstruent Clusters in English and Hungarian," in *Miscellanea di Studi Dedicati a Americo Varády* (Modena, 1966), pp. 197–201.
201. J. Lotz, A. Abramson, L. Gerstman, F. Ingemann, and W. Nemser, "The Perception of English Stops by Speakers of English, Spanish, Hungarian and Thai: A Tape-cutting Experiment," *Language and Speech*, 3 (1960): 71–77; K. Keresztes, "About the Problems of Hungarian Implication," *Ural-Altaische Jahrbücher*, 36 (1965): 39–45.
202. *American Slavic and East European Review* (hereafter cited as *ASEER*), 10 (1951): 157–159; 14 (1955): 149–51.
203. *American Speech*, 23 (1948): 261–62.
204. "A. Sauvageot, Esquisse de la langue hongroise," *Language*, 29 (1953): 98–100.
205. *The Uralic and Altaic Program of the American Council of Learned So-*

The use of Hungarian in America has been recorded and documented by sociolinguistic methods by Joshua Fishman of Yeshiva University,[206] and Elemér Bakó of the Library of Congress is carrying out a research project at a high scholarly level on Hungarian dialects in America, which is at the moment primarily in a text-collecting stage.[207] Linda Dégh of Indiana University is the primary investigator of another large-scale project of essentially ethnographic character but with a strong linguistic component. The report incorporating the linguistic results has not yet appeared.

VII

Closely connected with the study of the Southeast European languages is the exploration of the Balkan languages as a geographic and typological unity. While none of the American studies can match in importance the work of such pioneering explorers of the Balkan league as K. Sandfeld, G. Weigand, M. Małecki, A. M. Selishchev, and P. Skok, American linguists, and particularly American Slavists, have maintained and advanced the tradition of Balkan linguistics.

The most important contributions in this field are from the pen of Gołąb, who has examined the Balkanisms of the South Slavic languages,[208] some typically Balkan verbal categories and syntactic constructions of South Slavic,[209] and the role of Arumanian as a mediator in the diffusion of Balkan linguistic features.[210] A thorough analysis of all problems pertaining to the Balkan league (with a survey of the pertinent literature and some original conclusions) was given by Birnbaum.[211] Klagstad has posited the question of the morpho-syntactic parallelism in the Balkan languages.[212] Bidwell has probed into the

cieties (1959–1965), Indiana University Publications, Uralic and Altaic Series, vol. 63 (1966).

206. J. Fishman, Hungarian Language Maintenance in the United States, Indiana University Publications, Uralic and Altaic Series, vol. 62 (1966).

207. E. Bakó, "Hungarian Dialectology in the U.S.A.," Hungarian Quarterly, 1 (1961): 48–53; "Goals and Methods of Hungarian Dialectology in America," American Hungarian Dialect Notes, vol. 1 (New Brunswick, 1962).

208. " 'Balkanisms' in the South Slavic Languages," SEEJ, 6 (1962): 138–42.

209. "The Problem of Verbal Moods in the Slavic Languages," IJSLP, 8 (1964): 1–36; "Funkcja syntaktyczna partykuly da w językach pd.-słowiańskich" (The Syntactic Function of the Particle da in the South Slavic Languages), BPTJ, 13 (1954): 67–92.

210. "Some Arumanian-Macedonian Isogrammatisms and the Social Background of Their Development," Word, 15 (1959): 415–35.

211. "Balkanslavisch und Südslavisch," Zeitschrift für Balkanographie, 3 (1965): 12–63.

212. "Toward a Morpho-Syntactic Treatment of the Balkan Linguistic Group," Am. Contr. V, pp. 179–89.

relationship of Vulgar Latin and South Slavic in an important article which has a bearing on the chronology of the sound changes in Common Slavic.[213] The vicissitudes of the Slavic word "Slav" in the medieval European languages were traced by H. and R. Kahane.[214] Hamp has brought up the role of Albanian in the diffusion of Slavic place names in Greece,[215] and Stankiewicz has examined the place of Slavic and Balkan elements in Judeo-Spanish ("Džudezmo") of Yugoslavia.[216] The formation of Balkan literary languages was investigated by Skendi.[217]

VIII

Linguistic instruction in the East Central and Southeast European languages has shown constant expansion, especially within the last five years. Of the Slavic languages, Czech, Polish, and Serbo-Croatian are taught in most Slavic departments which have a graduate program, and in several other schools. Bulgarian is taught at Brown, Chicago, Harvard, Indiana, Stanford, Syracuse, Washington (Seattle), and Yale. The other Slavic languages — Slovak, Sorbian, Slovene, and Macedonian — are rarely taught in graduate departments except as reading or structure courses for Slavic linguists.

The University of Wisconsin publishes the only American journal dedicated to Slavic and East European linguistics and literature, *The Slavic and East European Journal* (editor-in-chief, Thomas J. Shaw).

Of the non-Slavic languages, modern Greek is taught at Bridgeport, University of Chicago, Columbia, Colorado, Illinois, Indiana, Minnesota, Ohio State, Seton Hill College, UCLA, and Wisconsin. Romanian is taught in several schools (e.g., Chicago, Columbia, Indiana, and Rice). Illinois publishes the *Journal of Rumanian Studies*, which accepts articles also on Romanian linguistics. Albanian is at present taught regularly only at Chicago. Indiana has been offering it, but has temporarily discontinued because of the lack of staff. Texas offers Albanian on a conference basis.

213. "The Chronology of Certain Sound Changes in Common Slavic as Evidenced by Loans from Vulgar Latin," *Word*, 17 (1961): 105–22.
214. "Notes on the Linguistic History of 'sclavus'," in *Studi in onore di Ettore Lo Gatto e Giovanni Maver* (Florence, 1962).
215. "The Albanian Diffusion of Slavic Toponyms in Greece," *Atti del VII Congresso Internazionale di Scienze Onomastiche e Memorie della Sezione Toponomastica*, 2 (1963): 137–44.
216. "Balkan and Slavic Elements in the Judeo-Spanish of Yugoslavia," *For Max Weinreich* (1964), pp. 229–36.
217. "The Emergence of the Modern Balkan Literary Languages; A Comparative Approach," *Südosteuropa Schriften*, 6 (1964): 303–21; "Studies on Balkan Slavic Languages, Literatures, and History in the Soviet Union during the Last Decade," *ASEER*, 16 (1957): 524–33.

Indiana and Columbia have extensive programs in Hungarian, which is also taught at Rutgers, Minnesota, California (Berkeley), UCLA, Washington (Seattle), and Western Reserve.

Indiana University has a large-scale program of instruction in all Hungarian subjects. Its center also publishes the Uralic and Altaic Series, which is a major outlet for Hungarian linguistic publications. About 10 percent of the more than 100 volumes published to date are devoted to Hungarian linguistics.

Graduate courses on the structure and/or history of the West and South Slavic languages are offered at each of the major Slavic graduate centers. Most of these courses have been initiated within the last three or four years. Several other schools (e.g., Illinois and Kansas) plan to initiate instruction in this area. The majority of these courses are intended to "broaden" and supplement the knowledge of Russian linguistics with the structure and/or history of a second or third Slavic language. Since 1959 only three schools have had more than one dissertation in West or South Slavic linguistics (Harvard, 10; Indiana, 5; Michigan, 5; see dissertation list below). A regular summer institute for Slavic studies was set up for the first time in 1967 under the auspices of the "Big Ten" and the University of Chicago (the CIC schools) for Slavists and area specialists. It is intended to offer courses in the languages, linguistics, and literatures of the area. The prime objective of the institute is to enable "area" students to fill in gaps in their regular curriculum and to provide a meeting ground for American and foreign scholars (which it hopes to invite in the future). The first summer institute was held at Indiana University.

Graduate courses in the structure and history of Hungarian are offered at Columbia and Indiana. No university has listed courses specifically on the history and structure of Romanian, but R. Austerlitz offered such a course during the summer session of 1967 at Columbia and repeated it in 1968.

Courses in the history and structure of Albanian and modern Greek are offered at Chicago. Of the "stateless" languages of East Central and Southeast Europe, Judeo-Spanish, Arumanian and Gypsy are everywhere neglected, despite their intrinsic linguistic interest and their relation to the other languages of the area. Judeo-Spanish and Arumanian can, however, be taken on a reading basis at the Balkan Center at Chicago.

Yiddish has been highly cultivated at Columbia, with its Atran chair for the Yiddish Language, Literature and Culture, which was occupied (until his death in 1967) by Uriel Weinreich and which is presently held by Marvin Herzog. Yiddish linguistics has also been taught at NYU.

The schools which offer linguistic courses at the graduate level on the history and structure of this area's languages are listed below, together with the names of the instructors (excluding foreign visitors). In most cases this information has been furnished by the schools directly, and in a few cases it has been excerpted from recent catalogue issues.

Brown
> W. Slavic — H. Kučera
> Bulgarian —R . Mathiesen

California (Berkeley)
> Comp. Slavic — F. Whitfield

Chicago
> W. Slavic — E. Stankiewicz, Z. Gołąb
> S. Slavic — H. Aronson (Bg.), Z. Gołąb, E. Stankiewicz (Slov.)
> Mod. Greek — K. Kazazis
> Albanian — E. Hamp

Colorado
> W. Slavic — R. Abernathy
> S. Slavic — H. L. Klagstad, Jr. (deceased; successor not yet named)

Columbia
> W. Slavic — G. Shevelov
> S. Slavic — R. Lenček
> Hungarian — R. Austerlitz
> Romanian — R. Austerlitz (not regularly scheduled)

Cornell
> W. Slavic — R. L. Leed
> S. Slavic — F. Foos

Harvard
> W. Slavic — H. Lunt
> S. Slavic — H. Lunt

Indiana
> W. Slavic — J. Sehnert, L. Newman, J. Maurer
> S. Slavic — J. Sehnert
> Hungarian —A. Raun, G. Bayerle

Michigan

W. Slavic — L. Matejka
S. Slavic — B. Stolz

North Carolina

W. Slavic —T. Gasinski
S. Slavic — T. Gasinski

Ohio State

W. Slavic — D. Robinson
S. Slavic — K. Naylor

Pennsylvania

W. Slavic — M. Zagórska-Brooks
S. Slavic — B. Šljivic-Šimšić

Pittsburgh

W. Slavic — C. Bidwell
S. Slavic — C. Bidwell

Syracuse

S. Slavic — J. Hursky, E. Levin

Texas

W. Slavic — J. Perkowski
S. Slavic — J. Perkowski

UCLA

W. Slavic — H. Birnbaum, G. R. Meyerstein
S. Slavic — A. Albin

Washington (Seattle)

W. Slavic — L. Micklesen
S. Slavic — L. Micklesen

Wisconsin

W. Slavic — L. Thomas (Pol.), H. Marquess (Cz.)
S. Slavic — J. Strmecki (S.-Cr.)

Yale

Polish — A. Schenker

IX

Following is a list of Ph.D. dissertations in the United States which deal with comparative aspects or with specific languages of the East Central and Southeast European countries:

Comparative studies

H. Rubenstein, "A Comparative Study of Morphophonemic Alternation in Standard Serbo-Croatian, Czech and Russian," Columbia, 1949.

T. F. Magner, "Consonantal Present Stems in Slavic," Yale, 1950.

M. Samilov, "The Phoneme *jat'* in Slavic," Columbia, 1960.

K. Kazazis, "Some Balkan Constructions Corresponding to Western European Infinitives," Indiana, 1965. (Greek, Albanian, Romanian, Bulgarian.)

D. Lockwood, "A Typological Comparison of Microsegments and Syllable Constructions in Czech, Serbo-Croatian, and Russian," Michigan, 1966.

Polish (including Kashubian)

D. L. Olmsted, "The Phonology of Polish," Cornell, 1950.

A. M. Schenker, "Polish Nominal Inflection," Yale, 1953.

C. A. Lewis, "Communication Patterns of Recent Immigrants: A Study of Three Nationality Groups in Metropolitan Detroit," Illinois, 1955.

C. G. Borkowski, "Kernel Sentences of Polish and Their Transformations," Pennsylvania, 1958.

F. Lyra, "English and Polish in Contact," Indiana, 1962.

M. Zagórska-Brooks, "An Acoustic Analysis of Nasal Vowels in Contemporary Standard Polish," Michigan, 1963.

J. L. Perkowski, "A Kashubian Idiolect in the United States," Harvard, 1965.

R. A. Rothstein, "Predicate Complementation in Contemporary Polish," Harvard, 1967.

Lower Sorbian

J. H. Cheek, Jr., "A Distinctive Feature Phonematic Analysis of Lower Sorbian," Harvard, 1959.

Upper Sorbian

J. A. Sehnert, "The Morphology of German Loanwords in Upper Lusatian," Indiana, 1966.

Czech

R. A. C. Goodison, "The Phonology of Czech," Cornell, 1952.

R. L. Leed, "A Historical Phonology of Czech," Cornell, 1958.

L. Newman, "A Generative Approach to the Czech Verb," Harvard, 1967.

Slovak

G. R. Piroch Meyerstein, "Selected Problems of Bilingualism among Immigrant Slovaks," Michigan, 1959.

Slovene

R. Zrimc, "Slovene Conjugation as Represented in the Dialect of Ljubljana," Harvard, 1961.

R. L. Lenček, "The Conjugational Pattern of Contemporary Standard Slovene," Harvard, 1962.

J. Paternost, "The Slovenian Verbal System, Morphophonemics and Variations," Indiana, 1964.

Serbo-Croatian

R. H. Ružić, "The Verbal Aspects in Serbo-Croatian," California, 1938.

A. Bormanshinov, "The Illyrian Movement as Reflected in the Serbo-Croatian Literature and Language," Pennsylvania, 1958.

T. Butler, "The Serbian Literary Controversy: 1814–1817," Harvard, 1963.

R. Harrington, "The Language of the Life of St. Symeon by Stefan Prvovenčani," Harvard, 1964.

A. L. Albin, "An Analysis of *Slavenno-serbskija vědomosti*," UCLA, 1966.

R. Beard, "The Suffixation of Adjectives in Contemporary Serbo-Croatian," Michigan, 1966.

M. Kantor, "Aspectual Derivation in Contemporary Serbo-Croatian," Michigan, 1966.

K. E. Naylor, "The Nominal Declension in the Čakavian Dialects," Chicago, 1966.

B. Šlijvić-Šimšić, "Deklinacija u paštroškim ispravama 16–18 veka," Harvard, 1966.

Bulgarian

H. I. Aronson, "Morphophonemic Patterns of the Bulgarian Inflection (Compared with Those of Russian)," Indiana, 1961.

J. A. van Campen, "Problems of Verbal Aspect and Inflection in Modern Standard Bulgarian," Harvard, 1961.

Romanian

P. M. H. Edwards, "A Basic Vocabulary of Rumanian," Pennsylvania, 1959.

E. S. Georges, "Studies in Romance Nouns Extracted from Past Participles," California, 1965.

Gretchen Buehler, "An Examination of the Debate on Rumanian Phonemics," Pennsylvania, 1966.

Albanian

R. W. Wescott, "A Comparative Grammar of the Albanian Language. Part I, Phonology," Princeton, 1948.

E. P. Hamp, "Vaccarizzo Albanese Phonology: The Sound System of a Calabro-Albanian Dialect," Harvard, 1954.

L. D. Newmark, "An Outline of Albanian (Tosk) Structure," Indiana, 1955.

D. Berberi, "Phonological and Morphological Adaptation of Turkish Loanwords in Contemporary Albanian Geg Dialect of Kruja: A Synchronic Analysis," Indiana, 1964.

B. Pogoni, "Albanian Writing Systems," Indiana, 1966.

Greek

P. S. Costas, "An Outline of the History of the Greek Language with Particular Emphasis on the Koine and the Subsequent Stages," Chicago, 1933.

G. Pappageotes, "The Partial or Complete Loss of the Infinitive and the Formation of the Future in the Balkan Languages with Special Reference to the Development and Disappearance of the Infinitive in Greek," Columbia, M. A. Thesis, 1952.

J. Macris, "An Analysis of English Loanwords in New York City Greek," Columbia, 1956.

A. Koutsoudas, "Verb Morphology of Modern Greek: A Descriptive Analysis," Michigan, 1961.

D. G. Moutsos, "A Stratification of a Segment of the Modern Greek Vocabulary," Chicago, 1963.

D. Sotiropoulos, "Noun Morphology of Modern Demotic Greek: A Descriptive Analysis," Michigan, 1963.

A. A. Katranides, "Conditional Constructions in Modern Greek: A Transformational Grammar," Indiana, 1965.

P. D. Seaman, "Modern Greek and American English in Contact: A Socio-Linguistic Investigation of Greek-American Bilingualism in Chicago," Indiana, 1965.

Irene Philippaki Warburton, "On the Verb in Modern Greek," Indiana, 1966.

Hungarian

T. A. Sebeok, "Finnish and Hungarian Case Systems: Their Form and Function," Princeton, 1945.

P. E. Szamek, "The Eastern American Dialect of Hungarian: An Analytical Study," Princeton, 1947.

W. J. Nemser, "The Interpretation of English Stops and Interdental Fricatives by Native Speakers of Hungarian," Columbia, 1961.

G. Bayerle, "A Detailed Register of the District of Novigrad of 1870," Columbia, 1966.

M.A. Theses on Hungarian

R. Austerlitz, "Phonemic Analysis of Hungarian," Columbia, 1950.
F. S. Jukász, "Constructive Features in Hungarian," Columbia, 1961.
J. Lázár, "Roumanian Loanwords in Hungarian," Columbia, 1962.
L. A. Rice, "Some Rules of Hungarian Vocalization," Indiana, 1965.

X

The following recommendations concern the promotion of graduate instruction and of research in the East Central and Southeast European (here designated as *area*) languages:

Graduate instruction

1. The introduction of area language courses should be encouraged in universities which are in any way involved in the development of East European studies.

2. Slavic departments with a strong commitment to Russian and Slavic literatures should be encouraged and advised to develop linguistic courses of a comparative character or pertaining to at least one Slavic language of the area.

3. Problems pertaining to the Balkan league should be investigated in all their aspects. The Balkan Center at the University of Chicago could be the logical place for the promotion of various facets of a Balkan program. Among its functions should be teaching, research, and publications.

4. Existing exchange programs with East European countries should be broadened to serve the needs of students and faculty.

5. Summer language programs of all types should be explored.

Research

1. There is a need for contrastive grammars prepared by linguists and stressing points of similarity between the area languages and Russian in the case of the Slavic languages, and between the area languages and English in the case of the non-Slavic languages. A beginning has been made in Hungarian and Greek.

2. Adequate scholarly dictionaries (of modest size) should be prepared for all languages of the area. Such dictionaries are presently in preparation for Serbo-Croatian-English (by Benson) and Slovenian-English (by Paternost).

3. Linguistic studies could be promoted to deal with diglossia, contact languages, and problems of linguistic interference. Some of these problems can be efficiently investigated at centers which are strong in linguistics of the area.

4. The fate and diffusion of the area languages in the United States can be studied by American linguists in conjunction with other specialists. Such studies would have a bearing on sociology, history of immigrant groups, development of rural and urban centers, cultural separatism, and acculturation. They would open new avenues for interdisciplinary research.

5. Special outlines (monographs and books) could be prepared to deal with the history of the literary languages of the area. Such outlines should also have introductions on the national and cultural developments of the respective countries insofar as these are connected with the history of the literary languages. These problems have been inadequately treated in Eastern Europe.

17/ SURVEY OF WEST AND SOUTH SLAVIC LANGUAGES

HOWARD I. ARONSON
University of Chicago

SCOPE

The present report has as its goal the determination of the nature and extent of offerings of instruction in American universities in the West Slavic (Polish, Czech, Slovak, Upper Sorbian, Lower Sorbian) and South Slavic (Bulgarian, Serbo-Croatian, Macedonian, and Slovenian) languages. Among the questions investigated are enrollment, regularity of offerings, goals, prerequisites, staffing, text materials, and integration into broader programs of Slavic and/or area studies. The basis for the report is the responses received from questionnaires sent to 166 addresses. The selection of potential informants was made first of all on the basis of the listing of foreign language offerings in the 1966 Directory issue of *PMLA*. In addition, state foreign language coordinators and editors of state foreign language bulletins were questioned, as were a large number of institutions listed in the *PMLA* directory as offering Russian. Of the responding institutions, thirty-six offered instruction in the relevant languages. There are probably about ten other institutions from which no response was received which also offer instruction in these languages.

It must be borne in mind that the present survey is concerned only with courses which have as their main goal the acquisition by the student of one or more of the four language skills: reading, writing, understanding, and speaking. Specifically excluded are those courses where the linguistic analysis of a given language is the main goal.

411

LANGUAGES OFFERED

Language instruction is offered currently in Polish, Serbo-Croatian, Czech, Bulgarian, Slovenian, and Slovak. No formal language instruction is offered in Upper Sorbian, Lower Sorbian, or Macedonian, although courses in the linguistic structure of all these languages are given.

Table 1 shows the number of institutions offering each of the relevant languages. Data is for 1965–67. Perhaps surprising is the relatively low

TABLE 1

Language	No. of Institutions	Percent
Polish	33	35
Serbo-Croatian	29	30
Czech	20	21
Bulgarian	9	10
Slovenian	3	3
Slovak	1	1
	95	100

position of Czech. The reason for this may be the small number of Czechs in the field of Slavic languages, since, as will be seen below, the vast majority of teachers of West and South Slavic languages (with the exception of Bulgarian) are native speakers of the language taught. This fact gives us an interesting insight into the history of the development of the teaching of these languages in the United States. There appears to be a direct correlation between the extent to which a given language is offered and the number of native speakers of that language who have entered the field of Slavic languages and literatures.

COURSE OFFERINGS

The ensuing discussion is based on the data from tables 3–8. For each institution the following information is given: (1) number of years of the language offered; (2) number of contact hours per week; (3) frequency of offering (1 = every year, 2 = every other year, 3 = every third year); (4) year first offered (if since 1959; the number is the first half of the academic year, e.g., 60 means academic year 1960–61); (5) major goals of the course (the order is significant only if preceded by the numbers 1, 2, etc.; courses with only one major goal have that goal underlined); (6) the basic methodology used in teaching ("G-T" stands for grammar-translation and "A-L" for audio-

TABLE 2
DISTRIBUTION OF LANGUAGES BY INSTITUTION

Institution	Pol.	S-Cr.	Czech	Bulg.	Sloven.	Slovak	Total
Boston Coll.		x					1
Boston Univ.	x						1
Brown			x	x			2
California (Berkeley)	x	x	x	x			4
UCLA	x	x	x				3
Chicago	x	x	x	x	x		5
Colorado	x	x	x	x			4
Columbia	x	x	x	x		x	5
Cornell		x	x				2
Duke	x						1
Florida State		x	x				2
Harvard	x	x	x				3
Holy Family	x						1
Illinois	x	x					2
Indiana	x	x	x	x	x		5
Kansas	x	x					2
Madonna	x						1
Massachusetts	x						1
Michigan	x	x					2
Minnesota	x	x					2
Nebraska			x				1
CCNY	x						1
SUNY (Buffalo)	x						1
North Carolina	x	x					2
Ohio State	x	x					2
Pennsylvania State	x	x					2
Pennsylvania	x	x		x			3
Pittsburgh	x	x					2
Portland State	x	x	x				3
Princeton	x						1
So. California		x			x		2
Stanford	x						1
Syracuse		x	x	x			3
Texas		x	x				2
Texas A. and M.			x				1
Tulane		x					1
Vanderbilt	x	x	x				3
Washington	x	x	x	x			4
Wayne State	x						1
Western Reserve	x	x	x				3
Wisconsin (Madison)	x	x	x				3
Wisconsin (Milwaukee)	x						1
Yale	x	x	x	x			4

lingual); (7) prerequisites for the course ("Russ" means "knowledge of Russian"; in those instances where there is a prerequisite, the additional words "or consent of instructor or department" should be understood). Columns 8 and 9 really belong with the next set of tables (students and requirements), but, for reasons which will be made clear below, they are included with this table. Column 8 indicates the percentage of students taking the course who have previously studied Russian; column 9 indicates the percentage of students taking the course who, because of family background, can be considered to have some prior background in the language from their homes.

A quick perusal of columns 8 and 9 should readily convince one that the South and West Slavic languages present a picture that differs greatly from the more usual languages offered in the university, for example, Spanish, French, German, and Russian. In most instances a majority of the students have previously studied Russian (or another Slavic language) or have heard the language spoken at home. Yet, again, in most instances, at least officially, the prerequisites to the course (column 7) do not take this into consideration. It is also clear that in a class where 50 percent of the students have previously studied Russian and 50 percent have not, one of the two groups will suffer: either those who have studied Russian will be held back, or those without such a background may not be able to keep up with the rest of the class. From the point of view of a Slavicist, it may seem that the solution to this problem is simple: make a background in Russian a prerequisite to the study of the West and South Slavic languages. This is the case at many institutions. But it must be borne in mind that for a student of Balkan history, or Habsburg history, or of German-Polish relations, or of similar areas of government or political science, economics, geography, etc., Russian may not be the most necessary language. If we are to develop Central and Southeast European studies independently of Russian studies, we must provide a way for potential specialists in the field to acquire the languages without insisting that they learn Russian first. One of the solutions to this problem would be to establish courses in Polish, Czech, Serbo-Croatian, Bulgarian, etc., specifically designed for social scientists without a background in Russian at precisely those institutions where programs in Central and/or Southeast European studies are already offered. However, the likelihood of Slavic departments inaugurating such programs must be regarded as remote. It will be more realistic to hope for the establishment of such courses in special summer workshops, especially workshops covering Slavic area courses. The creation of programmed textbooks for self-instruction would be another way of meeting this problem.

TABLE 3
Polish

	No. Yrs. (1)	Hrs./Wk. (2)	Frequency (3)	First Offered (4)	Goals (5)	Methodology (6)	Prereq. (7)	Percentage Knowing Russ. (8)	Percentage of Polish Background (9)	Notes (10)
California (Berkeley)	1	10	1	59	1 *Read* 2 Comp 3 Conv	G-T	none	90	10–20	
	2	4	1	59						
UCLA	1	4	2	68	*Read* Conv Comp Ling	G-T A-L	none	75	10–30	
	2	4	2							
Chicago	1	3	1	52	1 *Read* 2 Conv 3 Comp	G-T	none	50	20	
	2	3	1							
Colorado	1	5	1	59	1 *Read*	G-T	none	90	10	
	2	3	1							
Columbia	1	2½	1	59	1 *Read* 2 Conv 3 Comp	G-T	none	50–75	25	3d yr = Readings in Mod Pol Lit
	2	2½	1							
Duke	1	3			*Read*	G-T	2 yrs Russ	100	0	Inaugurated 1967–68
Harvard	1	4	1	59	1 *Read*	G-T	none	80	10–20	
	2	4	1	65						
Holy Family	1	8	1	60	*Read* Conv	A-L	UG	0	75	
	2	6								

TABLE 3 (continued)

	No. Yrs. (1)	Hrs./Wk. (2)	Frequency (3)	First Offered (4)	Goals (5)	Methodology (6)	Prereq. (7)	Percentage Knowing Russ. (8)	Percentage of Polish Background (9)	Notes (10)
Illinois	1	4	1	63	1 Read		none	G. 100	UG. 100	Methodology: 1st yr A-L, 2d yr G-T; no grad credit
	2	4	1		2 Conv					
Indiana	1	5	1	59	1 Read	G-T	Jr yr status	80	20-30	2d yr inaugurated 1965
	2	3	1		2 Comp					
					3 Conv					
Kansas	1	3½	1	63	Read	G-T	none	75	15-20	Russ recommended
Mass.	1	3	2	66	1 Read	A-L	none	25	90	Future PQ: Background in any other foreign lang
	2	3	2		2 Comp					
					3 Conv.					
Madonna		5	1	65	1 Conv	A-L	none	0	90	Offered only in summer sessions
					2 Read					
Minnesota	1	5	1	63	1 Conv	A-L	UG	10	50	3d yr offered when feasible
	2	3	1		2 Read					
	3	3			3 Comp					
CCNY	1	3		66	1 Read	—	Jr.-Sr. status	100	20	
					2 Comp					
					3 Conv					
SUNY (Buffalo)	1	4	1	63	1 Conv	A-L	none	10	80	
	2	3	1		2 Read					
					3 Comp					
North Carolina	1	3	2	64	1 Read	A-L	none	100	0	Russ recommended
					2 Ling					

TABLE 3 (continued)

	No. Yrs. (1)	Hrs./Wk. (2)	Frequency (3)	First Offered (4)	Goals (5)	Methodology (6)	Prereq. (7)	Percentage Knowing Russ. (8)	Percentage of Polish Background (9)	Notes (10)
Ohio State	1	3	2	62	1 Read	G-T	Russ	95	20	Contrastive analysis of Pol and Russ
	2	3	2		2 Conv					
					3 Comp					
Penn. State	1	3	2	61	1 Read	A-L	none	20	30	Knowledge of another Slav lang is helpful
	2	3		66	2 Conv					
Pittsburgh	1	4	2	62	1 Read	G-T	none	50	40	PQ: For Slav majors, Intermed Russ; for others, none
	2	4	2		2 Conv					
					3 Comp					
Penn.	1	4	1	61	1 Read	1st yr A-L	none	80	1st yr 0	
	2	4	1		2 Conv	2nd yr G-T			2nd yr 50	
					2 Comp					
Portland State	1	5	3	65	Read	A-L	none	50	25	3d yr inaugurated 1967–68
	2	5	3		Conv	G-T				
	3	3			Comp					
					Lit					
Princeton	1	6		66	Read	G-T	none	50	0	
Stanford	1qtr	5		61	1 Read	G-T	none	60	20	
					2 Conv					
Vanderbilt	1	3	2	62	Read	G-T	Grad	100	0	
Washington	1	5	2	61	Read	A-L	2 yrs Russ	75	25	
	2	5		64	Conv					

TABLE 3 (continued)

	No. Yrs. (1)	Hrs./Wk. (2)	Frequency (3)	First Offered (4)	Goals (5)	Methodology (6)	Prereq. (7)	Percentage Knowing Russ. (8)	Percentage of Polish Background (9)	Notes (10)
Wayne State	1	4	2	59	1 Read	A-L	UG	15	85	
	2	4	2		2 Conv					
	3	4			3 Comp					
Western Reserve	1	2/	1	64	Read	G-T	none	90	60	
					Conv					
					Comp					
Wisconsin (Madison)	1	4	1	59	Read	A-L	none	most	1.25	2-yr UG 4-skills course
	2	4	1	59	Conv				2.50	
					Comp					
	½				1 Read	G-T	3 yrs Slav lg.	100	10	1-sem course for grad students desiring reading knowledge
Wisconsin (Milwaukee)	1	4	1		1 Conv	G-T	none	50	50	Offered since 1932
	2	3								
	3	2								
Yale	1	5	1	61	Read	A-L	1 yr Russ	100	0	
					Conv					

TABLE 4
SERBO-CROATIAN

	No. Yrs. (1)	Hrs./Wk. (2)	Frequency (3)	First Offered (4)	Goals (5)	Methodology (6)	Prereq. (7)	Percentage Knowing Russ. (8)	Percentage of S-Cr. Background (9)	Notes (10)
Boston College	1	3	1	65	Read	G-T	none	100	0	Russ recommended
	2	3	1		Conv					
					Comp Lit					
California (Berkeley)	5qtrs			65	Read	G-T	none	50	33	1st qtr 10 hrs/wk; other 4 qtrs 4 hrs/wk
					Conv	A-L				
UCLA	1	5	2	62	Read	G-T	none	90	5	
	2	4	2		Conv					
					Comp					
Chicago	1	3	1	59	1 *Read*	A-L	none	75	25	A 1-qtr intensive reading course is also offered
					2 Conv					
Colorado	1	5	2	66	*Read*	G-T	none	90	10	
	2	3	2							
Columbia	1	5	1	59	1 *Conv*	A-L	none	50	0	3d yr readings in S-C lit also offered
	2	5	1		2 Read					
					3 Comp					
Cornell	1	3		62	Read	A-L	Russ	90	15	Advanced S-C on demand
					Conv					
Florida State	3	3	1	65	1 *Read*	G-T	none	80	0	
					2 *Comp*	A-L				
					3 Conv					

TABLE 4 (continued)

	No. Yrs. (1)	Hrs./Wk. (2)	Frequency (3)	First Offered (4)	Goals (5)	Methodology (6)	Prereq. (7)	Percentage Knowing Russ. (8)	Percentage of S-Cr. Background (9)	Notes (10)
Harvard	½	4	1	59	*1 Read* 2 Comp 3 Conv	G-T	none	85	5	
Illinois	1	4	2	62	Read Conv	A-L	none	100	0	No grad credit. 2d yr inaugurated 1967–68
Indiana	1 2	10 6	1 1	59	Read Conv Comp	G-T A-L	none	30	10–20	
Kansas	1	3	1	62	Read Conv	G-T	none	95	0	
Michigan	1 2	4 4	2 2	62	*1 Read* 2 Conv Comp	G-T A-L	Russ	70	30	
Minnesota	1	5	1	65	*1 Conv* 2 Read	A-L	none	50	25	
North Carolina	1 2		2 2	65	*1 Read* 2 Comp 3 Conv	G-T	none	80	0	
Ohio State	1 2	3 3	2 2	63	*1 Read* 2 Conv 3 Comp	G-T A-L	1 yr Russ	100	4	
Penn. State	1	3	2	62	Read Conv	A-L	none	50	33	

	No. Yrs. (1)	Hrs./Wk. (2)	Frequency (3)	First Offered (4)	Goals (5)	Methodology (6)	Prereq. (7)	Percentage Knowing Russ. (8)	Percentage of S-Cr. Background (9)	Notes (10)
Penn.	1	3	1	60	1 *Read*	A-L	none	90	0	2d yr inaugurated 1967–68
	2	3			2 Conv					
Pittsburgh	1	4	2	59	1 *Conv*	A-L		50	50	PQ: For Slav majors, 2 yrs Russ; for others, none
	2	4	2		2 Read					
					3 Ling					
Portland State	1	4	1	65	1 *Conv*	A-L	none	20	20	
	2	4	1		2 Read					
	3	3	1		3 Comp					
Southern Cal.	1	4		66	Read	A-L	none	50	25	
	2	4			Conv					
					Comp					
Syracuse	1	3	2	64	Read	—	none	80	20	
	2	3	2		Conv					
					Comp					
Texas	1	5		65	1 *Read*	—	none	100	0	
					2 Conv					
					3 Comp					
Tulane	1	2		64	Read	G-T	Grad Russ	100	0	
					Conv					
Vanderbilt	1	3		66	*Read*	G-T	none	100	0	Russ. recommended
Washington	1	5	2	62	Read	A-L	2yrs Russ	75	25	2d yr inaugurated 1965–66
	2	5			Conv					
Western Reserve	1	2	1	65	Read	G-T		50	60	PQ: Permission of Slavic Dept
					Conv	A-L				
Wisconsin	½	3	1	61	*Read*	G-T	3yrs Slav lg.	100	0	

TABLE 5
Czech

	No. Yrs. (1)	Hrs./Wk. (2)	Frequency (3)	First Offered (4)	Goals (5)	Methodology (6)	Prereq. (7)	Percentage Knowing Russ. (8)	Percentage of Czech Background (9)	Notes (10)
Brown	1	2	2	61	Read Ling	G-T	Grad Russ	100	0	
California (Berkeley)	1	10	1	63	1 *Read*	G-T	none	70–80	20	
	2	4	1		2 Conv					
					3 Comp					
UCLA	1	5	2	65	Read	G-T	none	99	10–20	
	2	4	2		Conv	A-L				
					Comp					
					Ling					
Chicago	1	3	1	61	Read	G-T	none	90	10	
	2	1								2d yr on demand
Colorado	1	5	2	59	Read	G-T	none	90	10	
Columbia	1	3	1	59	Read	G-T	none	60	20	
	2	3			Conv					3d yr by special request
Cornell	2	3	1		Read	G-T	Russ	90	15	Course offered 1960–61 to 1963–64
	1	3			Conv					
Florida State	2	3	1	65	1 *Read*	G-T	none	100	30	
					2 Comp					
					3 Conv					
Harvard	1	5	1	59	1 *Read*	A-L	none	50	5	
Indiana	2	3	1		2 Comv					
					3 Comp					

TABLE 5 (continued)

	No. Yrs. (1)	Hrs./Wk. (2)	Frequency (3)	First Offered (4)	Goals (5)	Methodology (6)	Prereq. (7)	Percentage Knowing Russ. (8)	Percentage of Czech Background (9)	Notes (10)
Nebraska	1	3	1	59	Read	G-T	none	0	50–60	Evening extension courses
	2	3	1		Conv					
	3	3	1		Comp					
Portland State	1	4	1	64	Read	G-T	none	25	25	
	2	4	1		Comp	A-L				
	3	3	1		Conv.					
					Lit					
Syracuse	1	3		65	*1 Read*	G-T	Russ	100	0	
					2 Comp					
					3 Conv					
Texas	3				*1 Read*	G-T	none	25	75	Offered since 1915
					2 Conv	A-L				
					3 Comp					
Texas A and M	1	3		65	*1 Conv*	A-L	none	2	70	
	2	3			2 Read					
					3 Comp					
Vanderbilt	1	3		65	Read	G-T	none	100	0	Russ recommended
Washington	1	5	2	64	Read	A-L	2yrs Russ	75	25	
	2	5	2		Conv					
Western Reserve	1	2½		67	Read	G-T	none	50	80	
					Conv	A-L				
Wisconsin	½	3		65	Read	G-T	3yrs Slav lg	100	0	
Yale	1	5		61	Read	A-L	Russ	99	10	2d yr on demand
	2			65	Conv					

TABLE 6
BULGARIAN

	No. Yrs. (1)	Hrs./Wk. (2)	Frequency (3)	First Offered (4)	Goals (5)	Methodology (6)	Prereq. (7)	Percentage Knowing Russ. (8)	Percentage of Bulgarian Background (9)	Notes (10)
Brown	1	2			1 Read 2 Ling	G-T	Grad Slav major	100	0	Inaugurated 1967–68
Chicago	1 qtr	3	2	62	Read	G-T	Grad 3 yrs Russ	100	0	
Columbia	1	5	2		Read	G-T	Russ	100	0	Combination of language and literature; inaugurated 1967; first offered in 1920s
Indiana	1	5	2	59	1 Read 2 Comp 3 Conv	G-T	none	80	20–30	
Penn.	1	2	1		Read	G-T	Russ	100	0	
Syracuse	1	3		65	1 Conv 2 Read 3 Comp	A-L	none	90	10	Offered 1959–60 to 1963–64
Washington	1	5		65	Read Conv	A-L	2 yrs Russ	75	25	
Yale	1			63	Read Conv	A-L	Russ	100	0	1st sem – 5 hrs/wk 2nd sem – 3 hrs/wk

TABLE 7
SLOVENIAN

	No. Yrs. (1)	Hrs./Wk. (2)	Frequency (3)	First Offered (4)	Goals (5)	Methodology (6)	Prereq. (7)	Percentage Knowing Russ. (8)	Percentage of Slovenian Background (9)	Notes (10)
Chicago	1 qtr	3		65	Read	G-T	Grad 3 yrs Russ	100	20	
Indiana	1	5		65	1 Read 2 Conv	A-L	none	100	0	
Southern Cal.	1	—		66	Read Comp	G-T	none	50	0	Directed readings

TABLE 8
SLOVAK

	No. Yrs. (1)	Hrs./Wk. (2)	Frequency (3)	First Offered (4)	Goals (5)	Methodology (6)	Prereq. (7)	Percentage Knowing Russ. (8)	Percentage of Slovak Background (9)	Notes (10)
Columbia	1	3	1		Read	G-T	none	0	50	Offered since 1930s

Another problem that exists concerns the question of goals. A very large percentage of the institutions offering these languages attempt to train their students in the traditional four skills — reading, composition, conversation, and comprehension. (Some, to be sure, place a greater emphasis on one or another of these skills, but nonetheless all four enter into the goals of the course.) The question then arises whether one can acquire reasonable speaking, reading, and writing skill in the amount of time a student has to devote to these languages.

TABLE 9

| | Number of Institutions | |
	Accepting	Not Accepting
Polish	14	17
Serbo-Croatian	12	17
Czech	6	10
Bulgarian	1	5
Slovenian	0	3
Slovak	0	1

Since a large number of institutions offer only one year of a given language and, in those where two years are offered, there is a sharp drop in enrollment in the second year, it is most likely that the four-skills approach would yield a lesser result than a one-skill approach. This is a question that calls for serious discussion from all concerned with the field.

If one checks the enrollment figures in tables 12–17, one will see that the majority of students studying these languages are graduate students in the fields of Slavic languages and literatures, general linguistics, and history. The justification for a four-skills approach seems to be even weaker, since the main need of these graduate students is to acquire the ability to read scholarly literature (and belles lettres) in their fields. The textbooks that are available are, for the most part, modeled after those used for first-year French, Russian, or German courses; that is, in addition to not taking the student's knowledge of Russian into consideration, they are designed basically for college freshmen, not for graduate students.

Some institutions have attempted to meet part of the problem by inaugurating intensive one-quarter or one-semester courses in a language, with a prerequisite of three or four years of Russian. Such courses are devoted solely to reading scholarly texts in the language in question, stressing vocabulary recognition and dictionary use.

Undergraduate enrollment in these languages tends to be made up largely of students whose families come from Poland, Czechoslovakia, Yugoslavia, or Bulgaria. Such students present special problems of their own. All too often they have to unlearn much of what they have heard at home. At the start of the course they tend to be far ahead of the other students; by the end, they tend to lag behind. The problems of teaching such students have received little attention in the past but should be considered in the future.

TABLE 10

| | Number of Institutions | |
	Accepting	Not Accepting
Polish	14	14
Serbo-Croatian	6	20
Czech	4	12
Bulgarian	1	4
Slovenian	1	2
Slovak	0	1

STUDENTS AND REQUIREMENTS

Tables 12–17 give the enrollments (1966–67) in language courses at individual institutions (column 1 in numbers with decimal points, the first number is the year of the course; the second, the number of students — for example, 2.4–5 means four or five students in the second-year course); the status of the majority of the students in the class (column 2; "UG" represents undergraduate, "G" — graduate, and the equal sign indicates that the class is about equally divided between graduates and undergraduates); the major fields of these students, or the reason for taking the course, are indicated in column 3. The following three columns indicate foreign language requirements which can be met by taking the language in question. Column 4 indicates whether or not the language meets an undergraduate foreign language requirement; column 5, whether it meets a graduate reading examination requirement; and column 6, whether it meets a Slavic department requirement for a second or third Slavic language. ("WP" means "with permission.") The last two columns indicate on what level a student can major in a given language (column 7) and on what levels he can minor in it (column 8).

One of the most striking facts comes from the enrollment figures. There is regularly a sharp drop in registration between the first- and second-year courses at those institutions where more than one year of the language is offered. Another interesting fact is that for Czech and Polish the number of institutions reporting an enrollment predominantly of graduate students is about equal to the number indicating a primarily undergraduate enrollment, while in the cases of the South Slavic languages, graduate enrollment predominates.

The overwhelming majority of students taking these languages are specializing in Slavic languages and literatures or in the social sciences

TABLE 11

| | Number of Institutions | | | | | |
| | Major | | | | Minor | |
	AB	MA	PhD	AB	MA	PhD
Polish	5	8	6	8	14	12
Serbo-Croatian	4	5	7	7	13	15
Czech	3	5	5	8	8	7
Bulgarian	0	0	1	2	4	3
Slovenian	0	0	0	1	2	2
Slovak	0	0	0	0	0	1

(mainly in history). On the undergraduate level there is a greater likelihood that a student studying one of these languages has been exposed to that language at home; that is, he is of South or West Slavic background.

Most institutions will not accept the South and West Slavic languages as meeting undergraduate foreign language requirements. These figures are summarized in table 9. In many institutions, the recognition of a given language as meeting undergraduate degree requirements allows students with a background in the language to fulfil the requirement by passing a proficiency examination.

Most institutions do not accept these languages for graduate reading examinations (table 10).

Requirements for a second and/or third Slavic language set up by departments can, almost without exception, be met by these languages.

Just as the majority of students studying the West and South Slavic languages are on the graduate level, so the majority of formal programs in these languages ("majors" and "minors") are on the graduate level. Table 11 summarizes columns 7 and 8 of tables 12–17.

TEXT MATERIALS

The following lists record the textbooks, readers, and dictionaries currently used by teachers of the languages under consideration. They are not intended to be a complete listing of all pedagogical material available.

TABLE 12
POLISH

	Enrollment (1)	Status (2)	Source (3)	UG FL Req. (4)	Grad. Read. Exam (5)	Slav. Dep. Req. (6)	Major (7)	Minor (8)
California (Berkeley)	no information	G	Slav	yes	no	yes	MA PhD	AB MA PhD
UCLA	1.10 2.4–5	=	Slav SocSci Family background	yes	no	yes	no	no
Chicago	1.7 2.9	G	Slav Soc-Sci	yes	no	yes	MA PhD	PhD
Colorado	1.7 2.5	G	Slav	yes	WP	yes	no	MA PhD
Columbia	1.8–10 2.2–3 3.4	G	Slav Hist Govt UG	yes	yes	yes	MA PhD	MA PhD
Duke	12–15	=	Slav Hist Govt	no	yes	yes	no	MA
Harvard	1.5–10 2.1–3	G	1 Slav 2 Russ Area 3 Linguistics	no	no	yes	MA PhD	MA PhD
Holy Family	5	UG	UG	yes	—	—	no	BA
Illinois	1.6 2.5	G	Slav	no	no	yes	no	PhD
Indiana	1.7–8 2.3–4	G	Slav Ling Hist	no	yes	yes	PhD	AB MA PhD
Kansas	6–10	G	Slav Hist Govt Slav-area	no	no	yes	AB	AB MA
Madonna	3–9	UG	Education	no	—	—	no	AB
Massachusetts			UG	yes	yes	yes	AB MA	—
Minnesota	1.8 2.4	UG	Hist	yes	no	—	no	no
CCNY	7–12	UG	Slav	no	no	no	no	no
SUNY (Buffalo)	1.25 2.10	UG	Slav Ling Soc-Sci	yes	yes	yes	AB	AB
North Carolina	8	UG	Slav Hist Govt	no	yes	yes	no	MA PhD
Ohio State	18	G	Slav Ling Family background	no	yes	yes	no	AB MA PhD

TABLE 12 (continued)

	Enrollment (1)	Status (2)	Source (3)	UG FL Req. (4)	Grad. Read. Exam (5)	Slav. Dep. Req. (6)	Major (7)	Minor (8)
Michigan	1.14 2.4	1-UG 2-=	Slav Ling Other	yes	no	yes	MA	no
Penn. State	1.10–15 2.2–5	UG G	Slav Other	yes	yes	yes	no	MA
Penn.	1.8 2.4	G	1 Slav 2 Ling 3 Hist	yes	yes	yes	MA PhD	MA PhD
Pittsburgh	23	G UG Eve	1 Slav 2 Govt 3 Other	no	WP	yes	no	—
Portland State	1.7 2.6	UG	Slav Ling Hist Govt Eng	no	no	yes	no	AB MA
Princeton	5	=	Slav Ling	no	no	yes	no	MA PhD
Stanford	10–12	G	Slav Ling Participants in Stanford-Warsaw-Exchange	no	yes	yes	no	no
Vanderbilt	9	G	1 Slav 2 Ling	no	no	yes	no	MA
Washington	1.7 2.5	G	Slav Ling Hist Govt UG	no	no	yes	no	no
Wayne State	38	UG	Slav, Social Work; FL requirement	yes	yes	yes	AB MA	AB MA
Western Reserve	6	G	Slav	no	no	yes	no	no
Wisconsin (Madison)	1.8 2.2	UG	Slav, native background	yes	yes	yes	AB MA PhD	PhD
Wisconsin (Milwaukee)	1.15 2.8 3.8	UG	Slav Other	yes	yes	yes	no	no
Yale	6	G	Slav	no	no	yes	no	PhD

TABLE 13
SERBO-CROATIAN

	Enroll-ment (1)	Status (2)	Source (3)	UG FL Req. (4)	Grad. Read. Exam. (5)	Slav. Dep. Req. (6)	Major (7)	Minor (8)
Boston Coll.	1.5 2.3	UG	Slav	no	no	—	no	no
California (Berkeley)	6–10	=	Slav Ling Anthro	yes	yes	yes	AB MA PhD	AB MA PhD
UCLA	20	UG	Slav Other	yes	no	yes	no	PhD
Chicago	3	G	Slav Hist Int Rel	no	no	yes	MA PhD	MA PhD
Colorado	1.7 2.4	G	Slav	yes	WP	yes	no	MA PhD
Columbia	5–6	G	Slav Econ Soc Int Aff	no	no	yes	no	no
Cornell	7	G	Slav Other	yes	yes	yes	MA PhD	MA PhD
Florida State	5–7	=	Slav	yes	yes	yes	AB AM PhD	AB AM PhD
Harvard	7	G	Slav, Ling Econ, Govt Hist, Anthro	yes	yes	yes	AB AM PhD	AB AM PhD
Illinois	8	G	Slav	no	no	yes	no	no
Indiana	4–8	G	Slav Hist	no	no	yes	PhD	MA PhD
Kansas	5	G	Slav Ling	no	no	yes	no	no
Michigan	1.8 2.3	G	Slav	yes	no	yes	PhD	—
Minnesota	8	=	Misc	yes	no	no	no	no
North Carolina	1.6 2.1	=	Slav Other	no	no	yes	no	MA PhD
Ohio State	1.15 2.7	G	1 Slav 2 Ling	no	WP	yes	no	AB MA PhD
Penn. State	7	=	Slav Other	yes	no	yes	no	no
Pennsylvania	6	G	Slav	no	no	yes	PhD	MA PhD
Pittsburgh	6–10	G	Slav Local community	no	WP	yes	no	—

TABLE 13 (continued)

	Enroll-ment (1)	Status (2)	Source (3)	UG FL Req. (4)	Grad. Read. Exam (5)	Slav. Dep. Req. (6)	Major (7)	Minor (8)
Portland State	1.15 2.12 3.13	UG	various	yes	no	yes	AB MA	AB
Southern Cal.	8	=	Slav Other	no	no	yes	no	AB MA
Syracuse	5	G.	Slav Other	yes	yes	yes	no	AB MA
Texas	8	G	Slav	yes	yes	yes	no	MA/PhD
Tulane	3–5	G	Slav	no	no	yes	no	no
Vanderbilt	1–10	G	Slav	no	no	yes	no	no
Washington	1.6 2.2	G	Slav Ling Hist Govt UG	no	no	yes	no	no
Western Reserve	6	UG	various	no	no	yes	no	no
Wisconsin	5–6	G	Slav, Ling	no	no	yes	no	PhD
Yale	6	G	Slav	no	no	yes	no	PhD

TABLE 14
CZECH

	Enrollment	Status	Source	UG FL Req.	Grad. Read. Exam Req.	Slav. Dep. Req.	Major	Minor
	(1)	(2)	(3)	(4)	(5)	(6)	(7)	(8)
Brown	8	G	Slav Ling	no	no	yes	MA PhD	AB MA PhD
California (Berkeley)	1.4–6 2.3–5	G	Slav	no	no	yes	AB MA PhD	AB
UCLA	1.10 2.5	=	Slav Family background	yes	no	yes	PhD	PhD
Chicago	4–8	UG	Slav Other	yes	no	yes	MA PhD	MA PhD
Colorado	3	G	Slav	no	no	yes	no	no
Columbia	5	G	Slav Ling Soc Sci	WP	yes	yes	MA PhD	AB(WP) MA PhD
Florida State	3	G	Slav	no	no	yes	MA	AB/MA
Indiana	4–8	G	Slav Ling Soc Sci	no	yes	yes	no	AB MA PhD
Nebraska	1.12–46 2.12–25 3.6–10		Evening extension class Family background					
Portland State	9	UG	Soc Sci; Part of area program	yes	no	yes	AB	AB MA
Syracuse	3	UG	Slav Ling	yes	yes	no	no	AB MA
Texas	13	UG	Native background	yes	yes	yes	AB	AB AM PhD
Texas A & M	1.16 2.5–12	UG	various	yes	WP	no	no	no
Vanderbilt	1–10	G	Slav	no	no	yes	no	no
Washington	6	G	Slav Ling Hist Govt UG	no	no	yes	no	no
Western Reserve	7	UG	Slav	no	no	no	no	no
Wisconsin	5	G	Slav	no	no	yes	no	PhD
Yale	5	=	Slav	no	no	yes	no	no

TABLE 15
BULGARIAN

	Enrollment (1)	Status (2)	Source (3)	UG FL Req. (4)	Grad. Read. Exam (5)	Slav. Dep. Req. (6)	Major (7)	Minor (8)
Chicago	5	G	1 Slav 2 Ling	no	no	yes	no	MA PhD
Columbia	2	G	Slav Educ	no	no	yes	no	PhD
Indiana	3–4	G	Slav Ling Hist	no	yes	yes	PhD	AB MA PhD
Penn.	5	G	Slav	no	no	no	no	MA PhD
Syracuse	8	G	Slav Other	yes	WP	yes	no	BA MA
Washington	5	G	Slav Ling Soc Sci UG	no	no	yes	no	no
Yale	2–4	G	Slav Ling Russ area	no	no	yes	no	no

TABLE 16
SLOVENIAN

	Enrollment (1)	Status (2)	Source (3)	UG FL Req. (4)	Grad. Read. Exam (5)	Slav. Dep. Req. (6)	Major (7)	Minor (8)
Chicago	5	G	Slav	no	no	yes	no	PhD
Indiana	5–10	G	Slav	no	yes	yes	no	MA PhD
Southern Cal.	6	=	Slav Other	no	no	yes	no	AB MA

TABLE 17
SLOVAK

	Enrollment		Status	Source	UG FL Req.	Grad. Read. Exam	Slav. Dep. Req.	Major	Minor
	(1)		(2)	(3)	(4)	(5)	(6)	(7)	(8)
Columbia	1–3		=	Native background	no	no	yes	no	PhD

Some interesting differences immediately appear between the text material used for the South and West Slavic languages and those used for French, German, Spanish, and, to a lesser extent, Russian. First, for the Slavic languages there is a much greater reliance upon materials published abroad. In some instances this raises a special problem of accessibility, as the works published in Poland, Czechoslovakia, Yugoslavia, and Bulgaria often go out of print or are difficult to order. Second, there is a real and a serious lack of readers. Many of the teachers questioned indicated that they rely upon Xerox copies of selections from collections of short stories, etc., or use newspaper and magazine articles. Others rely on readers used in the schools of the countries in question. There seems to be a real need for more readers with a full pedagogic apparatus, including notes, vocabulary, accents (where applicable), questions for discussion, etc. While dictionaries are available for all the languages, most teachers expressed dissatisfaction with them. The one exception was the Kościuszko Foundation Polish dictionary compiled by Bulas, Whitfield, and Thomas. One of the reasons for this dissatisfaction is the fact that, with the exception of the Kościuszko dictionary, all the dictionaries were prepared and published in the West and South Slavic countries and are intended for the use of native speakers of the Slavic language who are learning or reading English. These dictionaries tend not to give grammatical information; accents are often not marked; irregular forms are not given; etc. Whereas these dictionaries may give the principal parts of English verbs, the principal parts of the Slavic verbs are often lacking. All too often only one member of an aspectual pair is given. Forms of the genitive case (where relevant) or plural are not given. It is for this reason, perhaps, that many teachers rely on Soviet-prepared dictionaries such as Tolstoi's *Serbskokhorvatsko-russkii slovar'* or Bernshtein's *Bolgarsko-russkii slovar'*, which meet the criticisms enumerated.

The situation with audio-visual materials is also bad, although improving. A very large number of institutions teach the languages by an audio-lingual method. Most make some use of a language laboratory. But, with few exceptions (see bibliography, below), there are no programmed tape courses to accompany textbooks. Many teachers have the reading selections of the textbook they use recorded on tape, but, as is well known, the language laboratory is not used in the most efficient manner possible when the student is passively sitting and listening to a recording of what he has already read at home and in the classroom. The preparation of audio-visual materials is a very difficult task, one calling for a strong background in the language, in the psychology of learning, and in general and applied linguistics. It is very important, then, that more attention be paid to the production of effective tape materials to accompany textbooks.

POLISH

Textbooks

Bastgen, Z. *Let's Learn Polish.* Warsaw: Wiedza powszechna, 1961.

Birkenmayer, S., and Folejewski, Z. *Introduction to the Polish Language.* New York: Kościuszko Foundation, 1965.

Cienkowski, W. *Gramatyka języka polskiego dla cudzoziemców* (Polish Grammar for Foreigners). Warsaw: Uniwersytet Warszawski, 1966.

Corbridge-Patkaniowska, M. *Teach Yourself Polish.* New York: Roy, n.d.

Gladney, F. Y. *Materials for a Course in First-Year Polish.* Mimeographed. Urbana, Ill., 1963.

Klemensiewicz, Z. *Podstawowe wiadomości z gramatyki języka polskiego* (Basic Information on Polish Grammar). Warsaw: PWN, 1962.

Krotovskaia, Ia., and Gol'dberg, B. *Prakticheskii uchebnik pol'skogo iazyka* (Practical Textbook of Polish). Moscow: ILIIa, 1959.

Patkaniowska, M. *Essentials of Polish Grammar for English-Speaking Students.* Glasgow: Książnica Polska, 1944.

Schenker, A. M. *Beginning Polish.* New Haven: Yale University Press, 1966.

Szymczak, M. *Materiały do lektoratu języka polskiego* (Materials for Instruction in Polish). Warsaw: Uniwersytet Warszawski, 1965.

Teslar, J. A. *A New Polish Grammar,* 4th ed. Edinburgh: Oliver and Boyd, 1944.

Readers

Birkenmayer, S., and Krzyzanowski, J. *A Modern Polish Reader*. (In preparation.)

Kridl, M. *An Anthology of Polish Literature*. New York: Columbia University Press, 1957.

Milska, A. *Pisarze Polscy* (Polish Writers). Warsaw: Wydawn. Związkowe CRZZ, 1963.

Pietrkiewicz, J. *Polish Prose and Verse*. London: University of London, 1956.

Rowiński, C. *Wybór tekstów na użytek lektoratów języka polskiego dla cudzoziemców* (Selection of Texts for the Use of Language Instruction in Polish for Foreigners). Warsaw: Uniwersytet Warszawski, 1964.

Schenker, A. M. *Selected Polish Short Stories*. (In preparation.)

Sufin, S., *et al. Mowa ojczysta, Wypisy z ćwiczeniami, Dla klasy VII* (Native Language, Excerpts with Exercises, for the VII Class). Warsaw: PZWS, 1965.

In addition, selections are taken from the works of J. Andrzejewski M. Dąbrowska, Marek Hlasko, J. Iwaszkiewicz, J. Kaden-Bandrowski, L. Kołakowski, St. J. Lec, and Sł. Mrożek.

Dictionaries

Bulas, K., and Whitfield, F. J. *The Kościuszko Foundation Dictionary*, Vol. I: *English-Polish*. The Hague: Mouton, 1959.

Bulas, K.; Thomas, L. L.; and Whitfield, F. J. *The Kościuszko Foundation Dictionary*, Vol. II: *Polish-English*. The Hague: Mouton, 1961.

Grzebeniowski, T. *Słownik angielsko-polski i polski-angielski* (English-Polish, Polish-English Dictionary). Warsaw: PWN, 1961.

Stanisławski, J. *English-Polish and Polish-English Dictionary*. New York: Roy, n.d.

Tapes

Tapes accompany the textbooks of Schenker and of Birkenmayer and Folejewski.

Czech

Textbooks

Harkins, W. *A Modern Czech Grammar*. New York: King's Crown Press, 1953.

Kučera, H. *The Phonology of Czech*. The Hague: Mouton, 1961.

Kučera, Vl. *Conversational Czech*. Lincoln, Neb., n.d.

————. *Let Us Speak Czech.* Lincoln, Neb., n.d.

Lee, W. R., and Lee, Z. *Teach Yourself Czech.* London: English Universities Press, 1959.

Mikula, B. E. *Progressive Czech (Bohemian).* Chicago: Czechoslovak National Council of America, 1940.

Skrivanek, J. M. *Modern Conversational Czech,* Vol. I. (In preparation.)

Sova, M. *A Practical Czech Course for English-Speaking Students,* 2 vols. Prague: Státní pedagogické nakl., 1961–62.

Readers

Harkins, W. *Anthology of Czech Literature.* New York: King's Crown Press, 1953.

Kilianová, E., and Sirovátka, O. *Čarovné ovoce* (Enchanted Fruits). Prague: SNDK, 1965.

In addition, selections from the works of K. Capek, V. Dyk, V. Hálek, J. Hašek, B. Němcová, J. Neruda, J. Seifert, and J. Vrchlický are used.

Dictionaries

Čermak, A. *Nový kapesní slovník anglicko-český a česko-anglický* (New Pocket English-Czech, Czech-English Dictionary). Trebic: J. Lorenz, n.d.

Hais, K. *Anglicko-český a česko-anglický kapesní slovník* (English-Czech and Czech-English Pocket Dictionary). Prague, 1965.

Osička, A., and Poldauf, I. *Anglicko-český slovník* (English-Czech Dictionary). Prague: ČSAV, 1956.

Poldauf, I. *Česko-anglický slovník* (Czech-English Dictionary). Prague: SPN, 1965.

Procházka, J. *Czech-English and English-Czech Dictionary.* Prague: Orbis, 1952.

SERBO-CROATIAN

Textbooks

Arbuzova, I. V., Dmitriev, P. A.; and Sokal', N. I. *Serbokhorvatskii iazyk* (Serbo-Croatian). Leningrad: Leningradskii universitet, 1965.

Babić, Slavna. *Serbo-Croat for Foreigners.* Belgrade: Kolarac Peoples University, 1964.

Brabec, I.; Hraste, M.; and Žirković, S. *Gramatika hrvatskosrpskoga jezika* (Grammar of the Serbocroatian Language). Zagreb: Školska knjiga, 1961.

Bynum, David E. *Supplements to Beginning Serbocroatian.* Mimeographed. Cambridge, Mass., n.d.

Hodge, Carleton, and Jankovic, J. *Serbo-Croatian, Basic Course.* Vols. 1, 2. Washington, D.C.: Foreign Service Institute, 1965–.

Javarek, Vera, and Sudjić, M. *Teach Yourself Serbo-Croat*. New York: David McKay, 1964.

Leskovar, E., and Pranjić, K. *Hrvatskorsrpski audio-vizuelna globalno-strukturalna metoda* (Serbocroatian Audio-visual Global-structural Method). Zagreb: Jugoton, 1965.

Lord, Albert. *Beginning Serbo-Croatian*. The Hague: Mouton, 1958.

Magner, Thomas F. *Introduction to the Serbocroatian Language*. 2d ed. State College, Pa.: Singidunum Press, 1962.

Partridge, Monica. *Serbo-Croatian Practical Grammar and Reader*. New York: McGraw-Hill, 1964.

Readers

Barac, Antun. *Jugoslavenska književnost* (Yugoslav Literature). Zagreb: Matica Hrvatska, 1959).

Frangeš, I.; Šicel, M.; and Rosandić, D. *Pristup književnom djelu* (Introduction to Literature). Zagreb: Školska knjiga, 1964.

Javarek, Vera. *Serbo-Croatian Prose and Verse*. London: University of London, 1958.

Jurančić, J. *Srbsko in hrvaško berilo za osnovne šole* (Serbian and Croatian Reader for Elementary School). Ljubljana: Mladinska knjiga, 1966.

Kadić, Ante. *Croatian Reader*. The Hague: Mouton, 1960.

Šicel, M., and Rosandić, D. *Pregled književnosti sa čitankom* (Survey of Literature with a Reader). Zagreb: Školska knjiga, 1964.

Zaninović, V. *Čitanka sa pregledom jugoslavenskih književnosti* (Reader with a Survey of Yugoslav Literature). *Za III razred gimnazije; za IV razred gimnazije*. Zagreb: Školska knjiga, 1964.

In addition, many institutions make use of Xerox copies and locally edited editions of Yugoslav literature.

Dictionaries

Cvetanović, Ratomir J. *Rečnik englesko-srpskohrvatski i srpskohrvatsko-engleski sa engleskom gramatikom* (English-Serbocroatian, Serbocroatian-English Dictionary with English Grammar). (Sarajevo: Džepna knjiga, 1954.

Drvodelić, Milan. *Englesko-hrvatski rječnik* (English-Croatian Dictionary). Zagreb: Školska knjiga, 1954.

———. *Hrvatskosrpsko-engleski rječnik* (Serbocroatian-English Dictionary). Zagreb: Školska knjiga, 1953.

Filipović, Rudolf. *Englesko-hrvatski rječnik* (English-Croatian Dictionary). Zagreb: Zora, 1959.

Ristić, Svetomir, and Simić, Ž. *Englesko-srpskohrvatski rečnik* (English-Serbocroatian Dictionary). Belgrade: Prosveta, 1959.

Ristić, Svetomir; Simić, Ž.; and Popović, V. *Enciklopedijski englesko-srpskohrvatski rečnik* (English-Serbocroatian Encyclopedic Dictionary). Belgrade: Prosveta, 1956.

Tolstoi, I. I. *Serbsko-khorvatsko-russkii slovar'* (Serbocroat-Russian Dictionary). Moscow: GIINS, 1958.

Tapes

Audio-vizuelni kurs hrvatsko-srpskog jezika (Audio-visual Course in Serbocroatian). Zagreb University, Institut za fonetiku. Tapes and filmstrips.

Tapes are available to accompany the textbooks of Hodge and Magner.

BULGARIAN

Textbooks

Beaulieux, L. *Grammaire de la langue bulgare.* Paris: Institut d'études slaves, 1950.

Bezikovich, E., and Gordova-Rybal'chenko, T. *Bolgarskii iazyk* (Bulgarian). Leningrad: Izd. Leningradskogo universiteta, 1957.

Ghinina, St.; Nikolova, C.; and Sakazova, L. *A Bulgarian Text-Book for Foreigners.* Sofia: Naouka i Izkoustvo, n.d.

Hodge, C. T., and Associates. *Bulgarian: Basic Course.* Vols. 1, 2. Washington: Foreign Service Institute, 1961.

Lord, A. B. *Beginning Bulgarian.* The Hague: Mouton, 1962.

Stojanov, St. *Gramatika na bŭlgarskiia knizhoven ezik* (Grammar of the Bulgarian Literary Language). Sofia: Nauka i izkustvo, 1964.

Readers

Gornishkova, N.; and Karaleeva, L.; Marinova, M.; Mladenov, C.; Tsoneva, F. *Uchebnik-khristomatiia po bŭlgarski ezik za studenti chuzhdentsi* (Textbook-chrestomathy of Bulgarian for Foreign Students). 2d ed. Sofia: Nauka i izkustvo, 1960.

Hodge, Carleton T., ed. *Bulgarian Reader.* Washington, D.C.: Foreign Service Institute, 1962.

Lord, A. B., and Bynum, D. E. *A Bulgarian Literary Reader.* The Hague: Mouton, 1966.

Pinto, Vivian. *Bulgarian Prose and Verse.* London: University of London, 1957.

Walter, Hilmar, ed. *Wir lernen Bulgarisch sprechen.* Halle (Saale): VEB Verlag Sprache und Literatur, n.d.

Dictionaries

Bernshtein, S. B. *Bolgarsko-russkii slovar'* (Bulgarian-Russian Dictionary). Moscow: Sovetskaia entsiklopediia, 1966.

Chakalov, G.; Liakov, Il.; and Stankov, Zdr. *Bŭlgarsko-angliiski rechnik* (Bulgarian-English Dictionary). Sofia: Nauka i izkustvo, 1961.

Chukalov, S. *Bŭlgarsko-ruski rechnik* (Bulgarian-Russian Dictionary). Sofia: BAN, 1957.

Minkov, M., ed. *Bŭlgarsko-angliiski rechnik* (Bulgarian-English Dictionary). Sofia: Narodna prosveta, 1953.

Tapes, disks

A set of tapes to accompany Hodge's course is available. Records also accompany Walter Hilmar's *Wir lernen Bulgarisch sprechen.*

SLOVENIAN

Textbooks

Bajec, A. *Besedotvorje slovenskega jezika* (Derivation in Slovenian). Vol. 1. Ljubljana: Institut za slovenski jezik, 1950.

Bajec, A.; Kolarič, R.; and Rupel, M. *Slovenska slovnica* (Slovenian Grammar). Ljubljana: DZS, 1956.

Jakopin, F. *Slovene for You.* Ljubljana: Slovenska izseljenska matica, 1962.

Kopčavar, I. and C. *Jezikovna vadnica* (Language Textbook). Ljubljana: DZS, 1965.

Ramovš, F. *Morfologija slovenskega jezika* (Morphology of Slovenian). Ljubljana: DZS, 1952.

Svane, G. O. *Grammatik der slowenischen Schriftsprache.* Copenhagen: Rosenkilde und Bagger, 1958.

Readers

Pirjevec, D.; Mihelič, S.; and Kos, J. *Slovenska književnost* (Slovenian Literature). Vols. 1, 2. Ljubljana: Mladinska knjiga, 1964, 1965).

Dictionaries

Kotnik, J. *Slovene-English Dictionary.* Ljubljana: DZS, 1964.

Škerlj, R. *English-Slovene Dictionary.* Ljubljana: DZS, 1965.

Slikovni besednjak angleški in slovenski (English and Slovenian Picture Vocabulary). Ljubljana: Mladinska knjiga, 1963.

Slovenski pravopis (Slovenian Orthography). Ljubljana: DZS, 1962.

PERSONNEL

The following lists attempt to give the names of all persons teaching Polish, Serbo-Croatian, Czech, Bulgarian, or Slovenian (academic year 1966–67). Listings are by language, and, within each language, alphabetically according to institution. An asterisk next to a name indicates the language in question is either the native language of the teacher or a second language acquired in childhood at home. Also indicated is the highest degree earned by the teacher. For those holding the doctorate, the field of specialization is also indicated. The abbreviation "SLL" stands for Slavic Languages and Literatures. Other languages taught by the instructor are indicated within parentheses; (R), for example, stands for Russian. In many instances an instructor is working under the supervision of a senior member of the faculty.

One of the most striking facts that appears from the listing is the large number of native speakers teaching these languages. In the case of Polish and Czech the number approaches 100 percent. For Serbo-Croatian, approximately two-thirds of the teachers are native speakers, while one-third have learned the language on the university level. Only in the case of Bulgarian is there a larger number of non-native speakers as teachers. A very large percentage of the teachers of these languages are professional Slavicists, either already possessing a Ph.D. in Slavic languages and literatures or currently working on such a degree. The teacher of a West Slavic or South Slavic language is also more likely to be acquainted with linguistic methodology than, for example, his counterpart teaching French. Yet there is a problem in the area of staffing: non-natives must be trained in these languages if the field is to expand; they will be needed to form the future cadres of South and West Slavic language instruction. More will be said about this in the conclusions.

Polish

California (Berkeley)	*Najder, Zdzisław
UCLA	*Stone, Rochelle, M.A. (R)
Chicago	*Gołąb, Janina, M.A.
Colorado	*Foley, Edward, Ph.D. SLL
Columbia	*Krzyżanowski, Ludwik, Ph.D. Foreign Languages
Duke	*Krynski, Magnus Jan, Ph.D. SLL (R)
Harvard	*Weintraub, Wiktor, Ph.D. Polish
Holy Family	*Sister Margaret Mary Machowska, CSFN, M.S.
Illinois	*Gladney, Frank Y., Ph.D. SLL (R)
Indiana	*Maurer, Jadwiga, Ph.D. SLL
	Sehnert, James A., Ph.D., SLL (R, Bulg, Lusatian)
Kansas	*Krzyzanowski, Jerzy R., Ph.D. Comp. Lit. (R)

Madonna	*Sister M. Yolanda, C.S.S.F., M.A. (Latin, English)
Massachusetts	*Kosinski, Tatiana, A.M. (R., Cz.)
Michigan	Welsh, David J., M.A., Russ. Lit. (R)
Minnesota	*Zamojska, Danuta, M.A.
CCNY	*Von Wiren-Garczynski, Vera, Ph.D. SLL (R)
SUNY (Buffalo)	*Czerwinski, Edward J., Ph.D. SLL (R)
North Carolina	*Gasiński, Tadeusz A., Ph.D. Slav. Ling. (R)
Ohio State	*Koerner, Anna Ewa, M.A.
Pennsylvania State	*Birkenmayer, Sigmund S., Ph.D. SLL (R)
Pennsylvania	*Zagórska-Brooks, Maria, Ph.D. Linguistics
	*Giergielewicz, Mieczyslaw, Ph.D. Polish Lit.
Pittsburgh	*Mocha, Frank, M.A. (R)
Portland State	*d'Ermengard, M. Joseph P. (R)
Princeton	Baer, Joachim Theodor, Ph.D. SLL (R)
Stanford	*Szwede, Irena, M.A. (R)
Vanderbilt	*Majewska, Ewa, Cand. (R)
Washington	*Rieger, Anna, M.A.
Wayne State	Ordon, Edmund, Ph.D. SLL
Western Reserve	*Stanczak, Mark M., M.A. (R)
	*Maciuszko, Jerzy J., Ph.D. Library Science
Wisconsin (Madison)	*Gasiorowski, Xenia, Ph.D. SLL (R)
	Thomas, Lawrence L., Ph.D. SLL (R)
	*Zawacki, Edmund, Ph.D. SLL (R)
Wisconsin (Milwaukee)	*Napiorkowski, Thaddeus F. G., M.A. (R)
	*Gladecki, Leon, M.A.

Serbocroatian

Boston Coll.	*Taranovski, Vera, M.A. (R)
California (Berkeley)	Whyte, Robert E., Ph.D. Ling.
UCLA	Albin, Alexander, Ph.D. SLL (R)
Chicago	*Perković, Helenka, M.A.
Colorado	*Mayhanovich, Ljubo, M.A.
Columbia	Hannaher, William J., A.M.
Cornell	Leed, Richard L., Ph.D. Slav. Ling.
	*Veljković, Bogdan
Florida State	*Pribić, Nikola R., Ph.D. SLL (R)
Harvard	Bynum, David E., Ph.D. SLL
Illinois	*Dunatov, Rasio, Cand. (R)
Indiana	*Kadić, Ante, Ph.D. Phil. (R)

Kansas	*Jerkovich, George C., M.A.
Michigan	Stolz, Benjamin A., Ph.D. Slav. Ling. (R)
Minnesota	Sjoberg, Marilyn J., M.A. (R)
North Carolina	*Mihailovich, Vasa D., Ph.D. German (R, Ger)
Ohio State	Naylor, Kenneth E., Ph.D. SLL (R)
Pennsylvania State	*Kalogjera, Damir, Ph.D. Ling. (Eng)
Pennsylvania	Benson, Morton, Ph.D. SLL (R)
	*Šlivić-Šimšić, Biljana, Ph.D. SLL (R)
Pittsburgh	*Mila, Bruce, B.A.
Portland State	*Kovic, George B., M.A. (It., Sp.)
Southern California	*Mlikotin, Anthony M., M.A. (R)
Syracuse	Levin, Ephraim M., Ph.D. SLL (R)
Tulane	*Milivojević, Dragan, Ph.D. Ling. (R)
Vanderbilt	Porter, Richard N.
Washington	*Valčić, Sonja, M.A.
Western Reserve	*Yirka, Branko, M.A.
Wisconsin	*Strmecki, Joseph, Cand. SLL (R)
Yale	*Bennet, Simona M.K., Dip.

Czech

Brown	*Kučera, Henry, Ph.D. Sl. Ling. (R)
California (Berkeley)	*Zbořílek, Vladimir, Cand.
UCLA	*Meyerstein, Zlata P., Ph.D. Ling.
Chicago	*Součková, Milada, Ph.D. Phil.
Colorado	*Blom, Libor, M.A.
Columbia	*Nosco, Beatrice M., M.A. (German, Swedish)
Florida State	*Pribić, Elizabeth, Ph.D. SLL (R, German)
Indiana	*Beneš, Hana, Cand.
Nebraska	*Kučera, Vladimir, Ph.D. Czech
Portland State	Holling, Fred, M.A. (R)
Syracuse	*Kozak, Yitka R., M.A. (R)
Texas	Perkowski, Jan L., Ph.D. SLL (R)
Texas A. and M.	Skřivánek, John M. Ph.D. Philology (R., Sp.)
Vanderbilt	*Rysan, Josef
Washington	*Fryer, Ilona, B. S.
Western Reserve	*Nemecek, Jindrich, M.A.
Wisconsin	Marquess, Harlan E., Ph.D. SLL (R)
Yale	*Demetz, Hana, Maturita

Bulgarian

Brown	Mathiesen, Robert Christian, Cand. (R)
California (Berkeley)	Whitfield, Francis J., Ph.D. SLL
Chicago	Aronson, Howard I., Ph.D. SLL
Columbia	*Dimov-Bogoev, C.D., Ph.D.
Indiana	Sehnert, James A., Ph.D. SLL (Pol., Lusatian)
Pennsylvania	Salys, Anthony, Ph.D. Balto-Slav. Ling (R, Baltic)
Syracuse	Hursky, Jacob P., Ph.D. SLL (R, Pol., Ukr.)
Washington	*Ivanchukov, Alexey, B.A.
Yale	*Ganchev, Kamen, LL.M.
	Moser, Charles A., Ph.D. SLL

Slovenian

Chicago	Stankiewicz, Edward, Ph.D. SLL
Indiana	*Dekleva, Borut, M.A. (SCr., R)
Southern California	*Zrimc, Rudolf, Ph.D. SLL (R)

Slovak

Columbia	*Šimončič, Klement, M.A.

Although the teaching of the West and South Slavic languages in the United States can be said to form a thriving component of departments of Slavic languages and literatures, it must be admitted that these languages are not necessarily in the most secure position. The immediate postwar and post-sputnik development in the American universities was to establish Slavic departments, the center of interest in which was Russian; the so-called second Slavic languages were generally required for advanced degrees. It is hard to deny that it was this requirement that made the growth of the teaching of the West and South Slavic languages possible. At the present, however, one can discern the beginnings of a trend to allow alternative courses for these languages. Students are given the option of a second Slavic language, comparative literature, French, English, or German literature, Russian history, Russian government, etc. This development clearly threatens the future of the West and South Slavic languages within the Slavic departments of the country. This is especially true because the coming generations of Slavic department faculty are unlikely to contain as large a percentage of Czechs, Poles, and Yugoslavs as is presently teaching. It should be noted that the threat is greater in the field of literature than it is in the field of Slavic linguistics.

RECOMMENDATIONS

1. Offerings in one or another of the languages under consideration should be followed up with courses in literature or area studies. Students in such courses who have studied the language in question should be required to continue using that language (in background readings, for term papers, etc.).

2. One of the problems facing the teachers of the languages in question is the varied background of students taking the course or desiring to take the course. All too often, whether or not the course officially presupposes a knowledge of Russian, the majority of students registered will have completed at least three years of Russian. Students interested, for example, in Czech, Polish, or South Slavic history who have not studied Russian will find themselves at a distinct disadvantage in courses where the majority of students know Russian. On the other hand, students with a background in Russian will be held back if the given language course does not take this background into consideration. As a result, the following recommendations can be made:

a) There is a real need for two separate and distinct types of language courses: one for Slavicists with a background in Russian or another Slavic language, and one for students without such a background. The latter type of course could at first concentrate primarily on giving the student sufficient reading knowledge to read the scholarly literature in his field. In institutions offering more than one year of the given language, the two types of students could be brought together in the second year.

b) There is a need to develop textbooks for each of the two course types described above, one presupposing a good knowledge of a Slavic language, the other with no such presupposition. The latter type, because of the unlikelihood of the realization of (*a*) above, should be designed primarily for self-instruction.

c) It must be assumed that most Slavic departments will either not be in a position to offer such dual courses as outlined above or will not want to expand their offerings in a direction which would be mainly that of "service" courses for people outside the department. For this reason it is perhaps more important as well as more realistic to press for the offering of language courses for non-Slavicists at summer institutes, perhaps with NDEA support. Ideally, these institutes would be areal in nature.

3. Although there is a growing body of trained American teachers of the South and West Slavic languages, the majority of the teaching is done by native speakers. Since very often these are graduate students

in a Slavic department or some other department, their services often tend to be transient, and the regularity of offering suffers (see recommendation 4, below). It is therefore important to train American Slavicists to be able to teach these languages well. Much progress has been made in the training of Russian teachers through special NDEA institutes and through various university programs and courses in applied linguistics, contrastive analysis, etc. Such programs should be extended to the remaining Slavic languages. There is a need for pedagogical literature, contrastive analyses, etc., for the prospective teachers of these languages. Institutes should be inaugurated where teachers can learn how to teach both Russian and another Slavic language. Prospective teachers of Polish, Czech, Serbo-Croatian, etc., should have the opportunity to spend time in the country where their language is spoken, and to this end we should try to arrange special exchanges with the relevant countries so that American students can study with those people charged with the teaching of the local language to foreign students.

4. There is a real need for a tradition of continuity in offering the language at a given institution. Offerings should not be on the basis solely of whatever native speakers may happen to be on campus during a given year. The language course, as mentioned in recommendation 1, should be an integral part of a whole program of areal offerings.

5. Summer institutes should be available not only for the more commonly taught South and West Slavic languages but also for the rarer ones, such as Slovenian, Macedonian, and Lusatian. There should be some way for a student who knows neither Russian nor Serbo-Croatian, for example, but whose interest lies in the field of Slovenian history, to learn Slovenian. At the present, such courses tend to be directed mainly to the advanced Slavicists, particularly those who are working in the field of linguistics. Summer programs (and many are already being offered) are also important in that they allow the student to acquire the language during the summer and to begin the study of its literature, the history of the country, etc., during the following academic year. The inauguration of summer study tours to the country in question should also be recommended.

6. There is a real need for the development of graded readers for the languages in question. Although we have recommended the development of new types of textbooks (see 2b above), the greater need is for readers. Such readers should be oriented not only toward the potential student of the literature of the language in question but also to potential students of history, economics, geography, political

science, etc. Also necessary (and for the most part, generally unavailable) are reference grammars of the language in question.

7. Communication among teachers of the languages in question is not very well developed. National meetings of teachers of Slavic languages tend, quite justifiably, to be devoted primarily to the problems of teaching Russian. Further, there is great variety in the number of quarters or semesters or years of the so-called second Slavic languages offered and/or required; the goals of the course vary not only from institution to institution, but, within a given institution, from language to language; prerequisites for such courses also show great variation, often correlated with the goals of a given course. There is nothing inherently bad about such a situation, and in fact the great amount of variety can be viewed as a positive feature of the current American state of affairs in the teaching of these languages. But it also indicates that teachers have much to learn from each other. I would therefore suggest two steps: (1) that the national meeting of the AATSEEL consider the establishment of a new section devoted to the problems of teaching West and South Slavic languages, and (2) that a national conference to discuss the role of the West and South Slavic languages in the university be held at which questions of goals, methodology, prerequisites, etc., would be discussed. Such a meeting should also be attended by representatives of the social sciences concerned with the Slavic area, and the needs and special problems of their students should be brought forward.

8. Serious reconsideration of the question of goals is necessary. Languages taught in our universities are of necessity divided into "major" and "minor." Thus, for the vast majority of Slavicists, Russian will be the major language; but for specialists, in Habsburg history, for example, German most likely will be the major language. If the student studies three or four years of Russian or German, he will not have enough time for three or four years of Polish or Czech or Serbo-Croatian. The aim with these "minor" languages must be to give the student as much material as possible in a quite limited period of time. A graduate student, for example, in history cannot afford to spend three years studying a language. Even two years is a great amount of time, since it is likely that he will not be using the language as a tool during that period. One way of solving this problem is through summer programs (see recommendation 5), but the whole question of the four skills (reading, writing, speaking, and understanding) needs reconsideration. Such a four-skill approach is, of course, necessary for the potential teacher of the languages, but not necessarily for all students.

9. It must be recognized by all concerned with South and West Slavic studies that the future of these literatures within Slavic departments is intimately connected with the maintenance of second Slavic language requirements. The abolition of this requirement (or its weakening) can lead to a serious setback to the development of the area.

18/ SURVEY OF ALBANIAN, HUNGARIAN, MODERN GREEK, AND ROMANIAN LANGUAGES

Kostas Kazazis
University of Chicago

PURPOSE

This report attempts to determine the nature and extent of offerings of instruction in American colleges and universities in the Albanian, Hungarian, modern Greek, and Romanian languages. Among the questions investigated are enrollment, goals, prerequisites, staffing, and text materials. Inquiries were sent to about fifty institutions, and the present survey is based on the responses to those inquiries. Among the types of courses excluded from the survey are such courses having as their primary goal the linguistic analysis of a given language, rather than one or more of the four language skills: understanding, speaking, reading, and writing.

LANGUAGES OFFERED

Language instruction is currently offered in all four languages under consideration. As far as it could be determined, the situation for 1966–67 was as follows: Albanian was offered in one institution, Hungarian in five, modern Greek in ten, and Romanian in five, giving a total of twenty-one institutions.[1]

1. Indiana University has not been counted for modern Greek, although in 1966–67 it offered three years of instruction in that language. In 1967–68, however, modern Greek was entirely dropped at Indiana. This is by no means a rare occurrence, and it merely illustrates the precarious status of many minor languages in

TABLE 1
DISTRIBUTION OF LANGUAGES BY INSTITUTIONS

Institution	Alb.	Hung.	MGk.	Rom.	Total
Chicago	x		x	x	3
UCLA		x	x		2
Columbia		x		x	2
Indiana		x		x	2
Boston College				x	1
Bridgeport			x		1
California (Berkeley)		x			1
Dartmouth			x		1
Georgetown			x		1
Illinois			x		1
Ohio University			x		1
Portland State Colege		x			1
Seton Hill College			x		1
Texas			x		1
Washington				x	1
Wisconsin			x		1

DESCRIPTION OF OFFERINGS

Table 2 provides the following information for each institution: (1) number of years of instruction in the language offered; (2) number of contact hours per week; (3) major goals of the course — conversation, composition, or reading;[2] (4) the teaching method used;[3] (5) prerequisites for the course — wherever there is a prerequisite, the additional words ". . . or consent of instructor or department" should be understood. A dash indicates that information was not available.

STUDENTS AND REQUIREMENTS

Table 3 indicates the enrollment in language classes at various institutions (column 1),[4] the status of the majority of the students in

American universities. Offerings in a given minor language are often contingent upon the presence on campus of a specific faculty member — frequently a native speaker of the language in question. There may well be other instances of institutions reported herein as offering one or more of the relevant languages but which, in fact, discontinued instruction in those languages in 1966–67. Indiana's modern Greek program, however, is the only one that was brought to this writer's attention.

2. The order is significant only if preceded by the numbers 1, 2, and 3.

3. "G-T" stands for grammar-translation and "A-L" for audiolingual.

4. The first number stands for the year — first, second, or third. Thus, 1.8 means that there are eight students in the first-year course; 2.5 means five students in the second-year course.

TABLE 2
DESCRIPTION OF OFFERINGS

	No. Yrs. (1)	Hrs./Wk. (2)	Goals (3)	Method (4)	Prereq. (5)	Notes (6)
			Albanian			
Chicago	2	3	Conv Read	A-L	none	
			Hungarian			
California (Berkeley)	1 2	10 5	1 Conv 2 Read 3 Comp	A-L	none	
UCLA	1	—	Conv Read Comp	A-L G-T	none	4 quarters offered
Columbia	3	6	1 Conv 2 Read 3 Comp	G-T	none	
Indiana	1 2 3	5 3 3	1 Conv 2 Read 3 Comp	A-L G-T	none	Method: A-L 1st yr; G-T 2d/ 3d yr.
Portland State College	1 2 3	4 4 3	1 Conv 2 Read 3 Comp	A-L	none	
			Romanian			
Boston College	2	3	—	—	—	2d yr added 1967–68
Chicago	2	3	Conv Read	—	none	
Columbia	1	6	—	—	1 Rom. lg.	Began summer '67
Indiana	1 2	5 3	1 Read 2 Conv 3 Comp	G-T A-L	none	
Washington	1	5	1 Conv 2 Read 3 Comp	A-L	1 Rom. or Slav. lg.	

TABLE 2–(Continued)
DESCRIPTION OF OFFERINGS

	No. Yrs. (1)	Hrs./Wk. (2)	Goals (3)	Method (4)	Prereq. (5)	Notes (6)
			Modern Greek			
Bridgeport	1	—	Conv	A-L	none	
			Comp	G-T		
			Read			
UCLA	2	—	Read	—	none	
Chicago	2	5	Conv	A-L	none	
			Read			
Colorado	1	5	1 Conv	A-L	none	
	2	3	2 Comp			
			3 Read			
Dartmouth	1	4	1 Comp	A-L	none	
			2 Read	G-T		
			3 Conv			
Georgetown	2	5	1 Conv	A-L	none	
			2 Read			
Illinois	2	4	Conv	A-L	none	
			Read			
Ohio	2	5	Conv	A-L	none	
Seton Hill College	2	—	1 Read	A-L	none	
			2 Conv	G-T		
			3 Comp			
Texas	1	5	1 Read	G-T	none	
	2	3	2 Conv	A-L		
			3 Comp			
Wisconsin	1	4	Conv	A-L	none	
	2	3	Read	G-T		

the class (column 2),[5] and the percentage of students with a native background — such as Hungarian-American students in a Hungarian class (column 3) — for 1966–67. It also gives information on whether or not the language meets an undergraduate foreign language requirement (column 4), whether it meets a graduate reading examination requirement (column 5), and whether it meets a linguistics department requirement for a non-Western or, for Hungarian, non-Indo-

5. "UG" stands for undergraduate, "G" for graduate, and the equal sign means that the class is about equally divided between graduates and undergraduates.

TABLE 3
STUDENTS AND REQUIREMENTS

	Enrollment (1)	Students (2)	Percentage Native Backgr. (3)	UG FL Req. (4)	Grad. Read. Exam (5)	Ling. Dept. Req. (6)	Major (7)	Minor (8)
Albanian								
Chicago	1.1	G	0	no	no	no	no	MA
	2.1	G						PhD
Hungarian								
California (Berkeley)	1.3 2.3	UG	85	yes	—	—	no	MA
UCLA	12	=	40	yes	yes	yes	—	—
Columbia	15	=	15	no	WP	no	BA MA PhD	BA MA PhD
Indiana	1.7 2.4 3.4	G	30	yes	yes	yes	no	MA PhD
Portland State College	10	UG	0	yes	no	yes	BA	BA
Romanian								
Boston College	1.4 2.—	=	—	—	—	—	—	—
Chicago	1.2 2.0	G	0	no	no	no	no	MA PhD
Columbia	—	—	—	—	—	—	—	—
Indiana	1.7 2.1	G	0	no	no	yes	no	MA PhD
Washington	2	G	0	yes	yes	yes	no	BA MA
Modern Greek								
Bridgeport	8	UG	100	yes	no	no	no	no
Chicago	1.9	=	20	no	no	no	no	MA PhD
Colorado	1.12 2.2	UG	—	no	no	no	no	BA
Dartmouth	8	UG	30	no	—	no	no	no
Illinois	1.6 2.1	UG	60	yes	no	no	no	no

TABLE 3–(Continued)
STUDENTS AND REQUIREMENTS

	Enrollment	Students	Percentage Native Backgr.	UG FL Req.	Grad. Read. Exam	Ling. Dept. Req.	Major	Minor
	(1)	(2)	(3)	(4)	(5)	(6)	(7)	(8)
Ohio	4	G	25	yes	no	yes	MA PhD	—
Georgetown	7	UG	14	no	no	yes	no	BA
Seton Hill Coll.	1.8 2.7	UG	5–10	yes	—	—	BA	BA
Texas	9–15	UG	25–33	yes	yes	no	—	—
Wisconsin	1.13 2.10	UG	30	yes	yes	—	—	BA

European language (column 6).[6] The last two columns indicate on what level a student can major in a given language (column 7) and on what levels he can minor in it (column 8). Once again, a dash means that the information was not available.

It is often the case that a large percentage of the students taking a minor language are from families originating in the country where the language is spoken. At first sight this would appear to be a desirable thing, since such students more often than not have been exposed to the language in question. There are, however, difficulties, such as the fact that the variety of the language which the students may have heard at home is often very different from that taught at the university — respectively, local dialect vs. standard language. Whenever this is the case, the students have to unlearn in class much of what they have learned at home. There is a tendency for such students to be ahead of the rest of the class at the beginning. Later on, however, all but the most highly motivated of these students tend to lag behind. Little attention has been directed so far to the difficulties involved in teaching this type of student.

Table 3 shows that many institutions do not accept the languages covered by this survey as meeting undergraduate foreign language requirements. Table 4 gives the number of institutions which furnished information on this point.

---

6. "WP" means "with permission."

TABLE 4

| | Number of Institutions | |
	Accepting	Not Accepting
Albanian	0	1
Hungarian	4	1
Modern Greek	6	4
Romanian	1	2

Table 5 shows the number of institutions accepting the four languages for the purpose of graduate reading examinations.

Table 6 shows the number of institutions providing the possibility for students to major or minor in the languages under consideration.

INSTRUCTIONAL MATERIALS

Teaching materials for Albanian, Hungarian, modern Greek, and Romanian leave much to be desired. Many of them have been published abroad, often in the country where the language is spoken, which renders them less accessible. Dictionaries are almost invariably designed for the foreign student of English, rather than for English-speaking students learning the foreign language. They frequently record British usage, with a few "Americanisms" interspersed here and there. Some instructors have reported the availability of a language laboratory at their institutions, but have decried the lack of carefully prepared audio-lingual materials suitable for language-laboratory work. There is, moreover, an almost total lack of satisfactory readers for these languages. Occasionally, the effectiveness of an otherwise acceptable textbook will be severely limited by its failure to use stress marks, when (as in Romanian) the conventional spelling does not indicate them. Teaching materials are discussed in greater detail in the recommendations below.

TABLE 5

| | Number of Institutions | |
	Accepting	Not Accepting
Albanian	0	1
Hungarian	3	1
Modern Greek	2	6
Romanian	1	2

TABLE 6

| | Number of Institutions | | | | | |
| | Major | | | Minor | | |
	BA	MA	PhD	BA	MA	PhD
Albanian	0	0	0	0	1	1
Hungarian	2	1	1	2	3	2
Modern Greek	1	1	1	4	1	1
Romanian	0	0	0	1	3	2

The following lists contain the textbooks, readers, dictionaries, tapes, and records currently used by teachers of the language under consideration. They do not purport to be complete listings of all instructional materials available.

ALBANIAN

Textbooks

Newmark, Leonard, and Haznedari, Ismail. *Spoken Albanian*. Bloomington, Ind.: Air Force Language Training Program, Indiana University n.d.

Readers

None used.

Dictionaries

None used for class work.

Tapes, records

None used.

HUNGARIAN

Textbooks

Bánhídi, Z., Jókay, Z., and Szabó, D. *Learn Hungarian*. Budapest: Tankönyvkiadó, 1965.

Koski, Augustus, and Mihályfy, Ilona, *Hungarian Basic Course*. Vols. 1, 2. Washington: Government Printing Office, 1962, 1964.

Readers

Lotz, John. *Hungarian Reader* (Folklore and Literature). The Hague: Mouton, 1962.

Dictionaries

Országh, László. *Angol-magyar szótár.* Budapest: Akadémiai Kiadó, 1960.
————. *Magyar-angol szótár.* Budapest: Akadémiai Kiadó, 1963.

Tapes, records

There are tapes to accompany Koski and Mihályfy, *Hungarian Basic Course,* as well as locally produced tapes.

The University of California at Los Angeles reports using Hungarian records containing readings of prose and poetry — no further details available.

Modern Greek

Textbooks

Arpajolu, Ann. *Modern Spoken Greek for English-Speaking Students.* Thessaloniki, 1964.
Kahane, Henry and Renée, and Ward, Ralph L. *Spoken Greek.* New York: Holt, 1945.
Sofroniou, S. A. *Teach Yourself Modern Greek.* London: English Universities Press, 1962.

Readers

Sapountzis, P. and A., and Hodge, C. T. *Greek Intermediate Reader.* Washington, D.C.: Government Printing Office, 1961.

Dictionaries

D. C. Divry's *English-Greek and Greek-English Dictionary.* New York: Divry, 1964.
Kykkotis, I. *English-Greek and Greek-English Dictionary.* Several eds. London: Lund Humphries.
Pring, Julian T. *The Oxford Dictionary of Modern Greek* (Greek-English). Oxford: Oxford University Press, 1965.
Swanson, Donald C. *Vocabulary of Modern Spoken Greek.* Athens: John M. Pantelides, 1957.

Tapes, records

Records for Units 1–12 of Kahane, Kahane, and Ward, *Spoken Greek.*
Some institutions have reported using locally produced tapes with material from Kahane, Kahane, and Ward, *Spoken Greek,* and Arpajolu, *Modern Spoken Greek for English-Speaking Students.*

ROMANIAN

Textbooks

Cartianu, Ana; Leviţchi, Leon; and Ştefănescu-Drăgăneşti, Virgil. A
  Course in Modern Rumanian. Bucharest: Editura Ştiinţifică, 1958.
Guillermou, Alain. *Manuel de langue roumaine.* Paris: Klincksieck, 1953.

Readers

Indiana University reported using paperback texts for each author —
no further details available.

Dictionaries

Dicţionarul Limbii Romîne Moderne. Bucharest: Editura Academiei
  Republicii Populare Romîne, 1958.
Bogdan, Mihail, *et al. Dicţionar englez-romîn.* Bucharest: Editura
  Ştiinţifică, 1958.
Leviţchi, Leon. *Dicţionar romîn-englez.* Bucharest: Editura Ştiinţifică,
  1960.

Tapes, records

Indiana University reports using instructor's private collection of
Romanian literature and music on record and tape.

PERSONNEL

The following lists give the names of persons who teach Albanian,
Hungarian, modern Greek, or Romanian at American colleges and universities. Listings are by language, and within each language alphabetically according to institution. An asterisk next to a name indicates
that a person is either a native speaker of the language in question or
that he learned it as a second language at home during childhood. Also
indicated is the highest degree held by each person. For those holding the doctorate, the field of specialization is also given, if known.
Other modern languages currently taught by the instructor are enclosed
in parentheses.

Native-speaking instructors are often teaching assistants (graduate
students, student or faculty spouses, etc.), rather than regular faculty
members. In many instances such persons are working under the supervision of a senior member of the faculty. The presence of such
teaching assistants is partly responsible for the considerable turnover
of teaching personnel found in the minor languages. The lists given below are for the academic year 1966–67.

It is noteworthy that all teachers of Hungarian and the majority
of the teachers of modern Greek are native speakers of these languages.

This fact alone shows how urgent is the need for native American teachers of minor languages. This question is taken up again in the recommendations.

Albanian

Chicago	Hamp, Eric P., Ph.D., Linguistics
	Kazazis, Kostas, Ph.D., Linguistics
	(Modern Greek)

Hungarian

California (Berkeley)	*Sándor, András, B. Litt.
UCLA	*Birnbaum, Marianna, D., M.A.
Columbia	*Juhász, F., M.A.
	*Keresztes, K., M.A.
Indiana	*Bayerle, Gustav, Ph.D., Turkish Studies
	*Moravcsik, Edith, Ph.D., Classics
	*Virágos, Zsolt, B.A.
Portland State C.	*Ternay, Kálmán, Ph.D., Hungarian and Italian Literature, and Comparative Romance Linguistics

Modern Greek

UCLA	Mohr, Evelyn V., M.A.
Bridgeport	*Carovakis, Nicholas, A.B.
Chicago	*Kazazis, Kostas, Ph.D., Linguistics (Albanian)
Colorado	*Lafkidou, Aliki, Ptycheion
Dartmouth	Bien, Peter, Ph.D., Sociology
	*Choukas, Michael, Ph.D., Sociology
Georgetown	*Alatis, James E., Ph.D. English and Linguistics
Illinois	*Tsitsopoulos, Stamatis, M.A.
Ohio	*Panagos, Pery
Seton Hill College	*Stratigos, Harry D., B.A., B.S., (English)
Texas	Morgan, Gareth, D.Phil., Modern and Medival Greek
Wisconsin	*Tsimpoukis, Constantinos, M.S.

Romanian

Boston College	Moissiy, A., Ph.D.[7]

7. It was not indicated whether or not Professor Moissiy is a native speaker of Romanian.

Chicago	(Various visiting professors from Romania)
Columbia	Austerlitz, Robert, Ph.D., Linguistics
Indiana	Buehler, Gretchen H., Ph.D. Romance Linguistics (French)
Washington	Augerot, James E., Ph.D., Slavic Linguistics (Russian)

BASIC PROBLEMS AND RECOMMENDATIONS

CONSTRUCTION OF INSTRUCTIONAL MATERIALS

There is a great need for new instructional materials for all four languages, although admittedly this need is more or less acute depending on the individual language. As far as textbooks are concerned, the situation is worst in Albanian, modern Greek, and Romanian, where there is nothing available which would approach even remotely an up-to-date textbook. For Hungarian, there is the Foreign Service Institute's *Hungarian Basic Course*, by Koski and Mihályfy, but what we need are textbooks designed for use in colleges and universities, not works designed for specialized groups of people such as foreign service officers.

When we talk about "textbooks," we mean integrated courses including drills, tests, and tapes. These courses should be written preferably by a team of authors, not by a single individual (cf. the Modern Language Association projects which yielded *Modern French, Modern Russian,* and *Modern Spanish*). These otherwise audio-lingual textbooks should emphasize reading considerably more than is often the case today with similar materials (including the MLA textbooks).

For the four languages with which we are dealing, either there are no readily available readers at all (Albanian), or the available readers are not satisfactory (they either are not graded or are not representative of modern usage or lack a glossary; often these shortcomings are all combined in the same reader). There is an urgent need for elementary, intermediate, and advanced readers for all four languages. These readers should, of course, include a general glossary at the end. However, new words should also be glossed somewhat closer to the point at which they occur in the text. An excellent device is the marginal gloss. This system is naturally more space-consuming than listing the glosses at the bottom of the page, but footnoted glosses seem to be more time-consuming to use (and thus more distracting) than glosses listed in the margin. Still, both of the devices, as well as the additional one of listing new words on the facing page, are infinitely more effective than a simple glossary at the end of the reader.

In order to compile truly *graded* readers, it is necessary to have several word counts for all four languages. Thus we need a word count containing the 1,000 most frequent words of a given language, one with the 3,000 most frequent words, and so on. Otherwise we run the risk of including in our readers words that are relatively rare, and of excluding from them other words whose occurrence is much more frequent.

For Hungarian and Romanian, there are some good, invariably foreign-produced, dictionaries into and from English. However, these works were designed primarily with the needs of the foreign learner of English in view. So it is necessary to plan at least medium-sized dictionaries designed primarily for the English-speaking user, and where the needs of the beginner are paramount. The latter is important, since it is usually the beginners who suffer most from the lack of dictionaries designed for English speakers; people who have already acquired the rudiments of the target language can make do with less than adequate dictionaries. The same remarks apply to dictionaries from and into modern Greek and Albanian, except that here things are much worse. The few tolerably good large and medium-sized modern Greek–English and English–modern Greek dictionaries which exist are rather hard to get in this country. As far as Albanian is concerned, there is not a single good dictionary for the English-speaking user.

Recommendation 1. New textbooks are needed for all four languages. These should be prepared in accordance with the latest methods and preferably by a team of authors. They should be fully integrated courses, including drills, tests, and tapes. These otherwise audio-lingually oriented textbooks should emphasize reading considerably more than is the case with similar materials now available for other languages.

Recommendation 2. There is a pressing need for frequency word counts for all four languages. These word counts are indispensable for the construction of graded readers.

Recommendation 3. There is a need for graded readers at all levels and for all four languages. These should not only have a glossary at the end but should also provide glosses for new words closer to their occurrence in the text, preferably in the margin or on the page facing the text.

Recommendation 4. There is a need for dictionaries from these languages into English and conversely, with the needs of the English-speaking (not the foreign) user foremost in mind. In the preparation of dictionaries, the needs of beginners should be paramount, for it is they who suffer most from the unavailability of dictionaries designed for the English speaker.

SCARCITY OF TEACHERS

Some urgent measures should be taken to correct the current extreme scarcity of trained teachers in these four languages. The fact that so many of the teachers of these languages are native speakers emphasizes the need for training native Americans as replacements for the currently active personnel. Corrective measures could include summer language institutes on the model of NDEA institutes for the critical languages. The possibility of language-teacher exchanges with the countries where these languages are spoken should also be considered. As things stand now, of course, such exchanges would not include Albania, but they should not be impossible to arrange with the remaining three countries — Greece, Hungary, and Romania. An effort should be made to interest as many non-native speakers as possible, including second- and third-generation descendants of native speakers, in the teaching of these languages.

The scarcity of trained teachers is more or less severe depending on the language. Thus, as far as *trained* teachers (not merely native speakers) go, the situation seems to be worst for Albanian and Romanian. However, things are not much brighter with respect to the other two languages, Hungarian and modern Greek. To be sure, there are many native speakers of the latter two languages in this country, but teachers trained in current language-teaching techniques are extremely rare.

Recommendation 5. One measure for correcting the current scarcity of trained teachers in these four languages would be the setting up of summer language institutes, on the model of NDEA institutes for the critical languages.

Recommendation 6. Another measure to be considered for the purpose of training more teachers in these languages would be the exchange of language-teachers with at least Greece, Hungary, and Romania — and also with Albania as soon as the international political situation allows it.

Recommendation 7. Every effort should be made to interest non-native speakers, including second- and third-generation descendants of native speakers, in the teaching of these languages. Admitting these languages for undergraduate foreign language requirements and graduate foreign language reading examinations would probably prove excellent incentives. Other incentives might be to allow students to major or at least to minor in these languages, as well as to expand existing programs by introducing more years of instruction, courses in the literature of the language, in area studies, and the like (see also next section).

EXPANSION OF EXISTING PROGRAMS

It would, of course, be desirable for more institutions to begin offering courses in one or more of the four languages with which we are concerned. However, it is at least as important for institutions currently offering such courses to expand their programs. Such expansions should include, depending on the current situation, additional years of instruction in the language, introduction of courses in the literature and the linguistics of the language (structure, history, dialectology, etc.), as well as area courses in the history, economics, folklore, etc., of the country in which the language is spoken. There are at present several institutions offering one or two years of a given language, but giving no opportunity to their students to deepen their knowledge of the language or the people who speak it. Such a state of affairs could discourage all but the most highly motivated students from keeping up their interest in the foreign language and culture.

Recommendation 8. While more institutions should be encouraged to offer courses in one or more of the four languages, institutions currently offering such courses should be urged to expand their programs through the introduction of intermediate and advanced language courses, and courses in the relevant literature, linguistics, and area studies.

INDEPENDENCE FROM RUSSIAN PROGRAMS

When programs in any of the four languages are intimately connected with programs of Russian studies, it may sometimes happen that a person finds it difficult to specialize in the minor language or languages, rather than in Russian. Such a person may discover that the majority of required courses are in Russian literature, linguistics, or area studies. Since the importance of Russia or the Soviet Union in Hungary, Romania, and Albania is of relatively recent date, it might be preferable for programs in any of the four languages under consideration to be as independent as possible from Russian programs existing at the same institution. Where it would be administratively impossible to divorce the minor language program from the Russian one, then considerable flexibility should be exercised in setting up curricula for students who wish to specialize in the minor language and area.

Recommendation 9. Programs in any of the four languages should be made as independent as possible of Russian programs. It is by no means the case that a strong foundation in Russian studies is a prerequisite for non-Slavic Balkan or Hungarian studies, however desirable such a foundation might be otherwise. Too close a relationship between a program in any of these languages and a Russian program runs the risk of producing experts in Russian, rather than in the minor language for which it was set up.

POSTSCRIPT

Charles Jelavich

In this brief postscript it is not my purpose to comment upon the reports included in this volume. Each one speaks for itself. I believe that they constitute an accurate evaluation of the current state of the East European field and what needs to be done in it. My intention is to discuss the area as whole and the general impressions which I have gained in the three years during which I have been associated with this project.

The single predominant idea which comes from a study of the problems connected with the survey is the increasing significance of the area. Although Eastern Europe has been of great historic interest as a borderland where civilizations and cultures meet, it is today of prime importance for its new approaches and its social and economic experimentation. In other words, it is a laboratory where competing systems and principles can be observed.

Although the study of Eastern Europe was slow to begin in this country, our achievements, though still limited, have been truly impressive, given the obstacles which we have had to overcome. In research on economics, history, linguistics, political science, and international relations, American scholarship either leads the way or has offered new theories and viewpoints. We have organized institutes and centers in which the nations of the area can be studied either individually or as part of a wider organization. Our accomplishments gain more significance when it is remembered that it is only in the last three or four years that the Balkan states, for example, have undertaken to study their neighbors and their area as a whole, rather than concentrating solely on their own national life. In fact, East European scholars have themselves been most generous in their appreciation of what

467

American scholarship and teaching has done toward achieving a broader understanding of the area.

In the past, the problem of language seemed often insurmountable. No one today underestimates the continued difficulty in meeting this obstacle, but there is a conviction that much can be done through the regular summer language institutes which have been proposed. Today the graduate student entering the field is well aware that he must be prepared to devote an extra year or two of his graduate studies to becoming proficient in the language or languages of his research interest. He now recognizes that proper linguistic training is absolutely essential for teaching and writing about Eastern Europe. The recognition of the importance of language and the great increase in the availability of instruction is one of the major achievements of the period since World War II.

Every report, it will be noted, stresses the importance of expanding and improving the academic exchanges with all of the Eastern European countries. The necessity of research in the national archives of these countries, of discussions with their leading authorities and of gaining a direct knowledge of the land itself is recognized as essential to sound research and teaching. With the almost total removal of travel restrictions, it is now possible to travel freely in most of the countries. In the interwar period when such visits were allowed, only a few American scholars had the means or the interest. With the new opportunities available, our faculty and students are able to use many research and instructional facilities in the area of their principal concern. Equally important are the arrangements which have been made to enable East European scholars to visit the United States, and to offer lectures or courses. It has been strongly recommended that these visits be increased, and that foreign scholars be given the opportunity to offer semester courses and seminars in particular to graduate students and faculty.

The international political climate has been favorable not only for the exchanges but also for the establishment of close cooperation with foreign institutes or individual scholars on joint research projects. Throughout these reports, many suggestions of this nature have been made, such as translations of standard works, library acquisitions, publication of source books, compilation of dictionaries, preparation of instructional tools for language study, etc. Both the American and the foreign participants would benefit from this collaboration.

The survey also brought forth a clear expression of opinion by a majority of those who devote all their time to teaching and research in East European studies that this area should be separated from its previous close association with, and therefore subordination to, the Russian-Soviet field. Students should be trained in East European studies as they are now in the Russian-Soviet, Latin American, Middle Eastern, Asian, and African areas. To achieve this goal, centers or institutes should be established which are guided and administered exclusively by specialists in Eastern Europe, scholars who best know the problems and interests of their own field.

Although it was recognized that it could not be expected, nor was it desirable, that a great many such centers be established, there was virtually unanimous agreement that three to six should be formed and that they should be located in at least three different geographic areas in the United States. It was believed preferable that they should have a well-developed area-wide interdisciplinary program which would enjoy a major place in their universities' curriculum. In addition, it was agreed that they should receive the added financial stimulus which only a foundation or a federal grant can provide. The emphasis on the establishment of three to six major centers does not, of course, mean that other universities should not undertake to teach courses or conduct research on the area. On the contrary, all interested institutions should be encouraged to develop their interest in these lands. However, it was believed practical that these institutions concentrate on a few of the countries or on a particular region, rather than on the entire area. Here the problems of language training and library facilities are the determining factors in recommending a limitation in any proposed program.

The final point to be made concerns the role of the private foundations and the federal government in the continued growth and expansion of East European studies. Whereas the government's ability to subsidize the field is based upon congressional appropriations or the prevailing international political conditions, the private foundations are not limited by these factors. The foundations have largely stressed that their role was to provide "seed" money, to subsidize experimental projects, or to further research in new areas and fields. It is recognized by all that without this past financial support to universities, as well as through some of the foundations' independently administered programs, area studies in general would not enjoy the respect and success they have today. Although no one can, or should, expect that foundation support will continue indefinitely, it is obvious that some area programs are more advanced than others. Our area is still in need of assistance. It is hoped, therefore, that additional private support will be forthcoming to meet the scholarly and national needs for the next decade.

These comments cover, obviously, only a few of the many issues raised during the course of this project. We hope that the reader, whether he is or is not a specialist in Eastern Europe, will examine carefully the analyses of what has been accomplished in the field of East Central and Southeast European studies, what still remains to be done, and what course we should follow in the future. This survey should be a convincing demonstration of the great importance of this diverse region in the modern world and of the necessity of widening and deepening American research and study. These reports reveal that a base for the future has been laid, but the problems of a field encompassing nine modern nations — using at least a dozen languages — which are undergoing dramatic social, economic, and political experiments, are necessarily complex. At no period since 1945 have the scholarly, national, and international conditions been so favorable for an expansion of our study of that area. If the recommendations suggested in this survey are followed, the decade of the seventies should see East Central and Southeast European studies achieve the same degree of success now attained by Russian-Soviet studies.

INDEX OF AUTHORS

478   *Index*